Appreciation For *Withering Wind From Arabia*:

Richard Beswick, Campus Minister for many years at the University of Oregon, wrote: "For someone like me, whose major historical studies focused on American and European history (and I am fairly representative of one or more generations, I think), your manuscript [Withering Wind From Arabia] uncovers dimensions that such an education lacks for the Christian who wants to understand the phenomenon of Islam as a spiritual battle with Christianity and a worldly battle with Christendom. For these purposes, I have never read anything like it and for these reasons I find it very valuable! By taking us through different geographical arenas and bending the time line so we understand cause and effect in those areas, we can appreciate the tragic fate of brothers and sisters in Christ who saw their freedoms crushed and their faith tested—sometimes to the point of death!" – *Richard Beswick holds the B.A. Degree, with honors, in Religious Studies from the University of Oregon and a Master of Divinity Degree from Yale University. He teaches Apologetics and World Religions at both of Eugene's Christian Colleges.*

David Sowers, Campus Minister on the Columbia Missouri Campus of the University of Missouri, wrote: "I believe that this book would be a significant help to someone such as an international campus minister who is working in Muslim student evangelism. In addition, preaching ministers who serve in cities where there is an Islamic population would be helped by this book. Bible college professors teaching in missions or world religions classes could benefit greatly from this book." – *David Sowers holds a Bachelor of Ministry Degree from St. Louis Christian College, a Master of Divinity Degree from Cincinnati Christian Seminary and a Master of Theology Degree from Covenant Theological Seminary in St. Louis.*

Sarah Van Diest, leader of the review group at Last Chapter Publishing in Redmond, Oregon, who reviewed a much earlier and very incomplete edition of my manuscript, wrote, "You have compiled a vast amount of research and information on the subject of Islam The sheer amount of data you have collected shows a great accomplishment. Your dedication to seeing this project through to its current state is outstanding. There are few who can boast of such a feat in their entire lifetime."

Raouf Guirguis, Senior Pastor of the New Testament Arabic Church of Southern California sponsored by La Mirada Christian Church, wrote, "All the information in Withering Wind From Arabia [regarding Egypt] is accurate and well-written.... I congratulate you for this work. The three chapters I reviewed are perfect. I feel honored to be a part of it. I am waiting impatiently to see the book published." – *Dr. Raouf Guirguis is an Egyptian Christian.*

Grace Magney, forty-year veteran missionary in Afghanistan, wrote, "You have written a wonderful manuscript which is easy to read and very informative. Congratulations on a very timely book!" – *Grace Magney holds the M.A. degree from Syracuse University in New York.*

Other books by the author include:

Revelation, Verse by Verse

The Definitive Battle For Palestine, An Exposition of Ezekiel 38 and 39

God's Game Plan

Withering Wind From Arabia

*The Story of the Followers of Christ
Whose Countries Were
Conquered by Islam*

B. L. Turner

*Bachelor of Theology, 1947, San Jose Bible College
M.A. in South Asian Regional Studies, 1959, University of Pennsylvania
Ministered in the Muslim world for many years, beginning in 1960.*

Withering Wind From Arabia The Story of the Followers of Christ Whose Countries Were Conquered by Islam

Copyright © 2018, 2023 by B.L. Turner. All rights reserved.

Fig Press
3631 NE 102nd Avenue
Portland, OR 97220

ISBN: 978-1-961528-00-0

Unless otherwise indicated, biblical quotations are from the American Standard Version.

Scripture quotations marked (NIV) are taken from the Holy Bible, New International Version®. Copyright © 1973, 1978, 1984, 2011 by Biblica, Inc.®. Used by permission. All rights reserved worldwide.

Scripture quotations marked (ESV) are taken from the Holy Bible, English Standard Version® (ESV®). Copyright © 2001 by Crossway, a publishing ministry of Good News Publishers. Used by permission. All rights reserved.

Scripture quotations marked (NRSV) are taken from the New Revised Standard Version Bible, copyright © 1989 National Council of the Churches of Christ in the United States of America. Used by permission. All rights reserved.

All Koranic quotations, unless otherwise specified, are from <u>The Meaning of the Glorious Koran, An Explanatory Translation</u> by Marmaduke Pickthall, Alfred A. Knopf, New York, 1930.

Cover photo courtesy of http://pcwallart.com.

Photos were taken and copyrighted by B.L. Turner or Jonathan Turner, unless otherwise noted. All rights reserved.

Dedication

To Willard Vanderford,
(b. 4/28/14, d. 12/29/93),
a gifted teacher of young people
at the Orland First Christian Church.
After teaching me and leading me to faith in
Christ, he baptized me into the Savior in 1937
in Stony Creek at Orland, California.

Acknowledgment and Appreciation

It is impossible to adequately express the gratitude I have for the competent and generous assistance I have received in producing Withering Wind from Arabia. The Atlas has been skillfully produced by Jonathan Turner. Eugene Mitchell and Anna Wilson have rendered great service in the Key Communications library to confirm hundreds of quotations utilized in this book. I am deeply grateful to my secretary, Lisa DiVincenzo, for competently, patiently and graciously converting the dictated text of this book into the form which you are now reading. In addition to the textual work, she also designed the captivating cover of the book.

Gratitude

Rosalind W. Gwynne, Ph.D., Associate Professor of Arabic, Department of Religious Studies, University of Tennessee, retired, graciously received a manuscript copy of *Withering Wind From Arabia*. Finding it worthy of serious consideration, she spent hundreds of hours giving careful attention to every aspect of the document. Though she disagrees with some of the theological and historical emphases I have made in this book, she considers it to be a rewarding contribution to the understanding of the history and nature of Islam. Therefore, she devoted a huge block of her time to editing and proofreading the treatise. With deep appreciation, by this note I inadequately express my gratitude to Dr. Gwynne for her priceless contribution!

TABLE OF CONTENTS

Introduction 1

The International Background

Chapter   **Page**

1. Arabia and the Wider World.. 9
2. The Contest for Southwest Arabia... 23

The Life of Muhammad

3. Muhammad's Infancy to Early Manhood.. 39
4. From Marriage to the Beginning of Public Preaching............................. 47
5. Muhammad's Christology.. 51
6. Critical Deaths, the Hijra and the Fate of Yathrib's Jews....................... 65
7. From Victory Over Medina's Jews to Victory Over Mecca.................... 85
8. Ultimate Victory, Death and Important Early Post-Mortem Events....... 101

Islam's Expansion and Impact on the Church

9. Islam Expunges the Church in Arabia... 113
10. Muslim Arabs and Turks Bring a Great Reversal for the Gospel in Central Asia... 127
11. The Church Flourished in Afghanistan Till the Turks Embraced Islam......... 137
12. The Church Through the Centuries in Afghanistan............................... 147
13. The Church in Iran Before the Coming of Islam................................... 159
14. The Church in Iran, From Triumph to Eclipse...................................... 171
15. A Twofold Attack on the Church in Egypt.. 191
16. Egypt's Church Shows Amazing Resilience.. 195
17. Christianity Survives Tempestuous Centuries in Egypt........................ 203
18. North African Christianity, Candidate for Tragedy.............................. 215
19. The Death of Organized North African Christianity............................ 229

Photo Section..237

20. Muslims Enticed by Iberia, Gateway to Europe..........................251
21. The Islamic Advance Into Spain...259
22. Catholicism Competes With Islam for Spain................................265
23. Catholicism Altered by Confrontation With Islam........................275
24. Islam's Impact on the Eastern Seaboard of the Mediterranean......281
25. From Predominance to A Tiny Minority..291
26. Islam's Impact on the Churches in Turkey....................................301
27. The Ottoman Turks Invited Into Europe..309
28. Answering Skeptics...319
29. The Future..333

Appendices

Appendix A   The Geography of the Arabian Peninsula......................357

Appendix B   The Armenian Genocide...371

Appendix C   The Spread of Islam in Southeast Asia and Sub-Saharan Africa. 387

Appendix D   The Rise of Shi'ism..391

Appendix E   The Five Pillars of Islam..397

Appendix F   Did Muhammad Have Access to Christian Scripture?..........401

Appendix G   The Magi and the Church 407

Appendix H   Highlights of Iranian History...417

Glossary, Atlas and Indexes

Glossary...453

Atlas..467

    Map 1, Trajan's Canal...469

    Map 2, Trajan's Roads & Other Pre-Islamic World Trade Routes.........471

    Map 3, Ethiopia 473

    Map 4, Competing Empires...475

    Map 5, Arabian Peninsula – Political Divisions & Geographic Features...477

    Map 6, Arabian Peninsula – Notable Settlements...............................479

    Map 7, Bab-el-Mandeb..481

    Map 8, The Persian Conquest of Eastern & Southern Arabia...............483

Map 9, Yemen – Dominating Southwestern Arabia..................485
Map 10, Arabia and the Horn of Africa..................487
Map 11, Islam's Two Early Efforts to Win China..................489
Map 12, Muslim Invasions of India..................491
Map 13, William Carey – The Bible for Hindu India..................493
Map 14, Henry Martyn – The Bible for Muslim India & Iran..................495
Map 15, Central Asia & Far Western China..................497
Map 16, The Conquest of the Levant..................499
Map 17, Muslim Invasion of Iran..................501
Map 18, Egypt..................503
Map 19, North Africa at the Time of the Muslim Conquest..................505
Map 20, Spain's Future Role..................507
Map 20, The Islamic Empire – The First 75 Years..................509
Map 22, The Turkish Assault on Europe Through the Balkans..................511

Map Index..................515
Index of Koranic References..................525
General Index..................529
About the Author..................567

INTRODUCTION

In the recent past, Graham E. Fuller, former vice chairman of the National Intelligence Council at the C.I.A., wrote, "It was Europeans who visited their 'world wars' twice upon the rest of the world—two devastating global conflicts with no remote parallels in Islamic history."[1]

Fuller's assertion is grossly and breathtakingly misguided and misleading. Blithely, he has completely disregarded the record of the vast Muslim conquest, followed by centuries-long occupation and suppression of the people they had defeated. Even a brief resume of Islamic conquest will show how egregiously mistaken Mr. Fuller's analysis is. In 1734 George Sale pointed out in his epochal translation of the Koran into English in his message "To The Reader" that Muhammad was the "founder of an empire which in less than a century spread itself over a greater part of the world than the Romans were ever masters of."[2]

Initially, Islam came to be a daunting world power as the result of a seventy-five-year (636–711 A.D.) ceaseless, unremitting conquest of an area stretching from the present southwestern border of India to the Atlantic seacoast of Morocco, 5,700 miles! Muslim forces, having crossed the Pyrenees mountain range shortly after their triumph over Spain, were only denied victory over Western Europe by the dramatic defeat they suffered in 732 A.D. at the hands of Charles Martel (Charles "The Hammer") and his troops near Tours, France.

Central Asia was brought under the yoke of Islam as a consequence of the Muslims' stunning victory over a Tang Dynasty Chinese army in 751 A.D. on the Talas River, in present-day Kyrgyzstan. Subsequently, the boundaries of the Muslim world were further expanded by war in northern India. That expansion began in the year 997 A.D. with the first of seventeen devastating, plundering raids carried out by Mahmud of Ghazni and his band of daring marauders. In 1526, Babur, founder of the great Mogul Empire, won victory over northern India at the Battle of Panipat on the Yamuna River. The power of that Muslim empire was not broken till 1757 by Great Britain at the Battle of Plassey in Bengal.

Western Asia Minor was occupied by the Sunni-Muslim Ottoman Turks following the Seljuk Turks' decisive victory over the Byzantines at the Battle of Manzikert in 1071. From Asia Minor, crossing the Dardanelles, the Ottoman Turks made a centuries-long effort to conquer Europe by an invasion route which followed the Danube River all the way to Vienna. On their way to Vienna, the Ottomans took time to conquer and subdue the Balkan Peninsula. The Serbs courageously tried to stop the Muslim onrush toward Europe. But the Serbian army was utterly destroyed by the Turks at the Battle of Kosovo in 1389. Chronologically, the next major Turkish Muslim conquest was the siege, overthrow and occupation

---

1 Graham E. Fuller, *A World Without Islam*, Foreign Policy, January/February, 2008, p. 53.
2 George Sale, Translator, The Koran, (Philadelphia: J. B. Lippincott & Co., 1867), p. v.

of Constantinople (magnificent capital of the Byzantine Empire) on May 29, 1453. At that point, the Muslim Turkish war machine seemed completely dominant and invincible.

In 1526 the Hungarians very courageously tried to block the Muslim Turkish juggernaut only to be disastrously defeated at the Battle of Mohacs. Three years later, in 1529, the victorious Turkish Muslim military machine was poised for triumph at the gates of Vienna, capital of the Hapsburg Empire. Miraculously, at that desperate moment, a strong Shia-Iranian attack on the eastern border of the Sunni Ottoman Empire saved Vienna. "Suleiman had his eastern edge problems, too, namely the Safavids with their claims to Islamic supremacy. The unruly borderlands between the two Islamic powers defied Ottoman control."[3] However, in 1683 the relentless Turkish Muslim predators were back, again trying to capture Vienna—the eastern doorway to Muslim victory over Europe. Providentially, by that time, military obsolescence and flabbiness had undermined the Muslims' war-making ability. With European assistance, Vienna successfully defended herself. The high water mark of Muslim military aggression in the west was finally past, at least for the then foreseeable future.

Many years later, Abdul Rahman Azzam Pasha, Secretary-General of the Arab League, faithfully revealed the Muslim mind about war and conquest in a stern exhortation to Abba Eban, the famous Jewish diplomat. Upbraiding him, he harshly said, "The Arab world regards the Jews [in Palestine] as invaders. It is going to fight you. War is absolutely inevitable. If you win the war, you will get your state. If you get your state by winning a war, you have a chance that the Arabs will one day have to accept it, although that is not certain. But do not consider for a single moment that you will ever have a chance of our accepting you in advance. This is a question of historic pride. There is no shame in being compelled by force to accept an unjust and undesirable situation. It is shameful to accept such a fact without attempting to prevent it. This conflict has its roots deep in history. There will have to be a decision; and the decision will have to be by force." Eban's response was classic, one Graham E. Fuller should hear: "He [Azzam] was appealing to the martial tradition that had given Islam its original impetus in world history."[4]

Languages, cultures, national economic structures, political entities and religions on three continents were all deeply impacted and very often obliterated by Islam's unprecedented international conquest. *Withering Wind From Arabia* tries to call attention to the major changes Islam brought about in all these areas. Its main focus, however, is on the fourteen-centuries-long impact which Islam has had on the followers of Christ, both individually and corporately. It starts with the inquiry about Islam's impact on the church in Arabia, the country which was the epicenter from which the withering winds began to blow.

---

3   Jane Burbank and Frederick Cooper, <u>Empires in World History</u>, (Princeton, NJ: Princeton University Press, 2010), p. 144.

4   Abba Eban, <u>Abba Eban: An Autobiography</u>, (New York: Random House, 1977), p. 86.

Introduction

The rise of the Muslim empire was so dramatic and so epochal that any rational explanation of the phenomenon must focus considerable attention, as *Withering Wind From Arabia* does, on the unique geopolitical circumstances prevailing at the time Islam began its stunning career. Similarly, any understanding of the sudden appearance of the Islamic empire must also focus attention on the charismatic genius who gave the movement its initial dynamic impetus. Accordingly, *Withering Wind From Arabia* attempts to portray the essence of the unique personality of Muhammad, the Arabian Prophet through whose tireless efforts Islam was launched on its long and currently ongoing career of conquest and suppression.

Scores of sources, many out-of-print and hard to find, have been consulted to compile this account of the impact Islam has had on the church in the vast area stretching from India to the Atlantic Ocean. Those documents have brought to light inspiring—but mostly long forgotten—spiritual exploits of Christians which they rendered in the long period stretching from the late post-apostolic period till those Christian communities were carried away by the fierce withering wind blowing from Arabia.

Those interested in the dawn of Muslim evangelism and expansion in Southeast Asia will find it began approximately from the beginning of the fourteenth century. David Bentley-Taylor notes that epochal development by telling us, "When Marco Polo was in Sumatra in 1293, he observed that the inhabitants were 'all savage idolaters, a very cruel and very evil people,' but he also saw a new development at Parlak in the north-east corner of the island where 'all the people used to worship idols, but by reason of the many Saracen[5] merchants who frequent there with their ships, they have converted them all to the abominable law of Muhammad.'"[6]

Appendix C in this book briefly discusses the spread of Islam in Southeast Asia and Sub-Saharan Africa. Further, rich information on the expansion of Islam in Southeast Asia is given by Robert W. Hefner, <u>Civil Islam, Muslims and Democratization in Indonesia</u>, (Princeton University Press, 2000). In 2016, three important publications regarding the situation in Indonesia appeared. The first is <u>Islamisation and Its Opponents in Java: A Political, Social, Cultural and Religious History, c. 1930 to the Present</u> by M.C. Ricklefs. The second book is <u>Islam in

---

5 Tom Holland, drawing his information from the work of D. F. Graf and M. O'Conner, entitled, *The Origin of the Term Saracen and the Rawwafa Inscriptions*, informs us that, "It is telling that Roman authors, from the fourth century onwards, begin to use a new word to designate the Arabs, one that seems ultimately to have derived from [the Arabic word] *Shirkat*: 'Saracens.' Although the Romans themselves appear to have been wholly ignorant of the original meaning, and although the stereotype they had of the 'Saracens' remained the reassuringly traditional one, of nomads, bandits and savages, the use they made of the new name did nevertheless hint at a new and emerging order." – Tom Holland, <u>In the Shadow of the Sword: The Battle for Global Empire and the End of the Ancient World</u>, (London: Little, Brown, 2012), p. 236. Nigel Cliff says, "While Constantinople stood impotently by, the truculent desert tribesmen it disparagingly labeled Saracens – 'the tent people' – had taken all the lands it had so recently reconquered, at such great cost." In an end note, Cliff tells us, "The term [Saracens] *sarakenoi* or *saraceni* originally referred to the non-Arab peoples of northern Arabia, but it was subsequently applied to Arabs and then to all Muslims. Its etymology is unclear, but by the fourth century the historian Ammianus Marcellinus noted that it was used to refer to the region's desert nomads." – Nigel Cliff, <u>Holy War</u>, (New York: Harper Collins, 2011), pp. 16, 426.
6 David Bentley-Taylor, <u>The Weathercock's Reward, Christian Progress in Muslim Java</u>, (London: Overseas Missionary Fellowship, 1967), p. 9.

Indonesia: The Contest for Society, Ideas and Values by Carool Kersten. The third volume is Islam and Democracy in Indonesia: Tolerance Without Liberalism by Jeremy Menchik. Over all, probably Ricklefs' publication is the most helpful of the three.

Uncharacteristically, in comparison with its entrance into western China, Islam made an ambivalent entrance into eastern China. On one hand, during the century following the rise of Islam, the Tang Empire was weakened by Islamic pirate attacks on the eastern Chinese seaboard as far north as Hangchow (modern Hangzhou in southeast China). At the same time, very early in the Muslim era, at Guangzhou, previously known as Canton, Muslims built a mosque known as The Lighthouse Mosque because the minaret was used as a navigational reference point by those sailing in the Taiwan Strait. That mosque still exists, having been rebuilt many times. However, Islam never seemed to have made significant inroads into China from that early Muslim toehold.[7]

In contrast, in far western China, in today's Xinjiang Province, major inroads by Islam were made by zealous Turkish converts who penetrated the area following the Battle of Talas in 751 A.D. The current Chinese government is still trying to blunt that ongoing cultural-ethnic-religious thrust by displacing the Turkish Uygur (Uighur) Muslim people by overwhelmingly resettling the province with Han Chinese colonists. Currently under Communist rule, the Uighur people have very restricted civil liberties.

Those seeking information on Islam's current brutal push to the south in Sub-Saharan Africa should first read Appendix C in this book. That information is wonderfully complemented by Eliza Griswold's rewarding book, The Tenth Parallel, Dispatches From the Faultline Between Christianity and Islam, (New York: Farrar, Straus and Giroux, 2010).

In commenting on "the vast increase in numbers of the [Muslim] faithful in Africa and the Indies," Paul Kennedy reminds us by his sobering evaluation that "the proselytization by Christian missions paled in comparison"[8] to that carried out by Islam. One significant reason it was comparatively so much more effective is that economics played a major role in Islamic proselytization. Islam very cunningly and forcefully used its economic dominance as a proselytizing tool. The unprecedented conquests by Muslim armies created a contiguous economic trading block, more extensive than any which had ever existed. That made the unhindered move-

---

7 Without revealing his sources, Wells gives an interesting historical background to the building of the Lighthouse Mosque. He tells of a "remarkable embassy [which] also came to the court of Tai-tsung in the year 628, seven years earlier than the Nestorians. This was a party of Arabs, who came by sea to Canton in a trading vessel from Yanbu, the port of Medina in Arabia. ... These Arabs had been sent by that Muhammad we have already mentioned, who styled himself 'the Prophet of God,' and the message they brought to Tai-tsung was probably identical with the summons which was sent in the same year to the Byzantine emperor Heraclius and to Kavadh in Ctesiphon. But the Chinese monarch neither neglected the message as Heraclius did, nor insulted the envoys after the fashion of the parricide Kavadh. He received them well, expressed great interest in their theological views, and assisted them, it is said, to build a mosque for the Arab traders in Canton—a mosque which survives to this day. It is one of the oldest mosques in the world." – H. G. Wells, The Outline of History, (New York: Doubleday & Co. Inc., 1971), Vol. I, p. 489.

8 Paul Kennedy, The Rise and Fall of the Great Powers, (New York: Random House, 1987), p. 9.

ment of goods and services and travel for entrepreneurs possible on a scale never before seen. The Islamic economic triumph, growing out of unprecedented military success, was in itself highly evangelistic in its impact. Traders and businessmen were willing to embrace a theology stunningly at odds with Christianity in order to be welcomed into the thriving international market created by Islam's military prowess.

The stunning post-World War II Islamic expansion into Europe and North America by massive immigration is not covered in this account. Those interested in the situation in Europe will find Christopher Caldwell's Reflections on the Revolution in Europe, Immigration, Islam and the West, (Doubleday, 2009), very rewarding. Also, George Weigel, a brilliant Roman Catholic commentator, gives many cogent insights in his The Cube and the Cathedral, (New York: Basic Books, 2005). A very recent and richly rewarding analysis of the impact and future of Islam on and in Europe is given by Douglas Murray in his The Strange Death of Europe, Immigration, Identity, Islam (New York: Bloomsbury Continuum, 2017).

Those interested in the situation in North America as well as in Europe, will find Tony Blankley's book informative: The West's Last Chance, Will We Win the Clash of Civilizations? (Regnery Publishing, 2005).

The overriding concern of this historical inquiry is not only chronicling the birth and fourteen-centuries-long expansion of Islam in our area of concentration, but especially emphasizing what happened to Christians and organized Christianity throughout the entire vast area, from India to the Atlantic, as Islam became dominant.

Note: There are many instances of variations in the English spelling of Arabic words. All are considered acceptable. For example, Kaaba vs. Ka'ba; or Koran vs. Qur'an. When in a quote, I have used the quoted author's spelling. When not in a quote I have tried to use the simplest spelling consistently throughout the book.

Students who are curious about how battle plans and dates have been established for the earliest periods of Muslim conquest should read the Preface and the Author's Note in John Bagot Glubb's The Great Arab Conquests.

○ℜ

The International Background

Chapter 1

ARABIA AND THE WIDER WORLD

Rome's End Run Around Arabia

Well before the Prophet Muhammad's birth in 570 A.D., a new and desperate era had dawned for Arabia. It began when the Roman emperor Trajan, who reigned 98–117 A.D., learned that a navigational breakthrough had become possible for Rome, due to newly acquired understanding of the unique seasonal monsoon winds in the Indian Ocean.

Realizing the rich commercial potential of the discovery, Trajan took the bold initiative of reopening and rerouting the ancient canal which had previously connected the Nile River with the Gulf of Suez. (See map, Trajan's Canal.) That would allow Roman merchants via the Red Sea, the Gulf of Aden and the Indian Ocean to have direct maritime commercial contact with India. It would open a truly new era because "regular commercial contacts by sea between India and the Western world are not attested until the first century A.D."[9] However, while it would become a new era of prosperity for Rome, it would prove to be one of stringency, poverty and desperation for Arabia.

Trajan had probably learned about the Indian Ocean monsoon winds from the *Periplus*,[10] an ancient seaman's guide. The Guide recorded the observations of Hippalus that the southwest and northeast monsoon winds were periodic, enabling "Arab and Indian ships to sail directly, and thus more quickly, from the Red Sea to India and back again virtually eliminating Arabia."[11] The phrase, "virtually eliminating Arabia" helps us understand the economic catastrophe which the Roman utilization of the monsoon winds would shortly bring upon the inhabitants of the great Arabian desert peninsula.

Wanting to totally dominate the greatly expanded trade which he anticipated, Trajan took care in A.D. 106 to eliminate competition by conquering Petra, the fabled rose-red capital city of the Nabataean kingdom. "This was just after Hippalus had discovered the use of the monsoon winds [which] had opened up a direct route to

---

9 Patricia Crone, <u>Meccan Trade And The Rise of Islam</u>, (Piscataway, N.J.: Gorgias Press, 2004), p. 30.
10 Literally, from the Greek, to sail around. *Peri*, around + *plein*, to sail.
11 Wendell Phillips, <u>Unknown Oman</u>, (New York: David McKay Company, Inc., 1966), p. 189.

India."[12] From the Nabataean kingdom, Trajan created the Roman province of Arabia.

Role of Petra

"From the end of the fourth century (B.C.) on, Petra became a key city on the caravan route, linking spice-producing South Arabia with the consuming and marketing centers in the north. It commanded the routes to the port of Gaza in the west, to Busra [also Bosra and Bostra][13] and Damascus in the north, to Aila (the Nabataean port on the north shore of the Gulf of Aqaba about three kilometers east of ancient Ezion-Geber[14]) on the Red Sea, and to the Persian Gulf across the desert. In it [that is, in Petra] the relays of camels were provided."[15]

In addition to the Red Sea-Arabia trade, there was an important additional dimension of the trade through this once great entrepot. According to "evidence from Chinese sources of commerce with the West … in 128 and 91 B.C., it is clear that much, if not all of the Chinese silk was sent by sea from the Persian Gulf to the Nabataean Arabs at their ports on the Red Sea, and so to Petra and through to Palestine and Syria."[16] Petra was important not only economically, but also linguistically: "Arabic, a Semitic language, descends from Nabataean, the language spoken in ancient Petra."[17]

Wealth Allures

"Stories of the great wealth of Petra soon caused the Romans to cast covetous eyes in that direction. Two or three attempts to capture the city failed completely, though the Nabataeans as a nation were made to pay tribute. But with all its inaccessibility, it could not hold out against the might of Rome, and in A.D. 106 Petra with all its territory became a Roman Province. The Emperor Trajan built a great road, which passed through Petra, connecting Syria with the Red Sea. Under Roman rule Petra prospered greatly, and some of the finest monuments date from this period. … More and more wealth was lavished on the city, foreign craftsmen were brought in to embellish and beautify it, and it became one of the wonders of the world."[18]

But, "Rome … was getting ready to measure swords with that great Asiatic power, Parthia. No semi-independent power could be tolerated in between. All intermediary states must come within the full embrace of the empire. … In the following year [107 B.C.] Nabataea became a part of the Roman province of Arabia, with Busra as the leading city and later as the capital. Arabia Petraea was no

---

12 De Lacy O'Leary, History of Arabia Before Muhammad, (Lahore, Pakistan: Alliance Publishers, 1989), p. 181.
13 The ruins are near a village in SW Syria. Known to the Romans as Bostra, it became the capital of the Roman province of Arabia. (See Webster's New Geographical Dictionary.)
14 See Numbers 33:35-36 et al.
15 Philip K. Hitti, History of Syria, (London: Macmillan & Co., Ltd., 1957), p. 377.
16 George Every, Understanding Eastern Christianity, (London: SCM Press Ltd., 1978), p. 21.
17 Alexander Bevilacqua, The Republic of Arabic Letters, (Cambridge, MA: The Belknap Press, 2018), p. 116.
18 Author not given, Petra A Brief History & Some Photographs, (Amman, Jordan: Jordan Distribution Agency, 1973), pp. 31-32.

more. Its picturesque and opulent capital, 'a rose red city half as old as Time,' was pushed into the limbo of history, whence it had come. The east-to-west trade route shifted north to Palmyra, the south-to-north moved east to where the Moslem pilgrimage road and the modern Hijaz railway lie."[19] Petra's glory was past.

The eastern mouth of Trajan's Canal opened just opposite the port of Clysma (sometimes also called Qulzum/Culzum), situated at the north-east tip of the Gulf of Suez.[20] Except for its somewhat new route, Trajan's engineering essentially duplicated the work which had been done centuries earlier by the Persian emperor Darius I (550–486 B.C.) who had dug "a canal connecting the Nile with the Red Sea."[21]

Even before the Romans greatly enhanced their trade by their revolutionary utilization of the monsoon winds, "Roman trade with India was so great that Pliny the Elder [23 A.D.–79 A.D.] complained that India was draining Roman gold reserves. Sea routes then continued [from India] to the Malay Peninsula and the Indonesian Islands [where] traders searched for spices for the Roman market."[22]

The validity of Pliny's concern is made clear from the ruins of a Roman trading station near Pondicherry in India. There, "natives, digging around in the mud, still from time-to-time unearth fascinating fragments. ... One must have seen [those artifacts] and heard all of [the stories of] this [discovery] if one is really to understand the history of the exchanges between India and the Roman Empire in the first centuries of the Christian era."[23]

Both Parthian Persia and Arabia Impacted

Following the Battle of Actium in 31 B.C., Rome's ongoing eastward expansion, even more decisively, brought her face-to-face with the Parthian-Persian Empire (See Acts 2:9.). Romans found the Persians to be resolute, resourceful and an implacable enemy. Many thrusts against the Persians not only proved to be fruitless but often disastrous. The most unforgettable example of those disasters took place in 52 B.C., well before the Battle of Actium. It ended with the total defeat of the Roman army and the capture and execution of Crassus, the Roman Triumver under whom the Romans were waging that war.

---

19 Philip K. Hitti, <u>History of Syria</u>, (London: Macmillan & Co., Ltd., 1957), p. 382.
20 "Details of the construction of the first navigable canal linking the Nile with the Red Sea are lost in the mists of antiquity. Tradition claims that it was Sesostris, a Pharaoh of the Twelfth Dynasty (*circa* 2000 B.C.), who first set his hand to this enterprise. At intervals, certainly, during the next thousand years, such a canal was available to shipping: It is remembered as the Canal of the Pharaohs." – Hugh J. Schonfield, <u>The Suez Canal in Peace And War 1869–1969</u>, (Coral Gables, Florida: University of Miami Press, 1969), p. 3.
21 Ian Barnes & Robert Hudson, <u>The History Atlas of Asia</u>, (New York: Macmillan, 1998), p. 29.
22 Ian Barnes & Robert Hudson, <u>The History Atlas of Asia</u>, (New York: Macmillan, 1998), p. 37.
23 Auguste Toussaint, <u>History of the Indian Ocean</u>, (Chicago: The University of Chicago Press, 1966), p. 36. Wells concurs saying, "Roman Alexandrian merchants had numerous settlements in south India. At Cranganore on the Malabar Coast there was a temple dedicated to Augustus, and the settlement was defended by two Roman cohorts. Embassies were sent from the Emperor to various South Indian potentates." – H.G. Wells, <u>The Outline of History</u>, (New York: Doubleday & Co., Inc., 1971), Vol. 1, p. 325.

While several of Rome's thrusts against the land border with Iran proved to be costly failures, Trajan's decision to utilize the Indian Ocean monsoon winds became a major successful strategy against Parthian Iran. As Toussaint has pointed out, "The impact of Trajan's decision was not limited to Arabia, because by encouraging and developing sea trade, the Roman Empire diverted to its own channel the enormous revenue which the Parthians [had previously] derived from trade by land. Although Rome did not succeed in overthrowing the Parthians, she did, in this way deal them an indirect blow and seriously weakened them."[24]

In addition to the purely economic consequences which Rome's new Indian Ocean trade was destined to have on Arabia, this new "opening up of direct maritime relations between India and the Western world made Arabia [more] vulnerable to imperialism."[25] Fires of competition flared between the two "super powers" which bordered Arabia at that time, Parthian Iran and Western Rome. As Western Rome was later superseded in 330 A.D. by Byzantine Rome, similarly, in 226 A.D., Parthian Iran was supplanted by Sassanian Iran. However, these epochal changes in no way diminished the endemic East/West rivalry impacting Arabia.

Both Iran and Rome strove to bring Arabia into their respective orbits. For example, both empires salivated over rich silver deposits which had been discovered in the Najd area of Arabia. Also, the imperial fires of covetousness were further stoked by each empire's idolatrous desire to collect the rich rewards of being the main, or preferably the sole, middleman-merchant between East and West. The goal was to dominate or outflank Arabia. Additionally, both empires wanted to enhance that potentially extravagant income by also setting rates for and collecting lucrative tariffs on all East/West cargoes carried by others.

Pre-Islamic Arabia

For untold centuries prior to the birth of Islam, the energies of the tribes of Arabia were wasted on inter-tribal feudal warfare. Periodically, Arabian tribesmen also raided the sedentary people living in towns and villages both in Arabia and on Arabia's borders with the Persian and Byzantine Empires. This is not surprising because, "'intrigue and assassination, revolt and riot, and wars great and small' had haunted Arab history."[26]

That historic inter-tribal Arabian warfare, at least in part, stemmed from a long-standing quirk in the Arabian psyche. "The great Arab philosopher-historian Ibn Khaldun, himself a South Arabian by descent, said in the 14th century: 'Every Arab considers himself worthy to rule and it is rare to find one of them submitting to another, be it his father or brother or the head of his clan.' The unity generated against a commonly recognized foe—against, for instance, imperialism … breaks down when the reason for it disappears just as the unity generated by an idea

---

24 Auguste Toussaint, History of the Indian Ocean, (Chicago: The University of Chicago Press, 1966), p. 41.
25 Patricia Crone, Meccan Trade and the Rise of Islam, (Piscataway, N.J.: Gorgias Press, 2004), p. 45.
26 Michael B. Oren, Power, Faith, and Fantasy, America in the Middle East, 1776 to the Present, (New York: W.W. Norton & Company, 2007), p. 408.

does."²⁷ A former president of Syria confirmed Ibn Khaldun's analysis by saying, "Fifty percent of my people consider themselves leaders, twenty-five percent think they are prophets and ten percent think they are Gods."²⁸

The tendency noted by Ibn Khaldun and by the president of Syria was often exacerbated through greed, hatred and bravado. For example, during the Ottoman period of Arabian history, even bribery was ineffective in many cases in the attempt to wean the tribes away from pillaging raids against their fellow Arabs.

Great Empires Protected by Client Tribes

Arabian tribal raids on Byzantium and Sassanian Iran, the two empires to the north, were not a major concern to either Iran or Byzantium because those raids were routinely intercepted and deflected by client Arabian tribes on the borders of both empires. Specifically, "in eastern Syria and Damascus, the princely family of Beni Ghassan held sway, the head of the family enjoying the title of a Roman patrician. On the lower Euphrates, the Arab Lakhmids were subject princes of the Great [Persian] King. ... This system of Arab satellite princedoms guarding the desert flanks of both empires broke down, by a curious coincidence, a few years before the Muslim invasions."²⁹

The reason for the defection of the Arab tribes guarding Byzantium and Iran is well known. The Byzantine historian Theophanes (d. 818) wrote, "There were some of the nearby Arabs who received small money allowances from the emperors for guarding the 'gateways' of the desert. ... [On one occasion] a certain eunuch came to give their allowance to the soldiers, and the Arabs arrived to collect their stipend as usual. The Eunuch drove them away, saying that the ruler had scarcely enough pay for his soldiers, much less his dogs. ... Another Byzantine historian, Nicephorus, [wrote] ... He [one of the courtiers] induced Heraclius not to accede to sending the Saracens their customary allowance of thirty pounds of gold in commercial exchange [that is, in the form of commodities worth thirty pounds of gold] from the Roman government; henceforward they began to inflict outrages on Roman territory."³⁰

Simultaneously, a similar estrangement had alienated the client Lakhmid Arabs from their patron, the Sassanian Iranians. Thus, ominously, just at the time the tribes of Arabia, unified by Islam, surged out of their desert lair, the borders of both Iran and Byzantium were unprotected. The refusal of Sassanian Iran and Byzantine Rome to pay their clients grew out of their exhaustion from the twenty-six-year war they had waged against each other, from 602 to 628 A.D.

---

27 Harold Ingrams, <u>The Yemen Imams, Rulers & Revolutions</u>, (London: John Murray, 1963), p. 4.
28 Abram L. Sachar, <u>The Course of Our Times</u>, (New York: Alfred A. Knopf, 1972), p. 565.
29 John Glubb, <u>A Short History of the Arab Peoples</u>, (New York: Stein and Day, 1970), pp. 23-24.
30 F.E. Peters, <u>Muhammad and the Origins of Islam</u>, (Albany, New York: State University of New York Press, 1994), p. 232.

Energies Not Focused

Another significant reason why those perpetual raids historically had not been a major concern to either Persia or Byzantium was that the Arab tribes lacked the energy and dynamism that develops only from unity. They raided as single tribes or as ephemeral tribal alliances, consisting of only a few tribes. The lack of Arabian unity and national focus were ultimately overcome by the dynamic and charismatic leadership of the Prophet Muhammad. He unified Arabia for the first time in all history, transforming it into a major player in world affairs, impacting the destiny of many nations.

Unique Arabian Military Leaders Emerge

Despite Arabia's apparent total military insignificance, out of centuries of perpetual internal tribal warfare and border raids against the Persians and Byzantines, a cadre of elite militarily-capable Arabians emerged at the dawn of the early Islamic period.[31] They were skilled military leaders, largely inured to the sacrifices, sorrows and hardships of war, who could successfully lead large-scale operations. For example, in the year 629, "one of the most important results of Muhammad's increasing prestige ... was the conversion of Khalid ibn al Waleed, Amr ibn al Aasi and Othman ibn Talha. It was Khalid and Amr who ... were to become the greatest military commanders of the Muslims."[32]

Three Dominant Empires

At the dawn of Islam, world affairs were dominated by three great empires, two of which, Byzantine Rome and Sassanian Iran, shared borders with Arabia–Byzantium on the northwest and Iran on the northeast. Though having no common border with Arabia, China, the third world empire, controlled Central Asia and tried to block Islam's expansion into the vast, rich areas between the Pamir-Hindu Kush mountain complexes and the Caspian Sea. The area between those mountain ranges and the Caspian Sea is Central Asia.

The Byzantine Empire (330 A.D.–1453 A.D.), founded by Constantine, became heir and successor to the Western Roman Empire. It was a maritime empire with its capital, Constantinople, bounded on three sides by the sea: the Sea of Marmara to the south and east, the Golden Horn to the north and the Bosporus to the northeast. It dominated the shores of the Mediterranean and Black Seas along with those of their interconnecting waterways. Byzantium survived 1123 years, till

---

31 The rise of a martial people was indeed a great change. "After the rise of Roman power, covetous eyes were turned upon the wealth and trade which Arabia Felix had so long enjoyed. An invasion based on Egypt was organized under the Roman general Aelius Gallus in 24 B.C. According to the Greek geographer Strabo, no difficulty was anticipated because 'the Arabians, being engaged mostly in traffic and commerce, are not a warlike people.' Strabo reported further that 'the barbarians were entirely inexperienced in war and used their weapons unskillfully, which were bows, swords and slings; but the greater part of them used a double-edged ax.'" – Roy Lebkicher, George Rentz, Max Steineke, Aramco Handbook, (Arabian American Oil Company, 1960), p. 36.
32 John Bagot Glubb, The Great Arab Conquests, (London: Quartet Books, 1980), pp. 90-91.

conquered by the Muslim Ottoman Turks in 1453 who, after their stunning victory, renamed Constantinople as Istanbul and made it their capital.

The Sassanian Empire (226 A.D.–642 A.D.) was successor to the Persian Parthian Empire. Though it controlled the Persian Gulf, giving it access to the Indian Ocean, it did not fully utilize that great waterway. It was, therefore, principally, a land-based empire. It controlled the whole extensive region from the Indian border to the hinterland of the Mediterranean where it came up against the international border with Byzantium. Its moment on the stage of history lasted 416 years, till 642 A.D. when the Islamic lightning bolt, at the Battle of Nehawand, sent it reeling into oblivion.

The Sassanian capital was Medain. The name is the plural form of *medina*, the Arabic word meaning city. The plural form was appropriate because the capital consisted of two cities facing each other on opposite banks of the Tigris River, Ctesiphon on the east bank and Seleucia, former eastern capital of the Seleucid Empire, on the west bank. A large portion of the soaring brick-roofed vault and massive walls of the Sassanian emperor's magnificent palace, built in A.D. 550, located in present-day Iraq, are still standing.

The Tang Chinese Empire (618 A.D.–907 A.D.) was ruled from Chang'an, its principal capital city. At that time it was arguably the largest city in the world.[33] In the century following the rise of Islam, the Tang Empire was weakened because of incessant attacks by Turkish tribes from the north and, eventually, by Islamic pirate attacks on the eastern Chinese seaboard, as far north as Hangchow. Earlier, during a period of stunning expansion which lasted from 140 to 87 B.C., the Han military leader, "Ban Chao led an expedition [to the west] across the Pamirs, with the intention of establishing a direct contact with the Roman Empire. Although he failed in his mission, he nevertheless got as far as the Caspian Sea, the farthest point ever reached by the Chinese in their westward expansion."[34]

Amy Chua tells us that "by combining Turkic and Chinese forces, Taizong [Second Tang emperor, ruled 626–649 A.D.] extended Tang control throughout Central Asia and across the Pamir Mountains into modern-day Afghanistan. Samarkand, Bukhara, and Tashkent all became Chinese administrative districts. Tibet and Turkic tribes as far west as the Caspian Sea submitted to Chinese suzerainty. ... Taizong's successors further extended Tang rule, engulfing ... parts of present-day Iran."[35]

China's westward expansion seems to have been largely successful because "between 747 and 749, Chinese troops campaigned on the frontiers of India and claimed lordship over both Kabul and Kashmir; then, after 751, when Moslems

---

33 There seems to have been a fluctuating contest for the title of "largest city in the world." Burbank and Cooper write: "in Augustus's time, the city [of Rome] had a population of about a million—edging out the Chinese capital Chang'an (unknown to the Romans) as the most populous city on earth." – Jane Burbank and Frederick Cooper, Empires in World History, (Princeton: Princeton University Press, 2010), p. 35.

34 Ian Barnes & Robert Hudson, The History Atlas of Asia,, (New York: Macmillan, 1998), p. 47.

35 Amy Chua, Day of Empire, (New York: Doubleday, 2007), p. 68.

annihilated a Chinese expeditionary force in the battle of the Talas River, T'ang control of Central Asia collapsed."[36] (For further information on the Battle of Talas, please see Chapter 10, "A Plea to the Chinese" and also under "The Nestorian Monument" in Chapter 11.)

After their defeat on the Talas River, in present day Kyrgyzstan, China could not adequately seal its new western border, defined by the Pamir mountain range. Subsequently, Islamic ideology powerfully penetrated western China. Consequently, the predominant Uighur Turks in far western China's Sinkiang Province, who previously had embraced Manichaeism but before that had been "Christianized for several hundred years, were taken over by Islam. The Silk Road, along which Aluoben[37] and his delegation had traveled [to China], was now in hands unfriendly to Christianity."[38]

The Role of Ethiopia, a Second-Tier Empire

Leading up to the emergence of Islam, Ethiopia, though not in the same league as the Byzantine, the Sassanian and the Tang Empires, played a critical role in the affairs of Southwest Arabia.

Contest For Control of Bab-el-Mandeb (The Door of Tears)

The contest for control of Bab-el-Mandeb, the narrow strait connecting the Red Sea through the Gulf of Aden to the Indian Ocean, began when Yemen colonized ancient Ethiopia, then known both as Axum (Aksum) and Abyssinia. "In this case the colonists ['in the middle of the first millennium B.C.'] had crossed the [Red] sea from Yemen, bringing with them their language and culture, which likewise included an alphabetic script. ... The core of the Ethiopian population still speaks languages derived from that of the Yemenite colonists and uses a version of the script they brought with them from Yemen, where it died out more than a thousand years ago."[39] The surviving ancient Semitic-Yemenite-derivative language, spoken in both Ethiopia and Eritrea, is *Ge'ez*. Barthelemy d'Herbelot, in writing his great work *Bibliotheque Orientale* (the Oriental library), had access to Ge'ez manuscripts in the de' Medici's library in Florence.[40]

The invasion of Ethiopia by Yemen initiated a centuries-long back and forth, tit-for-tat contest for the control of the two-way sea traffic between the Indian Ocean and the Red Sea. All of that trade was destined to pass through a critical strait, a

---

36 William H. McNeill, <u>The Rise of the West, A History of the Human Community</u>, (Chicago: The University of Chicago Press, 1991), p. 463.
37 The name is also spelled Alopen. He was the first known Christian evangelist to take the Gospel to China. See additional descriptions in Chapters 11 and 13. While there are faint indications in history that the apostle Thomas sailed from southern India on an evangelistic trip to China, there is no solid evidence to corroborate such an assertion.
38 David Aikman, <u>Jesus in Beijing, How Christianity Is Transforming China and Changing the Global Balance of Power</u>, (Washington, DC: Regnery Publishing, Inc., 2003), p. 24.
39 Michael Cook, <u>A Brief History of The Human Race</u>, (New York: W.W. Norton & Company, 2003), pp. 108-109.
40 See Alexander Bevilacqua, <u>The Republic of Arabic Letters</u>, (Cambridge, MA: The Belknap Press, 2018), p. 115.

choke point, called Bab-el-Mandeb, Arabic meaning "door of tears." Sometimes in English it is called the Strait of Mandeb.[41]

Pre-Orthodox Ethiopia Invades Arabia

In or about the third century A.D., before the Byzantine form of Christianity had become their state religion, the tide turned and Ethiopia (ancient Abyssinia), invaded Yemen and, till about 523 A.D., controlled all of southwestern Arabia.[42]

Prior to that point, the city of Axum was the "capital of an ancient Ethiopian kingdom known as the Axumite Empire which was ruled by Himyaritic [i.e. Yemeni] emigrants from Arabia, in the 1st and 2nd centuries A.D."[43] In vengeance, the pre-Byzantine-Christian Ethiopians invaded South Arabia, presumably to wrest control of both sides of Bab-el-Mandeb, the eighteen-mile-wide strait separating southwestern Yemen from Africa.

Later, after having become Orthodox Christians, the Ethiopians again invaded South Arabia, in or about 525 A.D.[44] In between the first and second Ethiopian invasions of Yemen, a Jewish political entity, backed by Iran, had come to power in Yemen.[45] The reason for the second Ethiopian invasion of Yemen was not only to re-establish its control of sea traffic through Bab-el-Mandeb, but also to relieve the suffering and persecution of the Yemeni Christians being perpetrated by Dhu Nuwas, the Iranian-backed Jewish king of Yemen. Quite certainly, this second invasion had Byzantine support.

The Coming of Orthodoxy to Abyssinia

While Ethiopia was holding imperial sway in western and southwestern Arabia, the Orthodox form of Christianity was accepted as the empire's official religion by its rulers reigning from their capital at Axum. "The evidence is very strong that by the middle of the fourth century ... there was a Christian kingdom in Abyssinia."[46] That development ultimately brought the influence and impact of Orthodox Christianity to southwestern Arabia as well. That, however, was not the only impact of Orthodoxy on Yemen. The Byzantine Emperor, Constantius, also

---

41 For additional details about Bab-el-Mandeb see Appendix A.
42 This information comes from "a commercial traveler from Alexandria named Cosmas [who was] in Adulis [the sea port of Abyssinia] in 518 A.D. At the request of the then Abyssinian king he copied down an inscription on a throne there and published it in his *Christian Topography*. ... It seems likely that the inscription is Axumite and belongs to the era before the Christianization of Axum [ancient name of Abyssinia or Ethiopia as well as its capital city]. ... So by the third century, Axum was rich and powerful enough to possess a fleet and even overseas possessions in Arabia. Indeed, the Adulis inscription copied by Cosmas says quite clearly that the king of Axum had conquered and was taking tribute from the entire west coast of Arabia." – F.E. Peters, Muhammad and the Origins of Islam, (Albany, New York: State University of New York Press, 1994), pp. 41-42.
43 Webster's New Geographical Dictionary, (Springfield, Massachusetts: G.&C. Merriam Company, 1980), p. 19.
44 Consult Patricia Crone, Meccan Trade And The Rise of Islam, (Piscataway, N.J.: Gorgias Press, 2004), pp. 47-48.
45 "The Jews in Yemen in the fourth century strongly resisted Christian missionary propaganda and wielded considerable influence over the royal house. ... Stone tables discovered in Yemen indicate a gradual Judaization of the royal household, which reached its peak when the Jewish Tubba Dhu Nuwas, 'Lord of the Forelock,' ascended the throne." – Dana Adams Schmidt, Yemen, The Unknown War, (New York: Holt, Rinehart and Winston, 1968), p. 104.
46 F. E. Peters, Muhammad and the Origins of Islam, (Albany, New York: State University of New York Press, 1994), p. 44.

sent missionaries, who held diplomatic status, to bring the message of Orthodoxy to Southwest Arabia.

"By the sixth century, it was the Ethiopians who conducted most of the eastern trade of the Byzantines. ... The role of ... the Ethiopians [in the exchange of goods between Byzantium and the east] is well attested; and [the Ethiopian port of] Adulis [on the western shore of the Red Sea] was certainly far better known to the Greeks as an emporium than was Aden."[47] It is completely clear that in the immediate pre-Islamic period of history, Ethiopia was not the landlocked country it is today. Its Red Sea ports were allotted to Eritrea at the time of the separation of the two countries, May 24, 1993.

Prior to losing its sea ports to Eritrea, Ethiopia granted control of its sea port in Djibouti to France in a series of agreements beginning in 1897. The Republic of Djibouti became independent June 27, 1977. It now has a Chinese naval base and a U.S. Air Force base. Recently the Chinese rebuilt and modernized the railroad from the city of Djibouti to Addis Ababa, Ethiopia which had originally been built by France but had fallen out of service due to obsolescence and disrepair.

Byzantium's direct colonization in the Arabian Peninsula reached only to Tabuk, about 65 miles south of the present-day Jordanian border with northwest Saudi Arabia. However, "their sphere of influence was felt throughout western Arabia from the Syrian Desert where they had client kings [all the way] to the Yemen where their Ethiopian allies ruled [after they had defeated Dhu Nuwas] until they were outed by the Persians. Muhammad's Arabia had thus been subjected to foreign rule on a scale unparalleled even in modern times:"[48]

How Orthodoxy Came to Yemen

To further understand how the Byzantine concept of Christianity, known as Orthodoxy, came to Yemen, also called Himyar, we must rely upon "the fifth century Greek church historian, Philostorgius. ... [He recorded that] Constantius [emperor of Byzantium, who reigned 337–361 A.D.][49] sent ambassadors to the people once called the Sabeans and now named Himyarites. ... Its capital [was] Saba, whose queen once journeyed to visit Solomon. ... It was to them that Constantius sent an embassy with the intent of leading them to the true faith."[50]

While Christianity was found in many places in pre-Islamic Arabia, even in Mecca itself, Browne accurately tells us, "the most important Christian settlement in

---

47 Patricia Crone, Meccan Trade and the Rise of Islam, (Piscataway, N.J.: Gorgias Press, 2004), pp. 40-42.
48 Patricia Crone, Meccan Trade and the Rise of Islam, (Piscataway, N.J.: Gorgias Press, 2004), p. 246.
49 This was Constantius II, second son of Constantine the Great, ... had many conflicts with Persians; disastrously defeated by them (348) – Webster's New Biographical Dictionary.
50 F.E. Peters, Muhammad and the Origins of Islam, (Albany, New York: State University of New York Press, 1994), pp. 44-45. There is some disagreement about the date when Ethiopia embraced the Orthodox faith. For example, John Reader says, "The Aksum king's conversion to Christianity [took place] in the third century AD. The Orthodox faith adopted by the Aksumites is followed throughout Ethiopia to this day, unchanged by either the religious disputes of classical and medieval times, or the political upheavals of the twentieth century." [John Reader, Africa A Biography of the Continent, (New York: Alfred A. Knopf, 1998), p.208.] Reader gives no source for his date; probably the date based on Philostorgius' history should be accepted.

Arabia proper was [in] the town of Najran, on the northern border of Yaman [Yemen]. ... It is not clear how Christianity came to Najran. Though it does not seem that Ethiopian missionaries were the messengers, even so, the Najrani Christians did not refuse on the basis of color to cooperate with the black Ethiopians. Other places in Yaman [Yemen], and even in Hadramaut [Hadramawt/Hadhramaut],[51] had Christian communities. Muslim historians tell of a great church [building] at San'a, a city about halfway between Najran and Aden. The capital of the Himyarite kingdom had been moved to San'a from Ma'rib, probably in the fifth century when the great dyke of Ma'rib burst."[52]

A Four-Way Tug of War in Southwest Arabia

The Southwest Arabian Peninsula had become a vortex in which four contenders struggled for supremacy: (1) Ancient Ethiopia (Abyssinia) was expansionist and impacted Southwest Arabia both for Byzantium and on its own behalf. (2) Militant Judaism, which at this time was strong in Yemen, was also striving for a significant role. "The royal house of Himyar, and likely most of the nobility, was Jewish ... in the mid-fifth century."[53] (3) Opportunist Zoroastrian Iran, at the same time, sought to exercise significant influence in Yemen, while (4) Byzantium, working principally through its ally or client, Ethiopia, also sought control.

In addition to these national rivalries, the question of color or skin pigmentation also became an issue. The soldiers from Abyssinia were black and on that basis, in addition to being invaders, were hated by the Yemenis. That hatred spilled over to anyone who cooperated with Ethiopian black Christians, as Yemeni and Najrani non-black Arab Christians did.

Unexpected Developments

The eruption of Islam's powerful economic-religious-political-military movement out of the Arabian Peninsula proved to be a truly epochal development. However, the true nature of the Islamic entity was generally unrecognized even by most of those who suffered from its initial impact. One exception was Sophronius, patriarch of Jerusalem, who somehow understood that this was something far more significant than one of the perennial tribal raids which the areas bordering Arabia on the north had borne for centuries. These new incursions had made travel, even the short distance from Jerusalem to Bethlehem, impossible. From his pulpit, Sophronius named the invaders "Saracens" [see Introduction, footnote 5] and called attention to the widespread plunder already experienced by some monasteries and towns of Palestine. In a sermon on Christmas Eve in 634 he warned that the Saracens were boasting "that they would conquer the entire world."[54]

---

51 The ancient name for the eastern half of Yemen. Probably named after Hadoram, Genesis 10:27.
52 Laurence E. Browne, The Eclipse of Christianity in Asia From the Time of Muhammad Till the Fourteenth Century, (Cambridge: The University Press, 1933), p. 11.
53 F.E. Peters, Muhammad and the Origins of Islam, (Albany, New York: State University of New York Press, 1994), p. 49.
54 Dore Gold, The Fight for Jerusalem, (Washington DC: Regnery Publishing, Inc., 2007), p. 95.

Heraclius, emperor of Byzantium (reigned 610–641 A.D.), was in a position to have successfully confronted these new marauders and to have destroyed their power base, but he gave his attention to other concerns. Astonishingly, though a military genius, he continued to be distracted even after his forces had been decisively defeated by the Arabs in the Battle of Ajnadain in 634. Roughly, that battlefield was halfway between Hebron and the sea.[55]

The Islamic movement has proven to be the greatest peril the church has ever faced. Though waxing and waning during the long centuries which have elapsed since its birth, Islam clearly remains very much alive, in no way being a spent force. On the contrary, since World War II it has gained enormous strength and momentum. With renewed vigor it continues, worldwide, to threaten the church and its mission.

An Incontrovertible Reality

While many issues about Islam are controversial—such as the compilation of the Koran and the Hadith[56] and their interpretation—history proves, entirely beyond doubt, that in a mere 75 years an enormous Islamic empire had come into being, dominating the world scene. That empire stretched from the present western boundary of India all the way to the Atlantic coast of Morocco, engulfing vast areas from three continents (Asia, Africa and Spain in Europe)! From east to west it spanned a distance of some 5,700 miles, approximately twice the distance one travels crossing the United States of America!

That sprawling Islamic empire engulfed many of the greatest biblical and early post-biblical centers of Christianity, including Jerusalem, birthplace of the church, and Antioch, the base from which evangelism of the Western Roman Empire, north of the Mediterranean, was launched. Looking to the east, large numbers of well-established churches were to be found throughout the area covered by the present-day countries of Jordan, Iraq, Iran, Afghanistan and to some degree, in the five newly-independent Central Asian countries.[57] Those countries, formerly Soviet Republics, are: Kazakhstan, Kyrgyzstan, Tajikistan, Turkmenistan and Uzbekistan.[58]

Looking to the west from Antioch, along the northern shore of the Mediterranean, churches were well established all the way to and including Spain. On the southern seaboard of the Mediterranean, Christianity had come into an overwhelmingly dominant role all the way from Egypt to the Atlantic. Though there is no biblical account of the dramatic expansion of Christianity in North Africa, we do have the

---

55 For details on this battle, see John Bagot Glubb, The Great Arab Conquests, (London: Quartet Books, 1980), pp. 144-146.
56 The word *hadith* means tradition. Its meaning in Islamic history and theology is the account of the actions or sayings of Muhammad and his companions. Also, the whole body of sacred Tradition of the Muslims is called "*the hadith.*"
57 For those wanting information on Christianity in the five Central Asian "stan" countries, see Philip Jenkins, The Lost History of Christianity, (New York: Harper Collins, 2008), p. 45 ff.
58 The area covered by these five present-day countries didn't feel the full impact of Islam till after the Battle of Talas in 751. At that point the whole area was wrested from the Tang Dynasty of China which had up to that time exercised hegemony all the way to the Caspian Sea.

tantalizing account of men from Cyrene who came to Antioch and preached Christ to Greeks in that city. (Acts 11:20)

A series of stunning military triumphs made the new Islamic empire the dominant world power by the opening years of the eighth century. At that point, it had engulfed most of the Christian part of the world, except that segment north of the Mediterranean. Those triumphs took place in the brief period from the Second Battle of the Yarmuk in 636 A.D. to the occupation of Spain in the west and the province of Sindh in the east, now in southern Pakistan, both by 711 A.D.

As a consequence, churches by the hundreds died and extensive Christian communities shriveled and vanished! Reasons? Exorbitant and discriminatory taxes, extreme social and economic restrictions, unequal standing before the law, prohibition of Christian evangelism and heavy restrictions on the practice of one's Christian faith. The following chapters show that all of this resulted from the withering wind which blew from Arabia.

ଔ

Chapter 2

THE CONTEST FOR SOUTHWEST ARABIA

Superpower Contest Impacts Arabia

As long as Rome, governing either from the Tiber or from the Bosporus, dominated the Red Sea and Bab-el-Mandeb, the Door of Tears, (the bottle-neck connecting the Red Sea through the Gulf of Aden to the Indian Ocean), it controlled the critical choke point of the southern branch of the world's east-west maritime trade. Rome's control of the Red Sea-Indian Ocean route gave her an end-run around both Iran and Arabia. She also controlled the northern segment of international waterborne trade: the Black Sea/Bosporus/Dardanelles/Mediterranean route.

Iran, Byzantium's greatest imperial enemy, was left with control of only the middle portion of the fabled Silk Road, the multi-branched land-based trade route stretching all the way from China to the border of Byzantium. Until the rise of Islam, Arabia proved entirely incapable of breaking the Roman stranglehold on the southern branch of international seaborne commerce. But Iran, in defiance, set bold plans in motion to gain control of Bab-el-Mandeb, in an attempt to deny Rome its long-standing competitive advantage.

The Persian scheme was so urgent and intuitive that it was pursued by a succession of emperors over several centuries. Beginning to implement their strategic plan, "Ardashir I (226–241 A.D.) [the first emperor of the Sassanian Dynasty] subjected the [Persian] Gulf … [and] founded numerous cities on both sides [of that Gulf], [while the next Emperor] Shapur I (241–272 A.D.) formally incorporated Oman into his domains."[59]

Though Emperor Shapur I conquered Oman, it subsequently reasserted its independence. Then, "during the reign of the Sassanian King Anushiruwan, around A.D. 570, his General at-Tabari Wahraz embarked at Ubulla [near present-day Basra], first seizing Bahrain, then a dependency of Oman, and disembarked his thousands of Persian troops at Sohar to overrun the country of Oman. The Persian fleet then continued west along the Oman coast, conquering Dhofar and Hadhramaut [Hadramawt, Hadramaut] before taking Aden."[60]

---

59 Patricia Crone, <u>Meccan Trade and the Rise of Islam</u>, (Piscataway, N.J.: Gorgias Press, 2004), p. 46.
60 Wendell Phillips, <u>Unknown Oman</u>, (New York: David McKay Company, Inc., 1966), p. 185.

Other Means

The Persians were not content to rely solely on the interminably slow process of militarily subduing the whole Arabian coastline from Kuwait to Oman and on to Bab-el-Mandeb, to break the monopoly on world trade that Byzantium was maintaining with the help of its clients, the Ethiopians. Therefore, to break that monopoly, Persia began working through the large active Jewish population in Yemen. Those Jews had proselytized a leading member of the tribe which, before the coming of the victorious Ethiopians, had governed Yemen for a long time. Their rule had been snatched from them by the Byzantines working through their client, the invading Ethiopians.

Orthodox Abyssinia[61] Invaded Southwest Arabia

The Yemeni ruling house, now converted to Judaism, reasserted its authority. "By A.D. 525, Judaism had gained such an influence in the Himyarite kingdom that the rulers themselves were converted and began to persecute the Christian population."[62] Those Yemeni Jewish-convert leaders had gained renewed and enhanced power by acting as clients of the Sassanian Persians, somewhat as the Ethiopians/Abyssinians were clients of Byzantium. This Ethiopian-Christian vs. Yemeni-Jewish conflict was part of the larger struggle between the Sassanian Persians and the Byzantine Romans over control of that international trade route which traversed the Arabian Sea and the Red Sea to the Mediterranean.

The leading figure of the revived and re-established Yemeni royal house was Dhu Nuwas.[63] Not only was he a native Yemeni nationalist, he had also converted to Judaism. Each of these distinctions constituted a basis upon which to fight the EthiopianAbyssinian-Aksmuite Christian colonizers. For a patriotic citizen of Yemen, not only was living under foreign domination intolerable, but, now being a Jew, Dhu Nuwas also embraced Judaism's virulent anti-Christian stance as an operating principle.

The campaign to gain freedom from Ethiopia and reestablish Yemeni sovereignty was launched in winter, when Ethiopia could not send reinforcements to support their occupying troops. Consequently, Dhu Nuwas led his forces to a rapid and total triumph. He then turned his forces against the large vibrant Christian community at Najran in northwest Yemen. Besieging the town, he demanded that the

---

61 "The Aksum king's conversion to [Orthodox] Christianity [took place] in the third century AD. The Orthodox faith adopted by the Aksumites is followed throughout Ethiopia to this day, unchanged by either the religious disputes of classical and medieval times, or the political upheavals of the twentieth century." – John Reader, Africa A Biography of the Continent, (New York: Alfred A. Knopf, 1998), p. 208.

62 Maan Z. Madina, "The Arabs and the Rise of Islam," The Columbia History of The World, ed. John A. Garraty and Peter Gay, (New York: Harper & Row, Publishers, 1972), p. 255.

63 His real name was "Yusuf As'ar (better known by nicknames referring to his braids or ponytail: Dhu Nuwas, Dzu Nuwas, Dounaas, or Masruq)." – Christian History Institute. http://chi.gospelcom.net/DAILYF/2001/11/daily-11-25-2001.shtml "The prime mover in it [the persecution of the Christians in Najran] was Dhu Namas, or Dunaas, the Jewish king of the Himyarites. The name by which he is generally called is Masruq. Probably both are correct, Dhu Numas being a sort of surname, and Masruq the personal name." – John Stewart, Nestorian Missionary Enterprise, The Story of a Church on Fire (Edinburgh: T.&T. Clark, 1928), p. 56.

Christians deny the deity of Jesus. On their steadfast refusal, Dhu Nuwas had a large fire pit dug and forced hundreds of the Christians from Najran to jump into it, to a fiery death. His bestiality was so shocking that the martyrdom of the Christians in Najran is even memorialized in the eighty-fifth Surah of the Koran.[64]

Ethiopia Reclaims Rule in SW Arabia

The Byzantines simply would not allow Dhu Nuwas' victory to define a new status quo. Furthermore, the Abyssinians also were not willing to allow their own influence and economic advantages in southwest Arabia to be permanently overthrown. As a result, promising him support, the Imperial Byzantine Government encouraged Kaleb, King of Abyssinia, to undertake an expedition against Dhu Nuwas. Allowing for the time necessary to make arrangements, this expedition would not have taken place before A.D. 525, the traditional date assigned to it. "Dhu Nuwas was completely overthrown and put to death or, according to another less reliable account, threw himself into the sea and perished. [Thus,] Abyssinian overlordship in South Arabia was again established."[65]

A Vengeance Attack on Mecca

Another powerful motivation leading to Abyssinia's attack was repugnance generated by persecution of Christians in Yemen. That, "together with prodding from Byzantium[66]—which wanted to strike a blow at its ancient adversary, Persia—led to Christian Abyssinia's invasion of South Arabia. ... The Abyssinian governor, Abraha [whom King Kaleb had put in charge of the invasion], conquered South Arabia, then tried to move northward, but he failed to advance beyond Mecca."[67]

The campaign of Abraha (the Ethiopian general/governor/viceroy in Yemen) against Mecca was intended as a stroke of vengeance. He "had built a great Christian church [building] in San'a,[68] his capital, and sought to make this the center of pilgrimage for Arabia instead of the pagan Ka'ba at Mecca. This the Meccans resented, and one of them went to San'a and defiled the church. Incensed by this act of vandalism and contempt, Abraha gathered an army and marched to the Hijaz to

---

64 The pertinent verses are: (4.) (Self-)destroyed were the owners of the ditch (5.) Of the fuel-fed fire, (6.) When they sat by it, (7.) And were themselves the witnesses of what they did to the believers. (8.) They had naught against them save that they believed in Allah, the Mighty, the Owner of Praise, (9.) Him unto Whom belongeth the Sovereignty of the heavens and the earth; and Allah is of all things the Witness. (10.) Lo! They who persecute believing men and believing women and repent not, theirs verily will be the doom of hell, and theirs the doom of burning."
65 Richard Bell, The Origin of Islam In Its Christian Environment, (London: Macmillan and Co., 1926), pp. 37-39.
66 Abyssinia's [also called Aksum.] "rulers maintained close ties with the eastern Roman Empire, [Byzantium]." – John Reader, Africa A Biography of the Continent, (New York: Alfred A. Knopf, 1998), p.216.
67 Maan Z. Madina, "*The Arabs and the Rise of Islam*," The Columbia History of The World, ed. John A. Garraty and Peter Gay (New York: Harper & Row, Publishers, 1972), p. 255. "The Sixth-century king of Ethiopia, Kaleb, invaded the Himyarite kingdom when Dhu Nuwas was persecuting Christians. For a short time, Ethiopia ruled the Yemen, but it was displaced, first by the Persian conquest of Arabia, and later by the advent of Islam." – Elizabeth Isichei, A History of Christianity in Africa, From Antiquity to the Present, (Grand Rapids, Michigan: William B. Eerdmans Publishing Company, 1995), p. 33. "In 2009 another inscription concerning Abraha's military initiatives turned up in Bi'r Murayghan. It is undated but must follow the inscription of 552. ... The new inscription declares victory of Abraha that re-established his own authority over the Ma'add and enlarged his territories to the northeast and northwest, so as now to include Yathrib." – G. W. Bowersock, The Crucible of Islam, (Cambridge, Mass.: Harvard University Press, 2017), pp. 27-28.

destroy the Ka'ba. One of the things which impressed the Arab imagination was the presence of an elephant in this army. At the borders of the sacred territory of Mecca, however, the expedition was miraculously overthrown. The elephant refused to go forward, and flocks of birds appeared which pelted the army with stones. ...

"The date [of the elephant incident] was A.D. 570 or 571,[69] for by unanimous tradition Muhammad is said to have been born in 'the year of the elephant,' *i.e.* the year of Abraha's expedition. Abraha himself escaped from the disaster to his army, but did not long survive. Close upon his death appears to have followed the fall of the Abyssinian rule in Yaman.

"Mohammed alludes to Abraha's campaign [against Mecca] in Sura 105 in which the legend of the birds is related.[70] ... It proves that Mohammed originally shared the political sympathies of his people. Later, after he had broken decisively with his people, he made an alliance[71] with the [previously] hated Abyssinians."[72]

Empires at War

The prolonged struggle between Ethiopia and Yemen was an important factor in the destiny of Christianity in Southwest Arabia. Without doubt, it was also one of the most important aspects of the political background in the rise of Islam. That protracted, perennial contest was carried on by Sassanian Persia and the Byzantine Empire through their clients, in hopes of capturing and maintaining exclusive control of the fabulously rewarding east-west trade route which went through Bab-el-Mandeb.

In addition to their struggle to control the Mediterranean-Red Sea-Indian Ocean-trade route, just before Islam erupted out of the Arabian Peninsula, the Byzantines and the Sassanians became engulfed in a twenty-six-year all-out war, from 602 to 628 A.D. While the Persians initiated that war,[73] Byzantium ultimately triumphed.

---

68 "When Abraha saw that the Arabs were making their way to Allah's house in Mecca in droves at the time of the pilgrimage, he asked: 'Of what is this house made?' And received the answer: 'Of stone, dressed with striped material from Yemen.' Then he said: 'By Messiah! I will truly build you a better house!' He then built a church in San'a out of white, red, green, and black marble, the doors being covered with gold and studded with pearls and precious stones, and he caused incense to be burned within, and the walls to be sprinkled with musk, and then he told the people to make their pilgrimages to the temple." – Tor Andrae, <u>Mohammed the Man and His Faith</u>, trans. Theophil Menzel (New York: Harper Torchbooks, 1960), pp. 31-32.

69 Noldeke, *l.c.,* thinks this is much too late, and apparently discards the tradition that Muhammad was born in the year of Abraha's expedition.

70 Sura 105 is very short, having only five verses. It says: "In the name of Allah, the Beneficent, the Merciful. (1.) Hast thou not seen how thy Lord dealt with the owners of the elephant? (2.) Did He not bring their stratagem to naught, (3.) And send against them swarms of flying creatures, (4.) Which pelted them with stones of baked clay, (5.) And made them like green crops devoured (by cattle)?"

71 The alliance refers to his sending 83 of his followers to Abyssinia. He told his people, "'It might be better for you if you went to Abyssinia. ... The people there are friendly and the king rules with justice, for it is a Christian country. You could stay there until God relieves us of victimization in this country.'" – John Bagot Glubb, <u>The Life and Times of Muhammad</u>, (New York: Stein and Day/Publishers, 1970), p. 118.

72 Tor Andrae, <u>Mohammed the Man and His Faith</u>, trans. Theophil Menzel (New York: Harper Torchbooks, 1960), p. 32.

73 Professor Bowersock saw the death of the Byzantine emperor Maurice in 602 as the event which triggered the beginning of this war. "The Persians detected an opportunity for renewed conquest in opposition to the new government in Constantinople, and this enabled them to capture Jerusalem in 614." – G. W. Bowersock, <u>The Crucible of Islam</u>, (Cambridge, Mass.: Harvard University Press, 2017), p. 9.

However, that prolonged conflict left both empires utterly exhausted (see the last two paragraphs of Chapter 3), giving Muslims an unprecedented advantage in the initial phases of their war to conquer the vast area which stretched all the way from India to the Atlantic.

Though predictive prophetic passages in the Koran are scarce, yet through two of those rare prophecies which are found in Surah 30:2-5 and Surah 48:16, we know that Muhammad keenly followed the ebb and flow of the Byzantine/Persian war.

Plague Spreads

Just prior to Islam's successful simultaneous attack on both empires, Byzantium and Sassanian Persia had also been weakened by "a long-drawn-out natural catastrophe: from the 540s a major plague spread westwards through the empire and beyond, and it recurred right through to the eighth century. Population plummeted, including Constantinople itself, and the general impact can still be seen dramatically in Syria, until then an area of continuing vigorous Classical urban civilization, where town after town was sucked dry of life and was never reoccupied, leaving a series of ruins in semi-desert wilderness to the present day. Constantinople itself was a city of ruins, a ghost of its former self. This weakening of both Byzantine and Sassanian society by the plague must have been another reason why the Arabs found it so easy to overwhelm such large areas of mighty empires."[74] For a graphic description of the decimation caused by the plague, see Chapter 27 under "Plague Strikes."

It should also be noted that at the dawn of Islam the western shore of "the Persian Gulf was overwhelmingly Christian from the [delta of the] Tigris to Oman, and there was [also] a church of Nestorian Christians in Socotra."[75]

Iran's Power Base in Southwest Arabia

To understand the extent of the Sassanian Persian expansion into the Arabian Peninsula, it should be realized that "by about 570, the Sassanids ... had military colonies in Bahrayn [Bahrain/Bahrein], Oman, and the Yemen, as well as commercial colonies in both the Yemen and the Najd. With the exception of [the port of] Shihr, the successor of Classical Cane in the Hadramawt [Hadhramaut/ Hadramaut], they controlled all the major Arabian ports. ... The settlements of the Persians were protected by a string of client kings and other protegés, whose influence stretched from [the Persian border town of] Hira through central and eastern Arabia to the Yemen."[76]

---

74 Diarmaid MacCulloch, <u>Christianity, the First Three-Thousand Years</u>, (New York, Viking, 2010), p. 436.
75 Patricia Crone, <u>Meccan Trade and the Rise of Islam</u>, (Piscataway, N.J.: Gorgias Press, 2004), pp. 46-47. (Socotra is the island in the Indian Ocean just east of the point of the Horn of Africa.)
76 Patricia Crone, <u>Meccan Trade and the Rise of Islam</u>, (Piscataway, N.J.: Gorgias Press, 2004), pp. 48-49.

The Byzantine Reaction

The Byzantine Empire could not be indifferent to the major flanking move the Persians were making by their aggressive and prolonged expansion into Arabia. The Byzantine response, made principally through the agency of their client, Ethiopia, soon proved to be in vain because Abraha's "son, and second successor, lost South Arabia to Chosroes I, a Persian king of the Sassanid dynasty, and South Arabia remained a Persian province until the invasion of the Muslims."[77]

Persian Rule Detrimental to the Church

Though the prime motivation of Iran's prolonged push to capture Yemen and control Bab-el-Mandeb was economic, it also had a profound spiritual component. While Zoroastrianism was favored by Iran's Parthian Dynasty, the Sassanians who succeeded the Parthians in 226 A.D. made it the state religion from which point Christians were often persecuted. Therefore, it is not surprising that "Persia lent its aid to the native leaders against the hated blacks, and with their [i.e. the black Ethiopians] disappearance [ultimately] disappeared also the dominant influence of Christianity in the south-west of Arabia."[78]

An important exception to fading Christian presence in Yemen was the existence of the remarkably dynamic church in Najran. However, another blow to Christianity in Yemen fell "when the Persian satrap, Badhan, embraced Islam in A.D. 628. The area was thus opened to influence by the north Arabians, and Yemen became effectively absorbed into its cultural orbit. ... When the last Persian satrap of Yemen—Badhan—converted to Islam in A.D. 628, it seemed certain that much of Yemen would follow. Approximately half of the Yemeni tribes had converted by 630, and among the first to convert were those that had been proselytized by their fellow tribesmen residing in Medina. In that same year Muhammad recognized the son of the dead satrap as governor of San'a. The major attraction of Islam for the Yemenis was much the same as for most residents of the Arabian Peninsula: Islam was a regional phenomenon without foreign overtones. As such it had a special appeal for Yemenis who had undergone two successive foreign occupations."[79]

Agricultural Developments Related to the Rise of Islam

Coinciding with the birth of Muhammad, a calamitous agricultural crisis in Southwest Arabia arose due to a disaster in the very unique irrigation system in Yemen. There significant agriculture "depended on a series of dams, of which the largest

---

77 Maan Z. Madina, "The Arabs and the Rise of Islam," The Columbia History of the World, ed. John A. Garraty and Peter Gay (New York: Harper & Row, Publishers, 1972), p. 255. The Sassanian Empire came to an end as a consequence of the Battle of Nehawand in 642 AD.

78 Richard Bell, The Origin of Islam in its Christian Environment, (London: Macmillan and Co., 1926), pp. 40-41. "In Najran ... practically all the population was Christian." – John Bagot Glubb, The Life and Times of Muhammad, (New York: Stein and Day Publishers, 1970), p. 51. The church in Najran alone had 40,000 members. On the numerical strength of the church in Najran, see Chapter 9, footnote 272.

79 Richard F. Nyrop and associates, Area Handbook for the Yemens, (Washington D.C.: The American University, 1977), pp. 14-15.

and most famous was at Ma'rib. This dam broke twice, in 449 and 450 A.D. [Coon's second date is an error, probably typographical. It broke the second time in 570.], after which agriculture was no longer possible."[80] In part, at least, the destruction of the dam seems to have been the result of earthquakes. In any case, the failure of the Marib Dam, turned thousands of acres of lush cropland back into desert. Sadly, that marked the end of Arabia Felix, that is, *Happy Arabia*, the name the Romans used to describe those lush lands before the final collapse of the Marib Dam.

In between the two dam-related agricultural disasters, Abraha, Ethiopia's general/governor/viceroy, led in a successful repair project, enlisting the cooperation of many of the disaffected tribes for help in its restoration. He wrote of these events in a long inscription at Marib. In his inscription, "he records how he sought to harness the whole energies and resources of the country for the repair of the dam, including the spiritual: 'Now after they had appointed the time and the Arabs judged it propitious they went to the city of Märib and prayed at the church of Märib, which had a priest.' ... Later, mention is made of the sacrifices offered at the church and at the dam itself on the completion of the work. This restoration was the occasion for the despatch of a number of embassies and delegations to visit and congratulate Abraha, as recorded in the inscription."[81]

Abraha's repair project was amazing because in addition to administrative difficulties and many obstacles which had to be overcome, it would have been very difficult to duplicate the original workmanship. One traveler recorded, that the, "huge boulders [of the main dam] were so perfectly dressed that they fitted into each other like pieces in a jigsaw puzzle." A visitor's first-hand description tells us, " We saw no trace of mortar of any kind, yet we looked at portions of the wall that were more than fifty feet high, standing as they had when Sheba's great artisans built them about 2,700 years ago. ... As I saw with my own eyes, the massive northern and southern sluices are remarkably well preserved to this day. As the dam was probably intact until the end of the rule of Abraha in A.D. 570, the final collapse took place within a few years and probably was caused by a social rather than a natural breakdown resulting in repairs being delayed until it was too late. Thus ended the most celebrated construction in pre-Islamic Arabian history."[82] The main dam "was 660 yards long and sixty feet high, designed to control the waters of the river Adhanah in the Wadi Shibwan and its tributaries from scores of mountain-sides. ...

"Since those days [when Abraha repaired the dam] the Bedouin had removed the bronze bolts between huge blocks of granite and sand had drifted high around the base of the dam. Yet large sections are in such good condition still that one can imagine the dam readily restored, to transform the desert once more into per-

---

80 Carlton S. Coon, <u>Caravan: The Story of The Middle East</u>, (New York: Henry Holt and Company, 1956), p. 57.
81 J. Spencer Trimingham, "<u>Christianity Among the Arabs in Pre-Islamic Times</u>," (London, Longman Group Limited and Librairie du Liban, 1979), p. 300-301.
82 Wendell Phillips, <u>Unknown Oman</u>, (New York: David McKay Company, Inc., 1966), pp. 189-190.

fumed gardens and lush meadows. ... The collapse of the dam was one of the epoch-making events of the ancient world, for it marked the end of a great civilization built around economic resources derived from the Incense Trail."[83] The final disaster to befall the dam is probably referred to in Surah 34:15-19 where it is seen to have been divine judgment for the idolatry of the people.

Establishing the history of the Marib Dam was not easy. "When Thomas Arnaud, a French pharmacist, went to Marib in 1843 to collect tracings of ancient inscriptions, he was accused of being a sorcerer. On his flight over the mysterious 'white city' in 1934, Andre Malraux claimed that his aircraft was shot at. The Egyptian archeologist Ahmed Fakhry tried to prevent Yemenite officials from removing stones from Marib in 1947, but he received only insults for his efforts.

"In 1952–53, an American expedition led by Wendell Philips and W. P. Albright was threatened and forced to flee its Marib excavations, leaving its equipment behind. Nevertheless, enough archeological work has been accomplished to vindicate the story of a queen of Sheba."[84]

As a result of the deterioration and final collapse of the dam, there was a northward migration of a number of Yemenite tribes. Even much earlier, "one such community, bearing the name of Ghassan, seems to have reached the deserts of Syria about 250. ... At almost the same time as Beni Ghassan arrived in Syria, other Yemenite tribes appeared in the desert west of the lower Euphrates. In 268, Sapor I, King of Persia, appointed a certain Amr ibn Adi, of the tribe of Lakhm, as prince of the Arabs of the deserts west of the Euphrates."[85] These two tribes filled critical roles of defense against predatory tribal attacks on the Arabian borders both for Byzantium and for the Sassanian Empire.

Decline in Trade

"Agriculture, however, served mainly to feed people whose main interests lay in transport and trade. The South Arabians carried goods from India and points east overland from their landing spots on the shore of the Indian Ocean,[86] ... up to Mekka [Mecca], whence they went on to the Mediterranean."[87]

"Since Arabia had always been dependent on outside trade, events from without may be blamed [for the decline in economic activity in Arabia]. During this time the power of Rome declined, and the market for oriental goods shifted from Italy

---

83 Dana Adams Schmidt, Yemen, the Unknown War, (New York: Holt, Rinehart and Winston, 1968), p. 142.
84 Alex Mantoux, *The Land of the Queen of Sheba*, The World's Last Mysteries, (New York: The Reader's Digest Association, Inc., 1978), p. 48.
85 John Bagot Glubb, The Life and Times of Muhammad, (New York: Stein and Day Publishers, 1970), pp. 47-48.
86 One naturally wonders why the Indian Ocean ships which carried the Indian and Oriental cargoes for western markets didn't sail up the Red Sea and into the Gulf of Aqaba to the port of Aqaba (the modern Elat). Glubb gave the answer. He wrote, "But the majority of merchants avoided the navigation of the Red Sea, the waters of which were often infested with pirates, and the coasts deficient in harbors and difficult for navigation, due to the coral reefs off-shore. The greater part of the merchandise was therefore unloaded at Aden or on the coast of the Yemen, enabling the ships to profit by the return monsoon across the Indian Ocean." – John Bagot Glubb, The Great Arab Conquests, (Englewood Cliffs, New Jersey: Prentice-Hall, Inc., 1963), p. 22.
87 Carlton S. Coon, Caravan: The Story of the Middle East, (New York: Henry Holt and Company, 1956), p. 57.

to Byzantium. [However,] the Byzantines had their own trade routes to the east, over the oases of Turkestan to the Caspian shore, through the Transcaucasian Trough,[88] and along the southern waters of the Black Sea.

"With the dwindling of trade [as Coon emphasizes,] the cities grew weaker and probably less populous. Some of the erstwhile farmers of South Arabia turned to Bedouin life and moved north in search of pasture. Among these were the ancestors of the Beni Kalb and Tayyi' tribes of today. The oases with and without cities, needed by the nomads as trading centers and dry-weather havens for their camels, became so weak that the nomads forced them to pay tribute. Mekka [Mecca] was an exception. Thanks to its permanent spring, its holy and ancient pilgrim shrine, and the remnants of its caravan trade, the inhabitants of this city were able to maintain their independence."[89]

The situation of the Crusader states, which came into being much later in Palestine, helps one understand how important trade was in comparison to agriculture. There, just as in pre-Islamic Arabia, agriculture "was not the mainstay of the economy. The Crusader states grew wealthy from caravans that came from Damascus and beyond, bringing spices from the East to the royal ports of Tyre and Acre; it was a trade that provided enormous wealth and the Kingdom's customs men raked off a good percentage for their coffers. Pisans, Genoese and Venetians also did well as their ships carried most of the trade and Italian merchants were given their own self-governing 'trading estates' in the main ports."[90]

War And The Rise of Islam

In view of the account given so far, it is clear that Islam arose out of very turbulent conditions. **First**, there was war growing out of foreign aggression in southern Arabia. As already noted, "during the fourth century A.D. Ethiopians from Axum invaded southern Arabia, and [later] even made an attempt to take Mekka, [as] recorded in the Qur'an."[91]

Secondly, as noted earlier, there was a devastating clash-of-empires in the eastern Mediterranean. The Persians attacked and invaded Byzantium, initiating a war lasting from 602–628. That war "reduced the market for luxury goods [such as incense from Arabia] in the increasingly impoverished Roman Empire; then Persia gained control of South Arabia (threatening trade routes to India), and [**finally**] in the early eighth century Arab forces destroyed Adulis [main Ethiopian port]."[92]

---

88 Transcaucasian Trough is the valley of the Rioni-Kura rivers which stretches between the Black and Caspian Seas. In the spring of 1570 the Ottomans began work on a canal to join the Black and Caspian Seas through the Transcaucasian Trough. See Jason Goodwin's Lords of the Horizons, A History of the Ottoman Empire, (New York: Henry Holt & Co., 1998), pp. 161-162.
89 Carlton S. Coon, Caravan: The Story of the Middle East, (New York: Henry Holt and Company, 1956), p. 64.
90 Malcolm Billings, The Cross and the Crescent, A History of the Crusades, (New York: Sterling Publishing Co., Inc., 1988), p. 74
91 Carlton S. Coon, Caravan: The Story of the Middle East, (New York: Henry Holt and Company, 1956), p. 57.
92 John Reader, Africa, A Biography of the Continent, (New York: Alfred A. Knopf, 1998), pp. 218-219. Reader tells us that "Adulis probably was sited near the port of Massawa in the first century A.D. (p. 207) Massawa is today a seaport on the Eritrean coast of the Red Sea.

Poverty And The Rise of Islam

Just prior to the beginning of Muhammad's electrifying and epochal prophetic career, another event, a dramatic decline in the market for frankincense (the unique high-value export from Oman) conspired to bring poverty to many thousands of Arabians. In part, the cause of this economic collapse is thought to have been "the spread of Christianity. ... The new religion, it seems, had less need than pagan faiths for incense as a means of reaching heaven."[93]

"Rome's problem was to find a unifying bond in her vast and heterogeneous Empire. ... Rome saw in the spread of Caesar worship that very unifying principle which she needed; and so it became the law that once a year every Roman citizen should go to the temple of the Emperor, burn a pinch of incense to the godhead of Caesar, and say: 'Caesar is Lord.' Having done that, the citizen was given a written certificate to prove that he had made this act of worship. ... But the one thing no Christian would say was: 'Caesar is Lord.' For him Jesus Christ, and none other was Lord."[94]

Roman imperial persecution ended in 313 through a joint declaration by Constantine and Licinius which was made at Milan. That declaration is often erroneously called The Edict of Milan. They declared that "no man should be denied leave of attaching himself to the rights of the Christians, or to whatever other religion his might [that is, his strength] directed him."[95] That resulted in a greatly reduced use of frankincense in the Roman Empire. The failure of the frankincense trade not only decimated the economy in the growing areas in Oman but also in all the transhipment points throughout Arabia.

Undoubtedly, as just pointed out, the twenty-six year war between Sassanian Iran and the Byzantine Empire which disrupted trade in the eastern Mediterranean also devastated the international perfume trade and other trade upon which the normal economic well-being of Arabia depended. Further, as has previously been described, the acute negative economic impact caused by the disappearance of the fragrance market coincided with the tragic irredeemable collapse of the irrigation system in central Yemen. With that background in view, it is not surprising that, "Al-Kindi[96] ... explains that the campaigns of the Arabs were occasioned by their poverty, and were a punishment inflicted by God upon the Persians for their sins: They [the Arabs] were accustomed to eating lizards and chameleons, [they were] men of poverty and misery and wretched sustenance, in deserts and waste places; burnt up by the hot wind of summer and [frozen by] the intense cold of winter; exceedingly hungry, thirsty and naked.

---

93 Dana Adams Schmidt, <u>Yemen, the Unknown War</u>, (New York: Holt, Rinehart and Winston, 1968), p.101.
94 William Barclay, <u>The Revelation of John</u>, Vol. I, (Philadelphia: The Westminster Press, 1976), pp. 110-111.
95 Peter J. Leithart, <u>Defending Constantine: The Twilight of an Empire and the Dawn of Christendom</u>, (Downers Grove, IL: IVP, 2010), p. 99.
96 His full name was Yaqub ibn Ishaq as-Sabbah al-Kindi. He was called the Philosopher of the Arabs. He died in about 870 A.D. He flourished in Iraq under caliphs al-Mamun and al-Mu'tasim. Also, he was one of the first Arab students of Greek philosophers.

"So when there was brandished before them the vision of rivers of wine and milk, various kinds of fruits, abundance of meat and foods, and reclining on couches, and resting on carpets of silk and satin and brocade, and marriage with damsels like precious pearls, and being served by men-servants and maid-servants, and limpid water poured forth, and extended shade—like the description of the palaces of the Chosroes—this vision sunk into their minds [and some of them had already seen those luxuries in their travels and journeys to the land of Fars, that is Persia] and they leapt for joy, and when they heard of it they felt that they had already obtained it; and they seized it, and exerted themselves to fight against the people of Fars so as to take it from them and lay hold of it. ...

[In their judgment,] "they fought against an impure and filthy people who had revolted and rebelled against God, and the Most High gave them the sovereignty over them who had never paid heed to Him; so they slew them, and destroyed their houses, for that they had acted tyrannically and shed innocent blood. Thus was the command of God and His deed against a people of tyrants, and He took vengeance on some of them by the hands of others."[97]

The emergence of the epochal Islamic movement undoubtedly was, in part, the result of economic and sociological factors. Echoing the analysis of al-Kindi, in a book published in 1892, "Hubert Grimme, [1864–1942], championed the idea that Mohammed should be treated as a social rather than as a religious reformer. According to Grimme, the social injustices prevailing at the time in Mecca, where the wealthy merchants oppressed the poor and allowed them to perish in their misery, aroused the flaming wrath of the Prophet, and he arose to establish a new and better social order."[98]

Fortunately, the Oxford scholar, Paul Kennedy, helps us put that analysis in perspective when he warns us against uncritically over-estimating the power of economic determinism such as that expressed by Hubert Grimme. Kennedy wrote that one should not argue "that economics determines every event, or is the sole reason for the success and failure of each nation. There is simply too much evidence pointing to other things: geography, military organization, national morale, the alliance system, and many other factors [which] can all affect the relative power"[99] of a people or of a state.

However, though the leadership of both the Byzantine and the Sassanian Empires seemed to have been oblivious to the situation, Arabia "was ripe for a great national movement which would be entirely independent of foreign control, whether [Byzantine] Abyssinian or Persian. All that was needed was a leader who would be able to bring about a fusion of the different national parties and lead the way in

---

97 Laurence E. Browne, The Eclipse of Christianity in Asia From the time of Muhammad Till the Fourteenth Century, (Cambridge: The University Press, 1933), pp. 88-89.
98 Tor Andrae, Mohammed The Man And His Faith, trans. Theophil Menzel (New York: Harper Torchbooks, 1960), p. 74.
99 Paul Kennedy, The Rise and Fall of Great Powers, (New York, Random House, 1987), p. xxiv.

the formation of a homogeneous state. The rise of Muhammad furnished the leader required and coincided with a great national opportunity."[100]

While there is a common "profile of a typical militant, driven by economic desperation or by a sense of being marginalized,"[101] there are also wealthy men motivated to become militants. For example in modern times, "thousands of Saudis had fought in the jihad [in Afghanistan]. Largely funded and supported by their government, they came from [economically] good families, some immensely wealthy ones. ... But when these guys got there [Afghanistan], they met others and began to network; they found a whole new world out there. And despite their wealth, they were underemployed, frustrated, an accident waiting to happen—and it did."[102]

Shortly after Muhammad's death in 632 A.D., at the time when the first serious eruption of Islam into countries bordering Arabia occurred, undoubtedly the vast majority of the Arab fighters did fit the "profile of a typical militant, driven by economic desperation or by a sense of being marginalized." However, there were also some from families which were immensely wealthy. Some in this later category were attracted by the ideology, some by the prospect of incalculable wealth and others by fantasies of power and grandeur. Operating behind all these ostensible motives there seems to have been a sinister spiritual force which captivated thousands of Arabians and motivated them to join the jihad to conquer the world. (See "Evaluating the Withering Wind" at the end of Chapter 29.)

Far Flung Impact

In addition to the disastrous consequences which the Islamic military expansion had on the subjugated countries, a secondary, yet devastating, impact from the rise of Islam impoverished all of Europe. Previous to the rise of Islam, Europe fundamentally had a Mediterranean-based economy. "Where the Mediterranean world was united by a sea, India and the Near East were separated by one. The coasts on the way [to India] were barren, uninhabited, difficult of access due to coral reefs, rocks and mountain chains, lacking in natural harbors, and generally devoid of timber. Exceptional patches notwithstanding, it was not a coastline that encouraged cabotage, the leisurely trundling from port to port that soon gave the inhabitants of the Mediterranean the feeling of being frogs around a pond."[103]

Very soon after Alexandria, the main Byzantine naval base in the eastern Mediterranean, fell to the Islamic military assault, Muslims began to develop naval power and to gain control of the entire Mediterranean. In addition, Islam, by 711, controlled the eastern, the southern and the western shores of the Mediterranean. This deprived the Byzantines of the most important internal means of transportation in

---

100 John Stewart, <u>Nestorian Missionary Enterprise, The Story of a Church on Fire</u> (Edinburgh: T.&T. Clark, 1928), p. 70.
101 Mary Anne Weaver, <u>A Portrait of Egypt, A Journey Through the World of Militant Islam</u>, (New York: Farrar, Straus and Giroux, 2000), p. 274.
102 Mary Anne Weaver, <u>A Portrait of Egypt, A Journey Through the World of Militant Islam</u>, (New York: Farrar, Straus and Giroux, 2000), p. 191.
103 Patricia Crone, <u>Meccan Trade and the Rise of Islam</u>, (Piscataway, N.J.: Gorgias Press, 2004), p. 30.

their empire. The Mediterranean which was known prior to the Muslim conquest, as a "Roman Lake," became a "Muslim Lake." Its capture by Islam devastated the economy of Europe. Instead of connecting areas in which Christianity predominated, "the ancient Roman sea had become the frontier between Islam and Christianity. All the old Mediterranean provinces conquered by the Mussulman gravitated henceforth [first toward Medina, then toward Damascus and then] toward Baghdad."[104]

The Islamic conquests brought a vast economic community into existence which stretched from the Atlantic to India and China. But Europe was excluded from that huge integrated economic market. Consequently, European tax revenues dwindled to a pittance. The civic infrastructure such as roads, aqueducts and harbor facilities could not be properly maintained and fell into disrepair. Similarly, education shriveled and illiteracy spread. This disastrous set of circumstances, compounded by feeding upon itself, drove European society into a desperate situation which has appropriately been called the Dark Ages.[105] In Europe, churches along with civic organizations and the general population were impoverished. Consequently, for example, easy access to the Christian Scriptures became difficult. Only in the largest churches and in some of the monasteries could one have access to the Scriptures.

Islam not only had its own vibrant, very widespread economic community, but its own language and its own religion. Since the Germanic tribes, which earlier had infiltrated into Europe were quasi-Christian, they, their plundering of Rome notwithstanding, often sought to integrate with European culture. In stark contrast, the Muslims, with few exceptions, held the West, its culture, its language and its religion in utter contempt. Thus, the "great Arab conquests were not only battle victories but also revolutionary repudiations of the Roman and Persian world orders."[106]

ଅ

---

104 Henri Perenne, <u>Mohammed and Charlemagne</u>, (New York: Barnes & Noble Inc., 1968), pp. 162-163.
105 The Belgian historian, Henri Perenne (1862–1935), wrote a definitive history of the impact of the Muslim conquest on Europe. For bibliography see the preceding footnote.
106 Charles Hill, *Trial of a Thousand Years*, <u>Hoover Digest</u>, 2011, No. 3), p. 51.

The Life of Muhammad

Chapter 3

MUHAMMAD'S INFANCY TO EARLY MANHOOD

Early Childhood

"Did He not find thee an orphan and protect thee? Did He not find thee wandering and direct thee? Did He not find thee destitute and enrich thee?" This poignant passage is quoted from verses 6–8 of the brief 93rd Surah. With near universal agreement, the words are thought to refer to the very precarious early life of Muhammad.

The earliest surviving biography of Muhammad is that written by Ibn Ishaq (b. 85 A.H., d. 150/151 A.H.[107]). The great Arabist, A. Guillaume, who translated Ibn Ishaq's *Life of Muhammad* into English, says of Ishaq's biography of Muhammad, "no book known to the Arabs or to us can compare in comprehensiveness, arrangement, or systematic treatment, with Ibn Ishaq's work."

In deft strokes, Ibn Ishaq recorded the crucial events which substantiate the arresting and touching account given us in Surah 93. He wrote: "Abdullah the apostle's father died while his mother [Amina d. Wahb] was still pregnant. ... When he [Muhammad] was six years old his mother Amina died. ... Thus the apostle was left to his grandfather ['Abdul-Muttalib] for whom they made a bed in the shade of the Ka'ba. ... When the apostle was eight years of age, eight years after the 'year of the elephant,' his grandfather died. After the death of [his grandfather] 'Abdul-Muttalib, the apostle lived with his uncle Abu Talib, for (so they allege) the former had confided him to his care because he and 'Abdullah, the apostle's father, were brothers by the same mother, Fatimah b. 'Amr b. 'A'idh b. 'Abd b. 'Imran b. Makhzum. It was Abu Talib who used to look after the apostle after the death of his grandfather and he [Muhammad] became one of his family."[108]

Clan and Family Affiliation

Muhammad was born into the Beni Hashim clan of the Arab Quraish Tribe, in which the members of the Beni Umayya clan were their long-time rivals. Ultimately, out of the rivalry and animosity between those two clans, grew the great Sunni-Shia rift in Islam. (For additional details on the Sunni-Shia rift, please see Appendix D, The Rise of Shiism.)

---

107 A.H. stands for the Latin, Anno Hegirae, i.e. in the year of the Hegira (Hijra), Muhammad's flight from Mecca to Medina, which occurred in 622 A.D.
108 Ibn Ishaq, The Life of Muhammad, Trans. A. Guillaume, (Karachi: Oxford University Press, 1982), pp. 69, 73, & 79.

The Illiterate Prophet

Though Muhammad's uncle, Abu Talib, never became a Muslim, he remained until death completely and unfailingly loyal to his nephew. But, being a poor man he could not afford to give his nephew an education. Appropriately therefore, Surah 7:157, according to Pickthall's translation, calls Muhammad, "the Prophet who can neither read nor write." However, Yusuf Ali translated it: "The unlettered Prophet."

Yusuf Ali's translation makes one wonder if Muhammad was totally illiterate. Even more, Surah 96:1-5 raises the question whether Muhammad was, indeed, completely illiterate. The passage says, "Read: In the name of thy Lord who createth, createth man from a clot. Read: And thy Lord is Most Bounteous, Who teacheth by the pen, teacheth man that which he knew not."

The Muslim Brotherhood (arguably the largest and most influential Muslim social and political organization in the world till its power was ruthlessly broken by the military coup led by General el-Sisi in 2013) makes it clear that they understand Muhammad to have been completely illiterate. Their "Office of the General Council drew up the text of [an] invocation which was to be recited during the last prostration of each prayer: O God, … lift your fury and anger from us, you Lord of the Worlds and pray for Muhammad the illiterate prophet, his family and his companions and bless them."[109]

First Trip to Syria & Wider Christian Contact

In 582 A.D., probably to help Muhammad gain a marketable skill, "twelve year old Mohammed was taken on a mercantile journey as far as Syria. Here he came in contact with Christians and, according to tradition, met the monk Buhaira."[110] We cannot be certain whether, as Zwemer states, this was Muhammad's first contact with Christians. However, we do know there were numerous Christians of the Ebionite sect living in Mecca at the time Muhammad was born. (See Chapter 9 under "Impacting Muhammad.") Another scholar tells us that there was also a colony of Abyssinian Christians in Mecca at that time. Whether Muhammad had contact with any of those Meccan Christians before his trip to Syria, is not known.

Subsequent to his marriage to Khadija, Muhammad certainly had extended contact with Khadija's cousin, Waraqa bin Nawfal, who was the Ebionite church leader in Mecca. In addition to visits with Waraqa bin Nawfal, Muhammad used to sit for hours in the shop of a Christian named Jabr to discuss "the scriptural religions."[111] In fact, Muhammad spent so many hours there that he was accused of

---

109 Abd Al-Fattah Muhammad El-Awaisi, The Muslim Brothers and the Palestine Question, 1928–1947, (London: Tauris Academic Studies, 1998, p. 40.

110 Samuel M. Zwemer, Islam, A Challenge to Faith, (New York: Laymen's Missionary Movement, 1909), p. 35. For those wishing additional information about the Christian monk, Buhaira, see Barbara Roggema, The Legend of Sergius Bahira: Eastern Christian Apologetics and Apocalyptic in Response to Islam, (Leiden: Brill, 2009).

111 Ali Dashti, Twenty Three Years: A Study of the Prophetic Career of Mohammad, trans. F.R.C. Bagley (London: George Allen & Unwin, 1985), pp. 21-22.

getting his message from Jabr! Surah 16:103 records Muhammad's rebuttal of that damaging allegation: "And We know well that they say: Only a man teacheth him. The speech of him at whom they falsely hint is outlandish, and this [Koran] is clear Arabic speech." But again, we do not know that Muhammad communed with Jabr at any time before his trip to Syria and his meeting with Buhaira.

Regarding his meeting with Buhaira, "Muslim historians delight to relate that he was seen by a Christian monk in Syria, who allegedly foretold that one day he would be a prophet. The story may well record some meeting between the boy Muhammad and a Christian hermit, of whom there were many at this time on the border of the Syrian Desert.

"Muhammad appears to have been a serious child. The insecurity of his infancy may have made him quiet and thoughtful beyond his years. In such circumstances, it is not improbable that he may have engaged in conversation with a Christian recluse who, noticing his serious demeanor, may have foretold for him a life of exceptional quality."[112]

In any case, as Ali Dashti deftly summarized the issue, Muhammad seems to have been prompted "to meet and talk with Christian monks and priests on his Syrian journey. ... On his way back, through the lands of Medyan and the 'Ād and Thamud, he had heard the legends of the local people. In Mecca itself he had exchanged visits with followers of the scriptural religions. He had sat for hours in Jabr's shop near the hill of Marwa, and had been in constant touch with Khadija's cousin Waraqa b. Nawfal, who is said to have translated a part of the New Testament into Arabic. ... The biographies of the Prophet mention several other followers of the scriptures and possessors of knowledge with whom he exchanged visits before the start of his mission."[113]

The Hunafa

At some point in his youth, Muhammad was in fellowship with a loosely associated group of local monotheists known as the *Hunafa*. Though the Kaaba at that time "was still called the House of Allah, the chief objects of worship there were a number of idols which were called daughters of Allah and intercessors. The few who felt disgust at this idolatry, which had prevailed for centuries, longed for the religion of Abraham and tried to find out what had been its teaching. Such seekers of the truth were known as *Hunafa* (singular: *Hanif*), a word originally meaning 'those who turn away' (from the existing idol-worship), but coming in the end to have the sense of 'upright' or 'by nature upright,' because such persons held the way of truth to be right conduct. These *Hunafa* did not form a community. They were the agnostics of their day, each seeking truth by the light of his own inner consciousness. Muhammad, son of Abdullah, became one of these."[114]

---

112 John Bagot Glubb, The Life and Times of Muhammad, (New York: Stein and Day, 1970), pp. 70-71.
113 `Ali Dashti, Twenty Three Years: A Study of the Prophetic Career of Muhammad, Tr. F.R.C. Bagley, (London: George Allen & Unwin, 1985), pp. 21-22.

Muhammad's becoming a *Hanif* may have been the consequence of having been rebuked by one who probably belonged to the loose fellowship of the *Hunafa*. It is recorded that "a certain Zayd b. 'Amr upbraided him [Muhammad] for eating meat that had been sacrificed to idols and condemned idols as futile and impotent. This admonition had such an effect on Muhammad that he said that never again did he offer sacrifices to idols nor show them any honor. Unfortunately, the MS. [manuscript] does not tell us what Zayd's religion was. It simply says that he followed the religion of Abraham but was neither Jew nor Christian."[115] It is highly probable that Zayd b. 'Amr was a *Hanif*. In Surah 3:67 Abraham is said to have been a *hanif*. However, most English translations render the Arabic word *hanif* in this Koranic passage as "upright" or "upright man."

A Question of Dates

There is controversy over the dates in Muhammad's life. For example, A. Guillaume, writing the introduction to Ibn Ishaq's renowned biography of Muhammad, said, "We do not know Muhammad's age when he first came forth publicly as a religious reformer: some say he was forty, others say forty-five."[116] However, in this study, the year 570 is considered the date of Muhammad's birth. That year is often called the year of the elephant because of an elephant in Abraha's military forces during his campaign against Mecca.[117] (The very short 105th Surah recounts the incident of the elephant.) Also, this study takes 610 as the date of Muhammad's first vision.

---

114 Marmaduke Pickthall, trans., The Meaning of the Glorious Koran, an Explanatory Translation, (New York: Alfred A. Knopf, 1930), Introduction, pp. 1-2. Tariq Ramadan, highly controversial grandson of Hasan al-Banna, founder of The Muslim Brotherhood, in his panegyric, In the Footsteps of the Prophet, defines *hanif* as "pure." cf. p. 9.

115 Alfred Guillaume, New Light on the Life of Muhammad, (Manchester: Manchester University Press, n.d.), p. 7.

116 Ibn Ishaq, The Life of Muhammad, Trans. A. Guillaume, *Introduction*, (Karachi: Oxford University Press, 1982), p. xix.

117 "However, the statement that Mohammed was born in the 'elephant year' does not agree with other chronological facts in the life of the Prophet. According to a tradition which is often repeated in the earliest records of Islam, he received the prophetic call at the age of forty, thirteen years before his migration to Medina. Reckoning from this, then, Mohammed must have been born in the year 569, and he would have received his call in 609. On the other hand, there is complete agreement concerning the date of his emigration, 622, and the date of his death ten years later, in 632." Tor Andrae, Mohammed the Man and His Faith, trans. Theophil Menzel (New York: Harper Torchbooks, 1960), p. 33. John Bagot Glubb in The Life and Times of Muhammad, (New York: Stein and Day, 1970), p. 50 & p. 69, accepts 570 as the date of Muhammad's birth. Karen Armstrong, Muhammad a Prophet for Our Time, (New York: Harper Collins, 2006), p. 14, says "c. 570." Edith Holland, The Story of Mohammed, (London: George G. Harrap & Company, 1914, Reprinted in Pakistan in 1977 by Al-Biruni, Lahore), p. 30, says, "In that year [the year of the Elephant] was born Mohammed, the son of Abdallah, destined to be the Prophet of Arabia." The Sufi writer, Martin Lings, in Muhammad: His Life Based on the Earliest Sources (New York: Inner Traditions International, Ltd., 1983), pp. 21-22 accepts the year of the elephant as the date of Muhammad's birth. Tariq Ramadan, the controversial grandson of the Hasan al-Banna, founder of the Muslim Brotherhood, in his In the Footsteps of the Prophet, (New York: Oxford University Press, 2007), p. 10 says, "In his seminal book on the life of the Prophet Muhammad, Ibn Hisham informs us that Ibn Ishaq has clearly and precisely established the Prophet's birth date: 'The Messenger God's peace and blessings be upon him, was born on a Monday, on the twelfth night of Rabi al-Awwal, in the year of the elephant.' Other accounts mention other months of the year, but throughout history there has been broad acceptance of that date among scholars and within Muslim communities." Peters says, "Later Muslim authorities seem to give tacit recognition to the uncertainty of any of the chronological indications passed on about the Prophet's life at Mecca. They, like us, must have felt that the historical ground grew firm only at Muhammad's migration to Medina; it was that date, in any event, that they chose to begin the Muslim calendrical era." – F.E. Peters Muhammad and the Origins of Islam, (New York: State University of New York Press, 1994), p. 103. Haykal seems to agree with "Perceval [who] wrote in his book on the Arabs that after weighing the evidence, it is most probable that Muhammad was born in August, 570 C.E., *i.e.* 'The Year of the Elephant.'" – Muhammad Husayn Haykal, The Life of Muhammad, (Place of Publication not given: American Trust Publications, 1976), p. 48.

Infancy and Shepherd Life

Only a few facts are known about Muhammad's life between his birth and his employment by Khadija, the Meccan business woman, who later became his first wife. Custom tells us that Amina, Muhammad's mother, entrusted him to Haleema, a woman of the Sa'd ibn Bakr tribe, a nomadic desert tribal woman who suckled him till he was weaned. Muhammad, "used to say to his companions, 'I am the most Arab of you all. I am of the Quraysh and I was suckled among the Banu Sa'd ibn Bakr."[118] In harmony with Muhammad's experience, the Koran tells Muslims that, "If ye wish to give your children out to nurse, it is no sin for you, provided that ye pay what is due from you in kindness," (Surah 2:233)

While still with his temporary adoptive mother, at the tender age of five or six, just before he was returned to his mother, for a short time he followed flocks in the desert for his foster family. Muhammad is alleged to have said, "God sent no prophet who was not a herdsman ... Moses was a herdsman; David was also a herdsman; I, too, was commissioned to prophethood while I grazed my family's cattle at Ajyad."[119] If that tradition is factual, he probably also spent some time as a shepherd after he returned to his birth family.

Trip to Yemen

Muhammad's youth was not, however, an unvarying, uninterrupted schedule of tending flocks. "A tradition has survived telling us that he accompanied his uncle, Zubair, on a business journey to the Yemen."[120] If this tradition is true, Muhammad must have made the trip to Yemen while he was in his teens, for his first trip to Syria took place when he was twelve. Now, older and more aware of events, he probably could have assessed the political/military struggle taking place between Ethiopia, proxy of Byzantium, and Iran for control of Southwest Arabia and Bab-el-Mandeb, the door to the Red Sea. Later, this information probably helped shape his more comprehensive view of world affairs.

Participation in War

In his youth, well before he married Khadija, Muhammad learned to bear arms by participating in an erratic tribal conflict, known as the *fijar* war, which fitfully dragged on for five years. The word *fijar* means sacrilegious. The term was applied to that five-year series of tribal clashes because those pitched battles were fought during the "holy months," the months when all fighting had been banned by inter-tribal, Arabia-wide agreement. That ban had been enacted so people throughout Arabia could safely make pilgrimages to various shrines, the Kaaba being one of them, which housed their venerated idols. That ban on warfare also stimulated wide participation in the trade fairs associated with the pilgrimages to

---
118 F.E. Peters Muhammad and the Origins of Islam, (New York: State University of New York Press, 1994), p. 104.
119 Muhammad Husayn Haykal, The Life of Muhammad (8th ed.) trans. Isma'il Ragi A. al Faruqui, (North American Trust Publications, 1976), p. 58.
120 John Bagot Glubb, The Life and Times of Muhammad, (New York: Stein and Day, 1970), p. 72.

the various Arabian idol shrines. We do not know the extent of Muhammad's involvement in that protracted struggle. However, according to tradition he said, "I had witnessed that war with my uncle and shot a few arrows therein. How I wish I had never done so!"[121]

Reliability Leads to Employment and Marriage

Muhammad, reportedly, was so reliable in all that he did that he was known in Mecca as *al Amin*, the trustworthy or reliable one. It is not known when he first received that designation, but Ibn Ishaq tells us its propriety was greatly enhanced when he impartially adjudicated a heated quarrel which had arisen over the resetting of the Black Stone in the wall of the Kaaba during its rebuilding.[122] His well-known reputation for trustworthiness seems to have been one of the reasons why (in 595 A.D.) Abu Talib, Muhammad's uncle, suggested to Khadija that she hire his nephew to take one of her camel caravans to Damascus. Though she took him into her employ, even so, Khadija sent Maysara, one of her most trusted slaves along with Muhammad.

On that caravan trip to Damascus, the traditional story is that one day as he rode his beast in the intense noontime heat, "Maysara saw two angels shading the apostle from the sun's rays." At the end of the trip, when Muhammad delivered the merchandise to Khadija which he had acquired in Syria, she found it had been so well chosen that she was able to sell it for double her investment.

"Maysara for his part told her about the two angels who shaded him and of the monk's words. [This refers to another monk besides Buhaira whom Muhammad had met and who had predicted a bright future for him.] ... So when Maysara told her these things she sent to the apostle of God and—so the story goes—said: 'O son of my uncle I like you because of our relationship and your high reputation among your people, your trustworthiness and good character and truthfulness.' Then she proposed marriage."[123] After discreet negotiations through representatives, Muhammad accepted her proposal and the marriage was consummated in 595 A.D. During the twenty-four years of their marriage, Muhammad was strictly monogamous. However, following the death of Khadija (in 619), he became notoriously polygamous.

Observing International Developments

The business trip to Syria on Khadija's behalf was made when Muhammad was in the flower of manhood, being 24 or 25 years old. The trip took place in 594 or 595 A.D., at a time when Muhammad would have been able to evaluate some of the conditions which led to the outbreak of all-out war between Iran and Byzan-

---

121 Muhammad Husayn Haykal, The Life of Muhammad (8th ed.) trans. Isma'il Ragi A. al Faruqui, (North American Trust Publications, 1976), p. 57.
122 Ibn Ishaq, The Life of Muhammad, Trans. A. Guillaume, *Introduction*, (Karachi: Oxford University Press, 1982), p. 86.
123 Ibn Ishaq, The Life of Muhammad, Trans. A. Guillaume, *Introduction*, (Karachi: Oxford University Press, 1982), p. 82.

tium in 602 A.D. Since later Muhammad exhorts mankind to "travel in the land, and see the nature of the consequence for those who were before you!" ["the end of those before you"[124]] (Surah 30:42), it is difficult to think Muhammad would not have made substantive and penetrating evaluations of all that he was able to observe while on this business trip on behalf of his future wife.

It is obvious that the struggle between Iran and Byzantium was an issue of vital concern to Muhammad. Speaking in 618 A.D., while the war launched by Iran against Byzantium had been raging for sixteen years, in one of the very few prophetic passages in the Koran, he tells us, "The Romans have been defeated in the near land, and they after their defeat will be victorious, within ten years— Allah's is the command in the former case and in the latter—and in that day believers will rejoice." (Surah 30:2-4)

A series of extremely damaging battle losses were suffered by Byzantium in the beginning years of that war. They are clearly prophesied in the biblical book of Revelation in which the Byzantine Empire is called the "Beast who hath the stroke of the sword and lived." (Revelation 13:14)

The Roman victory, which Muhammad predicted would occur within ten years, took place in 628 A.D. when Heraclius, Byzantine Emperor, utilizing a fleet on the Black Sea, landed a Byzantine expeditionary force near Iran, far behind the battle front, forcing the Iranians to accept humiliating terms of surrender, leading to political chaos in Iran.

An arresting account of that military campaign has been given by Montefiore who wrote, "Heraclius sailed his army to the Caucasus via the Black Sea, and with his Khazar horsemen invaded Persia. He out-maneuvered the Persian forces, challenged and killed three Persian champions in duels, then defeated their main army, stopping just outside the Shah's capital. Khusrau's deluded intransigence destroyed him. He was arrested and placed in the dungeon, the House of Darkness, where his favorite son was butchered in front of him before he was himself tortured to death. The Persians agreed to restore the *status quo ante bellum*."[125]

That war, lasting from 602–628, left both empires exhausted and prostrate. (See Chapter 2 under "Empires at War.") Muhammad was probably astute enough to have anticipated the resulting vulnerability of the two exhausted empires. Such observations may have allowed him to visualize the possibility of his movement subsequently achieving world-wide triumph.

ෆ

---

124 A Summarized Version of the Qur'an by al-Hilali.
125 Simon Sebag Montefiore, Jerusalem: The Biography, (London: Phoenix Paperback, 1988), p. 164.

Chapter 4

FROM MARRIAGE TO THE BEGINNING OF PUBLIC PREACHING, 595–613 A.D.

Children and Grandchildren

Muhammad's marriage to Khadija in 595 A.D. produced two sons and four daughters. Very little is known about the two sons "Qasim and Abdullah except that they died before the coming of Islam, while still infants."[126] The four daughters, Zaynab, Ruqayyah, Umm Kulthum and Fatimah ultimately embraced Islam and followed their father to Medina.[127] Several of those girls eventually played important roles in the consolidation of the Muslim movement. Some of their careers are highlighted in Chapter 7.

The First Vision

Muhammad's marriage to the wealthy Khadija allowed him to pursue a lifestyle which previously he could never have sustained. Of special interest, he embraced a form of personal devotion, called in Arabic *tahanuth*. While some question the full ramification of the word, it is reliably defined as "'leading a solitary life' or 'acts of devotion,' or more specifically as 'an ascetic practice that the Meccans observed in [the month of] Ramadan on [Mount] Hira: [which involved] fasting and sexual abstention.'"[128] The term may reflect the Hebrew *tehinnoth*, 'prayers,' or *voluntary* devotions.

During the fifteenth year of his marriage, in the year 610, Muhammad went on a *tahanuth*-type devotional retreat near Mecca to a cave in Mt. Hira. Perhaps, going to the cave was itself a nudge from Allah who is recorded to have said, "We have inspired in thee this Qur'an though aforetime thou wast of the heedless." (Surah 12:3)

The historian Bukhari tells us that, "Suddenly, the Truth descended upon him while he was in the cave of Hira. The angel came to him and asked him to read. The Prophet replied, 'I do not know how to read.' The angel caught me (forcefully) and pressed me so hard that I could not bear it any more."[129] This was repeated

---
126 Muhammad Husayn Haykal, <u>The Life of Muhammad</u>, (Place of Publication not given: American Trust Publications, 1976), p. 68.
127 Cf. F.E. Peters <u>Muhammad and the Origins of Islam</u>, (New York: State University of New York Press, 1994), p. 137.
128 F.E. Peters <u>Muhammad and the Origins of Islam</u>, (New York: State University of New York Press, 1994), p. 129.
129 <u>The Translation of the Meanings of Sahih al-Bukhari</u>, trans. Muhammad Muhsin Khan (Beirut, Lebanon: Dar al Arabia Publishing, n.d.) Vol. I, The Book of Revelation, p. 3.

three times. On the third time the command came, "Read: In the name of thy Lord who createth, createth man from a clot. Read: And thy Lord is the Most Bounteous, Who teacheth by the pen, teacheth man that which he knew not."[130]

In great fear Muhammad "returned with the Inspiration and with his heart beating severely. Then he went to Khadija ... and said, 'Cover me! Cover me!' They covered him till his fear was over and after that he told her everything that had happened and said, 'I fear that something may happen to me.' Khadija replied, 'Never! By Allah, Allah will never disgrace you. You keep good relations with your kith and kin, help the poor and the destitute, serve your guests generously and assist the deserving calamity-afflicted ones.'"[131]

Assured by a Christian

When Muhammad told his wife "I fear that something may happen to me," he apparently feared that the message had come by demonic influence. Muhammad refers to this event in Surah 81:19-25. There he tells us, "This is in truth the word of an honored messenger. Mighty, established in the presence of the Lord of the Throne, (One) to be obeyed, and trustworthy; And your comrade is not mad. Surely he beheld him on the clear horizon. And he is not avid of the Unseen. Nor is this the utterance of a devil worthy to be stoned."

In Muhammad's statement, "your comrade is not mad," the Arabic word for "mad" is *majnun*, which means one in whom *jinn* (demons) dwell and exercise power. When Muhammad told his wife what he had seen, Khadija said to him, "'Rejoice, O son of my uncle, and be of good heart. Verily, by Him in whose hand is Khadija's soul, I have hope that thou wilt be the prophet of this people.' Then she rose and gathered her garments about her and set forth to her cousin Waraqa b. Naufal [Nawfal] ... who had become a Christian and read the scriptures and learned from those that follow the Torah and the Gospel. And when she related to him what the Apostle of God told her he had seen and heard, Waraqa cried, 'Holy! Holy! Verily by Him in whose hand is Waraqa's soul, if thou hast spoken to me the truth, O Khadija, there hath come unto him the greatest Namus[132] who came to Moses afore time, and lo, he is the prophet of this people. Bid him be of good heart.' So Khadija returned to the apostle of God and told him what Waraqa[133] had said."[134]

Shortly after Khadija's visit with him, Waraqa met Muhammad and personally confirmed the message he had conveyed through Khadija. From that point

---

130 Koran, Surah 96:1-5.
131 The Translation of the Meanings of Sahih al-Bukhari, trans. Muhammad Muhsin Khan (Beirut, Lebanon: Dar al Arabia Publishing, n.d.) Vol. I, The Book of Revelation, pp. 3-4.
132 "The Greek *Nomos*, in the sense of Divine Law or Scripture, here identified with the Angel of Revelation." – Martin Lings, Muhammad, His Life Based on the Earliest Sources, (New York: Inner Traditions International, Ltd., 1983), p. 44.
133 Mark A. Gabriel, in his Jesus and Muhammad, (Lake Mary, Florida: Charisma House, 2004), p. 241 gives convincing evidence that Waraqa was an Ebionite. (See quotes in Chapter 9 under the subtitle "Impacting Muhammad.") No doubt, Waraqa deeply influenced Muhammad's Christology.
134 Ibn Ishaq, The Life of Muhammad, Trans. A. Guillaume, (Karachi: Oxford University Press, 1982), pp. 73-79.

Muhammad never wavered in his conviction that he was the Prophet of God! It is one of the greatest ironies of all time that a Christian, even though of Ebionite conviction, persuaded Muhammad that, indeed, he was the Prophet of God!

The Visions Continue With Agony

Those occasions when Muhammad received revelation seem to have been physically trying and exhausting. "Some authorities tell of his very intense sufferings and purely physical pains at the time of an inspiration. 'When the revelations came to the Prophet they pressed hard upon him, and his countenance darkened.' It even happened 'that he fell to the ground as if intoxicated,' and that he 'groaned like a camel's colt.' Ayesha, [or Aisha, Muhammad's favorite wife, following Khadija's death] in a longer narrative, in which she plays the leading role, gives a noteworthy description, which is obviously both original and reliable: ... 'Allah's Apostle had his customary attack (the word here used is especially applied to attacks of fever, or rather to that stage of the attack in which the patient experiences intense heat), so that even though it was a very cold day, beads of perspiration rolled from his face.'"[135]

Taking the Message Public

During the initial periods of the Islamic movement, it seems that only Khadija and Waraqa bin Nawfal constituted the very limited inner circle with whom Muhammad shared his on-going visions. According to Ibn Ishaq, "three years elapsed from the time that the apostle concealed his state until God commanded him to publish his religion."[136] The command to go public with the message is recorded in Surah 15:94 which says, "So proclaim that which thou art commanded, and withdraw from the idolaters."

From the very beginning of his public preaching in 613 A.D., there was resistance to Muhammad's message. If the strict monotheism which Muhammad preached were embraced by fellow members of his Quraysh tribe, who were guardians of the Kaaba, all the hundreds of idols housed in that shrine would have to be destroyed. Naturally, those who gave ardent devotion to those idols resisted the idea that their personal deity must be renounced and abandoned. Further, should the idols housed in the Kaaba be destroyed, thousands of pilgrims from all over Arabia, who came yearly to renew their personal devotion to their particular idol, would no longer come to Mecca. Consequently, the trade fair held in conjunction with the pilgrimage would die, bringing death also to the economy of Mecca.

Though Muhammad obeyed the commandment to proclaim the message, the results were disheartening. "Ten years of the Prophet's teaching in Mecca resulted in only sixty or seventy converts, who were subjected to contempt, ostracism and sometimes even persecution, by the outraged citizens. Muhammad himself was

---

135 Tor Andrae, <u>Mohammed The Man And His Faith</u>, trans. Theophil Menzel (New York: Harper Torchbooks, 1960), p. 50.
136 Ibn Ishaq, <u>The Life of Muhammad</u>, Trans. A. Guillaume, (Karachi: Oxford University Press, 1982), p. 117.

mocked and humiliated, though fear of his clan, Beni Hashim, prevented his enemies from actually assassinating him."[137]

◌⃝

---

137 John Bagot Glubb, <u>The Empire of The Arabs</u>, (London: Hodder & Stoughton, 1963), p. 19.

Chapter 5

MUHAMMAD'S CHRISTOLOGY

In Chapter 4 the account of the Prophet Muhammad's life took us only to the beginning of his public preaching. At such an early point, it is quite certain that his Christology had not been fully developed. However, without question, Muhammad did have a rudimentary Christology even at the very beginning of his preaching. It is impossible to date when he became more aware of each element of his full and complete understanding of Jesus as it is recorded in the Koran. From his interchange with a delegation of Christians from Najran, we know that some very important concepts in his understanding about Christ came to him very late in his public ministry. (See Chapter 9 under "Najrani Christians Try to Win Muhammad.")

In addition to the impact on Muhammad's Christology which came from his dialogue with the Christian delegation from Najran, it is also quite likely that some points in his view of Christ, as expressed in the Koran, reflect the understanding of Waraqa bin Naufal [Nawfal]. (See Chapter 9 under the subtitle, "Impacting Muhammad.")

The Christology of the Koran may be summarized by fifteen Koranic statements about Jesus, eleven of which are in harmony with the biblical account, while four repudiate the biblical record. The source of the correct statements may well have been God directing Muhammad's utterances as he did for Balaam when he "put a word in Balaam's mouth." (Numbers 23:5)

Though the Koran positively affirms eleven crucial truths about Jesus, unfortunately the broad body of Muslims, the *umma*, lives in total ignorance of the full and true import of these remarkable, biblically-true Koranic statements. One of the greatest hopes for an eventual triumphant reception of the Gospel in the Muslim world is for Muslims to come to understand these positive affirmations. When Muslims truly understand the meaning of these Koranic statements, doubtless many will submit their lives to Christ! However, any Muslim who comes to a proper understanding of these true declarations about Jesus will have to do so in the face of resolute and subtle efforts by Islamic propagandists to distort the facts.

Miracle Worker

The first Koranic affirmation about Jesus which conforms to the biblical account declares that he performed miracles.[138] True miracles constitute one way in which God lets us know that a given development is a divine initiative or that a message has divine approval. Surah 2:87 tells us, "We gave Jesus the son of Mary Clear (Signs) and strengthened him with the Holy Spirit." (Yusuf Ali Trans.) These signs are to be equated with the "clear proofs" of Surah 5:110.

This assertion that Jesus performed miracles (signs) is again emphasized in Surah 2:253 which tells us, "Those apostles we endowed with gifts, some above others: To one of them Allah spoke; others he raised to degrees (of honor); To Jesus the son of Mary We gave Clear (Signs), and strengthened him with the Holy Spirit." (Yusuf Ali, Trans.)

The Koranic emphasis that Jesus worked miracles is in harmony with the entire Gospel account, which is summarized in John 20:30-31. There, John tells us that "Many other signs therefore did Jesus in the presence of the disciples, which are not written in this book: but these are written, that ye may believe that Jesus is the Christ, the Son of God; and that believing ye may have life in his name."[139]

The Koran's account presents a crescendo of three of the most significant signs or miracles Jesus performed. It says, "by My permission thou didst heal him who was born blind and the leper by My permission; and how thou didst raise the dead, by My permission." (Surah 5:110)

Some of Muhammad's contemporaries cast doubt on his legitimacy and integrity because, in glaring contrast to Jesus, he performed no miracles. Fortunately, the Koran has not only preserved their allegations but Muhammad's response. The doubters said, "If only some portent were sent down upon him from his Lord!" (Surah 13:7) **In the first answer** to this very dangerous objection, God is said to have told Muhammad: "Thou art a warner only, and for every folk a guide." (Surah 13:7) **The second rebuttal** was: "This Qur'an is not such as ever could be invented in despite of Allah; but it is a confirmation of that which was before and an exposition of that which is decreed for mankind—Therein is no doubt—from the Lord of the worlds." (Surah 10:38) **Muhammad's third argument** took the form of a challenge: "Or say they: He hath invented it? Say: Then bring a Surah like unto it, and call (for help) on all ye can besides Allah, if ye are truthful." (Surah 10:39) (See also Surah 81:19-21.) History has shown that it was extremely dangerous to rise in response to one of Muhammad's taunts like this. For example, "Abu 'Afak, a man of great age (reputedly 120 years), was killed because he had lampooned Muhammad. The deed was done by Sālem b. 'Omayr at the behest of the Prophet, who had asked, 'Who will deal with this rascal for me?' The

---

138 Signs, wonders, powers and miracles are all designations for the same reality. See Hebrews 2:3-4.
139 See also Hebrews 2:3-4.

killing of such an old man moved a poetess, 'Asmā b. Marwān, to compose disrespectful verses about the Prophet, and she too was assassinated."[140]

Strengthened by God's Spirit

The second Koranic statement about Jesus, which is in harmony with the biblical account, is that God strengthened him by the Holy Spirit. This affirmation is found in the two Koranic references just cited, that is, 2:87 and 2:253, both of which assert that God "strengthened him with the Holy Spirit." Please especially note the implicit Trinitarian connotation in these two Koranic references. They show God, Christ and the Holy Spirit working together in concert.

These Koranic affirmations are certainly in harmony with the Gospel record given by Luke in which he recorded, "When the devil had completed every temptation, he departed from him for a season. And Jesus returned **in the power of the Spirit** into Galilee." (Luke 4:13-14)

Identity With God's Spirit

The third Koranic assertion about Jesus which is compatible with the New Testament account is, that he is a Spirit from God. Surah 4:171 tells us, "The Messiah, Jesus son of Mary, was only a messenger of Allah, and His word which He conveyed unto Mary, and **a Spirit from Him.**"

The Koranic statement that Jesus is "a Spirit from Him" is in harmony with a New Testament affirmation about Jesus to which average Christians have given scant attention. Through inspiration, the apostle Paul said, "Now **the Lord is the Spirit**, and where the Spirit of the Lord is, there is freedom." (II Corinthians 3:17 NIV) The expression "the Lord is the Spirit" conveys the same truth which is also expressed in the phrase "the Spirit of life in Christ Jesus." (Romans 8:2)

Though not recognized by Muslims, this Koranic passage also clearly expresses the concept of the Trinitarian unity of God. Here, God ("Allah"), Christ ("Jesus son of Mary") and the Holy Spirit ("a Spirit from Him") work together as one deity. This plurality in unity in Koranic theology is also clearly seen in the use of the plural pronouns "we" and "us" in reference to God. For example, in reference to Jesus, the Koran quotes God as saying, "We may make of him a revelation for mankind and a mercy from Us." (Surah 19:21) It reminds one of the affirmation of the Trinity in Isaiah 48:16.

The Messiah

A fourth Koranic statement, which is gloriously in harmony with the biblical account, unequivocally and unambiguously calls Jesus the Messiah! For instance, in Surah 3:45 we read, "O Mary! Lo! Allah giveth thee glad tidings of a word from **Him, whose name is the Messiah, Jesus, son of Mary,** illustrious in the world

---
140 Ali Dashti, <u>Twenty Three Years: A Study of the Prophetic Career of Mohammad</u>, trans. F.R.C. Bagley (London: George Allen & Unwin, 1985), p. 100.

and the Hereafter, and one of those brought near (unto Allah)." The other references in the Koran to Jesus as the Messiah are: Surah 4:157, 4:171-172, 5:19, 5:72, 5:75 and 9:30-31.

Whether Muhammad had the true understanding of what the title "Messiah" means or not, it is completely certain that almost no present-day Muslim understands the significance of this term. However, Christians should clearly realize that the title "Messiah" means The Anointed One. The Old Testament term is "Messiah," while the New Testament translation is rendered by the Greek word, "Christ." (See John 1:41.) As Israel's prophets, priests and kings were anointed with special oil to set them apart for the work of their respective offices,[141] accordingly, Acts 10:38 records that "God anointed him [i.e., Jesus] with the Holy Spirit and with power: who went about doing good, and healing all that were oppressed of the devil; for God was with him." By anointing Jesus, God honored him with the offices of Prophet, Priest and King. (See also Hebrews 1:9.)

One New Testament account of Jesus being anointed by God records the fulfillment of a prophecy by Isaiah who ministered from 740 to 681 B.C. Looking forward to the work of Christ, Isaiah prophesied, "The Spirit of the Sovereign LORD is on me, because the LORD has anointed me to preach good news to the poor. He has sent me to bind up the brokenhearted, to proclaim freedom for the captives and release from darkness for the prisoners, to proclaim the year of the LORD's favor and the day of vengeance of our God, to comfort all who mourn, and provide for those who grieve in Zion—to bestow on them a crown of beauty instead of ashes, the oil of gladness instead of mourning, and a garment of praise instead of a spirit of despair. They will be called oaks of righteousness, a planting of the LORD for the display of his splendor." (Isaiah 61:1-3 NIV) This is the scripture which Jesus read to the people when he preached in Nazareth, his home town. On that occasion Jesus clearly pointed to himself as the one to whom the prophecy referred by saying, "Today hath this scripture been fulfilled in your ears." (See Luke 4:16-30.)

The Righteous One

The fifth Koranic affirmation about Jesus, which is in conformity with the biblical account, is that he was righteous. This assertion is made in two Surahs. First, Surah 3:46 says, "He will speak unto mankind in his cradle and in his manhood, and **he is of the righteous**." This Koranic declaration of Jesus' righteousness is again emphasized when, according to the Koran, the angel said to Mary, "I am only a messenger of the Lord, that I may bestow on thee a **faultless son**." (Surah 19:19)

In Christian theology, it is clear that Christ's sinlessness was utterly essential for him to be man's Savior. These Koranic statements of the righteousness and faultlessness of Jesus are in harmony with repeated affirmations in the New Testament

---
[141] For priests, see Exodus 40:13; for kings and prophets, see I Kings 19:15-16.

about Jesus' righteousness. There he is called, "Him who knew no sin." (II Corinthians 5:21) It is affirmed that in all points, he was "tempted like as we are, yet without sin." (Hebrews 4:15) Further it is stated that he was "holy, guileless, undefiled, separated from sinners." (Hebrews 7:26) He "did no sin, neither was guile found in his mouth." (I Peter 2:22) He was "manifested to take away sins; and in him is no sin." (I John 3:5) Jesus himself said, "Which one of you convicts me of sin? If I tell the truth, why do you not believe me? (John 8:46 ESV) His sinlessness made it possible for him to become "sin on our behalf; that we might become the righteousness of God in him." (II Corinthians 5:21)

In stark contrast to the sinlessness of Jesus, the Koran emphasizes Muhammad's sinfulness two times. First, he is ordered to pray for the forgiveness of his sin. Thus Surah 47:19 says, "So know (O Mohammad) that there is no god save Allah, and ask forgiveness for thy sin and for believing men and for believing women." Secondly, the sinfulness of Muhammad is also asserted in Surah 48:1-2 in which Muhammad is told, "Lo! We have given thee (O Mohammad) a signal victory, that Allah may forgive thee of thy sin that which is past and that which is to come, and may perfect His favour unto thee, and may guide thee on a right path."

The Word of God

Sixth in the remarkable biblically-true series of Koranic statements which acknowledge the utterly unique role of Jesus is the one which tells us that Jesus is the Word of God. The Koran says that Jesus is, "a messenger of Allah, and **His word** which He conveyed unto Mary." (Surah 4:171)

Everyone with biblical literacy surely can relate this statement to the well-known passages about Jesus in John 1:1 and 1:14. In those verses the inseparably intimate relationship of Christ and God is revealed by Christ being called the Word of God. As we cannot impugn the word of an individual without impugning the individual himself, so one cannot diminish the stature of Christ, the Word of God, without degrading the concept of God.

The Second Adam

The seventh Koranic affirmation about Jesus which is in harmony with the biblical account tells us, Jesus is like Adam! The Koran, quoting Muhammad, says, "Lo! The likeness of Jesus with Allah is as the likeness of Adam." (Surah 3:59) This echoes the biblical testimony that "the first man Adam became a living soul. The last Adam became a life-giving spirit." (I Corinthians 15:45) The biblical account further affirms that "death reigned from Adam until Moses, even over them that had not sinned after the likeness of Adam's transgression, who is a figure of him who was to come." (Romans 5:14)

Muhammad's acknowledgment that Jesus is as Adam came during an intense dialogue with a delegation of Christians from the city of Najran in southwestern Arabia. About seven years after Muhammad's epochal *Hijra*,[142] the church at Najran sent a delegation of leading Christians to Medina to meet Muhammad. (For further details, see Chapter 9.) The members of that delegation seemed to have had two objectives. First, they hoped to win Muhammad for Christ. But, even should that attempt fail, secondly, they wanted to negotiate a treaty, pact or covenant with Muhammad which would guarantee freedom for the Arabian church—especially for the church at Najran—to continue its existence. (On the location of Najran, see Appendix A.)

Though he had little or no formal education, Muhammad was a highly intelligent man. He must have realized at least some of the implications of the parallel which he had drawn between Adam and Christ. **First**, just as Adam was the source of life for the whole human race, so Christ must also be the source for universal life in an even more significant sense. **Second**, as Adam is related to all men, so Christ is the only truly universal messenger from God. Since Muhammad could claim neither of those distinctions for himself, he must have realized that Christ was far greater than he was. He should, therefore, have openly and contritely acknowledged the supremacy of Christ. Not to have submitted to Christ, knowing only these two obvious facts, was an enormous inconsistency.

Christ's similarity to Adam is obvious from three observations: (1) neither of them had a human father, (2) both are related to the whole human race and (3) both, in distinct ways, are fountains of life for every human being. Adam is the fountain through which everyone's physical life has flowed, while Jesus is the inclusive and exclusive fountain from which man's spiritual and eternal life flows. Though Muhammad may not have had a way to know, Christians know that Jesus is "the true light, even the light which lighteth every man, coming into the world." (John 1:9)

For Muslims, a further enhancement of the understanding of the relation between Christ and Adam comes from an interesting account in the Koran about the origin of Satan. Surah 17:61 says, "When We said unto the angels: Fall down prostrate before Adam and they fell prostrate all save Iblis [the Koranic title for Satan], he said: Shall I fall prostrate before that which Thou has created of clay?"

This narrative is so important that it is expounded in more detail in Surah 38:72-79 which says, "When thy Lord said unto the angels: lo! I am about to create a mortal out of mire, and when I have fashioned him and breathed into him of My spirit, then fall down before him prostrate. The Angels fell down prostrate, every one, saving Iblis; he was scornful and became one of the disbelievers. He said: O Iblis! What hindereth thee from falling prostrate before that which I have created with both My hands? Art thou too proud or art thou of the high exalted? He said: I am better than him. Thou createdst me of fire, whilst him Thou didst create of

---

142 *Hijra,* meaning flight, escape or emigration, is the Arabic term for Muhammad's flight from Mecca to Medina in 622 A.D., the event which marks the beginning of the Muslim Era.

clay. He said: Go forth from hence, for lo! thou art outcast, and lo! My curse is on thee till the Day of Judgement."

Since Muhammad proclaimed Jesus is as Adam, then shouldn't Jesus, the greater Adam, be worshiped as the lesser Adam was said to have been? And should not Muhammad himself, knowing this, have prostrated himself before Jesus? (See "God's Viceroy," Chapter 5.)

Virgin Born

In the eighth place, the Koran explicitly and unambiguously upholds the virgin birth of Jesus. The nineteenth Surah, consisting of ninety-eight verses, is named "Mary." There, the reality of the virgin birth is powerfully portrayed through Mary's perplexity. She asks the heavenly messenger, "How can I have a son when no mortal hath touched me, neither have I been unchaste? He said: So (it will be). Thy Lord saith: It is easy for Me. And (it will be) that We may make of him a revelation for mankind and a mercy from Us, and it is a thing ordained." (Surah 19:20-21)

We should thank God that Muhammad did not buy into the polemic attack made against Jesus by Celsus, an anti-Christian philosopher, who writing about 180 A.D. alleged that Jesus was the bastard son of Mary by a Roman soldier named Panthera. We know of the calumny of Celsus through a refutation written by Origen, (c.185–c. 254) a great Alexandrian Christian scholar.

Tragically, Jews incorporated Celsus' lie into the Talmud under the title *Toledot Yeshu*, turning thousands of Jewish people away from Jesus because of Celsus' grotesque and utterly false libel.

Revelation

The ninth concurrence between the Koranic portrayal of Jesus and that of the Gospels is that Jesus is a revelation. The Koran quotes God as saying of Jesus, "We may make of him a revelation for mankind." (Surah 19:21) This declaration is in harmony with the Koranic statement that Jesus is "Allah's messenger." (Surah 4:157) This is stressed also in Surah 4:171 in which Jesus is called "a messenger of Allah."

The Gospels make it clear that Jesus is not only the revelation of God himself, but also of the will and purpose of God at the most profound level. The Gospels quote Jesus as saying, "He that hath seen me hath seen the Father; ... the words that I say unto you I speak not from myself: but the Father abiding in me doeth his works. Believe me that I am in the Father, and the Father in me: or else believe me for the very works' sake." (John 14:9-11) It is in harmony with this profound God-Christ relationship that by the Holy Spirit Simeon said that Jesus was "a light for revelation to the Gentiles." (Luke 2:32 NIV) For additional confirmation, see John 15:15 and John 17:26.

Mercy

The tenth compatibility of the Koranic portrayal of Christ with that of the Gospel is the affirmation that Jesus is a mercy. In addition to being "a revelation for mankind," he is also destined to be "a mercy" from God. (Surah 19:21)

The Gospel account certifies that Jesus is not only himself the epitome of mercy, but the chief promoter of mercy as well. Thus, Jesus taught, "Blessed are the merciful: for they shall obtain mercy." (Matthew 5:7) When criticized for dining with tax collectors and sinful people, Jesus retorted, "They that are whole have no need of a physician, but they that are sick. But go ye and learn what this meaneth, I desire mercy and not sacrifice: for I came not to call the righteous, but sinners." (Matthew 9:12-13) He also taught that mercy should generate further mercy. In a parable, in reference to a rapacious person whose indebtedness had been forgiven, Jesus said, "Thou wicked servant, I forgave thee all that debt, because thou besoughtest me: shouldest not thou also have mercy on thy fellow servant, even as I had mercy on thee?" (Matthew 18:32-33) Jesus was consistently angry with those who refused to temper justice with mercy. He said, "Woe unto you, scribes and pharisees, hypocrites! For you tithe mint and anise and cummin, and have left undone the weightier matters of the law, justice, and mercy and faith: but these ye ought to have done, and not to have left the other undone." (Matthew 23:23)

God's Viceroy

Finally, in the eleventh place, in Surah 2:30 the Koran surprisingly calls Jesus, as the greater Adam, God's Viceroy on earth! The Arabic word in the Koran which has been translated Viceroy is *khalifa*. Normally, *khalifa* (caliph in English) means successor, but obviously the word cannot carry that significance here because God has not forfeited his sovereignty nor appointed a successor. God is still fully and actively sovereign though he has appointed a Viceroy, a vicegerent, one who shares his divine royalty.

This startling Koranic passage about Jesus says, "When thy Lord said unto the angels: Lo! I am about to place a viceroy [*khalifa*] in the earth, they said: Wilt Thou place therein one who will do harm therein and will shed blood, while we, we hymn Thy praise and sanctify Thee? He said: Surely I know that which ye know not and He taught Adam all the names, then showed them to the angels, saying: Inform me of the names of these, if ye are truthful. They said: Be glorified! We have no knowledge saving that which Thou has taught us. Lo! Thou, only Thou, art the Knower, the Wise. He said: O Adam! Inform them of their names, and when he had informed them of their names, He said: Did I not tell you that I know the secret of the heavens and the earth? And I know that which ye disclose and which ye hide and when We said unto the angels: Prostrate yourselves before Adam, they fell prostrate, all save Iblis. He demurred through pride, and so became a disbeliever. And We said: O Adam! Dwell thou and thy wife in the Garden, and eat ye freely (of the fruits) thereof where ye will; but come not nigh this tree lest ye become wrongdoers." (Surah 2:30-35)

If the angels were to prostrate themselves before the lesser Adam, should the command not apply also to the greater Adam, that is, to the Adam who is the "life-giving spirit"? (I Corinthians 15:45) Jesus Christ, the prophet, is greater than Adam because as God's Viceroy, he shares God's royalty. Jesus, being God's Viceroy, is clearly substantiated in Christian theology by the throne statements about him in the New Testament. They imply his divine sovereignty. The book of Hebrews tells us, "of the Son he saith, Thy throne O God, is forever and ever." (Hebrews 1:8) The writer of Revelation says, "he showed me a river of life, bright as crystal, proceeding out of the throne of God and the Lamb." (Revelation 22:1) This verse portrays only one throne which is simultaneously occupied by both God and the Lamb.

Four Negative Statements About Christ

In stark contrast to the eleven biblically-true Koranic affirmations about Jesus, amazingly, there are four Christological Koranic denials regarding him. These denials form the doctrinal stance concerning Jesus which Muslim clerics ordinarily emphasize. The intensity of their emphasis leads the average Muslim to think these denials frame the whole truth about Jesus!

Did Jesus Die?

In its first negative statement about Christ, the Koran says that Jesus did not die. The crucial Koranic statement is, "Their saying [is]: We slew the Messiah, Jesus son of Mary, Allah's messenger. They slew him not nor crucified, but it appeared so unto them; and lo! Those who disagree concerning it are in doubt thereof; they have no knowledge thereof save pursuit of a conjecture; they slew him not for certain." (Surah 4:157) In staunch rebuttal, Christians affirm the reality of his death every week through participation in the Lord's Supper.

This Koranic verse flagrantly and contemptuously challenges the historical testimony upholding the record of the death, burial and resurrection of Christ. Among many other accounts in the New Testament, a powerful and graphic summary is given in I Corinthians 15:3-8. By daringly alleging that Christians who affirm the reality of the crucifixion "have no knowledge thereof save the pursuit of a conjecture," the Koranic message not only undermines one of the essential affirmations of the Gospel of Christ, but also repudiates the bases of both the evidentiary process of Western legal systems as well as the process by which sound history may be established, that is, determining historical truth by the testimony of eyewitnesses.

When the Koran speaks about "those who disagree concerning it," it must be clearly emphasized that there was no disagreement between Jews, Roman officials and the followers of Christ about the reality of the death of Jesus. Their disagreement was over whether he had arisen from the dead. The testimony of eyewitnesses (Roman soldiers, Jews—officials as well as commoners—along with Christians) has always been united, testifying that Jesus really died by crucifixion. It requires great temerity for one living six centuries after the event to deny the united harmonious testimony of both the friends and enemies of Jesus who were present when and where he died.

Is Jesus God?

The Koran's second negative statement about Jesus repudiates the biblical assertion that Jesus is God! The Koran states that, "They surely disbelieve who say: Lo! Allah is the Messiah, son of Mary. The Messiah (himself) said: O Children of Israel, worship Allah, my Lord and your Lord. Lo! Whoso ascribeth partners unto Allah, for him Allah hath forbidden paradise. His abode is the Fire. For evil-doers there will be no helpers. They surely disbelieve who say: Lo! Allah is the third of three; when there is no God save the One God. If they desist not from so saying a painful doom will fall on those of them who disbelieve." (Surah 5:72-73) (See also Surah 9:31.)

The Biblical record is clear. God not only sent down, he came down! That is the import of Matthew 1:23 which says, "And they shall call his name Immanuel; which is, being interpreted, God with us." The deity of Jesus is confirmed by John's gospel in his message of "the Word." There, we learn that "the Word was God." (John 1:1) It was that same Word which became flesh. (John 1:14) See also Titus 2:13, Hebrews 1:8, I John 5:20 and Revelation 22:1.

Plurality in Unity

By denying the deity of Jesus, Islam not only repudiates the clear Koranic indications of the plurality in the unity of God, which have been carefully noted above, but it presents a monotheism so strict, so unitary and so monolithic that one cannot explore the fullness of the one God. It is a monotheism even more unitary than the mathematical number 1, whose values are factored out all the time by fractions such as 1/2 and 1/3. These fractions do not deny or compromise the unity of the numeral 1 which is written above the line. They simply affirm that within the unity of the numeral 1 are inherent values and factors which may be considered independently. To express this concept theologically, is to say that there is a fullness in the One, for "in him dwelleth all the fullness of the Godhead bodily." (Colossians 2:9)

Three Tests

In denying that Jesus is God, Islam repudiates even its own criteria for recognizing deity. According to the Koran there are three proofs of deity. The **first** proof is the power to create and the **second** is the power to reproduce creation. These criteria are found in Surah 10:35 which tells us, "Say: Is there of your partners (whom ye ascribe unto Allah) one that produceth Creation and then reproduceth it? Say: Allah produceth Creation, then reproduceth it. How then, are ye misled!"[143] The **third** proof of deity is whether the being under consideration is able to and actually does answer prayer. That criterion is given in Surah 7 which will be considered later.

Jesus Created

The Koran itself testifies that Jesus created. Therefore, Jesus meets the first Koranic criterion for being acknowledged as Deity. The Koran makes it very clear that Jesus created living organisms, not just lifeless matter. Surah 5:110 gives this account, "When Allah saith: O Jesus, son of Mary! Remember My favour unto thee and unto thy mother; how I strengthened thee with the Holy Spirit, so that thou spakest unto mankind in the cradle as in maturity; and how I taught thee the Scripture and Wisdom and the Torah and the Gospel and how thou did shape of clay as it were the likeness of a bird by My permission, and didst blow upon it and it was a bird by My permission, and thou didst heal him who was born blind and the leper by My permission; and how thou didst raise the dead, by My permission; and how I restrained the Children of Israel from (harming) thee when thou camest unto them with clear proofs, and those of them who disbelieved exclaimed: This is naught else than mere magic."[144]

The following three Koranic passages also assert that the power to create is one of the criteria by which we recognize or identify Deity. Surah 7:191-192: "Attribute they as partners to Allah those who created naught, but are themselves created, And cannot give them help, nor can they help themselves?" Surah 16:17: "Is He then Who createth as him who createth not? Will ye not then remember?" Surah 22:73: "O Mankind! A similitude is coined, so pay ye heed to it: Lo! those on whom ye call beside Allah will never create a fly though they combine together for the purpose. And if the fly took something from them, they could not rescue it from him. So weak are (both) the seeker and the sought!"

Biblical Testimony

Long before the Koran was ever known, the Bible made it clear that Jesus created. On the cosmic level, scripture tells us, "All things were made through him; and without him was not anything made that hath been made." (John 1:3; see also

---

143 To understand Surah 10:35 even more clearly, which was quoted from Marmaduke Pickthall's *The Meaning of the Glorious Koran*, consider it from the following translations: A.J. Arberry rendered it, "Say: 'is there any of your associates who originates creation, then brings it back again?' Say: 'God — He originates creation, then brings it back again." Sher Ali translated it, "Say, 'Is there any of your associate gods who originates creation and then reproduces it?' Say, 'It is Allah *alone* Who originates creation and then reproduces it." Yusuf Ali gives this rendering, "Say: 'Of your partners, Can any originate creation and repeat it?' Say: 'It is God who originates Creation and repeats it." N.J. Dawood's translation says, "Say: 'Can any of your idols conceive Creation, then renew it? Allah conceives Creation, then renews it."

144 This concept is so basic and fundamental that we should see how other translators have rendered it. N.J. Dawood translated the key assertion this way, "by My leave you fashioned from clay the likeness of a bird and breathed into it so that, by My leave, it became a living bird." Yusuf Ali has given it to us with equal clarity. His translation says, "And behold! thou makest Out of clay, as it were, The figure of a bird, By My leave, And thou breathest into it, And it becometh a bird." A.J. Arberry concurs with the other translators. His rendering is, "when thou createst out of clay, by My leave, as the likeness of a bird, and thou breathest into it, and it is a bird, by My leave."

Colossians 1:16-17.) On a more personal level, Jesus, through an act of creation, alleviated human hunger. This is seen in the miracle of the feeding of the 5,000 which is recorded in Matthew 14:13-21. The Koran may refer to this miracle in Surah 5:112-115. The essential part of Matthew's account says, "he [Jesus] directed the people to sit down on the grass. Taking the five loaves and the two fish and looking up to heaven, he gave thanks and broke the loaves. Then he gave them to the disciples, and the disciples gave them to the people. They all ate and were satisfied, and the disciples picked up twelve basketfuls of broken pieces that were left over. The number of those who ate was about five thousand men, besides women and children." (Matthew 14:19-21 NIV) It is obvious that without a miracle of creation, "the five loaves and the two fish" were utterly inadequate to have satisfied the hunger of that vast throng of people consisting of approximately 5,000 men, along with many women and children.

Jesus Restored Creation

The second Koranic criterion by which people may recognize Deity is whether a being is able to restore creation. We find this criterion in Surah 10:35 which puts the issue succinctly. It asks, "Is there of your partners (whom ye ascribe unto Allah) one that produceth Creation and then reproduceth it? Say: Allah produceth Creation, then **reproduceth** it. How then, are ye misled!"[145]

The Koran is very explicit that Jesus indeed did reproduce, repeat, bring back again, and renew creation! In Surah 5:110 it is recorded that Allah said to Jesus, "thou didst raise the dead, by My permission."

Jesus Answered Prayer

The **third** Koranic standard by which we may recognize Deity is whether a being which is under consideration is able and willing to help when we pray to him. This is clearly stated in Surah 7:191-194 which says, "Attribute they as partners to Allah those who created naught, but are themselves created, and cannot give them help, nor can they help themselves? And if ye call them to the Guidance, they follow you not. Whether ye call them or are silent is all one to them. Lo! those on whom ye call beside Allah are slaves like unto you. Call on them now, and let them answer you, if ye are truthful."

Jesus meets this criterion. We may call on him and he has the power and the love to respond positively. The Koran itself makes that clear. Surah 5:112-115, which we have already seen in another connection, asserts that Jesus answered the prayers of his disciples. When they called on him, saying, "We wish to eat there-

---

[145] To understand this passage even more clearly, consider the following translations: A.J. Arberry rendered it, "Say: 'is there any of your associates who originates creation, then **brings it back again**?' Say: 'God—He originates creation, then brings it back again." Sher Ali translated it, "Say, 'Is there any of your associate gods who originates creation and then **reproduces it**?' Say, 'It is Allah *alone* Who originates creation and then reproduces it." Yusuf Ali gives this rendering, "Say: 'Of your partners, Can any originate creation and **repeat it**?' Say: 'It is God who originates Creation and repeats it." N.J. Dawood's translation says, "Say: 'Can any of your idols conceive Creation, then **renew it**?' Allah conceives Creation, then renews it."

of," he fulfilled their request! The Koranic passage says, "When the disciples said: O Jesus, son of Mary! Is thy Lord able to send down for us a table spread with food from heaven? He said: observe your duty to Allah, if ye are true believers. (They said:) We wish to eat thereof, that we may satisfy our hearts and know that thou hast spoken truth to us, and that thereof we may be witnesses. Jesus, son of Mary, said: O Allah, Lord of us! Send down for us a table spread with food from heaven, that it may be a feast for us, for the first of us and for the last of us, and a sign from Thee. Give us sustenance, for Thou art the Best of Sustainers. Allah said: Lo! I send it down for you. And whoso disbelieveth of you afterward, him surely will I punish with a punishment wherewith I have not punished any of (My) creatures."

Though there are many biblical examples showing us that Jesus answers prayer (see Mark 2:5, Mark 10:51-52, Luke 17:12-17, John 5:6-8), I cite only Mark 4:35-41: "That day when evening came, he said to his disciples, 'Let us go over to the other side.' Leaving the crowd behind, they took him along, just as he was, in the boat. There were also other boats with him. A furious squall came up, and the waves broke over the boat, so that it was nearly swamped. Jesus was in the stern, sleeping on a cushion. The disciples woke him and said to him, 'Teacher, don't you care if we drown?' He got up, rebuked the wind and said to the waves, 'Quiet! Be still!' Then the wind died down and it was completely calm. He said to his disciples, 'Why are you so afraid? Do you still have no faith?' They were terrified and asked each other, 'Who is this? Even the wind and the waves obey him!'" (NIV)

In view of these facts, (1) Jesus creates, (2) Jesus recreates and (3) Jesus answers prayer, what should Muslims think of Jesus? He has met all the criteria set by the Koran to recognize deity, so every follower of the Koran should believe that Jesus is not only human but divine as well!

The Koran's third negative Christological denial is: There is no Trinity. The Koran puts it this way: "disbelievers are they surely who say: 'God is the third of the trinity;' but there is no god other than God the one. And if they do not desist from saying what they say, then indeed those among them who persist in disbelief will suffer painful punishment." (Surah 5:73 Ahmed Ali Translation)

As pointed out above in the paragraphs titled "Identity With God's Spirit" and "Plurality in Unity," the Koran itself has statements which imply the Trinitarian concept of God. Biblical Trinitarian statements depict not the association of three Gods but the profundity and fulness of the One God. The biblical concept of the Trinity, among many other references, is found powerfully presented in the following two passages: (1) "Come ye near unto me, hear ye this; from the beginning **I** have not spoken in secret; from the time that it was, **there am I**; and now **the Lord Jehovah** hath sent **me** and **his Spirit**." (Isaiah 48:16) (2) "And **I** will pray **the Father**, and he shall give you another Comforter, that he may be with you for ever, even **the Spirit of truth**: whom the world cannot receive; for it beholdeth him not, neither knoweth him: ye know him; for he abideth with you, and shall be in you." (John 14:16-17)

The Koran's fourth repudiation of biblical Christology is that Jesus is not the Son of God. In the Koran, Jesus is repeatedly called "the son of Mary," never "the Son of God." "And the Jews say: Ezra is the son of Allah, and the Christians say: The Messiah is the son [*ibn*] of Allah. That is their saying with their mouths. They imitate the saying of those who disbelieved of old. Allah (Himself) fighteth against them. How perverse are they! (Surah 9:30. See also Surah 19:35 and Surah 23:91.)

Chapter 9 relates the captivating account of a delegation of Christians from the Arabian city of Najran who traveled to Medina, hoping to negotiate an agreement with Muhammad which would allow their vibrant church to continue under Islamic rule. On that occasion, Muhammad tried to simplify the issue by attempting to convert the Christians to Islam. "When the two divines spoke to him [Muhammad] the apostle said to them, 'Submit yourselves.' They said, 'We have submitted.' He said: 'You have not submitted, so submit.' They said, 'Nay, but we submitted before you.' He said, 'You lie. Your assertion that God has a son, your worship of the cross, and your eating pork hold you back from submission.' They said, 'But who is his father, Muhammad?' The apostle was silent and did not answer them."[146] The silence of Muhammad has never been broken through all the centuries of Islamic history. Since Surah 19 of the Koran very strongly upholds the virgin birth of Christ, we are left with the insistent question which those delegates put before the great Prophet of Arabia, when they asked, "who is his father, Muhammad?" That demanding question is answered in the Biblical declaration that Jesus is the Son of God, which is summarized in Romans 1:1-4 and Hebrews 1:1-5.

Perhaps, one day in Muslim thinking, the eleven positive biblically-true affirmations in Koranic Christology will take precedence over the false statements about him found in the Koran. When that day arrives, it is nearly certain that there will be a massive turning of Muslims in obedience to the Gospel of Christ as clearly foreseen by the prophet Isaiah. (See Isaiah 19:19-25)

03

---

146 Ibn Ishaq, The Life of Muhammad, Trans A. Guillaume, (Karachi: Oxford University Press, 1967), pp. 271-272.

Chapter 6

CRITICAL DEATHS, THE HIJRA AND THE FATE OF YATHRIB'S JEWS, 619–623 A.D.

Trouble Compounded by Sorrow

In 619 A.D., opposition to Muhammad's message increased both in intensity and scope. At that critical juncture, his burdens were further compounded by the death of his wife, Khadija, as well as Abu Talib, his uncle and long-time protector. His season of sorrow began with Khadija's death. "Since his first Call, she had been his ever-ready confidante, his strengthener, his support and his first convert. He revealed all his doubts and his troubles to her, and her steadfast encouragement enabled him to persevere, in spite of seemingly endless difficulties and discouragements. He had remained for twenty-four years faithful to his middle-aged wife and he spoke of her with affection to the end of his life."[147]

That poignant moment when his beloved wife died soon became even more acute because "shortly afterwards, his uncle, Abu Talib, also lay dying. ... The Apostle made great efforts to persuade Abu Talib to repeat the Muslim witness of faith, but the old man only lay silent, making no response, until he passed away. ... He is not considered a hero by Muslims, for he died in unbelief. Nevertheless, if it had not been for the staunch courage with which he stood by his nephew, Islam might have died in its cradle."[148]

Converts Seek Refuge in Abyssinia

Abu Talib had given protection to his nephew, Muhammad, but he could not offer protection to those who had become converts to Islam. Peters, quoting Tabari,[149] tells us that when the level of persecution against the converts to Islam involved social pressure, economic boycott, and physical threats, Muhammad "commanded them to emigrate to Abyssinia. In Abyssinia there was a righteous king called the Negus in whose land no one was oppressed and who was praised for his righteousness. Abyssinia was a land with which the Quraysh traded and in which [they] found an ample living, security and a good market."[150] The number of Muslims

---

147 John Bagot Glubb, The Life and Times of Muhammad, (New York: Stein & Day Publishers, 1970), pp. 136-137.
148 John Bagot Glubb, The Life and Times of Muhammad, (New York: Stein and Day, 1970), p. 137.
149 This is Abu Ja'far Muhammad ibn Jarir Al-Tabari (839–926) who wrote a great Arab history. He is not to be confused with Ali ibn Sahl Rabban al-Tabari (ca. 783–858) who was a Christian convert to Islam and who wrote the first comprehensive work of Arabic medicine.
150 F.E. Peters Muhammad and the Origins of Islam, (New York: State University of New York Press, 1994), p. 173.

who took refuge in Abyssinia (ancient Ethiopia) is disputed, being between fifteen and eighty-three.

No Refuge Near Home

In Mecca, resistance to Muhammad's preaching continued and progressively became more threatening. Due to his death, the protection which his uncle had given had ceased. Therefore, Muhammad's situation had become much more precarious. Ibn Ishaq tells us, "Abu Talib died some three years before he [Muhammad] migrated to Medina, and it was then that Quraysh began to treat him in an offensive way which they would not have dared to follow in his uncle's lifetime. A young lout actually threw dust on his head."[151]

Urgently, Muhammad went alone[152] to the nearby hill town of Taif, home of the Thaqif tribe. (See "Taif" in Appendix A.) He hoped they might be more amenable to his message than his own Quraysh had been and would give him protection. There, too, he found only hostility. One man said, "'Could not God have found someone better than you to send?' Another said, 'By God, don't let me ever speak to you. If you are an apostle from God as you say you are, you are far too important for me to reply to, and if you are lying against God it is not right that I should speak to you!' So the apostle got up and went, despairing of getting any good out of Thaqif."[153] (Thaqif was a tribe living at Taif.)

Preparation for Muhammad's Hijra[154]

Eventually, a door of refuge for Muhammad from rejection and humiliation opened two-hundred-fifty miles north of Mecca in the major settlement of Yathrib, later known as Medina (meaning "city"). Jews were well established in Yathrib. They "seem to have been partly settlers from the north, of true Israelite descent, with an addition of Arab proselytes. As that may be, they had, to a great extent, adopted Arab customs and spoke a dialect of Arabic. They were divided into three tribes: the Qurayzah, the Nadir and the less important Qaynuqa.[155] There were in addition two dominant Arab tribes, said to be of Yemeni origin: the Aws and the Khazraj. Some other, smaller Arab tribes who had been there before them were closely connected with the Jews and partly Judaized."[156] Basically, it was strife between the Jews and Arabs of Yathrib, along with internecine strife among

---

151 Ibn Ishaq, The Life of Muhammad, Trans. A. Guillaume, (Karachi: Oxford University Press, 1982), p. 191.
152 One account says, "It was scarcely a fortnight after Abu Talib's death that Mohammed set out to walk to Taif. He was accompanied by Zaid, whom I have mentioned as an adopted son of the Prophet, and one of the earliest converts to Islam." – Edith Holland, The Story of Mohammed, (London: George G. Harrap & Company, 1914), p. 66.
153 Ibn Ishaq, The Life of Muhammad, Trans. A. Guillaume, (Karachi: Oxford University Press, 1982), p. 192.
154 Also spelled *hegira* and *hejira*. The word means flight or escape from danger or emigration.
155 Watt says concerning Banu Qurayzah and the Bunu 'n-Nadir, "While similar to their neighbors in many ways, these two groups adhered to the Jewish faith and vigorously maintained their creedal and ritual distinction. It is not clear whether they were of Hebrew stock or were judaized Arabs; possibly isolated Arabs had attached themselves to small groups of Hebrews." – W. Montgomery Watt, Muhammad at Mecca, (Oxford: The Clarendon Press, 1953), pp. 141-142. Some scholars trace the origin of the Jews in Arabia to Jews who had fled from Palestine following the Bar Kokhba rebellion against Rome in 135 A.D.
156 Maxime Rodinson, Mohammed, trans. Anne Carter, (New York: Pantheon Books, 1971), p. 139.

First Fruit From Yathrib

Hoping to find receptive listeners, it was Muhammad's incessant, unremitting practice to speak about himself and his religious views to devotees from all over Arabia, who not only came to Mecca to pay homage to one or more of the idols housed in the Kaaba, but also to attend the trade fairs which were held in the outskirts of Mecca during the annual hajj (pilgrimage) seasons. But consistently, he had found indifference, resistance and rejection.

In 620 A.D., that discouraging routine was broken at al-'Aqaba, near Mecca, where he spoke to a group of six pilgrims of the Khazraj[157] tribe from Yathrib. "The oasis town of Yatrib [Yathrib], with a flourishing agriculture, which Mecca wholly lacked, in addition to a substantial commerce, and with a relatively considerable degree of literacy in its population, thanks to the presence of three Jewish tribes, had attained a higher cultural and social level. Nevertheless Yatrib was generally placed second among the Hejazi towns after Mecca."[158] (See Appendix A under "Hejaz.")

When Muhammad told the pilgrims from Yathrib that he was a prophet of God, they said the Jews used to tell us, "A prophet will be sent soon. His day is at hand. We shall follow him and kill you by his aid as 'Ad and Iram perished.' So when they heard the apostle's message they said one to another: 'This is the very prophet of whom the Jews warned us. Don't let them get to him before us!' Thereupon they accepted his teaching and became Muslims, saying, 'We have left our people, for no tribe is so divided by hatred and rancor as they. Perhaps God will unite them through you. So let us go to them and invite them to this religion of yours; and if God unites them in it, then no man will be mightier than you.' Thus saying they returned to Medina as believers."[159]

The First Pledge of al-'Aqaba

In 621 A.D., during the next yearly hajj (pilgrimage) to the Kaaba, twelve men from Yathrib, including five of the original six plus seven others, met Muhammad at al-'Aqaba where the first converts from Yathrib had met him. One pilgrim's account of the meeting is preserved in the words of 'Ubada b. al-Samit. He said, "We gave allegiance to the apostle that we would associate nothing with God, not steal, not commit fornication, not kill our offspring, not slander our neighbor, not disobey him in what was right; if we fulfilled this, paradise would be ours and if

---

157 "During the sixth century, the Arab tribe of the Bani Qaylah had emigrated from South Arabia and settled in the [Yathrib] oasis, alongside the Jews. They then formed two distinct clans—Aws and Khazraj—which eventually became two separate tribes." – Karen Armstrong, Muhammad, A Prophet for Our Time, (New York: Harper Collins Publishers, 2006), p. 102.

158 Ali Dashti, Twenty Three Years: A Study of the Prophetic Career of Mohammad, trans. F.R.C. Bagley, (London: George Allen & Unwin, 1985), p. 77.

159 Ibn Ishaq, The Life of Muhammad, Trans. A. Guillaume, (Karachi: Oxford University Press, 1982), p. 198.

we committed any of those sins, we should be punished in this world and this would serve as expiation; if the sin was concealed until the Day of Resurrection, then it would be for God to decide whether to punish or to forgive."[160]

The giving of allegiance to Muhammad by these Yathribis is known as the First Pledge of al-'Aqaba. At that point it had become possible that the contact with the pilgrims from Yathrib might lead to the development of a refuge for the young Muslim movement. It was a toehold which should be enlarged and strengthened. Therefore, on their return to Yathrib, Muhammad sent Mus'ab with them who was "to read the Qur'an to them and to teach them Islam and to give them instruction about religion. In Medina, Mus'ab was called 'The Reader.' ... He [also] used to lead the prayers because Aws and Khazraj could not bear to see one of their rivals take the lead."[161]

In addition to being the reader, the *muezzin* (the one who calls the faithful to prayer), and the *imam* (the one who leads the faithful in prayer), Mus'ab also proved to be a persuasive missionary. When two enraged tribal leaders came to stop him from instructing the people, Mus'ab invited them to listen as he read. The first leader, laying aside his lance, listened to the recitation. Then, "his face changed. 'What wonderful and beautiful discourse this is!' he cried, 'What does one do to enter this religion?' After he had proclaimed his faith in Allah and prostrated himself in prayer, he went back to report to his chief. Sa'd was furious, grasped his own lance, and marched off to confront Mus'ab himself, only to be overwhelmed in his turn by the Qur'an. He then summoned his people and asked them to follow him; trusting his leadership implicitly, the entire clan converted en masse."[162]

The Second Pledge of al-'Aqaba

The following year, in 622 A.D., seventy-three men and two women came from Yathrib to al-'Aqaba to pledge their loyalty to Muhammad. Ibn Ishaq has preserved Ka'b b. Malik's account of the meeting: "When we had completed the *hajj* [pilgrimage] and the night came in which we had agreed to meet the apostle, there was with us ... one of our chiefs and nobles whom we had taken with us. We had concealed our business from those of our people who were polytheists. We said to him, 'You are one of our chiefs and nobles and we want to wean you from your present state lest you become fuel for the fire in the future.' Then we invited him to accept Islam and told him about our meeting with the apostle at al-'Aqaba. Thereupon he accepted Islam and came to al-'Aqaba with us, and became a *naqib* (leader).

"We slept that night among our people in the caravan until when a third of the night had passed we went stealing softly like sandgrouse to our appointment with the apostle as far as the gully by al-'Aqaba. There were seventy-three men with

---
160 Ibn Ishaq, The Life of Muhammad, Trans. A. Guillaume, (Karachi: Oxford University Press, 1982), p. 199.
161 Ibn Ishaq, The Life of Muhammad, Trans. A. Guillaume, (Karachi: Oxford University Press, 1982), p. 199.
162 Karen Armstrong, Muhammad, A Prophet for Our Time, (New York: Harper Collins Publishers, 2006), p. 106.

two of our women. ... We gathered together in the gully waiting for the apostle until he came with his uncle al-'Abbas who was at that time a polytheist;[163] albeit he wanted to be present at his nephew's business and see that he had a firm guarantee. ... He was the first to speak and said: ... 'If you think that you can be faithful to what you have promised him and protect him from his opponents, then assume the burden you have undertaken. But if you think that you will betray and abandon him after he has gone out with you, then leave him now. For he is safe where he is.' We replied, 'We have heard what you say [thus, turning to Muhammad they said], You speak, O apostle, and choose for yourself and for your Lord what you wish.'

"The apostle spoke and recited the Qur'an and invited men to God and commended Islam and then said: 'I invite your allegiance on the basis that you protect me as you would your women and children.' Al-Bara' took his hand and said, 'By Him Who sent you with the truth we will protect you as we protect our women. We give our allegiance and we are men of war possessing arms which have been passed on from father to son.'[164] While al-Bara' was speaking Abu'l-Haytham b. al-Tayyihan interrupted him and said, 'O apostle, we have ties with other men (he meant the Jews) and if we sever them perhaps when we have done that and God will have given you victory, you will return to your people and leave us?' The apostle smiled and said: ... 'I am of you and you are of me. I will war against them that war against you and be at peace with those at peace with you.'"[165]

The two pledges at al-'Aqaba and subsequent events at Medina substantiate the following statement attributed to Muhammad: "Amr ibn-Hammad ibn-abi-Hanifah from A'ishah: The Prophet said: 'All districts or cities were conquered by force, but al-Madinah was conquered by the Koran.'"[166]

The Hijra[167]

Mecca, Muhammad's home town, continued to resist him and his message and persistently ridiculed and harassed him and his small band of early followers. However, the Meccan response to Muhammad was not simply blind rage. On the

---

163 One challenging account states that "the whole incident of 'Abbas is probably to be rejected as a later invention to conceal the dishonorable treatment of Muhammad by the Banu Hashim at this juncture; on his return from at-Ta'if Muhammad was under the protection of the head of the clan of Nawfal." – W. Montgomery Watt, Muhammad at Mecca, (Oxford: The Clarendon Press, 1953), p. 147.

164 At this second pledge of al-'Aqaba those who pledged, "took an oath not merely to obey Muhammad but to fight for him—the Pledge of War, bay'at al-harb." – W. Montgomery Watt, Muhammad at Mecca, (Oxford: The Clarendon Press, 1953), p. 145.

165 Ibn Ishaq, The Life of Muhammad, Trans. A. Guillaume, (Karachi: Oxford University Press, 1982), p. 203.

166 al-Imam abu-l `Abbas Ahmad ibn-Jabir al-Baladhuri, The Origins of the Islamic State Being a Translation From the Arabic Accompanied With Annotations Geographic and Historic Notes of The Kitab Futuh al-Buldan, Trans. Philip Khuri Hitti (Beirut: Khayats, 1966), p. 21.

167 Also spelled Hijrah, Hidjra or in its Latin form, Hegira. "During the course of the calendar year Muslims celebrate a number of festivals and 'holy days.' In fixing the dates of these feasts they follow the Muslim calendar year, which begins with the Hijra. We must remember, however, that the Muslim era does not begin exactly on the day when Muhammad left Mecca for Medina. Its beginning was fixed by Umar in such a way that the year begins with Muharram and that the first day of that month keeps the date which it had in the year in which the Caliph put into force the new calculation. The Muslim era begins on the 15th (or 16th) of July 622." – Encyclopaedia Britannica, 11th Edition, Vol. IV, p. 1001.

contrary, it represented reasoned resistance. The economy of Mecca, for hundreds of years, largely depended on the annual pilgrimage of thousands of devotees from all over the Arabian Peninsula. They came to express their devotion to one or more of the hundreds of idols housed in the Kaaba, the ancient temple located in the center of Mecca. Those devotees never came empty handed. Along with other merchandise, depending on how close to Mecca they lived, they came driving flocks of goats, sheep or camels which they traded and bartered with other attendees in huge trade fairs sponsored and organized by the leaders of Mecca. Commissions levied by Mecca on this exceptionally vibrant trade generated much of the financial underpinning the city needed to survive. Muhammad's message, based on his assertion that there was only one God, if embraced, would bring the idol sanctuary to an end, thus stopping the pilgrimage and ruining the economy! Obviously, Muhammad and his movement could not be allowed to flourish!

Muhammad had searched desperately for a new center in which he and his disciples might live without opposition and from which he might propagate his message. Finally, he was successful when he came to amicable terms with the leaders of Yathrib, a city some 250 miles north of Mecca. That agreement, as previously mentioned, is known as The Second Pledge of al-'Aqaba, made in March of 622 A.D.

Finally, after nine long years of hostility and opposition from the Quraysh, a significant segment of a rival community had opened its arms to Muhammad, his message and his people. One of the reasons the message of monotheism, of only one God, did not arouse immediate hostility in Yathrib was because, in contrast to Mecca, there was no shrine there in which idols were venerated, drawing pilgrims from all over Arabia. On the other hand, Mecca saw that the message of *tawhid*, the stern unitary, monolithic monotheism preached by Muhammad, would totally exclude all the idols housed in the Kaaba which would end the annual pilgrimages and their related trade fairs. As stated before, that would have brought economic disaster on Mecca.

As soon as The Second Pledge of al-'Aqaba, also called the Pledge of War, was complete, the die was cast. The Muslims of Mecca would migrate to Medina. However, Muhammad was not the first to become a *muhajir*, an immigrant.[168] Rather, Muhammad oversaw the random departure of small groups of Muslims from Mecca on their way to Medina, collectively totaling about seventy persons in all. They were the *Muhajirun*, the Immigrants. Muhammad, Abu Bakr, who at Muhammad's death became the first caliph, and Ali, who was Muhammad's cousin as well as his son-in-law, delayed their departure. They wanted to give aid, direction and encouragement to the others, till essentially the entire tiny community had set out on its arduous and momentous emigration. It was a demanding journey, not only because of

---

[168] The one who goes on a *hijra*, an escape, a flight, is a *muhajir*. (The plural of *muhajir* is *Muhajirun*.)

traveling 250 miles through the desert by animal conveyance, but because the word *hijra* "has the connotation not [only] of geographical transference, but of separation from one's family and clan and attachment to others."[169]

The native resident Muslims of Medina received each group of *Muhajirun* and provided temporary housing and sustenance for them. Because of this, the Medinan Muslims were called *ansar*, Helpers.

Muhammad's Hijra

"It was about the middle of September [622 A.D.] before Muhammad himself was ready to set out. Shortly before he did so, the Meccan pagans are said to have become suspicious, and to have plotted to kill Muhammad himself."[170] Muhammad and Abu Bakr, along with a servant and a guide, took refuge in a cave for a couple of days and then surreptitiously, by little used roundabout tracks, aided by their guide, made their way to Medina, arriving on September 24, 622, A.D.[171]

In the Koran, Muhammad referred to this precarious experience in the graphic words of Surah 9:40: "Allah helped him when those who disbelieve drove him forth, the second of two; when they two were in the cave, when he said unto his comrade: Grieve not. Lo! Allah is with us. Then Allah caused His peace of reassurance to descend upon him and supported him with hosts ye cannot see, and made the word of those who disbelieved the nethermost, while Allah's word it was that became the uppermost. Allah is Mighty, Wise." At that juncture, no one could have guessed that Muhammad would return to Mecca just eight years later in complete military and spiritual victory!

The Muslim Era Begins

Muhammad's Hijra marks the beginning of the Muslim era. "As early as 643 A.D. we have documentary evidence that the Arabs were using an era beginning in 622 A.D."[172] Note that the passage of time in the Muslim era is based on a lunar calendar.

It is entirely appropriate that the Muslim era should be considered to have begun with Muhammad's Hijra because that event marked the first time that steps to initiate the concept of a Muslim state or empire could have been implemented. It is not certain, however, at which point Muhammad began envisioning the political

---
169 W. Montgomery Watt, Muhammad, Prophet and Statesman, (New York: Oxford University Press, 1974), p. 91.
170 W. Montgomery Watt, Muhammad, Prophet and Statesman, (New York: Oxford University Press, 1974), p. 90.
171 This is the date given by W. Montgomery Watt in his Muhammad, Prophet and Statesman, p. 91. But, there is confusion about determining the precise date. "Our confusion on the matter is that we cannot be sure how the later Muslims handled the dating of events that occurred before Muhammad forbade the practice of intercalation during his 'Farewell Pilgrimage' in March of 632 A.D. Did they retroject their own purely lunar calendar onto the years 622-632 or did they recall them according to the old intercalation system?" – F.E. Peters Muhammad and the Origins of Islam, (New York: State University of New York Press, 1994), p. 173.
172 Patricia Crone and Michael Cook, Hagarism, The Making of the Islamic World, (London: Cambridge University Press, 1977), p. 157. In addition, the authors state in their footnote 39 on page 157: "The dating 'year xvii' on the earliest Arab coins of Damascus presumably attests earlier use of the same era, but no corresponding Christian date is given."

and military aspects of his total concept. But, in any case, it was at Medina that he found the freedom and liberty as well as the resources to set about bringing his ideal into reality.

Islam "hitherto had been a religion within a state; in Medina it passed into something more than a state religion—it became the state. Then and there Islam came to be what the world has ever since recognized it to be—a militant polity."[173]

In his historical novel, Holland takes the position that "the judgment of God" about the supreme role of Muhammad in the Muslim world, and in the world at large, was not made clear till after the death of Mu'awiya, founder of the Umayyad Caliphate, in 680 A.D. Holland's contention is that the clarification came through one of the lieutenants of Ibn al Zubayr, a leader of the rebellion against Umayyad power. Sixty-four years after the Hijra in 685 or 686 A.D., Ibn al Zubayr "minted a coin in Persia with a novel and fateful message, 'Bismallah Muhammad rasul Allah,' it ran—'in the name God, Muhammad is the messenger of God.'"[174] But Holland's position is untenable because Crone and Cook (see footnote 172) give numismatic evidence that Muhammad's followers considered his Hijra to be the pivotal point of all history. For Muslims, after the Hijra, Christ was no longer to be the focal point of history. Beginning with the Hijra, B.C. and A.D. no longer had any validity for Muslims, only B.H. (Before the Hijra) and A.H. (Anno Hegirae, In the year of the Hijra) were to be used to mark historical epochs. No one in the Muslim world had dared to question the utilization and validity of the calendar based on the Hijra till Mohammad Reza Shah Pahlavi, defying Muslim sentiment, "had put it back to the foundation of the Persian Empire by Cyrus."[175] As soon as the Khomeini Revolution of 1979 took place, the Iranian calendar was readjusted to be based again on the Hijra.

Extent of Medina

At the time Muhammad arrived, only the most densely inhabited part of the oasis of Yathrib was known as *Medina,* the city. To honor Muhammad, that name was enhanced to *Medinat-un-Nabi,* The City of the Prophet. Now, by long standing usage, *un-Nabi* is dropped and the original form of the name, that is, Medina, is commonly used, referring to all of the old Yathrib, the entire oasis settlement.

Upon his arrival, there were eager appeals from many Muslims for Muhammad to take up residence in their part of Yathrib. To avoid the appearance of partiality, he gave his camel free rein telling everyone that where the animal voluntarily halted would be the location of his dwelling. "Eventually, she fell to her knees outside a *mirbad*, a place for drying dates, which belonged to

---
173 Philip K. Hitti, The Arabs, A Short History, (London: Macmillan & Co. Ltd., 1965), p. 27.
174 Tom Holland, In the Shadow of the Sword, (London: Little, Brown, 2012), p. 378.
175 Fereydoun Hoveyda, The Fall of the Shah, (New York: Wyndham Books, 1979), p. 47.

one of the Ansar. Muhammad got down, allowed his luggage to be carried into the nearest house and then began to negotiate with the owner for the sale of the land. Once the price was agreed upon, all the Muslims got to work to build the Prophet's residence, which would also serve as a place for prayer."[176]

Muhammad's Wives

The residence built for Muhammad in Medina, as soon as he arrived, was not only for the Prophet but separate rooms were built around the perimeter for each of his rapidly increasing number of wives. "Shortly after the death of Khadija Muhammad married Sawda, the wife of one of his followers who had gone to Abyssinia and died there. There was some question that the Prophet might have contracted to marry Aisha, the daughter of Abu Bakr, while they were both still at Mecca, but it seems likely that the marriage was not consummated till he had emigrated to Medina, when Aisha was reportedly only nine years old. At Medina he also married Umar's daughter Hafsa, Hind, Zaynab, daughter of Jahsh, Umm Salama, Juwayriyya, Ramla or Umm Habiba, Safiyya, and Maymuna. None of them bore him children, however, though he had a son, Ibrahim, by his Coptic concubine Mary. Ibrahim, too, died an infant."[177]

The Qibla Changed

The Arabic word *qibla* means the direction a Muslim should face when he prays. A *mihrab* is the mark, often an alcove in the mosque wall, showing the worshiper the direction, the *qibla*, to which he should face when he prostrates himself in prayer. At the beginning, the direction to which the Muslims in Yathrib prayed was toward Jerusalem. Probably that was a token of cordiality to the three Jewish tribes of Yathrib. But, seemingly in response to the increasing hostility expressed by the Jews, "in February 624 A.D., seventeen months after Muhammad's arrival in Medina, a revelation came [see Surah 2:142-150] bidding the Muslims make the sanctuary of Mecca the *qibla*."[178]

Making the Kaaba in Mecca, rather than Jerusalem, the direction in which Muslims should prostrate in prayer was, first of all, Muhammad's rebuke to the unbelieving Jews. It had become obvious that they would not, as he had hoped, acknowledge him as God's Prophet. Secondly, it was Muhammad's initial step in alleviating the fear of the leaders of Mecca that, if they accepted his religion, their

---

176 Karen Armstrong, Muhammad, A Prophet for Our Time, (New York: Harper Collins Publishers, 2006), p. 115. This was obviously the first mosque to be established following the Hijra. It is very doubtful that the extremely limited freedom enjoyed by Muhammad in Mecca would have allowed him to establish an earlier mosque. The institution of the mosque, in sharp contrast to the slow development of the synagogue among the Jews, came into full bloom from the very inception of Islam. Ideally, there was to be no divergence between the mosque and the center of political power. Historically, whenever the mosque has dared to defy Islamic political power, it has been put into a subordinate role by naked violence. A recent example is the Pakistan Army's attack on the Red Mosque in Islamabad, Pakistan.
177 F.E. Peters Muhammad and the Origins of Islam, (New York: State University of New York Press, 1994), pp. 178-179.
178 W. Montgomery Watt, Companion To The Qur'an, (London: George Allen and Unwin Ltd., 1967), p. 32.

shrine, thronged by worshipers from all over Arabia, would not be abandoned, marginalized, or possibly destroyed, bringing economic disaster on their town. Obviously, now Muhammad would not destroy the focal point toward which Muslims were to prostrate themselves in prayer. Muhammad's next overture to the leaders of Mecca, assuring them that he held their shrine in inviolable esteem, as we shall see shortly, was a pledge he took in March of 628 A.D. at Hudaybiyyah.

Holland takes the position that the change of *qibla* was from Jerusalem to some place, "between Medina and Palestine"[179] which he thinks was the mysterious place which the Qur'an in Surah 3:96 calls "Bakka" or "Becca."[180] If the very first *qibla* had been Jerusalem, there would have been no change of direction if the new *qibla* should be identified as some place "between Medina and Palestine." Also, Holland's position would require two changes of *qibla*, rather than only one.

Two Power Centers

At the point when Muhammad's Hijra was successfully carried out, there were suddenly two major power centers in Arabia. The first was the old religious-economic center of Mecca, based on its venerable idolatry along with its associated trade fairs. The second was Medina, based on the prophetic claims and the political-military genius of Muhammad. The destiny of Arabia lay in the outcome of the struggle for supremacy, which shortly ensued between these two competing centers of power, both striving to dominate the entire vast Arabian Peninsula.

In 625 A.D. the Meccans, at the Battle of Mount Uhud, delivered a decisive defeat to the Muslims, even seriously wounding Muhammad himself. They attacked Muhammad and his followers in retaliation because the Muslims had completely destroyed a 1,000-man military relief force which Mecca had sent to protect one of its large caravans returning from Damascus. That clash had taken place in 624 A.D. at a camel-watering place named Badr on the Red Sea coast. Because of their success at the Battle of Mount Uhud, it seems almost certain the Meccans could have occupied Medina and could have completely destroyed the nascent Muslim movement but, surprisingly, they did not capitalize on their victory!

Two years after the Battle of Mount Uhud, the Meccans tried again to destroy Muhammad and his movement. It proved to be their final effort. Bringing a ten-thousand-man army from Mecca, they besieged Medina for forty days. The effort is known as the Battle of the Trench because a Persian convert, hearing of the coming of the Meccan army, successfully urged Muhammad to have a dry moat dug in front of the exposed sections of Medina. After forty fruitless days' effort to breach the novel defense, the dispirited Meccan army withdrew. (These battles are discussed more fully in Chapter 7 under "Three Battles.")

---

179 Tom Holland, In the Shadow of the Sword, (London: Little, Brown, 2012), p. 385.
180 Tom Holland, In the Shadow of the Sword, (London: Little, Brown, 2012), pp. 330-331.

The failure to exploit the advantage gained by their victory at Mount Uhud proved to have been a fatal mistake on the part of the leaders of Mecca. Just five short years later, in January 630 A.D., from his power-base in Medina, only two years before his death, Muhammad led an overwhelming cavalry force of 10,000 soldiers to the gates of Mecca. The size of the Muslim army mimicked that of the Meccan force at the fruitless Battle of the Trench. Mecca's leaders, seeing their situation as hopeless, capitulated. At that point, both centers of Arabian power were solidly in Muslim hands. Immediately, important strategic changes were imposed under the direction of Muhammad's genius.

"In March 631 A.D., the greater pilgrimage [to the Kaaba in Mecca] was for the first time performed under Muslim control. Abu Bekr [Bakr] was sent to conduct the ceremonies. An announcement was made [by Ali], forbidding non-Muslims thereafter to perform the pilgrimage. It will be remembered that the annual pilgrim rites at the Kaaba had hitherto been carried out by idol-worshipers. Now, however, that the house of God had been cleansed of idols, only monotheists were to worship there."[181] (Note: On the "greater pilgrimage" see Appendix E under (5) The *Hajj*.)

The Kaaba was cleansed of all its idols except the Black Stone, a large stone thought to have been a meteorite. For centuries it had been lovingly venerated by the idol worshipers who thronged the Kaaba, especially during the annual pilgrimages. Though it was a total contradiction of his dictum that there is only one God, Muhammad left that Black Stone in its place, embedded in the wall of the Kaaba, to be idolized by generations of Muslims who succeeded him. After fourteen centuries, the adoring worshipful kisses of millions of Muslims have eroded the surface of the Black Stone till it is now deeply concaved.

One Center Shifted, the Other Remained Where it Was

The financial, political and military center of Islam was clearly Medina but, just as clearly, the spiritual-religious center was Mecca. Following the capitulation of Mecca to Muhammad, the financial power of Medina increased at Mecca's expense, for "one after the other, the great families migrated to Medina, now the [financial-political-military] capital of Islam. This tendency increased under the first three caliphs."[182]

Centers of Islamic Political Power

Following Medina's rise to power, the main financial-political-military capital of Islam changed locations many times. (It is worthy of special note that, in contrast, the spiritual-religious capital of Islam, Mecca, has never changed through the centuries!) First, the center of political power was snatched from Medina and taken to Damascus by Mu'awiya, Syria's rebellious governor. In

---
181 John Bagot Glubb, The Great Arab Conquests, (London: Quartet Books, 1980), p. 99.
182 H.A.R. Gibb and J.H. Kramers (ed's.), Shorter Encyclopaedia of Islam, (Ithaca, New York: Cornell University Press, 1974), p. 391.

657 A.D. he became the founder and first caliph of the break-away Umayyad Caliphate. Simultaneously, Ali, the fourth and final caliph of the initial sequence of caliphs, attempted to establish the political capital of Islam in Kufa, Iraq, but his effort ended with his assassination. (For details, see Chapter 19 under "Muslim Civil War.") That allowed the Umayyads to rule without competition till 750 A.D. when, through victory at the Battle of the Great Zab River,[183] the triumphant Abbasids[184] wrested power from the caliphs who had reigned from Damascus for nearly a century. "The Abbasids routed Marwan's[185] army, bringing to an end Umayyad rule. The deposed Caliph fled to Egypt, but was caught there and killed, and his head sent to the new Caliph as a present."[186] The only member of the former ruling Umayyad Dynasty to survive was the courageous and crafty Abd al-Rahman. (For additional details, see Chapter 22 under "Surviving Liberal Islam.")

The Abbasids established their initial capital at Kufa, capital of Ali's short-lived caliphate. Perhaps they did so as a perfunctory show of loyalty to Ali, the assassinated caliph, whose partisans had contributed greatly to the Abbasid success at the Battle of the Great Zab River. However, the location of Kufa was not conducive to efficient governance which would have to embrace the entire vast Muslim empire. Consequently, in 762 A.D. the Abbasids built a magnificent new capital, Baghdad on the Tigris.[187] (See Appendix H under B., The Abbasid-Caliphate Period of Iran's Muslim Era.)

Translation Center

It was at Baghdad, the splendid new Islamic capital, that an unprecedented expansion of learning in the Muslim world was initiated. It was centered in "an academy [The House of Wisdom] founded in 215/830 by [Caliph Harun al-Rashid] the [father of] Caliph al-Ma'mun (d. 218/833) for the purpose of

---

183 "The Battle of the Zab was one of the decisive battles of the world because it resulted in the orientalization of Islam. The Umayyad Empire had been a Mediterranean power. Damascus had been for a thousand years part of the Graeco-Roman world, as had Palestine, Egypt, North Africa and Spain. [Under Alexander the Great and for a time under his successors] Persia, the Punjab and Turkestan had been colonies of this Mediterranean empire. But the Abbasids had achieved power principally with the support of Persians. They made their [first] capital at Kufa in Iraq, which for more than a thousand years had been part of Persia." – John Glubb, A Short History of the Arab Peoples, (New York: Stein and Day, 1970), p. 93.

184 While the Umayyads were occupied with a number of difficulties, "there appeared a new revolutionary force that ultimately was to overthrow them. This was the Abbasid party, headed by a ruthless Muslim named Abbas, a descendant of an uncle of the Prophet. The center of the Abbasid movement was in Persia, where there was much ill feeling against the Umayyads; the Persians considered themselves heirs to a higher culture than these haughty Arab conquerors who treated them as inferiors." – Desmond Stewart, Early Islam, (New York: Time Incorporated, 1967), pp. 63-64.

185 This was Marwan II, the Umayyad's last caliph.
186 Desmond Stewart, Early Islam, (New York: Time Incorporated, 1967), p. 64.
187 "Baghdad was the creation of the Abbasids, the city which the second ruler of the dynasty had caused to be built on the west bank of the Tigris River, in that same valley which had furnished sites for some of the mightiest capitals of the ancient world. 'It is an excellent military camp,' he had remarked. 'Besides, here is the Tigris to put us in touch with lands as far as China and bring us all that the seas yield as well as the food products of Mesopotamia, Armenia and their environs. Then there is the Euphrates to carry for us all that Syria, al-Raqqah and adjacent lands have to offer.' It was a sagacious choice, and the new city— on the construction of which one hundred thousand labourers, craftsmen and architects worked for four years— instantly flourished." – Philip K. Hitti, The Arabs, A Short History, (London: Macmillan & Co Ltd, 1965), pp. 82-83.

translating Greek books on philosophy and the sciences into Arabic. Later, the Fatimids founded an academy in Egypt with a similar name, the 'Abode of Wisdom' (*Dar al-Hikmah*), for the propagation of Isma'ili doctrines."[188] The Academy in Baghdad "witnessed the most momentous intellectual awakening in the history of Islam and one of the most significant in the whole history of thought and culture. The awakening was due in large measure to foreign influences, partly Indo-Persian and Syrian, but mainly Hellenic, and was marked by translations into Arabic from Persian, Sanskrit, Syriac and Greek."[189]

Though the "official library named the *Bayt al-Hikma* (The House of Wisdom) was established in Baghdad under the Abbasid Caliph Harun al-Rashid (r. 786–809), it gained its reputation in the context of the translation movement during the reign of his son al-Mamun. Many of the acquired and translated scientific and philosophical works were collected in this library, and they were in turn made available to researchers and translators of the period.

"The most famous of these translators was a Nestorian (Christian) Arab by the name of Hunayn ibn Ishaq al-Ibadi (808–873). Together with a handful of students, he is responsible for the translation of most of the Galenic medical corpus, as well as many other Greek philosophical and scientific treatises. Hunayn left an autobiography in which he lists a large number of the works that he translated from Greek into Syriac or Arabic. He also describes some of the circumstances of his early career.

"Arabic science did more than simply preserve the Greek scientific legacy and pass it to its European heirs [through the Umayyads in Spain, supplementing the great work that Alcuin carried on at Aachen under Charlemagne]. The complex process of cultural transmission necessitated that this legacy, even as its texts were being translated, be reformulated and transformed. The final outcome of this transformation was a new science that was informed by (but not reducible to) its individual components.[190]

"The Abbasid era of translation lasted about a century after 750. Since most of the translators were Aramaic-speaking, many of the Greek works were first translated into Aramaic (Syriac) before their rendition into Arabic. Aramaic was the language Christ spoke.

"The translators into Arabic did not interest themselves in Greek productions of the literary type. No close contact was established between the Arab mind and Greek drama, Greek poetry and Greek history. In that field Persian influence remained paramount.[191] It was Greek philosophy as originated by Plato and Aristotle

---

188 Cyril Glasse, The Concise Encyclopedia of Islam, (San Francisco: Harper & Row Publishers Inc., 1989), p. 160.
189 Philip K. Hitti, The Arabs, A Short History, (London: Macmillan & Co Ltd, 1965), p. 88.
190 Adapted from Ahmad Dallal, *Science, Medicine, and Technology, The Making of a Scientific Culture*, The Oxford History of Islam, (Oxford: Oxford University Press, 1999), pp. 160-161.
191 The pinnacle of Persian poetry was achieved by the great epic poem *Shahnamah*, the story of the kings, by Firdausi.

and expounded by later Neo-Platonists, that served as the starting point of the voyage of intellectual discovery.

"The sheikh of the translators, as the Arabs express it, was Hunayn ibn-Ishaq (Johannitius, 808–873) [whom we have just previously mentioned], one of the greatest scholars and noblest characters of the age.[192] Hunayn was a Nestorian Christian from al-Hirah, and as a youth acted as dispenser to a physician. Taking as a challenge a chiding remark by the master that the people of Hirah had no business with medicine and that he had better go and change money in the bazaar, the lad left the service of his master in tears, but intent upon the study of Greek. Among other books in Arabic Hunayn is supposed to have prepared translations of Galen, Hippocrates and Dioscorides as well as of Plato's *Republic* and Aristotle's *Categories, Physics,* and *Magna Moralia*. Among these his chief work was the rendition into Syriac and Arabic of almost all of Galen's scientific output. The seven books of Galen's anatomy, lost in the original Greek, have luckily been preserved in Arabic. [Unfortunately,] Hunayn's Arabic version of the Old Testament from the Greek Septuagint did not survive.

"Hunayn's ability as a translator is affirmed by the report that he and other translators received about 500 dinars (roughly $1,200) per month and that al-Mamun paid him in gold the weight of the books he translated. But he reached the summit of his glory not only as a translator, but as a [medical] practitioner when he was appointed by the Caliph al-Mutawakkil as his private physician. His patron, however, once committed him to jail for a year for refusing the offer of rich rewards to concoct a poison for an enemy. When brought again before the caliph and threatened with death his reply was, 'I have skill only in what is beneficial, and have studied naught else.' Asked by the caliph, who then claimed that he was simply testing his physician's integrity, what prevented him from preparing the deadly poison, Hunayn replied: 'Two things: my religion and my profession. My religion decrees that we should do good even to our enemies, how much more to our friends. And my profession is instituted for the benefit of humanity and limited to their relief and cure. Besides, every physician is under oath never to give anyone a deadly medicine.'

"A modern French historian of medicine calls Hunayn 'the greatest figure of the ninth century.'"[193]

Subsequently, however, the Abbasid Caliphate slowly declined till in 1258 A.D the Mongols destroyed Baghdad and wrested power from the waning Abbasids. (See division V, section D in Appendix H.) A period of confusion about the location of the caliphate ensued, lasting 195 years, till finally the OttomanTurks conquered Constantinople in 1453, renamed it Istanbul and

---

192 Hunayn ibn Ishaq al Ibadi. Known in the West as Johannitius. 808–873. Arab scholar. Known for his translations into Arabic of works of Plato, Aristotle, Galen, and Neo-Platonists. – Webster's New Biographical Dictionary, p. 499.
193 Philip K. Hitti, <u>The Arabs, A Short History</u>, (London: MacMillan & Co., Ltd.,1965), pp. 90-92.

made it the imperial capital of the caliphate. It was recognized as such by most of the Muslim world and held that role till shortly after Turkish Ottoman power was broken at the end of World War I.[194]

"A tenuous, barely credible thread connects the Abbasid [caliphal] line with [that of] the Ottomans. After the Mamluk slave soldiers of Egypt beat off the Mongol threat in 1260, [See Chapter 17 under "Egypt's Christians Ruled by a Slave Dynasty."] a fugitive caliph [from the defeated Abbasids] became part of the Egyptian sultan's entourage, with 'no court of his own, no vizier, no military guard, just a tower in the citadel to live in and tutors to improve his religious education.' He was followed by a line of seventeen successors called caliphs, the last of whom was taken from Egypt to Istanbul by the Ottoman sultan Selim the Grim in 1517. The story that the last Abbasid had transferred the caliphate to the Ottoman sultan, Kennedy [author of Caliphate: The History of an Idea] writes, may have been 'no more than a piece of fiction concocted to justify the Ottomans' renewed interest to the caliphal title at that time.'"[195]

Political power in the Muslim world in the post World War I era was snatched by European powers in their rush to expand their colonial-imperial holdings by dividing the spoils of the defeated Ottoman Empire. In this they were following the earlier example set by the Portugese, the Dutch, the French and, especially, the British who had also much earlier, in 1757, by victory at the Battle of Plassey in Bengal, grabbed power in various portions of India at the disintegration of the Mogul Empire.[196]

In its turn, European colonial-imperial power was broken as one of the major consequences of World War II. The breakup of European imperialism forced those proud hegemonic powers to abandon their colonial-imperial acquisitions.[197] Thereafter, from that point, scores of Muslim areas regained political independence. However, those newly independent Muslim areas did not come

---

[194] "Even before the rise of the Turks, rival caliphates had arisen, fostered by the great distances within the various parts of the Muslim world. The Fatimids, who were not Sunnis at all but derived from the Isma`ili Shi`a (see later), ruled parts of North Africa and all of Egypt from 910 to 1171 A.D., numbering fourteen caliphs. In Spain the caliphate of Cordova, which later moved to Granada and which was an offshoot of the Umayyad line of Damascus, lasted from 755 A.D. to 1032. The later dynasties of Spain, which did not claim the caliphate, lasted until 1492, the year Ferdinand and Isabella expelled the last of the Muslims from the Iberian Peninsula." – Carleton S. Coon, Caravan: The Story of the Middle East, (New York: Henry Holt and Company, 1956), p. 97.

[195] Malise Ruthven, The Caliphate: From Grand to Sordid, The New York Review of Books, January 19, 2017, Vol. LXIV, No. 1, p. 36.

[196] As Dr. Pipes points out, the European expansion into Muslim lands was, perhaps, the greatest shock Islam had ever suffered. "To the extent that Muslims had always had to deal with kafir [pagan] conquests and alien cultural influences, Europe's armies and civilization fitted existing patterns. But prior challenges to the umma had been limited and had not prepared Muslims for unmitigated decline in the nineteenth century. Non-Muslims had previously conquered parts of Islamdom, to be sure, but never much of it; Turkish pagans from Inner Asia, Crusaders, and Spanish reconquistadors had torn off no more than fragments of the Muslim patrimony. Non-Islamic cultural elements had never threatened the Shar`i way of life. The worst pre-modern Muslim experience, that of the Mongol invasion, led to the loss of not much more than parts of the Middle East and involved rude barbarians eventually converted to Islam. Only portions of Islamdom had ever fallen and then not to peoples capable of challenging Islam culturally. In contrast, the modern Europeans conquered most of Islamdom, they enjoyed the highest civilization, and they threatened the Shar`i way of life." – Daniel Pipes, In the Path of God, Islam and Political Power, (New York: Basic Books, Inc. Publishers, 1983), p. 104.

under the authority of a caliph. Rather, a new phenomenon appeared, the Islamic-nation-state.

What form Islamic political and economic power may take in the future as the inconsistency between the concept of an imperial caliphate and the reality of independent Islamic-nation-states is resolved is not entirely clear.[198] "While the often Westernized nationalist leaders of the post-independence [World War II] period sought to hold on to the state and consolidate it; the new leaders hope to destroy it as a [despised] legacy of the [pagan] West and then re-create it in an Islamic mold. The former sought survival in a transitional world; the later demand purity in an impure one."[199]

The death struggle between the concept of a totalitarian world-wide Islamist State headed by a caliph, and on the other hand, multiple Islamic-nation-states in which individual liberties are guaranteed to some extent, underlies the present upheaval called "The Arab Spring." Starting in Tunisia, that upheaval quickly spread to Libya, Egypt, Syria, Bahrain and Yemen.[200]

Significance of the Spiritual Center Enhanced

In contrast to the drastic changes which came about in the location and nature of the centers of political-military power in the Muslim world, there has been great

---

197 The scope of this shift in power is startling. "In a quarter of a century [1948–1973] an average of one new nation was born every five months—more than sixty-five all told. [Christians should realize that the great majority of those sixty-five new countries were Muslim nation-states.] First to achieve independence were former British, French, and Dutch colonies along the southern periphery of Asia. As a result of postwar realignments, sixteen nations, including India, Pakistan, and Indonesia, gained their independence between 1943 and 1951. The second great surge of independence, from 1956 through 1960, ended foreign rule in most of Africa, as twenty-four more countries joined the community of nations. The third wave of independence has brought freedom to another two dozen countries scattered through Africa, southern Asia and the Caribbean." – Nancy L. Hoepli, ed., Aftermath of Colonialism (New York: The H.W. Wilson Company, 1973), p. 3.

198 It is quite clear, however, that the persistent clamor to impose the Sharia, Muslim canon law, on Muslim societies everywhere precludes a future form of government which could be considered a variety of constitutional liberalism enjoyed in the West as it is here defined by Zakaria: "In almost all of its variants, constitutional liberalism argues that human beings have certain natural (or 'inalienable') rights and that governments must accept a basic law, limiting its own powers, that secures them. Thus in 1215 at Runnymede, England's barons forced the king to abide by the settled and customary law of the land. In the American colonies these laws were made explicit, and in 1638 the town of Hartford adopted the first written constitution in modern history. In the 1970s, Western nations codified standards of behavior for regimes across the globe. The Magna Carta, the Fundamental Orders of Connecticut, the American Constitution, and the Helsinki Final Act are all expressions of constitutional liberalism." – Fareed Zakaria, The Rise of Illiberal Democracy, Foreign Affairs, November/December 1997, pp. 25-26.

199 Akbar Ahmed, Islam's Crossroads, History Today, June 1999, p. 24. In assessing the future political form that the Islamic movement may take, one has to consider the position of Hizb ut-Tahrir. "Extremist Islamist organizations such as al Qaeda [and ISIS] have become well known in recent years for trying to accomplish their objectives through terrorism and political violence. Less well known, however, are the complementary organizations devoted not to direct action but to ideological struggle. Of these, the most important has been Hizb ut-Tahrir (HT, or the Party of Liberation), a transnational movement that has served as radical Sunni Islamism's ideological vanguard. ... In 1953, deciding that the Muslim Brotherhood's ideology was too accommodating, one of its members, a Palestinian judge named Sheikh Taqiuddin al-Nabhani, left to form the more radical Hizb ut-Tahrir in what was then Jordanian-ruled East Jerusalem. Drawing on the work of Qutb and other Islamists, Nabhani rejected capitalism as exploitative and democracy as godless. He asserted that the only way to reestablish the kind of Islamic society promulgated by the Prophet was to liberate Muslims from the thoughts, systems, and laws of kufr ([blasphemy of] nonbelievers) and replace the Judeo-Christian-dominated nation-state system with a border-less umma ruled by a new caliph." – Zeyno Baran, Fighting the War of Ideas, Foreign Affairs. November/December 2005, pp. 68-70.

200 "If the Islamists can defeat the Middle Eastern states that seek to reform and work within the international system, we will be faced with another world war." – Charles Hill, Trial of a Thousand Years, (Hoover Digest, 2011, No. 3), p. 59.

stability in the spiritual-religious center of Islam. Through all the centuries that center has remained in Mecca and, more specifically, focused on the Kaaba. Originally, as noted earlier, Muhammad taught his followers to pray toward Jerusalem. However, when he saw that Jewish and Christian people refused to acknowledge him as the Prophet of God, he felt there was an unacceptable inconsistency in praying toward a center of Jewish and Christian devotion.

The Constitution of Medina

Shortly after arrival at Medina, Muhammad drew up a document now known as The *Umma* Document (literally, The Peoples' Document), also known as the Constitution of Medina. It specifies the liberties and responsibilities of the various tribes, clans and ethnic groups in Medina. The brief 39th article says, "Yathrib shall be a sanctuary for the people of this document." Brief though it is, it was very significant, for, "Article 39 of the document of Medina constitutes the oasis and its vicinity, the same kind of 'protected' enclave found elsewhere in Arabia. ... In this instance the sanctuary notion is constituted not around a shrine, as at Mecca, for example, but on the authority of a recognized 'holy man,' the Meccan *nabi* [prophet] Muhammad, now openly called in Article 42, *the Messenger of God.*"[201] The document clearly portrays a theocracy. Thus, Article 23 says "Whenever you differ about a matter it must be referred to God and to Muhammad."[202]

The Constitution and the Believers vs. Muslims Issue

Some scholars consider the term Muslim not to have been used from the very beginning of the movement inaugurated by Muhammad. For example, Donner says that the Koran, "differs from the traditional Muslim narratives and from modern scholarly practice, both of which routinely refer to Muhammad and his followers mainly as 'Muslims' (*muslimun*, literally, 'those who submit') and refer to his movement as 'Islam.' This later usage is, however, misleading when applied to the beginnings of the community as reflected in the Qur'an. ... Later Muslim tradition, beginning about a century after Muhammad's time, came to emphasize the identity of Muhammad's followers as Muslims and attempted to neutralize the importance of the many passages in which they are called Believers."[203]

The question whether the term Muslim was used from the inception of the movement to which Muhammad gave birth or was applied at a later date, is settled by the document known as The Constitution of Medina, now often referred to as The *Umma* Document. The document "exists in two recensions, one of Ibn Hisham (d. 833) from Ibn Ishaq (d. 767), the other Abu 'Ubayd

---

201 F.E. Peters Muhammad and the Origins of Islam, (New York: State University of New York Press, 1994), p. 201.
202 The Constitution quotations are from http://constitution.org/cons/medina/con_medina.htm. The full text is given by Fred M. Donner in Muhammad and the Believers, p. 227 ff.
203 Fred M. Donner, Muhammad and the Believers: At the Origins of Islam, (London: Harvard University Press, 2010), p. 57.

(d. 838) from Al-Zuhri (d. 742). The differences between them, however, consist only of minor scribal additions, omissions, and changes, and the document is generally considered to have been faithfully transmitted and to be what it says it is."[204]

The Constitution of Medina is, therefore, an inaugural document which faithfully portrays conditions at the very beginning of the great historical movement initiated through Muhammad. Its first clause states that, "This is a document from Muhammad the prophet (*al-nabi*), between the Believers and the Muslims of Quraysh and Yathrib and those who follow them and attach themselves to them and struggle alongside them. Verily they are one community (*umma*) to the exclusion of [other] people."[205] (For additional information about the initial use of the word "Muslim," see Chapter 9 under "Najrani Christians Try to Win Muhammad.")

The Fate of Medina's Jews

Of special interest in the enactments of The Constitution of Medina are the terms which were applicable to the Jews living at that time in the Yathrib oasis. While the Jews were guaranteed freedom of religion and full standing in the community (the *umma*), their duties to Muhammad and the *umma* were clearly specified. Muhammad, referring to The Constitution of Medina as a covenant, sternly exhorted the Jews to fulfill their responsibilities as defined by The Constitution. Quoting Allah he said, "O Children of Israel! Remember My favour wherewith I favoured you, and fulfill your (part of the) covenant, I shall fulfill My (part of the) covenant, and fear Me." (Surah 2:40) Those Jewish enactments were never amended because developments took place a bit later which impacted the Jews with utter finality.

"After the move to Medina, however, he [Muhammad] became a relentless warrior, intent on spreading his religion by the sword, and a scheming founder of a state. A messiah was transformed into a David."[206]

Accordingly, two of the main Jewish clans were expelled from the community. First was the Qaynuqa, who were expelled for killing a Muslim who tried to uphold the honor of a Muslim woman who had been insulted in a Qaynuqa shop. "They had to leave behind their arms and perhaps ... their goldsmith tools (though one might conjecture that by the latter are meant the tools used in making weapons and armor). The usual account is that they went to the Jewish colony at Wadi al-Qura, and after a month proceeded to 'Adhra'at in Syria."[207]

---

[204] Robert Hoyland, *Sebeos, the Jews and the Rise of Islam*, Ronald L. Nettler, (ed.), Medieval and Modern Perspectives On Muslim-Jewish Relations, (Luxembourg: Harwood Academic Publishers, 1995), p. 93.
[205] Fred M. Donner, Muhammad and the Believers: At the Origins of Islam, (London: Harvard University Press, 2010), p. 228.
[206] Ali Dashti, Twenty Three Years: A Study of the Prophetic Career of Muhammad trans. from Persian by F. R. C. Bagley, (London: George Allen & Unwin, 1985), p. 81.
[207] W. Montgomery Watt, Muhammad at Medina, (London: Oxford University Press, 1956), p. 209.

The Qaynuqa were followed in exile by the an-Nadir clan. The an-Nadir "departed proudly with a train of 600 camels for Khaybar [Khaibar], where they had estates."[208] Before leaving Medina, both clans were disarmed. There still remained several insignificant Jewish groups and one main clan, the Qurayzah. The accusation against the Qurayzah was that during the Battle of the Trench they had carried on clandestine contacts with the enemy, the attacking forces from Mecca. With Qurayzah's agreement, Muhammad appointed Sa'd b. Muadh, one of their old confederates, to be their judge. Surprisingly and shockingly, "he decreed that all the men of Qurayzah should be put to death and the women and children sold as slaves. The sentence was duly carried out, apparently on the following day."[209] That mass execution took place in April 627 A.D.

Before the destiny of the Jews of Yathrib had been so decisively and definitively sealed, they had been extended conditional constitutional rights. For example, Article 16 of the Constitution of Medina tells us, "To the Jew who follows us belong help and equality. He shall not be wronged nor shall his enemies be aided." And Article 25 declares, "The Jews of the B. 'Auf are one community with the believers (the Jews have their religion and the Muslims have theirs), their freedmen and their persons, except those who behave unjustly and sinfully, for they hurt but themselves and their families." Article 37 further specifies the rights and obligations of the Jews. It says, "The Jews must bear their expenses and the Muslims their expenses. Each must help the other against anyone who attacks the people of this document. They must seek mutual advice and consultation, and loyalty is a protection against treachery. A man is not liable for his ally's misdeeds. The wronged must be helped."

Identity of Medina's Jews

Who were the Jews of Yathrib? One "decisive fact [in identifying the Yathribi Jews] is the way in which the Prophet speaks in the Medina Suras to the Jews there. He apostrophizes [directly addressing an absent person] them as sons of Israel and reminds them that God has raised them above all men (ii.47, 122 [Koranic references]); he brackets them with the ancient Israelites as if they had taken part in the Exodus from Egypt (ii.49 *sq.*) Allah gave Moses the scriptures so that they might be rightly guided (ii.53); they break the laws which he bound them to observe at the treaty of alliance (ii.83 *sqq.*) etc. Such expressions suggest as clearly as possible that he regarded them as true descendants of the ancient Israelites. There must therefore have been in addition to the Judaized Arabs a stock of true Jews, and indeed it is obvious that without such there could have been no proselytes."[210]

---

208 W. Montgomery Watt, <u>Muhammad at Medina</u>, (London: Oxford University Press, 1956), p. 212.
209 W. Montgomery Watt, <u>Muhammad at Medina</u>, (London: Oxford University Press, 1956), p. 214.
210 F. Buhl, *Al-Madina*, <u>Shorter Encyclopaedia of Islam</u>, ed. H.A.R Gibb, J.H. Kramers, (New York: Cornell University Press, 1974), p. 292.

Perhaps even more decisive in identifying the Jews of Yathrib is the fact that "the Kuraiza [Qurayzah] and Nadir are frequently called the *Kahinani*,[211] the "two (tribes of) priests, which shows that the Jews knew their genealogy and laid stress upon their descent. ... The same thing is seen from the fact that the Nadirite [woman] Safiyya married by Muhammad is described as belonging to the family of Aaron (Ibn Sa'd, viii, 86)."[212]

After the expulsions and executions of the Jews of Medina, Jews in general are repeatedly stigmatized in the Koran. For example, of those Jews who allegedly broke the Sabbath, Allah said, "Be ye apes despised and hated!" (Surah 2:65) Accusing the majority of the "People of the Scripture" of being "evil-livers" it is said that, "Allah hath turned some to apes and swine." (Surah 5:59-60) To Jews who had allegedly digressed from the right path, Allah is quoted as saying, "Be ye apes despised and loathed!" (Surah 7:166) For further stigmata see the following Koranic references: 4:46, 4:160, 5:13, 5:51, 5:57, 5:82, and 7:169.

Though grievously stigmatized, mysteriously and surprisingly, the Jews, according to the Koranic scheme of things, still hold a unique place in the divine plan! Accordingly, Allah is quoted as saying, "O Children of Israel! Remember My favour wherewith I favoured you and how I preferred you to (all) creatures." (Surah 2:122 cf. 2:47) The Jews are exhorted to recall the time "when Moses said unto his people: O My People! Remember Allah's favour unto you, how He placed among you Prophets, and He made you kings, and gave you that (which) He gave not to any (other) of (His) creatures. O My People! Go into the holy land which Allah hath ordained for you. Turn not in flight, for surely you turn back as losers." (Surah 5:20-21) Again, Allah is quoted as saying, "We said unto the Children of Israel after him, dwell in the land; but when the promise of the Hereafter cometh to pass, we shall bring you as a crowd gathered out of various nations." (Surah 17:104)

One of the most amazing acknowledgments of the elevated role of Jews in the divine plan is given in Surah 29:27 where it is said, "We bestowed on him Isaac and Jacob, and We established the Prophethood and the Scripture among his seed." Almost as a review of the unique and pivotal role Jews are to play in the divine plan, we are told, "Verily We gave the Children of Israel the Scripture and the Command and the Prophethood, and provided them with good things and favoured them above (all) peoples; and gave them plain commandments. And they differed not until after the knowledge came unto them, through rivalry among themselves. Lo! thy Lord will judge between them on the Day of Resurrection concerning that wherein they used to differ." (Surah 45:16-17)

ଓଃ

---

211 *Kahin* is the Arabic for priest. It may also mean soothsayer.
212 F. Buhl, *Al-Madina*, <u>Shorter Encyclopaedia of Islam</u>, ed. H.A.R Gibb, J.H. Kramers, (New York: Cornell University Press, 1974), p. 292.

Chapter 7

FROM VICTORY OVER MEDINA'S JEWS
TO VICTORY OVER MECCA, 627–630 A.D.

Muslim Helping Muslim

The Yathribi converts to Islam were full of zeal for their new commitment. They had bound themselves, at the Second Pledge of al-'Aqaba (see Chapter 6), to fraternally receive and materially undergird their brethren in the faith who would shortly flee to Yathrib from the ongoing persecution in Mecca. Those benefactors are known in Arabic as *Ansar* (helpers), while the fleeing Meccan believers whom they helped were known as *Muhajirun* (those who participate in a *hijra*, flight or escape, thus: immigrants/refugees).

The Yathribi Muslims would temporarily supply housing and food till the new residents could maintain themselves. That assistance was essential because many of the immigrants "were penniless, having abandoned all their possessions in Mecca. Some men had been obliged to leave their wives and children behind them and found themselves in Medina, not only without money, but without shelter or family."[213] Though the Yathribi Muslims nobly and sacrificially fulfilled their commitment, they could not support their Meccan brothers indefinitely.

Razzia Versus Jihad

The pressing need to find a means of support was indeed a dire problem, but it also presented a cover under which the *Muhajirun* could indulge in a tempting opportunity. Muhammad knew the most lucrative thing he and his fellow newcomers to Medina, the *Muhajirun*, could do would be to indulge in an old Arabian practice of launching predatory raids (*razzia* in Arabic) on caravans passing near Medina. "A razzia was the [raiding] action of a tribe against another tribe. Even if two tribes were very friendly, their friendship might cool, and in a few years a razzia might be possible. *Jihad* [Holy War], however, was the action of a religious community against non-[Muslim] members of the community."[214]

If successful, Muhammad and his colleagues would be enriched by plundered money, sale or use of looted cargo and by ransom money received for release of

---
213 John Bagot Glubb, The Life and Times of Muhammad, (New York: Stein and Day, 1970), p. 169.
214 W. Montgomery Watt, Muhammad at Medina, (London: Oxford University Press, 1956), pp. 108-109.

anyone whom they might capture. Muhammad undoubtedly also knew that, should he and his marauders be successful, it would not only relieve the present stringency they were facing in their new home, but would become an enticement for other Arabs to join the Muslim movement, so they too might participate in future raids. Also, participation in raids would develop his followers militarily should conquest later be undertaken.

Also, "Muhammad cannot have failed to realize that, even if the raids were only slightly successful, the Meccans were bound to attempt reprisals. In these little raids, then, he was deliberately challenging and provoking the Meccans."[215]

Strategic Advantage

Undoubtedly, Muhammad became aware of the strategic advantage his geographic position at Medina had over that which was held by his Mecca-based opponents. Caravans, traveling between Mecca and Syria in either direction, were vulnerable to interdiction by any predatory force based in Medina. That was true whether a caravan attempted to slip past Medina along the Red Sea coast or tried furtively to outflank Medina by sneaking through the desert to the east.

Muhammad knew his movement could not dominate the Arabian Peninsula as long as he was successfully defied by the powerful trading cartels in Mecca. As mentioned in Chapter 6, at the point when the Hegira/Hijra had been successfully carried out, then there were two power centers in Arabia. First was the old economic-religious center of Mecca. Its strength was based on its camel caravan trade, along with the long-standing idolatry centered on the Kaaba and its associated trade fairs. Second was Medina, its dynamism now based on the charismatic-prophetic leadership and political-military prowess of Muhammad. The destiny of Arabia lay in the outcome of the struggle for supremacy which shortly erupted between these two competing power centers. Both were striving to dominate the whole vast Arabian Peninsula. Surely Muhammad knew success demanded that Mecca not only be humbled but brought into total acquiescence to Islam.

Between January and October 623 A.D., six or seven totally fruitless raids had been carried out. In June, for the first time, Muhammad personally participated in one of those *razzias*. "The futility of these first expeditions may be partly attributed to the instinctive hesitation of both sides to engage in fratricidal strife, for all the men of both parties were of Quraish."[216]

It seems quite certain that "the earlier *razzias* or [raiding] expeditions were enterprises of the Emigrants alone, in which the Medinan clans were not concerned as clans, even if a few individuals [may have] joined them. The presence of Sa'd ibn Mu'adh and over 200 Helpers at [The Battle of] Badr,

---

215 W. Montgomery Watt, Muhammad Prophet and Statesman, (London: Oxford University Press, 1978), p. 105.
216 John Bagot Glubb, The Life and Times of Muhammad, (New York: Stein and Day, 1970), p. 175.

however, following on the events of the last two months, indicates a change of policy on the part of the Helpers."[217]

In addition to the hesitancy of the *Muhajirun* to attack fellow-members of their Quraish Tribe, another reason for the failure of those early raiding forays grew out of the long-standing protection agreements the Quraish had with Bedouin tribes through whose territory their caravans passed. As long as those agreements were observed, not only would the Muslims have had to fight the men of the caravan but the protecting bedouins as well. To counter this adverse arrangement, Muhammad successfully began negotiations with some of the bedouin tribal leaders to induce them to break their protection agreements with the Meccan merchants. As an inducement to change their loyalty, Muhammad probably offered them a share in any future booty.

Plans for Broad Expansion

As one studies the intense raiding activity carried out in this period (624–632 A.D.), under orders from Muhammad, and sometimes (some say often) with his personal participation, it becomes clear that Muhammad had plans for international expansion for his theocratic movement (see "Two Exploratory Expeditions" below). Those raids eventually explored the defenses being maintained by Byzantium on Arabia's northwestern border, a daunting power blocking any attempt by Islam to expand to the west. Also, Muhammad certainly understood that any expansion beyond the Arabian Peninsula depended on achieving, as a first priority, triumph over Mecca, the long-standing epicenter of Arabian power.

One major hindrance to Muhammad's success was the inability of his raiding parties to conceal their plans and intentions. Consequently, to thwart spies and enemy informers, Muhammad began to send raiding parties out under sealed orders. The first to go with secret orders went in November 623 A.D. The leader's instructions directed him to set an ambush at Nakhla, a place between Taif and Mecca. Those marauders attacked and captured a small caravan loaded with raisins, hides and wine which they took to Medina as booty. Of the four men in charge of the caravan, one was killed, one fled and two were captured.

That attack had been carried out during one of the sacred or holy months during which, by long-standing, widespread agreement throughout Arabia, no attacks were to be made. However, concern about this inconsistency was quickly dispelled when Muhammad "received a revelation (2.214/217) to the effect that, while fighting in the sacred month was serious (with the connotation of sinful), keeping people from the way of God, and disbelief in Him, and the expulsion and persecution of His people are more serious than killing."[218]

---

217 W. Montgomery Watt, <u>Muhammad Prophet and Statesman</u>, (London: Oxford University Press, 1978), p. 119.
218 W. Montgomery Watt, <u>Muhammad Prophet and Statesman</u>, (London: Oxford University Press, 1978), p. 111.

Muhammad's Daughters

As noted in Chapter 4, Muhammad's daughters played significant roles in early Islamic developments. Fatimah was undoubtedly the most important of Muhammad's daughters. In harmony with that appraisal, "many revere Fatimah as the greatest Muslim woman who ever lived."[219] Her marriage with Muhammad's cousin 'Ali may have taken place in June 624 A.D. Her husband, Ali, was the son of Abu Talib, the uncle who, till his death in 619 A.D., had protected Muhammad. The first child of their marriage, Muhammad's grandson al-Hasan, was born early in March 625 A.D. Both of Fatimah's two sons, al-Hasan and al-Husain, became heroic figures in Shiite Islam.

Previously, in September 624 A.D., Muhammad had arranged the marriage of another daughter, Umm Kulthum, to 'Uthman who later became the third caliph. 'Uthman had previously been married to Umm Kulthum's sister Ruqayyah, but Ruqayyah had died about the time of the Battle of Badr. Thus, by this marriage, Uthman became Muhammad's son-in-law a second time. "Finally, about the end of January 625, Muhammad himself married Hafsah, the daughter of 'Umar, who became second caliph. This both forged a link with one of his most important lieutenants, and also provided for Hafsah, whose previous husband had been one of the handful of Muslims killed at Badr. These marriages, like all the marriages Muhammad contracted himself or arranged for his followers, had thus a definite political purpose, whatever else may have been involved."[220]

When thinking of the political implications of Muhammad's personal marriage arrangements, and those he arranged for his daughters, one should not forget that Aisha, Muhammad's favorite wife, was the daughter of Abu Bakr, not only Muhammad's companion during the Hijra, but the one who became the first caliph.

Ali became the fourth caliph[221] immediately following the assassination of Caliph Uthman. However, in his new caliphal capital at Kufa, located in present day Iraq, he was cut down as a martyr by one of his own disgruntled soldiers in a furious sword attack on January 24, 661, A.D. (See Appendix D, sixth paragraph.) The Shiites revere Ali as their supreme patriarch. The term Shi'ite is a contraction from the Arabic *Shi'at 'Ali*, The Party of Ali. Originally it referred to the large group of Arab Muslims who were united in the conviction that Ali should have been the first caliph following Muhammad's death. Now, the designation Shiite is also acknowledged by millions of non-Arab Muslim devotees.

Upon the death of Ali, Iraq "declared Ali's son, al-Hasan, the legitimate successor to the throne—with logic, since he was the eldest son of the slain caliph and Fatimah. ... But, unfortunately, this grandson of the Prophet had

---
219 Robin Wright, <u>Dreams And Shadows, The Future of the Middle East</u> (New York: The Penguin Press, 2008), p. 354.
220 W. Montgomery Watt, <u>Muhammad Prophet and Statesman</u>, (London: Oxford University Press, 1978), pp. 131-132.
221 The word "caliph" means successor, in this context, successor to Muhammad.

already sojourned too long among the fleshpots. His talents lay in fields other than administration—namely, in the boudoir. Though he died at the age of forty-five, he had by that time succeeded in making and unmaking no less than one hundred marriages and in winning a highly individual title for himself: 'the great divorcer.' Consistent, at any rate, in recognizing the true nature of his ability, he genially permitted Mu'awiya [founder and first caliph of the Umayyad Caliphate, ruling from Damascus] to buy him off as an aspirant to the caliphate, with a lifetime subsidy."[222]

By invitation of the people of Iraq, next in line to come to the caliphal eminence was Husain, Ali's youngest son. He was to become caliph after an 800-mile trip from Mecca to Kufa (September or October 680 A.D.). At that point, the rival Umayyad caliph, ruling from Damascus, was Yazid, Mu'awiya's unworthy son, who had succeeded to the throne at the death of his father. Husain was killed the same year near Karbala. (On the murder of Husain, see Chapter 24 under "Lust Skews Succession.")

Three Battles

The constant raiding carried out by the Muslims of Medina led to three serious battles, ultimately resulting in the consolidation and expansion of Muhammad's power and authority.

1. Battle of Badr in 624 A.D. West of Medina, on the Red Sea coast, were fresh-water springs known as the Springs of Badr. Camel caravans plying the coastal route between Mecca and Syria invariably broke their journey at this convenient place to refresh themselves and their camels.

Muhammad had learned that a major Meccan caravan, led by Abu Sufyan, was returning from Syria to Mecca. A razzia, consisting of three hundred armed Muslims from Medina, set out in January 624 A.D. to interdict that caravan. However, Abu Sufyan had somehow gotten word of the planned attack and, by a forced-nighttime march, passed the Springs of Badr safely. The leaders of Mecca also had learned of the Muslim's intentions and had sent a one-thousand-man posse to Badr to protect their caravan. When Muhammad and his three-hundred raiders arrived at Badr, it was not the caravan they met, but the one-thousand-man-armed posse from Mecca. "A battle ensued in which the Muslims were completely victorious, although outnumbered by three to one. As a result, Muhammad's prestige soared and more and more converts joined his religion."[223]

Muhammad's success at Badr enhanced his movement in at least four ways: [1] "Larger numbers of Helpers [Ansar] were now ready to take part in

---

222 Philip K. Hitti, The Arabs, A Short History (London: Macmillan & Co. Ltd., 1965), p. 59.
223 John Bagot Glubb, The Empire of The Arabs, (London: Hodder & Stoughton, 1963), p. 21. Those wishing more detail on the casualties encountered by both sides at the Battle of Badr should read John Bagot Glubb's The Life and Times of Muhammad, pp. 184-189.

Muhammad's expeditions. [2] The prospect of booty attracted to Medina poor nomads from the neighboring region. [3] Some of the leading men of Medina also began to think again. ... [4] [Soon also] all the Arab clans of Medina officially accepted Islam."[224]

Following the Battle of Badr, which was a severe blow to Meccan prestige, many of the tribes along the route, especially those near Medina, became more favorable to Muhammad than to the Meccans. Subsequently, to ensure the safety of a caravan, a very large accompanying armed force would be required. Even that did not rule out the possibility of a battle with the Muslims, since the larger the force the more difficult it became to keep its movements concealed. At that juncture, therefore, Abu Sufyan [Abu Sofian] judged it wiser not to dissipate his strength on caravan protection, but to concentrate on preparing a military expedition against Medina.

The soundness of Abu Sufyan's judgment became very clear when a group of Meccans, "rivals of Abu Sufyan [Abu Sofian], decided to risk sending a caravan by a route well to the east of Medina. They found a reliable guide, and despatched a caravan worth 100,000 (silver) dirhams. Unfortunately Muhammad got word of the caravan, and against it sent his adopted son, Zaid ibn Harithah, with a hundred men. They were successful in capturing the whole caravan. [November 624 A.D.]"[225]

2. Battle of Mount Uhud in 625 A.D. This battle is named for Mount Uhud, a small craggy peak about two miles north of Medina, where the conflict occurred. The Meccans came some 250 miles with the intent of destroying the dangerous marauding Islamic movement. Mecca's forces were led by the astute and wily Abu Sufyan who had successfully led the Meccan caravan which had eluded the Muslim ambush at Badr. Their forces consisted of three-thousand men, two-hundred of whom were mounted on horses, with the others traveling by camel.

Despite being grossly outnumbered, able to commit only seven hundred men and no horse to the fray, Muhammad, with no discernible thought of surrender, rose to Mecca's challenge. Perhaps he committed his meager forces to this dangerously unequal battle, thinking that Allah would give the Muslims victory, as he had in the uneven contest at Badr.

But at Uhud, the odds were even more unfavorable than they had been at Badr. There, the ratio had been 3.3 to 1 while here at Uhud the Muslims were outnumbered 4.3 to 1. Muhammad may well have thought that the notoriety of a Muslim victory against such overwhelming odds would bring most, if not all, of Arabia's tribes into the Muslim fold, as the victory at Badr had brought several to the Muslim side.

---

224 W. Montgomery Watt, <u>Muhammad Prophet and Statesman</u>, (London: Oxford University Press, 1978), pp. 127-128.
225 W. Montgomery Watt, <u>Muhammad Prophet and Statesman</u>, (London: Oxford University Press, 1978), p. 135.

One almost instinctively questions why so few Muslims volunteered to defend their home town. Apparently, there had been a failure to detect the military force coming against Medina. It seems the Muslims had been caught totally off guard. Men had no time to set their affairs in order so they might be free to take up arms. Also, apparently the attack came so suddenly and unexpectedly that Muhammad had no opportunity to rally his forces. Even regarding those who did join Muhammad in his determination to fight the Meccans at Uhud, he alleged that some of them "desired the world." (Surah 3:152) It was probably this lack of devotion to the Islamic cause which kept many, if not most, of the men in the Muslim community at Medina from joining Muhammad's warriors to oppose Mecca's attack.

However, at Uhud, in contrast to Badr, victory followed the odds. The Muslims were totally defeated, with Muhammad himself being badly wounded. The survivors, carrying their wounded leader with them, took refuge in the crevices and crannies of Mount Uhud. One of the Meccans loudly boasted that Muhammad had been killed. Though Abu Sufyan knew that boast to be false, still he acted as though it were true. He shouted to the Medinans, who were cringing in their crevices, "Today is in exchange for Badr, we will meet you again next year." Then he and his forces rode back to Mecca!

The true reasoning behind Abu Sufyan's retreat is inexplicable. One tenth of the Muslim force had been killed. Muhammad and his many wounded warriors were cowering in the folds of Mount Uhud, and Medina was totally undefended. The Meccans could have taken all the wives, children and cattle as booty. Or, they simply could have occupied Medina holding the Muslim's families and possessions hostage. Then, they could have negotiated from a position of overwhelming strength, forcing the wounded Prophet and his followers to meet their terms without compromise. A major turning point in world history offered itself to Abu Sufyan, but he turned away, with seeming incomprehension, taking his forces back to Mecca.[226]

Watts' analysis was that Abu Sufyan also had wounded men and horses and, therefore, thought it imprudent to press the battle further.[227] On the other hand, the Muslims were very badly shaken. They thought, "If Badr was a sign of God's favor, were their casualties at Uhud a sign of his disfavor? Or, was he [God] completely neutral with regard to them?"[228]

Glubb has correctly pointed out that verses 120-199 in the third Surah were revealed to allay the misgivings of the despondent Muslims.[229] Those verses give us the text of a post-battle oration Muhammad made to his shaken followers. First of all, Muhammad praises the virtue of tenacity. He told his

---

[226] For additional details see, John Glubb, A Short History of The Arab Peoples, (New York: Stein and Day, 1970), pp.37-38.
[227] For details see, W. Montgomery Watt, Muhammad Prophet and Statesman, (London: Oxford University Press, 1978), p. 141.
[228] W. Montgomery Watt, Muhammad Prophet and Statesman, (London: Oxford University Press, 1978), p. 143.
[229] John Bagot Glubb, The Life and Times of Muhammad, (New York: Stein and Day, 1970), p. 218.

troops, "If disaster strike you they rejoice thereat. But if ye persevere and keep from evil their guile will never harm you." (3:120) He further encouraged his defeated warriors by saying, "If ye persevere, and keep from evil, and (the enemy) attack you suddenly, your Lord will help you with five thousand angels sweeping on." (3:125)

Additionally, Muhammad argued that the purpose of the defeat they had sustained was to distinguish the believers from the unbelievers. He told his followers, "Faint not nor grieve, for ye will overcome them if ye are (indeed) believers. If ye have received a blow, the (disbelieving) people have received a blow the like thereof. [Here he probably is referring to the earlier Battle of Badr.] These are (only) the vicissitudes which We cause to follow one another for mankind, to the end that Allah may know those who believe and may choose witnesses [i.e., martyrs] from among you; and Allah loveth not wrong-doers. And that Allah may approve those who believe, and may blight the disbelievers." (3:139-141)

The ebb and flow of the Battle of Mount Uhud is reflected in the next segment of Muhammad's sermon to his dispirited warriors. He assured them, "Allah verily made good His promise unto you when ye routed them by His leave, until (the moment) when your courage failed you, and ye disagreed about the order and you disobeyed, after He had shown you that for which ye long. Some of you desired the world, and some of you desired the hereafter. Therefore He made you flee from them, that He might try you. Yet now He hath forgiven you. Allah is a Lord of Kindness to believers." (3:152)

Muhammad's post-battle oration to his warriors reached a crescendo when he told them, "And was it so, when a disaster smote you, though ye had smitten (them with a disaster) twice (as great), [he seems to refer to the victory at Badr] that ye said: How is this? Say (unto them, O Muhammad): it is from yourselves. Lo! Allah is Able to do all things. That which befell you, on the day when the two armies met, was by permission of Allah; that He might know the true believers; and that He might know the hypocrites, unto whom it was said: Come, fight in the way of Allah, or defend yourselves. They answered: If we knew aught of fighting we would follow you. On that day they were nearer disbelief than faith. They utter with their mouths a thing which is not in their hearts. Allah is best aware of what they hide." (3:165-167)

Muhammad's post-battle analysis reached its climax when he told his warriors, "Think not of those who are slain in the way of Allah, as dead. Nay, they are living. With their Lord they have provision." (3:169)

It was to make arrangements for the widows resulting from the seventy-four Muslim fatalities in the Battle of Mount Uhud that the general permission for polygamy is given in the early verses of the fourth Surah of the Koran. Like some Christians who, though having no stomach ailment, justify imbibing wine on the basis of Paul's therapeutic counsel to Timothy to drink a little wine for his chronic stomach problem (I Timothy 5:23), similarly many Muslims marry multiple wives even though the women were not widowed by war! Of course, not all of Muhammad's multiple wives were war widows. So his example would seem to give liberty to present-day Muslim polygamists.

As disheartening as the Battle of Mount Uhud undoubtedly had been to the average Muslim, Muhammad seemed to have understood that it was not the defeat that many of his disciples probably thought it had been. The Meccans' rash departure from Medina had left the position of Muhammad and the Muslims completely intact. Obviously, another battle would have to be fought, but it would be in the future, giving the Muslims time to prepare. Muhammad knew he would be "able to attract military support because his was a religious movement and because he was being carried forward in the stream of emergent social forces. The Meccans, on the other hand, were attempting to retain a position of privilege that was no longer appropriate in the new circumstances."[230]

Though the Meccans had failed to capitalize on their victory at Uhud, as we shall see later, amazingly once more, the Muslims, foolhardily it seems, made themselves vulnerable at Hudaybiyyah to the danger of a another fatal attack. But surprisingly, Mecca let that second and final opportunity to end the Muslim movement also slip from their hands. (See "First Pilgrimage, March 628 A.D." later in this chapter.)

3. The Battle of the Trench in 627 A.D. This battle was Mecca's second attempt to destroy the Islamic movement. It took place only two years after the Battle of Mount Uhud. The determination of Mecca, to recover from the folly of having turned their backs on the victory they had won at Uhud, is seen in the size of the force they brought to this encounter. It consisted of 10,000 men, including 600 horse-mounted cavalry. They clearly intended to destroy Muhammad and his movement. Negligently and surprisingly, however, the Meccans seem not to have utilized any military intelligence or surveillance. That is obvious since the dry moat the Muslims had dug (allegedly on the advice of a Persian convert) in front of the vulnerable sections of Medina, a many-months-long project, impossible to hide, was a complete surprise to the attackers. It was a situation for which they had made no preparation.

Alleged Jewish Conspiracy

Medina was besieged for three weeks by Meccan forces. Their efforts were thwarted by the dry moat the Muslims had dug. Then, "changing tactics, the Meccans camped outside Medina, negotiating with a Jewish clan inside the oasis to attack the Muslims from within. The negotiations broke down, however, and the weather turned cold. After 40 days the Meccans, now demoralized and short of supplies, went home. Muhammad, who had learned about

---
230 W. Montgomery Watt, Muhammad Prophet and Statesman, (London: Oxford University Press, 1978), p. 142.

the Jews' negotiations with the Meccans, dealt harshly with them: he sanctioned the decapitation of all the men—some 600 in number—and the enslavement of their women and children, and he allowed his followers to settle on their land."[231]

Two Exploratory Expeditions

In addition to the three battles out of which Muhammad's power base was consolidated (Badr, Uhud and The Trench), two notable expeditions reveal his far-flung aspirations for the future: first was his attack on Dumat al-Jandal and, second, his thrust against Mota. Both those centers were Byzantine Roman military strong points on Rome's frontier with Arabia which the Romans called *Limes Arabicus* (The Arabian Frontier). From those raids it became obvious that Muhammad wanted to test the strength and watchfulness of the Romans on their border with Arabia. Had Muhammad lived longer, it is very probable that he would also have conducted similar exploratory probing attacks against the Persian frontier.

From one of the very few predictive prophetic passages in the Koran, we know that Muhammad keenly observed developments in the two great empires bordering Arabia. Regarding the war which was raging between Iran and Byzantium, he said, as noted in Chapter 3, "The Romans have been defeated in the nearer land, and they, after their defeat will be victorious within ten years— Allah's is the command in the former case and in the latter—and in that day believers will rejoice in Allah's help to victory. He helpeth to victory whom He will." (Surah 30:2-5)

It seems clear, from another predictive passage, that Muhammad anticipated a Muslim military offensive against either Sassanian Iran or Byzantium, or both. He said, "Say unto those of the wandering Arabs who were left behind: Ye will be called against a folk of mighty prowess, to fight them until they surrender; and if ye obey, Allah will give you a fair reward; but if ye turn away as ye did turn away before, He will punish you with a painful doom." (Surah 48:16) Pickthall, the translator, in an explanatory footnote on this verse says, "This prophecy is taken to refer to the war with the Persian or the Byzantine Empire."

1. The expedition to Dumat al-Jandal. Dumat al-Jandal, often expressed simply as Dumah, was situated 500 miles due north of Medina. Some scholars believe that it was named for Dumah, a son of Ishmael, mentioned in Genesis 25:12-16. In modern times it is called Al-Jawf. In August and September 626 A.D., shortly before the pivotal Battle of the Trench (627 A.D.), Muhammad, surprisingly, led a 1,000-man force in an attack on this distant settlement.

---

231 Desmond Stewart, <u>Early Islam</u>, (New York: Time Incorporated, 1967), pp. 18-19.

Though the main purpose of the attack on Dumah seems clearly to have been to test the strength of that Roman Frontier fortress, Watt, on the other hand, speculated that Muhammad's "primary aim was to deter these northern tribes from joining the Meccan grand alliance against him [the alliance which resulted in the Meccan siege of Medina at the Battle of the Trench]; but what he now learnt about conditions in the north may have shown him the possibility of expansion in this direction. Certainly his rapid march with such a large force must have impressed all who heard of it. Despite [the setback at] Uhud, Muslim strength was clearly increasing."[232]

2. The first attack on Mota. This expedition also showed that Muhammad had aspirations far beyond only bringing Islam to Mecca and the Arabian Peninsula. In September 629 A.D., the first Muslim attack took place on Mota [Mu'ta, Mu'tah], located five miles south of Kerak, in present-day Jordan.

Only one year earlier, in 628 A.D., the twenty-six-year war between Sassanian Iran and Byzantium, a war initiated by the Sassanians, had finally been brought to an end with Byzantium's victory. At that point, Byzantium's victorious, battle-hardened forces could have projected power all the way to Medina, destroying the budding Muslim empire. It is impossible to think that the Romans, especially in light of the previous attack on Dumah and now on Mota, were totally unaware of the incipient danger which was brewing at Medina. But, Heraclius, military genius and emperor of Byzantium, was not paying attention. He was distracted, trying to work out a solution to the theological rift which violently divided his empire. The state-approved Orthodox Church viciously and persistently persecuted those groups, including the Copts of Egypt and the Nestorians of Syria, who dissented from Byzantium's "official" Christology.

The raid on Mota was led by Zaid ibn Harithah, the Prophet's freedman and adopted son. It was the largest raiding force so far assembled by the Muslims, consisting of three thousand men. At Mota they were surprised to encounter a force several times larger than their own. "Khalid ibn al Waleed, newly converted to Islam, was fighting in the ranks. ... He was nevertheless a more experienced commander than Zaid or Jafar [who had been appointed by Muhammad to take command should Zaid fall.] Assuming control at this moment of defeat, he [Waleed] succeeded in impressing his personality on the remnant of the raiders. A citizen of Medina planted the white banner in the ground and the Muslims gathered round. Then, by retiring methodically, the survivors, under Khalid's firm leadership, withdrew from the field. The enemy, perhaps severely mauled, neglected to pursue."[233]

Some think that one motive for the Mota raid was to take vengeance for the murder of a messenger whom Muhammad had sent to "one of the princes of

---

232 W. Montgomery Watt, Muhammad at Medina, (London: Oxford University Press, 1956), p. 35.
233 John Bagot Glubb, The Great Arab Conquests, (London: Quartet Books, 1980), pp. 92-93.

Beni Ghassan, who appears to have been the governor of Bosra in Syria. ... The messenger was set upon and killed on his way home, some say by the local tribes, others by order of another member of Beni Ghassan. ... The murder of Muhammad's emissary must have occurred in what is now the state of Jordan."[234]

The messenger may have been carrying a letter which invited Beni Ghassan's prince to acknowledge Muhammad as God's prophet and to accept Islam. If so, sending a punitive expedition would be a powerful message that anyone who might rebuff the invitation to join the growing Muslim Brotherhood would do so at great peril. This, the first Mota expedition carried out during Muhammad's lifetime, was a failure. Muhammad had put his adopted son, Zaid ibn Harithah, in charge and he, among others, was killed, losses not compensated by any gain. But Muhammad gave orders that the effort should be repeated, which it successfully was shortly after his death.

Perhaps another reason the Byzantine town of Mota was targeted was to secure a reliable source of superior weapons. "Swords were also manufactured at the Syrian frontier-town of Muta [Mota]. Highly esteemed especially were the Damascene swords—easily distinguishable by their wave-like form. This weapon they carried in a scabbard flung over the right shoulder."[235]

Mecca, Key to Success

Muhammad clearly understood it was utterly imperative that Mecca be won if Islam were to dominate Arabia and then, using Arabia as a power base, carry the message of Allah to the wider world. Accordingly, at this time, "by his raids on Meccan caravans he had blocked the path to the north for the Meccans, and alliances with the northern tribes would serve to tighten the blockade if Muhammad so desired."[236]

In his effort to win Mecca, Muhammad sought to allay one of the Meccans long-standing fears. They thought embracing Islam would bring economic disaster on their city, because Muhammad opposed the idolatry which was centered in the Kaaba. If the idols were destroyed no devotees would come and the lucrative accompanying trade fairs would cease.

We have already seen (Chapter 6) that Muhammad previously had made a very significant overture to the Meccans, in February 624 A.D., by changing the qibla from Jerusalem to Mecca, thus making the Kaaba the focal point of Muslim worship. Doubtless, that had carried a surprising but powerful message to the leaders of Mecca. It strongly implied that Muhammad would not destroy the Kaaba, because it had been declared the point toward which every Muslim was supposed to prostrate five times a day!

---

234 John Bagot Glubb, The Life and Times of Muhammad, (New York: Stein and Day, 1970), p. 289.
235 Von Kremer, The Orient Under the Caliphs, trans. S. Khuda Bukhsh (Beirut: United Publishers, 1973), p. 90.
236 W. Montgomery Watt, Muhammad Prophet and Statesman, (London: Oxford University Press, 1978), p. 180.

Daring Theological Inconsistency

To even further enhance his message to the Meccans about the sanctity of the Kaaba, Muhammad determined to lead hundreds of Muslims on a pilgrimage to that shrine. He was willing to run a fundamental theological risk in order to powerfully convey his message to the leaders and citizens of Mecca that Islam was not the enemy of the Kaaba. It entailed great risk because of the glaring theological inconsistency in making his proposed pilgrimage to the Kaaba while it still housed its full complement of idols. Obviously, to make a pilgrimage to the center of idolatry was a blatant contradiction of the stern monolithic monotheism which Muhammad insisted upon! Obviously, to make his point, political expediency would have to trump theology!

Muhammad's first attempt at leading a pilgrimage from Medina to the Kaaba took place in March 628 A.D. Such a pilgrimage is called *'umrah*—the lesser pilgrimage. It can be made in any month and is a minor pilgrimage in contrast to the *hajj*, known as the greater pilgrimage which can be performed only in the month of Dhu'l-Hijja. Muhammad "did not inaugurate these practices [of pilgrimages] but only assimilated them to his teaching. This he could do all the more readily as their original significance seems to have become but obscurely understood by his contemporaries. That he allowed them to persist at all is probably less to be attributed to his personal reverence for them than to his political instinct which made him respect the traditions of his conservative fellow-countrymen."[237]

First Pilgrimage, March 628 A.D.

Between 1,400 and 1,600 Muslims accompanied Muhammad. They took along a herd of seventy camels for sacrifice. When the men of Mecca heard of the Muslims' approach, assuming they were coming for an attack on Mecca, they sent a cavalry unit of 200 horse to stop them. The Muslims took an evasive track, bypassing the cavalry, and came to a halt at a place about eight miles west-northwest of Mecca called al-Hudaybiyyah.

"The Meccans had at this moment their last opportunity to destroy Islam and Muhammad once and for all. The Apostle's idea of a pilgrimage had placed him at the mercy of his enemies, bivouacked as he was outside Mecca with only a small force, armed with nothing but swords. If Quraish had been led by a single, determined commander, they could have seized this priceless opportunity to end the struggle in a few hours."[238]

---

237 R. Paret, 'Umra, Shorter Encyclopaedia of Islam, ed. H.A.R. Gibb and J.H. Kramers, (Ithaca, New York: Cornell University Press, 1974), p. 605.
238 John Bagot Glubb, The Life and Times of Muhammad, (New York: Stein and Day, 1970), p. 269.

The Muslim-Mecca Treaty

"The Meccans threatened to fight if Muhammad tried to perform the pilgrimage. Messengers came and went between them and him, and eventually a treaty was agreed on. This year the Muslims were to retire, but in the following year the Meccans were to evacuate their city for three days to enable the Muslims to carry out the various rites of the lesser pilgrimage. ... On the conclusion of the treaty Muhammad killed his sacrificial animal and had his hair shaved, and the Muslims, apparently after some hesitation followed his example. Then they set off home."[239]

The Second Pilgrimage, 629 A.D.

Without doubt, Glubb correctly analyzed the drama of Muhammad's *Umrah* by pointing out that his "idea of making a pilgrimage was a political masterstroke. Much of the opposition to him in Mecca had sprung from the belief that he wished to discredit the temple, on which the prestige of the city depended. Now he announced that the Kaaba was the House of God and had been built by Abraham, whose religion he was himself preaching. The Meccans had sinned by placing idols in the Kaaba and these must be removed. But when this had been done, the Kaaba would remain the House of God and pilgrimage to it would be a Muslim obligation."[240]

Treaty Violated

A treaty was negotiated to which the men of Mecca and Muhammad were signatories. It bound both sides to ten years of peace. However, only two years after signing, Muhammad, commanding an army of ten thousand, reminiscent of the number in the army with which Mecca besieged Medina at the Battle of the Trench, conquered Mecca! How can such a blatant violation of a treaty obligation be harmonized with honesty? For Muhammad and his followers the dilemma was solved by a timely revelation. The very first verse of Surah nine says, "Freedom from obligation (is proclaimed) from Allah and His messenger toward those of the idolaters with whom ye make a treaty."

The incident which triggered the Muslim attack on Mecca was a clash, resulting in fatalities, between the Quraish of Mecca and the Khuza'a tribe. Though not Muslims themselves, the Khuza'a had previously made a pact with Muhammad. Apparently Muhammad had unilaterally extended the meaning of the treaty he had signed with the leaders of Mecca to include not only the Muslims but also all who had a pact with them. The representative of the Khuza'a said to Muhammad, "I come to remind Muhammad of the old alliance between our fathers. ... Help us, now God guide you, and call God's servants to our aid. ... Verily Quraish have broken their promise to you, they

---

239 W. Montgomery Watt, <u>Muhammad Prophet and Statesman</u>, (London: Oxford University Press, 1978), p. 183.
240 John Glubb, <u>A Short History of the Arab Peoples</u>, (New York: Stein and Day, Publishers, 1970), p. 39.

have violated their pledged word."[241] We know that the representative's plea was not based on fact and truth, otherwise Muhammad would have had no need for the revelation in Surah 9:1 which declared him free from treaty obligations.

The plea of the representative of the Khuza'a was completely successful. Consequently, "in January 630 A.D., the Apostle of God once more called the Muslims to arms and, with ten thousand followers, set out for Mecca. Abu Sofian [Abu Sufyan], the victor of Uhud and the leader of the opposition, realizing that the game was up, met the advancing Prophet on the way and accepted Islam. Next day, the Muslims entered Mecca unopposed.

"Standing before the Kaaba, Muhammad ordered the idols to be cast down, broken and thrown away. A general amnesty was then proclaimed and the men and women of Mecca were made to swear loyalty. Although many of those who had formerly persecuted him were still living in the city, the Apostle won all hearts by his clemency on this day of triumph."[242]

Muhammad, in a stroke of genius, appropriated the center of Arabian pagan worship and made it the center of Islamic devotion. This reminds one of the construction of great Catholic cathedrals in Europe on sites of former pagan centers of worship. It is very doubtful, however, that Muhammad was in any way trying to follow that example, or that he even knew about it. In any case, the spiritual momentum which had been centered on the Kaaba had now been channeled into Islam. The sanctuary that had been the epicenter of Arabian paganism was now the spiritual epicenter of Islam. It was revealed that "Allah hath appointed the Kaaba, the Sacred House, a standard of mankind." (Surah 5:97) By keeping the Black Stone in the Kaaba sanctuary, new converts to Islam, whose devotion had previously been focused on one or more of the idols in the Kaaba, would not feel that the rededicated Kaaba had become completely foreign or hostile.

At the time Mecca was conquered, Muhammad received a vision which gave him an alleged history of the origin of the Kaaba. The Koranic record of Muhammad's vision tells us, "When We [i.e. God] made the House (at Mecca) a resort for mankind and a sanctuary, (saying): Take as your place of worship the place where Abraham stood (to pray). And We imposed a duty upon Abraham and Ishmael, (saying): Purify My house for those who go around and those who meditate therein and those who bow down and prostrate themselves in worship." (Surah 2:125)

Based on that alleged history, Muhammad conveyed a command to his people which he had received by another vision: "We have seen the turning of thy face to heaven (for guidance, O Muhammad). And now verily We shall make thee turn (in prayer) toward a *qiblah*[243] which is dear to thee. So turn thy face toward the Inviolable Place of Worship, [The Ka'ba at Mecca] and ye (O

---

241 Ibn Ishaq, The Life of Muhammad, Trans. A. Guillaume, (Karachi: Oxford University Press, 1982), pp. 542-543.
242 John Glubb, A Short History of the Arab Peoples, (New York: Stein and Day, Publishers, 1970), p. 39-40.

Muslims), wheresoever ye may be, turn your faces (when ye pray) toward it." (Surah 2:144)

As a result of those visions, approximately one-fifth of the world's population, presumably, prostrates itself five times each day in prayer toward Mecca. Consequently, in spite of the innumerable set-backs suffered by Islam during the past fourteen centuries, including deep rifts, sectarianism and violent, persistent disagreements, an underlying unity has persisted. One manifestation of that unity is seen when every Muslim faces the Kaaba in prayer. So far, that cohesion has prevailed over political and economic disparity, rivalry and conflict. Another display of that underlying unity is seen in the annual hajj, the reverent pilgrimage to the Kaaba, which —despite centuries of vicious rivalry—is ardently and simultaneously observed by both Sunnis and Shias.

"When Mohamed, towards the end of his career, entered victorious into his native town, which had fought against him so long and so strenuously, he acted with a clemency which, while surprising his opponents, annoyed his friends. But he was anxious to make his tribesmen his own again, and that as soon as possible, and the means to attain that purpose were such as with Arabs, or with most other men, work swiftly and surely. He made them first feel his power, he then won them over by mercy and generosity. This policy rarely fails in its effect, and to this may be attributed the easy and rapid acceptance of Islam by the Mekkans, for he gave them more than they [previously] had. ...

"Although [initially] they cared little for Islam, still they [soon] had every reason to be satisfied with the newly-created state of affairs. With the victorious campaigns and the extensive conquests of the Arab army, immense wealth poured into the two holy cities; infinitely more than the profit derived earlier through trade. And with the Caliph Othman the aristocratic party of Mekka succeeded in gaining the upper hand even in Medina, which had hitherto been the seat of extreme religious puritanism. Into their hands passed the entire government and the important governorships and all offices which yielded a large income. Thus within an incredibly short time the Mekkan patricians, to the utter vexation of the religious party, managed enormously to enrich themselves. Thus grew up a life of pleasure and luxury regardless and heedless of Islam and its moral precepts."[244]

ଓଃ

---

243 The word *qiblah* is Arabic and means the direction toward which Muslims turn their faces in prayer. Every mosque has a niche in the wall called a *mihrab* indicating the direction in which the worshipers are to prostrate themselves in prayer.
244 Alfred Kremer, The Orient Under the Caliphs, trans. S. Khuda Bukhsh (Beirut: United Publishers, 1973), pp. 31-33.

Chapter 8

ULTIMATE VICTORY, DEATH AND IMPORTANT EARLY POST-MORTEM EVENTS, 630–636 A.D.

The Kaaba Declared Off-Limits for Non-Muslims

As we have just seen, in January 630 A.D., as soon as Mecca had capitulated in face of the threat from his 10,000-man army, Muhammad ordered the Kaaba to be cleansed from its hundreds of idols, with the exception of the Black Stone. Not only were the idols to go but also the idol worshipers. From March of 631 A.D. only those who had acknowledged Allah, and Muhammad as his Prophet, were to be allowed to make a pilgrimage to the Kaaba.

The wording of the prohibition is given in Surah 9:17 and 9:28. The earlier passage says, "It is not for the idolaters to tend Allah's sanctuaries, bearing witness against themselves of disbelief. As for such, their works are vain and in the Fire they will abide." The second verse says, "O ye who believe! The idolaters only are unclean. So let them not come near the Inviolable Place of Worship after this their year. If ye fear poverty (from the loss of their merchandise) Allah shall preserve you of His bounty if He will. Lo! Allah is Knower, Wise." Muhammad gave the responsibility to his son-in-law, "Ali to announce in Mekka that no more idolaters would be permitted to make the pilgrimage, which from then on was reserved for Muslims."[245]

Revenge for the 629 Disaster at Mota

Muhammad chaffed under the defeat his forces had suffered at Mota. Had that defeat not been redressed it would have made Islam appear to be a toothless tiger. Therefore, "early in 632, Muhammad gave orders for an expedition to the Byzantine frontier. The more to emphasize that it was intended as revenge for Mota, he appointed Usama, the son of Zaid ibn Harithah [the previous commander] killed at Mota, to command the raid, though he was only twenty years old, a selection which aroused some resentment from more experienced commanders." [246]

In June 632, before the expedition could set out, Muhammad suddenly died. Almost immediately many tribal leaders throughout Arabia disavowed their commitment to Islam and returned to their previous loyalties and concerns. They had

---
245 Carlton S. Coon, Caravan: The Story of the Middle East, (New York: Henry Holt and Company, 1956), p. 93.
246 John Bagot Glubb, The Great Arab Conquests, (London: Quartet Books, 1980), p. 101.

sworn obedience to Muhammad, and now he was gone! This widespread defection has, with understandable logic, been called "The Apostasy." Many leaders among those who remained loyal to Muhammad's cause felt conditions demanded the campaign to Mota be cancelled. However, the elderly caliph, Abu Bakr, dispatched the expedition under the leadership of Usama holding that an order, issued by the Prophet, must be obeyed at all costs and under all circumstances. Usama, accordingly, started in command of 3,000 troops, a third of whom constituted his cavalry.

The Byzantines and the inhabitants of Mota had learned nothing from the previous Muslim attack. They apparently had never considered the possibility of a repeat attack. Mota's carelessness was indicative of Byzantium's blithe and disastrous indifference toward developments in Medina.

After arrival in the vicinity of Mota, Usama "sent out a scout, a Bedouin of the 'Udra tribe, who proceeded on a fleet camel to Obna (Jobna) to reconnoiter. He returned and reported that the inhabitants of the village were careless and without any resources and he counseled a swift attack."[247]

With the cry, "O Victors Slay," the town was completely overrun. Those who could not flee were taken captive. All the buildings were burned, smoke rising like heavy clouds. No doubt, with a great sense of satisfaction, Usama rode the same horse his father used when he was slain in the first attack on Mota. The Muslims suffered not a single casualty which made the division of spoils on the return home even more gratifying.

Death of Muhammad

When it finally came, death confronted Muhammad abruptly. However, that should not have surprised him because it was what he had requested. The details of Muhammad's death come from the *hadith*, a collection of traditional reports on the actions and sayings of Muhammad. These traditional reports were often carried forward in time only orally for several versions. However by the end of the first century of Islam, perhaps a bit earlier, "the main facts about the prophet's life were written down much as we have them in written works."[248] In accessing the *hadiths* one must use caution because many fabricated *hadiths*, concocted by unscrupulous people seeking to establish a point to achieve some end or goal, found their way into the Islamic historical accounts. The most widely accepted account is *Sirat Rasul Allah*, The Life of Muhammad, by Ibn Ishaq on which many of the following details about Muhammad's death are based.

Very late one night in the Arabic month of Rabi' al-Awal, in the year 632 A.D., Muhammad sent for Abu Muwayhiba, a former slave whom he had freed. He

---

247 Joseph Hajjar, "The Bible and Christian Witness in Islamic Countries," International Review of Mission, Vol. LXX. No. 279, July 1981, p. 165.
248 Ibn Ishaq, The Life of Muhammad, Trans. A. Guillaume, (New York: Oxford University Press, 1982) p. xv.

wanted him to be his companion on a trip to a cemetery in Medina where many fallen Islamic warriors were buried. There, as he addressed his fallen companions, Muhammad expressed the desire to join them because of great disappointments he was facing. "When he stood among them he said, 'Peace upon you, O people of the graves! Happy are you that you are so much better off than men here. Dissensions have come like waves of darkness one after the other, the last being worse than the first.'"

Apparently the disappointment which Muhammad expressed to his fallen warriors generated a death wish. Muwayhiba then reported that Muhammad turned to him and said, "'I have been given the choice between the keys of the treasuries of this world and long life here followed by Paradise, and meeting my Lord and Paradise (at once).' I urged him to choose the former, but he said that he had chosen the latter. Then it was that the illness through which God took him began."

Muhammad seemed to be aware of the imminence of his death. Though being tenderly nursed in the residence of Aisha, his favorite wife, as much as possible he urgently cared for important affairs during his last days. For example, there was growing resistance to his appointment of Usama to lead the second expedition to Mota. Though in severe pain he plead, "O men dispatch Usama's force, for though you criticize his leadership as you criticized the leadership of his father before him, he is just as worthy of the command as his father was."

Notwithstanding urgent affairs which were pending, death could not be held at bay any longer. On June 8, 632 A.D. (12th of Rabi al-Awwal), in the 11th year of the Muslim era, Muhammad "died ... in a small crowded hut, surrounded by his servants and his wives. ... Muhammadan historians proclaim that he died in blessedness and peace, confident in the knowledge that he had fulfilled his mission, but the words he uttered in the mosque suggest that he was aware of failure. 'O men, the fire is kindled! Rebellions come like the darkness in the night!'"^{249}

Filling the Void

Though previously he had pointed to Ali, his cousin and son-in-law as his preferred successor or caliph, in his last days he clearly indicated that Abu Bakr was his choice, though he did not formally appoint him before death called him away. Aisha, Abu Bakr's daughter, Muhammad's favorite wife, as well as his loving nurse in his dying days, probably influenced Muhammad to change his choice. Years earlier, Ali had implied to Muhammad that his young wife, Aisha, had been unfaithful to him. A revelation assured Muhammad that the aspersion was false. The consequent white-hot hatred for Ali in Aisha's heart never cooled. "Aisha said, When the prophet became seriously ill he ordered the people to tell Abu Bakr to superintend the prayers." The one who leads in prayer is the imam. "The Arabic word *imam* means 'leader

---

249 Payne, Robert, <u>The History of Islam</u>, (New York: Dorset Press, 1987), pp. 61-65.

of the community;' it is formed from the same root as the word for 'community' ('*umma*)."[250]

The imam is especially the leader of the community when the community is in prayer. Though the word, "imam properly means 'prayer leader,' in a wider sense it was also given to the head of state. A second title still used for the same office is *Amir ul-Mu'minin* or 'Commander of the Faithful.' Rightly or wrongly, the Imam of the Yemen so calls himself today. A third title is *Khalifa*, with its European rendition, Caliph. This is the term most commonly understood by non-Muslims. It means literally 'he who is left behind' and hence 'successor.'"[251]

After an acclamation in favor of Abu Bakr had taken place, those in attendance were exhorted by Umar, the man destined to become the second successor, or caliph, "Arise and swear fealty to him. [Abu Bakr's response allegedly was,] 'Obey me as long as I obey God and His apostle, and if I disobey them, you owe me no obedience.'"[252]

The choice of Abu Bakr as the first caliph was fortuitous. While he and his successor, Umar, were bonafide members of the Quraysh tribe, neither of them were members of either of the feuding Umayyad or Hashim clans. Thus their decisions did not stir up the old acrimonious clan rivalries which ultimately led to the Sunni-Shia split which has bedeviled Islam for almost fourteen centuries. (See Appendix D.)

Apostasy Suppressed by Khalid ibn al Waleed

During his ten-year rule in Medina (from his hijra to his death), Muhammad had for the first time in recorded history unified Arabia. However, upon his death that unity evaporated into renewed tribalism and widespread return to previous loyalties. That defection from Islam was considered apostasy, and as such it was intolerable. From June 632 to July or August 633 A.D., war to suppress apostasy was waged with great brutality and ferocity under orders of Abu Bakr, the first Caliph.

The Caliph and his advisers saw clearly that unless and until the unity of Arabia was restored, the energies of the people of that vast peninsula would be dissipated, as they had been previously for centuries, in local quarrels instead of international conquest. Like Mao Tse Tung, who many centuries later realized China would have no future unless it were unified, so Abu Bakr devoted himself to restoring and solidifying the unity of Arabia, because he knew the potential power of Arabia could only be harnessed if it were unified.

The Caliph gave command of the Muslim army to Khalid ibn al Waleed, the one who had saved most of the Muslim soldiers from death at the Muslim de-

---
250 Heinz Halm, The Shi'ites, A Short History, trans. Allison Brown, (Princeton: Markus Wiener Publishers, 2007), p. 3.
251 Carlton S. Coon, Caravan: The Story of the Middle East, (New York: Henry Holt and Company, 1956), p. 95.
252 Ibn Ishaq, The Life of Muhammad, Trans. A. Guillaume, (New York: Oxford University Press, 1982), p. 687.

feat during their first attack on Mota. Khalid proved to be one of Islam's greatest military leaders during the opening decades of the Muslim era. Glubb, himself a military leader, succinctly chronicled the rise of al Waleed to his pinnacle of power in early Islam. Though I have quoted Glubb's statement in Chapter 1, it is appropriate to reiterate his appraisal as we analyze this critical moment in Islam's history. He wrote, "One of the most important results of Muhammad's increasing prestige at this time was the conversion of Khalid ibn al Waleed, Amr ibn al Aasi and Othman ibn Talha. It was Khalid and Amr who had been responsible for the victory of Quraish at Uhud, by leading the mounted charge round the Muslim left flank. They were to become the greatest military commanders of the Muslims."[253]

The War of Apostasy, the *Ridda* War, lasted about fourteen months. "The Arabic term *ridda*, which is often deemed to be its [i.e., apostasy's] equivalent, does not correspond exactly to the English term 'apostasy.' Apostasy refers to a simple change in faith. *Ridda*, however is not and has never been plain and simple apostasy. The earliest usage of *ridda* was in the context of the political revolts that occurred during the reign of Abu Bakr, the first caliph, immediately after the death of the Prophet. The punishable offense in this case was the political rebellion and the act of disloyalty to the government in Medina, not renunciation of Islam. In fact, the tribes implicated in the *ridda* wars did not in fact apostatize (in the English sense of the word) but were deemed guilty of treason on account of their refusal to pay taxes to the state."[254]

It is extremely doubtful that the just-quoted distinction drawn by Asma Afsaruddin between treason and apostasy was valid even for the opening years of Islamic history. It should be made very clear that today simple defection from Islam, not the refusal to pay taxes to a Muslim government, is considered a capital crime in much, if not most, of the Islamic world.

The Battle of Yemama and Defeat of Musailama, 632 A.D.

The no-holds-barred ferocity of The War of Apostasy comes clearly before us in the record of the vicious Battle of Yemama. It was a battle against Musailama who was one of those deemed by Muhammad and his followers to be a false prophet, working in opposition to and in defiance of Islam. Probably no one has captured the drama and suspense of that battle better than Glubb has, in the following paragraph.

"A furious sword-slashing melee swayed to and fro, made even more exhausting by a hot south wind blowing up the sand in the faces of the Muslims. At length, after several hours of battle, Beni Haneefa began to waver. The battle must presumably have been fought by one of the many small oases in

---
253 John Bagot Glubb, <u>The Great Arab Conquests</u>, (London: Quartet Books, 1980), pp. 90-91.
254 Asma Afsaruddin, *Making The Case For Religious Freedom Within The Islamic Tradition*, <u>Faith & International Affairs</u>, Volume 6, Number 2, Summer 2008, p. 58.

this area, for the retreating enemy took refuge in a walled garden of date palms, barricading the door behind them. At last Beraa, the first of the twelve leaders from Medina who had pledged loyalty to the Prophet at the second al-'Aqaba, and Abu Dujana, who had fought with the Prophet's sword at Uhud, were hoisted on to the wall near the door by their companions. Jumping down into the midst of the enemy, Abu Dujana was slashed to death in a few seconds. Beraa, however, was able to reach the door and open it. The Muslims poured in like a torrent and a desperate sword battle ensued round the trunks of the palm trees in the cramped garden. Beni Haneefa, penned in and unable to withdraw further, were fighting literally with their backs to the wall. At last they were overwhelmed, those in the garden being exterminated to a man."[255]

The victor in the fourteen-month-long vicious war was clearly Caliph Abu Bakr and his army. Just as the victory was decisive, so were the consequences. "When the rebels were defeated by Khalid with great slaughter, the authority of Medina was much more firmly established than it ever had been in the days of Muhammad himself."[256]

The War of Apostasy Ends and the Wars of Conquest Begin

When the War of Apostasy ended victoriously for the Muslims, once again "all Arabia was united under one firm rule, and the Muslims burning with zeal for religion, honor and plunder were casting their eyes around for fresh and more distant fields to conquer."[257]

The Wars of Muslim Conquest began with victory over those Arabs who, as clients to their imperial patrons, had protected Byzantium on Arabia's northwest and Sassanian Iran on its northeast. The first Persian outpost to fall to the Muslim onslaught was the border town of Hira, inhabited by "Christian Arabs, ... [who] belonged to the Nestorian Church with whom the Meccans were in specially vital contact."[258] Hira was located on the Euphrates River, about four miles southeast of the modern town of An Najaf. "Besieged within their walls and without tribal support, the citizens were glad to come to terms, especially as the sum of money demanded by the Arabs, though it appeared large to the bedouins, was trivial in comparison with the wealth of the city. In return for this payment, the Muslims undertook to protect the town, the inhabitants of which, though Arabs, refused to renounce their Christian religion in favor of Islam. This agreement was probably signed in May 633 A.D., [the year following the death of Muhammad] while the last embers of the apostasy were being stamped out in the Yemen."[259]

---

255 John Bagot Glubb, The Great Arab Conquests, (London: Quartet Books, 1980), pp. 113-114.
256 John Bagot Glubb, The Great Arab Conquests, (London: Quartet Books, 1980), p. 124.
257 John Bagot Glubb, The Great Arab Conquests, (London: Quartet Books, 1980), pp. 118-119.
258 Tor Andrae, Mohammed The Man And His Faith, trans. Theophil Menzel (New York: Harper Torchbooks, 1960), p. 90.
259 John Bagot Glubb, The Great Arab Conquests, (London: Quartet Books, 1963), p. 128.

As mentioned before, just prior to the launching of Islam's wars of conquest, "both the Byzantine Emperor and the King of Persia had abolished [dismissed] their local Arab dynasties and attempted to rule their frontier provinces direct. Consequently the Arabs along their borders, who for centuries had defended the marches of both empires, had become hostile to their former sovereigns."[260]

The Second Battle of the Yarmuk (August 20, 636 A.D.)

One of the most astounding features of the Muslim Wars of Conquest is the fact that they unleashed their armies simultaneously on Sassanian Iran in the east and the Byzantine Empire in the west. It is extremely doubtful that Alexander the Great, had he been directing these wars, would have had the audacity to fight such a two-front war. His carefulness to destroy Persian naval power in the Mediterranean before launching his knock-out blow against Persia was a clear reflection of his caution against the hazard of having to battle in opposite directions at the same time. As earlier noted, Muhammad maintained careful military intelligence about conditions in both the Byzantine Empire and Sassanian Iran. Perhaps, Caliph Abu Bakr and his generals, carrying on similar intelligence operations, had information indicating that both empires were vulnerable to defeat should an all-out Muslim attack be launched simultaneously against them.

The initial battles against Byzantium were fought on the upper reaches of the Yarmuk River, the largest eastern tributary to the Jordan. The waters of the lower Yarmuk flow through a very precipitous gorge across which no army could launch an attack. On the upper Yarmuk, just before the waters drop into the gorge, there is level ground between the beginning of the gorge and the huge boulders of a vast lava field to the east. These two geographical features define a bottleneck or a narrow gateway, known as the Deraa Gap, through which armies moving north or south on the eastern side of the Jordan River must pass. Here, two times the Byzantine army faced Muslim armies trying to push north through this constricting passageway.

The first contest at Deraa, known as The First Battle of the Yarmuk, took place in 634 A.D. Through this battle, the Muslim armies temporarily wrenched Syria and Palestine from the grasp of Byzantium. In 636 A.D., setting the stage for a second battle on the Yarmuk, "a fresh Byzantine army marched southwards to reconquer Syria and Palestine. The Arabs abandoned most of their conquests and fell back to the south of Deraa. On 20th August, 636 A.D., a general battle took place on the Yarmuk, in which the Byzantine army was annihilated. The Arabs re-occupied the whole of Syria and the Emperor Heraclius retired behind the Taurus Mountains, abandoning Syria and Palestine forever."[261]

---

260 John Bagot Glubb, The Great Arab Conquests, (London: Quartet Books, 1980), p. 124.
261 John Bagot Glubb, The Empire of The Arabs, (London: Hodder & Stoughton, 1963), p. 26.

"Damascus and the main towns of Syria surrendered even before the decisive battle on the river Yarmuk between the forces of Emperor Heraclius and the Muslim army in August 636 A.D., when—it is said, twelve thousand Ghassanid Arabs went over to the Muslim ranks, being mercenaries with little love for Byzantium."[262]

The Second Battle of the Yarmuk in 636 A.D. marked the beginning of a spectacular epochal change. "For seven centuries, the line of the Syrian Desert and the upper Euphrates divided the Middle East between Roman and Iranian sovereignties. This frontier proved remarkably stable. Despite innumerable wars, it underwent no permanent shift from 64 B.C., when Pompey fastened Roman control upon Palestine, Syria, and Anatolia, until 636 A.D., when Khalid ibn al-Walid defeated a Byzantine army at the [Second] Battle of the Yarmuk and drove the Roman frontiers back into Anatolia."[263]

With the Second Battle of the Yarmuk, Muslim conquest began in earnest. Their effort was crowned, both in the East and the West with startling success. In just seventy-five years, from the Second Battle of the Yarmuk in 636 A.D. to 711 A.D., Islam had triumphed militarily and politically all the way from the present southwestern border of India to the Atlantic Ocean, carving out an empire spanning approximately 5,700 miles, east to west!

How should we evaluate the Muslim conquest? It is appropriate to repeat a quote from Graham E. Fuller, former vice chairman of the National Intelligence Council at the CIA. He wrote, "It was Europeans who visited their 'world wars' twice upon the rest of the world—two devastating global conflicts with no remote parallels in Islamic history."[264] In making that egregiously erroneous statement, Mr. Fuller completely disregarded the record of the vast Muslim military conquest.

From the very beginning of the conquest there were "indications of a marked hostility towards Christianity on the part of the invaders. The converted Jew of the *Doctrina*[265] protests that he will not deny Christ, the son of God, even if the Jews and Saracens catch him and cut him to pieces. The Christian garrison of Gaza put the same determination into practice, and was martyred for it. A contemporary sermon includes among the misdeeds of the Saracens the burning of churches, the destruction of monasteries, the profanation of crosses, and horrific blasphemies against Christ and the church."[266]

---

262 Kenneth Cragg, The Arab Christian, A History in the Middle East, (Louisville, Kentucky, Westminster/John Knox Press, 1991), p. 53.
263 William H. McNeill, The Rise of the West, A History of the Human Community, (Chicago: The University of Chicago Press, 1993), p. 417.
264 Graham E. Fuller, *A World Without Islam*, Foreign Policy, January/February, 2008, p. 53.
265 This refers to the document known as Doctrina Jacobi ("Teachings of Jacob"). It purportedly was composed in Africa in July 634. For details see Robert G. Hoyland, Seeing Islam As Others Saw It, A Survey and Evaluation of Christian, Jewish and Zoroastrian Writings on Early Islam, (Princeton: The Darwin Press, Inc., 1997), p. 55 ff.
266 Patricia Crone and Michael Cook, Hagarism, The Making of The Islamic World, (London: Cambridge University Press, 1977), p. 6.

Professor Donner thinks the contemporary testimony of Christians telling of the destruction wrought by Islamic armies, which he calls the "violent conquest model," is nullified because, "archeological evidence has turned up little or no trace of destructions, burnings, or other violence in most localities, particularly in geographical Syria, which is the area both most fully described by the literary sources and most thoroughly explored by the archeologists."[267] Be sure to evaluate this issue in light of the information given in Chapter 28, "Answering Skeptics."

It seems that the historically-certified destruction and oppression characterizing the Muslim conquest of Syria, Palestine and Egypt was ameliorated by Caliph Mu'awiya, founder of the Umayyad Caliphate. He "was concerned principally to woo, not his Jewish but his Christian subjects. That the Arabs, in their original assault on Palestine, had fought in alliance with Jews was now, to the new 'King of the Holy Land', something of an embarrassment. Both his tax base and his bureaucracy, after all, were composed primarily of Christians."[268]

As emphasized before, "When the Arab Muslims conquered a number of Roman provinces in the Levant and North Africa and Europe, they did not act like the Christianized barbarians from the north, who struggled to preserve something of the Roman state and its laws and made use of the Latin and Greek languages in which their laws and scriptures were written. The Muslims brought their own scripture, in their own language, and created their own state, with their own sovereign institution and their own holy law."[269]

---

267 Fred M. Donner, Muhammad and the Believers: At the Origins of Islam, (London: Harvard University Press, 2010), p. 107.
268 Tom Holland, In The Shadow Of The Sword, (London: Little, Brown, 2012), p. 365.
269 Bernard Lewis, What Went Wrong?, (New York: Oxford University Press, 2002), p. 101.

Islam's Expansion and Its Impact on the Church

Chapter 9

ISLAM EXPUNGES THE CHURCH IN ARABIA

During Muhammad's lifetime, there was a remarkable Christian church and community at Najran in Southwest Arabia. (See Appendix A for the location of Najran.) Those Christians experienced individual and cumulative changes in their living situation growing out of a series of portentous and ominous developments.

First, ever since the Palestinian Jewish Christians, in obedience to Jesus' instructions (Matthew 24:15-18), had refused to join in the Jewish anti-Roman rebellions, either in 70 or 132 A.D., a poisonous anti-Christian hatred and revulsion began to dominate Jewish corporate life. "In such a severe social context, the curse [of Jewish enmity] on the Christians had everyday consequences, not least the expulsion from the synagogues of those Christians of Jewish origin who still went to these common places of worship. [See James 2:2-4.] The last remaining places of contact after the destruction of the temple had become inaccessible."[270] Eventually, that raging hatred had worked its way internationally through the web of interconnected synagogues, till the Jews of Southwest Arabia also had come to look upon the Christians in their area with lethal enmity.

Further, Persia's centuries-long effort to conquer the western shore of the Persian Gulf all the way south to Oman and then west along the coast of Oman to Hadhramaut and, eventually, along the southern shore of Yemen to snatch control of Bab-el-Mandeb from Byzantium's client, the Ethiopians, finally succeeded. Initially, the Persians worked through Dhu Nuwas, a member of the indigenous Yemeni ruling class who had shortly before converted to Judaism. Du Nuwas not only drove the Ethiopians back to Africa, but then, viciously persecuted the Christians of Najran. (See Chapter 2 under "Orthodox Abyssinia Invaded Southwest Arabia.")

The Ethiopians counterattacked and once again gained control of Yemen and Bab-el-Mandeb, but their triumph proved ephemeral. Ethiopian hegemony ended when the Persians again gained control of Yemen, and imposed governance on the area by a series of ruling satraps (governors). In 628 A.D., as pointed out previously,

---

270 Carsten Peter Thiede and Matthew D'Ancona, Eye Witness to Jesus, (New York: Doubleday, 1996), p. 51. The definitive rupture of Christian-Jewish relationships growing out of the Christians' flight from Jerusalem led to "the final separation of Judaism and Christianity." – Paul Johnson, A History of the Jews, (New York: Harper Perennial, 1988), p. 143.

Badhan, the Persian satrap, converted to Islam throwing the area open to evangelism by Muslims from northern Arabia.

Previously, pagan Mecca had blocked Muslim missionaries from expanding their work to the south, but in 630 A.D. Mecca capitulated to Muhammad with his ten-thousand-man army and embraced Islam. From that point, the vibrant church in Najran had to directly face the full brunt of triumphant, expanding Islam.

Scripture-possessors at Mecca "had on God's advice [to Muhammad] been politely answered and not threatened (anymore than the common people) with future punishment for failure to embrace Islam, because the Prophet's function was solely to convey the message to them. [In sharp contrast, they] were ordered in the year 10 A.H. to choose between the alternatives of conversion, payment of tribute and acceptance of inferior status, or condemnation to death. The edict comes in verse 29 of Sura 9: 'Fight those who do not believe in God and the last day and do not prohibit the things which God and His apostle have prohibited! And (fight) possessors of scriptures who do not accept the religion of truth (i.e. Islam) until they pay tribute by hand, being inferior!' With the passage of the years, these scripture-possessors had become the 'worst creatures' (Sura 98, verse 6).

"Muhammad's announcement of this edict after the elimination of the Medinan Jews, the seizure of the Jewish villages of Khaybar [Khaibar] and Fadak, and the conquest of Mecca, indicates that with Islam in power, polite and rational discussion with dissentients was no longer deemed necessary. The language of future discourse with them was to be the language of the sword."[271]

The leaders of the church in Najran knew the time had arrived when they must come to terms with Islam, a burgeoning, dynamic, spiritual, political-military movement. They also knew that any accommodation reached through negotiation with local leaders of Islam, at best, would have only temporary and limited validity. There remained only one viable option, negotiation with the leader and founder of this looming theocracy, Muhammad himself.

Consequently, late in the year 630 A.D. or early in 631 A.D., a delegation of 60 men, official representatives of the 40,000-member[272] Arabian church in the city of Najran, made its way north through the desert, 560 miles to Medina, to consult with Muhammad, the Prophet of Islam. Perhaps a small preliminary group from the church had previously made the same journey to arrange an appointment with Muhammad for the main delegation.

---

271 Ali Dashti, <u>Twenty Three Years: A Study of the Prophetic Career of Muhammad</u> trans. from Persian by F. R. C. Bagley, (London: George Allen & Unwin, 1985), p. 85.

272 This stunning number is from two sources: (1) "The reduction of the number of Christians of Najran from 40,000 to 4,000 in the space of about eighty years is one of the few definite details we have of the diminution of Christians under Islam." – Laurence E. Browne, <u>The Eclipse of Christianity in Asia From the time of Muhammad till the Fourteenth Century</u>, (Cambridge: The University Press, 1933), p. 36. (2) "The people of Najran having increased in number to 40,000." – *The Origins of the Islamic State, Being a Translation From the Arabic of Kitab Futuh Al–Buldan of al-Imam abu-l 'Abbas Ahmad ibn-Jabir al-Baladhuri*, trans. Philip Khuri Hitti (Beirut: Khayats, 1966), p. 103.

We may be able to partially grasp the determination of that delegation if we translate those 560 desert miles in terms of the gait of a camel. A modern Irani cameleer claims a good riding camel can travel at a ten-mile-an-hour clip for 12 hours and repeat the performance after only a two hour rest.[273] Another cameleer gives us more realistic statistics which help us understand the arduous nature of the journey made by the delegation of Christians from Najran. He tells us, "Before I left Kutum I had some of the finest riding camels in the Sudan, for I bought the best that I could find. ... On one of the camels I rode 115 miles in twenty-three hours, and a few months later I rode from Jabal Maidob to Omdurman, a distance of 450 miles, in nine days."[274] According to the second testimony, provided the Najrani delegation traveled without breaks, their journey would probably have taken ten or eleven days, one way.

Muhammad not only knew about the Najrani church, but seemingly had great admiration for it. In 525 A.D., fifty years before Muhammad was born, a Yemeni Jewish ruler (not only out of hatred for all Christians but additionally and mistakenly thinking that the Najrani Christians were complicit with the Abyssinian-Christian military forces against whom he was fighting) forced hundreds of Najrani Christians to leap to their deaths in a huge roaring fire pit. The Koran, as mentioned earlier, extols and memorializes the Najranis' courage and faithfulness. It says, "(Self-)destroyed were the owners of the ditch of the fuel-fed fire, when they sat by it, and were themselves the witnesses of what they did to the believers. They had naught against them save that they believed in Allah, the Mighty, the Owner of Praise, Him unto Whom belongeth the Sovereignty of the heavens and the earth; and Allah is of all things the Witness. Lo! They who persecute believing men and believing women and repent not, theirs verily will be the doom of hell, and theirs the doom of burning." (Surah 85:4-10).

"The majority of Qur'anic exegetes take it [that is, Surah 85:4-10] to be a reference to the martyrs of Najran. If true, then this *sura* becomes a diminutive Arabic martyrology in Islam's Holy Book on the passion of Najran, revealed in the second decade of the seventh century, and it will be of course an important document for a Christian-Muslim dialogue."[275]

Fiery Trials

Whether we read the Muslim account of persecution in Najran, or the Christian account, both remind us vividly of Peter's exhortation. He wrote, "Beloved, think it not strange concerning the fiery trial among you, which cometh upon you to prove you, as though a strange thing happened unto you: but insomuch as ye are partakers of Christ's sufferings, rejoice; that at the revelation of his glory also ye may rejoice with exceeding joy." (I Peter 4:12-13)

---

273 William Graves, "Iran Desert Miracle," National Geographic Magazine, Vol. 147, No. 1 (January 1975), p. 41.
274 Wilfred Thesiger, Arabian Sands, (London: Readers Union Longmans, Green & Co., 1960), p. 13.
275 Irfan Shahid, The Martyrs of Najran: New Documents, (Bruxelles: Societe Des Bollandistes, 1971), p. 193.

While the Koran tells us of the fire pit which Dhu Nuwas and his forces used to persecute the Christians in Najran, Christian sources tell also of a burning church building having been deliberately torched to impede Christianity in Southwest Arabia. The Christian account tells us, "The king sent his three army commanders with their forces to the city of Najran to fight with the Najranites. And the Najranites marched out against them with a few men, put them to flight, killed many of them with the power of Christ, and returned to the city of Najran, not one of them injured in any way. And for the second time he sent others equal to them in numbers, and again the Najranites killed many of them. Finally the king himself came with one hundred and twenty thousand soldiers and laid siege to Najran for many days. And when he saw that it was not to be reduced by war, he sent Jewish priests from Tiberius, bearing the Torah of Moses and a letter of oaths with the seal of this Jewish king; and he swore to them by the Torah, the Tablets of Moses, the Ark, and by the God of Abraham, Isaac, and Israel, that no harm would befall them if they surrendered the city willingly and came out to him.

"And the Najranites put trust in the oaths and about three hundred of their leaders went out to him. And he received them gladly and cordially, and again swore to them in person the very same oaths that he had sent them written in the letter, namely, that no harm would befall them, that he would not ask them to deny their Christianity, and that no one would be oppressed because of their Christianity; and so they broke bread with him. And when they came out to him the following day, he ordered them distributed among his chieftains—fifty men to each chieftain. and he secretly instructed them that each chieftain should guard the men who were to come to him, and that when these had broken bread they were to be bound by their hands and legs and their weapons were to be taken away from them.

"And when they had done this to them and had made sure that all their leaders had been bound, they immediately sent to Najran the Jews and the pagans who thus captured the Christians of the city and asked them to show them the bones of the martyrs. And they gathered together all the bones of the martyrs and those of Mar [a term of great respect and honor, sometimes translated, lord] Paul, the bishop, who had been consecrated the first bishop of Najran by the holy Mar Aksenaya who is called Philoxenos—the bishop of Hierapolis; for this Mar Paul had won the crown of martyrdom by stoning—as had Stephen the first martyr—at the hands of the Jews from Tiberius, in the city of Zafar, the Royal City of the Himyarites. But now they burnt also his bones with fire together with the holy Mar Paul, the other bishop who was consecrated the second bishop of the city of Najran by the very same Mar Aksenaya, the bishop of Hierapolis.

"And the Jews thus brought all their bones together into the church and heaped them in the center of the church; and they brought in the presbyters, the deacons, the sub deacons, the readers, the sons of the covenant and the daughters of the covenant, and the laity, both men and women, some of whose names we intend to write at the end of our letter; and they filled the whole church from one side to the other, with the Christians all of whom came to be about two thousand, as those who came from Najran have said. And they brought wood and surrounded the church from the outside and threw fire into it and burnt it together with all that were found in it."[276]

Scant Records

The description, just given, of the burning of the Najrani Christians comes from one of the few surviving accounts, written by Christians, of the day-to-day life of the vibrant Najrani church. Though it is utterly inconceivable that such an energetic and accomplished people would not have kept copious records, aside from several brief epigraphic inscriptions, we are dependent upon only two literary sources from Christians. They are the *Book of the Himyrites* and the *Letter of Simeon* which have been expertly and competently made available by Irfan Shahid of Georgetown University in The Martyrs of Najran: New Documents, published in 1971 by the Societe Des Bollandistes in Bruxelles.

When the Najrani Christians were later expelled from Arabia, probably most of their historical accounts had to be left behind and were destroyed by the Muslims who occupied their homes and church buildings. Except for the *Letter* and the *Book of the Himyarites* we are totally dependent upon Muslim historical sources. Fortunately, the Muslims initially were so deeply and favorably impressed by the life and activities of the church that almost nothing negative is recorded.

The exuberant life of the Najrani church implies the existence of paid ministers and a considerable support team. The necessary financial base required to create and maintain such arrangements could be generated because Najran "was on the trade route from the East which came up through South Arabia and then ran parallel with the coast [of the Red Sea] through Mecca to Syria. The Christian community in Najran was probably connected with this trade route."[277]

The prosperity derived through trade was reflected in the highly developed infrastructure of the city of Najran. "The *Book of the Himyarites* had recreated daily life in Najran, as a sixth century Arabian city, and the *Letter* supplements this picture with many vivid details: the topography of the city is illuminated by reference to such details as its gates, walls, market, the canal under the walls, and the tamarisk tree."[278]

---

276 Irfan Shahid, The Martyrs of Najran: New Documents, (Bruxelles: Societe Des Bollandistes, 1971), pp. 45-47.
277 Laurence E. Browne, The Eclipse of Christianity in Asia From the time of Muhammad till the Fourteenth Century, (Cambridge: The University Press, 1933), p. 11.
278 Irfan Shahid, The Martyrs of Najran: New Documents, (Bruxelles: Societe Des Bollandistes, 1971), p. 39.

Impacting Muhammad

The resolute Najrani Christians may have thought, even now it may not be too late to bring Muhammad to a position closer to the biblical truth about Christ. They probably knew Muhammad had taken much of his Christology from the large Ebionite church which had been "founded in Mecca by Othman Bin Al-Huweirith. The next pastor of this church was Khadija's cousin, Waraqa bin Neufel [Nawfal]."[279] It was he, ironically, a man professing to be a Christian, along with Khadija, who persuaded Muhammad that his first visions, which had begun in 610 A.D., were revelations from God, not satanic messages as Muhammad had initially feared. (See Chapter 4 under "Assured by a Christian.")

"The doctrine [of the common Ebionites,] may be reduced to the following proposition: Jesus is, indeed, the promised Messiah, the son of David, and the supreme lawgiver, yet a mere man, like Moses and David, sprung by natural generation from Joseph and Mary. The sense of his Messianic calling first arose in him at his baptism by John, when a higher spirit joined itself to him."[280]

If Muhammad had, indeed, gotten his understanding of Christ from Waraqa the Ebionite, he certainly had not accepted all of the Ebionite dogma for, as mentioned before, according to Surah 19, Muhammad clearly and resolutely believed that Jesus was born of the virgin Mary. That Surah tells us, "She [Mary] said: How can I have a son when no mortal hath touched me, neither have I been unchaste? He [the angel] said: So (it will be). Thy Lord saith: It is easy for Me. And (it will be) that We may make of him a revelation for mankind and a mercy from Us, and it is a thing ordained. And she conceived him, and she withdrew with him to a far place."[281]

On their way north to Medina, as they passed through Mecca, did members of the delegation from Najran try to interact with any of the Christian and quasi Christian people living in that former pagan pilgrimage capital of Arabia, which had only recently pledged loyalty to Muhammad? Though it would be enlightening to know, the sources are silent. In any case, the delegation probably could not have tarried long in Mecca for they still had 250 more miles to travel to meet Muhammad in Medina.

A Copy of Scripture

It is difficult to imagine that the delegation of Christians from Najran would have traveled to Medina without taking a copy of Scripture with them, though no mention is made of it in the available sources. Presumably they would have wanted to

---
279 Mark A. Gabriel, <u>Jesus and Muhammad</u>, (Lake Mary, Florida: Charisma House, 2004), p. 31.
280 Philip Schaff, <u>History of the Christian Church</u>, (Grand Rapids, Michigan: Wm. B. Eerdmans Publishing Company, 1910), Vol. II, *Ante-Nicene Christianity*, p. 433.
281 <u>The Meaning of The Glorious Koran, An Explanatory Translation</u>, trans. Marmaduke Pickthall (New York: Alfred A. Knopf, 1930), Surah 19:20-22.

have a copy of Scripture with them for devotional and study purposes as well as for reference during discussions with Muhammad who had become the undisputed hegemon of Arabia. The Najrani Christians undoubtedly knew that Muhammad had extensive biblical knowledge. For example, there are many references to gospel narratives in the Koran, though many of them are badly distorted.

"We have seen that the [Arabian] Prophet was not only acquainted with the main outlines of the Christian doctrines of judgment, retribution and good works, but also that he reproduced in detail the interpretations of these doctrines which were prevalent in the churches of the Orient, and at times he even employs a style and expressions which must have had a Christian origin. This riddle can be solved only in one way. At some time [perhaps multiple times] Mohammed must have heard a Christian missionary sermon."[282]

Andrae's conclusion that Muhammad had heard Christian preaching or teaching is in harmony with the significant Christian presence in Mecca. Historical references to the spread of Christianity in the vast Arabian Peninsula, prior to the rise of Islam, are fairly abundant. However, until recently, few archaeological remains of Christian communities in Arabia proper were known.[283]

Multiple Channels for Biblical Knowledge

One of the most puzzling questions about the spread of Christianity in Arabia is whether the Bible, especially the New Testament, had been translated into Arabic before 622 A.D., the date at which the Muslim era began with Muhammad's Hijra. If the delegation from Najran did take a copy of scripture with them, it probably would have been in Arabic because not only was it the language commonly used in Najran, it was also the liturgical language of the Najrani church. "The use of the Arabic language as a devotional medium can, therefore, be assumed without much hesitation, especially since this particular language, unlike those of newly converted barbarians to Christianity [in western Rome], had reached a very high level of literary expressiveness, which enabled it to accommodate easily the religious concepts of the new faith."[284]

"Although the language of Najran was Arabic, Najran moved in the cultural orbit of the Himyaritic South and it is not unreasonable to assume that the Arabs of Najran adopted the Sabaic 'musnad' [the ancient Yemeni alphabet] as the script of written Arabic."[285] (On the question of whether the Bible had been translated into Arabic before Muhammad's birth, please see Appendix F.)

---

282 Tor Andrae, Mohammed The Man And His Faith, trans. Theophil Menzel (New York: Harper Torchbooks, 1960), p. 91.
283 In the far north, in Dura-Europos, on the right bank of the Euphrates River, so far north one can hardly count it part of Arabia, archaeologists much earlier uncovered a church building dating to about 232 A.D. See Kenneth Scott Latourette, A History of Christianity, (New York: Harper & Row, Publishers, 1975), Vol. I, p.79.
284 Irfan Shahid, The Martyrs of Najran: New Documents, (Bruxelles: Societe Des Bollandistes, 1971), p. 248.
285 Irfan Shahid, The Martyrs of Najran: New Documents, (Bruxelles: Societe Des Bollandistes, 1971), p. 97.

Aside from the debatable issue of whether and when the gospel account of Christ was translated into Arabic, literate Nabataean Arabs (See "Rome's End Run Around Arabia" in Chapter 1.), who had used Aramaic for their inscriptions and commercial transactions, could have had access to the message of Jesus. "Bilingualism was common, and in the same way as the Nabataean Arabs had used Aramaic for their inscriptions and commercial transactions, so Syriac served all ecclesiastical purposes."[286] Also, any literate Arab who may have stepped inside a church building would often have been exposed to the written story of Christ because "Kufic [an angular form of the Arabic alphabet later used in making fine copies of the Koran] had also attained a special status by being employed for inscribing scriptural verses on the walls of churches."[287]

Those inscriptions of biblical scripture inside church buildings may well have been the model, as well as the inspiration for the anti-Christian Koranic inscriptions inside The Dome of The Rock in Jerusalem. The builder, Abd al-Malik, "placed 800 feet of inscriptions that denounced the idea of the divinity of Jesus with a directness that hints at the close relationship between the two faiths of monotheists: they shared much [doctrinally] but not the Trinity. The inscriptions are fascinating because they are our first glimpse at the text of the Koran which Abd al-Malik was having collated into its final form."[288]

Those anti-Christian Koranic quotations displayed inside the dome of Islam's most famous structure, have had a centuries-long impact because, "The Dome of the Rock in Jerusalem [is] the oldest surviving Islamic monument. Built and decorated in the ornate Byzantine tradition, the mosque is surmounted by a gilded dome[289] that shimmers in the sun, among the hills in which it rests, like a crown of burnished gold. To Muslims this splendid structure, built in 691 A.D., had [and still has] both religious and political importance. ... By building what they intended to be the most magnificent shrine in Jerusalem over this hallowed rock, the Muslims [thought to have] honored God and the Prophet; and by putting an Islamic shrine on a spot holy to the Jews [and Christians], they demonstrated their political and spiritual superiority over non-Muslims."[290] It is, then, "a symbol of Muslim strength replacing both Judaism and Christianity."[291]

Najrani Christians Try to Win Muhammad

That a delegation from the church in Najran visited Muhammad is beyond question, being related in several Muslim historical sources. What is not clear

---

[286] J. Spencer Trimingham, Christianity Among the Arabs in Pre-Islamic Times, (New York: Longman, 1979), p.163.
[287] J. Spencer Trimingham, Christianity Among the Arabs in Pre-Islamic Times, (New York: Longman, 1979), p. 228.
[288] Simon Sebag Montefiore, Jerusalem, the Biography, (London: Orion Books Limited, 2011), pp. 182-183.
[289] That dome had been confiscated from a church building in Baalbek. See Chapter 24 under "Distorted Theology."
[290] Desmond Stewart, Early Islam, (New York: Time Incorporated, 1967), p. 102.
[291] Alan M. Guenther, *The Christian Experience and Interpretation of the Early Muslim Conquest and Rule*, Islam and Christian-Muslim Relations, Vol. 10, No. 3, 1999, p. 371.

is how many members made up the delegation. The lowest figure cites two delegates.[292] The highest figure says there were sixty.[293] Perhaps, while the entire delegation was comprised of sixty Christians, only two were appointed to represent their cause in discussions with Muhammad.

Having completed their epic trek to Medina, the spokesmen for the Najrani delegation were finally brought face to face with Muhammad. One Muslim historical source gives so much detailed information that from it considerable insight may be gained regarding the development and maturity of the church in Najran. In part it says, "A deputation from the Christians of Najran came to the apostle. There were sixty riders, fourteen of them from their nobles of whom three were in control of affairs, namely (a) the *Aqib,* the leader of the people, a man of affairs, and their chief adviser whose opinion governed their policy, 'Abdu'l-Masih by name; (b) the *Sayyid,* their administrator who saw to transport and general arrangements, whose name was al-Ayham; and (c) their Bishop, scholar, and religious leader who controlled their schools, Abu Haritha b. 'Alqama. ...

"The first three named above spoke to the apostle. They were Christians according to the Byzantine rite, though they differed among themselves in some points, saying He is God; and He is the Son of God; and He is the third person of the Trinity, which is the doctrine of Christianity. They argue that he is God because he used to raise the dead, and heal the sick, and declare the unseen. ...

"When the two divines spoke to him [Muhammad] the apostle said to them, 'Submit yourselves.' They said, 'We have submitted.' He said: 'You have not submitted, so submit.' They said, 'Nay, but we submitted before you.' He said, 'You lie. Your assertion that God has a son, your worship of the cross, and your eating pork hold you back from submission.' They said, 'But who is his father, Muhammad?' The apostle was silent and did not answer them. So God sent down concerning their words and their incoherence the beginning of the sura of the Family of 'Imran"[294]

When the two delegates said to Muhammad, "Nay, but we submitted before you," it was because the word Muslim, which means "one who has submitted," was a name which the Christians in Najran had previously used to define themselves. By using that name they meant to affirm that they had submitted to God through Christ. Muhammad seemingly had plagiarized the name for his budding movement and by the time the men from Najran were visiting him the name had been infused with the meaning of submitting to Muhammad and

---

292 That is the figure given by abu-l `Abbas Ahmad ibn-Jabir al-Baladhuri, The Origins of The Islamic State, tr. Philip Khuri Hitti (Beirut: Khayats, 1966), p. 99.
293 This is the figure given by Ibn Ishaq, The Life of Muhammad, Trans A. Guillaume, (Karachi: Oxford University Press, 1967), pp. 271-272.
294 Ibn Ishaq, The Life of Muhammad, Trans A. Guillaume, (Karachi: Oxford University Press, 1967), pp. 271-272.

his doctrine. Of course, the delegates from Najran had not and would not submit in that sense.[295]

When the Christians from Najran asked, "But who is his father, Muhammad?," they confronted Muhammad with the central truth of the gospel, the identity of Christ, the true biblical Christology! Muhammad could not answer their inquiry. But that night he had a vision which is recorded in the 59th verse of the third Surah of the Koran which says, "Lo! the likeness of Jesus with Allah is as the likeness of Adam. He created him of dust, then He said unto him: Be! and he is." Though this statement in no way subverts the affirmation that Jesus is the Son of God, still, because of it, Muhammad seemingly felt exonerated in his refusal to submit to Christ. (For additional details see Chapter 5, "Muhammad's Christology.")

Permission Granted and Canceled

When it became obvious that their attempt to convert Muhammad would not bear fruit, the Najrani delegation turned to its second matter of concern. They wanted a covenant which would guarantee the safety and continuance of the church in Najran. The Najrani Christians "offered to sign a pact of alliance. The pact, as cited by Hamidullah, consists of four paragraphs. The first paragraph spells the terms of financial obligation imposed on the Christians of Najran, the second defines their religious and social rights, the third explains the economic matters and the fourth states the abiding clause of the pact."[296]

The outcome of the negotiations resulted in Muhammad issuing an order "that the ... Christians in Najran should be allowed full protection. Umar [the second caliph or successor following the death of Muhammad] simply disregarded the treaties signed by Muhammad and expelled [the Najrani Christians] to Syria, having come to the conclusion that only Muhammadans should be permitted to live in Arabia."[297] In practical terms, the prohibition which had previously been announced against non-Muslims entering Mecca is ruthlessly enforced to the present day.

One hadith, attributed to Aisha, states that Muhammad's very last injunction was, "Let not two religions be left in the Arabian Peninsula."[298] It is claimed that Umar's expulsion order was in conformity to this, Muhammad's final injunction.

In contrast to the statement by Payne, Hitti points out that, "The second caliph, `Umar, deported (A.D. 635–6) to al-`Iraq those of them who had failed to embrace

---

[295] The shift in the use of the name Muslim has also been noted by others: "In the Qur'an *muslim* basically means 'monotheist' and it could therefore be applied to Christians, Jews and other monotheists but, ... gradually, the Qur'anic term *muslim* underwent a kind of shrinkage, so it applied now only to those monotheists who followed Qur'anic law and no longer applied to Jews and Christians." – Fred M. Donner, Muhammad and the Believers, (London: Harvard University Press, 2010) p. 204.

[296] Muhammad Khalid Masud, *Minorities In Islamic History: An analytical Study Of Four Documents*, "The Pact of Najran," Al Mushir (The Counselor), Vol. 40, No.2, 1998, pp. 52, 53. Note: Masud is commenting on the Najran Treaty as given in M. Hamidullah, *Majmu'ah al-Watha'iq al-Siyasiyyah* (Cairo: Lajnat al-Talif wa'l-tarjumah wa'l-nashr, 1956), pp. 111-112.

[297] Robert Payne, The History of Islam, (New York: Dorset Press, 1990), p. 105.

[298] Ibn Ishaq, The Life of Muhammad, Trans A. Guillaume, (Karachi: Oxford University Press, 1967), p. 689.

Islam."²⁹⁹ Probably, they were deported to a location on the border between Syria and Iraq. If so, both assertions, the one by Payne and the one by Hitti, are in agreement. In any case, "The reduction of the number of Christians of Najran from 40,000 to 4,000 in the space of about eighty years is one of the few definite details we have of the diminution of Christians under Islam."³⁰⁰

No Reprieve

At the time the Christian delegation from Najran made its way to Medina to interview Muhammad, it had become obvious that the spiritual tide in Southwest Arabia was flowing strongly in favor of Islam. To this day, Muhammad's covenant has never been restored. The order given by Caliph Umar has stood through the centuries. The net result is grim. "Christians are prohibited from holding religious services in Saudi Arabia (foreign embassies and companies organize discreet weekly 'lectures' for their nationals); supermarkets that have tried to import Christmas trees have had their consignments burned as infidel totems; ... and all these, and many more, manifestations of the Wahhabi spirit in the age of the computer and of the silicon chip are maintained by 'Committees for the Propagation of Virtue and the Prevention of Vice' whose bearded representatives patrol streets with canes. As twilight descends over Riyadh and the robed old men shuffle round the dusty alleys of the *souq*, beating on the windows and calling out '*Salaat*!' ('Prayer!'), the shutters come rattling down and you may well wonder just what century you are living in."³⁰¹

A Wasteland

Today, as far as the gospel of Christ is concerned, Saudi Arabia is a barren wasteland. Not a single congregation of those who are followers of Christ exists within the boundaries of that huge anachronistic kingdom. Today, most of the peninsula is ruled by Saudi Arabia, named for the house of Saud which came to power through brutal warfare, beginning with Ibn Saud's³⁰² bold overthrow of the governor of Riyadh in 1901.³⁰³ It currently, as of 2016, has a population of thirty-two-and-a-third million.

The bleakness of Christianity's situation in Saudi Arabia came to light in "the 2011 State Department Religious Freedom Report [which] offers a revealing distillation of the problem as it exists in Saudi Arabia. There, one al Qaeda-linked Islamic gang of murderers went on a rampage against personnel of a Western (probably petroleum) company. 'We began to comb the site looking for infidels,'

---
299 Philip K. Hitti, The History of the Arabs, (London: Macmillan, 1968), p. 61.
300 Laurence E. Browne, The Eclipse of Christianity in Asia From the time of Muhammad till the Fourteenth Century, (Cambridge: The University Press, 1933), p. 36.
301 Robert Lacey, The Kingdom, (New York: Harcourt Brace Jovanovich, Publishers, 1981), p. 59.
302 His full name was Abdulaziz ibn Abdul Rahman ibn Faisal ibn Turki ibn Abdullah ibn Muhammad Al Saud. His military conquest of Arabia was intended to revive and rejuvenate Wahhabism, a Muslim extremist movement.
303 One of the best books on the rise and stance of Saudi Arabia is by Robert Lacey, The Kingdom, (New York: Harcourt Brace Jovanovich, Publishers, 1981). Another very rewarding book is by Karen Elliott House, On Saudi Arabia, Its People, Past, Religion, Fault Lines—and Future, (NY: Alfred A. Knopf, 2012).

crows one gang member. 'We found Filipino Christians. We cut their throats and dedicated them to our brothers the Mujahideen in the Philippines. We found Hindu engineers and cut their throats, too. Allah be praised. That same day, we purged Muhammad's land of many Christians and polytheists.' After this orgy of murder, the group decided to cap the day's events with a Koran study.

"The problem in Saudi Arabia is not confined to citizen perpetrators. The State Department report points out that 'freedom of religion is neither recognized nor protected under Saudi Law and is severely restricted in practice.' The Saudi government also fails to define, 'private religious worship for all.' It permits its religious police, called the Commission for the Promotion of Virtue and Prevention of Vice (also known as the *mutawwa),* as well as personnel from the Ministry of the Interior to raid with impunity entirely private, non-Muslim religious gatherings. Almost all of these are Christian. In response to complaints about the steady drumbeat of anti-Christian propagandizing by official Saudi media outlets, the Saudi regime has said that its clerics condemn terrorism, even as statements on Saudi national television continue to call for the killing of Jews and Christians and the ultimate take over of the United States by Islamic forces."[304]

Was Extinction God's Judgment?

The church in Arabia, in Afghanistan, in Iran, in Central Asia, in the entire eastern seaboard of the Mediterranean and all across North Africa withered from the stunning impact of triumphant Muslim armies sweeping through those extensive areas. Islamic Arabia was the source of the withering wind which desiccated and enfeebled the churches not only in Arabia itself, but in vast regions where the gospel of Christ had previously flourished. Shortly after the rise of Islam, the church in Arabia quickly shriveled and then died out completely.

Some scholars have taken the view that the death of the church where Islam triumphed, was God's judgment on a corrupt church. One of those scholars tells us that the church in Muslim lands had fallen into such bitter controversy over utter trivialities, "that at length having wearied the patience and long-suffering of God, in thus turning this holy religion into a firebrand of hell for contention, strife, and violence among them, which was given them out of his infinite mercy to the quite contrary end, for the salvation of their souls, by living holily, righteously, and justly in this present world, he raised up the Saracens to be the instruments of his wrath to punish them for it."[305]

Parochial Analysis

One of the problems with that analysis is its gross parochialism. If God brought fatal judgment on churches in the Middle East and Central Asia, as well as on both

---

304 David Aikman, *The Worldwide Attack on Christians*, Commentary, February 2012, pp. 38-39.
305 Arthur Penrhyn Stanley, Lectures On The History of The Eastern Church, (New York: E.P. Dutton & Co., 1861), p. 258.

the Donatist and Catholic churches in northern and in northwestern Africa, because of their apostasy, why has he not visited comparable wrath upon churches in the West whose departure from the purity of the message of Christ has, in many cases, been even much more flagrant?

An example of a grossly corrupt church in the West is "the Romanian Orthodox Church [which] proclaimed [Corneliu Zelea] Codreanu a 'national saint.'"[306] It was that Codreanu who formed the Legion of the Archangel Michael. On January 21, 1941 those Legionnaires "burnt down seven synagogues and went from house to house in the Jewish quarter, raping and torturing women to death in front of their husbands and children. ... The following night, the Legionnaires rounded up an additional 200 Jews and took them to the municipal slaughterhouse, where they stripped them naked and put them through all the stages of animal slaughter on a conveyor belt."[307]

Churches in the Balkan Peninsula have shown a degree of apostasy from New Testament norms exceeding any comparable divergence by the Eastern or North African churches. "Only against the backdrop of Tito's grim, industrial feudalism and the steel jaws of his Serbian secret police could the legacy of Habsburg Austria-Hungary and the Roman Catholic Church—and by extension, of Pope John Paul II—look so benign. Indeed, the aspect of Croatian nationalism that saw itself as culturally superior to the Serbs—the very nationalist tradition that had inspired Stepinac's original desire to see the Serbs converted [by the most brutal methods imaginable] to Catholicism—could not have come about without the active incitement of the Habsburg court and the Vatican."[308]

Time and Chance

The blanket indictment which states that the church went into extinction under Islamic rule only as a divine judgment on the church's wickedness, also ignores the possibility of external factors.

By God's Spirit, Solomon informs us that there may be a random factor, both in life and in history. He wrote, "the race is not [always] to the swift nor the battle to the strong, ... but time and chance happeneth to them all." (Ecclesiastes 9:11)

For example, if a Christian community had happened to have food and fodder needed by a Muslim army which had just run short of those supplies, the Muslim commander very probably would not have hesitated to plunder and ravage those Christians' possessions to achieve his military goal.

Further, if a Muslim military commander felt he needed to put an area in fear by brutally destroying a Christian community as an example, as certainly happened in

---

306 Robert D. Kaplan, Balkan Ghosts, A Journey Through History, (New York: St. Martin's Press, 1993), p. 95.
307 Robert D. Kaplan, Balkan Ghosts, A Journey Through History, (New York: St. Martin's Press, 1993), p. 97.
308 Robert D. Kaplan, Balkan Ghosts, A Journey Through History, (New York: St. Martin's Press, 1993), p. 23.

Egypt, undoubtedly—under similar circumstances—many others also would not have hesitated to plunder Christians to extinction.

Fatal Exposure

Another problem with the traditional analysis of the cause for the extinction of organized Christianity in much, if not most, of the Muslim world, is the theological error of the analysis. Though persecution to extinction may at times have been divine judgment because of the church's excessive wickedness, at other times, quite the opposite view may reasonably be taken. Holding closer to the teachings of Christ may make churches which do so more vulnerable than those which have apostatized. Jesus himself said, "A city on a hill cannot be hidden." (Matthew 5:14) His words imply exposure and vulnerability. Such distinguishing and exposing visibility was also stressed by the apostle Paul when he said, "in the midst of a crooked and perverse generation ... ye are seen as lights in the world, holding forth the word of life." (Philippians 2:15-16)

It is faithfully holding forth the word of life which usually brings the opposition of the world. Such a development is in harmony with Jesus' own experience. He said, "The world cannot hate you; but me it hateth, because I testify of it, that its works are evil." (John 7:7) Any church which has departed from true Christianity, till it has blended into a surrounding dissolute society, has become far less vulnerable to opposition, persecution and extinction. The operative principle is, the corrupt churches "are of the world: therefore the world heareth them." (I John 4:5) In contrast, the faithful church cries out, "he who is not of God heareth us not." (I John 4:6)

The withering wind from Arabia blew simultaneously both east and west. Surprisingly, both Egypt and Iran were defeated by 642 A.D. From this brief account of the church in Arabia, our attention will next be focused toward the east, on Central Asia.

CR

Chapter 10

MUSLIM ARABS AND TURKS BRING A GREAT REVERSAL FOR THE GOSPEL IN CENTRAL ASIA

One evening shortly before a spark ignited the Balkans and began a conflict which drew almost the whole human race into the vortex of World War I, a group of German scholars and archaeologists were relaxing around a campfire after a day of exploring the desert ruins of Turfan in far western China. The day had been rewarding because, among other things, they had retrieved an ancient book written in the Syriac script. However, the discovery was also frustrating because though the book had been written using the Syriac orthographic system which they knew well,[309] that script had been used to transcribe a language which none of them understood.

Because of an 1899 scientific report by two Russian scholars, those German specialists had been drawn to the sand-covered ruins of the ancient caravan town of Turfan, which is now in western China's Sinkiang Province.[310] Through that report it had become known that this site had been a major Buddhist center for many years and that rich archeological treasures lay buried beneath its sands. Because of that information, several German expeditions between 1902 and 1914 had extensively explored those ruins. Their investigations had focused on a part of the area often called Chinese Turkestan. The ruins of Turfan are situated about 90 miles southeast of Urumchi (capital of present-day Sinkiang Province) at the foot of the Tien Shan mountain range. That ancient city had flourished because it was an important junction on one of the major branches of the fabled Silk Road, a main artery of commerce between China, the Middle East and Europe, far to the west.

Crossroads of Culture

"North Asia's greatest cultural and intellectual communities evolved at the crossroads of intersecting caravan trails. At Turfan, Dunhuang, Kashgar, and other cities, travelers exchanged ideas and religious creeds along with their

---

[309] "The Syriac characters as used by the Nestorians gave rise to many Central Asian and Far Eastern alphabets such as the Mongolian, the Manchu, and the Sogdian. The existing characters of the two former groups of languages are lineal descendants of the original Uighurian forms which were certainly derived from the Nestorian Syriac characters, under the influence of the civilized Christian community of Uiguria." – A. Mingana, *The Early Spread of Christianity in Central Asia and The Far East; A New Document*, Bulletin of The John Rylands Library, (Nendeln, Liechtenstein: Kraus Reprint Limited, 1967), Volume 9, 1925, p. 338. Alphonse Mingana, while Assistant Keeper of Manuscripts in The John Rylands Library, was a special lecturer in Arabic in the University of Manchester. Three-quarters of a century after his research into the history of Central Asia, scholars are still richly rewarded by his work.

[310] See Samuel N.C. Lieu, Manichaeism in Central Asia and China, (Boston: Brill, 1998), p. 3.

merchandise. Despite frequent raids by nomads, many of these oasis communities prospered for centuries as centers of artistic and intellectual achievement."[311] Scholars knew that among those who participated in the caravan trade on this artery of commerce between China and the West had been a people known as the Sogdians. They, "through their mercantile activities, were the earliest Iranians to be in prolonged contact with China."[312] The language of the Sogdians, "was the pre-Islamic lingua franca of Central Asia, with its center in Samarkand. It was replaced by Turkish languages in the New Iranian period [i.e. from the ninth century A.D. to the present]."[313] However, up to the time the German archaeological team was relaxing around its campfire, no one in modern times had been able to decipher Sogdian, that once common language.

That evening, as one German scholar casually but carefully turned those ancient pages, suddenly a name leapt up at him, recognizable because it had been spelled normally in a known alphabet. It was a name from the genealogy of Jesus as recorded in the gospel of Matthew. At that moment the German scholars knew they had the key to understanding Sogdian, after many years' efforts during which no one had been able to unlock its secrets.

Responsive Readings in Sogdian

What had been retrieved was not Matthew's gospel as such but "some leaves and parts of leaves of a Gospel Lectionary[314] written, using Syriac letters, in the Sogdian language, a dialect of Middle-Persian."[315] Thus, that lectionary became a kind of Rosetta Stone, facilitating understanding of the Sogdian lan-

---

311 George E. Stuart, (ed.), *North Asia From 8000 B.C. to A.D. 1500, The Restless Frontier*, Peoples and Places of the Past, The National Geographic Illustrated Cultural Atlas of the Ancient World, (Washington, D.C.: The National Geographic Society, 1983), p. 277.
312 C.E. Bosworth, The Medieval History of Iran, Afghanistan and Central Asia, (London: Variorum Reprints, 1977), Chapter XIX, p. 12. "**Sogdiana**, ancient name for a region of Central Asia centering on the fertile valley of the Zeravshan, in the modern Uzbek Soviet Socialist Republic [now Uzbekistan]. Excavations have shown that Sogdiana was probably settled between 1000 and 500 BC and that it then passed under Achaemenian rule. It was later attacked by Alexander the Great and may have been included in the Bactrian Greek kingdom until the invasions of Saka and Yueh-chih peoples in the 2nd century BC. Sogdiana remained a prosperous center until the Mongol invasions. Under the Samanid dynasty (9th-10th centuries AD) it was an eastern focal point of Islamic civilization." – The New Encyclopaedia Britannica, 15th Edition, Micropedia, Vol. IX, p. 324.
313 Richard N. Frye, *Pahlavi Rule*, Colliers Encyclopedia, Vol. 13, 1971, p. 237.
314 The word lection derives from Latin, meaning a reading. Thus a lectionary is "A book or list of lections to be read at church services during the year." The American Heritage Dictionary of The English Language, Third Edition. The fragments and leaves of that lectionary "contain sixteen quotations from Matthew, nineteen from Luke, fifteen from John, three from I Corinthians, and one from Galatians, and all are in almost complete agreement with the sacred text used by the Nestorian Church." – A. Mingana, *The Early Spread of Christianity in Central Asia and The Far East; A New Document*, Bulletin of The John Rylands Library, (Nendeln, Liechtenstein: Kraus Reprint Limited, 1967), Volume 9, 1925, p. 338.
315 F. C. Burkitt, The Religion of the Manichees, (Cambridge: At The University Press, 1925), p. 119. Surprisingly, a tiny group still speak a derivative of Sogdian. "The East Iranian dialects and languages, superseded by Farsi, have remained only in the most remote regions of the western Pamirs, in the territory of the present Gorno-Badakhshan Autonomous Republic (as part of Tajikistan): Yazgulami, Shugni, Ishkashimi, Roshani, and some others, constituting the Pamiri group of the East Iranian languages, and Yagnobi (in the Yagnob valley of Zeravshan), descending from the Sogdian language (with only 2,500 people speaking that language today)." – Vitaly V. Naumkin, Central Asia and Transcaucasia, (Westport, Connecticut: Greenwood Press, 1994), pp. 11-12.

guage once again.[316] Beyond the linguistic interest the discovery aroused, that lectionary also provides a testimony to the strength of the Christian thrust into China and Central Asia from the church in Sassanian Iran. (See Appendix H.) It is also certainly possible that the Iranian church had begun that gospel outreach during the days of the earlier Parthian Empire which had been supplanted in 226 A.D. by the Sassanian Empire. Those early Christian evangelists not only had taken the message of Jesus to Central Asia and the Far East, they had also translated the scriptures into the language of those people! The existence of a lectionary indicates the presence of a congregation of Christians who used it in their worship.

Over a millennium ago, Central Asia, when The Church of the East evangelized there, was a turbulent area, as it still is today. For example, a letter written by Thomas, Bishop of Marga,[317] tells of the Central-Asian area into which a number of bishops, newly ordained by the Patriarch Timothy, had been sent.[318] According to Thomas, the bishops were ordained "to the countries of the savage peoples, who were devoid of every understanding and civilization. No missionaries and sowers of truth had till then gone to their [particular] regions, and the teaching of the Gospel of our Savior had not yet been preached to them; but why should I say the teaching of the Christ, our Lord, while they had not even received, like the Jews and the rest of the Gentiles (i.e., Muslims), the knowledge of God, Creator and Administrator of the worlds, but were worshiping trees, graven wood, beasts, fish, reptiles, birds and such-like, along with the worship of fire and stars. These were the Bishops who preached the teaching of Christ in those countries of the Dailamites and Gilanians, and the rest of the savage peoples beyond them, and planted in them the light of the truth of the Gospel of our Lord."[319]

"The Caspian provinces of Gilan and Mazandaran ... were inhabited by a hardy, warlike and independent people, for long regarded by the Iranians of the plateau as alien and dangerous. In ancient times, the rulers of Iran had never been able effectively to subjugate them, and even the Sassanids had found it necessary to maintain border fortresses as defensive bastions against their incursions."[320]

---

316 The first time I learned of the thrilling account of the Turfan Christian scripture portions and the exciting implications for both linguistics and understanding of the spread of the message of Jesus was at the University of Pennsylvania in 1958 during the lectures of the late Professor Dr. Mark J. Dresden, an outstanding scholar of Persian history and culture and a specialist in the Sogdian language.
317 Marga was located near Adiabene, between the Great Zab and the Little Zab Rivers on the east of the Tigris. Thomas wrote in the 860s A.D.
318 Patriarch Timothy served from May 7, 780 to January 9, 823 A.D.
319 A. Mingana, *The Early Spread of Christianity in Central Asia and The Far East; A New Document*, <u>Bulletin of The John Rylands Library</u>, (Nendeln, Liechtenstein: Kraus Reprint Limited, 1967), Volume 9, 1925, p. 307. While the Dailamites and Gilanians inhabited the area south and southeast of the Caspian Sea, those described as "the savage peoples beyond them" seems to point to the turbulence of Central Asia as a whole.
320 Bernard Lewis, <u>The Assassins</u>, (New York: Oxford University Press, 1967), p. 41.

In spite of the ignorance, violence and turbulence which prevailed in Central Asia, Christianity triumphed in that vast area between the Caspian Sea on the west, the Oxus River on the south and a line on the east from the Pamir Mountains to the Tien Shan Mountains, an area encompassing the current nations of Uzbekistan, Turkmenistan/Turkestan, Tajikistan, Kyrgyzstan, eastern Kazakhstan and Sinkiang Province in western China.[321]

Extent of Triumph

"There are no grounds whatever for denying the incontrovertible fact that the glory of converting the peoples of Central Asia and of the Far East to the Gospel of Christ, and the merit of implanting among them the Western civilization, based on the teaching of Jesus of Nazareth, belong entirely to the untiring zeal and the marvelous spiritual activities of the Nestorian Church, which is by far the greatest missionary Church that the world has ever produced. ... In the teeth of the strong opposition and the terrible vengeance of the wizards of Shamanism and the mobeds of Zoroastrianism, [they] literally explored all the corners of the Eastern globe in order to sow in them the seed of what they firmly believed to be the true religion of God."[322]

Christianity triumphed to the point that, as Toynbee observed, an "embryonic Far Eastern Christian Civilization in a Nestorian chrysalis was germinating in the Oxus-Jaxartes basin before it was rendered abortive; and the blow which robbed it of its chance of coming to life was the definitive annexation of the region to the Arab Empire in A.D. 737–41. Before this conquest, all the local conditions in the area appeared to be in favor of the genesis of a new civilization there. There had been a long and thorough intermingling of cultures: Iranian and Syriac and Hellenic and Indic. There had been an equally long and thorough intermingling of races: an indigenous Iranian peasantry had been overlaid by a deposit of Iranian-speaking nomads in the second century B.C., and by two further layers of Turkish-speaking nomads in the fifth and sixth centuries of the Christian Era. This fruitful diversity of the human element was preserved and accentuated by the character of the physical environment. The concentration of the sedentary inhabitants into a number of separate fortified oases had resulted in the social articulation of the country into a number of politically independent but economically and culturally inter-connected city-states. These maintained good relations with their Ephthalite and subsequent Turkish overlords, who had the sense to realize that the prosperity of master and subject alike derived from the transit-trade along the East-West caravan route, and hence depended upon the guarantee of safe and unobstructed passage through their dominions. To these beneficial human and physical conditions was added the religious stimulus of a vigorous Nestorianism,

---

321 Anyone wanting to read of current conditions in this vast volatile area will find The Resurgence of Central Asia, Islam or Nationalism? by Ahmed Rashid, published by Oxford University Press in 1994 very rewarding.
322 A. Mingana, *The Early Spread of Christianity in Central Asia and The Far East; A New Document*, Bulletin of The John Rylands Library, (Nendeln, Liechtenstein: Kraus Reprint Limited, 1967), Volume 9, 1925, p. 347.

carried into Central Asia and as far as China by the adherents of the faith who had fled from persecution in the Roman Empire.

Cause For Extinction

"In the middle of the seventh century of the Christian Era the new embryonic civilization in Transoxania had every prospect of coming to birth. The cause of its premature extinction is to be found in its failure to respond [adequately] to the menacing challenges presented by the Muslim Arabs' intrusion. A prolonged resistance to the Arab invaders and the devastating intervention of the Turgesh (Western Turkish) Nomads threatened to produce conditions of such intense anarchy that the trade-routes could not have been kept open; and, once these were cut, the life-blood of Transoxania would flow out unstaunched. The Arabs offered a choice between an unmitigated economic catastrophe and a moderated form of political servitude in which the loss of local independence was made more tolerable by the prospect of access to the markets of the Arab Empire, spanning a hinterland from Khurasan to the Atlantic. By accepting, as they did, a peace that was not an unconditional surrender, the Transoxanians escaped the alternative of economic annihilation; but at the same time their acquiescence in being incorporated in an alien universal state had the inevitable effect of stifling the embryo of their own civilization. In this case, the price of response to the challenge had been prohibitively high."[323]

To repeat for emphasis, Toynbee asserted that "the cause of its premature extinction is to be found in its failure to respond to the menacing challenges presented by the Muslim Arabs' intrusion." But he also pointed out that the part of Central Asia known as Transoxania was not politically unified. As just noted, he also accurately observed that "the concentration of the sedentary inhabitants into a number of separate fortified oases had resulted in the social articulation of the country into a number of politically independent but economically and culturally interconnected city-states."

It should be realized that there was often staunch resistance to Islam's onslaught, that withering wind from Arabia. However, that resistance was neither unified nor coordinated. The resistance was probably best shown in the area now known as Afghanistan. It, adjacent to the southernmost part of Central Asia, demonstrated the resolute defense which was made in the face of repeated attacks by Arab Muslims. "The indigenous rulers of northern and eastern Afghanistan ... resisted fiercely the Arabs' attempts at domination, and it was not until the coming of the Turkish slave commanders of the Samanids to such centers as Bust, Ghazna and Gardiz that Islam was implanted there; even then, the inaccessible central province of Ghur remained pagan till the eleventh cen-

---

[323] Arnold Toynbee, A Study of History, (New York: Portland House, 1988) pp. 125-126.

tury, and it is less than a century now that Kafiristan [land of blasphemers], modern Nuristan [land of light], had Islam imposed upon it."[324]

Similarly, in the very heart of Central Asia, the Sogdians tried valiantly to resist the Muslim juggernaut. This came to light when, "in 1933, Soviet scholars found several paper documents among 76 Sogdian, Arabic and Chinese texts discovered at Mount Mug, the mountain stronghold, near Pendzhikent in Tajikistan, where Devastich, lord of Panch, had attempted to escape from the Arab invaders in 722–723, some three decades before the Battle of Talas. Pendzhikent, just east of Samarkand, is only 500 kilometers (300mi) from Talas."[325]

Not only followers of Christ in Central Asia, but many Christians in other localities tried to flee from the engulfing Muslim war of conquest. However, the Muslim conquest was so vast that escape was most often not possible. In one case, the Roman emperor under threat from the Muslim caliph forced a 4,000-member tribe which had escaped from the Islamic territory to return to Muslim captivity. (See footnote 639.) Also, the Louata Tribe of Berbers fled before the Muslim onslaught in North Africa. The record of their flight takes us only as far as Morocco. Ominously, we have no record of their fate beyond that point. (See Chapter 18.)

A Plea to the Chinese

In lieu of political unity, the best alternative available to small kingdoms singlehandedly engaging the Muslims in combat was to appeal for help to the acknowledged hegemon of Central Asia, the great Chinese Tang Dynasty. "It was the Ixsid [the title of the ruler] of Fargana who called in the Chinese army which [accordingly] invaded Transoxania."[326] To gain further understanding of China's role in Central Asia at this time, see "The Tang Chinese Empire" in Chapter 1.

Iran had capitulated to Arab Muslim forces in 642 A.D. as a consequence of the decisive Battle of Nehawand. Byzantium had lost the Levant, Egypt and all of North Africa to the Arabs by 711 A.D. At that point, the remaining imperial giants of the world were the Arabs and the Chinese. "As the Arabs moved east and the Chinese west, the two empires were on a collision course.

By 741 A.D. Arab armies threatened Tibet. Alarmed at the prospect that Arab and Tibetan armies might unite in an alliance against him, the Chinese emperor

---

324 C.E. Bosworth, The Medieval History of Iran, Afghanistan and Central Asia, (London: Variorum Reprints, 1977), Introduction, p. 3.
325 Jonathan M. Bloom, *Revolution by the Ream, A History of Paper*, Aramco World, May/June 1999, p. 29.
326 C.E. Bosworth, The Medieval History of Iran, Afghanistan and Central Asia, (London: Variorum Reprints, 1977), Chapter XX, p. 6. For a more detailed account of the Chinese invasion see H.A.R. Gibb, The Arab Conquests in Central Asia, (New York: AMS Press, Inc., 1970), pp. 96-97. This certainly was not the first incursion of Chinese military forces into western Central Asia. "The first raids into Central Asia by Chinese princes took place around 100 BC and for a time they captured the Ferghana valley and imposed an annual tribute of 1,000 stallions on their victims." - Ahmed Rashid, The Resurgence of Central Asia, Islam or Nationalism?, (Karachi: Oxford University Press, 1994), p. 11.

Hsüan-tsung [of the Tang Dynasty] sent his trusted general, a Korean named Kao Hsien-chih, racing east to forestall the union. Marching his troops across the high heart of Central Asia in one of the most extraordinary campaigns of Asiatic history, General Kao drove his men north and west of the Pamirs across the mountainous heart of the continent. There, in 747 A.D., he successfully broke up the Arab-Tibetan coalition."[327]

Astonishingly, the tenacious Muslim forces successfully renewed their attack against the Chinese Tang Dynasty in 751 A.D., this time on the banks of the remote Talas River, now in Kyrgyzstan. Consequently, China was forced to withdraw to the eastern side of the Pamir mountains, where its western border remains till this day. At that juncture, with the exception of the peripheral Jewish kingdom of Khazaria, all of Central Asia had been brought under Muslim hegemony, which ultimately led to the conversion of the entire area to Islam.

Evaluating the Church of the East

As noted in footnote 316, the Christians of Turfan recited the New Testament scriptures in their church meetings. In the copy of their lectionary, which was recovered from the ruins at Turfan, were fifty-four excerpts from nine of our New Testament books. In their worship services they probably utilized their lectionary somewhat in the fashion with which many American churches use responsive readings from scripture during times of congregational worship.

The Christians at Turfan made up just one of the countless number of congregations of Christians who dwelt in the vast territory stretching from Mesopotamia to the capital of the Chinese Tang Dynasty and to far-western China. Collectively, from their beginning, those congregations were known as The Church of the East. When the Nestorian controversy erupted, those churches did not agree that Nestorius, by order of the Roman emperor, should have been censored and forced into exile in a very remote Egyptian monastery/citadel. Nestorius, while Bishop of Constantinople, had taken the position that in referring to Mary, the mother of Jesus, it was better to call her the one who was pregnant with Christ *(Christotokos)*, rather than the one who was pregnant with God *(theotokos)*. He fully believed that Christ was Emanuel, "God with us," (Matthew 1:23) but for his preference of names for the virgin Mary he was humiliated and exiled. His purpose had been to stave off the rise of a cult centered on Mary. From a remark attributed to the famous British statesman, Benjamin Disraeli, it is clear that Nestorius failed. Dis-

---

[327] Samuel Hugh Moffett, A History of Christianity in Asia, Vol. I: Beginnings to 1500 (2nd ed. rev.; Maryknoll, New York: Orbis Books, 1998), pp. 297-298.

raeli said: "Half of Christendom worships a Jewish man, and the other half a Jewish woman."[328]

Nestorius "is reputed to have died the day before a message arrived inviting him to participate in the Council of Chalcedon; regardless of this impulse to reconciliation, the emperor then ordered Nestorius' writings burned. ... His last and most extensive work, written in prison, a dignified defense of all that he had done, was only rediscovered in a manuscript in 1889 in the library of the East Syrian Patriarch, whose Church's separate status originated in its unhappiness with the results of Chalcedon."[329]

Because The Church of the East sympathized with Nestorius' anti-Mariolatry stance, they came to be known as The Nestorian Church. There was a powerful reason The Church of the East wanted to be known for their anti-Roman government stance. By seeming to endorse Nestorius, who was in exile as a Roman prisoner, they demonstrated that they were not pro-Roman. This saved them from being considered Roman agents working to overthrow the Sassanian-Persian government. In Chapter 13 under the title "State Preference for Episcopal Hierarchy," you will find one record of the terrible persecution The Church of the East suffered from the Persian Sassanian government when the church was thought to have been pro-Roman.

The Fate of the Christians

Following the Muslim conquest, those Christians who kept their faith were severely penalized. For example, "Muhammad ibn Ja`far relates from Hatim the [Muslim] Jurist, that when Qutayba came to Bukhara the fourth time and seized the city, he made peace on condition that every year 200,000 *dirhams* be sent to the caliph, and 10,000 to the amir of Khurasan. They had to give half of their houses and fields to the Muslims, and fodder for the horses of the Arabs, firewood, and whatever was levied in taxes."[330]

It is no wonder that "although not all Moslem [sic] rulers were anti-Christian, most of them were, and the disqualifications under which Christians were placed led either to wholesale secessions to Muhammadanism on the part of the nominal Christians, or to the migration to other lands of many of the more genuine followers of Christ."[331]

---

328 Victor Buksbazen, Miriam the Virgin of Nazareth, (Philadelphia: The Spearhead Press, 1963), p. 178.
329 Diarmaid MacCulloch, Christianity, the First Three-Thousand Years, (New York, Viking, 2010), p. 227.
330 Narshakhi, The History of Bukhara, Translated from a Persian Abridgment of the Arabic Original by Narshakhi, trans. Richard N. Frye (Cambridge, Massachusetts: The Medieval Academy of America, 1954), p. 53. Note: "The History of Bukhara was written in Arabic and presented to the Samanid amir Nuh ibn Nasr in 332/943 or 994. The author was Abu Bakr Muhammad ibn Ja`far ibn Zakariya ibn Khattab ibn Sharik al-Narshakhi from the village of Narshakh, in the vicinity of Bukhara. Nothing is known of the life of Narshakhi, and it seems this was the only work he composed. The book was translated into Persian by Abu Nasr Ahmad al-Qubavi in 522/1128-9. On the first page it is stated that the work was translated because people did not wish to read the Arabic original. Qubavi also omitted unnecessary and tiresome passages in the book, and brought the history down to 365/975." – From the introduction to Frye's translation. (See also the letter from Ishu 'Yab to the Christians in Merv in Chapter 14. This testimony from a Muslim jurist certainly confirms the statement by Patriarch Ishu 'Yab III.)

In contrast to the degrading fate of Christians who submitted to the rapacious Muslims, those who resisted the Islamic military advance were simply eliminated. For example, when "the Khwarizmians rose in revolt ... after the capture of Samarqand [Samarkand], a strong force under al-Mughira b.'Abdullah could be sent to effect a re-conquest. Qutayba's retribution on this occasion exceeded even the terror of Paykand and Shuman. ... the educated classes and more cultured elements in Khwarizm were slaughtered almost to extinction."[332]

The harsh treatment of Christians is frequently cited even in Muslim historical accounts. For example, "When you enter the city [i.e. the city of Bukhara] proper the first quarter to the left is called the 'quarter of the rogues.' [The word *rogue* refers to the Zoroastrians whom the Muslims called fire worshipers.] Before this time a Christian church was there, but now it is a mosque called the mosque of the Bani Hanzala."[333]

A New Economy, a Resurgent Islam

Today, the once vibrant economy supported by trade along the branches of the ancient Silk Road no longer exists. "With the discovery of the sea route to India, the importance of the Silk Route had declined and, semi-forgotten, Central Asia slipped into a limbo."[334] "Since 1917 Central Asia, the land of the greatest trading routes in history, had become little more than an economic colony for Moscow, producing cotton, metals and other raw materials for the Soviet economic powerhouse."[335]

Now that vast oil and gas resources have been discovered, Central Asia has become the focal point of an international chess game played by the world's largest nations and their client states, along with the largest multinational oil and gas companies.

The most daunting condition which 21st century Christian evangelists have to face is the withering wind from Arabia in the form of a powerful resurgent Islam. (Please read the author's booklet, *The Drama of Islam in World History*, available by request from feedback@keycom.org.) "The first sign of this independent spirit in the Islamic revival was the building of new mosques. By October 1990 there were [sic] a total of 50 new mosques in Kyrgyzstan compared to 15 in 1989, 30 in Turkmenistan compared to 5 before, 40 in Tajikistan compared to 17 before, and 90 in Kazakhstan compared to 37 before. In Tashkent city there were 30 new mosques compared to just 2 in 1989. A year later, by

---

331 John Steward, Nestorian Missionary Enterprise, (Edinburgh: T.&T. Clark, 1928), p. XXXIII. For examples of others who tried to flee from the withering wind from Arabia, see Chapter 19 under "Christian Numerical Decline."
332 H.A.R. Gibb, The Arab Conquests in Central Asia, (New York: AMS Press, Inc., 1970), p. 43.
333 Narshakhi, The History of Bukhara, Translated from a Persian Abridgment of the Arabic Original by Narshakhi, trans. Richard N. Frye (Cambridge, Massachusetts: The Medieval Academy of America, 1954), p. 53.
334 Ahmed Rashid, The Resurgence of Central Asia, Islam or Nationalism?, (Karachi: Oxford University Press, 1994), p. 16.
335 Ahmed Rashid, The Resurgence of Central Asia, Islam or Nationalism?, (Karachi: Oxford University Press, 1994), p. 4.

October 1991, there were over 1,000 new mosques in every republic and a new mosque was being opened every day. Converted homes, schools, social centers and even abandoned factories were turned into mosques, paid for largely by public donations from the local community. By October 1992 thousands of mosques had been set up in each republic."[336]

No one should ever imagine that the Islamic resurgence which is taking place in Central Asia is a revival of some sort of benign Islam. This reality became unmistakably clear in a news dispatch from Reuters dated August 16, 2000. It said, "Dozens of Islamic rebels crossed into the former Soviet republic of Kyrgyzstan from neighboring Tajikistan today and waged fierce battles with government troops, the Kyrgyz president, Askar Akayev, said. In a television broadcast, he said that more than 150 gunmen had also massed near the border, threatening a step-up in a week of fighting that has killed dozens of troops and rebels and drawn in three former Soviet Central Asian republics."[337]

The militant nature of the current Islamic thrust in Central Asia is confirmed by the fact that "the Clinton administration added the Islamic Movement of Uzbekistan to its list of foreign terrorist organizations, saying the group has ties to the Saudi financier Osama bin Laden. ... The stated goal of the Islamic Movement, a coalition of several thousand Islamic militants from Uzbekistan and other Central Asian states, is to overthrow the secular government in Uzbekistan and establish a Taliban-style Islamic state there and in other former Soviet republics of Central Asia, whose population is about 85 percent Muslim."[338]

☙

---

336 Ahmed Rashid, The Resurgence of Central Asia, Islam or Nationalism?, (Karachi: Oxford University Press, 1994), p. 45.
337 *Islamic Rebels Make War in Central Asian Region*, The New York Times, August 17, 2000, p. A8.
338 Judith Miller, *U.S. Puts Uzbek Group on Its Terror List*, The New York Times, September 15, 2000, p. A3.

Chapter 11

THE CHURCH FLOURISHED IN AFGHANISTAN TILL THE TURKS EMBRACED ISLAM

Historical Note: Islam came to Afghanistan during the Iranian dynasty known as the Saffarids who reigned in eastern Iran and western Afghanistan from 869 to 1015 A.D. The Saffarids get their name from the occupation of Yaʻqub, the founder of the dynasty, who was a coppersmith which is expressed in Farsi by the word *saffar*, thus, the Saffarids—literally, "the coppersmiths." In the year 870 A.D. "he turned again toward the east and acquired the glory of a warrior of the faith by spreading Islam to Afghanistan."[339] Afghanistan gained its political independence "by the Treaty of Paris, signed in 1857, [under which] Iran withdrew from Herat and recognized the independence of Afghanistan."[340] "King Amanullah Khan, [was] the country's ruler for a decade until 1929. Khan introduced Afghanistan's first constitution and first national budget."[341]

Beginning with a trickle after World War II, the number of pilgrims, students and tourists traveling to Afghanistan from around the world grew to throngs till the flow was cut off by the Russian invasion on Christmas day 1979. Those visitors had come seeking opportunity, either out of religious devotion, academic interest or simple curiosity to behold marvelous monuments erected centuries earlier by devotees to some of the world's great religions.

Muslim visitors might well have made their way to an extremely remote valley in the over eleven-thousand-foot-high Safed Kuh (the white, i.e. snowy mountains), in the center of Afghanistan. They would have gone there to marvel at the slender, gently tapering, Minaret of Djam [Jam], built between 1163 and 1203 AD.[342] It is an exquisite masterpiece of the brick mason's art, reaching 197 feet into the pristine mountain air. It is the only remaining structure of what was once the capital city of the vast Muslim Ghurid Empire whose domain ultimately reached all the way to Delhi.

A Buddhist visitor would undoubtedly have had the Bamian [Bamiyan] Valley on his/her itinerary. In that verdant valley, carved in the side of a perpendicular cliff were the world's two largest statues of the Buddha. One was eleven stories high, the other thirteen. Those gigantic statues were there until the year 2000 when, despite a worldwide outcry, the Taliban destroyed them. When were those marvels

---

339 Carl Brockelmann, <u>History of the Islamic Peoples</u>, (New York: Capricorn Books, 1960), p. 135.
340 Donald N. Wilber, <u>Iran Past and Present</u>, (Princeton: Princeton University Press, 1963), p. 78.
341 Nikhil Kumar, *Afghanistan is the Front Line*, <u>Time</u>, June 12, 2017, p. 40.
342 According to <u>The World Atlas of Archaeology</u>, Christine Flon, ed., (Boston: G.K. Hall & Co. 1985), p. 151, the minaret was "built in 1194 by the *Ghorid* Ghiath al-Din."

crafted out of the sheer cliff? While the exact date may be debated by scholars, we know they were there when the Chinese Buddhist monk Hsüan-tsang beheld them in 630 AD as he came through Bamian on his pilgrimage to Buddhist sites in India. (See Photo 4.)

A Hindu would have been able to visit stunning Hindu shrines unearthed by western archaeologists. And though the Jewish population in Afghanistan dwindled from some 40,000 down to just two feuding Jewish men resident in Kabul, a Jewish visitor might still have wanted to visit the decaying synagogue in the Afghan capital.

But what site could a Christian visit in Afghanistan that would proclaim that there had once been a significant Christian period of Afghan history? There is not even a single Christian monument in the entire country! In modern times only one church building existed. It was near the Russian embassy in Kabul but was destroyed on June 14, 1973. Even its foundations were bulldozed out of the ground. Now only a barren vacant lot awaits anyone who might know where that beautiful building once stood.

Without a single monument testifying that once Christianity was present, one might well ask, did the gospel of Christ ever reach the area now known as Afghanistan in any significantly influential way? The Old Testament prophet Zechariah predicted that one day "a fountain [would be] opened to the house of David and to the inhabitants of Jerusalem, for sin and for uncleanness." He further predicted that the living waters from that fountain would "go out from Jerusalem; half of them toward the eastern sea, and half of them toward the western sea: in summer and in winter." (Zechariah 13:1 & 14:8). We know from the book of Acts and the New Testament epistles that the living water from that fountain did indeed flow copiously to the west. But there is no New Testament document which tells us of those waters flowing to the east. Was Zechariah's prediction accurate? Did those waters flow to the east? If so, did they reach Afghanistan? Impeccable evidence allows us to answer both of those questions with a resounding "Yes!"

One might also ask if the movement of living waters was so different from those of Hinduism, Buddhism and Islam that its thrust was expressed by changed lives rather than monuments and shrines. Also, it is possible that the physical evidence of Christian presence in Afghanistan might have been obliterated, like the church building in Kabul (in modern times the only church building in all of Afghanistan), through deliberate attempts to erase all evidence of that segment of Afghan history.

Lack of awareness of Christ's church in Afghanistan prevails not only because there is no Biblical account of the coming of Christ's gospel to the area, and no existing Christian-related monuments; but also because there is an acute scarcity of post-Biblical Christian historical documents. Among scholars, the reasons for the scarcity of such source materials are well-known. For example, "from the third century there were long periods of persecution which involved the ruthless destruction of churches and monastic institutions and other [places having] depositories of invaluable historical documents."[343] The persecutions which began in the third century were inflicted upon the church by Zoroastrianism while those from the seventh century till the present have been carried out by Islam.

The destruction of church buildings in the Islamic period, some of which were converted into mosques, is confirmed even by Muslim authors. For example, the Muslim historian, traveler and geographer Abul-Qasim Muhammad Ibn Hauqal (Hawqal), who flourished from A.D. 943 to 977, graphically confirms this when he mentions that, in the 10th century, just north of Afghanistan, at Barki in the Syr River watershed [The ancient name of this river was Jaxartes.], now in Tajikistan, there was a "Friday mosque that had originally been a (Nestorian) Christian church."[344]

Also, congregations and church property were swept away by destructive invasions which periodically overwhelmed the area. Typical of such occurrences was the church in southwestern Afghanistan at Seistan (Sistan). When the Mongol conqueror Timur (Tamerlane, Tamburlaine[345]) appeared with his hordes between 1383–1385 A.D., "the capital of Sistan [Zaranj] closed its gates, and declined to surrender. After a short siege it was taken by storm, all its inhabitants who could be found were massacred, its walls were then razed and its houses destroyed. Since that time Zaranj has come to be a nameless ruin."[346]

Vestigial evidence of the strong presence of Christian witness has sometimes survived in spite of repeated destruction. Though "Genghis Khan [1162–1227] ruthlessly slaughtered one million people in Afghanistan's Herat Valley, a strong center of Christianity in the thirteenth century, even today one of Herat's suburbs is called *Injil,* which means gospel."[347] There are also other surviving witnesses to the presence of Afghan churches in the past. "Crosses, still woven in Afghan carpets, witness to the past Christian era, and old coins bear the legend 'In the name of the Father, Son, and Holy Ghost, one God.'"[348]

---

343 Gordon H. Chapman, *Christianity Comes to Asia*, The Church in Asia, ed. Donald E. Hoke (Chicago: Moody Press, 1975), pp. 182-183.

344 G. Le Strange, The Lands of the Eastern Caliphate; Mesopotamia, Persia, and Central Asia, from the Moslem Conquest to the Time of Timur (Cambridge: The University Press, 1905), p. 487.

345 "Tamerlane's name means approximately 'man of iron': but *timur* was not actually iron itself, rather the quality of hardness which made it so difficult to bend." – Jason Goodwin, Lords of the Horizons, A History of the Ottoman Empire, (New York: Henry Holt & Co., 1998), p. 140.

346 G. Le Strange, The Lands of the Eastern Caliphate; Mesopotamia, Persia, and Central Asia, from the Moslem Conquest to the Time of Timur (Cambridge: The University Press, 1905), p. 338. From the time Le Strange wrote, Zaranj has experienced a renewal. In 1984 it had a population of 7,100. It is the capital of Nimruz province and is located on the banks of the Dor River, a tributary of the Helmand River.

347 J. Christy Wilson, Jr., Afghanistan, The Forbidden Harvest, (Elgin, Illinois: David C. Cook Publishing Co., 1981), p. 69.

348 J. Christy Wilson, Jr., Afghanistan, The Forbidden Harvest, (Elgin, Illinois: David C. Cook Publishing Co., 1981), p. 68.

Approximately two hundred miles due north of the Afghan city of Herat are the ruins of the ancient city of, Merv now often called Mary. Though now in Turkmenistan, in New Testament times and well into the Muslim era Merv was located in Khorasan (Khurasan), the ancient Iranian province in which all of the northern half of present-day Afghanistan is situated. Surviving pastoral letters from the Patriarch Ishu 'Yab III, dated between 650 and 658 A.D., tell of the conditions in the church in Merv.[349]

Not only do we have testimony that Christianity was present, but there is also clear evidence that Christianity in pre-Islamic times was strong in the area now known as Afghanistan and also in what is now northern Pakistan. First, it is likely because of the active Afghan church in this area that Buddhism altered its doctrine. In the concept of Mahayana Buddhism, which arose in the area stretching from Rawalpindi, Pakistan to Bamiyan, Afghanistan, man needs a savior. This concept is an abrupt and radical departure from the much older Hinayana form of Buddhism surviving in Sri Lanka (Ceylon). The savior in this case is called a Bodhisattva. He is one who has achieved the right to enter nirvana but voluntarily refuses entrance into that state of blissful non-existence in order to suffer on behalf of others so they too may be "saved."

"The suffering Bodhisattva so closely resembles the Christian conception of the God who gives his life as a ransom for many that we cannot dismiss the possibility that the doctrine was borrowed by Buddhism from Christianity, which was vigorous in Persia from the 3rd century A.D. onwards."[350] Persia at that time included what is now Afghanistan and northern Pakistan.

But why should Buddhism want to borrow a theology from Christianity which was radically different from its historic doctrine? The best answer is, it needed to do this to compete with the new faith which was winning many converts from Buddhism in that very area.

The Muslim historian Ibn Hauqal, mentioned above,[351] "tells of a Christian church in Herat, but makes only slight mention of Christianity in Samercand [Samarkand, also Samarqand]; yet we know ... that Christianity had many followers in Central Asia beyond the Oxus [the river now known as the Amu Darya] at this very time."[352] He also records that in the hills some "two leagues" north of Herat in the 10th century A.D. was a fire temple "called *Sirishk*. A

---
349 See the first two paragraphs of Chapter 14 for details of those letters which show the presence of the church in Afghanistan.
350 A.L. Basham, The Wonder That Was India, A Survey of the Culture of the Indian Sub-Continent Before the Coming of the Muslims, (London: Sidgwick and Jackson, 1954), p. 276.
351 Ibn Hawqal "Flourished c. 943–977. ... He left Baghdad and began his travels in 943. He met al-Istakhri probably c. 952 and at the latter's request revised the maps and text of his geography. He then rewrote it and republished it under his own name, with the title 'Book of Roads and Provinces' ... not before 977." – George Sarton, Introduction to the History of Sciences, (2 Vols. Baltimore: Carnegie Institute of Washington, 1927–1931), Vol.1, p. 674.
352 C.R. Beasley, The Dawn of Modern Geography, (3 Vols. London: Vols. 1 & 2, 1897–1901, Oxford: Vol. 3, 1906), Vol. 1, p. 454.

Christian church also stood at a place lying halfway between this fire temple and the city."[353]

Political or economic conditions in the area often forced churches to adopt organizational models which departed from the New Testament pattern. While those Afghan Christians organized their corporate life in a somewhat hierarchical manner, under monarchical bishops, there is no evidence that they ever modified the fundamental basics of the gospel message.

A bishop for Christians on both sides of the Amu River, the northern border of present-day Afghanistan, was sent by the Nestorian Patriarch in 549 A.D.[354] Because records of early Christianity in the area have been largely destroyed, knowledge of the church in what is now Afghanistan comes mostly through intriguing historical vignettes. However, from writings dating to about 650 A.D., it is clear that there was a church in Balkh and enough Christians "in the upper Oxus[355] valley" to require appointment of bishops.[356] At the same time there was in Merv a "'falling church' because of a slow but steady defection of the faithful to Islam." But still, "in 850 we find the line of metropolitans still continuing in Merv."[357] And there is evidence that about 893 A.D. there was a metropolitan see based in Seistan.[358]

A testimony to the strength of Christianity in Afghanistan is found in the history of its penetration into China with Christ's Gospel. That Gospel thrust not only came through, but came from the area that is now Afghanistan. In part, at least, it was made by utilizing the Sogdian language. "Sogdian was the pre-Islamic lingua franca of Central Asia, with its center in Samarkand. It was replaced by Turkish languages in the New Iranian period."[359] Thus, in a language of northern Afghanistan, which had died out by the Islamic period, the message of Jesus was taken by Afghan-based Christians to western China. The exciting account of Christian evangelism which was carried on by means of the Sogdian language has been given in Chapter 10.

In addition to linguistic evidence that Christianity was once strong in the area which is now Afghanistan, that fact is confirmed by the history of Christian

---

353 G. Le Strange, The Lands of the Eastern Caliphate; Mesopotamia, Persia, and Central Asia, from the Moslem Conquest to the Time of Timur (Cambridge: The University Press, 1905), p. 408.
354 Kenneth Scott Latourette, A History of the Expansion of Christianity, Vol. 2: The Thousand Years of Uncertainty (Grand Rapids: Zondervan Publishing House, 1976), p. 273.
355 This is the older name for the Amu River.
356 C.R. Beasley, The Dawn of Modern Geography, (3 Vols. London: Vols. 1 & 2, 1897–1901, Oxford: Vol. 3, 1906), Vol. 1, pp. 212-213. Obviously, Christians and Christianity did not instantly vanish with the military and political victories of Islam. For example, "the majority of the inhabitants of Syria and lower Egypt were still Christian in the ninth century, and Baghdad itself is stated to have had as late as 900 a Christian population of 40-50,000." – George E. Kirk, A Short History of the Middle East, (New York: Fredrick A. Praeger, 1959), p. 23.
357 C.R. Beasley, The Dawn of Modern Geography, (3 Vols. London: Vols. 1 & 2, 1897–1901, Oxford: Vol. 3, 1906), Vol. 1, pp. 219-220.
358 C.R. Beasley, The Dawn of Modern Geography, (3 Vols. London: Vols. 1 & 2, 1897–1901, Oxford: Vol. 3, 1906), Vol. 1, p. 242.
359 Richard N. Frye, *Iranian Languages,* Colliers Encyclopedia, Vol 13, (Crowell-Collier Educational Corporation, 1969), p. 237.

missions. Alopen, the first Christian missionary known to have taken Christ's message to China,[360] arrived in the capital (Chang'an, now Xi'an) in 635 A.D. It seems he not only came through what is now northern Afghanistan, but had probably been helped on his way by communities of Christians in that area. This assertion is based on the fact that in a Chinese imperial edict Alopen is called a "Persian monk."[361]

It should be remembered that Afghanistan was continually part of Persia during all four of Persia's great historic dynastic periods: (1) the Achaemenian period (559 B.C.–330 B.C.), (2) the Greek period beginning with the Greek invasion under Alexander the Great and the subsequent period of colonization which took place 330 B.C.–248 B.C., (3) the Parthian, (248 B.C.–224 A.D.), and (4) the Sassanian, (224 A.D.–642 A.D.).

A tenth century Persian geography[362] clearly puts Herat in the Persian province of Khorasan/Khurasan. It says that Herat's "cathedral mosque is the most frequented in all Khorasan."[363] In fact, "Khurasan as a province of medieval Persia may conveniently be held to have extended only as far as the Oxus on the northeast, but it still included all the highlands beyond Herat, in what is now the north-western part of Afghanistan."[364]

The Nestorian Monument

That the early expansion of Christianity into China did come, in part at least, from support by Christians and Christian congregations in the area constituting present-day Afghanistan is also confirmed by the discovery in 1623 in Hsianfu, China of a monument, often called the Nestorian Monument. It had been erected in 781 A.D. near the capital city Chang'an (Xi'an) "to commemorate the munificence of a Christian who had come from Balkh,[365] in the ancient Bactria in the vicinity of the Oxus [River], had risen to high favor in the Chinese government, and had been generous in the use of his wealth in caring for the poor and in restoring and enlarging monasteries and churches."[366]

The vitality of Afghan Christianity is further revealed by the fact that "so successful were the [Christians'] missionary efforts that it appeared that Christianity might become the dominant faith in the whole region between the Caspian Sea and Sinkiang [Province] in Northwest China. The largely animistic and polytheistic religions there offered little or no effective resistance to the higher faith. Moreover, Islam at first made little headway in that area, and the dualistic

---

360 See Chapter 13 for additional information on Alopen.
361 William G. Young, Patriarch, Shah and Caliph, (Rawalpindi: Christian Study Centre, 1974), p. 172.
362 The anonymous *Hudud al-Alam* [The Boundaries or Regions of The World]
363 Hudud al-Alam, 'The Regions of the World,' A Persian Geography 372 A.H.– 982 A.D. translated by V. Minorsky. (London: Luzac & Co., 1937), pp. 103-104.
364 G. Le Strange, The Lands of the Eastern Caliphate; Mesopotamia, Persia, and Central Asia, from the Moslem Conquest to the Time of Timur (Cambridge: The University Press, 1905), p. 382.
365 The ruins of Balk are in present-day Afghanistan.
366 Kenneth Scott Latourette, A History of the Expansion of Christianity, Vol. 2: The Thousand Years of Uncertainty, (Grand Rapids: Zondervan Publishing House, 1976), pp. 277-278.

faith of Manichaeism with its headquarters at Samarkand also had scant appeal. Christian Turks visiting Ctesiphon [then the capital of Persia] in connection with the election of a new metropolitan about this time [the seventh century] were described as people of clean habits and orthodox beliefs and as readers of the Scriptures in both Syriac and their own language."[367]

Many of the Turkic people, some before and some after having migrated into the area, had been responsive to the message of Jesus. However, their close ethnic non-Christian Turkic relatives, who also had migrated into the area, were a dynamic and martial people. Many of them, if not the majority, could easily embrace the monotheistic Koranic form of militarism which Islam offered as an alternative to the message of Christ.

Persian sovereignty over the area ended completely when Muslim Arab forces overwhelmed the Iranian army in 642 A.D. at the decisive Battle of Nehawand. Those victorious Muslims could not immediately rule the entire area of the former Persian empire because they still had to destroy the surviving remnants of the Persian army. Consequently, for a brief time no one exercised hegemony in Afghanistan. However, that vacuum was quickly filled by China, governed at that time by the Tang Dynasty, which was friendly to Christianity.

As soon as the Arab Muslims delivered the *coup de grace* to Persia's fleeing army, made up of units which had escaped destruction at the Battle of Nehawand, the withering wind from Arabia blew into the Afghan area with gale force. "Arab power was at its height, and ... in 751 A.D., [by a decisive battle] at Talas in what is now the isolated central Asiatic Republic of Kirghistan [Kyrgyzstan], ... [the] Chinese army was defeated. The encounter, although fought in an area remote from the centers of Chinese and Arab power, was one of the most fateful battles of history. It marked the end of Chinese control over Central Asia and the beginning of five centuries of steady military decline for the Chinese Empire. It also marked the beginning of the Arab conquest of Central Asia. Soon the area was permanently converted to Islam."[368] (For discussion of the extension of Chinese power into Afghanistan and the Caspian area, see Chapter 1 under "Three Dominant Empires.")

These developments ultimately led to a mass conversion of Turks to Islam in the eleventh century.[369] Consequently, by the thirteenth and fourteenth centuries Islam dominated the area. Obviously then, Islam had reached critical mass, an ominous development for the church in Afghanistan.

---

367 Gordon H. Chapman, *Christianity Comes to Asia*, The Church in Asia, ed. Donald E. Hoke (Chicago: Moody Press, 1975), pp. 194-195. See more on the Nestorian Monument in Chapter 13 under the subtitle "Evangelism."

368 Samuel Hugh Moffett quoting E.O. Reischauer in A History of Christianity in Asia, Vol. I: Beginnings to 1500, (2nd ed. rev.; Maryknoll, New York: Orbis Books, 1998), p. 298.

369 "In Transoxania ... the Turkic Karakhanid dynasty and its subjects converted [to Islam] in mass. The Karakhanids' conversion marked a critical phase in the Islamization of Inner Asia. However, because they were sited north of the Amu Darya (Oxus River), this did not [yet] mark a new phase in the creation of a Turkish-Muslim presence *inside* the Middle East." – Carter Vaughn Findley, The Turks In World History, (New York: Oxford University Press, 2005), p. 66. See also Appendix B.

Those new Turkic converts to Islam were filled with zeal to promote the cause they had just embraced. "Islam gave a religious justification to this way of life [the *ghaza* way of life, i.e. border raiding]—in addition to earthly booty, a promise of heavenly reward, a promise that probably helped win converts to Islam."[370] First, they established their brand of Islamic rule in Afghanistan, making it the base from which they projected Muslim military power, both east and west. After Afghanistan was secure, they brought Islam to what is today northern Pakistan and India by the power of the sword. This feat was one which the Arabs, who in 711 A.D. had subjugated the southern drainage basin of the Indus River, the provinces of Sindh[371] and Baluchistan, did not have the residual dynamism to carry out. Names of some of the outstanding Turkic Muslim marshal leaders are Sabuktigin, Sabuktigin's son Mahmud of Ghazni, and Babur. These and many others were imbued with military genius. For example, "Babur, the founder of the Mughal dynasty, was descended from Genghis Khan and Timur (Tamerlane) and was another instance of the extraordinary military potency of Central Asia, Gibbon's source of 'barbarian' vitality."[372]

An example of that vitality was seen when "in 997 the Muslim warlord Mahmud of Ghazni stormed through the Khyber Pass and wreaked devastation through the rich provinces of Punjab and Sindh. His Turkic cavalrymen looted all that lay in their path, desecrating temples and smashing sacred idols in their pious, pitiless iconoclasm.[373] There would be 16 more attacks over the next three decades."[374] Those raids took Mahmud's plunderers, in 1026, all the way to the seashore of the Kathiawar Peninsula where they plundered the famous and extremely rich Hindu temple at Somnath.

How fabulously rewarding Mahmud's plundering raids were can be assessed by the recent evaluation of the treasure in just one of the vaults beneath the ancient Sri Padmanabhaswamy Temple in Trivandrum, India. "The inspection of these vaults took place on June 30, 2011 ... The treasure in Vault A could radically transform the city of Trivandrum and, indeed, the state of Kerala. If the horde in Vault A turned out to be half the twenty-billion-dollar estimate, it would likely earn enough interest in one year to cover the cost of the major projects in the state's 2012 budget, including new waste-processing plants, cargo ports, ambu-

---

370 Carter Vaughn Findley, <u>The Turks In World History</u>, (New York: Oxford University Press, 2005), p. 68.
371 Muhammad ibn-al-Qasim, advancing in 710 at the head of a considerable army, of which 6,000 were Syrians, this son-in-law of al-Hajjaj subdued Makran, pushed on through what is now termed Baluchistan and in 711–12 reduced Sind, the lower valley and delta of the Indus (Sindhu). – Philip K. Hitti, <u>History of The Arabs</u>, (London: Macmillan, 1968), pp. 210-212. "The Arabs were in Makran almost 3-quarters of a century before Muhammad al-Qasim conquered Sind and established the first Muslim settlement on the Indus. Adjacent to the Persian province of Kirman, a western extension of coastal Sind, Makran was first invaded in 644 A.D., the 23rd year of the Hijra, toward the end of the caliphate of Umar." – Andre Wink, <u>Al-Hind, the Making of the Indo-Islamic World</u>, (Boston: Brill Academic Publishers, Inc., 2002), p. 129.
372 Jeremy Black, <u>War and the World, Military Power and the Fate of Continents, 1450–2000</u>, (New Haven: Yale University Press, 1998), p. 24.
373 The reach of these plundering raids is seen in the fact that "Mahmud of Ghazna, who swept down in Gujarat from eastern Afghanistan and in 1026 utterly destroyed the sea side Hindu Temple of Somnath." – Robert D. Kaplan, <u>Monsoon</u>, (New York: Random House, 2010), p. 102.
374 Jonah Blank, *Words into Swords*, <u>U.S. News & World Report</u>, August 16/August 23, 1999, p. 55.

lances, office parks, hospital trauma units, and a modern laboratory for monitoring food and drug quality. And there would still be a three-hundred-and-fifty-million-dollar surplus, which could be used to help Kerala's poor."[375]

It was easy for these Turkic Muslim despots to tyrannize the Christians of Afghanistan. According to Islamic dogma, those Christians had two choices: either convert to Islam or accept the status of *dhimmis*. *Dhimmitude* is a social position which is granted only to Jews and Christians who wish to retain their religion. Muslims are exhorted to "Fight against such of those who have been given the Scripture as believe not in Allah nor the Last Day, and forbid not that which Allah hath forbidden by His messenger, and follow not the religion of truth, until they pay the tribute readily, being brought low."[376] It is obvious that not only did the Christians and Jews have to pay a repressive tax, they had to be humiliated, "brought low."

"It is the duty of a Muslim, wherever he may be, to bring the faith to the unbelievers. ... It is, however, strictly forbidden to a *dhimmi* to try to convert a Muslim to his religion, and if by any mischance he succeeds, the penalty for apostasy is death. From a Muslim religious point of view, this discrepancy is both logical and proper. To promote the true faith is a divine commandment. To abandon it, or to persuade another to do so, is both a mortal sin and a capital crime."[377]

Severely repressed both economically and socially and forbidden to evangelize, only the vitality of the church in Afghanistan allowed it to persist as long as it did. If it should be difficult for a twenty-first-century Western Christian to give credence to the assertion that it was the mass conversion of Central Asia's Turks to Islam which led to the eclipse of Christianity in that whole area, then consider what happened to Christianity in Asia Minor following the Turkish rise to power and dominance there!

○ℜ

---

[375] Jake Halpern, *The Secret Of The Temple*, The New Yorker, April 30, 2012, p. 56.
[376] Marmaduke Pickthall, The Meaning Of The Glorious Koran, An Explanatory Translation, (New York: Alfred A. Knopf, 1930), Surah 9:29, p. 195.
[377] Bernard Lewis, Islam And The West, (New York: Oxford University Press, 1993), p. 53.

Chapter 12

THE CHURCH THROUGH THE CENTURIES IN AFGHANISTAN

Gordon Chapman points us to the very portentous and ominous fact that "there was a mass conversion of Turks to Islam in the eleventh century."[378] By the thirteenth and fourteenth centuries, Islam, having reached critical mass among those Turks, dominated Central Asia, the whole area east of the Caspian Sea all the way to the western border of China. It was a foreboding development for the then beleaguered church. Consequently, during the ensuing centuries the number of Christ's followers, especially in Central Asia, dwindled precariously.

Imperial Confrontation

Conditions were rendered even more desperate by political developments in the nineteenth and early twentieth centuries which exacerbated anti-Christian sentiment in Afghanistan. At that point, India was the jewel of the British Empire, producing much of its vigorous economic success and serving as a rich pool of manpower for its armies. But British India was put in jeopardy by the inexorable militarily-backed expansion of Tsarist Russia following victory over Napoleon at Moscow. Their conquering armies had reached the Amu River, the northern border of Afghanistan. Great Britain and Tsarist Russia had reached an agreement which was recorded in "the Convention of St. Petersburg in August 1907 whereby, among other things, they agreed to a division of Iran into three zones: a Russian zone of influence in the north, a British one in the south, and a narrow central buffer zone under the control, at least nominally, of the Teheran government. They still pledged, however, to respect the territorial integrity and independence of Iran."[379] However, Russia apparently did not feel bound to respect the independence of Afghanistan. As noted at the beginning of Chapter 11, "by the Treaty of Paris, signed in 1857, Iran withdrew from Herat and recognized the independence of Afghanistan."[380] Even after Afghanistan received its independence, ominously, Tsarist diplomacy had won the cooperation of their clients in northern Iran. Their armies were trying to penetrate Afghanistan from the west by attacking Herat.[381] British strategists and diplomats saw this

---
378 Gordon H. Chapman, *Christianity Comes to Asia*, The Church in Asia, ed. Donald Hoke (Chicago: Moody Press, 1975), pp. 194-195.
379 Amin Saikal, The Rise and Fall of the Shah, (Princeton, NJ: Princeton Univ. Press, 1980), p. 14.
380 Donald N. Wilber, Iran Past and Present, (Princeton: Princeton University Press, 1963), p. 78.
381 According to the terms of the Anglo-Russian Convention of 1907, "The northern part of Persia was recognized as a Russian sphere of influence, the southern part as a British sphere, and the central part as a neutral zone where the two powers pledged themselves not to interfere except by mutual consent." – Hutton Webster, World History, (New York: D.C. Heath & Co., Publishers, 1921), p. 552.

two-pronged Russian advance as a direct threat to the British *Raj* in India. To protect its great Indian colony from danger, Great Britain launched three disastrous wars to ensure that Kabul did not fall under the control of Russia, the powerful British enemy.

The First Afghan War began in 1839 (eighteen years before Afghanistan had gained its independence), the second in 1879 and the final one in 1919. Those wars left a heritage of animosity, disdain and hatred against the presumed premier "Christian" country at that time and, by easy association, against everything Christian. This only accentuated and intensified the Koranic anti-Christian animus which had, for centuries, been active in Afghanistan.

The Second Afghan War was fought when Edward Robert Bulwer Lytton was Governor General of India (1876–1880). Lytton's instructions to Major General Frederick Roberts, who led the central front in the war, express the reciprocal hatred engendered by those invasions of Afghanistan. Writing in the first person, Lytton said, "'Every Afghan brought to death I shall regard as one scoundrel the less in a nest of scoundrelism.' Some rough and ready authority such as a drumhead Court Martial might be necessary to satisfy English sentiment, but the enquiries should in each case be limited 'to the question of whether the exacters of retribution are satisfied that it is desirable that the alleged culprit should be put to death.' Retribution, not justice, was to be the watchword. The object was to strike terror swiftly rather than set up a reign of terror."[382]

Conflicting Lifestyles

There is evidence that during the First Afghan War some kind of Christian missionary activity was being carried out in Afghanistan. It may have consisted only of the spontaneous testimony of genuinely believing Christian soldiers in the British forces rather than formal missionary activity. In any case, in view of the death and destruction being inflicted by the British upon the Afghans, it was an extremely poor context in which to introduce the message of the love of Christ! A Muslim analyst tells us, "The Christian missionaries accompanying the occupation forces meddled in the religious life of the Afghans. They distributed everywhere the Bible translated into Persian—'a proselytism that was more injurious than profitable to them.'"[383]

In addition to the barbarity and ruthlessness of those wars, there was the added provocation of sexual corruption practiced by the invading forces. Governor General Lytton "had noted ... that 'immaculate chastity is not one of the many virtues of the British soldier' and there was certainly some anxiety among the British authorities lest there be a repeat of the indiscretions which had caused such animosity during the First Afghan War."[384]

---
382 T.A. Heathcote, The Afghan Wars, (London: Osprey Publishing Limited, 1980), p. 118.
383 N.D. Ahmad, The Survival of Afghanistan, (Lahore: People's Publishing House, 1973), p. 55.
384 T.A. Heathcote, The Afghan Wars, (London: Osprey Publishing Limited, 1980), pp. 119-120.

British sexual laxity, to say the least, was unpopular among Afghans. "It was still more unpopular when tales spread that Afghan girls were being seduced, even abducted, into the households of members of the British occupation forces. … In particular, the recently-knighted dashing young Assistant Envoy, Sir Alexander Burnes, was said to be a great lady-killer. There were tales of carousing and music at the house of this British *elchi* [ambassador], of nocturnal visits by dark-eyed Afghan damsels, and indeed of flagrant immorality involving British officers and the wives of Afghan gentlemen."[385]

In such a highly charged adversarial environment it is extremely surprising that "a small church reappeared in the capital of Kabul in the nineteenth century and ministered to a refugee Armenian community. But, tragically, British military forces destroyed this group in 1896, and its adherents were exiled shortly thereafter. Then for a time there were no known Christians in Afghanistan."[386]

Residual Influence

In April 1978, just a few months before the Russian invasion of Afghanistan, which began Christmas day 1979, I was in Kabul to visit a few friends on my return from a visit to Christians in Pakistan. My taxi driver and I were visiting in a combination of English, Urdu and my very limited and broken Dari. Over the din of his rickety Russian-built *Moskava* taxi he suddenly asked me if I knew Mr. Christy Wilson.

J. Christy Wilson Jr. was a Presbyterian minister with many years of service in Afghanistan. I had met Christy and his gracious wife Betty and had become quite well acquainted with them in 1971 during a six-month stay in Afghanistan. My family and I had evacuated from Pakistan to Afghanistan in anticipation of the war which shortly afterward erupted between Pakistan and India. When I assured my driver that I knew Mr. Wilson quite well, he became ecstatic. He told me that Mr. Wilson had been his teacher and he was always glad to meet and serve his acquaintances and friends. I learned later that the roster of Afghans who have reached out in friendship to Westerners because of the influence of Christy Wilson was a long one.

---

385 T.A. Heathcote, The Afghan Wars, (London: Osprey Publishing Limited, 1980), pp. 50-51. It is ironic that this same ambassador helped Dr. Joseph Wolff, who was the converted son of a Bavarian Jewish rabbi and probably the earliest Christian missionary to enter Afghanistan in comparatively modern times. Between 1831 and 1834 he preached his way across Afghanistan. In one village he was commanded to repeat the Muslim confession of faith. He refused to do so and as punishment he was robbed of all he had and was sent out of the village in rags. When Lieutenant Alexander Burns heard of his plight he "assured Dr. Wolff that he would receive every assistance and invited him to stay with the British party during his Kabul visit." – J. Christy Wilson, Jr., Afghanistan, The Forbidden Harvest, (Elgin, Illinois: David C. Cook Publishing Co., 1981), p. 71. "The Englishman Joseph Wolff, [was] a rabbi's son who had first converted to Catholicism before becoming an Anglican and marrying the daughter of an Oxford earl." He was a "converted British Jew, who tried to persuade him [George English who had converted to Islam, and adopted the name Muhammad] to return to Christianity." – Michael B. Oren, Power, Faith, and Fantasy, America in the Middle East, 1776 to the Present, (New York: W.W. Norton & Company, 2007), pp. 93 & 104. For much greater detail see: Google's cache of http://www.cwi.org.uk/Heralds/Archives/Joseph%Wolff.htm, pp. 1-5.

386 Anonymous, *Afghanistan*, The Church In Asia, (Chicago: Moody Press, 1975), Donald E. Hoke, ed., p. 64.

Christy Wilson was certainly not the first nor the last dedicated follower of Christ to live and work in Afghanistan in modern times. However, despite the deviations from New Testament norms enshrined in Presbyterianism, during his twenty-two years' residence in that country Christy had shown forth the excellencies of Christ more powerfully and more meaningfully than any other single individual follower of Christ in Afghanistan whom I knew. Having known Christy Wilson, I find it appropriate that Gordon-Conwell Theological Seminary in Hamilton, Massachusetts named their Center for World Missions in his honor.

A Brave and Congenial King

Under the benign and enlightened rule of King Zahir Shah who reigned 1933–1973, the doors of Afghanistan, which had slammed shut and had remained closed to Western influence since the First Anglo-Afghan War in 1839, began to open. The king understood that the years of Afghan isolation had left his land-locked, Texas-size country benighted and uncompetitive in the modern world. As the King gradually opened the doors to his country, phalanxes of Westerners, many of them Christians, began careers there as agronomists, as engineers, as researchers, as teachers, as nurses and in many other roles. Through the recommendation of Howard Larsen, an American who had become principal of Kabul's Habibia High School, the oldest secondary school in Afghanistan, the Afghan Ministry of Education invited Christy Wilson to join the faculty in 1951 as a teacher of English.

Because Christy had been born to missionary parents in Mashhad, Iran and had spent his boyhood days there, he spoke fluent Farsi, the more refined form of Dari, the main language of the fifty-two languages spoken in Afghanistan. His linguistic fluency made it easy for him to verbalize the love of Christ, which was obviously in his heart and life, so compassionately that many of his students bonded with him. That resulted in a heritage, a reservoir of good will, which I encountered in my taxi driver and which continues to this day.

Three years after joining the faculty at Habibia, Christy was asked to serve as acting principal in Mr. Larsen's absence. In that role, he recounted, "Governmental order could stop me from verbally sharing my testimony, but no governmental order can stop a person from living a Christian life before the students he comes to know and love. My witness to the students included being their friend and helping when they had a problem."[387]

Ministry Embraced and Expanded

Since in the early 1950s Christy Wilson was the only ordained Protestant minister resident in the capital of Afghanistan, members of the American and other expatriate communities reached out to him to officiate at weddings and funerals. With that record of loving Christian service, it is not surprising that in 1952 he was asked to preach to the newly organized Community Christian Church in Kabul.

---

387 J. Christy Wilson, Jr., Afghanistan, The Forbidden Harvest, (Elgin, Illinois: David C. Cook Publishing Co., 1981), p. 98.

He continued in that role for 20 years. He took a cut in salary from the Ministry of Education to have time to preach and teach adequately on Sundays.

But the church grew so dramatically that soon he could no longer do justice both to the church work and to his teaching responsibilities at Habibia. That created a serious dilemma because his residence visa had been granted on the basis of his work of teaching at Habibia. However, Howard Larsen, who initially had been instrumental in bringing Christy to Habibia, had subsequently become the acting resident representative for the United Nations in Afghanistan. Mr. Larsen, in his new capacity, appealed to the Afghan Government to give Christy a visa as a full-time chaplain to the international community. That appeal was granted. At that point Christy was free to spend all his energies on just one endeavor and he threw himself afresh into his Christian ministerial work.

By the time Christy and Betty had to leave Afghanistan, in March of 1973, they had led in and participated in a surprising number of Christian outreach ministries in Kabul and beyond. In 1958 Betty was instrumental in the founding of Ahlman Academy, a Christian school for children. It not only taught children their academic subjects but the curriculum was kept centered on Christ until the school had to close in 1980 following the Russian occupation. Betty also led in establishing a remarkable school for the blind.

The Wilsons cooperated with and encouraged the staff of the Afghanistan Institute of Technology Incorporated (AITI) which established a school of engineering in Kabul, originally staffed mostly by Christian professionals.

They were also deeply involved in the founding of the International Afghan Mission (IAM) in 1965. That effort led to outstanding Christian doctors like Doctor Howard Harper coming to Afghanistan. In 1966 Dr. Harper "made fifty-seven visits to the Ministry of Health. As a result, the protocol agreement with the Afghan government for the National Organization of Ophthalmic Rehabilitation (NOOR, 'light'), an arm of the International Afghan Mission (IAM), was signed in April of 1966."[388]

A Christian medical team comprised of Dr. Rex Blumhagen and his wife, Dr. Jeanne Blumhagen, former U.S. Embassy doctors in Kabul, led in establishing MAP (Medical Assistance Program) which concentrated on bringing medical help to the isolated areas of the country. They, in cooperation with the Afghan Ministry of Health, established a medical center and a large hospital at Nyak in the remote, predominately Shia, Hazarajat region of Afghanistan. The Christian personnel in all these service ministries shared their knowledge of Christ with their Afghan colleagues as well as with those to whom they ministered. These

---

[388] J. Christy Wilson, Jr., <u>Afghanistan, The Forbidden Harvest</u>, (Elgin, Illinois: David C. Cook Publishing Co., 1981), p. 113.

ministries flourished till 1973. At that point, "IAM had 119 members from 14 nations, representing 21 supporting agencies."[389]

International Relations Intrude

It seemed the door to Afghanistan for Christian outreach had finally and irreversibly opened.[390] But Satan had been at work. King Zahir Shah had to travel to Italy for medical treatment. In his absence the Prime Minister, Mohammed Daoud, seized control of the country. He then sought military aid from America. But American diplomats knew a modernized Afghan military would be used against Pakistan because of Daoud's commitment to a scheme called Pashtunistan. It was a plan to give independence to the Pathan people, the Pashtuns. That would have violently taken major areas away from Pakistan.

America's refusal to grant military aid to Afghanistan drove Kabul to seek that aid from the Soviet Union. In that development, Mohammed Daoud was the pivotal figure, first as prime minister under King Zahir Shah and then, after usurping power on July 17, 1973, as president. During his term as president he sought the support of Afghan Marxists to consolidate and enhance his own power. However, Daoud knew the danger of his policy and resorted to it during his presidency only after another rebuff from America.

Feeling driven to seek their help, Daoud thought he was shrewd enough to exploit the Marxists without giving them an opportunity to build a power base. History has proven how tragically mistaken Mohammad Daoud was. He was overthrown and killed in a coup led by Marxist Nur Muhammad Taraki in April, 1978. The Taraki coup set the stage for the betrayal of Afghanistan into the hands of the Soviet Union in 1979.

Donald Rumsfeld, former U.S. Secretary of Defense, has recorded the grim story of the ten-year occupation of Afghanistan by the Soviets and the egregious U.S. foreign policy mistakes following the departure of the Soviets. He wrote, "The legacy of the decade-long Soviet misadventure would not be erased easily. The Soviets had brutalized the country's people, killing one million and displacing five million more. They had also destroyed much of the land, stripping its forests of trees. The prospects of survival for the puppet regime they left behind in Kabul were exceedingly poor. Once the Soviets withdrew, opposition forces, known collectively as Mujahideen, ('holy warriors' in Arabic, literally those who wage *jihad*, holy war), quickly closed in on Kabul and seized power.

---

[389] J. Christy Wilson, Jr., Afghanistan, The Forbidden Harvest, (Elgin, Illinois: David C. Cook Publishing Co., 1981), p. 116.

[390] The optimistic view of conditions in Afghanistan from the Christian point of view was buttressed by a secular evaluation which called that short time a "brief flowering of social liberalism. Kabul was known as the Paris of the East and visitors could travel freely. Girls in miniskirts made their way to school, people left the city at the weekend to stay at ski lodges, and the equestrian set amused themselves with dressage competitions." – Jon Boone, The Defender of Kabul, Financial Times, Weekend, February 15, 2009, p. 1.

"For most of the 1980's the U.S. government [to force the Soviets out of Afghanistan] channeled funds and material to various Mujahideen groups as part of the largest covert operation in CIA history. As the Soviets completed their retreat, the CIA station in Islamabad, Pakistan, cabled the headquarters at Langley, Virginia, 'We won.'

"Not long afterward, American activities in Afghanistan ended. After the disintegration of the Soviet Union [December 25/26, 1991], the administrations of George H. W. Bush and Bill Clinton turned their attention away from Cold War preoccupations. In the chaos and civil war that consumed the country after the Soviet departure, the United States Embassy in Kabul closed its doors. As America lost interest in Afghanistan, Saudi Arabia and Pakistan poured in millions of dollars to fund roads, clinics, radical Wahhabi madrassas [mosque schools] and mosques. The Pakistani government cultivated Afghanistan's Pashtun war lords, and beginning in 1986, supported the regime that became known as the Taliban. None of this caused any noticeable concern at the senior levels of the U.S. government. Few American policy or intelligence officials imagined that they would ever have to concern themselves again with that distant, poor, and abused land."[391]

After the Soviets were driven out by the American-trained and American-armed Mujahideen, Afghanistan was subsequently taken over by the radical Muslim organization known as the Taliban.[392] It was the Taliban who gave Osama bin Laden his Afghan hideout from which he directed his demonic minions to make their September 11, 2001 attack on America. However, well before the rise of the Taliban and the occurrence of 9/11, other radical Muslims had been at work in ways detrimental to the growth of Christianity in Afghanistan.

Eulogy for a Vibrant Church

The Wilsons had patiently pursued a request made to the Afghan government, during the reign of King Zahir Shah, to permit the construction of the first and only church building in Afghanistan in modern times. Oral permission was ultimately granted and a beautiful church building rose on land about three blocks from the Soviet Embassy. Even before the building was entirely completed, it was dedicated on May 17, 1970. Nearly a year later, in April 1971, the government finally granted permission to complete the building. The inscription on the cornerstone read:

TO THE GLORY OF GOD
"Who loves us and has freed us
from our sins by His blood"
THIS BUILDING IS DEDICATED AS

---

391 Donald Rumsfeld, <u>Known and Unknown, a Memoir</u>, (New York: Penguin, 2011), pp. 365-366.
392 The word *Taliban* (students) is the plural form of the Persian (Farsi) word *Talib,* meaning a student. It refers to the many thousands of students in mosque schools known as *madrassahs* where those students were instructed to offer themselves as *mujahideen,* those who fight in a Jihad, a holy war.

"A house of prayer for all nations"
IN THE REIGN OF H. M. ZAHIR SHAH
MAY 17, 1970 A.D.
"Jesus Christ Himself
being the chief cornerstone"

Unfortunately, only two years later, hard-core Muslims had gained ascendancy in the government and, "Dost Mohammed Fazl, acting mayor of Kabul, sent the church board an expropriation notice." It read, "From the morning of Wednesday, June 13, 1973 the roof of the church will be destroyed by the Kabul Municipality."[393] Every effort of highly placed resident expatriate Christians to have that order rescinded was in vain and on June 14, 1973 the bulldozers began to raze the building. Even the foundations were uprooted; so not a trace of the building remains.

The continued increase of Muslim opposition also forced the closure of many Christian outreach ministries. The great NOOR (*"light"*) ministry to the blind and the optically impaired was summarily closed, driving highly committed and talented personnel from Afghanistan. No longer able to minister there, Dr. Herb Friesen, a highly gifted ophthalmologist with long experience, and his lovely wife, Ruth, were so committed to outreach to Muslims in the name of Christ that after a brief ministry in a clinic in Hunza in extreme northern Pakistan, they opened an eye clinic in conjunction with Gordon and Grace Magney's work in an Afghan refugee camp. Dr. Friesen served in that camp near Peshawar, Pakistan till his untimely death. Earlier, driving through Afghanistan, my son, Jonathan, and I needed to make repairs to our jeep. The Friesens hosted us in their home for three days while we took care of that work. We both were deeply impressed by the loving and godly atmosphere of the Friesen home.

As a result of Daoud's coup which overthrew King Zahir Shah, the rise of Muslim hardline zealots, the destruction of the only church building in Afghanistan, the overthrow of the Daoud regime by the Marxists, the Russian invasion and occupation and the victory of the Mujahideen followed by the takeover by the super-fundamental hardline Taliban party, the door of the country tightly closed once again to outsiders and to Christian witness. Further, the few Afghan Christians are again cruelly stigmatized as traitors both to Islam and to Afghanistan.

How can the current situation for the cause of Christ in Afghanistan be summarized most succinctly? Initially that is probably best done by quoting from a letter dated April, 1999 from a friend, who must remain anonymous. Fluent in Dari and with profound knowledge of Afghan life and culture, he tried for decades to spread the gospel in Afghanistan. Though one of the most optimistic people I have ever known, still, he didn't fail to point out the prevailing somber conditions which highlighted the desperate situation prevailing in Afghanistan in the closing

---

393 J. Christy Wilson, Jr., <u>Afghanistan, The Forbidden Harvest</u>, (Elgin, Illinois: David C. Cook Publishing Co., 1981), p. 65.

days of the twentieth century. He wrote, "Afghanistan poses the greatest challenge to fulfilling the vision of 'a church for every people and the Gospel for every person by the year 2000.' Everywhere, work among the Afghans is under heavy attack."

In another letter from my friend, dated July 2, 1999, he told me of a young Afghan couple, Bibi Gul and her husband. Because they believed in Jesus and tried to share their devotion to him, they had been forced by animosity to move several times during their brief married life. In June of that year, Bibi Gul invited more than a dozen neighbor ladies to watch the *Jesus* film. Before the showing of the film was half over, "an angry man came into the room. The women scattered. He caught Bibi Gul around the neck and choked her to death. Her father claimed the body and threatened to kill her husband, who went into hiding in another city. Their house was looted of all possessions. The police had no interest in finding the killer, since she was only a woman and an apostate to boot."

Conditions Worsen

The withering wind from Arabia, which has shriveled Gospel efforts and decimated Christian fellowships in Afghanistan, is blowing once more with increased intensity. The following six paragraphs are taken from an open letter from the Afghan Christian community to the body of Christ worldwide.

The letter "addresses recent events inside Afghanistan that have unfolded since May 27th, 2010 after an incendiary documentary showing photos and videos of secret 'Afghan Christian Converts' aired on Noorin TV, an independent TV station based in Kabul. The documentary was the first of its kind to ever air publicly on national TV in Afghanistan, a country that considers itself to be 100% Muslim. The controversial content, revealing names and faces of supposed Afghan Christian converts, sparked riots and demonstrations throughout Afghanistan in the days that followed.

"During the ensuing protests, demonstrators called on President Hamid Karzai and the Afghan government to take strong and decisive actions against these exposed Afghan Christian converts by enforcing the Afghan constitution, based on Islamic Sharia law, which clearly calls for the arrest and public execution of anyone who leaves Islam for another religion.

"According to an online report by the Associated Free Press dated June 1, 2010, Abdul Sattar Khawasi, deputy secretary of the Afghan lower house in parliament, called for the execution of Christian converts from Islam saying, 'those Afghans that appeared in this video film should be executed in public, the house should order the Attorney General and the NDS (intelligence agency) to arrest these Afghans and execute them.'

"In another reported statement, Qazi Nazir Ahmad, a lawmaker from Herat, declared that killing a Muslim who converts to Christianity is 'not a crime.' Waheed Omar, the spokesman for the President, told reporters that President Hamid Karzai himself was 'personally' taking an interest in this case, and had ordered his interior minister and the head of the country's spy agency to do a full investigation and 'to take immediate and serious action to prevent this phenomenon.'

"Reports from inside Afghanistan already tell of many arrests in recent days, frequent and ongoing searches of homes and businesses, as well as claims of torture by those under arrest in an effort to forcibly extract the names of other Afghan Christian converts and the locations of secret Afghan Christian 'churches' and underground fellowships throughout the country."[394]

America's interest in Afghanistan did not revive till September 11, 2001. After the horrible attack on the Trade Center Towers in New York, which killed over 3,000 American citizens, our intelligence services quickly traced the perpetrators of that disaster to Osama bin Laden who had found refuge in Afghanistan. By late September 2001, "the first of the CIA teams had entered Afghanistan and linked up with the northern alliance."[395] On December 22, 2001, just 102 days after the catastrophe of 9/11, America installed Hamid Karzai to serve as chairman of an interim authority. Former President, George Bush, wrote, "Afghanistan was the ultimate nation building mission. We had liberated the country from a primitive dictatorship and we had a moral obligation to leave something better. We also had a strategic interest in helping the Afghan people build a free society."[396] Unfortunately, President Bush's vision did not include freedom of religion.

Unless those demonic powers which now have Afghanistan in their grip are brought down, the message of Jesus will not have free course among the approximately thirty-two-million people who comprise the population of Afghanistan.

In spite of the dire conditions for Gospel outreach in Afghanistan, brave, committed followers of Christ have courageously continued to make Christ known in that extremely hostile environment. One example was the work of Gordon and Grace Magney, to whom mention was made earlier. Both Gordon and Grace had completed the M.A. degree at Syracuse University in New York studying under Frank Laubach, founder of a very successful and unique system to help illiterates learn their own language. In addition, Gordon earned a master's degree in Dari, the national language of Afghanistan. Both Gordon and Grace devoted themselves to outreach to Muslim people.

Years earlier, at a lovely dinner in the Magney home in Kabul, I had the high privilege of meeting a totally blind Uzbek young man. Though blind, he had committed large sections of the Bible to memory so he could share the message of Jesus

---

394 Email from Morning Star Development, daniel@msdev.org, June 25, 2010.
395 George W. Bush, Decision Points, (New York: Crown Publishers, 2010), p. 197.
396 George W. Bush, Decision Points, (New York: Crown Publishers, 2010), p. 205.

with his fellow Uzbeks to lead them out of Islam to Jesus. At that dinner, I asked that young man about the roots of the Uzbek people. Jocularly, he replied, "We are descendants of Job, who was of the land of Uz!" Because that courageous blind Afghan would not refrain from testifying for Jesus, he was later tortured to death because of his faith.

The work of the Magneys extended to the Afghan refugee camps which were established in Pakistan following the Russian invasion and occupation of Afghanistan. During that period, Gordon became ill and died, leaving Grace to carry on. Boldly, she again made Kabul her base and oversaw a very extensive outreach, showing the love of Christ to Muslim women by providing them with solar cookers and teaching them how to utilize them in their family cooking (over 22,000 of those cookers were distributed!). Grace continued in that ministry till her neighborhood was targeted by Muslim killers, determined to drive the kafir (blasphemous) Christians from Kabul.

The mortal struggle still goes on for the miniscule Christian community in Afghanistan. Jason Mandryk, editor of *Operation World*, "estimates Afghan Christians to now number in the hundreds. 'The increase of Afghan believers is impossible to document, yet undeniable,' he said. (The State Department estimates the number of Christians in Afghanistan between 800 and 5,000.)"[397]

It is essential that we always remember that "the weapons we fight with are not the weapons of the world. On the contrary, they have divine power to demolish strongholds. We demolish arguments and every pretension that sets itself up against the knowledge of God, and we take captive every thought to make it obedient to Christ." (II Corinthians 10:4-5 NIV)

☙

---

[397] Mindy Belz, *Holding Fast*, World, November 19, 2011, p. 54.

Chapter 13

THE CHURCH IN IRAN BEFORE THE COMING OF ISLAM

Note: Before reading this chapter, you may find it helpful to carefully read "Appendix H" to gain context and background.

The Birth of the Church

Some two thousand years ago, in 33 A.D., Jews from several areas in Iran traveled to Jerusalem to participate that year in the annual Jewish Feasts of Passover and Pentecost. In his record of that epochal pilgrimage season, Luke identified the Jews in that vast throng, who unexpectedly heard Peter's message about Jesus of Nazareth, by the areas from which they had come. Among many others, he tells us there were "Parthians and Medes and Elamites, and the dwellers in Mesopotamia."[398] At the time of that memorable celebration of Pentecost, all those people lived in areas which were administrative districts of Parthian Iran. With the exception of Mesopotamia, all those areas were located within the borders of present-day Iran. Unexpectedly, that festival of Pentecost proved to be the occasion during which Christ's church was born. While it is certainly correct to say that the birth of the church was unexpected, if there had been any significant cross-fertilization between the Iranian Zoroastrian Magi and Iranian Jews, it might have alerted those Jews to expect something extraordinary since the King of the Jews had appeared! (Matthew 2:2.)

The Iranian Parthian Dynasty had come to power in 250 B.C., bringing Greek rule over Iran to an end and putting Iranians back in control of their own country! The Parthians continued to govern till 226 A.D. when they were overthrown and replaced by the Iranian Sassanian dynasty. The Sassanian torch burned brightly, but with varying intensity, for some four centuries till it began to flicker badly just before it was blown out at the Battle of Nehawand in 642 A.D. by a withering wind from Muslim Arabia. That gale not only swept the Sassanian dynasty away, but deeply and adversely impacted the Iranian church as well. However, to appreciate the impact of Islam, it is necessary first to get some insight into the life of the church in Iran prior to the Islamic conquest.

It is beyond reasonable doubt that some, perhaps many, of those Iranian Jews who heard Peter preach on that exceptionally significant Pentecost Day in 33 A.D. became followers of Christ. On their return to their homes, those initial

---

398 Acts 2:9

Iranian Christians constituted the charter members of the church in Iran. Shortly after that landmark Pentecost, we get glimpses of the vitality of Christ's church in the extensive Parthian Empire. Unfortunately, "the term 'Nestorian Church' has become the standard designation used by [many] church historians for that ancient oriental church which called itself simply, 'The Church of the East.'"[399]

Church Music

That the church in Iran was vibrant is seen, first, in the spiritual music it composed. *The Odes of Solomon,* produced by the church in Iran, is the world's oldest surviving Christian hymn book. Surprisingly, it was only discovered by Western scholars in 1909. Internal evidence in the hymns points to its composition in the late Apostolic Age, between 80 and 100 A.D. It seems to have been the hymn book used especially by the Jewish Christians in and around Edessa, today called Urfa. Though in early Christian times that town was in Iran, today it is in eastern Turkey. In the first and second centuries it was one of the great Iranian Christian centers in far western Iran, on the border with the Byzantine Roman Empire.

In *The Odes of Solomon,* "scriptural quotations and allusions abound, drawn from most of the canonical books of the New Testament and much of the Old, with references from the Gospel of John leading all others by far."[400]

As Nehemiah reminded the servants of God in his day, "the joy of the Lord is your strength,"[401] one wonders if joy expressed in the hymns of the Iranian Christians, in part, explains the incredible exuberance and resilience of the Iranian church during the dynasties of both the Parthians and the Sassanians. (See Appendix H for portrayal of these two Iranian empires.)

Evangelism

The vitality of the early Iranian church is further seen in its phenomenal missionary activity. Taking Christ's message in 635 A.D., a Persian/Afghan Christian missionary, whose Chinese name was Alopen,[402] reached Chang'an (modern Xi'an), the capital city of the Chinese Tang (T'ang) dynasty. That epochal achievement is documented by a great stone memorial discovered in 1623 by workmen who found the long-forgotten ancient monument during an excavation. The monument, usually called the Nestorian Monument, is a black granular limestone pillar over nine feet tall, "beautifully inscribed in Chinese characters beneath a design at the top centering around a cross rising from a lo-

---

399 S.P. Brock, The *'Nestorian' Church: A Lamentable Misnomer,* Bulletin of The John Rylands University Library of Manchester, Volume 78, Number 3, Autumn 1996, p. 23.
400 Samuel Hugh Moffett, A History of Christianity in Asia, Vol. I: Beginnings to 1500 (2nd ed. rev.; Maryknoll, New York: Orbis Books, 1998), p. 53. Just two pages later, Moffett tells us that, according to the *Odes,* "Initiation [into Christian fellowship] is through the 'crown' of baptism; and here again a striking picture of the primitive church emerges—believers in white robes were prepared for the solemn ceremony that marked them as Christians; crowns of leaves, green with 'living water,' were placed symbolically on their heads as the initiates came near the baptismal waters."
401 Nehemiah 8:10 (NIV)
402 Reference was made to this in Chapter 11.

tus blossom. ... It was a monument erected in 781 telling of the arrival of a Nestorian missionary in the Chinese capital in 635 A.D."[403]

Quite possibly, Christian missionaries from Iran had previously reached far western China as early as 455 A.D. However, there is no incontrovertible evidence dating that earlier missionary effort like that which exists for Alopen's remarkable mission. (Be sure to read Chapter 10 which highlights the great Persian missionary outreach to Western China, present day Xinjiang Province.) Obviously, there was great vitality and dedication motivating Christian missionaries from Iran who took the message of Christ to China. Commendably, they also took the message to the Turkic and Mongol tribal people, who dominated vast areas between Iran and China, which we now call Central Asia. Their commitment becomes obvious when we realize that "more than forty-five hundred miles of incredibly difficult land travel and an even greater distance by sea separated Seleucia-Ctesiphon [the Iranian dual-city imperial capital] and Baghdad from Chang'an."[404]

"By the year 225 [or 226] A.D., as the Parthian Dynasty fell before the Persian Sassanids, Christian missionaries had planted communities of the faith from the Euphrates to the Hindu Kush and from Armenia to the Persian Gulf."[405] In fact, as mentioned in Chapter 10, a "Far Eastern Christian Civilization in a Nestorian chrysalis was germinating in the Oxus-Jaxartes[406] basin before it was rendered abortive; and the blow which robbed it of its chance of coming to life was the definitive annexation of the region to the Arab Empire in A.D. 737–41."[407] Taking the whole scope of the expansion of Christianity in view, which emanated from the church in Iran, it is no surprise that one scholar stated: "Geographically, and possibly even numerically, the expansion of this church outstripped that of the church in the West in the early centuries."[408]

Christian Literature Production

Another remarkable development in Iranian Christianity was the emphasis which it placed on Christian literature production and theological study. These two emphases undoubtedly helped stoke that evangelistic fervor which carried their missionaries as far as China. From their efforts we know certainly that at

---

403 Samuel Hugh Moffett, A History of Christianity in Asia, Vol. I: Beginnings to 1500 (2nd ed. rev.; Maryknoll, New York: Orbis Books, 1998), p. 288.
404 Samuel Hugh Moffett, A History of Christianity in Asia, Vol. I: Beginnings to 1500 (2nd ed. rev.; Maryknoll, New York: Orbis Books, 1998), p. 296.
405 Samuel Hugh Moffett, A History of Christianity in Asia, Vol. I: Beginnings to 1500 (2nd ed. rev.; Maryknoll, New York: Orbis Books, 1998), p. 79.
406 These are the modern-day names for the Amu and Syr Rivers which flowed into the Aral Sea before Communist Russia diverted their waters to irrigate vast new areas of cotton production. Consequently, the Aral Sea has almost dried up.
407 Arnold Toynbee, A Study of History, (New York: Portland House, 1988), p. 125.
408 Gordon H. Chapman, *Christianity Comes to Asia*, The Church in Asia, ed. Donald Hoke (Chicago: Moody Press, 1975), p. 185.

least eleven congregations of Christians came into being, while there are historical hints of many more.[409]

One widely influential Iranian Christian publication was the *Diatessaron* by Tatian whose home was on the east side of the Tigris River. It was the first harmony of the Gospels in the history of the church, either East or West. Tatian's "*Diatessaron* (literally, 'through four' [gospels], but it is also a musicological term meaning 'choral' 'harmony'), which was a life of Christ compiled from all four Gospels but based on the outline and structure of John. ... [It] was used until the 5th century and influenced the Western Church even after four separate gospels were established."[410]

"A significant shift took place in 489, A.D., when the Byzantine Emperor Zeno in his drive to placate Miaphysites [See Glossary.] finally closed the school of the Persians in the city of Edessa (now Urfa in Turkey). This had been the major centre of higher education for Christians throughout the East, both within and beyond the empire, but now a school was established little more than 150 miles eastwards in Sassanian territory, in the city of Nisibis (now Nusaybin in the extreme southeast of Turkey), ready to take on the duty of training Dyophysite [See Glossary.] clergy. In Nisibis, Greek works could be translated and expounded to Syriac-speakers: the Church was concerned to preserve even the works of pre-Christian Greek philosophy so that they could be used as intellectual tools for arguments with Chalcedonian [See Glossary.] and Miaphysite Christians. This was of huge importance for a wider future. Moreover, the flow of knowledge to Nisibis was not just from the west. It was a Christian scholar from Nisibis, Severus, with a Persian surname, Sebokht, abbot and bishop of a monastery on the Euphrates, who in the mid-seventh century first described a system of mathematical signs invented by Indians, which were then absorbed into Islamic culture and are therefore known to us as Arabic numerals."[411]

Higher Christian Education

The church in Iran also established and supported great Christian theological schools. These helped prepare students to participate both in local church life and in the great evangelistic outreach which sprang from the Iranian church to non-Christian people. Records indicate that sometimes these schools had student bodies of as many as 1,000 students. Three schools are particularly worthy of mention which were located at Edessa, at Nisibis and at Seleucia-Ctesiphon, the dual-city capital of the Sassanian Empire. The school at Edessa fell back and forth under the political control of the Sassanians and the Byzantines as the border fluctuated between the two empires during the interminable wars in which they "fought each other to exhaustion." Edessa was especially coveted by

---

409 For additional information, see Samuel Hugh Moffett, A History of Christianity in Asia, Vol. I: "Beginnings to 1500 (2nd ed. rev.; Maryknoll, New York: Orbis Books, 1998), p. 293.
410 H. Grady Davis, *Biblical Literature*, The New Encyclopaedia Britannica, (Chicago: Encyclopaedia Britannica, Inc. 1979), Vol. 2, p. 940.
411 Diarmaid MacCulloch, Christianity, the First Three-Thousand Years, (New York, Viking, 2010), p. 246.

both empires because it was situated where important strategic North-South and East-West trade routes crossed. Had those two great empires not squandered their strength in debilitating wars fought against each other, especially "in those critical first decades of the seventh century, there might have been no Arab Armageddon in the desert, no victory for Islam."[412]

Jesus said of his church, "the gates of Hades will not overcome it." (Matthew 16:18 NIV) Yet, over the entire fourteen-centuries-long panorama of Islamic opposition to the gospel of Christ in the vast Muslim world, the church has in many places struggled to survive and locally has very often utterly disappeared. Two current examples, from many cases which could be cited of countries where the church—once strong—but has now completely disappeared, are Saudi Arabia and Afghanistan. Though organized Christianity in present-day Iran has not completely vanished, it is struggling for existence. Before the withering wind of Islam began to blow upon it, great vibrance and resilience had been shown by the Iranian church in the face of stunning and appalling opposition.

Church Organization, The Testimony of Bardaisan

In the year 179 A.D as Bardaisan, a native young man, resident of Edessa, "happened" to walk by the church building he heard Hystaspes, an elder, expounding the Scripture. "He believed and was baptized. He proved to be a zealous convert and was soon made a deacon, earning a reputation for himself as a defender of the faith against the heretics in which Edessa abounded. His high position at the court of the king must have quickly marked him for leadership in the church. He excelled in everything he touched."[413] Bardaisan's succinct account of the church in Iran gives us rich insights into how those Christians lived in his time. He said, "We are all called Christians, by the one name of Christ, wherever we may be found. On the day of Sunday we come together, and on the appointed days we fast."[414]

Further Extant Records

One of the most important documents by which a picture of the early church in Iran may be seen is the *Chronicle of Arbil*. It was written between 541 and 569 A.D. by Mashiha-zakha, a native Christian of the province of which Arbil was the capital. Arbil is today called Erbil and currently serves as the capital of the Kurdish people. It is located in present-day northern Iraq some 50 miles east of Mosul. According to the *Chronicle*, "Up to about 180 A.D. only two orders of ministers are mentioned—bishops and deacons. This accurate reflection of primitive Christianity would not have been invented in the 6th century [when the

---

412 Samuel Hugh Moffett, A History of Christianity in Asia, Vol. I: Beginnings to 1500 (2nd ed. rev.; Maryknoll, New York: Orbis Books, 1998), p. 241.
413 Samuel Hugh Moffett, A History of Christianity in Asia, Vol. I: Beginnings to 1500 (2nd ed. rev.; Maryknoll, New York: Orbis Books, 1998), p. 65.
414 Samuel Hugh Moffett, A History of Christianity in Asia, Vol. I: Beginnings to 1500 (2nd ed. rev.; Maryknoll, New York: Orbis Books, 1998), p. 94.

Chronicle was written], and gives us confidence that Mashiha-zakha is using early sources."[415]

Change in Church Leadership

"There is very little reliable evidence of a developed episcopate in Persia until much before the year 300.[416] It is apparent from the evidence in other parts of the Persian border regions, notably Edessa and Arbela (Adiabene), that ever since about the end of the second century the church had slowly been moving in the direction of greater centralization of authority and that in the third and fourth centuries the process accelerated. ... It was only with the first Persian synods of the fifth century, beginning with the Synod of Isaac in 410, that national authority was established and given to the bishop of the capital city, Seleucia-Ctesiphon. ... [In sharp contrast,] The epistles of Ignatius of Antioch, written about 110, portray churches [in the West] in which the bishop was supreme, a ruling officer and a spiritual authority higher than either presbyter (priest, elder) or deacon."[417]

State Preference for Episcopal Hierarchy

The Persian Sassanian imperial government seems to have favored the centralization of authority in the church. In general it made it easier for the state to control the church. "The Church was recognized as a permitted religious community, or *millat* [nation], in a State whose official religion was Zoroastrianism."[418] Basically, this same arrangement was adopted by Islam when it later replaced the Sassanian Zoroastrian Persian government. Even today, the church in a Muslim country, as the Copts in Egypt, where it is allowed to exist at all, is only tolerated and must bear many adverse impositions on its freedom and liberty.[419]

However, there were Iranian bishops who dared to defy the authority of the state when it was exercised against the people of Christ. For example, in the reign of the Sassanian Emperor Shapur II who ruled from 309 to 379, the Christians were falsely accused of collusion with Byzantium during one of Constantine's attacks against Iran. Informers accused Bishop Simon (whose principal

---

415 William G. Young, Patriarch, Shah and Caliph, A Study of the Relationships of the Church of The East with The Sassanid Empire and the Early Caliphates up to 820 A.D. with special Reference to Available Translated Syriac Sources, (Rawalpindi, Pakistan: Christian Study Center, 1974), p. 9.

416 An episcopate is that form of church government in which a solitary bishop is distinguished from and raised above the elders to a position of supreme authority.

417 Samuel Hugh Moffett, A History of Christianity in Asia, Vol. I: Beginnings to 1500 (2nd ed. rev.; Maryknoll, New York: Orbis Books, 1998), p. 117.

418 William G. Young, Patriarch, Shah and Caliph, A Study of the Relationships of the Church of The East with The Sassanid Empire and the Early Caliphates up to 820 A.D. with special Reference to Available Translated Syriac Sources, (Rawalpindi, Pakistan: Christian Study Center, 1974), p. 1.

419 "The Catholicos [the title given to the national reigning bishop in Iran] was made responsible for the behavior of his people and the Christian community became a kind of state within a state, not unlike the position of the religious minorities in the Turkish Empire which persisted into the twentieth century." – Kenneth Scott Latourette, A History of The Expansion of Christianity, Vol. I: The First Five Centuries (Grand Rapids, Michigan: Zondervan Publishing House, 1970), p. 229.

office was in Seleucia-Ctesiphon, the Sassanian dual-city capital) of conveying state secrets to the Romans. "Shapur II's response was to order a double tax on Christians and to hold the bishop responsible for collecting it. ... [The Emperor gave the following order to his officer], 'When you receive this order ... you will arrest Simon, the chief of the Nazarenes. You will not release him until he has signed this document and agreed to collect the payment to us of a double-tax and a double tribute for all the people of the Nazarenes who are found in the country of our godhead and who inhabit our territory. For our godhead has only the weariness of war while they have nothing but repose and pleasure. They live in our territory [but] share the sentiments of Caesar our enemy.' Bishop Simon refused to be intimidated. He branded the tax as unjust and declared, 'I am no tax collector but a shepherd of the Lord's flock.'"[420]

This defiance led to Bishop Simon's death on Good Friday, April 17, 341 A.D., and, as we shall see shortly, it also led to the persecution of the church. In fact on the same day Simon was put to death, "about 100 other Christians, including many clergy and some monks and nuns, were put to death."[421]

Controversy About Christ

Even though at times the church in Iran was drawn into theological controversies about the nature of Christ, those controversies really were centered more in the church in the West. They were struggles principally between theologians in Rome, in Constantinople, in Antioch and in Alexandria.

The earliest major Christological controversy, the Arian Controversy, was a very heated dispute over the relation of Christ to God. Arius, a presbyter of a church in Alexandria, Egypt denied the eternity of Christ, thus denying that he was deity. A great theological storm broke out over this issue which resulted in Emperor Constantine convening the Nicene Council in 325 A.D. That council produced the Nicene Creed, later modified by the Council of Constantinople in 381 A.D.

Even though the church in Iran agreed with the conclusions of those two Councils, they were spared the fiery assaults of the Arian protagonists. Later however, Islam embraced a Christology very similar to the Arian heresy and promoted it zealously. (See Chapter 5, "Four Negative Statements About Christ.") Islam fully backed its theological zeal with political and military power, the power with which they destroyed Persia's Sassanian Empire and annexed Iran into the then vast and rapidly growing Islamic empire. From that point the church in Iran has continually had to face Islam with its enhanced, empowered, very aggressive and stifling form of Christology, which essentially mimics Arianism.

---

420 Samuel Hugh Moffett, A History of Christianity in Asia, Vol. I: Beginnings to 1500 (2nd ed. rev.; Maryknoll, New York: Orbis Books, 1998), p. 140.
421 Robin E. Waterfield, Christians in Persia, Assyrians, Armenians, Roman Catholics and Protestants, (London: George Allen & Unwin Ltd., 1973), p. 19.

Controversies Over the Relationship of the Humanity and Deity of Christ

The cycle of debate about Christ became even more subtle, arcane and obscure than the original issue in the Arian contention. It became a deep speculative philosophical controversy over the relationship of the divine and the human elements in Christ's being. It developed into an argument over whether the divine predominated over the human, or vice versa, or whether the two were in balance.

"A vexing, unanswered question [was] raised by the statement in the Nicene Creed that Christ is God and that he is also man. In that case, said some Christians, he must be two persons, one divine and one human. Then what becomes of his unity? Is he a split personality? On the other hand, if he is only one whole person, how can one contain two wholes ('wholly God and wholly man')?"[422] It was a controversy so deeply philosophical and so extremely speculative that then, as now, few Christians could or can grasp the full significance of its subtle propositions and counter proposals.

The Nestorian Controversy

The church in Iran had little participation in the debates and controversies which raged in the western church over their highly speculative Christological issues. In spite of being on the margins of the rancorous and sometimes violent clashes in the western church,[423] the church in Iran was labeled Nestorian by the church in the West. Then, on the basis of that inaccurate and unjust appellation, the church in the West considered the church in Iran to be apostate!

As theologians in the Roman Empire argued against the doctrine of Arianism, to emphasize the deity of Jesus they began to call the virgin Mary "the Mother of God." However, Nestorius, who had become patriarch in Constantinople in 428 A.D., "disliked the use of the term *theotokos* (God-bearer) [that is, carrying God in embryonic form in the womb] as a name for the Virgin Mary because it seemed to exalt her unduly. He offered the word *Christotokos* [Christ-bearer] as an alternative, arguing that Mary was only the mother of the human side of Christ. ... Christ was in effect only a perfect man who was morally linked to deity. He was a God-bearer rather than the God-man. Leaders of the Church gathered at Ephesus in 431 A.D. and condemned this doctrine."[424]

---

422 Samuel Hugh Moffett, <u>A History of Christianity in Asia</u>, Vol. I: <u>Beginnings to 1500</u> (2nd ed. rev.; Maryknoll, New York: Orbis Books, 1998), p. 170.

423 "Christians in the Syriac-speaking regions [at this time Syriac was one of the main languages of the church in Iran] long lived their lives somewhat apart from the currents which disturbed the Graeco-Latin sections of the Church. Although Gnosticism vexed them, in general on most of the disputed issues they remained in doctrinal accord with the majority of Christians until about the close of the fifth century. In the sacraments, too, they differed little in essentials from Greek and Roman Catholics. Yet the Arian controversy which brought such upheaval among their brethren of Greek and Latin speech seems not to have loomed large on their horizon. In the fourth century their Christianity had changed less from that of the second than had that of the Greek world. They developed, too, a Christian literature in their own tongue." – Kenneth Scott Latourette, <u>A History of The Expansion of Christianity</u>, Vol. I: <u>The First Five Centuries</u> (Grand Rapids, Michigan: Zondervan Publishing House, 1970), p.356.

424 Earle E. Cairns, <u>Christianity Through The Centuries</u>, Rev. ed., (Grand Rapids, Michigan: Zondervan Publishing House, 1967), p. 146.

Consequently, Nestorius was exiled and his followers persecuted. Historically, this kind of rapacious outcome always ensues when ideology or theology is backed by political or military/police power. (We will shortly see that the same virulent mixture was previously at work when the Sassanian Empire threw its muscle behind Zoroastrian ideology/theology.) All of the followers of Nestorius who could fled to the Sassanian Empire where the church gave them refuge. Because of the presence of those refugees, the whole Iranian church in the Sassanian Empire was unjustly labeled the Nestorian Church! This name was assigned to the Iranian church even though the Christians in Iran, as noted before, called themselves simply, The Church of the East. To read the Coptic/Nestorian Creed, please see page 212.

Persecuted by the Successors to the Magi!

The martyrdom of Simon, the bold and courageous Bishop, previously mentioned, who ministered from the Sassanian dual capital city of Seleucia-Ctesiphon, triggered the first period of intense persecution of Christians in pre-Islamic Sassanian Iran, the persecutions of the fourth century.

By that time, Zoroastrianism had become the official state religion under the Sassanians.[425] "It was with this powerful, highly organized state religion that the little Church of the East eventually found itself in direct conflict. ... For the first hundred years of the new [Sassanian] dynasty, Christians, though harassed by the *mobeds* [the magi], were not often persecuted by the state. ... [In fact, there is] little evidence of any persecution of minority religions like Christianity during the reigns of the first eight Sassanian monarchs."[426]

Caught Between Two Imperial Giants

"When Rome became Christian, its old enemy Persia turned anti-Christian. ... As long as Roman emperors considered Christians to be enemies of Rome, Persian emperors were inclined to regard them as friends of Persia. It was about 315 [A.D.] that an ill-advised letter from the Christian emperor Constantine to his Persian counterpart Shapur II seemed to have triggered the beginnings of an ominous change in the Persian attitude toward Christians. Constantine believed he was writing to help his fellow believers in Persia but succeeded only in exposing them [to mortal danger].

"He wrote to the young shah: 'I rejoice to hear that the fairest provinces of Persia are adorned with ... Christians. ... Since you are so powerful and pious, I commend them to your care, and leave them in your protection.' ... Faced with what seemed to be a double threat, a threat not only to national security but to the national religion as well, Persia's priests and rulers cemented their alliance

---

425 It was emperor "Ardashir [b. 180, d. 242 A.D.] who made Mazdaism the state religion." – Donald N. Wilber, Iran Past and Present, (Princeton: Princeton University Press, 1963), p. 31.
426 Samuel Hugh Moffett, A History of Christianity in Asia, Vol. I: Beginnings to 1500 (2nd ed. rev.; Maryknoll, New York: Orbis Books, 1998), p. 107-108.

of state and religion in a series of periods of terror that have been called the most massive persecution of Christians in history, 'unequaled for its duration, its ferocity and the number of martyrs.'"[427]

Waves of Persecution

Shortly after the first period of great persecution ended, "around the year 401 the historian Sozomen, who lived near enough to that time of tribulation to remember the tales of those who had experienced it, wrote that the multitude of martyrs had been beyond enumeration. One estimate is that as many as 190,000 Persian Christians died in the terror. It was worse than anything suffered in the West under Rome, yet the number of apostasies seemed to be fewer in Persia than in the West, which is a remarkable tribute to the steady courage of Asia's early Christians."[428]

One would have thought such butchery would have quenched the blood lust of the Zoroastrian hierarchy which carried out its evil by means of the Sassanian state. Regrettably, such was not the case. Iranian Christians went through three additional distinct periods of severe Zoroastrian persecution: (1) 419–420 A.D., (2) 420–422 A.D. and (3) the third period which was in two phases 445–448 and 454–456 A.D.

"On 24 and 25 August 446 A.D., Christians from a number of provinces, including the bishops, senior clergy and many members of distinguished families, were collected at Karka (modern Kirkuk) [center of the Kurdish quasi state in present-day northern Iraq] and put to death. They met their martyrdom with great courage. The way in which one of the Christian women, Shirin, and her two sons met their death so touched the King's officer in charge of the proceedings that he too confessed faith in Christ and on 25 September was himself crucified. ... The persecution ... was so fierce that it has remained in the minds of Christians up to the present day. The little Christian community in Kirkuk still gathers together year by year to celebrate the faith and courage of their martyred forebears."[429]

"The most appalling of the slaughters that marked the renewal of persecution in Persia occurred in northern Mesopotamia in 448 A.D. This was the frightful bloodletting at Kirkuk ... which was one of the original metropolitanates, beyond the Tigris and east of Arbela. There on a mound outside the city masses of Christians were systematically butchered for days—10 bishops and an incredible 153,000 believers!"[430]

---

427 Samuel Hugh Moffett, A History of Christianity in Asia, Vol. I: Beginnings to 1500 (2nd ed. rev.; Maryknoll, New York: Orbis Books, 1998), pp. 137-138.
428 Samuel Hugh Moffett, A History of Christianity in Asia, Vol. I: Beginnings to 1500 (2nd ed. rev.; Maryknoll, New York: Orbis Books, 1998), pp. 144-145.
429 Robin E. Waterfield, Christians in Persia, Assyrians, Armenians, Roman Catholics and Protestants, (London: George Allen & Unwin Ltd., 1973), p. 26.
430 Samuel Hugh Moffett, A History of Christianity in Asia, Vol. I: Beginnings to 1500 (2nd ed. rev.; Maryknoll, New York: Orbis Books, 1998), p. 161.

Marvelous Resiliency

The period of fierce persecution in Zoroastrian Iran lasted till 456 A.D. Hundreds of thousands of followers of Jesus Christ were killed. Nevertheless, during the next two centuries, the church survived, revived and prevailed. The proof of this noteworthy rebound can be seen in the church's amazing evangelism. As we have seen, the Iranian church evangelized Central Asia and, as mentioned earlier, an evangelist from the church in Iran/Afghanistan even took the gospel to China, arriving in the Chinese capital city of Chang'an (modern Xi'an) in 635.

Is it possible for such a vibrant church to be turned back? Can such a committed church be brought to the brink of extinction? Zoroastrianism could not do it. Sassanian imperial power could not do it. But ominous developments were generating ferocious winds in Arabia, which ultimately would not only shrivel the church in Iran but would cripple the cause of Christ all the way from India to Spain and all the way from Egypt to China!

Just thirteen years before the Afghan/Iranian evangelist Alopen reached Chang'an, the Arabian Prophet Muhammad had reached Medina, having fled there secretly from Mecca in 622 A.D. That move, known as the Hijra (Hidjra, Hejirah) in Islamic history, gave Muhammad the first opportunity to develop the political and military backing, which were inherent necessities for Islam, his new religious/political system. The names "Islam," which means submission and its derivative "Muslim," which means one who has submitted, were both usurped. They previously had been names used by the Christians in the northern Yemeni city of Najran (now in southern Saudi Arabia near the border with Yemen).[431] From Muhammad's surreptitious migration (the Hijra was begun at night) sprang the movement which became the bane of Christ's people throughout the vast expanses of the very extensive Muslim empire which was, with surprising speed, welded together by the victorious armies of Islam. There was a menacing element, like a withering wind, in the new movement which has usually shriveled and often eliminated the church in many national venues.

෴

---

[431] On the meaning of the terms "Islam" and "Muslim" be sure to read Chapter 9 under "Najrani Christians Try to Win Muhammad." Please also see the Glossary under "Islam" and "Muslim."

Chapter 14

THE CHURCH IN IRAN FROM TRIUMPH TO ECLIPSE

Letters Tell the Story

Shortly before 600 A.D. a son was born to Bastomag, a Christian-Persian nobleman who owned lands near the village of Kufalana on the banks of the Great Zab River.[432] That son, at an unrecorded age, joined a Christian monastery on the opposite side of the river from his home. Showing great ability, complete integrity and honesty, after some intermediate appointments he was so highly respected that he ultimately became Patriarch of the East in 650 A.D.[433] As patriarch he was known officially as Ishu 'Yab III. Though his term of service was short, having served as patriarch for only eight or nine years before his death in 658 or 659, twenty-one of his pastoral letters have survived. They give invaluable insight into the cause of Christ in Iran (Persia) during his patriarchate.[434]

One of his letters was addressed to a leader of the church in the ancient city of Merv. It was written shortly after Arab Muslim armies had conquered the region. He showed deep concern because some of the Christians in that great center of Persian Christianity were leaving the church. Out of obvious anxiety Ishu 'Yab wrote, "Why then do your *Mrwnaye* [a Syriac word meaning *people of Merv*] reject their faith on a pretext of theirs? And this when the *Mrwnaye* [people of Merv] themselves admit that the Arabs have not compelled them to abandon their faith, but only asked them to give up half of their possessions in order to keep their faith.[435] Yet they forsook their faith, which is forever, and retained the half of their wealth, which is for a short time."[436]

That defection of Christians in Merv marked the turning point when the Iranian church, previously vibrant and evangelistic, went into centuries of decline. It also coincided with the beginning of triumph for Islam in Iran (Persia). Those events marked the point after which the cause of Christ struggled to maintain even a toehold in that great country. Today, as the withering wind from Arabia continues to

---
432 The main tributary flowing into the Tigris from the northeast, just south of Mosul.
433 On the rise of episcopacy in The Church of the East, please refer to Chapter 13 under "State Preference for Episcopal Hierarchy."
434 For these details on the life of Ishu 'Yab III I am indebted to Dr. William G. Young for the fine resume given on page 85 in his Patriarch, Shah and Caliph, A Study of the Relationships of the Church of the East with the Sassanid Empire and the Early Caliphates up to 820 A.D., (Rawalpindi, Pakistan: Christian Study Centre, 1974).
435 See the report from Hatim the Jurist in Chapter 10.
436 Robert G. Hoyland, Seeing Islam As Others Saw It, A Survey and Evaluation of Christian, Jewish, and Zoroastrian Writings on Early Islam, (Princeton, New Jersey: The Darwin Press, Inc., 1997), p. 181.

blow in an Iranian Shiite configuration, Christians in that environment survive only precariously and tenuously.

A Brief Review

Islam has now been dominant in Iran for over 1300 years. This figure dates the beginning of Islam's dominance from 652 A.D., the date of the death of the fugitive, Yazdegerd III, the last Sassanian emperor. Previously, Sassanian Iran's military power had been destroyed at the Battle of Nehawand in 642. To understand what has happened to the cause of Christ in Iran it will be helpful to very briefly review the development of Muslim power and the conquest of Iran by Muslim forces. (Be sure also to study Appendix H.)

Following its conception, Islam went through a very difficult time of incubation. During that early period, Muhammad and his small band of followers were rejected and harassed in Mecca, their home town, the place where the concept of the Islamic movement had its birth. It was fortunate for the movement that in Medina, some 250 miles to the north, a number of citizens had yielded their allegiance to Muhammad. Subsequently, the Prophet's small band of harassed Meccan devotees were able to surreptitiously flee to that haven. Later, in 622 A.D., emulating his disciples, Muhammad himself made his personal *hijra* (flight or escape) to Medina where he was enthusiastically welcomed. Afterward, the Muslims in Medina were besieged on two occasions by hostile forces from Mecca. (See the index under "Battle of the Trench" and "Battle of Mt. Uhud.") After surviving those sieges, Muhammad (with his Medinan Muslims) turned the tide and was finally triumphant through the military conquest of Mecca in 630 A.D. Shortly afterwards, all of Arabia was brought to submission. At that point of triumph, the Prophet, who had so dramatically and unexpectedly made his appearance on the Arabian desert scene, began planning expansion for his movement far beyond the borders of Arabia.

Ambient War

Almost simultaneously with the period from Muhammad's first prophetic vision (in 610 A.D.) to his military victory over Mecca (630 A.D.) two of the world's three leading empires, both bordering Arabia on the north, were locked in a wasting, all-out war lasting twenty-six years (602–628 A.D.). Not surprisingly, at the conclusion of those hostilities, both the Byzantine Empire on the northwestern border of Arabia and the Sassanian (Persian) Empire on its northeastern border were exhausted and enfeebled. That highly significant development occurred just as the new Islamic movement was gaining momentum and direction under a Koranic mandate for world conquest.

Since some people question whether there actually is a Koranic mandate for Muslim world conquest, the following four Koranic references and notes taken from

The Study Quran (edited by Seyyed Hossein Nasr, published by Harper Collins in 2015) answer that question definitively.

First, that mandate is given to us in Surah 9:33 where we are told, "He it is Who sent His Messenger with guidance and the Religion of Truth to make it prevail over all religion, though the idolaters be averse." In the marginal note we are told that "prevail over ... can also mean to manifest, show, or make something known. Moreover, *all religion* can also be understood as 'all religions' or '[the peoples] of all religions.'"

Second, in the 28th verse of Surah 48, which is entitled "Victory," it is recorded that "He it is Who sent His Messenger with guidance and the Religion of Truth to make it prevail over all religion. And God suffices as a Witness." The accompanying note says, "The majority of commentators interpret *Religion of Truth*, or 'the True Religion' *(din al-haqq)*, here and in 9:33 and in 61:9 as a reference to Islam itself and thus see all three verses as a reference to the triumph of Islam over all other religions."

Third, it is recorded in Surah 61:9 that "He it is Who sent His Messenger with guidance and the Religion of Truth to make it prevail over all religion, though the idolaters be averse." In the accompanying note we are told that this verse "is repeated verbatim in 9:33 and 48:28. *Guidance* can here be seen as a reference to the Quran or to the truth itself. *All religion* is understood to mean all religions; see 9:32-33c; 48:28c. Almost all classical commentators interpret *Religion of Truth* here and in 9:33 and in 48:28 as a reference to Islam and thus see all three verses as a reference to the triumph of Islam over all other religions."

Fourth, the very short 110th Surah says "When God's Help and Victory come and you see mankind entering God's religion in throngs, hymn the praise of thy Lord, and seek forgiveness from him. Truly He is Ever Relenting." In an explanatory note we are told that "when read in the future tense, this verse is seen by many as an allusion to the conquests by which Islam spread beyond the borders of Arabia after the death of the Prophet."

In addition to those Koranic statements indicating that Muslims were acting under a mandate for world conquest, as will be pointed out again, the Prophet Muhammad repeatedly sent diplomatic messages to world rulers demanding them to bring their countries into the realm of Islam: "It was at this period, the year 628, that the Prophet [Muhammad] despatched messages to the King of Persia, the

Byzantine Emperor, the Governor of Egypt and the Prince of Abyssinia, summoning them to accept the Muslim religion."[437]

The diplomatic messages from the Prophet Muhammad went out globally to world rulers, advising them to give loyalty to the message of Islam. In addition to summons to Western leaders, one of those diplomatic missives was also delivered to the emperor of China as mentioned in footnote 7 in the Introduction.

Early Success

On the northern borders of Arabia, "several minor Arab kingdoms had [previously] been established. ... Both powers [Byzantium and Sassanian Persia] trained and subsidized these border Arabs to fight for them as mercenaries, but when their treasuries had been depleted by fighting each other [in the protracted war of 602–628 A.D.] they withdrew the subsidies and imposed taxes on the Arabs to [help] pay for the wars. When Islam finally burst out of its Arabian cocoon, the oppressed border peoples looked to the arriving Muslims more as liberators than as conquerors, and many joined them to fight against their former masters."[438]

Conquest of Persia/Iran Begins

The first Persian outpost to fall to the Muslim onslaught was the border town of Hira, capital of an Arab Christian kingdom which had been tributary to the Persian Sassanian Empire.[439] Hira was located on the Euphrates River, about four miles southeast of the modern town of An Najaf. It was a strategic location, being only seventy miles from the Persian imperial capital at Medain.[440] "Besieged within their walls and without tribal support, the citizens were glad to come to terms, especially as the sum of money demanded by the Arabs, though it appeared large to the bedouins, was trivial in comparison with the wealth of the city. In return for this payment, the Muslims undertook to protect the town, the inhabitants of which, though Arabs, refused to renounce their Christian religion in favor of Islam. This agreement was probably signed in May 633, [the

---

437 John Bagot Glubb, The Great Arab Conquests, (London: Quartet Books, 1980), pp. 89-90. Note: The precedent set by the Prophet Muhammad was followed by his second successor, the caliph Umar ibn al Khattab, simply called Umar for short. Agapius, the Christian bishop of Manbij, a town northeast of Aleppo in Syria, stated in a history which he wrote about 940 A.D., "He ['Umar] wrote for Leo the king [of the Byzantine Empire] a letter summoning him therein to Islam and, moreover, disputed with him about his religion." – Robert G. Hoyland, Seeing Islam As Others Saw It, A Survey and Evaluation of Christian, Jewish and Zoroastrian Writings on Early Islam, (Princeton, NJ: The Darwin Press, Inc. 1997), p. 490. For a discussion of the earliest doctrinal debates between Islam and Christianity see David Thomas, Christian Doctrines in Islamic theology, (Leiden: Brill, 2008).

438 Desmond Stewart, Early Islam, (New York: Time Incorporated, 1967), p. 54.

439 Today the ruins of Hira are located in Iraq but then it was part of the Persian Empire.

440 Medain is the plural form of the Arabic word *medina*, a city. The name, therefore, means "Twin Cities." It was the Arab name for two cities sited opposite each other on the Tigris River. They were "Seleucia on the west bank of the Tigris and Ctesiphon on the east. Seleucia had been founded in B.C. 312 by Seleucus Nicator, one of the Greek rulers [generals] who inherited portions of the empire of Alexander the Great. ... Ctesiphon was established two hundred years after Seleucia, on the opposite bank of the Tigris, and became the capital of the [Persian] Sassanid dynasty in the second [should read third] century A.D. At the time of the Arab conquests, the Persian court, palaces and government were in Ctesiphon, on the east bank." – John Bagot Glubb, The Great Arab Conquests, (London: Quartet Books, 1963), p. 201.

year following the death of Mohammad] while the last embers of the [Arab] apostasy[441] were being stamped out in the Yemen."[442]

Amazingly, as mentioned before, in Chapter 8, in the initial explosive expansion of Islam, the Arab Muslims simultaneously unleashed war on both the Byzantine and Sassanian Empires and were victorious on both fronts! However, for tactical reasons, Hira, in that section of Persia west of the Zagros Mountains, had to be abandoned by the Arabs several times before its final capitulation took place.

Omitting details of the Battle of the Bridge (in October 634 A.D.), which was lost by the Muslims, and the Battle of Buwaib (in November 635 A.D.), which was lost by the Persians largely because Christian Arab tribes fought on the side of the Muslims, there were three main stages in which the forces of Islam overwhelmed Persia. To a large extent, victory resulted from the tenacious determination of the Muslim general Muthanna, conqueror of Hira, wounded in the Battle of the Bridge, who nevertheless led the Muslims to victory in the Battle of Buwaib before he succumbed to his wounds. He was replaced by forty-year old Sa'ad, (in autumn of 636 A.D.) who became the new Muslim commander-in-chief on the Persian front.

Just before the Muslim offensive began, Persia had been further weakened by the annihilation of its imperial family, a consequence of enmity and chaos growing out of its defeat in its disastrously long war (602–628 A.D.) with Byzantium. That military humiliation came despite having earlier achieved striking triumphs that had carried victorious Persian arms to the shores of the Mediterranean (614 A.D.), to Alexandria, Egypt (616 A.D.) and to Chalcedon (617 A.D.).

The humbled Persian Sassanian dynasty fell into confusion and deadly internecine fighting. The Persian war against Byzantium had been lost during the reign of Khosrow II (Chosroes II), emperor from 590 to 628 A.D. Ironically, at the pinnacle of his reign he had been called "the Victorious." But "he lived, however, to witness unparalleled vicissitudes of fortune."[443] Finally, he suffered the ultimate humiliation, being the victim of patricide inflicted by Siroes, one of his sons!

At the same time Siroes killed his father, he also killed 18 of his brothers and half brothers. Then, "to secure his position, the parricide caused all the male descendants of the great Chosroes Anushirvan[444] to be sought out and murdered, with the object of leaving no member of the royal family alive capable of disputing the throne with him. These savage massacres were, however, of no avail, for Siroes himself was murdered after a reign of only eight months. The

---

441 Following the death of Muhammad in 632 A.D. many tribes in Arabia returned to their former tribal and religious loyalties. Arabia was brought back to the Muslim fold by a one-year vicious war waged by those who had remained loyal to the vision of Muhammad. That war is known as the War of Apostasy.
442 John Bagot Glubb, The Great Arab Conquests, (London: Quartet Books, 1963), p. 128.
443 Carl Hermann Ethe, Persia, The Encyclopaedia Britannica, (New York: The Encyclopaedia Britannica Company, 1911), Vol. XXI, p. 223.
444 Also known as Chosroes I. He was greatest of all the Sassanid emperors. Chosroes II was the grandson of Chosroes I.

whole of Persia was then abandoned to anarchy and torn between rival factions. All the male members of the royal family having apparently been put to death, no legitimate successor to the Crown could be discovered."[445]

Surprisingly, in 632 A.D., Yazdegerd, a fifteen-year-old boy alleged to be of the royal lineage, was proclaimed king. Being an inexperienced boy incapable of wise imperial decisions, it was fortunate that during his novitiate, Rustem, a great Persian general, served as his regent. However at the next critical juncture in the war with the marauding Muslim armies, Yazdegerd overruled his regent and forced him to adopt a foolhardy military strategy. The Muslims wanted to entice Persian forces to attack in the desert where their horses and elephants would be unable to cope with the sand but where Arab camels could maneuver at will. In contrast, Rustem wanted to lure the Muslims to attack in the cultivated areas on the east side of the Euphrates where Arab camels would be at a disadvantage but Persian steeds would be on congenial and familiar ground.

Not only did Rustem want to lure the Arabs into an advantageous battlefield, he also thought if battle could be postponed long enough, "Arab enthusiasm might die down or internal dissensions might divide them. Rustem's plan therefore was to wait on the east bank of the Euphrates and see what happened. The young [Persian emperor] Yazdegerd held diametrically opposite views. With haughty impatience, he urged his general to sweep this desert scum from the frontier of his dominions and then to follow them into their own country and chastise them for their insolence in daring to molest the subjects of the King of kings."[446]

Persia, West of the Zagros Mountains, is Overwhelmed

<u>The first stage in the Arab conquest</u> of Sassanian Persia was completed by victory in the decisive battle which took place at Qādisiyyah. Due to incessant pressure put on the battle-proven Rustem by the impetuous Yazdegerd, the great Persian army was obliged in the spring of 637 A.D. to cross the Euphrates River to meet the challenging Arab forces in the desert, the very scenario Rustem had tried to avoid. The battle raged for three days but on the third night the Arab warriors spontaneously launched an all-night attack, called in Muslim accounts "the night of fury." On the morning of the fourth day, fresh Arab troops, which had arrived from Syria a day earlier after a 600-mile forced march, joined the battle giving the advantage to the Muslim forces. Exhausted Persian ranks, which had fought all night, now not only had to face the augmented Arab troops but also a brisk desert wind sprang up blowing sand in the faces of the Persian soldiers.[447] The center of the Persian defense line collapsed allowing a determined band of Arabs to thrust, hack and slash its way through Rustem's personal body guard to kill the renowned Persian general.

---

445 John Bagot Glubb, <u>The Great Arab Conquests</u>, (London: Quartet Books, 1963), p. 129.
446 John Bagot Glubb, <u>The Great Arab Conquests</u>, (London: Quartet Books, 1963), pp. 193-194.
447 That put them at the same disadvantage that the Byzantine soldiers had experienced at the Second Battle of the Yarmuk in 636 A.D.

Notwithstanding the widespread rout which ensued, "thirty 'regiments' of Persians, however, stood fast disdaining flight and were killed to a man. No sooner was the fighting ended than the Arab-tribes women and their children [who had accompanied the Arab army] spread over the field. Carrying clubs and weapons in one hand and goatskins of water in the other, they assuaged the thirst of the wounded and dying Muslims and despatched the disabled Persians to hell-fire. ...' The Persian army, which only ten years before had been hammering on the gates of Constantinople, had been destroyed beyond recovery by the rude but hardy tribesmen of Arabia."[448]

With the exception of the dual capital city of Seleucia-Ctesiphon, called Medain from the plural form of the word *medina*, meaning city), the Arab forces had subdued the whole region of Persia west of the Tigris River. "The remaining Christian Arab tribes of the north hastened to make their submission and, in some cases, to embrace the Muslim religion,[449] by means of which their Bedouin brothers of Arabia had achieved such incredible glory and wealth. The settled Christians made their submission and paid the poll tax prescribed."[450]

The town of Hira became the headquarters of Muthanna, a tribal sheikh of the Beni Bekr tribe who led the attack on Persia even after half his forces had been ordered to Syria to help in the military offensive there. Muthanna was not a member of the ruling Quraish, the tribe from which Muhammad sprang and the tribe which was "determined to monopolize all authority and limit high command to themselves."[451]

In the second stage of the Arab conquest, the Persian capital was overwhelmed. After the loss of the Battle of Qādisiyyah and the death of Rustem, the Persians realized that the oldest half of their dual capital, Seleucia, on the west side of the Tigris River, was totally indefensible. Therefore, they surreptitiously abandoned that 1000-year-old city, leaving behind magnificent treasures of art which could not easily be transported across the Tigris. The Persians were reasonably confident that, because of the natural bulwark of the river, they could hold Ctesiphon, the eastern half of their dual capital. However, an Iranian traitor told the Arabs of a ford across the Tigris. The first Arab fording party crossed with only one casualty despite a rain of arrows from a Persian force defending the location. Then, hordes of Arab horsemen, seeing the success of their fellow warriors, spurred their steeds into the river and established a beachhead on the eastern shore of the Tigris. That vanguard of Arabs could not be overwhelmed by the weakened Persian defenses.

---

448 John Bagot Glubb, The Great Arab Conquests, (London: Quartet Books, 1963), p. 199-200.
449 The Taghlib tribe was an exception which remained Christian for a long time. "The most powerful Christian tribe seems to have been the Taghlibs who were stretched out from Oman and the banks of the Tigris to the valley of the Orontes and Damascus." – The Early Christian-Muslim Dialogue, A Collection of Documents from the First Three Islamic Centuries (632–900 A.D.), Translations with Commentary, (Hatfield, Pennsylvania: Interdisciplinary Biblical Research Institute, 1993), N.A. Newman (ed.), p. 44.
450 John Bagot Glubb, The Great Arab Conquests, (London: Quartet Books, 1963), p. 200.
451 John Bagot Glubb, The Great Arab Conquests, (London: Quartet Books, 1963), p. 148.

"The garrison of Ctesiphon seems to have been surprised by this daring operation. Such as had time to get away fled eastward to the [Zagros] mountains. The remainder submitted without resistance [in April 638 A.D.] and agreed to pay tribute in return for protection. The luxuries of Seleucia proved to have been but a mild foretaste of the splendors of the court of the King of Kings in Ctesiphon. [See Photo 1.] ... The Arabs became possessed of immense wealth, as, on the old raiding system, the plunder was immediately distributed to the men of the army after the subtraction of the orthodox fifth, which was to be sent to the Khalif in Medina."[452]

The third and final dramatic phase of the catastrophic Persian defeat was assured by two events. The young Sassanian emperor not only embraced folly once more, but, on this occasion, compounded it.

First, after the fall of Seleucia-Ctesiphon the old Caliph Umar (Omar), leader of the victorious Muslim world, sent word from Medina, his capital in Arabia, to Sa'ad, his general then in charge of the Persian campaign, not to push further east, which would involve crossing the daunting Zagros mountain range. He indicated that the fertile Tigris-Euphrates plains were sufficient for the Arabs.

Though news of that decision seems to have been conveyed to the Persian emperor, Yazdegerd persisted in building up offensive forces, hoping to recapture Persia's lost territories. Thus the Arab army, in defense of their newly won territory, had to attack Yazdegerd's forces which were centered on the city of Nehawand located on the edge of the great Persian plain just south of Hamadan. The Arabs lured the Persians into an ambush. Though they gave a spirited and resolute fight, inflicting heavy casualties on the Arabs, the Persian ranks ultimately broke and fled in panic and disorder just at sunset. The Persian army was completely destroyed and the commander of the Persian forces himself was killed. Following the Battle of Nehawand in 642, though local resistance continued for several years, the Persians could never again put an army in the field to fight a major battle.

Secondly, at that somber juncture, Yazdegerd became a fugitive. Even then he was contemptuous of the very ones who gave him succor. "No misfortune seems to have been sufficient to reduce the arrogance of the fugitive monarch."[453] Near the ancient city of Merv, Yazdegerd was murdered and his body thrown into a river. "With the death of Yazdegerd in 652, resistance [to Muslim conquest and domination] in Persia virtually came to an end."[454]

The expansion of Islam into Persia stands in stark contrast to the earlier expansion of Christianity, not only in Persia/Iran but with the advance of Christianity both east and west. One Iranian Christian, shortly after grievously

---

452 John Bagot Glubb, The Great Arab Conquests, (London: Quartet Books, 1963), p. 203.
453 John Bagot Glubb, The Great Arab Conquests, (London: Quartet Books, 1963), p. 292.
454 John Bagot Glubb, The Great Arab Conquests, (London: Quartet Books, 1963), p. 292.

suffering in his home country for his faith during the 1979 Khomeini Revolution, accentuated this contrast by noting that "in the first century, Christian missionaries represented a small, poor, oppressed minority who carried their message to the most powerful and richest state in the world, the Roman Empire."[455] Those first-century Christians had no armies, no swords and no political power. When they went into countries to preach, they did not strip them of their wealth and treasures to be divided among themselves.

Three Classifications

The manner in which Islam first expanded gave unmistakable evidence that from its very inception it was neither a congenial nor a benign movement. Under Islam, "the world was divided into [1] *Dar al-Islam*, the House of Islam, and [2] *Dar al-Harb*, the House of War, or lands under infidel rule, and between the two there was a perpetual state of war, interrupted only by truces, and preordained to end with the incorporation of the whole world into the House of Islam. Besides the *Harbi* or infidel beyond the frontier, [the one against whom war was to be waged] there was also [3] the *Zimmi* (from Arabic *Dhimmi*), the protected non-Muslim subject of the Muslim state, whose position was determined by the *dhimma*, or pact, between his community, called *millet*, and the dominant community of Islam.

"The fundamental aim of Islamic policy was to incorporate the *Dar al-Harb* into the *Dar al-Islam*, and to turn the *Harbi* infidels into Muslims or, if that were not possible, into *Zimmis*. The essential classification—political, social, even economic—was Muslim, *Zimmi*, *Harbi*. This tripartite distinction between the believer, the subjugated unbeliever, and the hostile unbeliever was far more important than such divisions as Turks, Greeks, and Slavs in the Balkans or Turks, Persians, and Arabs in Asia."[456]

"The first types of limits imposed on Christians and the other *dhimmi* [*Zimmi*] were religious. They could follow their own religion but were forbidden from engaging in any kind of missionary activity, while Muslim missionary activity was encouraged. In addition, the various Muslim law schools drew up different laws regarding the practice of the Christian religion, but all limited its public expression. Hence processions, displaying Christian symbols in public, and bell-ringing were all forbidden. Very strict laws were also written for the building of new churches or the restoration of old ones. The second type of restrictions were mainly social and clearly stated the inferiority of non-Muslims, both socially and legally. The latter were not allowed to hold any kind of political or military power and were subject to heavier taxes. Besides taxes on land and on different kinds of assets, they also had to pay a special per capita tax, the *jizya*[457], considered compen-

---

455 H. B. Dehqani-Tafti, The Hard Awakening, (New York: The Seabury Press, 1981), p. 18.
456 Bernard Lewis, The Emergence of Modern Turkey, (New York: Oxford University Press, 1968), pp. 238-239.
457 One scholar has poignantly expressed the taxation imposed on Christians saying, "they [were] generally granted religious freedom [to exist] in exchange for higher taxes. [It was a] system of taxed tolerance." – Elif Batuman, Ottomania, The New Yorker, February 17 & 24. 2014, p. 51.

sation for protection given to them by the Muslim political powers. Muslim superiority was also guaranteed in family matters. The special laws regarding mixed marriages allow only one kind of mixed union: that of a Muslim man with a Christian or Jewish woman, whose offspring must be brought up as Muslims. A non-Muslim man wanting to marry a Muslim woman is required to convert to Islam. This particular system of laws seems to have played a very important role in the substitution of the Christian population with a Muslim one during the first centuries of the Muslim empire."[458]

The Current Situation

That brief description of the conditions Muslim rule places upon individual Christians and upon the church should help one understand the dire condition for Christians in present-day Iran. "The church in Iran is harshly persecuted. Nominal churches serving Iran's traditionally Christian Armenian population are [grudgingly and barely] tolerated, but Farsi-speaking churches that reach out to Muslims are usually closed, their members threatened, and leaders imprisoned. [According to] White[459] ... anyone caught with a Farsi-language Bible 'is in a lot more trouble than someone with an Armenian one,' he said. Most Farsi-speaking congregations meet secretly in private homes. At least 10 Christian pastors and lay leaders have been martyred since 1979. The Islamic government uses radical Muslim groups to terrorize and threaten Christians, Ghaffari[460] said. Three were killed in 1994 and another in 1996, he said. At least 20 Muslim converts baptized in local churches were reported missing last year and most are presumed dead, he said."[461]

"In spite of a more moderate [Iranian] president[462] in office, the persecution of Muslim-convert Christians continues. Ordinary Christian believers who have turned from Islam are routinely questioned, threatened, arrested and beaten. At least ten have been killed in the past ten years, and a number of others have simply disappeared."[463]

Going all the way back to the rise and expansion of Islam, the animus against Christians in the whole broad spectrum of the Muslim world has been extreme. For example, Shah Abbas found a community of Armenian Christians living in Julfa in the extreme northwest corner of Iran. He was attracted by their diligence and acumen in trade and industry. He felt their presence in large numbers would help ensure the economic vitality of his new capital at Isfahan. So in 1604 he forced some twelve thousand families to move to an adjacent area southwest of his

---

458 Andrea Pacini (ed.), Introduction, Christian Communities in the Arab Middle East, The Challenge of the Future, (Oxford: Clarendon Press, 1998), pp. 3-4.
459 This refers to Tom White of *The Voice of the Martyrs*.
460 This refers to Abe Ghaffari of *Iranian Christians International*.
461 Quoted from the *Current Feature Story* by the Editors at Religion Today.com on October 7, 1999.
462 He refers to the 53-year-old Mohammed Khatami who won in the 1997 election with 69 percent of the 29 million votes cast. Persecution continued through 2017, with no end in sight.
463 Newsletter from *Radio Voice of Christ* dated November 1999. Currently, the ministry is called *Voice of Christ Media Ministries* and broadcasts exclusively in the Farsi language into Iran by radio, internet and other media. www.VoiceofChristMedia.org

capital, Isfahan.⁴⁶⁴ One method of coercion was seizing and closing their sources of irrigation water.⁴⁶⁵ In their new location, the Armenians had to build their own city. They called their new town, which eventually merged into Isfahan, Julfa, in memory of their old home. In their new home the Armenians prospered, in some cases too much for their own good. "Their industry appears to have provoked a certain amount of jealousy, for Fryer tells us that at the end of the century they were forbidden to enter the city with their servants 'bearing after them their Kelyans, or Glass Vessels out of which they smoke tobacco,' but were allowed to appear only as merchants." ⁴⁶⁶

However, one advantage Shah Abbas bestowed was official permission to build church buildings. Today in the Julfa section of Isfahan the Armenian Cathedral (built between 1606 and 1654) and several church buildings are the focal points of the religious activity of this ancient Christian community. They were zealous to provide scripture for their people and in this interest installed the first successful printing press in the Middle East. The original press, type molds, and many samples of early scripture portions in Armenian are on display in the very modern museum building in the Cathedral compound. (See Photo 9.)

It is amazing that—following the usurpation of the Abbasid Caliphate by the Seljuk Turks and then the Caliphate's utter destruction by the Mongols—not only did Islam survive as the guiding ideology of Iran but Islam in its Shi'ite form.

Resilient Nationalism

Surprisingly, even during Iran's most tumultuous times, the spark of a distinct Iranian nationalism was never snuffed out, though its guardians were divided by deathly contention in their inter-relationships. "Through triumph and defeat the culture and the way of life of the Persians have unified the population of the country more than political or even religious forms unless they too were integrated into the heritage of Persia."⁴⁶⁷ In contrast, much of the Arab world had no significant history before Islam. "The Arabs before the time of Mohammad had been a collection of rival tribes or clans, excelling in the savage virtues of bravery, hospitality and even chivalry, and devoted to the pursuit of booty."⁴⁶⁸ While the Arab

---

464 An additional comment on this may be of interest. Frye points out that Shah Abbas had a "policy to mix population and separate possibly troublesome peoples. ... The policy of moving possibly rebellious tribes or groups of people from one part of the country to another is, of course, an ancient one in the history of Iran." – Richard N. Frye, Iran (New York: Henry Holt and Company, 1953), p.10-13. While the forced migration of the Julfa Christians may have been carried out under that policy, it seems the main consideration was the contribution Shah Abbas hoped they would make to the success of Isfahan, his new capital.

465 A later reading note made me realize Shah Abbas had been, relatively speaking, very lenient with those Christians. "But, for all his genius and many sterling qualities, Abbas, like many absolute rulers, possessed a streak of excessive cruelty that placed him in the same league as his infamous contemporary, Ivan the Terrible of Russia. It was this weakness in his make-up that contributed largely to the later decline and fall of the Safavids. Fearing that his sons might sooner or later attempt to usurp the throne, he ordered the death of his eldest child and blinded his two remaining sons. Abbas was often quoted as claiming he would gladly kill 100 children to reign alone for a single day. There seemed no reason to doubt that he meant it." – Jon A. Teta, Iran in Pictures (New York: Sterling Publishing Co., 1973), p. 29-30.

466 Roger Stevens, The Land of the Great Sophy, (London: Methuen & Co. Ltd., 1962), p. 186.

467 Richard N. Frye, The Heritage of Persia, (New York: The World Publishing Co., 1963), p. 223.

468 Stanley Lane-Poole, quoted by John Bagot Glubb, War in the Desert (London: Hodder and Stoughton, 1960), p. 19.

people feel Islam has given them their history, Iran, in contrast, looks back to pre-Islamic times for its greatest period of glory. This is probably the very reason why Khomeini, at one point after coming to power, threatened to have the magnificent ruins of Persepolis totally destroyed! He wouldn't want such powerful testimony to continue which shouts that Iran was truly great, long before Islam!

After the fall of the Abbasid Caliphate, some of its successor political entities were grand but others were trivial. For example, the dynamic Safavid Dynasty (1501–1735 A.D.) ruled powerfully from Isfahan, often challenging the Ottoman Empire. However, during the Saffarid Dynasty (869–1015 A.D.), despite being a lesser entity, "occurred an event of [great] cultural significance, when the secretary of Ya'qub composed the first poetry in Persian."[469]

Corresponding to that literary triumph, tragically, at that time no Christian in Iran produced a contemporary Persian (Farsi) translation of the Bible. That is not surprising if we keep in mind the terrible pogroms bordering on genocide which the Persian Christians had endured during the Sassanian and the Islamic periods which followed. Such a translation to update or replace the then no longer widely useful antecedent translations[470] had to wait till the great work of Henry Martyn. (See following.) However, Christians continued to express their hope of bliss in the presence of God even during those bleak times in Iranian Christian history. This comes out incidentally in a quotation from the great poet, Hafiz [1325–1389 A.D.]. Expressing the hopelessness of Islam, he wrote, "'If Muhammadanism be that which Hafiz holds, Alas if there should be a tomorrow after today.' On being accused of heresy, Hafiz attributed this verse to a Christian whom he heard in passing a wine shop."[471]

Following her victory over France and Spain at the Battle of Trafalgar in 1805, Great Britain was one of the two dominant world powers (the other being Russia after her great victory over France in 1812). Being at that pinnacle of power, Great Britain was able to substantially influence conditions in Iran. Even so, an adequate translation of the New Testament in Farsi, the name of modern Persian, did not exist. Two translations existed at that time but "neither that of Mr. Colebrook, the great Sanskrit scholar, nor of the Serampore [India] missionaries, had quite the idiomatic freedom that was needed."[472] Apparently there were in Iran at that time neither the highly trained, dedicated and capable scholars in the roster of Iranian Christians, nor the resources or freedom to undertake such a needed and demanding enterprise. However, one should not forget the earlier work of the Christian translator in Harun al-Rashid's academy, known as The House of Wisdom, which was founded in Baghdad in 830 A.D. His name was Hunayn ibn Ishaq al-Ibadi (808–873 A.D.). Among the many medical and scientific documents he translated, he also translated an Arabic version of the Old Testament from the Greek Sep-

---

469 Donald N. Wilber, Iran, Past and Present, (Princeton, NJ: Princeton Univ. Press, 1963), p. 39.
470 Like those in Sogdian (see Chapter 10), the Persian of the *Odes of Solomon*, or that used in Tatian's *Diatessaron*.
471 Richard N. Frye, Iran, (New York: Henry Holt & Co., 1953), p. 23.
472 Constance E. Padwick, Henry Martyn, Confessor of the Faith, (London: Inter-Varsity Fellowship, 1959), p. 102.

tuagint, but, unfortunately, that translation did not survive. One wonders why Hunayn did not translate the Old Testament into the Persian current in his time.

To fill that plaguing and limiting lacuna or gap, God raised up Henry Martyn, a man about whom Padwick said that few men knew the Muslim outlook upon life and God as Martyn did because he had made the effort "to learn the religious mind of Islam."[473]

God placed a burden on Martyn's heart to make the Gospel of Christ known in India, which at that time was governed by the British East India Company. Martyn had been appointed chaplain to British troops in India, giving him "a handsome salary and the obligations of Government service."[474] The large convoy in which Martyn's ship belonged set out to sea on August 28, 1805, only two months before the history-making Battle of Trafalgar (which occurred October 21, 1805) in which Great Britain destroyed a combined French and Spanish war fleet to become the world's dominant sea power. Martyn's ship reached Madras/Chennai, India on April 21, 1806. "They sailed from Madras in dreadful heat. 'Exertion seemed like death, indeed absolutely impossible.' Reaching the Hooghly River on the western edge of the vast delta of the Ganges, they edged their way cautiously eighty miles upstream to Calcutta [now, Kolkata]. On 16 May, Henry went ashore at daylight and with some difficulty found William Carey."[475] It was a meeting of two of the world's most prolific linguists. First was Carey, the cobbler, who translated scripture into several of the languages of Northeast India. In dramatic contrast, Martyn, prize-winning graduate of Cambridge University, shortly proved to be "one of the most talented Christian linguists there ever had been."[476]

On March 25, 1811, just two months less than five years after his arrival, Martyn departed from India, sailing from Bombay (now Mumbai). During his five-year stay in India, he had completed work on new translations of the New Testament, both into Urdu and into Farsi. Martyn (though by that time very sick and weak) made his way to Shiraz, Persia (Iran), where he spent another eleven months perfecting the Farsi translation under the scrutiny of highly critical and contentious Muslim scholars who disdained his religion but were deeply moved by the quality of his translation. However, "barely had he settled into Shiraz when Henry realized that he would have to scrap the Persian New Testament on which he and Sabat had worked in Cawnpore [now, Kanpur, India] and produce an entirely new one with the aid of [his Muslim informant] Seid Ali. This time there were no British regiments to minister to, so he gave himself utterly to that one task, diverted only by the heated discussions with the Muslim intelligentsia."[477] "On 12 Feb-

---

473 Constance E. Padwick, <u>Henry Martyn, Confessor of the Faith</u>, (London: Inter-Varsity Fellowship, 1959), p. 107.
474 Constance E. Padwick, <u>Henry Martyn, Confessor of the Faith</u>, (London: Inter-Varsity Fellowship, 1959), p. 61.
475 David Bentley-Taylor, <u>My Love Must Wait, The Story of Henry Martyn</u>, (Leicester, Great Britain: Universities & Colleges Christian Fellowship, 2nd ed, 1978), p. 63.
476 David Bentley-Taylor, <u>My Love Must Wait, The Story of Henry Martyn</u>, (Leicester, Great Britain: Universities & Colleges Christian Fellowship, 2nd ed, 1978), p. 74.
477 David Bentley-Taylor, <u>My Love Must Wait, The Story of Henry Martyn</u>, (Leicester, Great Britain: Universities & Colleges Christian Fellowship, 2nd ed, 1978), p. 129.

ruary 1812, the Persian New Testament was finished. Three weeks later, the Book of Psalms was also completed."[478]

In May of 1812, having completed his translation of the New Testament in Persian, he set out from Shiraz to Tabriz to give it to the British Ambassador who would formally present it to the Shah. "Twelve days' hard riding brought him to Isfahan."[479] It would have been another 1,500 miles from Tabriz to Constantinople. Having begun that extremely long journey, on or about October 16, 1812, Henry Martyn died at Tokat, Turkey and was buried by Armenians in their cemetery. His death coincided with Napoleon's retreat from Moscow in which tens of thousands of French soldiers died from hunger, sickness and exposure. Today, as the withering wind from Arabia continues to blow fiercely in Iran, Martyn's great translation and its succeeding editions have been prohibited from distribution in Iran since the Khomeini Revolution in 1979. In April 1990, the Iranian Bible Society was shut down and has not been able to reopen, despite repeated appeals. Surprisingly, the Bible Society had operated openly for ten years after the Islamic revolution, but then the government prohibited printing of Scripture portions and banned the importation of Bibles, New Testaments and portions. The executive secretary was subjected to repeated harassment and he fled the country. Finally, the Society was closed, its files confiscated and its staff locked out of the premises.

Though currently the Farsi Bible may not be printed and distributed in Iran, God has worked out an alternative method. This became clear during late March and early April 2017 in a rather secretive conference in the Netherlands. There, Christian technicians told how they had developed new technologies to penetrate difficult or closed areas of the world with the biblical message. One organization told the attendees that they had distributed close to one-half million digital Bibles to people in Iran. Roughly, that is one Bible for every 160 Iranians!

Overthrow of Mosaddegh, Iranian Prime Minister

Along "with Great Britain, the U.S. had funded and arranged the 'counter coup' of 1953 [led by Kermit Roosevelt] in which the democratically elected prime minister, Mohammed Mosaddegh, had been displaced and the autocratic rule of the shah affirmed. ... This school of thought, skeptical of the possibilities of Islamic democracy, tends to see the 1979 revolution as a deviation from a process of secularization that began with the introduction of constitutional monarchy in 1906. The shah and his father before him may have been autocrats, but they knew that the future of Iran depended on secularization and contact with the West. They improved education, liberalized the position of women in society, and drove Iran into relative prosperity in the modern world. Opinions are divided within this school of thought on whether the overthrow of Mosaddegh saved Iran from tilting toward

---

[478] David Bentley-Taylor, <u>My Love Must Wait, The Story of Henry Martyn</u>, (Leicester, Great Britain: Universities & Colleges Christian Fellowship, 2nd ed, 1978), p. 137.
[479] Robin E. Waterfield, <u>Christians in Persia</u> (London: George Allen & Unwin Ltd., 1973), p. 93.

communism or represented a deviation from democratic development. But there is broad agreement that the Islamic revolution [led by Khomeini in 1979] was a disaster for modern Iran."[480]

The late Shah of Iran was indeed repressive. However, his record in this area should not be assessed only by comparison with concepts of freedom in the U.S.A., but must be evaluated by comparison with the historic situation in Iran. Was it from that perspective an improvement or a regression? Also, the Shah's record should be assessed not only by comparison with the historic situation in Iran but with contemporaneous regimes in the Middle East. Such a comparison is flattering to the Shah for "most Middle Eastern rulers were cruel and by their standards he was a liberal."[481]

Two powerful Iranian vested interests conspired to defeat the Shah: the secular feudal landlords and the religious feudal landlords, i.e. the mullahs. (See Glossary.) Any land reform which broke up the vast estates controlled by feudal landlords and feudal Muslim religious organizations in favor of private ownership by the land-tilling peasants would, inevitably, be hated and opposed. The mullahs could easily enlist the uninformed and unenlightened peasantry in violent protests under the banner of loyalty to Islam. Thus the peasantry sided with a system which would ensure the continuation of their own captivity in serfdom!

The Shah attempted, as it were, to mix oil and water but never achieved a stable emulsion. He tried to blend the Iranian cultural heritage, Islamic theology, and Western democracy. From the Iranian cultural heritage he stressed, particularly, the idea of macro-monarchy, that is, the emperor-king ("God-king" is closer to the historical reality), known in Iranian history as "King of kings." But, Islamic theology has its own inherent concepts of polity and economics. The Shah failed to recognize, until far too late, that the mixture not only was incompatible but impossible. In 1979, the year of the Khomeini Revolution in Iran, General Zia-ul-Haq, president of Pakistan by a military coup, expressed the reality of the situation with far greater understanding, clarity and accuracy. He said, "Pakistan's present political edifice is based on the secular democratic system of the West, which has no place in Islam. ... This country was created in the name of Islam and in Islam there is no provision for Western type elections."[482]

Obviously, one also wonders what part democracy would have in a society dominated by a monarch. The Shah spoke of "imperial democracy"! He said, "The union of these two words should not be surprising. According to Iran's constitution, be it that of 1906 or 1950, although the Emperor submits his projects for acceptance by the government, he nevertheless remains a constitutional monarch. He

---

[480] Noah Feldman, <u>After Jihad, America and the Struggle For Islamic Democracy</u>, (New York: Farrar, Straus and Giroux, 2003), pp. 92-93.
[481] Paul Johnson, <u>Modern Times, The World From the Twenties to the Eighties</u> (Harper & Row Publishers: New York, 1983), p. 704.
[482] "Islam Takes Over," <u>Asia Week</u>, November 2, 1979, p. 16.

reigns but does not rule."⁴⁸³ Further, the Shah's answer was "that by 'political democracy' he meant the blend of the Western principle of [a] parliamentary [system] with the Persian monarchical tradition!"⁴⁸⁴

The Shah apparently was committed to drastically altering the concept of the monarchy. He said, "Threatening developments [during the Allied occupation of Iran during World War II] could not easily scare me into abandoning the principles of such men as Thomas Jefferson, principles I was determined to follow."⁴⁸⁵

In harmony with his commitment to democracy, the Shah seemed to feel he should be an elected sovereign. However, his concept of election was farfetched. He considered the enthusiastic popular support for the monarchy at the close of Mosaddegh's attempt to bring Iran under communism an election! He wrote, "I returned to Tehran where I was greeted with popular enthusiasm. Throughout Iran the people were undeniably behind the crown. Before, I had been no more than a hereditary sovereign, but now I had truly been elected by the people."⁴⁸⁶ (See Photo 12, the Tehran Freedom Tower.)

Just three years before the Khomeini Revolution, my son, Jonathan, and I extensively explored Iran. The evidences of prosperity were visible everywhere. It seemed inconceivable that chaos, religious persecution, revolution, mob rule, and widespread killing could engulf the country as they did.

The adverse economic consequences of the 1979 Khomeini Revolution were highlighted by contrasting statistics. In 1980 the exiled Shah evaluated the economic progress which had taken place during his reign. He wrote, "When Mosaddegh was in power, Iran's budget was around $400 million. Our last budget was $57 billion, of which approximately $20 billion came from oil revenues and the rest from taxes that the people could now afford; in 1963 our per capita income was $174, in 1978, the last year of my reign, it was $2,540. And all of this was accomplished at a time of great population growth, from 27 million in 1968 to 36 million in 1978. And our social programs were developing under the White Revolution at a remarkable rate."⁴⁸⁷

The successes during the Shah's regime notwithstanding, institutional Christian mission outreach in Iran began to suffer terminal trouble between the overthrow of the Mosaddegh Government and the Khomeini Revolution. A testimony to this is found in the June 1975 edition of *The Bulletin of the Fellowship of Faith for Muslims*. It called attention to the situation in Mashhad, which at that time had a population of 750,000⁴⁸⁸, by telling us that "Mashhad, a city of pilgrimage for many Shi'ite Muslims in Iran, is situated near the Afghan border. Five years ago this

---

483 Mohammad Reza Pahlavi, Answer to History (New York: Stein and Day Publishers, 1980), p. 129.
484 Amin Saikal, The Rise and Fall of the Shah (Princeton: Princeton University Press, 1980), p. 80.
485 Mohammad Reza Shah Pahlavi, Mission For My Country (London: Hutchinson & Co. Publishers, Ltd., 1974), p. 77.
486 Mohammad Reza Shah Pahlavi, Mission For My Country (London: Hutchinson & Co. Publishers, Ltd., 1974), pp. 90-91.
487 Mohammad Reza Pahlavi, Answer to History, (New York: Stein and Day Publishers, 1980), p. 176.
488 In 2016 the population had risen to 2.95 million.

place had a thriving church of over 100 members, then the hospital closed and the missionaries left. Today there is no pastor, and only a handful of people. Do please pray." (See Photo 11, the Shrine at Mashhad.)

H. B. Dehqani-Tafti, Iranian Bishop of the Episcopal Church in Iran, which has been severely persecuted since the Khomeini Revolution, gives an evaluation of institutional missions such as the hospital in Mashhad. Regarding the earlier trouble experienced by the Episcopal Church during the crisis when Prime Minister Mosaddegh nationalized the Anglo-Iranian Oil Company (the expropriation law was approved by the Majlis on April 19, 1951), Bishop Dehqani-Tafti wrote, "Looking back nearly thirty years, it is easy to say that we ought to have read the writing on the wall and accommodated ourselves to the spirit which brought about the oil crisis. Instead, it seemed to us to be God's will that the hospital should remain in the hands of the church. I am sure now that the right thing would have been somehow to have 'nationalized' our hospitals and indeed our other institutions. The American Presbyterians, who perhaps saw better the signs of the times, closed, handed over, or sold all their seven hospitals in the north of the country. We were reluctant to close down good and useful establishments, but we would have been wise to negotiate with the government or groups of interested doctors, and divest ourselves of the immense responsibilities of running these big organizations."[489]

A Gripping Account

Having escaped to Cambridge after amazingly surviving a point-blank pistol attack, Bishop Dehqani-Tafti began receiving reports of attacks on members of his staff still resident in Iran. The Bishop's portrayal will help us grasp the poignancy in which he received one account after another of attacks on his co-workers. He tells us, first "came the news of Jean Waddell's arrest in Isfahan. I could not believe it at first. We had heard to our great satisfaction that Jean had recovered from her bullet wound and was hoping to return to Britain, and we were looking forward to meeting her again. However, problems she had faced for some time in leaving Iran culminated in a summons to answer questions before the Revolutionary authorities in Isfahan. Accompanied by an official of the British Embassy, she traveled to Isfahan on 5 August to report to the Revolutionary Court. There she was arrested, and the Embassy official was refused permission to see her. From that day to the time of writing (November 1980), she has seen no one from the outside world, though a consular official was on one occasion permitted to send her a few books and simple necessities.

"Four days later, on 9 August, three British missionaries who were running the Nur Ayin home for blind girls were summoned to the Ministry of National Guidance. They were Margaret Knill, a CMS missionary, Libby Walker, a short-service worker sponsored by CMS, and Anne White, of the Bible and Medical Missionary Fellowship. Dimitri Bellos went with them in his capacity as Diocesan

---
[489] H.B. Dehqani-Tafti, The Hard Awakening (New York: The Seabury Press, 1981), pp. 20-21.

Administrator. The women were given forty-eight hours to leave the country, and Dimitri was arrested there and then. No one has heard from him since. His wife, Joka, who is expecting their third child, continues to help at Nur Ayin.

"On the following day, John and Audrey Coleman, had to go to Tehran, to the Ministry of National Guidance, to see about their residence permit. They too were immediately arrested. No reason for their detention has ever been given, and no one has heard from them or seen them since.

"A week later, on 17 August, members of the Revolutionary Guard went to St. Luke's vicarage in Isfahan, which stands next to the church, and arrested Iraj Muttaheddeh in the presence of his wife and three children. No one has been allowed to see him since. …

"In the meantime, allegations and slanders against our church continue over Tehran radio and television, and in the revolutionary press. Government ministers have joined in the slander. A junior official of the Department of Education in Isfahan, who was in charge of the fanatical *Tablighat-e Islami* organization in that town and is now deputy speaker of the Majlis, has publicly, and with no respect for truth, accused me and the diocese of being involved in espionage. The deputy Information Minister talks wildly about the diocese having received 500 million dollars from the CIA for distribution to officers in the army, and 300 kilogrammes of T.N.T. explosives from the British ambassador, Sir John Graham, to be given to conspirators plotting a *coup d'etat*. No amount of denial seems to stop them from making these ridiculous and devilish allegations which have not an atom of truth behind them."[490] Shortly after these events, Bishop Dehqani received word that his only son had been executed in Iran by murderers.

From a summary of conditions of Christians in Iran since the Khomeini Revolution, given by the Middle East correspondent for *Morning Star News*, it is appallingly clear that persecution for Christians in Iran continues unabated. His report tells us that "the government has left only a few if any Farsi-language churches open. … Christians have no other option but to hold meetings in homes, which are illegal and heavily persecuted. … There is nowhere they can go … [where] they can freely worship the Lord." Christians are accused of "actions against national security, being present at an illegal gathering and collusion with foreign entities. … The leadership of the house church movement has been gutted. Many of the leaders have been imprisoned and increasingly Iran has been forcing pastors into a form of self-enforced exile by harassing and pressuring them to leave. One of the big problems is most of the mature leaders have been forced out of the country."[491]

Perhaps the plight of Christians in present-day Iran can be highlighted by a few succinct insights from the recent past about conditions for a segment of another re-

---
490 H.B. Dehqani-Tafti, The Hard Awakening (New York: The Seabury Press, 1981), pp. 90-91.
491 Email from Morning Star News (http://morningstarnews.org.) April 1, 2016,

ligious minority group, thirteen members out of the 30,000-member Iranian Jewish community, the oldest in the Middle East. Those thirteen Jews, whose trial took place in Shiraz, were charged with espionage and treason. During the days of Ayatollah Ruhollah Khomeini, "though not as brutally treated as the Iranian Baha'is, who had committed the unforgivable sin of founding a new faith and thereby denying the finality of the Prophet Mohammad's mission, Jews were regularly harassed and always viewed suspiciously by officials. In a revolutionary Islamic society, where religion is the primary identity and basis for fraternity and loyalty to the state, Jews [as well as Christians] are in a very precarious position. ... [They] are constantly under suspicion because of their religion, which is clearly marked on their identity papers. ...

"If you'd taken a long look at Iran's 'reformist' newspapers—before they were shut down by the hard-liners—you would have rarely found even a tepid, let alone full-throated, denunciation of the trial. ... This case shows clearly that Mr. Khatami is, at best, indifferent to the Jews' [and the Christians'] fate. He has said very little and what he has said isn't encouraging. ...

"The speaker of Iran's parliament told a British newspaper that the defendants would be treated leniently. But the Islamic Republic is quite capable of hanging one or more of these Jews. Prison sentences are certainly in their future. And the Western response to the trial hasn't so far been muscular."[492]

No one should imagine that the withering winds from Arabia have stopped blowing in Iran. A news bulletin from *Compass Direct News* dated December 6, 2005 reported, "The United States has approved emergency resettlement for a family of four Iranian Christians left stranded in Turkey since an October deportation order. Widow Zivar Khademian, together with her daughter Fatemeh Moini, 19, and sons Hossein and Kazem Moini, both in their early 30s, had fled [from Iran] to Turkey in January 2003. After arriving in Turkey, the family was twice refused UNHCR refugee status, despite their status as former Muslims who had converted to Christianity. Under Iran's strict Islamic laws, anyone who abandons the Muslim faith faces the death penalty."

On April 1, 2016, *Morning Star News* (http://morningstarnews.org) reported that "in the face of a crack down that has crippled Iran's house-church leadership, an imprisoned convert from Islam has managed to sneak a message of encouragement to Iran's Christians. With Iran's house churches mushrooming even as the government has imprisoned or harassed most pastors into exile, a Christian held in Rajai Shahr Prison in Karaj last week exhorted Iranian Christians to expect persecution but to continue proclaiming Christ."

Morning Star News in a release dated October 29, 2016, stated that "Three Iranian Christians sentenced to receive 80 lashes for drinking wine during a communion service filed an appeal Wednesday (October 25) to have their case overturned, a

---

492 Reuel Marc Gerecht, *Who Will Defend Iran's Jews?*, The Wall Street Journal, June 7, 2000, p. A-2.

noted advocacy group reported. In a trial that lasted a mere 10 minutes, the three converts from Islam, Mohammedreza Omidi, Yasser Mossayebzadeh and Saheb Fadaie, on September 10 were all sentenced to receive 80 lashes for drinking wine. It was the second time that Fadaie and Omidi have been sentenced to flogging for taking communion."

Evaluating the Khomeini Revolution

Christian leaders will benefit from the following analyses by secular analysts who have evaluated and categorized the multifaceted upheaval resulting from the Khomeini Revolution.

"The 1979 Iranian Revolution is one of the signature events of modern history, akin to the 1917 Russian Revolution, and the U.S. has never figured out how to deal with it."[493]

"The movement inspired by the charismatic leadership of Khomeini and led by the mullahs of Iran was by far the most effective of these Islamic movements—if not perhaps in the attainment of its ultimate objectives, then surely in the mobilization of support. But it was far from being the only such movement. In virtually every country in the Islamic world, as well as among Muslim minorities elsewhere, there were powerful and passionate movements of Islamic resurgence."[494]

"What none of the U.S. embassy archives predicted was the brutality of the Iranian Revolution, the extraordinary cruelty that manifested itself among the so-called judges and jurists who were predisposed to torture and kill out of whim rather than reflection. At the end of the eight-year Iran-Iraq War, this would meet its apogee in the mass hangings of thousands of opposition prisoners. But its characteristics were clearly evident within days of the Shah's overthrow; and no one emphasized them more chillingly than Chief Justice Khalkhali, who had told me in December 1979 how he intended to 'string up' the Shah. When he said that, and despite his ferocious reputation, I thought at first it was a joke, a cliche, an idle remark. Of course, it was nothing of the sort."[495]

"The word *revolution* has been much misused in the modern Middle East, being applied to—or claimed for—many events which would more appropriately be designated by the French *coup d'etat*, the German *putsch*, or the Spanish *pronunciamiento*. The political experience of the English-speaking peoples, interestingly, provides no equivalent term. What happened in Iran was none of these but was in its origins an authentic revolutionary movement of change. Like its predecessors, it has in many ways gone badly wrong, leading to tyranny at home, terror and subversion abroad."[496]   ☙

---

493 David Brooks, *The Reality Situation*, <u>The New York Times</u>, May 30, 2008, p. A23.
494 Bernard Lewis, <u>Islam and the West</u>, (New York: Oxford University Press, 1993), p. 40.
495 Robert Fisk, <u>The Great War for Civilization, The Conquest of the Middle East</u>, (New York: Alfred A. Knopf, 2005), pp. 111 & 130.
496 Bernard Lewis, <u>The Crisis of Islam, Holy War and Unholy Terror</u>, (New York: The Modern Library, 2003), pp. 20-21.

Chapter 15

A TWO-FOLD ATTACK ON THE CHURCH IN EGYPT

Note: Definitions for the doctrinal terminology relating to the debates about the nature of Christ are given in the Glossary.

The oldest mosque in Egypt, in fact one of the oldest in the entire Muslim world, is the lavish Amr ibn al-As mosque in Cairo. It was built in honor of Amr ibn al-As, the Arabian Muslim general who on behalf of Islam conquered Egypt, a vitally important Byzantine-Roman province. Because of its exceptional crops of wheat, Egypt had been the "bread basket" of the Byzantine Empire.

At the end of January 640, with a tiny cavalry force of only 3,500 men, Amr audaciously attacked and destroyed the fortress city of Pelusium, located at the mouth of the eastern branch of the Nile. "The Arabs not only burnt the shipping and dismantled the fortress, but also, like the Persians [before them], destroyed the remnant of the churches in Pelusium."[497]

A Seditious Bishop

Under Cyrus, who had been appointed by the Byzantine-Roman Emperor Heraclius to be "simultaneously both [Orthodox] Patriarch of Alexandria and also civil governor of Egypt,"[498] the government in Alexandria did nothing to relieve Pelusium during the one month it was under siege by Amr and his troops. Cyrus' total dereliction of duty has fueled speculation ever since about what motivated him to sacrifice one position after another to the Arabs. His total inaction has prompted many to ask, "Had he already formed in his mind the plan for rendering the patriarchate of Alexandria independent of Constantinople by an alliance with the Arabs against the Empire?"[499]

Mercy is For the Birds

Following the stunning Muslim victory at Pelusium, the major Egyptian fortress city of Babylon (near present-day Cairo) surrendered on April 9, 641 A.D. Next on the schedule of conquest was Byzantium's great cultural-hub and naval-base city of Alexandria. When Amr's soldiers began to take down their general's tent to move northwest for the siege of Alexandria, they found that a

---
[497] Alfred J. Butler, <u>The Arab Conquest of Egypt and the Last Thirty Years of the Roman Dominion</u>, (Oxford: At The Clarendon Press, 1902), p. 211.
[498] John Bagot Glubb, <u>The Great Arab Conquests</u>, (Englewood Cliffs, New Jersey: Prentice-Hall, Inc. 1963), p. 223.
[499] Alfred J. Butler, <u>The Arab Conquest of Egypt and the Last Thirty Years of the Roman Dominion</u>, (Oxford: At The Clarendon Press, 1902), p. 213.

dove had built a nest on it and was sitting on her eggs. "The tent was left behind, sooner than disturb the bird, Amr stating that she had taken refuge in his tent and was therefore under his protection."[500]

While that act of mercy might seem to indicate that Amr was a man of compassion, in reality he was a ruthless, pitiless warrior. On the way to Alexandria, unable to conquer the city of Faiyum, the Arabs attacked "a town called Bahnasa, which they took by storm and slaughtered all before them—men, women, and children."[501] That despicable act became a policy, carried out several times as Amr's Arabs ravaged Egypt.[502]

The brutality of Amr ibn al Aasi and his pillaging Arabian soldiers was not the first savagery which Egypt's followers of Christ[503] had been fated to endure. The Muslim invasion was part of a long period of unparalleled trouble for Egypt. In 602 A.D. Sassanian Iran launched an all-out war against Byzantium, which lasted till 628 A.D. During that horribly destructive twenty-six-year war, the Iranians occupied the country of the Nile from 617 to 628 A.D. Though the Persians did not persecute the Coptic Church as such, they "committed many and terrible atrocities during their conquest."[504] Now, only thirteen years after the Persian army was forced to withdraw from Egypt, Arab Muslim forces were pillaging the country.

Distracted by Theology

Antedating both the Persian and Muslim Arab invasions of Egypt, the unity of the Byzantine Empire had been shattered by bitter and prolonged Christological debates between the clergy of the official state "Orthodox" Church[505] and the leaders of the monophysite[506] Coptic Church. In 628 A.D., finally free from the Persian war, Heraclius devoted himself to finding some balm which would stimulate healing in the empire. The emperor's concentration on how to solve this theological conundrum drew his attention away from the rising danger of Muslim power in Arabia.

---

500 John Bagot Glubb, The Great Arab Conquests, (London: Quartet Books, 1963), p. 237.

501 Alfred J. Butler, The Arab Conquest of Egypt and the Last Thirty Years of the Roman Dominion, (Oxford: At The Clarendon Press, 1902), p. 223.

502 Glubb recorded that, "The Byzantine forces, which had successfully defended Faiyum against the raid of Amr ibn al Aasi, now abandoned the whole province and taking ship on the Nile, passed Babylon and took refuge in the town of Nikiou, forty-five miles north-west of the fortress. Amr immediately detached a force, which took Faiyum by assault and massacred the inhabitants. The whole province thereupon surrendered without resistance." Again he says, "The city [of Nikiou], though surrounded with fortifications, was not defended and the Arabs charging into it, put many of the inhabitants to the sword. This massacre took place on 13th May, 641." – John Bagot Glubb, The Great Arab Conquests, (London: Quartet Books, 1963), pp. 230 & 238.

503 The majority of Egypt's Christians were Copts, a word derived from the name Egypt. So, if we speak of Coptic Christians, we are simply saying, Egyptian Christians. The Coptic Christians stood in opposition to the state church, called Orthodox or Melkite. The word Melkite comes from the Arabic word *malik* which means ruler. Thus, it was another term for the state church.

504 John Bagot Glubb, The Great Arab Conquests, (London: Quartet Books, 1963), p. 223.

505 To reiterate, it was also called the Melkite Church from the Arabic word *malik* meaning ruler since it held the doctrine which was endorsed and enforced by the authority of the emperor of the Byzantine Empire. Thus, they were also called Caesar-Christians.

506 From μονος (monos) + φυσις (phusis)—a single nature. Used of those who hold that there is but a single nature in Christ or that the human and divine in Him constituted but one composite nature.

The theological standoff had resulted from decisions reached by some 600 participants in the Council of Chalcedon, convened in 451 A.D. They had condemned the Egyptian Christians "because they taught that the two natures in Jesus Christ had been fused into one, the human lost in the divine as a wine drop in the sea. Leo [Bishop of Rome] declared that the union was perfect, but the natures remained perfectly distinct; this contradiction in terms became the orthodox position. The monks and peasants of Egypt and the populace of Alexandria solidly supported their patriarch [in opposition to the official position]."[507]

"From the time of Justinian [Byzantine emperor who reigned 527–565 A.D.] the doctrine of the two natures may be said to have been supreme in the Roman Empire, both eastern and western. The Monophysites, being no longer tolerated in the established church, now became a schismatical party, with church organization, bishops, and patriarchs of their own."[508]

The Coptic Church responded to the decision of the Council of Chalcedon with "deplorable deeds of violence ... [which] again stained the record of the Church in Egypt. The network of monastic settlements now enmeshed much of the country, and the cry 'One Nature!' became indeed a battle-cry of these fierce ascetics.[509] ... Persecution of Coptic Christians by the official Orthodox party, with the Emperor's power behind them, both in the reign of Justinian and of his successors, left a rankling resentment that persisted for many a generation.[510] Such was the unhappy state of the Church in Egypt at the time when a new national force and religious faith were coming to birth in Arabia—a rival power that Egyptians would soon hear hammering at the gate."[511]

New Christology Unacceptable

Realizing that this destructive confrontation between Christians in the Roman Empire had to be brought to an end, Heraclius, with the assistance of a committee of three bishops,[512] devised the Monothelite concept as a middle position between the warring camps, a position both could hopefully accept without

---

507 Elias J. Bickerman, *Late Roman Society and Culture*, The Columbia History of the World, (New York: Harper & Row, Publishers, 1972), eds. John A. Garraty & Peter Gay, p. 244.
508 Albert Henry Newman, A Manual of Church History, (Philadelphia: The American Baptist Publication Society, 1933), Vol. I, pp. 349-350.
509 "In the fourth century, as Christianity emerged as the official religion of the Roman Empire, the number of monasteries in Egypt grew at a phenomenal rate. Thousands of men and women abandoned the world for a life of the spirit, until 'the desert grew full of monks.'" – William Lyster, *Coptic Egypt and the Holy Family*, Be Thou There, The Holy Family's Journey in Egypt, ed. Gawdat Gabra (Cairo: The American University in Cairo Press, 2001), p. 10.
510 Groves, quoting T.W. Arnold says that "Justinian is said to have had 200,000 Copts put to death in the city of Alexandria alone." – C.P. Groves, The Planting of Christianity in Africa, (London: Lutterworth Press, 1964) V. I, p. 46.
511 C.P. Groves, The Planting of Christianity in Africa, (London: Lutterworth Press, 1964), V. I, p. 46.
512 They were: (1) Sergius of Constantinople. "With him originated the formula of compromise adopted by Heraclius, whereby it was settled to dismiss the question whether our Lord's nature was single or twofold, but to pronounce positively that there was but one will or operation." – Alfred J. Butler, The Arab Conquest of Egypt and the Last Thirty Years of the Roman Dominion, (Oxford: At The Clarendon Press, 1902), p. 136. (2) Paulus, an Armenian church leader and (3) Cyrus, a Nestorian bishop from Phasis in the Caucasus. This is Cyrus who later became simultaneously Patriarch of Alexandria and civil governor of Egypt.

feeling they had compromised. The Monothelite view was "the confession of two natures and *one energy* [or *one will*] in Christ."[513]

"To persuade the Egyptian Christians to accept the new dogma, Heraclius unfortunately chose Cyrus, bishop of Phasis in the Caucasus,[514] who was made simultaneously both Patriarch of Alexandria and also civil governor of Egypt. ... The Monophysites rejected the emperor's new formula, probably without understanding it. Perhaps, with the passage of time, they might have been won over, for the new formula was thought by some people to have been very nearly a surrender to Monophysite doctrine.

"The Copts, however, were not prepared to listen and Cyrus was quite ready to use force. Without waiting to observe the healing effects of the new formula, he inaugurated an active persecution of all who refused to conform. Early in 632, the year of Muhammad's death in Medina, violent measures were adopted against all heretics in Egypt. Menas, brother of Benjamin, the Coptic Patriarch, was seized, his body burned in many places with torches and his teeth pulled out. He was then put in a sack weighted with sand, and rowed out to sea. Three times he was offered his life if he would acknowledge the Orthodox formula. As he still refused, he was thrown into the sea in his weighted sack.

"Parties of soldiers were sent to Monophysite monasteries to demand the signatures of their abbots to the creed of the Orthodox Church and to flog, torture or imprison the recalcitrant. Many Copts submitted, others fled, while many continued to worship in secret according to the creed of the Monophysites. On the whole, as has so often happened, the persecution probably strengthened the Coptic Church. It also severed the last strands of political loyalty and affection for Byzantium."[515]

Reflecting on the Greek church when the Ottomans captured Constantinople, one scholar noted, "The triumph of the Ottomans might have been expected to mark the end of the Greek Orthodox Church, but this did not happen."[516] A similar predictive death knell might easily have been sounded for the Coptic Church in Egypt, some seven centuries earlier, when Arab-Muslim forces overran Egypt. Though in the rest of northern Africa the church did come to an end shortly after the arrival of the Muslims, yet surprisingly, against all reason, the church survived in Egypt.

CR

---

513 Albert Henry Newman, A Manual of Church History, (Philadelphia: The American Baptist Publication Society, 1933), Vol. I, p. 351.
514 Phasis is now known as Poti. It is a seaport town in the west of the Republic of Georgia situated on the eastern shore of the Black Sea at the mouth of the Rioni River. The ancient Greek colony was established in the 6th century B.C. The present town was developed in the 1880s.
515 John Bagot Glubb, The Great Arab Conquests, (London: Quartet Books, 1963), pp. 223-224.
516 David Brewer, The Greek War of Independence, The Struggle for Freedom From Ottoman Oppression and the Birth of the Modern Greek Nation, (New York: The Overlook Press, 2001), p. 4.

Chapter 16

EGYPT'S CHURCH SHOWS AMAZING RESILIENCE

From Mary and Joseph to the Council of Chalcedon

Overwhelmingly, Christianity, of one persuasion or another, was the dominant religion in North Africa at the time Islam began its march from Egypt to Morocco. As mentioned in the final paragraph of Chapter 15, shortly after the triumphant Muslim forces' arrival at the Atlantic in 711 A.D., churches quickly began to vanish from Africa's Mediterranean shore—except in Egypt! Estimates are that from 900 to well over 1,000 churches went into extinction in Mediterranean Africa because of the victorious Islamic offensive and subsequent Muslim occupation.

In evident amazement because of this phenomenon Durant wrote, "The most striking of all effects produced by the Arab conquest of North Africa was the gradual but almost complete disappearance of Christianity. ... Doubtless economic considerations entered: non-Moslems paid a head tax, and converts [to Islam] were for a time freed from it. When in 744 A.D. the Arab governor of Egypt offered this exemption, 24,000 Christians went over to Islam. Occasional but severe persecutions of Christians may have influenced many to conform to the [new] ruling faith. In Egypt, a Coptic minority held out bravely, built their churches like fortresses, maintained their worship in secret, and survive to this day. But the once crowded churches of Alexandria, Cyrene, Carthage, and Hippo were emptied and decayed; the memory of Athanasius, Cyril, and Augustine faded out; and the disputes of Arians, Donatists, and Monophysites gave way to the quarrels of Sunni and Ismaili Mohammedanism."[517]

The Arab-Muslim oppression must have been especially ironic and galling to the Coptic followers of Christ because they had, in two cases at least, actively helped the invading Muslim forces win Egypt for Islam! Their active assistance to the Muslims was a mistaken effort to end the oppression which the Melkite Church, the Imperial Church, had heaped upon them. (The word Melkite is derived from the Arabic *malik*, king or ruler, thus, official or state-approved.) What they had really done was jump from the frying pan into the fire! In any case, The Monophysite followers of Christ in Egypt, "received the

---

517 Will Durant, The Age of Faith, A History of Medieval Civilization—Christian, Islamic, and Judaic—from Constantine to Dante: A.D. 325–1300 (New York: Simon & Schuster, 1950), p. 289.

Moslems with open arms, helped them to take Memphis, guided them into Alexandria."[518]

However, not only have the Copts survived as the largest body of the followers of Christ in Africa, north of the Sahara, but in the 21st century, "the Coptic Church is by far the largest body of Christians in the Middle East."[519] While the official Egyptian census states that the Christian segment of the population is only 6 percent, at least 14.2 percent wear the name of Christ while some claim the percentage to be 20![520]

Resilient Christianity

How do we account for the stunning, unique fourteen-centuries-long resiliency of those in Egypt who have upheld the name of Christ? Why were the followers of Christ so buoyant in Egypt compared to those in the rest of North Africa? There are many stark reminders that the once-vibrant Christianity west of Egypt has died out. For example, "the columns of the basilica of Carthage stand empty in the coastal sands of modern Tunisia."[521] Was it because Christ's followers in Egypt had learned under imperial Byzantine persecution how to endure suffering for Christ's sake before Islam subjected them to a new phase of persecution? That cannot be the answer because the churches in the rest of North Africa which had not submitted to the creedal demands of the imperial church also suffered as did the Christians in Egypt. For example, where the celebrated Augustine held sway, "the laws against Donatists became coercive in the true sense of the word: they punished laymen for *not* becoming Catholics. In 405, the Donatist Church had merely been 'disbanded' [which means]: it had been deprived of its bishops, of its churches, and of its funds; its members lost certain civic rights. From 412, by contrast, a tariff of exceptionally heavy fines was applied to laymen of all classes who failed to join the Catholic Church."[522]

The Origin of Egyptian Christianity

Though we know very precisely how Islam came to Egypt, surprisingly, in contrast, we have only very tantalizing and incomplete information about how the message of Christ first came to Egypt and to the rest of North Africa.

Joseph and Mary lived in Egypt for some time with baby Jesus, whom they had brought to that country to protect him from Herod's schemes to assassinate him. As scripture tells us, God always prepares a place which becomes "the

---

518 Will Durant, The Age of Faith, A History of Medieval Civilization—Christian, Islamic, and Judaic—from Constantine to Dante: A.D. 325–1300, (New York: Simon and Schuster, 1950), p 282.
519 Patrick Johnstone & Jason Mandryk, Operation World, 21st Century Edition, (Waynesboro, Georgia: Paternoster, 2001), p. 234.
520 Patrick Johnstone & Jason Mandryk, Operation World, 21st Century Edition, (Waynesboro, Georgia: Paternoster, 2001), p. 204.
521 Brian Moynahan, The Faith, A History of Christianity, (New York: Doubleday, 2002), pp. 65-66.
522 Peter Brown, Augustine of Hippo (Berkeley: University of California Press, 2000), pp. 334-335.

way of escape." It says, "There hath no temptation taken you but such as man can bear; but God is faithful, who will not suffer you to be tempted above that ye are able; but will with the temptation make also <u>the way of escape</u>, that ye may be able to endure it." (I Corinthians 10:13) While in Egypt, did that godly couple share the story of Jesus' birth with the Egyptian people with whom they had found protection? When Egyptian citizens pressed them to explain why they had come to Egypt, as surely some of them must have, it would have given Mary and Joseph a wonderful opportunity to give a pre-gospel message about Christ. Did they tell the Egyptians that they had been commanded to name the child "Jesus" because it was he who should save his people from their sins? (Matthew 1:21) Presumably they did. In any case, "many Copts[523] believe that even prior to the beginning of the public ministry of Jesus Christ, Egyptians accepted the Divine Child as Lord over their lives."[524]

Thousands of visitors to Jerusalem are mentioned in the second chapter of Acts of the Apostles who had come to the holy city to participate in the observance of Israel's annual national feasts of Passover and Pentecost. Some of those who participated in those feasts are described as "residents of … Egypt."[525] Undoubtedly some of those Egyptian Jewish worshipers were part of the throngs who heard Peter preach the very first gospel message. It is also reasonable to believe that some of those Egyptian Jews who heard Peter's gospel sermon yielded their lives to Christ when men and women were invited to respond to the message to find pardon and become recipients of the Holy Spirit. "There is good reason to believe that at least some of these Egyptians returned to their homes where they established Christian congregations."[526]

Mark's Egyptian Ministry

Though the church in Egypt had a very early start, beginning shortly after the first feast of Pentecost following Jesus' resurrection when people from Egypt (Acts 2:10) heard the Gospel, still, the influence of the gospel of Christ in Egypt appears to have been limited and spotty till the coming of John Mark. At that point we seem to be on more solid ground, for there is quite strong tradition which states that Mark carried the message of Jesus to Egypt.

Atiya tells us that "St. John Chrysostom (ca. 347–404) states that it [Mark's Gospel] was originally composed in Egypt in the Greek language." Then he goes on to say, "It is certain that St. Mark brought his Gospel with him to Alexandria; and though the Greek version could have fulfilled his purpose in that city, the suggestion is made that another version in the Egyptian language

---

523 Copt is an Arabic word from Greek, meaning Egyptian. Ultimately it came to mean the native Church of Egypt.
524 Otto F.A. Meindarus, <u>Christian Egypt Ancient And Modern</u>, (Cairo: The American University in Cairo Press, 1977), p. 2.
525 Acts of the Apostles 2:9-10 (NIV).
526 Otto F.A. Meindarus, <u>Christian Egypt Ancient And Modern</u>, (Cairo: The American University in Cairo Press, 1977), p. 2.

was prepared for the benefit of native converts who were not conversant with Greek."[527]

The early use of the Gospel of Mark in Egypt has recently been highlighted by the discovery of a manuscript, possibly from the lifetime of Mark. "Daniel B. Wallace, a New Testament professor at Dallas Theological Seminary, claims to have discovered a first-century fragment of the Gospel of Mark, along with other early manuscripts in Egypt. [The portion from the Gospel of Mark] ... is 'a very small fragment, not too many verses but it's definitely from Mark,' and he [Wallace] added, 'to have a fragment from one of the Gospels that's written during the lifetime of some of the eye witnesses of the resurrection, is just astounding.'"[528]

Following the military triumph of Alexander the Great over Egypt in 332 B.C., the Greek language began to predominate in the major cities of Egypt, especially in the new Greek city of Alexandria. Thus, undoubtedly there was a significant Greek-speaking church in metropolitan Egypt from the beginning of gospel outreach in the country. However, in Egypt's vast rural countryside the Greek language did not replace local languages. But there, too, positive response to the gospel of Christ was significant. "In 303 [A.D.] Athanasius writes of more than one hundred bishops scattered about Egypt. Harnack estimated a fourth-century Egyptian church of a 'million strong' with many of that number found in towns and villages along the Nile."[529]

Eusebius (263-339 A.D.) confirms the account of Mark's evangelistic trip to Egypt. He recorded, "The same Mark, they also say, being the first that was sent to Egypt, proclaimed the gospel there which he had written, and first established churches at the city of Alexandria. And so great a multitude of believers, both of men and women, were collected there at the very outset, that in consequence of their extreme philosophical discipline and austerity, Philo has considered their pursuits, their assemblies, and entertainments, and in short their whole manner of life, as deserving a place in his descriptions."[530] "A much earlier fragment [earlier than Eusebius' account] from Clement [also] refers to Mark's presence in Alexandria."[531]

"As the Christians in the city [of Alexandria] multiplied, so did rumors that they were defiling and overthrowing pagan deities. A mob descended on them

---

527 Aziz S. Atiya, A History of Eastern Christianity, (Millwood, N.Y., Kraus: 1980), p. 26.
528 Editor, *Quick Reads*, Bible Editions & Versions, April-June, 2012, p. 20. Wallace's announcement has been met with great skepticism. Simon Gathercole, Editor of the *Journal For The Study of The New Testament*, at Cambridge University says, "I won't believe it until I see it." – Gordon Govier, *Sensation Before Scholarship*, Christianity Today, May 2012, p. 12. In an email dated 1/5/17 asking Prof. Wallace for clarification, I received this answer: "I'm afraid that I can't comment on it; I've signed a nondisclosure agreement."
529 Mark R. Shaw, The Kingdom of God in Africa, A Short History of African Christianity. (Grand Rapids, Michigan: Baker Books, 1996), p. 35.
530 Eusebius Pamphilius, The Ecclesiastical History, trans. Christian Frederick Cruse (Grand Rapids: Baker Book House, 1979), p. 65.
531 Elizabeth Isichei, A History of Christianity In Africa From Antiquity to the Present, (Grand Rapids, Michigan: William B. Eerdmans Publishing Company, 1995), p. 17.

while they were celebrating Easter in [the year] 68. Mark was dragged around the streets on a rope to be bled and bruised to death; a violent storm saved his body from being burnt by his tormentors and the Christians secretly buried it in a tomb carved beneath the altar of their church."[532]

Egyptian Christianity Expands

Mark Shaw, a lecturer at Nairobi Evangelical School of Theology and editor of *Africa Journal of Evangelical Theology,* affirms "that by the late second century Christianity was thriving in Egypt. Bishop Demetrius (189–231 A.D.) makes an abrupt appearance on the historical stage as the supervisor of a number of churches and subordinates as well as the patron of a rising theological school. The star of Egyptian Christianity shone almost as brightly as in Rome."[533]

"By 211 there were twenty Coptic bishops. Fragments of papyrus show that the new faith had moved far up the Nile Valley within a century; it then slowly penetrated south of the first cataract at Syene, modern Aswan, to the Nubian kingdoms and Ethiopia."[534]

The theological school to which Shaw makes reference was called the *Didascalia*. The name is Greek which simply means "teaching." It referred to the famous Catechetical School located in Alexandria. "The first great scholar who served as head of the *Didascalia* was Pantaenus. ... [He] came to Alexandria about the year 180 A.D. when he was appointed head of the School of Catechumens and remained there until he died shortly before 200 A.D.[535] He was followed by Clement of Alexandria, the most illustrious pupil of Pantaenus.

"The most important theologian and extensive author was Origen ... [who] joined the Catechetical School at an early age where he listened to the lectures of Pantaenus and Clement. ... For twenty-eight years, from 204–232 A.D., Origen worked in Alexandria. It was during this time that he traveled to Rome, Arabia, Antioch and Palestine. In Palestine ... he was ordained presbyter, an act which [Bishop] Demetrius of Alexandria interpreted as an infringement of his own right. Demetrius convened two synods; the first gathering resolved to banish Origen from Alexandria, the second determined that he was to be deprived of his ordination. In 232 A.D., after having settled in Caesarea, Origen established a flourishing school."[536]

---

532 Brian Moynahan, The Faith, A History of Christianity (New York: Doubleday, 2002), pp. 66-67.
533 Mark R. Shaw, The Kingdom of God in Africa A Short History of African Christianity. (Grand Rapids, Michigan: Baker Books, 1996), p. 27.
534 Brian Moynahan, The Faith, A History of Christianity (New York: Doubleday, 2002), p. 67.
535 Pantaenus, who was head of the renowned theological school of Alexandria, Egypt was appointed before 190 AD to preach the gospel in India. "Eusebius says that Pantaenus found among the Christians there a copy of the Gospel according to St. Matthew in 'Hebrew' characters, which was said to have been left by St. Bartholomew, who had preached in that country. St. Jerome, who repeats this, evidently understood the India in question to be our India, for he added that Pantaenus, who was a philosopher, was sent 'to preach Christ among the Brahmins and philosophers of that nation.'" – Cyril Bruce Firth, An Introduction to Indian Church History, (Madras: The Christian Literature Society, 1961), p. 19
536 Otto F.A. Meindarus, Christian Egypt Ancient And Modern, (Cairo: The American University in Cairo Press, 1977), pp. 3-4.

"Origen of Alexandria was one of the earliest Church Fathers to accept the 27 books of the New Testament as the complete Canon. Thus, both Old and New Testament Canons were established in Alexandria, Egypt."[537] The first church council to recognize the canon was at Bone, in what is now Algeria, in 393 A.D. (See also the sixth paragraph of Chapter 18.)

Theological Struggles

In contrast to notable scholars like those mentioned above who strengthened Egyptian Christianity, Arius,[538] a highly gifted but particularly notorious heretic, arose promoting a blasphemous teaching about Christ. He vigorously, adroitly and winsomely contended that Christ was not divine but totally human. When determined attempts by Egyptian church leaders and theologians to discredit and silence him failed, Emperor Constantine convened the Council of Nicaea in 325 A.D. as a supreme attempt to discredit Arius and stop the pernicious doctrine he espoused.

Though it exiled Arius, the Council of Nicaea was not successful in thwarting the continued growth of the heretical Christology conceived and propagated by him. In addition to spreading among German tribes east of the Rhine, (they ultimately rejected the Arian view as a false doctrine), ironically a Christology similar to that of Arius was embraced by Muhammad, the Arabian Prophet. It continues to be the Christology of Islam which has persuaded one-fifth of the human race that Jesus is not divine! Tragically and dogmatically, mediated through Islam, the heresy of Arius has triumphed in the hearts of not only eighty percent of the people of Egypt, but also among the 1.2 billion Muslims worldwide!

While "by 639 [A.D.], the majority of the Christians had accepted the dogmatic decisions of [the council of] Chalcedon [held in 451 A.D.], the Coptic population [of Egypt] followed its leaders in refusing to accept the decisions of the Council of Chalcedon and held to the Monophysite views."[539]

The Monophysite dogma has been the Christological cornerstone of Coptic Christians for many centuries. "The Egyptians, like their opponents, [except Arius] acknowledged, and acknowledge, that Christ was God and Man. They only say that both natures were united in Him, instead of being coexistent in Him, and that therefore it is irreverent to speak of two natures, as that implies imperfect union, whereas in Him there was no imperfection, the two natures were absolutely one God-Man."[540]

---

537 Sobhi Z. Ouida, *God's Heart is in Egypt* (unpublished Ph.D. dissertation, Western Conservative Baptist Seminary, Portland, Oregon), p. 17.
538 For additional discussion about Arius, see Chapter 13 under "Controversy About Christ."
539 Sobhi Z. Ouida, *God's Heart is in Egypt* (unpublished Ph.D. dissertation, Western Conservative Baptist Seminary, Portland, Oregon), p. 18.
540 Shawky F. Karas, <u>The Copts Since The Arab Invasion: Strangers In Their Land</u>, (Jersey City, New Jersey: The American, Canadian, and Australian C. Coptic Associations, 1985), p. 6.

Bible Translation

Underpinning, strengthening and enhancing gospel outreach in rural Egypt was an active program of Bible translation. "Beginning in the late third century and continuing well into the eighth century a periodic stream of translations in the major Coptic languages (Sahidic, Bohairic, and Bashmuric) were produced. With vernacular translations and the multiplication of local churches, the roots of the faith began to sink deeper into Egyptian soil."[541] This wide distribution of Scripture in the local languages of Egypt is probably what strengthened the church in Egypt enough to withstand the withering cyclonic storm of Islamic conquest, oppression, suppression and persecution.

CR

---

541 Mark R. Shaw, The Kingdom of God in Africa A Short History of African Christianity. (Grand Rapids, Michigan: Baker Books, 1996), p. 35.

Chapter 17

CHRISTIANITY SURVIVES TEMPESTUOUS CENTURIES IN EGYPT

Saladin, the great Muslim conqueror, shown in a stylized-idealized-almost canonized form, giving a ruling while seated on an Oriental (South Asian) throne. – Courtesy of Wikimedia Commons

From his capture of Crusader Jerusalem on October 2, 1187 till now, Saladin has been the unrivaled darling of the Muslim world. For example, in the decade of the 1950s, Egypt's "Abdel Nasser invoked [the memory and example of] Saladin continually in his efforts to forge the United Arab Republic."[542] More recently, "During a video address in front of his Afghan cave, Osama bin Laden ... called for 'a new battle, similar to the great battles of Islam, like [those of] the conqueror of Jerusalem.'"[543]

One of the greatest affronts anyone may fling in front of the Muslim world is to disdain the achievements of Saladin, their great conqueror. An example took place "in July 1920, when the French general Henri Gouraud took charge of Damascus [under a mandate from the League of Nations]. He strode to Saladin's tomb next to the Grand Mosque and exclaimed, to the everlasting disgust

---

[542] James Reston, Jr., Warriors of God, (New York: Doubleday, 2001), p. xviii.
[543] Angus Konstam, Historical Atlas of the Crusades, (New York: Thalamus Publishing, 2002), p. 6.

of modern Arabs, 'Saladin, we have returned. My presence here consecrates the victory of the Cross over the Crescent.'"[544]

General Gouraud's foolish boast notwithstanding, the power of the memory of Saladin's prowess is so strong that, "in the seemingly endless struggle of modern-day Arabs to reassert the essentially Arab nature of Palestine, Saladin lives, vibrantly, as a symbol of hope and as the stuff of myth."[545] The adoration of Saladin is still a living issue for many Muslims. Recently, Egyptian scholar and philosopher Youssef Zeidan called Saladin "one of the most despicable figures in human history." By doing so, he has brought a storm of protest on his own head.[546]

Saladin was born of Kurdish parents in 1137 A.D. in Tikrit, the home town of Saddam Hussein, recent dictator of Iraq. His birth took place just thirty-nine years after the knights and the rabble of The First Crusade had captured Jerusalem, massacring seventy thousand unresisting Muslim and Jewish inhabitants, thus bringing perpetual infamy upon themselves and upon the cause of Christ! "William of Tyre wrote, 'and even the sight of the victors covered with blood from head to foot was also a ghastly sight' ... That evening, 'full of happiness and weeping for joy,' the Crusaders went to worship Christ in the church of his Holy Sepulcher."[547]

Egypt's Christians Survive Transition from Fatimids to Ayyubids

It was that fabled Saladin who wrenched control of Egypt from the Fatimids[548] and forced the Muslims in the country of the Nile to renounce Shi'ism, which the Fatimids had imposed, and again to embrace Sunni Islam.

One may understand what a turning point that was, not only in Egyptian Muslim history but in the history of all Islam, when he understands that "the Fatimids ... were moved by more than personal or dynastic ambition; they were the heads of a great religious movement—the Isma'ili branch of the Shi'ah sect —and as such aimed at nothing less than the overthrow of the existing religious and political order in all Islam. Unlike their predecessors [who had ruled Egypt], they [the Fatimids] refused to offer even nominal recognition to the Abbasid Caliphs, whom they rejected as usurpers. ... The coming of the crusaders indirectly sealed its [the Fatimid Caliphate's] fate, for in the great 12th-century contest between Islam and Christendom there was no room for a schis-

---

544 James Reston, Jr., Warriors of God, (New York: Doubleday, 2001), p. xvii.
545 James Reston, Jr., Warriors of God, (New York: Doubleday, 2001), p. xiv.
546 https://english.alarabiya.net/en/variety/2017/05/14/Egyptian-scholar-in-hot-water-for-calling-historical-Muslim-leader-Saladin-despicable-.html Accessed 7/14/17.
547 Brian Moynahan, The Faith, A History of Christianity, (New York: Doubleday, 2002), pp. 238-239.
548 The Fatimids ruled Egypt from 969 to 1171 A.D. They "appeared as successors to the sixth imam, even managed to occupy Egypt in 969 and establish themselves in Cairo, their newly founded residence. Although the Fatimid caliphs were not Twelver Shiites but Ismailis (they were descendants of Ismail, a son of the sixth imam, Jafar), the establishment of a Shia caliphate in Egypt served as a powerful impetus for Shiism in general. The tenth century could almost be characterized as the 'Shia century.'" – Heinz Halm, The Shiites, A Short History, (Princeton NJ; Markus Wiener Publishers, 2007), pp. 96-97.

matic caliphate on the Muslim side. ... In 1171, as the last [Fatimid] caliph lay dying in his palace, Saladin, who as nominal vizier [prime minister] had become the real master of Egypt, allowed a preacher to recite the bidding prayer [the call to prayer, the azaan] in the name of the Abbasid caliph of Baghdad. The Fatimid caliphate, already dead as a religious and political force, was now formally abolished. After more than two centuries, Egypt had returned to the Sunni fold."[549]

Saladin "succumbed to a fever and died in 1193. ... [but his] descendants were to rule over Egypt until 1250. ... The Ayyubids [named after Saladin whose full name was Salah al-Din al-Ayyub, but known in the West as Saladin] were good rulers; they improved the irrigation system, extended canals, dykes and dams, ensured public security so that travelers and commerce were not interfered with, and founded a number of scholarly institutions which were to make Egypt a great intellectual center."[550]

Egypt's Christians Ruled by a Slave Dynasty

Next to the last Ayyubid ruler of Egypt, Al-Salih Ayyub, because he doubted the loyalty of his own army, bought "enough slaves to make up a regiment. These slaves, known as *mamluks*, an Arabic word meaning 'owned,' were both to save his kingdom and destroy his dynasty at one and the same time."[551]

"These slaves, who had initially formed a caste, became a growing power in the Ayyubid army and eventually overthrew the ruler, naming one of their own officers as Sultan. ... The Bahrite Mamluks [so named because their barracks were on the bank of the Nile River, the *bahr* in Arabic] brought back to Egypt the grandeur it had lost since antiquity. They successfully defended Syria against the Mongols, expelled the last Crusader states from the Syro-Palestinian littoral and extended their empire to the upper Euphrates and Cilicia."[552]

"From 1250 to 1517 A.D. Egypt was ruled by the Mamluk dynasties, upstart slaves and soldiers of the guard. Under such as these, in 1301, Christians were made to wear the blue turban and Jews the yellow turban. In 1321 fanatical Muslim conspirators destroyed all of the principal churches of Egypt after looting them. In revenge the Copts fired many mosques, palaces, and private Muslim houses. There were mass executions without trial in which both Copts and Muslims perished. Finally the Sultan yielded to the vast and dangerous mob, and there was a massacre of Christians without parallel. Christians were for-

---
549 Bernard Lewis, *Fatimids*, The New Encyclopaedia Britannica, (Chicago: Encyclopaedia Britannica, Inc. 1979), Vol. 7, pp. 193-195.
550 Afaf Lutfi al-Sayyid Marsot, A Short History of Modern Egypt, (Cambridge: Cambridge University Press, 2002), pp. 23-24.
551 Afaf Lutfi al-Sayyid Marsot, A Short History of Modern Egypt, (Cambridge: Cambridge University Press, 2002), p. 24.
552 Youssef Courbage and Philippe Fargues, Christians and Jews Under Islam, trans. Judy Mabro (New York: I.B. Tauris Publishers, 1998), p. 18.

bidden to ride horses or mules, or even asses unless they sat facing backward. The blue turban was again made obligatory. A bell had to be worn about the neck when entering a [public] bath. Copts were expelled from all public offices and from the employ of Muslim dignitaries. As a result there were in 1354–1355 A.D. vast [numbers of] conversions [to Islam] accompanied by the destruction of churches in Upper Egypt."[553]

The great achievement of the Mamluks, in the broader context of world history, was their defeat of the Mongols. "The Assassins [the infamous Muslim terrorist sect whose main headquarters were at Alamut in northern Iran] were exterminated and Baghdad [capital of the waning Abbasid Caliphate] fell early in 1258. [Both had succumbed to the forces of the Mongol Hulagu.] After the death of Mongke [Hulagu's brother who was fighting against China] in 1259, armed conflict broke out between rival claimants, causing Hulagu to concentrate the bulk of his troops in Azerbaijan leaving only a skeleton force in Syria. This soon became known at Cairo, and the Mamluk sultan took the opportunity to march against the pagan [Mongol] enemies of the faith. At Ayn Jalut [the Springs of Goliath] near Nazareth on 3 September 1260, the superior Mamluk army inflicted a crushing defeat [on the Mongol military machine]. This battle was a turning point in history. The Mongol advance in the West was never seriously renewed, and the spell of their invincibility [had been] shattered forever."[554]

"The local Christians [in Syria], mainly Armenians, [had] made common cause with the [Mongol] khan [Hulagu] and even provided him with soldiers. ... When they emerged victorious over the Mongols at Ayn Jalut in 1260, the Mamluks, who by this time had overthrown the Ayyubids, made the Christians pay for this collaboration. Eschewing the tolerance shown by their Fatimid and Ayyubid predecessors who, despite the two Crusader invasions of Egypt, had not made life particularly hard for the Christians, they devastated the Armenian Kingdom of Cilicia and the Principality of Antioch without bothering to distinguish between [the Crusader] Franks and indigenous Christians. ... The new masters of Egypt and Syria, as recently converted military slaves, were armed with the neophyte's zeal and contributed greatly to the degradation of the conditions of life of its Arab Christian and Jewish subjects. Initially limited in scale, their extortions were soon directed at all Arab Christians, who for three centuries were exposed to a general hardening of Islam."[555]

"The Copts realized that they had to give up many material privileges in order to retain their spiritual heritage. Before the crusades, however, they adapted themselves to the conditions of Islamic rule without the loss of their way of life, and were generally accepted and often very highly revered by the caliphs.

---
553 William H. Worrell, A Short Account of the Copts, (Ann Arbor: University of Michigan Press, 1945), pp. 47-48.
554 Geoffrey Barraclough (ed.), Harper Collins Atlas Of World History, (Ann Arbor, Michigan: Borders Press, 2001), pp. 128-129.
555 Youssef Courbage and Philippe Fargues, Christians and Jews Under Islam, trans. Judy Mabro (New York: I.B. Tauris Publishers, 1998), p. 54.

They were the clerks, tax-collectors and treasurers of the caliphate ... The Crusades, being the Holy Wars of the Cross, antagonized the followers of Muhammad toward all worshipers of the Cross, whether Latin, Greek or Coptic, and so a new agonizing chapter began in the Copts' unending patience."[556]

The Christian character of the Copts, who worked in the internal revenue service of the Muslim sovereigns of Egypt, sometimes entangled them in contradictory inconsistencies with the nature of the work as it was visualized by the rulers. For example, a Copt whose name was Girgis became treasurer during the regime of Muhammad Ali. Girgis was "a leading figure in the Coptic bourgeoisie who attracted the sympathy of the people with his gentleness in fiscal matters, but whom the governor had to get rid of for the same reason."[557]

Egyptian Christians Come Under the Ottoman Turks

(See Appendix H, division V, section C.)

Far to the north, ominous developments were taking place which would prove fatal to the Mamluk empire. The Abbasid Caliphs, whose capital was Baghdad, would trust neither the Arabs nor the Persians to lead and staff their armies. Their solution consisted in hiring thousands of Turkish soldiers of fortune to whom, ultimately, the caliphs became captive. Constituting the leading branch of those Turks were the Seljuks, followed by a junior branch, the Ottomans. Ultimately, it was the Seljuks who dominated the Abbasid Caliphs. The fortunes of both branches of the Turks were immeasurably enhanced by their victory over Byzantium in the Battle of Manzikurt [Manzikert, Malazgirt, Malaskirgt] (now in eastern Turkey, about 25 miles NW of Lake Van) in 1071 A.D. "Manzikurt was the worst disaster ever experienced by the Byzantines until the final fall of Constantinople to the Turks in 1453. [It was so overwhelming that] the imperial army had virtually ceased to exist and the whole of Asia Minor lay open to the Turkman invaders."[558] We should note that this victory allowed the Turkification of Anatolia to begin. Anatolia is the major land area controlled by the current Turkish government.

Following the Battle of Manzikert, the Seljuks allowed their junior partners, the Ottomans, to migrate into western areas of Asia Minor while in Baghdad they retained their dominating oversight of the Abbasid Caliphate, a role ultimately disastrous to the Seljuks. As previously mentioned, in 1258 the Mongol Hulagu, grandson of Genghis Khan, led his wolves in an almost totally destructive attack on Baghdad, destroying the Abbasid Caliphate and simultaneously breaking the power of the Seljuk Turks. Those events opened the door of opportunity for the Ottoman Turks who, seizing it, founded their empire in 1299 A.D. They continued

---

556 Aziz S. Atiya, A History of Eastern Christianity, (Millwood, New York: Kraus Reprint, 1980), pp. 92-93. (Note: The historian Aziz Suryal Atiya founded the Institute of Coptic Studies in Cairo.)
557 Youssef Courbage and Philippe Fargues, Christians and Jews Under Islam, trans. Judy Mabro (New York: I.B. Tauris Publishers, 1998), p. 73.
558 John Bagot Glubb, The Course of Empire, (London: Hodder and Stoughton, 1965) pp. 207-210.

to gain strength, which prepared them to face the Egyptian Mamluks with overwhelming power in a decisive battle on August 24, 1516 at Marj Dabiq, just north of Aleppo, Syria.

"In the Ottoman-Mamluk conflict, the Mamluks were severely hampered by their sneering disdain for firearms, which they refused to carry, regarding them as effeminate innovations. Unlike the Ottomans, they never fully made the transition to the gunpowder age and unwisely relegated their guns and cannons to inferior units. Consequently they paid a staggering price in battle, despite their celebrated valor and martial elan."[559]

"Described as the most brilliant cavalry of the age, the Mamluks entered battle expecting to face the enemy in a normal hand-to-hand combat at which they excelled, and for which they had been trained. Instead they were met by a deadly hail of gunpowder that decimated their ranks before they even got within hailing distance of the enemy. Mamluks who were captured alive raged at the Ottomans, asking them to give them a fighting chance, to fight like men in hand-to-hand combat instead of aiming these fire-spewing instruments at them. The Ottomans, who were not fighting a war for fun, but for profit, contemptuously laughed at the Mamluks who believed there was a code of honor in fighting a war which had to be respected or the soldier disgraced. The Ottomans won the day through superior technology."[560]

The Ottomans, after their history-changing victory at Marj Dabiq (just north of Aleppo) over the Mamluks, rather contemptuously, utilized the surviving Mamluk administrative cadres in Egypt to carry out the imperial governance of their new territory on the banks of the Nile. Because of those residual cadres being used by the Ottomans to help them govern Egypt, one often finds it was still being referred to as Mamluk Egypt, but it is very clear that the ultimate authority resided in Istanbul, the capital of the Ottoman Empire, not within Egypt itself.

Egyptian Christians Under Napoleon

The Ottoman period of Egyptian history was interrupted by two remarkable leaders. First was Napoleon who led a French expeditionary force through the Mediterranean and conquered Egypt by his stunning victory at the Battle of the Pyramids in July 1798. "Napoleon's 'orders' from the Directory, were 'to clear the English from all their oriental possessions which he will be able to reach, and notably to destroy all their stations in the Red Sea; to cut through the Isthmus of Suez and to take the necessary measures to assume the free and exclusive possession of that sea to the French Republic.'"[561]

---

559 Peter N. Stearns (ed.), The Encyclopedia of World History, (New York: Houghton Mifflin Company, 2001), p. 129.
560 Afaf Lutfi al-Sayyid Marsot, A Short History of Modern Egypt, (Cambridge: Cambridge University Press, 2002), p. 37.
561 Lord Kinross, The Ottoman Centuries, The Rise and Fall of the Turkish Empire, (New York: Morrow Quill Paperbacks, 1977), p. 424.

The strategic importance of Napoleon's Red Sea military goal becomes clear when we realize that, Great Britain's "East India Company sent more than one expedition in the 1770s from India to Suez, whence the freight was transported under Egyptian guarantee to the Mediterranean for shipment to England. By opening up this route, which foreshadowed the speeding-up of communications in the following century, Calcutta was brought within two months of London, as compared with five months by the Cape Route."[562]

This part of Napoleon's grand scheme was brought to utter disaster on August 1, 1798 when British Admiral Nelson's naval squadron found the French fleet at anchor in Abukir Bay, a few miles east of Alexandria, and totally destroyed it. The coup de grace to the ill-fated French eastern thrust for power and glory was given in 1799 by the defeat of Napoleon's army by a combined British and Ottoman force at the fort of Acre, in Palestine, near the point where Mt. Carmel meets the sea. Following those two disasters, Napoleon with his personal staff secretly returned to France where, surprisingly, he raised yet another army to carry out the rest of his grand design. That effort ended in total disaster in Belgium at the Battle of Waterloo on June 18, 1815.

"In 1798, Girgis Al-Gauhari wrote an appeal to Napoleon ... to lift the disabilities of the Copts and grant them a full measure of equality with their Muslim brethren. Napoleon's initial response was favorable, though he never sacrificed the interest of the Muslim majority for the sake of the Coptic minority; and we have to remember that numerous French soldiers, including Napoleon at the head of the list, posed as Muslims. ... Though the Copts were not in any way favored by their French co-religionists, the fact remains that they were not subjected to repression."[563] In Egypt, the withering wind from Arabia was only briefly assuaged, not ended.

"The French expedition of 1798–1801 offered the Latin missionary more freedom of movement in the country, and a few Copts seem to have had no objection to union with Rome, until the bishop of Girga, Anba Yusab al-Abahh, known for his sanctity and eloquence, rose to defend Coptic doctrine and silence Roman propaganda."[564]

Egypt's Christians Live Under an Albanian Genius and His Successors

The second outstanding personality who looms large in Egyptian affairs during the Ottoman period of Egyptian history was Muhammad Ali, born in Albania in 1769. "With no education but endowed with ability amounting to genius, [he] landed [in Egypt] as a soldier of fortune in the Ottoman army. By 1805 he had become pasha, or governor, and soon secured virtual independence and founded a dynasty that ruled the country until 1952. With the help of French

---
562 George E. Kirk, A Short History of the Middle East, from the Rise of Islam to Modern Times, (Washington, D.C.: Public Affairs Press, 1949), p. 72.
563 Aziz S. Atiya, A History of Eastern Christianity, (Millwood, New York: Kraus Reprint, 1980), p. 101.
564 Aziz S. Atiya, A History of Eastern Christianity, (Millwood, New York: Kraus Reprint, 1980), p. 112.

and other foreign advisers, he established a modern army and navy and the most efficient government in the region and started a process of rapid economic and social development."[565]

To prevent Muhammad Ali from turning his Egyptian-based empire into a competitive world power, able to thwart their own designs, Britain, France and Russia cooperated to reverse his military successes in Greece and Syria. However, he was allowed by those European powers to establish a hereditary regime in Egypt. Almost exactly one century after Muhammad Ali's death in Alexandria on August 2, 1849, King Farouk (the last of Muhammad Ali's line of ruling descendants to sit on the throne of Egypt) was deposed and sent into exile in 1952 in a coup led by Mohammed Naguib and Gamal Abdel Nasser.

It was during the years of the Muhammad Ali dynasty that Protestant missions came to Egypt. The Anglicans began working in 1815 and renewed their efforts in 1882. The United Presbyterian Church of the United States of America began their work in 1854. It has grown till now the Presbyterians constitute the largest Protestant church in Egypt.

From the extreme but abortive effort of Egyptian President Nasser to establish a united Arab empire, events take us to the very courageous but tragic rule of Anwar el-Sadat, Nasser's successor. Sadat boldly dared to make peace with Israel, a step for which he was assassinated on October 6, 1981. On Sadat's death his vice-president, Hosni Mubarak automatically became president. Precariously, until January 29, 2011, Mubarak ruled without having appointed a vice-president. On that very late date he named Omar Suleiman as his vice-president.

Egypt became engulfed in the widespread Arab uprisings known as "The Arab Spring" which began in Tunisia on December 18, 2010. One of the important aspects of that movement "has been a persistent call for Arab governments to become independent of foreign influence. [Should that happen, the withering wind from Arabia would blow even more fiercely.] Dictators such as Egyptian President Hosni Mubarak were upbraided by protestors as 'agents' of foreign powers, especially the United States and Israel."[566]

"Mubarak was ousted after 18 days of demonstrations during the 2011 Egyptian Revolution, when, on 11 February, Vice President Omar Suleiman announced that Mubarak had resigned as President and transferred authority to the Supreme Council of the Armed Forces."[567]

Immediate Consequences

On websites such as YouTube, one could witness "Muslim mobs that began throwing rocks at Coptic Christians on October 8, 2011. These young Copts

---
565 Charles Issawi, *The Near East*, The Columbia History of the World, ed. John A. Garraty and Peter Gay (New York: Harper & Row, Publishers, 1972), p. 819.
566 Augustus, Richard Norton, *Arab Revolts Upend Old Assumptions*, Current History, January 2012, p. 16.
567 https://en.wikipedia.org/wiki/Hosni_Mubarak, p. 1.

had been protesting the burning of a Coptic church in Aswan and the failure of the Egyptian authorities to respond satisfactorily. Frustrated with the traditional Coptic adoption of a *dhimmi* (subordinate religion) status toward Egypt's Muslim majority, the young Copts defiantly left Coptic sections of Cairo to march through Muslim neighborhoods. After the first rocks were thrown, the army came in to suppress the demonstration and ran down protestors with large military vehicles."[568]

The atrocity goes on unabated. On May 26, 2017, "heavily armed Islamists in Egypt ambushed a youth pilgrimage to a monastery, shooting dozens of bus passengers to death and leaving more to succumb to their wounds on a desert road. Up to 28 people have been reported dead in the attack in Minya Province, with another 23 injured, though casualty numbers are still being confirmed."[569]

Skipping and Focusing

This account has not included the construction of the Suez Canal, the period of British dominance in Egypt, Nasser's nationalization of the Suez Canal or Egypt's role in the repeated Arab-Israeli wars. However, in pursuit of our main purpose, we must take a brief further look at the current situation for Egypt's Copts. "Disappointment in the political institutions ... has spurred the Copts to strengthen their community, in order to make their voice heard more effectively in politics, again with the aim of national integration. The fact that this goal has still not been achieved is shown by the persistence of a whole series of laws which in practice do not recognize the same rights for Copts as for other citizens. One example is the law in force at present regarding the building and restoration of places of Christian worship. Permission for this is only obtainable by special decree from the President of the Republic, which is only issued upon satisfaction of a whole series of requirements, which include a minimum distance from the nearest mosque. No such conditions are necessary for the building or restoration of mosques. Besides this example regarding places of worship, there are ... [many] legal and social practices which tend to favor affiliation to Islam. These include the law by which Arabic is only taught by Muslim teachers at school, the public funding of the Muslim school system, under the authority of Al-Azhar [University], while the Christian schools receive no funds from the State, and the clear and significant decrease in the number of Copts employed in all sectors of public administration, where Muslims seem to have preference. ...

"As a part of their campaign in favor of an Islamic State ruled by the shari`a, these movements often commit acts of violence against the Copts, who, according to some of their leaders [i.e., Egypt's Muslim leaders], should be relegated again to the status of *dhimmi*. Since the spread of Islamic ideology, there have been numerous religious conflicts, both in the country and in the towns and universities, particularly in the area of Assiut, which traditionally has a

---

568 David Aikman, *The Worldwide Attack On Christians*, Commentary, February 2012, p. 37.
569 Email from www.MorningStarNews, May 30, 2017.

large Coptic population. The interesting aspect of the Copts' response to political and cultural developments in Egyptian society is that in defending their rights, they do not insist on the fact that they are a minority whose rights must be defended, but on the State's responsibility to guarantee equal rights to all citizens."[570]

Doctrinal Stance

Survivors of centuries of discrimination and persecution, the Copts have held to their faith in Christ. A testimony to that fact is their current creed which states, "Truly we believe in one God, God the Father Almighty, Creator of heaven and earth, of all things visible and invisible.

"We believe in one Lord Jesus Christ, the unique son of God, begotten of the Father before all times, light of light, very God of very God, begotten not made, being of one substance with the Father by whom all things were made. Who for us men and for our salvation came down from heaven, and was incarnate by the Holy Ghost and of the Virgin Mary, became man, and was crucified for us under Pontius Pilate. He suffered, and was buried and the third day he rose again according to the Scriptures and ascended into heaven. He sitteth on the right hand of the Father, and He shall come again with his glory to judge the quick and the dead, whose kingdom shall have no end.

"And we believe in the Holy Ghost, the Lord and Giver of life, who proceedeth from the Father, who with the Father and the Son together is worshiped and who speaks through the prophets.

"And we believe in one catholic [i.e., universal] and apostolic Church, we acknowledge one baptism for the remission of sins. And we look for the resurrection of the dead, and the life of the world to come."[571]

It is very regrettable that some of these biblically sound positions are carried out in blatantly anti-biblical ways. For example, in violation of a New Testament principle that "all shall know me, from the least to the greatest" (Hebrews 8:11), the Copts practice infant baptism! Obviously, those infants do not yet know the Lord.

Do Western Christians Care?

"Since the late 1990s, Islamists in Egypt have killed more than 1,300 Christians, according to Operation World. The U.S. war on terrorism has led to a

---

570 Andrea Pacini, ed., Christian Communities in the Arab Middle East, The Challenge of the Future, Introduction, (New York, Oxford University Press, Inc., 1998), pp. 15-18. In addition to the totally adverse prejudice against the building or repair of church buildings the internal sloth in the state bureaucracy is so bad that "Cairenes like to say, more bodies are at rest [in the bureaucracy] than in all the tombs of ancient Egypt." – Milton Viorst, Sandcastles, The Arabs in Search of the Modern World (New York: Alfred A. Knopf, 1994), p . 83.
571 Bishop Athanasius, The Doctrines of The Coptic Orthodox Church of Alexandria, (Egypt: 1977), pp. 29-30.

crackdown on Islamic extremists in U.S.-friendly Egypt—but the level of persecution against Christians remains, on balance, unchanged."[572]

"Aside from evangelical Protestants, most Western churches are uninterested in defending the rights of their co-religionists in the Islamic world. Most mainline protestant churches, from the Anglican Church and its U.S. and international branches to the Methodist, Baptist, Mennonites and other churches have organized no sustained efforts to protect or defend the rights of Christians in the Muslim world."[573]

Those who wear the name of Christ in the great historic country of Egypt have withstood the withering wind from Arabia for many centuries. Pray that the Lord's church may soon flourish again, bearing much fruit as a result of the courageous stand countless followers of Christ have made through many historic vicissitudes in the country of the Nile.

From Saladin's Victory in Cairo to the Beginning of European Colonialism in North Africa

The Shia Fatimid General Jawhar gained control of Egypt in 969 A.D. and founded Cairo as a new Fatimid capital. The Fatimids held the Abbasid caliphs in Baghdad in utter and total contempt. At the peak of their power, the Fatimids ruled from Tunisia to Syria. When Saladin, in 1171, brought Egypt back into the Sunni fold, it ended two-hundred-two years of Fatimid rule over North Africa, Egypt and the Levant. Following Saladin's victory in Egypt, there was continued but declining regional Fatimid influence from their capitals to the west, at Raqqada, Mahdia and al-Mansuriya.

In 1258, only eighty years following Saladin's victory at Cairo on behalf of the Abbasids and Sunni Islam, the Abbasid Caliphate and its capital at Baghdad were destroyed by the Mongols. Following the destruction of Baghdad the Sunni cause was carried forward by the Ottoman Turks. The Ottomans had three main goals: <u>The first goal</u> was the capture of Constantinople, which they finally achieved in 1453 A.D. <u>The second goal</u> was to capture Vienna, gateway to the conquest of Europe. In 1529 after conquering the whole Balkan Peninsula, with the exception of Greece, the Ottoman army was poised at the gates of Vienna to deliver the death blow. At that critical moment, the Iranian Safavids, whose capital was Isfahan, attacked the Ottomans' eastern border making it urgently necessary for the Ottomans to move their troops from Vienna to face the new peril. <u>Finally, the third goal</u> was to reclaim North Africa for Sunni Islam. In this cause, utilizing the barbarity of the buccaneer Barbarossa brothers, they captured Algiers in 1516.

Algeria. For three centuries, from 1516 to France's conquest of Algeria in 1830, the Ottomans—working through the Barbary pirates—governed Algeria and captured non-Muslim shipping throughout the Mediterranean. They confiscated car-

---

572 *Egypt, Heightened Hostilities*, <u>Christianity Today</u>, December 9, 2002, p. 58.
573 Malcolm Hedding, *The Enemy Within*, <u>The Jerusalem Post, Christian Edition</u>, November 2011, p. 43.

goes and enslaved non-Muslim crews and passengers. Additionally, those pirates made many enslaving raids on European islands and coastal areas in the Mediterranean.

Tunisia. In a fifty-year period, from 647 to 697 A.D., during Islam's early expansion, the Muslim military forces of the Ummayad Caliphate conquered Tunisia. Subsequently however, the Fatimids wrenched Tunisia from Sunni governance. Following the destruction of the Abbasid Caliphate, the arduous work of bringing North Africa back under Sunni control fell to the Ottoman Turks. In just fifty years, 1534 to 1574, the Ottomans gained sovereignty over Tunisia, which they held until 1881 when France conquered Tunisia.

Libya. By an effort beginning as early as 647 A.D. under the caliphate which ruled from Medina and was consummated during the Ummayad Caliphate ruling from Damascus, Libya was brought into the fold of Islam. In 750 A.D., rule over Libya passed to the victorious Abbasid Caliphate which ruled from Baghdad. The Fatimids, on their way to conquer Egypt, snatched control of Libya and invited the ravaging Arab tribes of Beni Hilal and Beni Sulaim (Sulaym) into Libya. (See Chapter 19 under "More Arab Predators.") In 1517, by conquest, Libya was brought into the Ottoman Empire. Subsequently, in 1911 it was conquered by Italy.

Morocco. Arabs of the Ummayad Caliphate, ruling from Damascus, conquered Morocco in 683 A.D. Most of the indigenous Berbers converted to Islam, though they maintained their ethnic identity, never merging with the Arabs.

Whether the international capital of Islam was Damascus, seat of the Umayyad Caliphate, or Baghdad, capital of the Abbasid Caliphate, it was extremely difficult to govern Islam's far-flung western territories. To ameliorate that persistent problem, Kairouan, now in Tunisia, was established. It was the capital city for the personal representative of the reigning caliph. Extreme harshness was used whenever a governor or general in far-western North Africa was thought to have shown independence or insubordination. When Baghdad was destroyed by the Mongols in 1258, the Ottoman Turks found it very difficult to immediately put efficient and effective government control in the remote regions of North Africa. One conspicuous evidence of that difficulty is seen in the fact that the Ottomans were never able to occupy Morocco, however, Morocco was vulnerable to European influence. "In the nineteenth and twentieth centuries Britain, France, and other powers proclaimed 'protectorates' over some areas—Morocco, Tunisia, parts of coastal east Africa, and parts of Vietnam—under the fiction that the local ruler, while remaining sovereign, had voluntarily ceded some of his powers to the protecting empire."[574]

CR

---

[574] Jane Burbank & Frederick Cooper, Empires in World History, (New Jersey: Princeton University Press, 2010), p. 17.

Chapter 18

NORTH AFRICAN CHRISTIANITY, CANDIDATE FOR TRAGEDY

The ruins of a church building at Latrun, Libya, near Apollonia (Arabic Al Athrun). It is one of over a thousand known ruins of church buildings in North Africa. The churches which used those buildings died mainly as a result of the Muslim conquest.
– Photo by Galen R. Frysinger

In discussing the history of Christianity in North Africa, we are at a great disadvantage. There is no contemporary account of the initial Gospel triumph in this enormous area comparable to the record in the book of Acts which documents Gospel triumph in the countries situated north of the Mediterranean. However, there are two intriguing historical vignettes which may give us clues about how the church began in North Africa.

First, just as Gospel evangelism in the regions north of the Mediterranean began from the church in Antioch, it is probable that North African evangelism got its initial impetus from the church in Alexandria, Egypt. There is strong historical evidence that the Alexandrian church was committed to evangelism. In Chapter 16, under the title "Egyptian Christianity Expands," (footnote 535) we have already encountered the career of Pantaenus whom the Alexandrian church sent on a mission trip to southwest India. Since Pantaenus was the head of the catechetical school in Alexandria, it is reasonable to assume he inspired men in that student body with great evangelistic zeal. It may have been some of his disciples who initially carried the message of Jesus across North Africa. Whatever influence Alexandria may have initially had in western North Africa, it was later completely overshadowed by the dominating spiritual and ecclesiastical influence emanating from Rome.

Secondly, Luke tells us that on the day of Pentecost, when Peter preached the sermon which brought the church into being, there were among those who heard that history-making message some from "the parts of Libya about Cyrene." (Acts 2:10) Did some of those men respond positively to Peter's exhortation to repent and "be baptized everyone of you in the name of Jesus unto the remission of your sins" that they might receive the gift of the Holy Spirit? If so, when they returned to Libya they would have constituted Christ's initial church in that area. The vitality of the North African church is certainly reflected in the fact that Lucius, a Christian brother from Cyrene, became prominent among the leaders of the church in Antioch. His name appears in the list of the prophets and teachers in that church. (Acts 13:1) One wonders if Lucius had been sent to Antioch by the church in Cyrene to assist in bringing that church to higher levels of spiritual attainment.

"Cyrenian Jews are referred to in the book of Acts (2:10; 6:9; 11:20; 13:1). In one place (6:9) the Alexandrians are coupled with them. An Alexandrian Christian, Apollos, appears in Corinth and Ephesus as a missionary preacher, but when and where he became a Christian is unknown (Acts 18:24-19:1)."[575]

In any case, up to the time Islamic military forces—flushed by their series of stunning victories—raced to the west, following their brutal conquest of Egypt, "the Levant[576] and North Africa [had] constituted the heartlands of Christianity, with most of its population, key institutions, and cultural centers."[577]

The assertion that North Africa had been one of the two areas constituting the heartland of Christianity is supported by the fact that "at Bone [modern Annaba in Algeria], 125 miles east of Bougie, [modern Bijaya/Bejaia,] ... in the year 393 a council of bishops[578] ... first recognized the canon of the New Testament."[579] Though this seems to have been the first church council to have recognized the canon, Origen and the church in Alexandria had recognized it earlier. (See Chapter 16 under "Egyptian Christianity Expands.") Also, "in his monumental survey [entitled] *The Provinces of the Roman Empire*, the great historian Theodor Mommsen once remarked of [African] Christianity that, 'if it arose in Syria, it was in and through Africa that it became the religion of the world.'"[580]

The most conspicuous development which made North African Christianity especially noteworthy was the ministry of Bishop Augustine of Hippo. Through his writings it may honestly be said that Christianity, as Peter Brown affirmed

---

575 C. P. Groves, The Planting of Christianity in Africa, (London: Lutterworth Press, 1964), Vol 1, p. 34.
576 Levant from Italian *levante,* the east (where the sun rises). The Levant, derivative of the Latin levare, to raise. The EAST: Orient. Specifically, the countries washed by the eastern part of the Mediterranean and its contiguous waters.
577 Daniel Pipes, In The Path of God, Islam and Political Power, (New York: Basic Books, Inc., Publishers, 1983), p. 83.
578 This is the council which church historians usually call the Council of Hippo. The ruins of Hippo or, as it was also called, Hippo Regius, are only one mile to the south of Annaba.
579 Rick Atkinson, An Army at Dawn, The War in North Africa, 1942–1943, (New York: Henry Holt and Company, 2002), p. 175.
580 Peter Brown, Augustine of Hippo, A Biography, (Berkeley: University of California Press, 2000), p. 461.

in his biography of Augustine, "became the religion of the world." The most touching of Augustine's writings is found in Confessions but his writing carrying the greatest ecclesiastical impact is The City of God. However, it should be clearly recognized that Augustine's basic concept of the church, as expounded in The City of God, violates Jesus' clear teaching of the separation of church and state. (See Matthew 22:21.) This led, even during Augustine's lifetime, to the Roman Catholic Church becoming a persecuting power. (Augustine's war against the Donatists has been briefly discussed in Chapter 16 under "Resilient Christianity.")

Two other North African church leaders, Tertullian (c.155–c.240 A.D.) and Cyprian (c.200–c.258 A.D.), also left their mark on Christian thinking. Knowing this helps us understand the validity of the assertion that—through North Africa—Christianity became the religion of the world.

"Tertullian is the first known major Christian theologian who thought and wrote in Latin. He came from the important North African city of Carthage, which [under Hannibal] in the third and second centuries BCE had nearly succeeded in ending the steady rise of the Roman Republic. Its conquest, destruction and refoundation as a Roman colony had been so thoroughgoing that it was now a center of Latin culture, with its own flourishing schools of advanced education; it is likely that a Latin-speaking Christian church emerged first here rather than in Rome."[581]

Cyprian also strengthened the North African church. He "was an ardent admirer of Tertullian, and may be regarded as his disciple. Cyprian became bishop of the Carthaginian church so shortly after his conversion as to cause much dissatisfaction among the presbyters.[582] But the Christian community had become so impressed with his sanctity and his fitness for the highest position in the North African Church, that he was enthusiastically appointed notwithstanding the opposition. ... He transferred the life and theology of Tertullian into the Catholic Church. Though a man of great holiness, Cyprian may be said to have done more for the development of hierarchical views than any man of his age. ... Cyprian was the first to establish clearly the [anti-biblical] distinction between presbyters and bishops, and the primacy of the Roman church as the *Cathedra Petri*."[583]

Historian Moynahan called North Africa "an ancient bastion of the faith." He noted, however, that it "had been softened up by schism and heresy." He concluded that, ultimately, its standing was totally nullified because "no remnant was to survive [since] it did not withstand the [withering wind of the]

---

[581] Diarmaid MacCulloch, Christianity, the First Three-Thousand Years, (New York, Viking, 2010), p. 144.
[582] During the apostolic era of church history, the words 'elder' and 'bishop' referred to a single position in the organization of the church. Compare Acts 20:17 with Acts 20:28.
[583] Albert Henry Newman, A Manual of Church History, (Philadelphia: The American Baptist Publication Society, 1933), Vol. I, pp. 265-266.

Moslems."[584] Through this survey, the collapse of Christianity all across North Africa is one of the realities we seek to understand more fully. Hopefully, clarity will result from reviewing events and participants leading up to the stunning and ultimate disappearance of any organized expression of Christian faith in this extensive and highly strategic region.

Immensity of North Africa

North Africa matters, not only because it was at one time a major part of the heartland of Christianity, but also because it embraces a sweeping geographic expanse, inhabited by millions, whose activities have dominated millennia. The vastness of the Great Libyan Desert, for example, helps one grasp the gargantuan size of North Africa. That desert "extends 1,100 miles from east to west and over 1,000 from north to south, covering an area roughly equivalent to the entire Indian subcontinent."[585]

Perhaps North Africa's immensity comes into focus, even more clearly, with a brief glance at the geographical extent of Algeria, just west of Libya. There, "one gropes inadequately for the right adjectives to describe the country. Distance never ceases to amaze; from Algiers to Tamanrasset in the barren, lunar mountains of the Hoggar is 1,300 miles, or roughly the same as from Newcastle to Algiers; from Algiers to Oran, a flea's hop on the map of North Africa, is little short of 300 miles by road. [Algeria is] four times as big as metropolitan France, with its land area unchanged since the colonial era, present-day Algeria is the tenth largest country in the world."[586]

Scattered over this vast area are "the remains of churches [which] can be numbered at well over a thousand."[587] Without doubt, the ruins of countless other church structures have been quarried through the centuries to provide stone for other building projects and, consequently, no longer appear in the census of former places of Christian worship.

North Africa's Past Intrudes

In North Africa the past often impinges powerfully upon the present. For example, one who visits the ancient city of Cyrene will probably learn that it was the birthplace of Hannibal, the great Carthaginian general whose troops and war elephants had once threatened Rome. But, ironically, it was also in North Africa that Hannibal "had been smashed at Zama [southwest of Carthage] by Scipio Africanus to close the Second Punic War in 202 B.C."[588] A visitor is also reminded of North Africa's earlier glory when he drives past Roman

---

584 Brian Moynahan, The Faith, A History of Christianity, (New York: Doubleday, 2002), p. 182.
585 John Bierman and Collin Smith, The Battle of Alamein, Turning Point, World War II, (New York: Viking, 2002), p. 19.
586 Alistair Horne, A Savage War Of Peace, Algeria 1954–1962, (New York: The Viking Press, 1977), p. 44.
587 W.H.C. Frend, The Donatist Church, A Movement of Protest in Roman North Africa, (Oxford: The Clarendon Press, 1971), p. 77.
588 Rick Atkinson, An Army at Dawn, The War in North Africa, 1942–1943, (New York: Henry Holt and Company, 2002), p. 253.

"aqueducts dismembered during the Vandals' century of anarchic misrule and now [are] bleaching like stone bones in the sun."[589]

One would also have been reminded of the intrusion of the past if in Tunis he should have visited the Council Chamber of Habib Bourguiba, first President of post-colonial Tunisia. There, Bourguiba kept "busts of the four historic heroes of Tunis—Jugurtha, Hannibal, St Augustine ['*Augodjin* in Arabic] and Ibn Khaldoun."[590] Of course, all of these were "dominated by an immense portrait of the President."[591] Obviously, President Bourguiba wanted to be compared favorably with the exceptional leaders from an extremely long period of North African history whose likenesses he displayed. Both Jugurtha (King of the Roman North African province of Numidia, who died in a Roman prison in 104 B.C.) and Hannibal (the great Carthaginian general who lived 247–183 B.C.) carried out their exploits on the stage of history before the coming of Christ. The second pair of historic giants represent the periods of North African history about which we are trying to gain understanding, the Christian and Muslim eras. Specifically, we are asking, what impact on the cause of Christ did the coming of Islam, that withering wind from Arabia, have through its subjugation of North Africa?

The Real Natives of North Africa

"The whole of North Africa from the Atlantic to Egypt had been included in the Roman Empire at the time of its power. With the collapse of the Western [Roman] Empire in the fourth century, however, the Vandals, a tribe of northern barbarians, had crossed from Europe and occupied Carthage.[592] Here they had established an independent kingdom, which extended from modern Algeria to Libya, and included Majorca, Minorca [in the Mediterranean Balearic Islands], Corsica and Sardinia. In the year 532, however, the Byzantine emperor Justinian sent an army to Carthage. Under the command of the famous Belisarius, one of the few great soldiers of the decline of the empire, the Byzantines had defeated the Vandals and North Africa had returned to the empire of Constantinople [capital of the Byzantine Empire]. The population of these territories was extremely mixed. The early Carthaginians, the Romans, the Byzantines and the Vandals had occupied only the coastal plains. The moun-

---

589 Rick Atkinson, <u>An Army at Dawn, The War in North Africa</u>, 1942–1943, (New York: Henry Holt and Company, 2002), p. 168.
590 His full name was Abu Zayd 'Abd ar-Rahman ibn Khaldun. He lived from 1332 to 1406. He was an Arab philosopher, historian and sociologist. Two of his outstanding works are *Muqaddimah*, a work on the theory of history and sociology and *Kitab al-'ibar* a definitive history of Muslim North Africa.
591 Alistair Horne, <u>A Savage War Of Peace, Algeria 1954–1962</u>, (New York: The Viking Press, 1977), p. 248, footnote.
592 Only because of the treachery of a Roman general were the Vandals enabled to invade North Africa. "Count Boniface, embittered by the attitude of the Augusta … had decided to call in the help of the Vandals. … Boniface sent to Gonderic, the king of the Vandals, who was encamped in Spain, a trusted messenger charged with an offer to hand over to him, in return for his aid, a third of the Roman possessions in Africa. Gonderic's death placed Genseric, his son, at the head of the Vandal army (mixed with Goths and Alans), estimated as numbering eighty thousand fighters. Through the Strait of Gibraltar they passed from Spain into Africa in May 428, Boniface having placed at their disposition a large part of his navy." – Jacques Chabannes, <u>St. Augustine</u>, trans. Julie Kernan (New York: Doubleday & Company, Inc., 1962, p. 197.

tains of the interior were the home of the Berbers,[593] the real natives of the country, who had resisted absorption into the successive races which had conquered the coast."[594] In fact, "the Berbers of the interior were never influenced by a spread of [either] Punic[595] or Latin influence inland from the long-established coastal towns."[596]

Enigmatic Berber Personality

As has just been noted, going west from Egypt, one immediately encounters the Berbers, "the real natives of the country." They, "through history have been a warlike and unruly people; as far back as 950 B.C. they are chronicled as fighting the Pharaohs on the Nile; they provided two Roman Emperors,[597] Septimus Severus and Caracalla, and were with the vanguard of the Muslim conquest of Spain. But they tended to be as unsuccessful at ruling as being ruled. Revolt, and revenge in the Corsican fashion, were honored occupations from time immemorial. Like the Scots they are a people imbued with intense national and regional pride; they are not great smilers, but if you tell a Kabyle [a branch of the Berbers] waiter in Algiers that you have been to Tizi-Ouzou, his face will explode with pleasure. Jean Amrouche, the Kabyle writer, characterizes his people as swinging between extreme enthusiasm, when inspired by an idea, and an apathetic withdrawal when that idea has lost its charm."[598]

There is ample evidence to support Horne's assertion that the Berbers "have been a warlike and unruly people." This was true even for some of the Christian Berbers who made up the Donatist church. North Africa's Christians were sharply divided between the Donatists (founded by the Berber Bishop Donatus Magnus) and the Roman Catholics. "The Catholics were fatally implicated in their record of persecution at the 'Time of Macarius'; and Augustine could get around this awkward memory only by publicizing the sporadic brutalities of an extreme wing of the Donatist church, the Circumcellions."[599] However, there is certainly also countervailing testimony. For example, "the attitude of defiance and rebellion was developed to an extreme degree in Africa. The powers of evil seemed to be personified in the Roman officials and magistrates. Yet the

---

593 "It is thought by some [though it is very questionable] that the Berbers are descended from Jews who fled Israel after the destruction of the Temple by the Romans in A.D. 70." – John W. Kiser, The Monks of Tibhirine Faith, Love, and Terror in Algeria, (New York: St. Martin's Press, 2002), p. 182. However, since the Berbers were in North Africa since 950 B.C., it is certain their origin is not to be traced to Jews scattered by Roman suppression in 70 A.D.
594 John Bagot Glubb, The Great Arab Conquests, (London: Quartet Books, 1980), pp. 260-261.
595 Punic is from the Latin word *punicus* or *poenicus*. It was the name given by the Romans to the Carthaginians, in allusion to their Phoenician descent.
596 W.H.C. Frend, The Donatist Church A Movement of Protest in Roman North Africa, (Oxford: The Clarendon Press, 1971), p. 27.
597 Not only did the Berbers produce two Roman emperors but the celebrated Christian theologian Augustine as well. Augustine, "was born to African parents of Romanized Berber origins in Tagaste in Numidia (modern Algeria) in 354." [David F. Wright, Augustine of Hippo, Tim Dowley (ed.), Eerdmans' Handbook To The History of Christianity, (Carmel, New York: Guideposts, 1977), p. 198.] Augustine's mother was Monica. "Monica's forebears had been Christians for several generations and they too belonged to the Kabyles, a division of the Berber race." – Jacques Chabannes, St. Augustine, trans. Julie Kernan (Garden City, New York: Doubleday & Company, Inc., 1962), p. 18.
598 Alistair Horne, A Savage War of Peace, Algeria 1954–1962, (New York: The Viking Press, 1977), p. 49-50.
599 Peter Brown, Augustine of Hippo, A Biography, (Berkeley: University of California Press, 2000), p. 225.

[Berber] Christians did not take up arms against their enemies. Martyrdom was their means of victory, in itself an act of vengeance, for martyrdom gave them hope of revenge hereafter, as the judges of the pagans."[600]

Constantine's Efforts to Bring Peace

Emperor Constantine was so troubled by the fighting between the Berber church and the Catholic Church in North Africa that he called two councils in an attempt to bring peace. "Unfortunately, the bishops were not as interested in concord as Constantine was. By the time the bishops assembled in Rome in early October 313, Donatus—'charismatic, eloquent, tireless, and utterly convinced of the justice of his cause'—had taken over as the 'shadow bishop' of Carthage. In the meantime, Miltiades had done what he could to ensure the outcome by stacking the court with anti-Donatist bishops. Unsurprisingly, they decided against Donatus, particularly condemning his practice of re-baptizing those who had been baptized by *traditores* or those consecrated by them. Perhaps aware of Miltiades' manipulation of the decision, Constantine felt compelled the following summer to call bishops to a second council at Arles [on the Rhône River in France]. In summoning them, he offered imperial transport and issued an exhortation. He reviewed his efforts to settle the controversy at Rome and his hopes that the Donatist dispute could be put to rest."[601]

"In the 314 [A.D.] letter summoning bishops to Arles, he [Emperor Constantine] repeatedly referred to 'Christ our Savior' and warned that the 'mercy of Christ' has departed from hardened Donatists. He expressed surprise that the Donatists had appealed to him to judge in this case, since he himself was under judgment, awaiting the 'judgment of Christ.' An assembly of bishops would heal the division, he hoped, since bishops could speak or teach nothing but what they learned from the 'teaching of Christ.' He accused the Donatists of being traitors to the church and wondered what their behavior said about their regard for 'Christ the Savior.'"[602]

Most Berbers Untouched by the Gospel

It is important to understand the role of the Berbers in the church in North Africa and their interaction with the Muslims at the time of the Islamic invasion and later. Fundamental to such understanding is the fact that "the Berbers had been little influenced by the Mediterranean civilizations which established outposts on or within their borders. In spite of successive alien dominations,

---

600 W.H.C. Frend, <u>The Donatist Church A Movement of Protest in Roman North Africa</u>, (Oxford: The Clarendon Press, 1971), p. 107-108.
601 Peter J. Leithart, <u>Defending Constantine, The Twilight of an Empire and the Dawn of Christendom</u>, (Downers Grove, IL: InterVarsity Press, 2010), p. 158. **Traditore** plural: *traditores* (Latin), is a term meaning 'the one(s) who had handed over' and defined by Merriam-Webster as 'one of the Christians giving up to the officers of the law the Scriptures, the sacred vessels, or the names of their brethren during the Roman persecutions.'" – Wikipedia; accessed 11/06/17
602 Peter J. Leithart, <u>Defending Constantine, The Twilight of an Empire and the Dawn of Christendom</u>, (Downers Grove, IL: InterVarsity Press, 2010), pp. 88-89.

mainly affecting coastal zones, the Berbers remained *imazigan*, 'free men.'"[603] This implies, obviously, that the main body of the Berber people were never given the opportunity to yield their lives to Christ and, consequently, did not in significant numbers become part of the church. This was one of the great weaknesses of the church in North Africa, making it vulnerable to the Muslim onslaught.

A major contributing factor which hindered the Berbers from coming to Christ was the fact that, prior to the Muslim invasion, the Bible had not been translated into any of the Berber dialects. Tragically, there was no one in North Africa who followed the example of "the Greek brothers Cyril and Methodius [who] ... evangelized Moravia and translated the Bible ... into Slavonic. The Cyrillic alphabet of the Slavs is named for Cyril."[604]

The majority of those Berbers who did become Christians, in spite of the scarce opportunities to do so, subsequently became part of the Donatist movement. However, "the Donatists used the Old Latin Bible in use in Cyprian's time."[605] It seems quite obvious, in view of these facts, that for the majority of Berbers, the choice when Islam came was not between Christ and Muhammad but between their paganism and Muhammad's call to Allah.

Haunting Clues to a Christian Past

Even though the gospel did not penetrate the Berber people with the strength and depth with which it should have, there are some tantalizing vestigial practices which seem to point back to a time when some branches of the Berbers (who are not now Christians) had among them family or tribal members who had yielded their lives to Christ. "The Tuareg [a branch of the Berbers], whom the Arabs sometimes call the Christians of the Desert, are Muslims, but they retain many beliefs belonging to an earlier religion. There is a considerable body of evidence pointing to their having once been Christians. In spite of now being Muslims they are monogamous and their favorite motif in ornament is the cross. Their shields often bear the cross-crosslet[606] of heraldry, depicted rising out of a sea of glory. Their swords are cross-hilted, the great pommels of their camel saddles take the form of a cross, and the same symbol is much used by their leather– and metal–workers. It is also found in the T'ifinagh script.

---

603 J. Spencer Trimingham, The Influence of Islam upon Africa, (London: Longmans, 1968), p. 8.
604 Brian Moynahan, The Faith, A History of Christianity, (New York: Doubleday, 2002), p. 207.
605 W.H.C. Frend, The Donatist Church, A Movement of Protest in Roman North Africa, (Oxford: The Clarendon Press, 1971), p. 25, footnote 2. Cyprian became bishop of Carthage in about 248 A.D. During the persecutions under Valerian he was beheaded at Carthage in 258 A.D. "All the early popes were Greek speakers; although the Bible had been translated into variants of Old Latin by the end of the second century, it was not until 382 that the Western scholar Jerome began to translate the definitive Latin or Vulgate version of the Testaments from the Greek and Hebrew originals. To learn Hebrew he had to travel east, to Syria." – Brian Moynahan, The Faith, A History of Christianity, (New York: Doubleday, 2002), p. 68.
606 Cross-Crosslet: A cross seen especially in medieval heraldry, the cross-crosslet is a combination of four Latin crosses placed at right angles like the points of the compass. The four points are said to represent the four Gospels or the four Evangelists, Matthew, Mark, Luke and John. – https://www.osv.com/OSVNewsweekly/Story/TabId/2672/ArtMID/13567/ArticleID/2259/Crosssection-of-crosses-and-their-significance.aspx (accessed 11/6/17)

There are several words in the Temajegh language which suggest a Christian origin."[607]

However, one should not give too much weight to these vestigial remnants of the Tuareg's possible former Christian faith because "the transfer of outward religious allegiance has never meant in North Africa the complete abandonment of previously held convictions."[608] Also, we may understand the nature of Christianity in North Africa more accurately "if we examine the acceptance of Christianity by large numbers of North Africans from the point of view of a transformed popular religion, rather than that of conversion to a new religion. The Christian message may have sounded to many as the restatement of age-old beliefs and hopes that were tending to become lost in the syncretist paganism of the third century."[609]

Unique Features of Berber Christianity

Generally, Berber Christianity was equivalent to Donatist Christianity, for the Berbers were the ones who embraced the Donatist cause. Surprisingly, the Donatist-Berber Christians venerated the Bible. When driven before magistrates who condemned them to a martyr's death, they carried the writings of the apostle Paul with them, even though they had no translation of the Bible or portions of the Bible in any Berber language. This is in sharp contrast to the situation in Egypt where the Gospel of Mark followed by the New Testament was translated into Coptic, seemingly, in the Apostolic period. However, "in their church services the Donatist clergy used the same Bible, the Old Latin text, as that in use in Cyprian's time [200–258 A.D.]. The Latin Vulgate [translated by Jerome in the late fourth century] was read only by the Catholics in Africa."[610]

"If Berber-speaking peasants from Numidia [now Algeria and part of Tunisia] predominated in Donatism, their Latin-speaking masters dominated the Catholic party."[611] But, as has just been emphasized, the Berber-speaking peasants had no access to Christian scripture in their own language. In contrast, the Catholic party had the Latin Vulgate but did not, in general, look to it for their final source of authority and inspiration because of the generally held teaching that the clergy's voice was the voice of the church. Inevitably this separation

---

607 E. W. Bovill, The Golden Trade of the Moors, (London: Oxford University Press, 1961), pp. 51-52.
608 W.H.C. Frend, The Donatist Church A Movement of Protest in Roman North Africa, (Oxford: The Clarendon Press, 1971), p. 78.
609 W.H.C. Frend, The Donatist Church A Movement of Protest in Roman North Africa, (Oxford: The Clarendon Press, 1971), p. 98.
610 W.H.C. Frend, The Donatist Church A Movement of Protest in Roman North Africa, (Oxford: The Clarendon Press, 1971), p. 320.
   For a very complete discussion of the Latin translations of the Bible and the New Testament which were used in North Africa, see Jean Danielou, A History of Early Christian Doctrine Before The Council of Nicaea, Vol. III: The Origins of Latin Christianity, trans. David Smith and John Austin Baker, (London & Philadelphia: Darton, Longman & Todd The Westminster Press, 1977), pp. 5-15.
611 W.H.C. Frend, The Donatist Church A Movement of Protest in Roman North Africa, (Oxford: The Clarendon Press, 1971), p. 327.

from the Word of God weakened both groups so neither of them stood when ultimately confronted by the withering wind from Arabia—the spiritual, theological, economic, military and political challenge of Islam.

Mass-Movement Christians

Those Berbers who did convert to Christianity from their former worship of Saturn seem to have done so in some kind of a mass movement, in contrast to individual conversions resulting from careful personal teaching, the process which is so clearly implied in Hebrews 8:11. "On the High Plains [of maritime North Africa, i.e., north of the Aures Mountains] something like a real conversion en masse of the country population seems to have taken place."[612] Frend stresses that what had happened was a "mass conversion of the native peasantry from the worship of national deities to Christianity."[613]

That mass movement among the Berbers occurred between A.D. 240 and 275 and brought about the cessation of Saturn worship. "At that point, there was a sudden and complete break. The next datable inscriptions are Christian. The mass of population seems to have changed its religious allegiance with startling suddenness."[614] The number of people who had ostensibly given their allegiance to the cause of Christ was so great "that in the first half of the fourth century Donatus was able to gather 270 bishops for a Council at Carthage."[615] This should not surprise us when we realize that "Christianity was the one religion of the day that welcomed the sinner, and opened salvation to all men without distinction of birth, occupation or race. ... One of the commonest representations of Christ in the third century is as the Good Shepherd, the friend of sinners, and guide to paradise. Brotherly love, a desire to live and worship as a community, a real regard for the sufferings of the poor, a pacifist outlook in an age characterized by perpetual wars, these were some of the features of the nobler minds who accepted Christianity."[616]

Surprisingly, "it is uncertain, even, how Christianity first penetrated the province [of Carthage], whether direct from Rome, or step by step by way of the Jewish colonies in the coastal towns of Tripolitania and Tunisia. There is no mention of any Christian community whatsoever before A.D. 180, and no Bishop of Carthage is recorded prior to Agrippinus at the turn of the third century."[617]

---

612 W.H.C. Frend, The Donatist Church, A Movement of Protest in Roman North Africa, (Oxford: The Clarendon Press, 1971), p. 84.
613 W.H.C. Frend, The Donatist Church, A Movement of Protest in Roman North Africa, (Oxford: The Clarendon Press, 1971), p. 86.
614 W.H.C. Frend, The Donatist Church, A Movement of Protest in Roman North Africa, (Oxford: The Clarendon Press, 1971), p. 83.
615 W.H.C. Frend, The Donatist Church, A Movement of Protest in Roman North Africa, (Oxford: The Clarendon Press, 1971), p. 93.
616 W.H.C. Frend, The Donatist Church, A Movement of Protest in Roman North Africa, (Oxford: The Clarendon Press, 1971), p. 96.
617 W.H.C. Frend, The Donatist Church, A Movement of Protest in Roman North Africa, (Oxford: The Clarendon Press, 1971), p. 87.

North African Christianity Divided

When Islamic armies came with their radically different theology, backed by fearsome military power, they confronted a Christianity in North Africa which was badly divided and in conflict, often mortal, between its two main divisions, Donatist and Roman Catholic. It was a house divided against itself which, ultimately, could not withstand the withering wind from Arabia.[618] It was a body of believers who were biting and devouring one another. (See Galatians 5:15.) The energy of organized Christianity in North Africa was not used for strengthening the body of Christ. Before they ultimately would have been devoured by each other, they were consumed by the conquering armies of Islam, the first gales from the withering wind from Arabia.

Ironically, the division among the followers of Christ in North Africa was not over deep doctrinal differences. "Except for the question of the validity of sacraments dispensed by non-orthodox clerics, no serious theological difference separated them [the Donatists] and the Catholics. There was no difference even of ecclesiastical organization, and it had been proved more than once that they had no legal case against their opponents. It was a matter of schism rather than heresy. But despite centuries of repression by the authorities and the compelling logic of St. Augustine and other Catholic writers they [the Donatists] remained defiant."[619]

Every Rooster on His Own Dung Hill

"The rivalry of Donatist and Catholic led to the spectacular increase in the number of bishops we find at the beginning of the fifth century, the total given by Harnack being from 500 to 700. The learned Father Mesnage, who has examined the evidence with care, points out that while the Catholics occasionally declined to compete in the race for bishoprics (as at the Council of Carthage in 390), yet it was too much to expect that such self-restraint should persist, with the opposing party growing so rapidly. Thus in 397 the Catholic primate of Carthage admitted having an episcopal consecration almost weekly. There is also evidence (from a document of 411) of bishops being placed not only in villages, but also on the estates of landed proprietors. Mesnage concludes that there was nothing to choose between the two parties in this matter. Indeed, they would set up two, three, or even four bishops to oppose one, to such a length did the competition run. Suitable episcopal candidates naturally ran short, so that the less worthy, to state it mildly, were appointed; best of all was

---

618 The controversy between the Donatist Church and the Roman Catholic Church, headed in Africa by Augustine, became so vicious that Emperor Constantine was drawn in. At one point, he "ordered Donatists' property be confiscated and their churches closed. He imprisoned Donatist bishops, and some were tortured and put to death. The precedent was not lost on Augustine. ... For their own sake, they should be forced back into communion with the true church, 'compel them to come in.' Constantine, who had ascended to the throne as *liberator ecclesiae*, had begun to persecute Christians—schismatic Christians, but Christians." – Peter J. Leithart, Defending Constantine, (Downers Grove, IL: I. V. Press, 2010), p. 161.

619 W.H.C. Frend, The Donatist Church A Movement of Protest in Roman North Africa, (Oxford: The Clarendon Press, 1971), pp. 2-3.

to secure your opponent's priest and ordain him bishop. One Donatist bishop stigmatized the priest he lost in this way as his Absalom."[620]

Instead of edifying, informing and uplifting Christians, and instead of reaching out with the Gospel to non-Christians, the leadership of both Catholics and Donatists were competing in a sordid, degraded competition to claim the most bishops! The situation had become so despicable that the appeal of Islam, though offered by threatening military force, seemed preferable! This was only one of the abhorrent conditions which ultimately led to the extinction of any form of organized Christianity in the western part of North Africa.

The Point of Extinction

The scholar who has written most definitively on Christianity in North Africa and its related issues is undoubtedly Professor Frend from whose writings I have frequently quoted in this chapter. He wrote, "Christianity itself lasted only a relatively short time in North African history, between A.D. 200 and 700."[621] Though his research has led to very rich insights about Donatist belief and the Catholic Church in North Africa, Frend is probably wrong in saying that Christianity in North Africa lasted only till 700 A.D.

"The last references to an indigenous Christianity go back to 1049 in Libya, 1091 in Tunisia, 1150 in Algeria and 1300 in Morocco. A turning-point in the disappearance of these Christianities was the reign of the founder of the Almohad dynasty, Ibn Tumart, a [Muslim] fundamentalist who in 1121 established a small state in the south of Morocco and proclaimed himself the Mahdi, the Muslim Messiah. The Almohads conquered the whole of Morocco in 1130, then invaded Algeria in 1147 and Tunisia in 1160. They carried with them the puritanical teachings and intolerance of their founder and although their empire did not last for long it had a devastating impact on the Christian communities it encountered.

"Among the regions to the West of the Nile, Islam spread most rapidly in Libya which the Muslim armies entered in 640 A.D. The country lost the core of its Christian population when a Berber tribe, the Louata, departed with its bishop to Morocco. All traces of them had been removed by the time the [vicious Arab tribe[622] known as] Banu Hilal passed through in their march towards the west.

"In Tunisia, Christianity seems to have survived until the eleventh century. Carthage, formerly a prestigious bishopric in which the last of a long line of Councils was held in 646, was conquered by the Arabs in 698 A.D. However, the [Roman Catholic Holy] See was maintained there for several more centuries even if the recollections of Europe and the Maghreb have together put this distant memory under seal. The [Shia] Fatimid Dynasty, which during the

---
620 C. P. Groves, <u>The Planting of Christianity in Africa</u>, (London: Lutterworth Press, 1964), Vol. 1, pp. 62-63.
621 W.H.C. Frend, <u>The Donatist Church A Movement of Protest in Roman North Africa</u>, (Oxford: The Clarendon Press, 1971), p. xviii.
622 See reference to this tribe in Chapter 19 under "More Arab Predators."

first half of the tenth century was centered on Kairouan, [Qayrawan/Kairwan] was probably as tolerant in its North African phase as it was in Egypt until the time of al-Hakim. Certainly in 990, the church in Carthage once again had a demographic and spiritual foundation sufficient for it to send a bishop to be consecrated in Rome. Letters dated 1053, 1073 and 1076 addressed by the pope to the bishops of Carthage, bear witness to Christian activity. Another source which attests to it is Constantine the African, a Benedictine monk born in Tunisia in about 1015 who has given us numerous translations in Latin of Arabic medical texts. However, in 1270, when Saint Louis died in front of the besieged Tunis, Christianity had been almost extinguished for two centuries. The first blow came with the Norman conquest of Sicily (1072–91), after which the ruthless intolerance endured by the Muslims of the island [of Sicily] led to the elimination of Berber Christianity in response. By 1159 it only remained for the Almohad conqueror, Abd al-Mu'min, to raze the See of Carthage and force the remaining Christians into exile or apostasy."[623]

Youssef Courbage's evaluation, which has just been cited, is confirmed by the research of Roger Le Tourneau who wrote, "There are many indications that Christian communities continued to exist in North Africa until the seventh [Muslim]/twelfth [Christian] century. They were certainly still important, although docile, even after Musa b. Nusayr's policy of Islamization."[624]

"After the invasion by Arab Muslims in the seventh century, North African Christianity faded out. Baur [J. Baur, 2,000 Years of Christianity in Africa] refers to Arab writers who 'mention a few Christian villages still existing in 1400 and a solitary Christian community in Tunis, the new Carthage, in 1500.'"[625]

Though Frend is wrong about the date of the final disappearance of organized Christian life in North Africa, unfortunately he is absolutely on target when he tells us, "the splendid ruins of Roman cities, with their churches and temples, serve as a reminder of the eventual failure of both Christianity and classical culture to survive over large areas where they had once prevailed. ... All efforts to win it back, either by St. Louis' crusaders or by the missionaries of more recent times,[626] have been unsuccessful."[627] The withering wind from Arabia has been terribly desiccating!

⊗

---

623 Youssef Courbage and Philippe Fargues, Christians and Jews Under Islam, trans. Judy Mabro (New York: I.B. Tauris Publishers, 1998), pp. 39-40.
624 Roger Le Tourneau, North Africa To The Sixteenth Century, The Cambridge History of Islam, ed. P. M. Holt (Cambridge: At The University Press, 1970), Vol. II, p. 214.
625 Steven Paas, Christianity in Eurafrica, A History of the Church in Europe and Africa, (Washington, DC: New Academia Publishing, 2017), p. 293.

626 One example of a modern effort to see some form of Christianity rooted again in North Africa is that of Charles Lavigerie who was appointed Roman Catholic Bishop of Algiers in 1867. "He saw himself in the chain of church fathers leading back to Saint Augustine. His task, he declared at his investiture ceremony, was to make Algeria again the cradle of a Christian nation 'of another France, and to spread the light of civilization of which the Gospels are the source, and the law.' ... There was no need to rush to convert Muslim souls to the light of Christianity. Lavigerie was confident they would see for themselves the light shed by Christian good works. But Muslims did not see the light, not enough to convert. ... Muslims accepted the good works but not the faith." – John W. Kiser, The Monks of Tibhirine Faith, Love, and Terror in Algeria, (New York: St. Martin's Press, 2002), p. 184-185. For an even more modern effort, read Kiser's account of how in the spring of 1996, militants of the Armed Islamic Group, today affiliated with Osama bin Laden's al Qaeda network, broke into a Trappist monastery in war-torn Algeria. Seven monks were taken hostage, pawns in a murky negotiation to release imprisoned terrorists. Two months later, the severed heads of the monks were found in a tree not far from Tibhirine. For an informative and winsome introduction to Roman Catholic mission work among the Kabyle Berbers in the late nineteenth century, see Fadhma A.M. Amrouche, My Life Story, The Autobiography of a Berber Woman, (New Brunswick, NJ, Rutgers University Press, 1989.)

627 W.H.C. Frend, The Donatist Church A Movement of Protest in Roman North Africa, (Oxford: The Clarendon Press, 1971), p. 1.

Chapter 19

THE DEATH OF ORGANIZED NORTH AFRICAN CHRISTIANITY

All across North Africa church spires have been replaced by mosque minarets, like this one in Tripoli, Libya. – Courtesy of Wikimedia Commons.

Light from any kind of organized indigenous Christian presence emitted its last glimmer at various times and from diverse locations across the vast northern expanse of the continent of Africa.[628] As we have seen in the previous chapter, the demise in each area finally resulted from the Muslim conquest and occupation of North Africa. That series of eclipses took place in "1049 in Libya, 1091 in Tunisia, 1150 in Algeria and 1300 in Morocco."[629]

North Africa as a whole is known to the Arabs as "'Jezirat al Maghrib,' or 'The Island of the Sunset.'" They consider it an island because it is bounded by the waters of the Nile on the east, of the Mediterranean on the north, by the Atlantic on the west and by a great sea of sand on the south. Colloquially the term, Jezirat al Maghrib, is now shortened simply to Maghrib. In the Maghrib, immediately adjacent to Egypt on the west, "were the people whom the Egyp-

---

[628] The name Africa has an interesting origin. After the Romans destroyed Carthage "they were gradually extending their hegemony in the Maghrib. They had at once annexed the districts which the Carthaginians had directly administered, and had made of them a province which they called 'Africa,' from a Punic root meaning 'cut off'; this presumably referred to the fact that Carthage had been 'cut off' from its motherland of Phoenicia, and the word was eventually extended to cover the whole of the continent." – Geoffrey Furlonge, The Lands of Barbary, (London: John Murray, 1966), p. 73.

[629] Youssef Courbage and Philippe Fargues, Christians and Jews Under Islam, trans. Judy Mabro (New York: I.B. Tauris Publishers, 1998), p. 39.

tians called 'Libyans' and the Romans 'Barbari'—whence our words Berber and Barbary—and they [still] form one [very important] component of the population of today. ... The Roman appellation 'Barbari, meaning 'uncultured,' was obviously a term of contempt."[630]

Byzantine Defenses Collapse

Egypt had been the Byzantine defensive bastion against any land attack on the Maghrib, i.e., North Africa, launched either from Palestine to the north or from Arabia to the east. At the same time, the Mediterranean maritime defense of North Africa was provided by the unrivaled Byzantine navy based principally on Alexandria. At the time of the Islamic assault on the Maghrib, Egypt "supported a population of perhaps six or seven million, and was provided with a number of fortified cities. The many canals and branches of the Nile made military operations difficult, while Alexandria itself, if resolutely defended [which it was not], was capable of defying any army of the period, probably for several years. Thus any invader who had conquered Egypt would find the occupation of Libya little more than child's play. To this rule, Amr ibn al Aasi [the military commander who had conquered Egypt] proved no exception. In the spring of 643, he appears to have occupied Barqa[631] without opposition, the people agreeing to pay poll-tax [jizya] and tribute."[632]

Military Motivation

Some historians have speculated that Muslim military forces pushed on west after Egypt capitulated, not because of lust for additional conquest but because Egypt was indefensible unless vast areas of North Africa to the west were conquered. However, that analysis is not supported by competent military analysts. In discussing the World War II Battle of El Alamein, John Bierman and Colin Smith wrote, "In all the North African desert, nowhere fitted Auchinleck's requirements for a defensive battle better than the position which started on the shores of the Mediterranean around the little railway halt of El Alamein and ended some forty miles to the south at the northern cliffs of the Qattara Depression. This 7,000-square-mile basin sinks to almost 450 feet below sea level; a large part of its surface consists of deceptively sand-encrusted saline lakes and marsh, punctuated by small, table-topped hills and weird sand sculptures chiseled by centuries of arid wind. There were tracks through it, but it was difficult for camels, let alone tanks, and wheeled vehicles stood a very good chance of getting bogged down."[633]

---

630 Geoffrey Furlonge, The Lands of Barbary, (London: John Murray, 1966), pp. 1-4.
631 Barqa appears on many maps as Al-Marj, about 60 miles northeast of Benghazi, in the province of Cyrenaica, now in Libya.
632 John Bagot Glubb, The Great Arab Conquests, (London: Quartet Books, 1980), p. 261.
633 John Bierman & Colin Smith, The Battle of Alamein Turning Point, World War II, (New York: Viking, 2002), p. 202.

Worthless Guarantees

There is no definitive historical record of how or when Christians became prominent in Cyrenaica. "'Simon of Cyrene' is mentioned in three of the four Gospels as carrying the Cross through the Via Dolorosa, and 'men of ... Cyrene' are mentioned in the Acts as preaching Christianity in Antioch [Acts 11:20], but there is no record of a Bishop from Cyrenaica before the third century, and even in the fourth, when there were Bishops in the Pentapolis cities,[634] Cyrene itself seems to have still been a center of pagan cults."[635] Though the account of the spread of the gospel of Christ has eluded historians, there is no doubt that the followers of the Messiah were very numerous in Cyrenaica at the time Islam's withering wind from Arabia in the form of conquering hordes thundered into the area.

In exchange for paying the humiliating, demeaning and impoverishing poll-tax (called *jizya* in Arabic), theoretically the Christian community was to be protected by their Muslim conquerors and allowed to exist, albeit with severe restrictions but without molestation. Notwithstanding the fact that the Christians accepted that very detrimental set of conditions which had been imposed upon them, "in Cyrenaica [where Barqa was located] there is archaeological evidence of the deliberate destruction of churches by the conquerors."[636]

Christian Numerical Decline

It is probable that the Muslims' breach of their contractual obligation to the Christian community led to the beginning of the marked decline of organized Christian presence in Libya. In any case, as mentioned in Chapter 18 under "The Point of Extinction," "the country lost the core of its Christian population when a Berber tribe, the Louata, departed with its bishop to Morocco. All traces of them had been removed by the time the Banu Hilal [a very destructive Arabian Muslim tribal group] passed through [some four centuries after the initial Arab-Muslim invasion] in their march towards the west."[637] It is likely that the Louata Berber tribe could not have imagined that after a short time following their flight, Islam would also inundate their Moroccan refuge! Did they flee again? If so, the only direction by land, which offered refuge from the Islamic juggernaut, would have been very far to the south.

The Louata Tribe of the Berber people was certainly not the only Christian group to flee in face of the Muslim onslaught on North Africa. Soon after the conquest of Egypt, the Arabian war machine gained naval forces on the Mediterranean, which were commandeered "from the naval resources of Egypt

---

634 The five cities of the Pentapolis in Cyrenaica were: Apollonia, Arsinoe, Berenice, Cyrene, and Barka.
635 Geoffrey Furlonge, The Lands of Barbary, (London: John Murray, 1966), pp. 18-19.
636 Patricia Crone and Michael Cook, Hagarism, The Making of The Islamic World, (London: Cambridge University Press, 1977), p. 156, note 33. Crone and Cook quote, (W.M. Widrig and R. Goodchild, 'The West Church at Apollonia in Cyrenaica' in Papers of the British School at Rome 1960, p. 71, note).
637 Youssef Courbage and Philippe Fargues, Christians and Jews Under Islam, trans. Judy Mabro (New York: I.B. Tauris Publishers, 1998), pp. 39- 40.

and Syria."[638] Those Muslim naval forces quickly became dominant. "The Arab naval supremacy in the Mediterranean at the time forced the Byzantines to evacuate their remaining possessions on the Maghribi coast, taking their Christian inhabitants to the islands of the Mediterranean."[639]

Meaning of Human Tribute

As we attempt to understand the causes for the disappearance of organized Christian presence in North Africa, following the Muslim invasion and colonization of the area, it is instructive to realize more fully the situation faced by the Louata Christians. The Muslim conquest of the Maghrib west of Libya was not a pushover. "By 640 both Palestine and Syria were in Muslim hands; Alexandria fell to the Arabs in 642, and with Egypt as a base the conquerors crept slowly along the North African coast. Here they encountered more effective resistance, and it was not till the close of the seventh century that the capture of Carthage laid open the way to Spain."[640]

Muslim leaders believed it was due to Berber perfidy that they had experienced such difficulty in the conquest of the Maghrib. "This belief served after the conquest as a justification of the extortionate policy adopted by the Arab rulers, one of whose most heinous aspects was the levying of human tribute upon the Berbers. Human tribute was a means through which the conquerors obtained slaves, especially slave girls, to cater for the pleasures of the Arab ruling class. This practice seems to have been initiated at the beginning of the conquest. ... Upon conquering Cyrenaica in 642 or 643 'Amr b. al-'As [the Arab military commander who was also governor of conquered Egypt] fixed the jizya to be paid by its Berber tribes at 13,000 Dinars. From the Lawata [Louata] tribe he demanded that they should 'sell' to the Arabs a number of their 'sons and daughters' to the value of their share of the total jizya. ... About Musa b. Nusayr, ... during his term as amir of Ifriqiya his son and nephew, each commanding a column of troops, raided Berber settlements and took captives who were treated as war booty and taken into slavery. The caliph's share of the Berber slaves captured during Ibn Nusayr's amirate, according to the rule that he was entitled to one-fifth of the booty won by the Muslim army, is said to have amounted to 20,000."[641]

---

638 Norman H. Baynes and H. St. L. B. Moss (ed's.) Byzantium, An Introduction to East Roman Civilization, (Oxford: The Clarendon Press, 1953), p. 12.

639 Jamil M. Abun-Nasr, A History of the Maghrib in the Islamic Period, (Cambridge: Cambridge University Press, 1987), p. 31. Other cases of Christians trying to flee before the conquering Muslim armies come from Mesopotamia and Central Asia. For example, in 634, "on the conquest of the upper Mesopotamia a small tribe, consisting of some 4,000 souls, professing Christianity, fled to the Roman territory. Omar, thereupon, wrote to the Greek Emperor: An Arab tribe has forsaken my territory and fled to thine. I swear by God that if thou dost not deliver them to me, I shall expel every Christian from my territory to thine. The Greeks did not hesitate to send back the fugitives, and Omar distributed them in the adjoining provinces of Mesopotamia and Syria." Von Kremer, The Orient Under the Caliphs, trans. S. Khuda Bukhsh (Beirut: United Publishers, 1973), pp. 121-122.

640 Norman H. Baynes and H. St. L. B. Moss (ed's.) Byzantium, An Introduction to East Roman Civilization, (Oxford: The Clarendon Press, 1953), p. 12.

641 Jamil M. Abun-Nasr, A History of the Maghrib in the Islamic Period, (Cambridge: Cambridge University Press, 1987), p. 34.

Probably the Ottomans later used this example of enforced slavery as the role model they followed in conscripting teenage boys for their Janissaries, the new shock troops they raised to conquer and hold Asia Minor and the Balkans. The formation of the Janissary corps is discussed in Chapter 27 under "Institutionalized Kidnapping."

More Arab Predators

Toward the end of organized Christian presence in North Africa, the Christians had to face a new peril. "In the eleventh century came disaster, when Cyrenaica was invaded ... by two nomad Arab tribes, the Beni Hilal and the Beni Sulaim, who reduced its cities to ruins and its interior to grazing for their flocks. Thereafter it lay under the long-range domination of the rulers of Egypt, the Fatimids and their successors the Ayyubids."[642] For more information on the Fatimids, see Chapter 18 under "Point of Extinction."

Muslim Civil War

Following the Muslim conquest of Libya, which began while the caliphate still had its capital at Medina, it became difficult for the Caliphs, whether the Umayyad Caliphs ruling from Damascus, or, later, the Abbasid Caliphs ruling from Baghdad, to govern the Maghrib. The difficulty was, in part, a consequence of the Battle of Siffeen[643] which was fought in July of 657 A.D. That battle was fought because of the murder in Medina of Othman, the third caliph. That war was the method of determining whether Mu'awiya, who had been appointed by Caliph Othman to be governor of Damascus and who was a relative of the murdered caliph, would become the next reigning caliph or Ali. Ali was "one of the most respected of all Muslims. He was the son of Muhammad's uncle, Abu Talib, who had raised the Prophet, and the husband of Muhammad's daughter Fatimah, who bore him two sons."[644]

That war intensified the Sunni-Shia factional split in Islam. The term "Shia" is a shortened form of the Arabic *"Shi'at 'Ali"* which means "a partisan of Ali." Those who supported Ali in this confrontation with Mu'awiya were the initial Shia party. Those who sided with Mu'awiya ultimately became the Sunni branch of Islam. Mu'awiya objected to Ali becoming caliph because Ali had refused to seek and to prosecute the murderers of Caliph Othman. Both sides concluded that the only way to resolve the stalemate was a resort to war. During the ensuing battle, the Battle of Siffeen, the forces of Ali were winning which led Mu'awiya to call for a negotiated settlement based on the Koran.[645] Ali accepted the proposal and by doing so forever lost the opportunity for a de-

---
642 Geoffrey Furlonge, The Lands of Barbary, (London: John Murray, 1966), pp. 19-20.
643 Siffeen was located a little north of Ragga (Raggah/Rakka) which is on the west bank of the Euphrates near where the Balikh River flows into the Euphrates.
644 Desmond Stewart, Early Islam, (New York: Time Incorporated, 1967), p. 59.
645 Most probably, the Koran in its final rendition, did not exist at this early date. However, "that does not mean, of course, that a proto-Qur'an did not exist in some form or another, prior to that point." Andrew Rippin, *Forward*, In John Wansbrough Quranic Studies, (Amhurst, New York: Promethius Books, 2004) p. xvii.

cisive military decision in his favor. This so dismayed and angered some 12,000 of his troops that they defected from Ali's army and "formed an independent community in northern Arabia. In 658 A.D. most of them were killed and the remnants dispersed."[646] (For additional information on the Sunni-Shia split in Islam and the Battle of Siffeen, see Appendix D).

Seceders Bring Grief

Those defectors, one of whom murdered Ali, are known as *Kharijites*, an Arabic word meaning "seceders." Among those who were dispersed was also an appreciable contingent who came to the Maghrib where they very successfully advocated that the Muslims of North Africa obey none of the caliphs reigning in the East. Their appeal resonated strongly with the Berbers of the Maghrib, a people over whom, for centuries, outside conquerors had tried vainly to exercise rule, first the Phoenicians, followed by the West Romans, the Vandals, the Byzantines and, finally, the Arab Muslims.

One result of the successful Kharijite campaign was that, ultimately, Christians in North Africa were exposed to the "mercy" of a multitude of North African Muslim political-religious regimes. Before that, they had been exposed one after the other to the rapacious policies of the vicious Arab caliphates. The oldest caliphate had ruled from Medina where it was operative till 657 A.D. Then the caliphate shifted to Damascus and ultimately to Baghdad. Complicating the situation even more, Morocco had "a tradition of renegade dynasties that remained outside the control of the great Islamic empires, from the Abbasids to the Ottomans."[647] Paralleling those "renegade dynasties" were "two Berber [Muslim] empires, the Almoravids and Almohads [which] during the late eleventh, twelfth and early thirteenth centuries, controlled Andalus [southern Spain]."[648]

Causes of Death

It was the Almohads who gave the final blow to the church in North Africa. Surprisingly, the philosopher Ibn Rushd, known as Averroes[649] in the West, found enough tolerance in Almohad, Spain to teach and write. That is astonishing because, "the self proclaimed Mahdi who began [the Almohad political] process was intolerant to excess."[650] That intolerance was recorded by the Arab historian al-Raqiq. He wrote of Musa ibn Nusayr that, "He pursued them [the Berbers who had fled out of fear of the Arabs] and slaughtered savagely and took a large number of them captive. He reached the nearer Sus [the valley

---

646 Carlton S. Coon, Caravan: The Story of the Middle East, (New York: Henry Holt and Company, 1956), p. 120.
647 Matti Friedman, *The End of Morocco's Mosaic of Tolerance*, The Jerusalem Report, July 14, 2003, p. 23.
648 Isabel O'Connor, *The Fall of the Almohad Empire in the Eyes of Modern Spanish Historians*, Islam and Christian-Muslim Relations, Vol. 14, Number 2, April 2003, p. 149.
649 The full name of Ibn Rushd was Abu al-Walid Muhammad ibn Ahmad ibn Muhammad ibn Rushd. He lived from 1126 to 1198. He was trained in medicine and became chief *qadi* (religious judge) in Cordoba. He wrote books on medicine, philosophy and Muslim religious law.
650 H.T. Norris, The Berbers in Arabic Literature, (London: Longman, 1982), p. 183.

above Agadir between the high-Atlas and the anti-Atlas Mountains] without meeting any resistance. When the Berbers beheld the suffering which they endured they asked for *aman* [peace] and they submitted."[651]

The records tell us that "it is likely that Jews played a part in the resistance to the Muslim conquerors. There is no indication that the Christians of Africa, as Christians, did the same; this phenomenon is not peculiar to the Maghrib, since neither in the Fertile Crescent nor in Egypt did the Christians resist the Muslims in defense of their faith. But there are many indications that Christian communities continued to exist in North Africa until the seventh/twelfth century. They were certainly still important, although docile, even after Musa b. Nusayr's policy of Islamization."[652]

Unfortunately, Christianity in North Africa before the Muslim conquest was much like that in Hungary and the Balkans where there were "quarrels that sapped much of the nation's ability to organize Christian resistance against the Muslim invasion."[653]

On to the Atlantic

The Muslim avalanche did not wait for the last glimmer of organized Christianity in North Africa to die out before resuming its seemingly inexorable onward rush. "Amr's nephew Uqba rode farther west, adding Tunisia's pastures to Islam, then all the way to the foothills of the Atlas Mountains, sweeping over farms long fortified against local raiders. Stopped by the Atlantic in 681, he rode impatiently into the surf, exclaiming to Allah: 'Were I not hindered by this sea, I would go forward to the unknown kingdoms of the West ... subduing those nations who worship other gods than Thee!'"[654] In a few short years, the withering wind from Arabia, moved by that same impatient impetus, was ready to blow violently across the Strait of Gibraltar into Spain.

⊗

---

651 H.T. Norris, The Berbers in Arabic Literature, (London: Longman, 1982), p. 63.
652 Roger Le Tourneau, *North Africa to The Sixteenth Century*, P.M. Holt, Ann K.S. Lambton, Bernard Lewis (eds.), The Cambridge History of Islam, (Cambridge: The University Press, 1970), Vol. 2, p. 214.
653 Stanford J. Shaw, History of the Ottoman Empire and Modern Turkey, Volume I, Empire of the Gazis, The Rise and Decline of the Ottoman Empire, 1280–808, (Cambridge: Cambridge University press, 1977), p. 18.
654 Desmond Stewart, Early Islam, (New York: Time Incorporated, 1967), p. 70. Some believe the account of Uqba ibn Nafi riding his charger into the sea is fable or folklore. "Did he ever ... ride his charger into the Atlantic with a zealot's oath of absolute dedication to the cause of Islam? Alas, we cannot be sure, and there are some who would wish to shorten the range and narrow the focus." – H.T. Norris, The Berbers in Arabic Literature, (London: Longman, 1982), pp. 47-48. One thing is absolutely sure. That is, Muslims, by 710, had conquered all of Mediterranean maritime North Africa and were ready to launch their attack on Spain in 711.

Photos

Photo Index

Photo 1:	The Palace of Shapur at Ctesiphon	239
Photo 2:	Ruins of Petra	240
Photo 3:	Ruins of Palmyra	241
Photo 4:	Buddha Statue, Bamiyan, Afghanistan	242
Photo 5:	Victory Tower at Ghazni	243
Photo 6:	Minaret in Herat	244
Photo 7:	Green Mosque in Balkh	245
Photo 8:	Lutfallah Mosque in Isfahan	246
Photo 9:	Armenian Cathedral in Isfahan	246
Photo 10:	Royal Staircase at Persepolis	247
Photo 11:	Mashhad Shrine	247
Photo 12:	Freedom Tower, Tehran	248
Photo 13:	Tomb of Cyrus the Great at Pasargadae, Iran	249

Photo 1: The Palace of Shapur at Ctesiphon – Courtesy of Wikimedia Commons

Photo 2: A glimpse of the magnificent ruins of Petra as one enters through the narrow gorge, called the Siq.

Photo 3: The magnificence and grandeur of Palmyra was obvious in the many acres of stately ruins before being destroyed by forces of ISIS, the pseudo caliphate.

Photo 4: At Bamiyan, Afghanistan, a 1500-year-old 13-stories-tall witness to the power of Buddhism.

Photo 5: One of Mahmud's victory towers at Ghazni, his capital city which he built by loot.

Photo 6: Beautiful turquoise blue faience work on a very old minaret in Herat.

Photo 7: The ancient "Green Mosque" (from green tiles on the dome), in Balkh, the home city of the Christian evangelist memorialized on the Nestorian Monument.

Photo 8: The Lutfallah Mosque at Isfahan.

Photo 9: The Armenian Cathedral in Isfahan

Photo 10: The Royal Staircase at Persepolis

Photo 11: The shrine at Mashhad (place of martyrdom, i.e., becoming a shahid). Imam Reza (the 8th Imam) was martyred here. Today Mashhad has a population of over 3 million and millions of devotees visit on pilgrimages annually..

Photo 12: The magnificent Freedom Tower which straddles the western entrance to Tehran.

Photo 13: The tomb of Cyrus the Great at Pasargadae, Iran, first capital of the Achaemenian Empire.

Chapter 20

MUSLIMS ENTICED BY IBERIA, GATEWAY TO EUROPE

The modern-day harbor of Ceuta on the western Mediterranean shore of North Africa, just opposite Gibraltar. It was from this harbor that Islam launched its invasion of Spain. – Courtesy of Wikimedia Commons

In the year 711 A.D., a mere 8.9 miles of water must have seemed trivial to the Muslim conquerors, flushed with their victory over North Africa, as they gazed covetously across the Strait of Gibraltar to the Spanish shore. "In the first place, the Peninsula was close to Africa, and the Arab conquerors or their Berber subjects must have known about the fertility and beauty of the country and the possibility of securing handsome booty. Furthermore, the Peninsula was undergoing serious sociopolitical crises, and that, too, must have been known to the Arabs through their effective espionage system."[655]

More Distant Goals

Looking beyond Spain itself, they knew conquest of the Iberian Peninsula would put them on the southwest threshold of Europe. This could make it possible to compensate for the failure of Mu'awiya[656] (the first caliph of the Umayyad dynasty who ruled from Damascus) to conquer Europe from the southeast. Utilizing a flotilla of warships, in vain he had "besieged the capital

---

655 Anwar G. Chejne, <u>Muslim Spain, Its History and Culture</u>, (Minneapolis: The University of Minnesota Press, 1974), p. 7.
656 His Arabic name is represented by various spellings in English.

[Constantinople] for seven years (672–678 A.D.)."[657] It is entirely possible, having seen the resolute defense which was thrown up by the Byzantine emperors in Constantinople, that the current caliph may have concluded that a western attack on Europe, launched through Spain, would ultimately prove to be the most fruitful and successful way to subjugate Europe.[658]

In any case, the war had to go on, for the caliphs, the generals and the Muslim body politic (the *ummah* [umma] in Koranic terms) could never forget that "Islam is a militant religion, which makes perpetual war incumbent on the Muslim community until the whole world is subjected to its rule. The conquered nations which had a revealed religion had to pay a special tax and to live in abject subjection to the followers of Islam."[659]

Crossing the Strait

Like other narrow straits such as the Bosporus or the Dardanelles, crossing the 8.9-mile-wide Strait of Gibraltar had historically presented little trouble to determined conquerors or desperately fleeing groups of persecuted and oppressed people seeking refuge on its opposite shore.

The earliest known people group to have crossed the Strait of Gibraltar, perhaps as early as 3,000 B.C., for reasons which are not known, were the Iber people, making their way from Africa to Spain. It was from these people that the Ebro River and Iberia itself have been named.[660] As this energetic people surged northward they encountered the Celtic people pushing determinedly south over the Pyrenees. "During the sixth century B.C. Iberia was invaded from the north by large tribes of Celts. ... Rivers and mountains, and possibly lack of resistance, led the Celts to concentrate in the north and west, where some of their vocabulary and their bagpipe music may still be heard. In the center of the peninsula they mingled with the Iberians to form Celt-Iberian [Celtiberian] tribes, while in the east there is little or no trace of them."[661]

While the Muslim military leaders probably knew nothing of the crossing of the Strait by the Iberians, it is quite likely, however, that they did know about the exploits of the great Carthaginian general Hannibal. He not only ferried his hordes,

---

657 H.G. Wells, The Outline of History (Garden City, New York: Garden City Books, 1949), Vol. I, p. 620.
658 At the outset, the Caliph may have been ambivalent about the conquest of Spain. According to one source, "The Governor of Africa, Musa ibn Nusayr, ... sought instructions from the Khalif, Walid. The Khalif thought the undertaking too perilous. 'Explore Spain with some light troops,' he replied, 'but do not, at any rate for the present, expose a large army to the dangers of an expedition beyond the seas.'" – Reinhart Dozy, Spanish Islam A History of the Muslims in Spain (New Delhi: Goodword Books, 2002), p. 230.
659 S.D. Goitein, Jews and Arabs Their Contacts Through the Ages, (New York: Schocken Books, 1967), p. 66.
660 Other names for Spain may be of interest. "When the Greeks arrived on Spanish soil, around 600 B.C., they referred to the peninsula as Hesperia, which means 'land of the setting sun.' When the Carthaginians came around 300 B.C. they called the country Ispania (from Sphan, 'rabbit'), which means 'land of the rabbits.' Strangely, the long-eared, timid creature appears on the early Iberian coins. The Romans arrived a century later and simply adopted the Carthaginian name of the country, calling it Hispania. ... The Hebrew name for Spain was Sepharadh, hence Jews from Spain are known as Sephardim." – John A. Crow, Spain The Root and the Flower, (3rd ed. expanded & updated; Berkeley: University of California Press, 1963), pp. 7 & 120.
661 Ruth Way, A Geography of Spain and Portugal, (London: Methuen & Co. Ltd. 1962), p. 76.

but his war elephants as well, from Africa to Spain across the Strait which we call the Strait of Gibraltar.

Dangerous Betrayal

Without any doubt the Muslim generals had learned that, before their own arrival, the Vandal minions had crossed the Strait from Spain to Africa. Even though the Byzantine General Belisarius had wrested North Africa from the Vandals in 532 A.D., it was in memory of those Vandals that the Muslims named a part of the Iberian Peninsula which they conquered and occupied. For phonetic reasons they dropped the initial "V" from the name Vandal and called their newly conquered area Al-Andalus. The name survives today in Andalusia, the name of Spain's southern province.

Obviously, no army could cross that Strait, narrow though it is (8.9 miles wide), without an adequate flotilla. Ironically, the required ships for both the Vandals, and later, the Muslims, were provided through treachery. The Vandals had been given the use of Roman ships because Boniface, an offended imperial general, wanted to take vengeance on the empire. Succinctly the story is this: "Count Boniface, embittered by the attitude of the Augusta which was fostered, as we know, by the intriguer Aetius, had decided to call in the help of the Vandals.

"Partly from anger and partly from fear, Boniface sent to Gonderic, the king of the Vandals, who was encamped in Spain, a trusted messenger charged with an offer to hand over to him, in return for his aid, a third of the Roman possessions in Africa. Gonderic's death placed Genseric, his son, at the head of the Vandal army (mixed with Goths and Alans), estimated as numbering eighty thousand fighters. Through the Strait of Gibraltar they passed from Spain into Africa in May 428, Boniface having placed at their disposition a large part of his navy."[662]

Augustine, the great Roman Catholic Bishop, boldly and sternly exhorted Boniface to reverse course and save North Africa from the depredations of the Vandals. At great personal risk a priest named Paul delivered Augustine's letter to Boniface in which the great but traitorous general was confronted starkly with his responsibility for the disaster and his duty to rise against the Vandals. Augustine first asked, "You say you have just reasons for your action?" Without waiting for an answer Augustine turned to accusation. "'What shall I say of Africa's devastation by the barbarians which is met by no resistance? You do nothing to prevent this calamity! Who could have believed such a thing! They ravage, pillage, change into a desert this prosperous and populous land. Not even a single fruit tree remains standing. But, you reply, these things should be blamed on those who have offended you, those who have repaid your loyalty

---

[662] Jacques Chabannes, St. Augustine, trans. Julie Kernan (Garden City, New York: Doubleday & Company, Inc., 1962), p. 197

with bitter enmity. ...' But Boniface was committed to the rebellion he had begun—too proud to denounce it, too involved to withdraw."[663]

Equally repugnant perfidy made the initial Muslim invasion of Spain possible. "The Goths [who ruled Spain after the withdrawal of Rome's forces] maintained a fortress in northern Africa at Ceuta [as modern Spain does today], the mountain which is opposite Gibraltar.[664] This stronghold was in the command of Count Julian, general of the Visigoths. Legend has it that Julian's daughter, who lived at the court in Toledo, had been seduced by the Gothic king, Roderick. To revenge himself Julian is said to have allied himself with the Arabs, inviting them to undertake the conquest of Spain."[665] It was the traitor Julian who, as Boniface had done for the Vandals, supplied the ships to Tariq, first Muslim invader and conqueror of Spain, to cross the Strait!

However, the treachery of Julian did not stop with providing boats for the Arab forces. He and his troops joined the Gothic forces in the plains of Jerez, on the banks of the Guadalete, in the battle against the Muslim invading army. "The two armies fought to a standstill for many hours, but finally there was a defection among the Christians in that part of the army led by Count Julian; [then] the Arabs broke the ranks of the Visigoths and routed them in dismay."[666]

For their invaluable cooperation, the Muslims enriched and honored the traitors. "The role of Julian of Ceuta and that of Oppas, Bishop of Seville, could not be overestimated. They continued their cooperation with the conqueror and were handsomely rewarded. Some of Julian's descendants enjoyed the favors of the court of Cordova, and were accomplished scholars and administrators."[667]

The Gospel Comes to Spain

Since the purpose of this chapter is to trace the impact sustained by the churches and the people of Christ in Spain which were engulfed by the rise of the Islamic empire and desiccated by the withering wind from Arabia, let us, at this point, briefly review the history of those in Spain who professed loyalty to Christ.

The sole Biblical clue about the origin of Christianity in Spain[668] comes from the apostle Paul's statement in Romans 15:28 in which he shared with the Roman Christians his desire to go to Spain. He wrote, "So after I have completed this task and have made sure that they have received this fruit, I will go to Spain and visit you on the way." (NIV)

---

663 Jacques Chabannes, St. Augustine, trans. Julie Kernan (Garden City, New York: Doubleday & Company, Inc., 1962), pp. 198-199.
664 The two mountains, Ceuta and Gibraltar, are thought to have been the fabled Pillars of Hercules.
665 John A. Crow, Spain The Root and the Flower, (3rd ed. expanded & updated; Berkeley: University of California Press, 1963), p. 41.
666 John A. Crow, Spain The Root and the Flower, (3rd ed. expanded & updated; Berkeley: University of California Press, 1963), p. 46.
667 Anwar G. Chejne, Muslim Spain Its History and Culture, (Minneapolis: The University of Minnesota Press, 1974), p. 27.

Did Paul actually get to Spain? To answer this question consider a statement by Clement of Rome in his Epistle to the Corinthians, written in the year 95 A.D., shortly after Paul had died. Clement wrote, "Paul by his example pointed out the way to the prize for patient endurance. ... After he had been seven times in chains, had been driven into exile, had been stoned, and had preached in the East and in the West, he won the genuine glory for his faith, ... having taught righteousness to the whole world and **having reached the farthest limits of the West**. [Bolding added.] Finally, when he had given his testimony before the rulers, he thus departed from the world and went to the holy place, having become an outstanding example of patient endurance."[669]

On the basis of this almost contemporaneous account regarding Paul's ministry, it is quite certain that Paul really did reach "the farthest limits of the West." This undoubtedly refers to Spain, because Spain and the Azores were probably as far west as geographical knowledge went at that time.

Rome Comes to Spain

Unfortunately, like Paul's ministry in Arabia (Galatians 1:17), in Illyricum (Romans 15:18-19) and his probable work in Dalmatia (II Timothy 4:9-10), we have no details concerning his ministry in Spain. However, we do know that Spain was a part of the Roman Empire at the time Paul made his visit. "The incorporation of Hispania into the empire was a long, slow process, lasting from 218 B.C. to 19 B.C.[670] (Though the greater part was incorporated by 133 B.C.). This was a much longer time than was required to subjugate other major portions of the Mediterranean littoral."[671] Roman expansion into Spain was necessitated by the war against Carthage. Hannibal, the great Carthaginian general, used Spain as a highway to bring his troops from the south over the Pyrenees to attack Italy from the north.[672]

---

668 Though there is not the slightest Biblical support for it, there is a widely believed Roman Catholic tradition that James the son of Zebedee took the message of Christ to Spain and that his mortal remains are buried in a cathedral built in his honor at Santiago. Not only is there no Biblical support for a visit by James to Spain, "history adduces almost no evidence in support of the miraculous events which gave rise to the cult of St. James, but in this case historic evidence is unimportant. What is important is that the story was believed, and this belief became so militant that it moved men to accomplish incredible deeds." – John A. Crow, Spain, The Root and the Flower, (3rd ed. expanded & updated; Berkeley: University of California Press, 1963), p. 83. Anyone who might wish to examine the evidence for the Roman Catholic tradition will find a rich source in William Steuart McBirnie's The Search For The Twelve Apostles, Chapter Five.

669 J. B. Lightfoot and J. R. Harmer, The Apostolic Fathers, The Letter of the Romans to the Corinthians (I Clement), (Grand Rapids, Michigan, Baker Book House, 1956), p. 31.

670 It was, "under Augustus (19 B.C.), that the last of the restless and impressionable Spanish tribes were conquered and a true *Pax Romana* prevailed throughout the peninsula. Augustus himself was forced to come to Spain to direct the final campaign against the indomitable mountaineers of that 'wild Cantabrian land which will not bow to the Roman yoke' of Horace's famous ode." John A. Crow, Spain The Root and the Flower, (3rd ed. expanded & updated; Berkeley: University of California Press, 1963), p. 28.

671 Stanley G. Payne, A History of Spain and Portugal (Madison, Wisconsin: The University of Wisconsin Press, 1976), p. 4.

672 There were actually three wars, known as the Punic Wars. The word Punic refers to "the dialect of Phoenician spoken in ancient Carthage." [The American Heritage Dictionary of The English Language, (Boston: Houghton Mifflin Company, 1992, 3rd ed.), p.1468] "Carthage was eventually destroyed by the Roman Empire following the three Punic Wars, fought in 264–261 B.C., 218–201 B.C., and 149–146 B.C." – Encarta World English Dictionary (New York: St. Martin's Press, 1999), p. 1457.

If one inquires how the Carthaginians came to be in Spain in the first place, the answer goes back to the sixth century B.C. That was when "the city of Cadiz was attacked from the north and sought aid of the Carthaginians from across the straits. Carthage had been founded about 300 years before by people from Sidon and was therefore of Phoenician origin. The Carthaginians came to help Cadiz and remained to conquer. They set up a sterner regime and centered their rule in New Carthage, now called Cartagena."[673]

In Spain of the apostolic period, undoubtedly Paul would have centered his evangelistic efforts in one or more of the flourishing Roman cities. Though we do not know the fruit which God gave him for his labor, we do know that "Christianity spread through Roman Hispania during the second and third centuries. There, as elsewhere, it was a predominantly urban religion. Large portions of the countryside remained for a long time almost untouched, as did most of Cantabria and almost all the Basque region.

Christianity Takes Root

"By the beginning of the fourth century, however, Hispania apparently had a Christian minority at least as large proportionately as that of the empire as a whole—upwards of 10 percent. After the official recognition of the church early in the fourth century, its following greatly increased, until almost the entire peninsula had become Christian. The pattern of Hispanic church organization was similar to that of most other parts of the empire: bishoprics became coterminous with the urban-centered civitas units and archepiscopal sees were established in provincial capitals. By the fifth century there had developed a distinctively Hispanic church, whose individual religious culture was most evident in the use of the special Hispanic rite (later inaccurately called the Mozarabic[674] rite) in its services until the eleventh century. Theologically the Hispanic church was Orthodox Catholic, though the Priscillian heresy of the late fourth century originated in Galicia (the northwestern corner of the peninsula) and Donatism was temporarily widespread in the fifth century. Yet the Orthodox Hispano-Catholic Church became increasingly strong and well organized, and provided spiritual and cultural leadership and identity which a faltering imperial government could no longer offer."[675]

The condition of the Spanish church at this period may, in part, be judged by the fact that Hosius, bishop of Cordoba/Cordova, advised emperor Constantine on church matters. At the Council of Nicaea (325 A.D.), "Constantine freely took part in the discussions and had great influence in the council. Two outstanding bishops who were present were Eusebius of Caesarea from the East,

---
673 Nicholson B. Adams, <u>The Heritage of Spain An Introduction to Spanish Civilization</u>, (rev. ed.; New York: Holt, Rinehart and Winston, 1959), p. 3.
674 Mozarab is the term which was used to refer to a Christian who lived in Moorish Muslim territory in Spain and had adopted the Arab life style.
675 Stanley G. Payne, <u>A History of Spain and Portugal</u> (Madison, Wisconsin: The University of Wisconsin Press, 1976), pp. 7-8.

and Hosius of Cordova from the West, both of whom were special counselors of the emperor. Hosius was likely the president of the council."[676]

That Hosius did not forfeit his autonomy to the Roman government in order to hold his high position of prestige became clear during the reign of Emperor Constantius, Constantine's son. He "banished Hosius, his father's old adviser, and the bishop railed angrily from exile. 'Do not intrude yourself into church matters, nor give commands to us concerning them,' he wrote. 'God has put into your hands the kingdom; to us he has entrusted the affairs of the Church.'"[677]

Rome Leaves a Heritage

By the time the Muslim invasion of Spain occurred (711A.D.), Roman rule had long been terminated to be followed by a period of turmoil during which the Alani, the Vandals and the Suevi rampaged through the peninsula. That tumultuous period ended when the Vandals migrated to North Africa, the Alani and the Suevi were dispersed within the Iberian Peninsula and a powerful branch of the Visigoths[678] poured over the Pyrenees from Gaul to establish a government and bring order once again out of a chaotic period of Spanish history.

During the Roman period: (1) Roman law was adopted, (2) Christianity was bequeathed to the people of the Iberian Peninsula, and (3) the beginnings of the Spanish language were discernible, derived from Latin. However, "it must be made clear that the inhabitants of Spain were not yet really 'Spaniards' in their ways of thinking, in their feelings, or in their actions. Certainly, there were notable differences between these people and the Spaniards who conquered the Moors and discovered and colonized the New World. Hispanic culture was still in a state of flux. The language spoken in Spain in 400 A.D. would have to undergo many radical changes before it eventually became Spanish. Roman law, too, would be considerably altered by the Visigothic code and by the Moors. Spanish Christianity, after many centuries of contact with Moslems and Jews, evolved a church and a concept of religion vastly different from those of the fourth century A.D."[679]

The story of the coming of the Visigoths to the Iberian Peninsula is another tale of betrayal and sedition. The Roman emperor, "Theodosius had already, on his deathbed in 395, divided the empire into east (Byzantium) and west (Rome) under his two sons. Honorius, aged eleven when he succeeded to the western inheritance, soon saw his authority challenged by one Constantine, nominee of the legionaries in Britain. This was the threat he sought to counter in 406 by the desperate measure of allowing three Germanic peoples, the Alans, Suevi,

---

676 Elgin S. Moyer, Great Leaders of The Christian Church, (Chicago: Moody Press, 1951), p. 111.
677 Brian Moynahan, The Faith, A History of Christianity, (New York: Doubleday, 2002), p. 108.
678 Though we usually think of them as the western Goths, their name seems to mean "valiant people."
679 John A. Crow, Spain The Root and the Flower, (3rd ed. expanded & updated; Berkeley: University of California Press, 1963), p. 35.

and Vandals, to cross the Rhine and stream over Gaul. Constantine, not seriously impeded thereby, was able to march his legions south, unseat his rival, and overrun the Peninsula. The road to Rome he found barred by the fact that the Goths had already swarmed over northern Italy. But it mattered little thereafter who ruled in Rome. Roman Spain, defenseless, lay at the mercy of the invading hordes, now invited across the Pyrenees by Constantine's own general in a personal bid for power."[680]

These events bring us to the Gothic period in Spain's history which proved to be a pivotal period for Christianity, for Spain, for Islam and for Europe.

ଔ

---

[680] William C. Atkinson, A History of Spain and Portugal, (Baltimore: Penguin Books Inc., 1960), p. 35.

Chapter 21

THE ISLAMIC ADVANCE INTO SPAIN

Near Cadiz, on the south coast of Spain, the waters of the Guadalete River flow into the Atlantic Ocean past mud flats where today salt is extracted from sea water by evaporation. But on July 19, in the year 711 A.D., on the banks of that rather insignificant stream, an epochal battle was fought. It proved pivotal not only for Spain and the cause of Christ in that country, but for the whole world.

Flamboyant Beginning — Craven Ending

For background, read about "the treachery of Julian" on p. 256. The initial struggle was between the Visigothic army under King Roderic and invading Muslim Berbers from nearby Africa, led by Tariq, lieutenant to Musa bin Nusayr, the Umayyad Caliph's viceroy in North Africa. "Following an old Gothic tradition, Roderic arrived in an ivory chariot, wearing a purple mantle, a gold crown, and silver boots. At the height of the fray, he abandoned the chariot and mounted a white horse. The Visigoths, despite enormous courage, could not hold out against the Arab onslaught. Screaming Berber horsemen, mounted on small, long-tailed steeds, swooped down from every direction, their broad burnooses flowing and scimitars whirling above their turbaned heads. Amidst guttural cries, the whir of arrows, the neighing of horses, and the clash of armor, the Goths took flight. When night fell on Jerez [a nearby town] the Berbers raised the green standard of the Prophet. In vain did they look for Roderic. The only trace of him was his white bemired horse and, close to it, a silver boot."[681]

Many Influences

Long before Islam's stunning victory on the banks of the Guadalete, which ultimately very materially impacted the cause of Christ in Spain, that cause had already been subjected to profound and wrenching influences.

"By 200 the church had been ... growing in both Spain and Gaul [the area of modern France]. Its members belonged to a vibrant organization that boasted its own leaders, properties, and rituals. But as the church grew stronger, the empire was beginning to weaken."[682]

---

681 Jean Descola, <u>A History of Spain</u>, trans. Elaine P. Halperin, (New York: Alfred A. Knopf, 1963), p. 96.
682 Gayla Visalli (ed.), <u>After Jesus The Triumph of Christianity</u>, (New York: The Reader's Digest Association, Inc., 1992), p. 148.

Those who followed Christ in Spain suffered from state persecution as did those in other areas of the Roman Empire. For example, "On September 14, [258 A.D.] Cyprian became Africa's first bishop-martyr. The persecution spread to Spain, where Fructuosus, bishop of Tarragona, and two of his deacons were burned alive."[683]

Not only were the followers of Christ harassed by Roman imperial persecution, they were deeply divided by powerful and basic deviations from Biblical doctrinal norms. The outstanding case of flagrant doctrinal deviation is that of the concept contrived by Priscillian, bishop of Avila [west-northwest of present day Madrid] in Spain. However, "there was a lively Christian Church in Gallaecia before Priscillianism gained the importance that it achieved from the late fourth to the end of the sixth century, and ... Roman and Christian cultural influence had been very efficient in converting Gallaecia's intelligentsia."[684] "Somewhat like the Gnostics before him, Priscillian taught that the spirit is good and all matter, including the human form, is evil. In this notion detractors discerned an implication that Jesus could not have been truly human."[685] This affair led to blatant state interference in church matters. Under Emperor Maximus, Priscillian was taken to Germany for trial, falsely accused of sorcery and executed.

"The episode was traumatic for the church; it had permitted the state to interfere dramatically in ecclesiastical affairs. After Priscillian's death, the bishops who had accused him were excommunicated. Soon afterward, Theodosius overthrew Maximus, rescinded all the former emperor's orders, and deposed the guilty Spanish prelates. Galicia (in northwest Spain) remained Priscillianist until 400, when most Priscillianist bishops in that province were reconciled to the church at the first ecclesiastical Council of Toledo."[686]

Visigoths Bring Heresy

One of the most serious and destructive theological events which happened to Spanish disciples of the Messiah, before the coming of Islam, was the imposition of Arianism upon their homeland. This happened because of the Visigothic conquest of Iberia beginning in 415 A.D. "The [Roman] empire maintained a shadow existence [in Spain] for another twenty years: only in 475, the year before its demise, did it formally recognize Visigothic sovereignty [over

---

[683] Gayla Visalli (ed.), <u>After Jesus The Triumph of Christianity</u>, (New York: The Reader's Digest Association, Inc., 1992), p. 177.
[684] Alberto Ferreiro (ed.), <u>The Visigoths Studies in Culture and Society</u>, (Leiden: Brill, 1999), p. 67.
[685] Gayla Visalli (ed.), <u>After Jesus The Triumph of Christianity</u>, (New York: The Reader's Digest Association, Inc., 1992), p. 253. There is controversy over Priscillian's actual doctrinal position. For example, "From the Tractati, which seem to have been written by Priscillian himself, we know that they used apocryphal Scriptures in the teaching of the faith, which took place in a community of master and disciples. More importantly, however, the texts seem to reveal orthodox and not heretical doctrines." – Alberto Ferreiro (ed.), <u>The Visigoths Studies in Culture and Society</u>, (Leiden: Brill, 1999), p. 70.
[686] Gayla Visalli (ed.), <u>After Jesus The Triumph of Christianity</u>, (New York: The Reader's Digest Association, Inc., 1992), p. 254.

Spain]."[687] It was a sovereignty exercised by committed adherents to Arian Christology who, under King Athanagild, settled on Toledo as their Spanish capital about the year 554.

The Visigoth invaders carried a Gothic translation of the Bible with them as they flooded into Gaul and Spain. For it they owed a great debt of gratitude to Ulfilas, 'Apostle of the Goths,' who lived from 311–381 A.D., for providing them with the Scripture in their own language. Ulfilas, had "led his Christian converts [south] across the Danube into the land now known as Bulgaria, but then as the Roman province of Moesia. There he translated the Bible into their language."[688] Their Bible was complete except for "the books of Samuel and Kings [which] were not translated because the translator believed that these books were 'too warlike to be transmitted' to the Gothic tribes."[689]

How far Ulfilas' Arianism may have skewed his translation is a matter of debate. "Perhaps the only certain trace of the translator's dogmatic bias is found in Phil. ii.6, where reference is made to the pre-existent Christ in terms of being *galeiko guda* (= 'similar to God'), whereas the Greek *isa theo* should have been rendered *ibna guda* [= 'being in very nature God']."[690]

Western Europe and NW Africa in 490 A.D.

"The Vandals [had] crossed the Pyrenees to occupy northern Spain while the Visigoths passed through Italy to Gaul, plundering Rome on the way. After the Visigoths had moved on, other barbarian generals ruled in Italy until they were defeated by the Ostrogoths, who took possession of Italy. Meanwhile the Visigoths had driven the Vandals from Spain and the latter had taken control of North Africa. Thus by A.D. 490 the Ostrogoths held Italy, the Visigoths southern Gaul and Spain, and the Vandals the African coast."[691] "Although the states created by the Vandals in North Africa and by the Ostrogoths in Italy were comparatively short lived, that of the Visigoths in Spain lasted some 300 years."[692]

Mutual Enmity Finally Ends

The Visigoths and the much more numerous indigenous Hispano-Roman Catholic population lived for many years with reciprocal enmity. "The fighting between the [Visigothic] invaders frequently led to violence against the Catholics and to the pillage and destruction of their churches."[693] It was "the

---

687 William C. Atkinson, A History of Spain and Portugal, (Baltimore: Penguin Books, Inc., 1960), p. 37.
688 F.F. Bruce, The Books and the Parchments How We got our English Bible, (Old Tappan, New Jersey: Fleming H. Revell Company, 1984), p. 207.
689 Norman L. Geisler & William E. Nix, A General Introduction to the Bible, (Chicago: Moody Press, 1968), p. 324.
690 Paul D. Wegner, The Journey from Texts to Translations The Origin and Development of the Bible, (Grand Rapids, Michigan: Baker Academic, 1999), p. 258.
691 Sidney Painter, A History of the Middle Ages – 284–1500, (New York: Alfred A. Knopf, Inc., 1960), p. 25.
692 Sidney Painter, A History of the Middle Ages – 284–1500, (New York: Alfred A. Knopf, Inc., 1960), p. 65.
693 Alberto Ferreiro (ed.), The Visigoths Studies in Culture and Society, (Leiden: Brill, 1999), p. 104.

religious cleavage that more than anything else divided Arian conquerors from Catholic conquered."[694]

Finally, the Visigothic King Reccared, whose mother was a Catholic and whose brother (Hermenigild) had been executed for previously adopting Catholicism, realized the futility of harassing the majority community and consequently converted to Catholicism in 587 A.D.

Baptism Changed

Prior to the mass conversions following King Reccared's embrace of the Catholic Church, it seems baptism had been correctly acknowledged to be immersion. A basilica and baptistry dating from the sixth century "reveals the baptismal customs in Lusitania [Western Spain], thus confirming what texts ... tell us about the first appearance in Hispania of the problem of triple immersion versus simple immersion in the baptismal rite."[695]

At the time of the mass conversion of the Visigoths to the Catholic Church, the Pope compromised the form of baptism. "His friend Leander, the archbishop of Seville, who was weaning the Spanish Visigoths from their Arianism, asked what method of baptism should be used; Gregory replied that 'where there is one faith, a diversity of usage does no harm to the Church. He preferred to adapt heathen practices to Christianity rather than destroy them.'"[696] Obviously, then, it certainly was not only the Muslim invasion and Islam's centuries-long occupation of much of Spain which adversely impacted the church!

Anti-Semitism

Catholics and the Visigoths (during both the Arian and Catholic periods of their Spanish kingdom) were both anti-Jewish. "Hostility against the Jews was always present in Catholic society during the Visigothic monarchy, even among the kings who paid no attention to the Jewish problem. ... [The kings' attitudes] were determinant in creating an atmosphere of social-aggression and hate towards the Jews in Visigothic Spain. ... In the actual writings of the Visigothic Fathers we can find specific references to the desire for a totally Christian society without the presence of unfaithful Jews. ... And Julian of Toledo ... thought that Judaism 'had to be cut off, since it was like the cancerous part of the body, before this harmful disease could be passed on to the healthy parts.'"[697]

More specifically, "The Sixth Council of Toledo proclaimed: 'No one in the royal kingdom will be tolerated who is not a Catholic.' Since the Arians were [then] no longer a threat, this was aimed principally at the Jews. ... It was [the Visigothic] King Sisebut who initiated the policy of anti-Semitism which, for

---

694 William C. Atkinson, A History of Spain and Portugal, (Baltimore: Penguin Books, Inc., 1960), p. 39.
695 Alberto Ferreiro (ed.), The Visigoths Studies in Culture and Society, (Leiden: Brill, 1999), p. 113.
696 Brian Moynahan, The Faith A History of Christianity, (New York: Doubleday, 2002), p. 197.
697 Alberto Ferreiro (ed.), The Visigoths Studies in Culture and Society, (Leiden: Brill, 1999), pp. 124-128.

so many centuries, was pursued by the Catholic kings. Brief indeed were the periods of relaxation or reconciliation! Although Isidore had already warned the Seventh Council that conversion was a matter of free will, and had censured the Gothic monarch for 'using violence instead of persuasion to bring people to the Church,' he could not prevent Sisebut from persecuting the Jews."[698]

Faulty Political System

The political weakness of the Visigothic kingdom resulted from the faulty method of choosing a successor to any given king. "The elective nature of the Visigothic monarchy, the king being but a noble chosen by his peers, did not make, it is true, for social peace or stability; in the end it would lead to the ignominious collapse of the regime and the overrunning of the land anew, this time from Africa."[699]

Three factors entered into the election or appointment of a king: heredity, popular acclaim by the nobles and the will of the army. The Catholic Church had great influence as well. Depending on where they saw expediency calling, they might side with the nobles or with the army or, even, with the king. This led to inconclusive decisions. If the occupant of the throne did not win the approval of all three power bases, his legitimacy would likely be challenged and contested by the one who had received lesser support. In fact, this was precisely the situation which prevailed in 711 A.D. when the Muslims invaded Spain.

King Witiza "was preparing the way when he died [in 710] for his son Achila to follow him. This proved too much for the nobles, who promptly elected one Roderic, and again civil war broke out, provoked by Achila and his uncle Oppa, archbishop of Seville."[700]

As we have just seen, "supporters of Witiza's clan refused to accept the election of a rival candidate, Roderic, in 710, and sought assistance from the newly established Muslim overlords of North Africa. The Visigothic dissidents obviously failed to appreciate the dynamism and integrative potential of the Islamic culture that had swept [like a withering wind] out of Arabia only a few generations earlier. Their miscalculation was probably due in part to [their knowledge of] the considerable difficulty encountered by the Muslims in subduing the Berber Kabyles of the Maghreb [northwest African coastal area] during the

---

698 Jean Descola, A History of Spain, trans. Elaine P. Halperin, (New York: Alfred A. Knopf, 1963), p. 86. Note: "The Spanish Jews under Egica (687–702) continued to meet with new restrictions. They were forbidden to own land and houses, to trade with North Africa, to transact business with Christians. In the end, on the pretext that the Jews were plotting with the Moors, the whole population was virtually sentenced to slavery and their children of seven years and upwards were handed over to Christians to be brought up in their faith. Fortunately, this state of affairs came to an abrupt end when Egica's second successor, Roderic (711–113), the last Visigothic king in Spain, was defeated and killed by the Muhammadans in the autumn of 713. It is of no mean significance that during the occupation of Spain by the Saracens the Jews enjoyed a period of peace and security, with the exception of the persecution started by the Caliph of Damascus, Omar II, in 720." – Jakob Jocz, The Jewish People and Jesus Christ, (London: S.P.C.K., 1949), p. 81.
699 William C. Atkinson, A History of Spain and Portugal, (Baltimore: Penguin Books, Inc., 1960), pp. 38–39.
700 William C. Atkinson, A History of Spain and Portugal, (Baltimore: Penguin Books, Inc., 1960), p. 43

preceding half-century."[701] "Although the Berbers living near the plains have adopted Islam through contact with the Arabs, the majority of the highlanders have no religion at all, only revering their 'marabouts.' Daumas and Fabar, in the 1840s, carry this process of deislamicisation [sic] to its limit, writing that if one scratches the Moslem exterior, the Christian essence appears, symbolized by the cross which figures in their facial tattoos. The Kabyles are thus not only Nordic in origin, but even originally Christians forcibly converted to Islam."[702]

The Era of Spanish Islam Begins

The Roman period of Spanish history was supplanted by the Visigothic period which began in 415 A.D. The end of the Visigothic period, as we have just seen, was brought about decisively and suddenly in 711 A.D. by the beginning of the Arab-Berber-Muslim period of Spanish history at the battle on the banks of the Guadalete. The Muslim period of Spanish history lasted 781 years, from 711 to 1492. Chapters 22 and 23 explore the impact of Islam on the cause of Christ in the Spanish Peninsula.

By the time the Muslim era began in Spain, the visible church had already gone far away from the Biblical concept of Christ's church. Unfortunately, it was still to go much further away from the Biblical pattern. One last glimpse of the life and structure of the visible church will perhaps prepare us to pick up the sobering account of the visible church's life during the centuries when Islam both dominated Spanish affairs and then went into decline.

"As the clergy grew in number and importance, it [the clergy] tightened its grip on the civil power. National synods usurped the functions of a parliament or council of state. Provincial synods claimed jurisdiction over every problem submitted to them. Bishops controlled the public administration. Judges and tax collectors were supervised by the heads of dioceses. Moreover, it was the councils that trained the members of the revenue and law-enforcement agencies and instructed them in their duties. Thus, the Church moved imperceptibly first from the legislative to the judiciary, then to the executive. Its tendency toward despotism led it to foster, deliberately or unwittingly, a hunger for wealth and a spirit of revenge. This is the grave danger of too close an alliance between church and state."[703]

ϾԲ

---

701 Stanley G. Payne, <u>A History of Spain and Portugal</u>, (Madison, Wisconsin: The University of Wisconsin Press, 1973), p. 15.
702 Ann Tomson, <u>Barbary and Enlightenment, European Attitudes Toward the Maghreb in the 18th Century</u>, (NY: E.J. Brill, 1987), p. 110.
703 Jean Descola, <u>A History of Spain</u>, trans. Elaine P. Halperin, (New York: Alfred A. Knopf, 1963), p. 87.

Chapter 22

CATHOLICISM COMPETES WITH ISLAM FOR SPAIN

The Great Mosque of Cordoba. Of the 3000 mosques which eventually adorned the city, this was the greatest and most celebrated. It began as a commandeered church building. After negotiations with the Christians the church was razed by order of Abd al-Rahman I to make way for this mosque which continued to be remodeled and renovated into the reign of Abd al-Rahman III. – Photo courtesy of Steve Fazzio

A new mosque has recently been built in the city of Granada, last bastion of Islam before Muslims were totally expelled from Spain at the end of the fifteenth century. It is "the first [mosque] built here in more than 500 years. The row of men kneeling in prayer at the city's new mosque are not modern-day Moors; they are well-educated European converts. 'We've come to offer society the only alternative that exists to lead it out of chaos,' declared one of the community's founders, Hajj Abdulhasib Castineira. ...

"While immigration is gradually spreading Islam across Europe[704], a homegrown movement is giving it added momentum in Spain, where a generation of post-Franco intellectuals are reassessing the country's Moorish past and recasting Spanish identity to include Islamic influences rejected as heretical centuries ago. ... Spain's Muslim converts now number in the tens of thousands. ... Today, the whitewashed brick mosque blends seamlessly into the increas-

---

[704] "Owing to migration from North Africa, Turkey and the Middle East there are 11.8 million Muslims in Western Europe. This includes 5 million in France, 3.1 million in Germany, 2 million in the UK, and the rest in other countries such as Belgium, the Netherlands, and Switzerland." – *Idea via Mission Net*, Pulpit Helps, Vol. 29, Num. 1, January 2004, p. 31. According to the U.S. National Intelligence Counsel (NIC), "there are already as many as 18 million Muslims in Western Europe or 4.5% of the population. The percentage is even lower for the 27-country European Union as a whole. The future will certainly see an increase, but it's hard to imagine that Europe will even reach the 10% mark (except in some countries or cities). For one thing, as the same NIC study indicates and demographers agree, fertility rates among Muslims are sharply declining as children of immigrants gradually conform to prevailing social and economic norms. Nor is immigration still a major source of newly minted European Muslims. Only about 500,000 people a year come legally to Europe from Muslim-majority countries, with an even smaller number coming illegally—meaning that the annual influx is a fraction of a percent of the European population." – Justin Vaisse, *Eurabian Follies*, Foreign Policy, January/February, 2010, p. 88. This note was written before the massive influx of Muslim refugees from North Africa and war-stricken Syria flooded into Europe in 2016. As of 2016, the total population of the twenty-eight EU countries was 505.3 million. This means the Muslim population was 4%. However, that percentage is not uniform among all the nations of the EU. For example, the United Kingdom has 4.6%, Belgium has 6% and Bulgaria has 13.4%. www.muslimpopulation.com, accessed 9/29/17.

ingly gentrified neighborhood. Hundreds of tourists visit the garden each day and Mr. Castineira said a few people convert to Islam there each week."[705]

Obviously, the contest between Catholicism and Islam in Spain is not finished; it is current as well as historic. That raises the question whether Roman Catholicism is capable of successfully resisting the power of the new Islamic resurgence. George Weigel, a very perceptive Catholic analyst, points to some of the most important issues. He wrote, "Why European Christianity was particularly vulnerable to the siren song of atheistic humanism raises another, deeper set of questions. ... Answers to those questions will certainly require carefully probing the Catholic Church's identification with the political forces most resistant to the democratic project in late-eighteen- and nineteenth-century Europe."[706] Weigel makes a further even more sobering observation in which he tells us, "the radicalization of Islam that seems to be a by-product of some Muslims' encounter with contemporary, secularized Europe, could eventually produce a Europe in which Polish King Jan III Sobieski's victory at Vienna in 1683 is reversed, [See the Introduction and Chapter 25 under "Turkish Decline."] such that the Europe of the twenty-second century, or even the late twenty-first, is a Europe increasingly influenced, and perhaps even dominated, by militant Islamic populations, convinced that their long-delayed triumph in the European heartland is at hand."[707]

The extremely crucial Spanish contest between Catholicism and Islam began at the Battle of Guadalete in 711 A.D., when the first Muslim intruders invaded Spain from North Africa. The battle has been named for the tiny river on whose banks the seven-day struggle between the Muslim invaders and the Visigothic-Catholic-Spanish defenders took place. That dramatic struggle was briefly described in the previous chapter.

A Bridge Becomes a Wall

With the Muslim attack on Spain in 711 A.D. Islam had, unmistakably, traversed the entire length of the Mediterranean. The consequences of Islam's dash to the Atlantic and to Spain were epochal. "The coming of Islam in the seventh century transformed the Mediterranean from a link to a barrier. In Roman times, even in the chaotic years toward the end, Egyptian monks could journey to northern Ireland while Gauls could visit Syria or Cyrenaica. But after the coming of Islam, Europe was isolated ... and its intellectual nutriment was of the sparest."[708]

---

705 Craig S. Smith, *Where the Moors Held Sway, Allah Is Praised Again*, The New York Times, International, October 21, 2003.
706 George Weigel, The Cube and the Cathedral, Europe, America, and Politics Without God, (New York: Basic Books, 2005), p. 52. In Alan Posener's book *Benedict's Crusade*, he "argues that [Pope] Benedict's activist agenda is a brand of fundamentalism that has more in common with Islamist radicalism than it does with any kind of contemporary Christian democracy." – Paul Hockenos, *The Pope and the Chancellor*, Foreign Policy, January/February, 2010, p. 92.
707 George Weigel, The Cube and the Cathedral, Europe, America, and Politics Without God, (New York: Basic Books, 2005), p. 134.
708 Desmond Stewart, The Alhambra, (New York: Newsweek Book Division, 1974), p. 82.

From the battle on the Guadalete in 711 until the Battle of Musara on May 15, 756[709] which assured Abd al-Rahman I's rule, Muslim Spain had been hectic and seething. It had been torn by struggles for power, by premature attempts to bring France under Muslim rule before Muslim forces had even fully finished bringing all of Spain to its knees. It had also been torn by natural disasters and by Catholic attempts to reverse the series of misfortunes which had brought vast areas of Spain under Muslim rule.

Liberal Islam?

It is important to evaluate the Muslim period of Spanish history, not only because of its impact on Spanish Christianity but because it is claimed that "Islamic Spain, the Emperor Akbar's rule in Mughal India, and the Abbasid Caliphate are the best-known historical examples of liberal Islam. These regimes [the writer goes on to assert] practiced religious tolerance, promoted educational and scientific achievement, and made pluralism a state as well as a social value."[710]

To help evaluate the pro-Islamic panegyric cited in the preceding paragraph, consider a Jewish scholar's evaluation of the religious tolerance of Islamic Spain. He wrote, "Sectarian Islam, ... was responsible for forced mass conversion of adults. The most notorious example of this was the Almohad movement [See below.], ... which during the twelfth century conquered North Africa and Spain, countries which at that time harbored some of the most flourishing Jewish communities. Those congregations which refused to accept Islam, the town of Fez [in Morocco], for instance, were put to the sword. Those who accepted Islam had no easy life either. The fanatical Almohads understood well that the forced confession of the Muslim faith had little value and therefore put the converts under strict supervision. They had to wear a special garment—described in detail in the sources—and were treated more or less as outlaws. Even those who endeavored to show their zeal for the new religion were brought to court on the slightest pretext, and in many cases the converts were executed, their property confiscated and their wives turned over to Muslims. All the horrors of the Spanish Inquisition were anticipated under Almohad rule."[711]

Dr. Goitein's analysis is confirmed repeatedly by Dario Fernandez-Morera in The Myth of the Andalusian Paradise, his 2016, 240-page, historical analysis of the specious claim that Muslim rule in Spain was benign.

---

709 This is the date given by Thomas Ballantine Irving, Falcon of Spain, A study of Eighth-Century Spain, with special emphasis upon the life of the Umayyad ruler 'Abdurrahman I 756–788, (Lahore, Pakistan: Orientalia Publishers & Booksellers, 1954), p. 49.
710 M. A. Muqtedar Khan, *Radical Islam, Liberal Islam*, Current History, A Journal of Contemporary World Affairs, December 2003, p. 418.
711 S.D. Goitein, Jews and Arabs, Their Contacts Through the Ages, (New York: Schocken Books, 1967), p. 80.

Islam's Political Center Goes East

The Muslim invasion and occupation of Spain took place under the oversight of the waning Damascus-based Umayyad Caliphate. Just thirty-nine years after Tariq, the Muslim general, and his victorious troops set foot on Spanish soil, the Umayyad Caliphate, in 750 A.D., after a ninety-two-year existence, was sent into oblivion by the victorious Abbasids at the Battle of the Great Zab River. "The Battle of the Zab was one of the decisive battles of the world because [as mentioned earlier] it resulted in the orientalization of Islam."[712]

Also, the Battle of the Zab moved the center of political power in the Muslim world from the Mediterranean, at Damascus, to Baghdad[713] on the Tigris in Asia. Marwan II, was the last Umayyad Caliph. On 25th January 750, in the decisive battle at the Great Zab, a branch of the Tigris in northern Iraq, "the Abbasids routed Marwan's army, bringing to an end Umayyad rule.[714] [As noted before], the deposed Caliph fled to Egypt, but was caught there and killed, and his head sent to the new Caliph as a present."[715] Those stunning events left a total political vacuum in Spain which invited eager aspirants to repeatedly lunge for power.

Subordinating the Subordinate

Prior to the demise of the Umayyad Caliphate there had been an ongoing power struggle between Kairwan (Qayrawan/Kairouan) in North Africa and Damascus. Kairwan had been "founded in 670 as a base of operations and administrative center for that Far West of the Arab empire."[716] Damascus was the caliphal capital of the entire Umayyad empire. The dispute was over how the conquest and occupation of Spain were to be carried out.

It was a deadly contest. The Muslim invasion of Spain was carried out under the oversight and direction of Musa, the caliph's deputy and governor of North Africa. He appointed his son 'Abd al-Aziz to be the first ruler (the emir) of newly conquered Spain. However in Damascus Caliph Suleyman heard reports that the young ruler was living in an extremely ostentatious manner. Consequently, he ordered him to be assassinated! Shortly after that assassination, "Caliph 'Umar II made ['Abd al-Aziz's successor] Samh's appointment [as

---

712 John Glubb, <u>A Short History of the Arab Peoples</u>, (New York: Stein and Day, 1970), p. 93.
713 In 762 A.D., Mansur, brother of Abbas, "was looking for a site for a new capital. Abbas' capital in Hashimiya had two major drawbacks: from a military point of view it was not strategically located, and it was too near to Kufa, long a center of rebellion. But Mansur had another motive for establishing a new capital: he wanted it to be a magnificent symbol of Abbasid power. The Caliph is said to have made many journeys through Iraq before finally finding a suitable location. He chose an ancient village named Baghdad, approximately 20 miles northwest of the former Persian capital of Ctesiphon." – Desmond Stewart, <u>Early Islam</u>, (New York: Time Incorporated, 1967), p. 79.
714 The Umayyad Caliphate had been founded in 658 A.D. In that year Syrian Governor Mu'awiya annexed Egypt and declared himself Caliph. Mu'awiya ruled Syria, Palestine, and Egypt from Damascus. Ali ruled Iraq and Persia from Kufa for a very short time. Thus, Islam was briefly divided with two opposing caliphs.
715 Desmond Stewart, <u>Early Islam</u>, (New York: Time Incorporated, 1967), p. 64.
716 Thomas Ballantine Irving, <u>Falcon of Spain, A study of Eighth-Century Spain, with special emphasis upon the life of the Umayyad ruler 'Abdurrahman I 756–788</u>, (Lahore, Pakistan: Orientalia Publishers & Booksellers, 1954), p. 2.

ruler of Spain] independent of Qayrawan, in order to bring the new province under the closer supervision of Damascus."[717]

This contest became so severe that ultimately it led to the caliph's deputy, Musa, being called from Spain to Damascus to be utterly humiliated. When caliph Walid was succeeded by his brother Suleyman, the new caliph, "inflicted even greater humiliation upon the proud conqueror: he decreed that Musa should lose all his property and titles and be executed. Court influence saved his life, but he was nevertheless punished physically by exposure to the summer sun, which indeed nearly killed him because he was subject to asthma. The conqueror of Spain died a beggar in the Hijaz after the crowning humiliation of being handed the decapitated head of his son 'Abd al-Aziz."[718]

Surviving Liberal Islam

The dynastic revolution of 750, resulting from the Battle of the Zab, in which the Umayyad Caliphate was supplanted by the Abbasid Caliphate, resulted in the execution of the reigning Umayyad family members. They were, "violently overthrown by [the new] rival and, with one exception, exterminated in wholesale massacre. The [lone] survivor [Abd al-Rahman] a youth of nineteen born of a Berber slave-woman, after an adventurous [and perilous] five years made his way to Al-Andalus [as the Muslims called their part of Spain], was there welcomed by the many partisans of his house, and after some fighting entered Cordoba in triumph in 756."[719]

Their brutal extermination of the Umayyad ruling family gives us a characteristic peek at the Abbasid Caliphate which Muqtedar Khan ironically, brazenly and falsely alleges "practiced religious tolerance ... and made pluralism a state as well as a social value."[720] The facts are quite the opposite. "The first Abbasid caliph referred to himself as *al-saffah*, 'the bloodshedder', which became his sobriquet. The fact was ominous. The incoming dynasty depended upon force in the execution of its policies. For the first time in the history of Islam the leathern spread beside the caliph's seat, which served as a carpet for the executioner, became a necessary adjunct of the imperial throne."[721]

---

717 Thomas Ballantine Irving, Falcon of Spain, A study of Eighth-Century Spain, with special emphasis upon the life of the Umayyad ruler 'Abdurrahman I 756–788, (Lahore, Pakistan: Orientalia Publishers & Booksellers, 1954), pp. 21-22.
718 Thomas Ballantine Irving, Falcon of Spain, A study of Eighth-Century Spain, with special emphasis upon the life of the Umayyad ruler 'Abdurrahman I 756–788, (Lahore, Pakistan: Orientalia Publishers & Booksellers, 1954), p. 20.
719 William C. Atkinson, A History of Spain & Portugal, (London: Penguin Books, 1960), p. 48.
720 As we have already seen, Muqtedar Khan also claims that Islamic Spain is among "the best-known historical examples of liberal Islam." It is alleged to have, "practiced religious tolerance, ... and made pluralism a state as well as a social value." For an evaluation of Mr. Muqtedar Khan's claim I refer the reader to: Edward Rothstein, *Was the Islam Of Old Spain Truly Tolerant?*, The New York Times, September 27, 2003, p. A15. Especially see Dario Fernandez-Morera, The Myth of the Andalusian Paradise, (Wilmington, DE: ISI Books, 2016).
721 Philip K. Hitti, The Arabs A Short History, (London: Macmillan & Co. Ltd., 1965), p. 82

A Mountain Lair

After the Visigothic-Catholic forces had been defeated in the Battle of Guadalete, many of their survivors made their way to Asturias in the remote and mountainous far north-central Spain to try another day to recoup the staggering loss which they had suffered at the Guadalete.

It had been the Muslim general Musa's plan to cross the Pyrenees and conquer Gaul (France) at the earliest possible moment. Though Musa, as we have just seen, was deposed and humiliated, his vision captivated the Muslim military decision makers who followed him. Both in 717 and in 719, under the leadership of an Arab general named Hurr, France was invaded. Samh, the new emir actually took the French town of Narbonne in 720. "This he made into an army base, because it lay on the Mediterranean and could be easily provisioned from the sea in case of siege."[722]

Fourteen years before the military catastrophe which the Muslims suffered in France from the battle known as the Battle of Tours, though nearer to Poitiers than to Tours, the Muslims did make one attempt in 718 A.D. to defeat the Catholic forces which had taken refuge in the Asturian wilderness of the Cantabrian Mountains. Surprisingly, the Muslim force, "was defeated by the Asturian chieftain Pelayo, who is also regarded as the first king of Asturias. The vale of Covadonga is marked as the place of this legendary Spanish victory, so widely celebrated in song and story. ... The Moors [the collective name for the people who made up the multinational Muslim invasion force], did not seek further penetration into these wild mountains, and it was from this primitive nest that the reconquest of Spain began."[723]

Crucial Battles

Two other key battles took place on Catholicism's long campaign to expel Islam from Spain. They were, (1) The Battle of Simancas in 939 A.D. in which Abd al-Rahman III's army of 100,000 men was utterly broken. "Abd al-Rahman fled, leaving on the field a priceless Koran that had accompanied him everywhere, and, back in Cordoba, crucified for cowardice 300 of his officers. He never thereafter led his armies in person."[724] (2) The second great Catholic victory took place at the Battle of Las Navas de Tolosa in 1212 A.D. which really broke the back of Spanish Islam's military power.

Had Muslim leadership "been alive to the danger of leaving even one area, however apparently insignificant, unsubdued, the Spanish Peninsula might still today be an Arab-speaking Mohammedan country. Instead the invaders, their impetus not yet spent, crossed the Pyrenees. In fourteen years they streamed as

---

722 Thomas Ballantine Irving, Falcon of Spain, A study of Eighth-Century Spain, with special emphasis upon the life of the Umayyad ruler 'Abdurrahman I 756–788, (Lahore, Pakistan: Orientalia Publishers & Booksellers, 1954), p. 22.
723 John A. Crow, Spain The Root and the Flower, An Interpretation of Spain and the Spanish People, (Berkeley: University of California Press, 1985), p. 48.
724 William C. Atkinson, A History of Spain & Portugal, (London: Penguin Books, 1960), p. 51.

far north as Poitiers, there to suffer in 732, in one of the decisive battles of history, a crushing reverse at the hands of Charles 'the Hammerer' which saved Gaul for Europe. The [Spanish] Peninsula was never wholly lost to Europe in the centuries that followed, but it was a profoundly altered Peninsula that would one day re-emerge to play its full part anew in that context."[725]

The great Muslim emir, Abd al-Rahman I, after coming to power in Cordoba following his 5-year flight and narrow escape from the Abbasid death squads, sent aid to the Muslim outposts in France which had survived after the major Muslim defeat at the Battle of Tours. However, the relief, "expedition was defeated in the Pyrenean passes in 140/758. The following year [759 A.D.], the Muslim lands held in Gaul fell to the Gauls and the Franks, so that the Arabs lost everything beyond the Pyrenees."[726]

Thus, not only did the Muslim military thrusts into Gaul ultimately prove totally futile, they gave the small Visigothic-Catholic forces which had taken refuge in the mountains of Asturias, time to become a more credible military factor in the future of Spain.

A Fatal Withdrawal

The northwestern and the north-central part of Spain, bordering on Asturias where the Visigothic-Catholic Spaniards had taken refuge, had been given to the Berber contingents of the Muslim invasion forces. It was less desirable land compared to the southeast section of Spain which the Arab Muslims kept for themselves. "In 750 there occurred a great drought, and the remaining Berbers in northern Spain abandoned their holdings and returned to Africa. ... The Arabs [then] had to withdraw their authority to the south of a line stretching from Coimbra in Portugal through Coria, Toledo, Guadalajara and Tudela to Pamplona by the Pyrenees. The Christians now held Asturias, Santander, Burgos, and parts of Leon and Galicia under Pelayo's son-in-law, Duke Alfonso of Cantabria; between them and the Arabs lay a No-Man's-Land."[727]

In the year 719, only eight years after the Battle of Guadalete, General Samh, who had come to power in Spain by direct appointment from Damascus, shifted the capital of Muslim Spain from Seville to Cordoba on the Guadalquivir River. It was in and from Cordoba that Abd al-Rahman I began his rule in 756. His ascension to power, though challenged many times, overall brought the chaos in the Muslim part of the Spanish Peninsula to an end. In succession, the three main centers of Islamic civilization in Spain were Cordoba (756–1013), Seville (1013–1248) and Granada (1248–1492).

---

725 William C. Atkinson, A History of Spain & Portugal, (London: Penguin Books, 1960), p. 46.
726 Mahmoud Makki, *The Political History of Al-Andalus (92/711–897/1492)*, The Legacy of Muslim Spain, Vol 1, ed. Salma Khadra Jayyusi (Leiden/Boston: Brill, 2000), p.16.
727 Thomas Ballantine Irving, Falcon of Spain, A study of Eighth-Century Spain, with special emphasis upon the life of the Umayyad ruler 'Abdurrahman I 756–788, (Lahore, Pakistan: Orientalia Publishers & Booksellers, 1954), p. 27.

Summary of the Muslim Era

The nearly eight-centuries-long Muslim period of Spanish history may be summarized under five eras: (1) The era of chaotic Umayyad rule from 711 to 756 when Abd al-Rahman I came to power in Cordoba. (2) The era of the Umayyad Emirate-Caliphate, from 756 to 1013. Abd al-Rahman I did not call himself a caliph but an emir. It was Abd al-Rahman III who took the title of caliph. This era stretched from the ascension of Abd al-Rahman III to the ruthless general al-Mansur's placing his totally unworthy son, on the caliphal throne at Cordoba, which led to a revolt and Hisham II sacking the city in 1013. These events ended the Umayyad-Emirate-Caliphate period of Spanish-Muslim history and led to political chaos and disintegration. (3) The era of Petty Muslim Kingdoms. The sacking of Cordoba was followed by a period during which Muslim Spain was divided among some 26 petty or splinter kingdoms (*taifas* in Arabic). "Left to themselves the *taifas* were doomed, and knew it. ... (4) The Almoravide era. Across the straits [of Gibraltar], as it happened, the recent acceptance of Islam by some Berber tribes of the Sahara had created the conditions for a new crusade. These Almoravides ('vowed to God [for holy war]')[728] were filled with the fanaticism of the newly converted and, knowing nothing of the civilized values of the Arab way of life, cared nothing for them."[729] (5) Finally, there was the era of the Almohads whose exploits are given briefly below.

Desperation and Decline

The desperation of the Spanish Muslim's situation was made dramatically clear by the capture of Toledo in 1085 by Catholic forces. Subsequently, "Toledo was incorporated into Castile."[730] The significance of the loss of Toledo was obvious to the taifa-king al-Mutamid whose capital was Seville. It had become, "the second city of Andalusia, and its size, influence, and opulence were growing constantly. After the decline of Cordoba, Seville moved into the limelight. In the second half of the eleventh century, under al-Mutamid, it became a rendezvous of scholars and artists."[731] However, al-Mutamid understood that "for all their militance, the Muslims of Andalus were clearly outmatched by the resurgent Christians. Faced with the possibility of losing his throne to the Muslims of North Africa if he sought their aid or the certainty of losing it to the Christians if he did not, al-Mutamid of Seville [in 1086] called in his co-religionists. He did so, he noted wryly, because he preferred to be a camel driver

---

[728] These new Berber converts to Islam called, "themselves al-murabitun ('united for holy war'), the Arabic has been westernized as Almoravids." – Stanley G. Payne, <u>A History of Spain and Portugal</u>, (Madison, Wisconsin: The University of Wisconsin Press, 1973), p.61.

[729] William C. Atkinson, <u>A History of Spain & Portugal</u>, (London: Penguin Books, 1960), p. 54.

[730] Stanley G. Payne, <u>A History of Spain and Portugal</u>, (Madison, Wisconsin: The University of Wisconsin Press, 1973), p. 62.

[731] John A. Crow, <u>Spain The Root and the Flower</u>, (3rd ed. expanded & updated; Berkeley: University of California Press, 1963), p. 65.

in North Africa than a swineherd in Castile. (He died, destitute, in Morocco, the unwilling guest of the Almoravide Berber who displaced him.)"[732]

"The invitation to do battle in support of the emir of Seville against [Catholic] Castile was accepted by the Almoravid leaders as a logical extension of their jihad. As usual, Alfonso VI seized the initiative, meeting the Almoravids on Muslim territory at Sagrajas (near Badajoz). ... At Sagrajas the forces from Seville bore the brunt of the formidable Castilian charge while a mobile portion of the Almoravids flanked the Castilian host and struck their camp from the rear. Defeated, the Castilians retreated in fairly good order, and the Almoravids retired to Africa without exploiting their victory."[733]

As was just said, "Yusuf went back to Africa, but four years later returned and made himself master of all Moslem Spain except Saragossa, which was won by his successor. Meanwhile, another fierce Moslem sect arose in Africa, the Almohads.[734] In the century after Yusuf, the Almoravides themselves became soft and sybaritic; the country was again split into *taifas* and was ripe for invasion. The Almohads fell upon the Peninsula in 1146 and in a quarter of a century had non-Christian Spain in their power. The Almohads were fierce and fanatical Berbers, and persecuted the Arabs and Jews as they did the Christians (Mozarabs). Their leader Yakub defeated Alfonso VIII of Castile in 1195, but the Christians had their revenge in the great Battle of Las Navas de Tolosa (1212) in which the power of the Almohads was broken. The little Moslem states were conquered one by one, except Granada, which managed to maintain itself for two and a half centuries."[735] Muslim power in Granada was finally snuffed out in 1492 by the armies of Ferdinand and Isabella.

೧೩

---

732 Desmond Stewart, The Alhambra, (New York: Newsweek Book Division, 1974), p. 102.
733 Stanley G. Payne, A History of Spain and Portugal, (Madison, Wisconsin: The University of Wisconsin Press, 1973), p. 62.
734 "The Almohads (al-muwahhidun, 'asserters of religious unity') preached a more sophisticated and mystical version of Islam in place of the simple, anthropomorphic religion of the Almoravids." – Stanley G. Payne, A History of Spain and Portugal, (Madison, Wisconsin: The University of Wisconsin Press, 1973), p. 71.
735 Nicholson B. Adams, The Heritage of Spain, An Introduction to Spanish Civilization, (New York: Holt, Rinehart and Winston, 1959), p. 18.

Chapter 23

CATHOLICISM ALTERED BY CONFRONTATION WITH ISLAM

A partial scene of the devastation caused by bombs allegedly detonated by Islamic terrorists. At least 200 people were killed in commuter trains in Madrid on March 11, 2004. Some observers feel the Prime Minister Elect's statement that he would pull Spanish troops out of Iraq may have sent a signal that terrorism can achieve its political goals. -- Photo by Getty Images

Certain elements in the cascade of events in Spanish history had a deteriorating impact on Spanish Catholic doctrine and practice as well as on Catholicism as a whole. For example, "The church did not originally look with favor on holy men[736] taking arms, but with the invasion of [Spain by] the [Muslim] Moorish Almoravides ('those vowed to God') in 1086, the blending of religion and war among the Moors, the concept of Muslim Jihad or 'holy' war, was again brought to the attention of Spanish Catholics who could not help realizing the effectiveness and appeal of the idea.

Holy War?

"Holy war, therefore, became the mission of the Church Militant. Among these orders were the Knights of Santiago, Calatrava, Alcantara, the Knights Templar, and the Hospitalers. The primary duty of the Knights of Santiago was to

---

[736] The term "holy men" is not equivalent to the New Testament term "saints." Rather, it refers to those who have been inducted into religious orders. Roughly, those orders were the medieval equivalent of today's para-church organizations but were, generally, under the control of the papacy.

keep the pilgrim road free of bandits and evildoers. Later they became a core group in the Moorish wars. At the end of the fifteenth century, under Ferdinand and Isabella, such core groups constituted the bone and sinew of the Christian army."[737]

The Northern Diversion

As was noted in the previous chapter, Muslim military thrusts into Gaul (the area of modern France) diverted Islamic military forces from completely conquering the Spanish hold-out groups. This gave the militant Catholics under Pelayo and his successors essential breathing space. In addition, those thrusts by Muslim military forces north of the Pyrenees sparked French reprisal raids into Spain to punish and, hopefully, totally destroy the Muslims. The dedication and violence with which those thrusts were made and the infinite antipathy between the forces of Islam and Christendom become startlingly graphic when one reads the legendary French epic, *The Song of Roland*. The epic account memorializes several French heroes, especially Roland, who died in battle on August 15, 778 at Roncevaux in the defiles of the Pyrenees Mountains as Charlemagne's forces were withdrawing from Spain to confront the Saxons who were invading France in the north.

Though the Battle of Roncevaux took place in 778, "the poem itself, as we know it, would appear to have achieved its final shape towards the end of the eleventh century. It is not difficult to see why the legend should have taken the form it did, nor why it should have been popular about that time. The Saracen menace to Christendom became formidable about the end of the tenth century, and led to a number of expeditions against the Moors in Spain with a definitely religious motive."[738]

Since we are trying to determine, among other issues, the impact of Islam on Christianity in those countries which were invaded and occupied by Muslim forces, the portrait of Spanish and French Christianity given in *The Song of Roland* at approximately 1100 A.D. is invaluable.

Ultimatum to Accept Christ

By the end of the eleventh century, French Christendom, next-door neighbor to Spanish Islam, had adopted the Prophet Muhammad's practice of giving ultimatums to neighboring rulers to submit to the dictates of Islam. The only difference was the ruler of French Christendom issued an ultimatum to submit to Catholicism. None of us should need to be reminded that there are light years of difference between an invitation to accept Christ and a bellicose ultimatum to yield to the doctrine of Christendom!

---

[737] John A. Crow, Spain The Root and the Flower, An Interpretation of Spain and the Spanish People, (Berkeley: University of California Press, 1985), p. 88.
[738] Introduction, The Song of Roland, trans. Dorothy L. Sayers (Baltimore: Penguin Books Inc., 1959), pp. 8-9.

Perhaps recounting what Muhammad had done will help us understand the source of the practice adopted by Christendom: "It was at this period, the year 628, that the Prophet [Muhammad] despatched messages to the King of Persia, the Byzantine Emperor, the Governor of Egypt and the Prince of Abyssinia, summoning them to accept the Muslim religion."[739]

The comparable practice in Christendom is clear from section 33 of The Song of Roland:

> "King Charlemagne, the Great, thus sends you word:
> You must receive the faith of Christ Our Lord,
> And as your fief half Spain he will award.
> If you refuse to accept this accord,
> You shall be taken and fettered by main force,
> And hauled away to Aix, into his court,
> There to be doomed and done with once for all;
> There shall you die in shamefulness and scorn."[740]

"Holy War"— A Guarantee of Heaven?

On the French expedition during which the Battle of Roncevaux took place, the French regimental chaplain was Archbishop Turpin. Full of bravery and courage, he stayed with the doomed rear guard in order to minister to those men in that most critical moment, ultimately sharing their fate. Both the crusading ideal, parallel to Islamic Jihad, and the guarantee of heaven for the warrior who falls in battle on behalf of his faith, whether borrowed from Islam or not, are nearly identical to the Muslim concepts. "Among the [Spanish] Muslims, circumstances changed during the hegemony of al-Mansur, and the jihad was preached with great intensity during the Almoravid invasion.

"As for the Christians, the explicit ideal of the crusade as a holy war against Muslim usurpers was introduced from France and Italy during the Catholic religious renewal of the eleventh century. It was a consequence of the expanding population, military strength, and assertive spirit of western Europe, and of the increased power of the Hispanic kingdoms.

---

739 John Bagot Glubb, The Great Arab Conquests, (London: Quartet Books, 1980), pp. 89-90.
  The precedent set by the Prophet Muhammad was followed by his second successor, the caliph Umar ibn al Khattab, simply called Umar for short. Agapius, the Christian bishop of Manbij, a town northeast of Aleppo in Syria, stated in a history which he wrote about 940 A.D., "He ('Umar) wrote for Leo the king [of the Byzantine Empire] a letter summoning him therein to Islam and, moreover, disputed with him about his religion." – Robert G. Hoyland, Seeing Islam As Others Saw It, A Survey and Evaluation of Christian, Jewish and Zoroastrian Writings on Early Islam, (Princeton, NJ: The Darwin Press, Inc. 1997), p. 490. For a discussion of the earliest doctrinal debates between Islam and Christianity see David Thomas, Christian Doctrines in Islamic theology, (Leiden: Brill, 2008).
740 All quotes from The Song of Roland are from Dorothy L. Sayers' translation published by Penguin Books Inc. in 1959.

A Spanish Crusade

"The primary target of the western crusades was the Holy Land, but the struggle against the Muslims in the [Spanish] peninsula also received attention. As early as 1064, nearly three decades before the First Crusade to Palestine, the papacy promised indulgences to French knights who volunteered to assist an Aragonese campaign against the Muslims."[741] And now, hear Archbishop Turpin:

> "He calls the French and preaches them a sermon:
> 'Barons, my lords, Charles picked us for this purpose;
> We must be ready to die in our King's service.
> Christendom needs you, so help us to preserve it.
> Battle you'll have, of that you may be certain,
> Here come the Paynims[742] — your own eyes have observed them.
> Now beat your breasts and ask God for His mercy:
> I will absolve you and set your souls in surety.
> If you should die, blest martyrdom's your guerdon;
> You'll sit on high in Paradise eternal.'"[743]

> "'Barons, my lords, these shameful thoughts put by;
> By God I charge you, hold fast and do not fly,
> Lest brave men sing ill songs in your despite.
> Better it were to perish in the fight.
> Soon, very soon we all are marked to die,
> None of us here will see tomorrow's light;
> One thing there is I promise you outright:
> To you stand open the gates of Paradise,
> There with the holy sweet Innocents to bide.'
> His words so fill them with courage and delight
> There's none among them but shouts 'Mountjoy' on high."[744]

---

[741] Stanley G. Payne, <u>A History of Spain and Portugal</u>, (Madison, Wisconsin: The University of Wisconsin Press, 1973), pp. 66-67.
[742] The name used in the Epic for Muslims.
[743] Section 89, <u>The Song of Roland</u>.
[744] Section 115, <u>The Song of Roland</u>.

Conversion or Death

A final quote from The Song of Roland will let us know that Christendom had also at that point borrowed the concept of forced conversion, as well as other grave errors, from Islam.

> "The day is past, the dark draws on to night,
> Clear is the moon, the stars are shining bright;
> All Saragossa lies in the Emperor's might.
> Some thousand French search the whole town, to spy
> Synagogues out and mosques and heathen shrines.
> With heavy hammers and with mallets of iron
> They smash the idols, the images they smite,
> Make a clean sweep of mummeries and lies,
> For Charles fears God and still to serve Him strives.
> The Bishops next the water sanctify;
> Then to the font the Paynim folk they drive.
> Should Carlon's orders by any be defied
> The man is hanged or slain or burned with fire.
> An hundred thousand or more are thus baptized
> And christened,—only the Queen fares otherwise:
> She's to go captive to fair France by and by,
> Her would the King convert by love to Christ."[745]

Yielding to the Opposition

"Spanish Christianity, after many centuries of contact with Moslems and Jews, evolved a church and a concept of religion vastly different from those of the fourth century A.D. ... Visigothic Spain was on its way to becoming a Visigothic-Romanic-Hispanic nation. Had this process of history been allowed to continue, Spain would have stayed in the main current of European history and culture. The Moors [i.e., Muslims] prevented it; they remained in the peninsula for nearly eight centuries, altering radically the very bedrock of the beliefs, character, and psychology of the people."[746]

"Christian society in the south and east [of Spain] was completely unable to hold its own. The independent Christians of the north came to call their counterparts in the south Mozarabs, derived from the Arabic *musta'rib*, meaning Arabized or Arabic-speaking. Mozarab culture became fossilized, its post-conquest literature for example rhetorical and usually mediocre, deficient in dia-

---

[745] Section 266, The Song of Roland.
[746] John A. Crow, Spain The Root and the Flower, An Interpretation of Spain and the Spanish People, (Berkeley: University of California Press, 1985), pp. 35 & 38.

lectic and analysis. Of course it must be recognized that Mozarab culture was placed under increasing pressure [from Islam] and not able to develop in full freedom.

"Limited tolerance never meant equality, and Christians were never permitted to dispute publicly the teachings of Islam. Religious practice and cultural opportunity were increasingly circumscribed. It is true that some towns had Christian majorities for a century or more, that most Mozarab dioceses were able to continue an uninterrupted line of episcopal succession for nearly three hundred years, that all Mozarab church councils were occasionally called, and that some religious and cultural contacts were maintained with other parts of western Christendom.

"Nonetheless, the strength and influence of Islam was increasingly felt. From about the beginning of the ninth century pressure mounted; taxes were raised and new restrictions were introduced while the Muslim proportion of society steadily increased. One response to latent and then mounting persecution was the Christian 'martyrs of Cordoba' movement of 850–859 in the course of which several score Christian spokesmen, confronting Islam directly were put to death. A more common response was Mozarab emigration to the Christian principalities in the northern mountains. The Muslim state did not embark on a policy of extreme persecution until late in the tenth century, however, and the Mozarab minority persisted, in ever-dwindling numbers, until almost the end of Al-Andalus [as the major part of Muslim Spain was called]."[747]

A Rising Tide

"Despite the success of the Iberian Christian states in ending Muslim rule in their own backyards, and eventually evicting from the peninsula all Muslims who did not convert to Christianity, they had only chipped away at the western edge of the Muslim world. In the meantime their gains were being dwarfed by the menacing expansion of Muslim rule in the Balkans under the Ottomans.[748] Indeed for Busbecq, a Fleming who was sent on an embassy to Istanbul in the mid sixteenth century, an Ottoman conquest of the core territories of Europe did not seem far away. Under such conditions, any attempt to mount a massive attack on the Islamic world by land was likely to prove expensive and futile. The question, then, was whether the [Spanish] peninsular peoples could use their maritime resources to outflank their Muslim enemies."[749]

CR

---

[747] Robert Payne, The History of Islam, (New York: Dorset Press, 1990), p. 22.
[748] On the Muslim advance into the Balkans, see Chapters 26 & 27.
[749] Michael Cook, A Brief History of the Human Race, (NY: W.W. Norton & Co., 2003), p. 302.

Chapter 24

ISLAM'S IMPACT ON THE EASTERN SEABOARD OF THE MEDITERRANEAN

This chapter explains how the majestic Dome of the Rock in Jerusalem was built and is maintained to convey a theological challenge to every Jewish and Christian person. To guarantee that the proud affirmation implicit in this Islamic shrine is maintained, the Muslim world gives high priority to regaining control of Jerusalem. – Pixabay.com

In just two military contests, the wily and ecstatic Muslim Arab armies wrested from the Byzantine Empire all the land bordering the east coast of the Mediterranean. The Byzantines had been exhausted by a twenty-six-year war with the Persians which finally ended in A.D. 628. That was only six years before Islam unleashed its minions against that nearly prostrate empire. Both battles took place on the banks of the upper Yarmuk River, the largest tributary flowing from the east into the Jordan River. In September 634 A.D., just one month after the death of Abu Bakr, the first caliph or successor to Muhammad, the Muslims fought against the Byzantine army of Emperor Heraclius at the First Battle of the Yarmuk. Though indecisive, later it became clear that "the doorway to Syria had been forced open"[750] as John Bagot Glubb stated in his assessment.

---

[750] John Bagot Glubb, A Short History of the Arab Peoples, (New York: Stein and Day, Publishers, 1970), p. 47.

Plunging through that door, an Arab force shortly arrived at Damascus, a city guarded by massive walls. Instead of futilely flinging themselves to certain destruction against the impregnable fortifications of Damascus, the Arabs relied upon conspiracy. In the summer of 635 they developed a liaison with a disgruntled Christian bishop. It seems that the bishop held Monophysite views (see Glossary) for which he and his followers were being harassed and persecuted by the Byzantine state church, known as the Orthodox Church. The bishop and his accomplices provided two scaling ladders for the Muslims and informed them of a gate which would be virtually unguarded due to a celebration in the city on a certain night. On that night, just before morning, chosen Arabs, scaled the wall, overpowered the skeleton guard and flung the gate open through which the main Muslim army flooded in to overpower the entire city. After the capitulation of the city, the magnificent cathedral of St. John was divided by a wall so the victorious Muslims could use one side as a mosque.[751] That was only a trivial token of the coming impact which Islam would have on the lives of those who wore the name of Christ.

Recovery Thwarted

Two years after the First Battle of the Yarmuk, which had been fought in September 634 A.D., Emperor Heraclius, who had made a strategic retreat far to the north with the remnants of his battered army, now having regrouped and having raised thousands of new troops, many of them Armenians, now marched south. His new army swept the Muslim forces before it. The Muslims, abandoning Damascus and other northern cities they had occupied, in the face of Byzantium's new juggernaut fell back to their former position on the Yarmuk River. Biding their time, the Muslim forces knew that circumstances were in their favor on August 20, 636 when a strong hot desert wind began blowing sand in the direction of the Byzantine army. Heraclius' troopers had to close their eyes as they confronted the Arabs who attacked from the same direction from which the raging sand storm was blowing. But the Arabs, with their backs to the storm, could attack with their eyes wide open. The Byzantine army was exterminated. Even Emperor Heraclius' brother was killed!

The Emperor, knowing that everything on the east coast of the Mediterranean, the Levant, had been lost, pulled whatever tattered remnants of his forces he could salvage to the north side of the great Taurus Mountain complex. For many subsequent years, that daunting mountain range served as the boundary between Dar ul-Islam (The Muslim World) and Sultanate ur-Rum (Arabic for The Roman Empire). In fact, "the calamity inflicted by the Arabs, ... nearly proved mortal. Syria, Palestine, and [shortly thereafter] Egypt were lost permanently, and with them went huge tax revenues, lucrative trade centers, vast food supplies, and large reservoirs of human resources."[752] After the Byzantine military disaster at Yarmuk, only a few cities held out against the Muslims. Most prominent were Jerusalem and Caesarea. Spiritually, the most important

---
751 John Bagot Glubb, A Short History of the Arab Peoples, (New York: Stein and Day, Publishers, 1970), p. 48.
752 Dennis P. Hupchick, The Balkans, from Constantinople to Communism, (New York: Palgrave, 2002), p. 31.

of these two was Jerusalem which capitulated in 638. "Already in December 634 Sophronius, patriarch of Jerusalem, could speak of 'the wild and barbarous Saracen, which is filled with every diabolical savagery'"[753]

Byzantine Syria

How should we designate the area on the eastern seaboard of the Mediterranean? It currently includes Syria, Lebanon, Israel, Palestine, Gaza, Jordan and the Sinai Peninsula, all the way to the Egyptian border. Some scholars, among whom is Fred McGraw Donner in his *The Early Islamic Conquests*, when referring to the entire region at the time of the Islamic conquest, lump it all together collectively as "Byzantine Syria," which secular geographers call the "Levant." It is an area which should fascinate all Christians because it was home to many of the significant developments of early Christianity. Of extreme importance among many key places in the area was Jerusalem where, on the first Jewish festival of Pentecost following the crucifixion, the identity of Jesus as the Son of God was made known to thousands of Jews. In response, those with honest hearts gave their full allegiance to Christ, thus bringing the church into existence. Subsequently, multitudes of churches on the eastern seacoast of the Mediterranean gave Islam almost countless points at which to make a damaging, and, in many cases, a ruinous impact on the cause of Christ.

Development of the Church

For over a decade after its founding, the Jerusalem church was an entirely Jewish church. No wonder then that Philip Schaff called the church in Jerusalem "the mother church of Jewish Christendom."[754] As God manifested himself in Jerusalem, to initiate the Gospel Age, he subsequently opened the door to the gospel for the inclusion of all people by the miraculous conversion of Cornelius and his Gentile family. (See Acts 10:1-48.) Following that, he motivated and led the church in Antioch of Syria to launch the first concerted and sustained effort to take the gospel to the Gentile world. (See Acts 13:1 ff.) Appropriately, Schaff called the church in Antioch "the mother church of Gentile Christendom."[755] Schaff probably used the term "Christendom" to refer to those in whose hearts Christ had dominion. He does not seem to have used it in the sense in which Kierkegaard, the Danish philosopher, did when he said, "We must disassociate Christianity from Christendom so we may reintroduce Christianity into Christendom."

When we talk about the Christians living on the eastern seaboard of the Mediterranean, we are talking about "a Christian presence whose roots are fully embedded in the Middle East and that to all intents and purposes belongs to

---
[753] Robert G. Hoyland, Seeing Islam As Others Saw It, (Princeton, New Jersey: The Darwin Press, Inc., 1997), p. 58.
[754] Philip Schaff, History Of The Christian Church, Vol. I, (Grand Rapids, Michigan: Wm. B. Eerdmans Publishing Company, 1978), p. 247.
[755] Philip Schaff, History Of The Christian Church, Vol. I, (Grand Rapids, Michigan: Wm. B. Eerdmans Publishing Company, 1978), p. 279.

Inception of Islamic Division

In 644 A.D., only three years after he had been acclaimed as the third caliph, Uthman began in 647 to favor the Umayya, his own branch of the Arab Quraish Tribe, the tribe which had dominated the leadership of Islam from the very inception of the new faith. Out of this favoritism he appointed his blood relative Mu'awiya to be governor of conquered Byzantine Syria. Damascus became the governor's capital. In 656 Uthman was murdered and Ali, who was both cousin and son-in-law of the Arabian Prophet Muhammad, was appointed to be the next, that is the fourth, Caliph in Medina.

Ali called for the immediate resignation of all the political appointees whom Uthman had put in power. Persistently, Mu'awiya refused to resign because Ali would not bring the murderers of Uthman to justice. Mu'awiya believed, therefore, that Ali somehow had been complicit in the murder of Caliph Uthman. Two years later, in 658 A.D., Governor Mu'awiya annexed Egypt and declared himself Caliph, beginning the Umayyad Caliphate, named after the Umayya branch of the Quraish Tribe. At that point, Mu'awiya ruled Syria, Palestine and Egypt from Damascus. At the same time Ali ruled Iraq and Persia from Kufa, having moved the political center from Medina which, up to that point, had been the supreme seat of Muslim political power. From that rupture, for a short time, Islam was divided, having two opposing Caliphs.

Lust Skews Succession

In 661 A.D. Ali was murdered by one of his own soldiers in protest because he had chosen to determine the outcome of the Battle of Siffeen by negotiation rather than by war. Ali's eldest, but extremely sensual son, al-Hasan (See Chapter 7, "Muhammad's Daughters"), was rightful heir to his father's caliphate. Though it was very early in the history of Islam, even at that point the succession to the caliphate had become hereditary, replacing the previous practice of filling the position by acclamation. The crass carnality of al-Hasan made it easy for Mu'awiya to bribe him so he would renounce his right to the caliphate. For him the choice was reflexive, he preferred the pleasures of the fleshpots, to which he had become habituated, rather than the rigors of leading the incipient Islamic empire. Ali's youngest son, Husain, was tragically assassinated by Mu'awiya's soldiers while on his way to Kufa to become caliph in place of his murdered father. At that point Damascus became the sole political center for the entire Muslim world. It remained so till 750 A.D. when the Umayyad Caliphate was overthrown by the Abbasids through victory in a momentous battle on the banks of the Great Zab River in Iraq.[757]

---

[756] Andrea Pacini (ed.), Christian Communities in the Arab Middle East, The Challenge of the Future, (Oxford: Clarendon press, 1998), p. 2.

[757] For the significance of the Battle of the Great Zab River, see footnote 183 in Chapter 6.

Islam's Impact on the Eastern Seaboard of the Mediterranean ~ Chapter 24

Overlooked Significance

In some ways it seems the Muslims, in those opening years of their movement, understood more of the significance of some events in the development of Christianity than did the Christians themselves! For instance, they understood that the church had come into being in the Jewish temple in Jerusalem. In view of the last two verses of the Gospel according to Luke, there can be no doubt that the epochal events culminating in the birth of the church, events which Luke recorded in the second chapter of the Acts of Apostles, took place in the Jewish temple in Jerusalem which had become a dazzling structure through a forty-six year renovation and augmentation project financed and overseen by Herod the Great. (See John 2:20.) As we all know, because of a Jewish rebellion Roman legions, under the generalship of Titus, completely destroyed that temple in 70 A.D. Surprisingly, however, the site of the temple was never in any way memorialized or hallowed by Christians as the physical or geographical spot where Christ's church had come into being. Amazingly, on the contrary, in 638 A.D. when the city of Jerusalem capitulated to the army of Caliph Omar/Umar (the second caliph), the citizens of Jerusalem, overwhelmingly Christian, whether of one persuasion or another, were using that site as a common garbage dump!

Enmity Backfires

The late Barbara W. Tuchman has pointed out the reason for the Christians' disdain for the site on which the church came into being. She wrote, "Omar, the conqueror of Jerusalem, paid a visit of respect to the Holy Rock where Abraham had prepared to sacrifice Isaac and where the Temple of Solomon had once stood. Having cleaned it of the filth with which the Christians of that time had defiled it to show their resentment of the Jews, he adopted the site as a Mohammedan place of worship. There the Mosque of Omar was built, and thenceforward Mahomet was supreme where David had reigned and Jesus preached."[758]

Deep Regret

Sophronius, patriarch of Jerusalem, had deep regret about the adoption of the Temple Mount by the Muslims. His words have been conveyed to us by archdeacon Theodore: "The godless Saracens entered the holy city of Christ our Lord, Jerusalem, with the permission of God and in punishment for our negligence, which is considerable, and immediately proceeded in haste to the place which is called the Capital. They took with them men, some by force, others by their own will, in order to clean that place and to build that cursed thing, intended for their prayer and which they call a mosque (*midzgitha*)."[759]

---

[758] Barbara W. Tuchman, Bible and Sword, How the British Came to Palestine, (London: MacMillan, 1985), p. 25.
[759] Robert G. Hoyland, Seeing Islam As Others Saw It, (Princeton, New Jersey: The Darwin Press, Inc., 1997), p. 63.

Four years before Omar seized the Temple Mount for construction of Muslim places of worship, Sophronius saw the omen of the future after he had experienced grievous restrictions on Christian access to Bethlehem. He wrote, "The army of the godless Saracens has captured the divine Bethlehem and bars our passage there, threatening slaughter and destruction if we leave this holy city and dare to approach our beloved and sacred Bethlehem."[760]

An Eye on History

Caliph Omar immediately recognized the significance of the site of the former Jewish temple. He, as Tuchman noted, had all the garbage hauled away and the site cleansed. Then Omar had a crude temporary mosque constructed on that site.[761] Subsequently, under the oversight of the Umayyad Caliph Abd al-Malik, the Muslims replaced that impromptu mosque by the magnificent Dome of the Rock. It was dedicated in 691 and today it is the oldest surviving Islamic monument in the world! But more significantly, as Alan M. Guenther has pointed out, The Dome of the Rock was built "as a symbol of Muslim strength replacing both Judaism and Christianity."[762]

Distorted Theology

An expression of that self assumed and self-perceived Islamic supremacy is captured by the historical novelist Kanan Makiya in the presumed words of Umar when he said to his adviser, "Face the fact, old man—the torch has passed over the heads of those who were favored of old; it has been passed to the sons of Ishmael, not Ishaq [Isaac]."[763] In harmony with the theological message that the building of The Dome of the Rock was alleged to convey to the world, as Schick has pointed out, Muslims did not hesitate or scruple to take the gilded copper dome from a church building in Baalbek to adorn their splendid Dome of the Rock![764]

Paying the Price

From that point on, Christians in Jerusalem couldn't avoid noticing that stunning, triumphant and dominating architectural monument which reminded them of the Muslim taunt that Christians belonged to an out-dated and superseded religion. For persistently and obstinately continuing in that allegedly discarded and repudiated system, Christians would have to pay a price.

---

760 Robert G. Hoyland, Seeing Islam As Others Saw It, (Princeton, New Jersey: The Darwin Press, Inc., 1997), p. 70.
761 "A Syriac chronicle of the mid-eighth century maintains that the work was commissioned by the caliph 'Umar when he came to the city, a journey that is assigned by most Muslim sources to AH 17/638." – Robert G. Hoyland, Seeing Islam As Others Saw It, (Princeton, New Jersey: The Darwin Press, Inc., 1997), p. 64.
762 Alan M. Guenther, *The Christian Experience and Interpretation of the Early Muslim Conquest and Rule*, Islam and Christian-Muslim Relations, Vol. 10, No. 3, 1999, p. 371.
763 Kanan Makiya, The Rock, A Tale of Seventh-Century Jerusalem, (New York: Pantheon Books, 2001), pp. 146-147.
764 Robert Schick, The Fate of the Christians in Palestine During The Byzantine-Umayyad Transition, A.D. 600–750, (Chicago: A Dissertation Submitted to the Faculty of The Division of The Humanities in Candidacy for the Degree of Doctor of Philosophy, The University of Chicago, 1987) Vol. I, p. 179.

The price which Christians would have to pay for their refusal to embrace Islam, and for their stubborn persistence in clinging to their old outmoded and discarded ways, was outlined in a famous document drawn up by the Caliph to whom Jerusalem had capitulated. That document is known as the Pact of Umar (Omar). It is sometimes also called The Covenant of Umar. Irshad Manji, the courageous Canadian Muslim author says, whether Umar was the author or not, the Pact of Umar consists of "thoroughly supremacist diktats. And ... the question comes up yet again: Why did Muslims choose intolerance over tolerance through the Pact of Umar?"[765]

The Pact in Detail

The Pact was imposed first in Byzantine Syria because it was the first Christian-majority area to come under Muslim governance. The stipulations of the Pact were ultimately imposed over the entire vast Islamic empire which stretched nearly 6,000 miles east to west in only 75 years after The Second Battle of the Yarmuk which occurred in 636 A.D.!

Perhaps Meron Benvenisti, a former Deputy Mayor of Jerusalem, who administered both East Jerusalem and the Old City, captures the essence of The Pact of Umar most succinctly. He wrote that Christians, "were forbidden to ring the church bells, to wear crosses, or to conduct religious ceremonies in public; non-Muslims were forbidden to bear arms or ride horses; a head tax was imposed, and they were even obliged to shave the front of their heads."[766]

A couple of important restrictions not mentioned by Benvenisti should be noted to help all of us understand why Christianity has shriveled wherever it has had to exist through the centuries under the withering winds from Arabia. Jane I. Smith says Christians "were not, however, allowed to give testimony concerning a Muslim in a court of law. The recruiting of new Christians was forbidden, as was an insult about Islam or its Prophet."[767] Of course, it was the Muslims who decided what was an insult and what was not.

The restrictions on Christians giving testimony concerning Muslims are currently incorporated in Pakistan's code of law. One of Pakistan's former military presidents, General Zia-ul-Haq, who ruled from 1977 till he was killed in the crash of a Pakistani Air Force plane in 1988, decisively molded Muslim corporate life in Pakistan. He "associated the strengthening of Pakistan's Muslim identity with the steady erosion of the rights of its dwindling non-Muslims. His most decisive moves in this direction were contained in a series of judicial reforms (known as the Law of Evidence), announced in 1984. They barred non-Muslims from giving evidence against Muslims in newly established Is-

---
[765] Irshad Manji, The Trouble With Islam, A Muslim's Call for Reform in Her Faith, (New York: St. Martin's Press, 2003), p. 63.
[766] Meron Benvenisti, City of Stone, The Hidden History of Jerusalem, (Berkeley: University of California Press, 1996), p. 14.
[767] Jane I. Smith, *Historical, Cultural, and Religious Interaction From The Seventh To The Fifteenth Centuries*, The Oxford History of Islam, ed. John L. Esposito, (Oxford: University Press, 1999), p. 308.

lamic courts (so-called *sharia* courts), and obliged them to accept that their evidence in such courts would be worth half that submitted by a Muslim, thus making it easier for Muslims to pursue legal proceedings against non-Muslims. ... Benazir Bhutto failed to roll back discriminatory legislation against non-Muslims, while Nawaz Sharif [recently deposed prime minister of Pakistan] moved further to extend Zia's Islamization programme by formalizing the application of *sharia* law."[768]

How Long, Oh Lord!

The yoke of Islam is heavy and galling. It has had to be borne for centuries by Christian communities on the eastern seaboard of the Mediterranean and throughout the Muslim world, by those who have dared to wear the name of Christ. Up till the Catholic Crusades, Christians living in former Byzantine Syria had endured the yoke of Islam for 460 years. After Saladin brought the Crusader period to an end by the capture of Acre in 1291, Christian families and communities have borne that yoke for another 725 years. With the exception of the Crusader period, as Tuchman has pointed out, "Palestine [and all of Byzantine Syria] remained under one form or another of Moslem rule, through a bewildering succession of Abbasid and Fatimite caliphates, [and] Seljuk and Ottoman Turks, until 1918."[769] The only respite was enjoyed in the Mandate areas during the Mandate Period following World War I. During that period, Britain and France respectively held sway in two areas. Palestine and Iraq were given to Britain, while Syria (including Lebanon) was given to France.

Richard Bell summed up the situation well when he said "The populations of the provinces were subjected to much hardship under Omayyad [Umayyad] governors. The tribute demanded from conquered territories could, as already pointed out, be increased, and most governors made their offices a source of personal enrichment. But that can hardly be called persecution of Christians as such. It did, however, help to accentuate the situation which we shall see was the main motive for the conversion of these populations [to Islam].

The Balance Changes

"There may have been cases of real conversion. There were keen missionaries of Islam as a religion even in these days. Discussion and arguments between members of the two religions seem to have been fairly frequent. The fact that John of Damascus and other Christian writers composed dialogues, which are essentially handbooks of guidance to Christians as to how to meet the arguments of their opponents, shows that the appeals of Moslems to reason and argument were not without effect.

"But if we consider the position of these Christians (and members of other faiths) under Moslem rule, and the social and monetary advantages of adopting

---
768 Farzana Shaikh, Making Sense of Pakistan, (New York: Columbia University Press, 2009), pp. 76-79.
769 Barbara W. Tuchman, Bible and Sword, How the British Came to Palestine, (London: MacMillan, 1985), p. 24.

Islam, we will not require much further explanation of the fact that, as time went on, Islam increased and Christianity decreased. Islam was in the position of the ruling faith. Though at first Christians, Jews, and others found employment pretty freely in the Government service, yet the tendency to dispense with them soon began to show itself. In any case, they could only occupy subordinate positions. Career was open only to Moslems, and in fact under the Omayyads [Umayyads], only to Arabs, or to those who, adopting Islam, managed to secure the patronage of some powerful Arab. The social pressure to adopt the new faith must have been very strong, even though not consciously exerted. Aspiring spirits among the subject peoples would naturally desire to have some share in the dazzling wealth and brilliant careers which the progress of conquest was setting before the eyes of their Arab and Moslem neighbors."[770]

The withering wind from Arabia not only impacted Christians, but Jews as well. The great Jewish scholar and statesman, Abba Eban, wrote graphically and incisively of the disparity in the standing between Muslims and non-Muslims living under Muslim rule. He wrote, "Even in the best of past ages, the relations between Arabs and Jews were not equal. The Arabs were on top as the masters of power. The Jews were below, sometimes tolerated, sometimes not, but never on an equal level. Arabs and Moslems thus find no incentive in history for regarding the Arab-Jewish relationship as anything but an encounter between a dominant empire and its subject citizens. The idea that non-Arabs or non-Moslems are legitimate carriers of independence in the Middle East requires the Arab mind to make an effort at innovation, not of memory."[771]

ଔ

---

770 Richard Bell, <u>The Origin of Islam in its Christian Environment, The Gunning Lectures Edinburgh University, 1925</u>, (London: Macmillan and Co., Ltd., 1926), pp.186-187.
771 Abba Eban, <u>Abba Eban, An Autobiography</u>, (New York: Random House, 1977), p. 19.

Chapter 25

FROM PREDOMINANCE TO A TINY MINORITY

The fire-ravaged ruins of the Christian quarter in Damascus, Syria left by a 3-day massacre that began on July 9, 1860. The Islamic suppression of Christians throughout the eastern seaboard of the Mediterranean is briefly recounted in this chapter.
– Wikimedia Commons

The cradle in which the Christian era had its infant care was located on the eastern seaboard of the Mediterranean. At its completion, the Christian era, will have been the climactic and culminating period of all human history, having stretched from its inauguration at the first Feast of Pentecost following Jesus' resurrection all the way to the end of time.

That assertion about where and when the Christian era began is clearly substantiated by Jesus' prophecy that, repentance and forgiveness of sins, central concepts of the Christian era, would be preached in his name to all nations, **beginning at Jerusalem**. (Luke 24:47) The prediction that the Christian era would continue till time ends, is obvious from Jesus' promise to everyone who promotes that era's message that he would be with them till the end of the age. (See Matthew 28:18-20)

The apostle Peter also made the span of the Christian era clear when he stated that the message of forgiveness through Christ would prevail as long as God was calling people to himself. He, rather incidentally, revealed the scope and duration of the Christian era when he responded to desperate inquirers who wanted to know what they should do about their sins. He told them, "Repent and be baptized, every one of you, in the name of Jesus Christ so that your sins may be forgiven. And you will receive the gift of the Holy Spirit. The promise is for you and your children and for **all who are far off—for all whom the Lord our God will call**." (Acts 2:38-39 NIV)

Since the message of how to obtain forgiveness of sins and, thus, reconciliation to God, is the defining message of the entire Christian age, the place and occasion of its inauguration should be clearly noted, since no other message can have comparable importance.

The expression "the eastern seaboard of the Mediterranean," refers to the area which is defined by the Taurus Mountains on the north, the Sinai Peninsula on the south all the way to the Egyptian border, and the Syrian Desert on the east. It is the same area which Fred McGraw Donner, as we saw in the previous chapter, called "Byzantine Syria." Other scholars have called it Greater Syria.

Robert Haddad, who called the area "Geographic Syria," vividly informs us that through the many centuries of its recorded history the area has been "generally less favorable to the administrator than to the outlaw and heretic."[772] In spite of that unsavory characterization, there could have been no more favorable place than Jerusalem and its adjoining areas on the eastern seaboard of the Mediterranean to begin proclaiming a message, if the goal was to internationalize that message. By using the words, "all nations" recorded in Luke 24:47, Jesus clearly indicated that his message was, indeed, to be internationalized. Jerusalem is the hub where three continents (Europe, Asia and Africa) meet and from which those continents could efficiently be evangelized. This pivotal location of Jerusalem is, undoubtedly, why it is called "the gate to the nations" in Ezekiel 26:2.

Critical Region

Islam's conquest and occupation of Greater Syria had a devastating impact on the cause of Christ, for it was here where many epochal events which were utterly central to the progress of the gospel of Christ had taken place. It was here, for example, that the people of Christ's time could say of Jesus that he "dwelt among us and we beheld his glory, glory as of the only begotten from the Father, full of grace and truth." (John 1:14) It was here that the Christian era was inaugurated by Peter's inspired sermon on Pentecost. (Acts Ch. 2) Also, it was here that God dramatically endorsed the reception of the whole Gentile world into the Christian fel-

---

772 Robert M. Haddad, <u>Syrian Christians in Muslim Society, An Interpretation</u>, (Westport, Connecticut: Greenwood Press, Publishers, 1970), p. 6.

lowship by the spectacular events which took place at the house of Cornelius, a God-fearing Roman centurion. (Acts 10:1-48) It was here that the followers of Christ were first called Christians. (Acts 16:26) It was from this special area, from the church in Antioch, to be precise, that the first missionaries to Asia Minor, and to Europe were sent out. (Acts 13:1-3)

It is in this area, too, that the church experienced some of the most spectacular growth in all Christian history, growth seldom exceeded even up to the 21st century. For instance, Edward Gibbon wrote that, "Under the reign of Theodosius [emperor from 379–395 A.D.]… the ancient and illustrious church of Antioch consisted of one hundred thousand persons, three thousand of whom were supported out of the public oblations."[773]

Also, Christianity was overwhelmingly dominant in Byzantine Syria at the advent of Islam. Robert Schick tells us that, "Churches [were] found in every village and town; some country towns, such as Umm al-Jimal and Umm al-Rasas, had a dozen or more churches for just a few thousand inhabitants, and smaller towns and villages, such as Khirbat al-Samra and Rihab could have a half dozen or more."[774]

"The solidly Orthodox character of the Christian population, coupled with the presence of smaller groups, remained a feature of the Christians in Palestine throughout the period under study."[775] Obviously then, "Christians were the overwhelming majority of the population, but Jews still formed a sizable group, forming something around ten to fifteen percent of the population of Palestine in the sixth century."[776]

Drastic Decline

Following the Islamic conquest and occupation of the area which had served as the cradle of Christianity, the numerical decline of Christians was precipitous and severe. Many Christians migrated to live once again in an area which was still governed by the Byzantines. As S. D. Goitein tells us, "Palestine, of course, was a special case. Large parts of its Christian population, especially that of the Greek towns, emigrated after the Muslim conquest to the Greek Christian empire of Byzantium."[777] We know, too, that it was not just Greek Christians who migrated but Arab Christians as well.

Schick highlights a crucial early period in the numerical decline of Christians in this area. He tells us, "by the Abbasid revolution in A.D. 750 their numbers

---

773 Edward Gibbon, Christianity And The Decline of Rome, (Volume I of The Decline and Fall of the Roman Empire abridged and edited by Jacob Sloan), (New York: Collier Books, 1962), p. 135.
774 Robert Schick, The Fate of The Christians in Palestine During The Byzantine-Umayyad Transition, A.D. 600–750, Ph.D. dissertation, Department of Near Eastern Languages and Civilizations, University of Chicago, 1987 pp.13-14.
775 Robert Schick, The Fate of The Christians in Palestine During The Byzantine-Umayyad Transition, A.D. 600–750, Ph.D. dissertation, Department of Near Eastern Languages and Civilizations, University of Chicago, 1987, pp.14-15.
776 Robert Schick, The Fate of The Christians in Palestine During The Byzantine-Umayyad Transition, A.D. 600–750, Ph.D. dissertation, Department of Near Eastern Languages and Civilizations, University of Chicago, 1987., p. 17.
777 S.D. Goitein, Jews And Arabs, Their Contacts Through the Ages, (New York: Schocken Books, 1967), p. 113.

had declined sharply. The evidence is unmistakable: Christians were using only half or fewer of the churches and monasteries in A.D. 750 that they had used in A.D. 600, and even where Christian communities were still present, this one hundred and fifty year period was disruptive."[778]

For a later period Andrea Pacini defines the disastrous situation statistically. She wrote, "From the tenth to the seventeenth centuries the Arab Christians declined: in 1570, when the first census of the Ottoman Empire was carried out, they were reduced to just ... 8 per cent of the whole population of the Empire."[779]

Haddad succinctly tells why the precipitous decline in the number of Christians took place. He said, "At few times in the course of the Muslim centuries was it other than perfectly clear to the non-Muslim that most mundane interests would be served by conversion to the faith of the Prophet. Only apostasy [from one's previous religion] offered the full range of possibility. Most non-Muslims were to take that step."[780]

A Parochial Church

The consequences have been summarized poignantly by Joyce Napper who tells us, "It is small wonder that each Christian community could be described as 'a static, encysted minority.' Very conservative, defensive, determined to preserve the Traditions, the Faith as they had received it, Christians opposed anything that might cause the break-up of their Community. Innovation was out. Community solidarity, religious and social, was all important. This heritage of local-Church-community solidarity (whether or not all its members cared about the Church's faith) is still an important factor in many aspects of life in Middle East countries. Since Christian schools [she refers especially to theological schools] were rarely allowed, clergy could not be educated or trained. Even where the Bible was available, few could read it. Inevitably, ignorance and stagnation lay like a deadly pall almost everywhere."[781]

How deadly that pall was is illustrated by some of the matters the British government had to deal with during the days of their Mandate Government. Utter trivialities were given great importance. For example, "The stairs leading to the Chapel of St. Mary's Agony in the Church of the Holy Sepulcher are Latin property. The question was, whose right was it to sweep the lowest step, situated only slightly above the level of the church forecourt, or parvis, which was common property. In 1901, a bloody dispute broke out between the Greeks and the Latins over this issue. Today the arrangement is that the Latins sweep the

---

778 Robert Schick, <u>The Fate of The Christians in Palestine During The Byzantine-Umayyad Transition, A.D. 600–750</u>, Ph.D. dissertation, Department of Near Eastern Languages and Civilizations, University of Chicago, 1987, p. 369.
779 Andrea Pacini (ed.), <u>Christian Communities in the Arab Middle East, The Challenge of the Future</u>, (Oxford: Clarendon Press, 1998), p. 5.
780 Robert M. Haddad, <u>Syrian Christians in Muslim Society, An Interpretation</u>, (Westport, Connecticut: Greenwood Press, Publishers, 1970), pp. 8-9.
781 Joyce Napper, <u>Christianity in the Middle East</u>, (Larnaca, Cyprus: Middle East Christian Outreach, 1996), p. 12.

step at sunrise, while the Orthodox sweep it when it is their turn to clean the parvis. ... In 1924, there was a clash over the right to clean the dust from the door leading to the Copts' room between columns 10 and 11. The Armenians claim full possession of the area and of the room, and argued, therefore, that they had the right to clean the dust from the doors, while the Copts demanded this right for themselves."[782]

Napper's evaluation was also substantiated by Haddad when he wrote, "The intellectual and aesthetic impulse of the Syrian Christians [was] gradually reduced to commentary and compilation (and these only irregularly pursued), even as their numerical preponderance was reduced from a substantial majority in the eleventh, and even as late as the thirteenth, century to perhaps some 30 percent of the population in the sixteenth. The sustained play of the creative impulse is not characteristic of the beleaguered community. For the Christians who remained, communal preservation was all."[783]

Education Revived

The deplorable and shocking educational deprivation found widely among those who wore the name of Christ, as Pacini points out, began to be ameliorated by the coming of Western missionaries, both Catholic and Protestant, into the declining Ottoman Empire. "The missionaries established a network of health institutions and schools through which they contributed enormously towards cultural development and the improvement in the standard of living of Arab Christians in particular, who were offered access to modern education locally. An analysis of data regarding the rate of schooling in some provinces of the Arab area of the Ottoman Empire at the end of the nineteenth century shows that everywhere Christians had a much higher rate of schooling than Muslims and often, with the exception of Aleppo and Basra, than the Jews."[784]

Salvation Through Political Action?

In modern times some of the Christians on the eastern Mediterranean seaboard have tried desperately to break out of their marginal and subordinate status through political activism. They "strove for the dissolution of an Islamic order which, if true to its own canons, could only affirm for Christians that marginal status which had been theirs for over a thousand years. Hence the effort of Syrian Christians in the late nineteenth and [well into the] twentieth century to create essentially secular nationalisms which would be blind to confessional distinctions or, as in the case of Lebanese nationalism, would even incline to-

---

782 Meron Benvenisti, City of Stone, The Hidden History of Jerusalem, (Berkeley: University of California Press, 1996), pp. 95-96.
783 Robert M. Haddad, Syrian Christians in Muslim Society, An Interpretation, (Westport, Connecticut: Greenwood Press, Publishers, 1970), p. 13.
784 Andrea Pacini (ed.), Christian Communities in the Arab Middle East, The Challenge of the Future, (Oxford: Clarendon Press, 1998), p. 7.

ward Christian predominance."⁷⁸⁵ "Thus, Ba'athist doctrine, [the political doctrine of the late Saddam Hussein of Iraq and of the late Hafez al-Assad of Syria] as articulated by its most influential exponent, the Damascene Greek Orthodox [Christian] Dr. Michel Aflaq, held that Muhammad, the Prophet of Islam, was also ipso facto the founder of the Arab nation, and was to be venerated as such by every Arab Nationalist, whether Muslim or not."⁷⁸⁶

Various Centers, A Single Policy

The five major phases of Islamic rule over the Christian lands on the eastern shore of the Mediterranean are:

(1) Rule from Medina by the first four Caliphs, 636 to 658. The year 636, it should be noted, was the date of the fateful Second Battle of the Yarmuk which gave Muslims permanent control of the entire eastern seaboard of the Mediterranean.

(2) Rule from Damascus under the Umayyad Caliphs, which prevailed from 658 to the destruction of the Umayyad Caliphate by the Abbasids in 750. "The destruction of the Umayyads signaled an acceleration of the process of institutionalization of the theoretic Islamic theocracy, and the passing of Syrian Christianity from its creative age to a twilight age of transmission."⁷⁸⁷

(3) Rule from Baghdad under the Abbasid Caliphs, 750 to 1258. "Violently snatched by the Abbasids, in 750 [in a decisive battle on the Great Zab River] the central political power was moved from [Damascus in] Syria to Iraq, leaving the former in the hands of foreign garrisons, some of them tyrannical. Islam won over a part of the population by ... the coercion exercised by the Abbasid caliph al-Mutawakkil (847–61)."⁷⁸⁸ In 1258 the Mongols conquered Baghdad bringing the Abbasid Caliphate to an end. The only interruption of Muslim rule over Christians in the eastern Mediterranean was the brief two-year rule by the non-Muslim Mongols, from 1258 to 1260.

(4) Rule from Cairo under the Mamluks (also spelled Mamelukes), from 1250 to 1516/17. The Mamluks were Turkish slave troops hired by the renowned Saladin's successors who were known as the Ayyubids, after Saladin's last name, Ayyub. "The last Ayyubid sultan built a powerful contingent of Turkish slaves, hoping thereby to give himself the military advantage, but upon his death in 1249 these slave troops seized power for themselves, marking the be-

---

785 Robert M. Haddad, <u>Syrian Christians in Muslim Society, An Interpretation</u>, (Westport, Connecticut: Greenwood Press, Publishers, 1970), p. 5.
786 Elie Kedourie, <u>Islam in the Modern World and Other Studies</u>, (New York: Holt, Rinehart and Winston, 1980), p. 55.
787 Robert M. Haddad, <u>Syrian Christians in Muslim Society, An Interpretation</u>, (Westport, Connecticut: Greenwood Press, Publishers, 1970), p. 12.
788 Youssef Courbage and Philippe Fargues, <u>Christians and Jews Under Islam</u>, trans. Judy Mabro (New York: I.B. Tauris Publishers, 1998), p. 11.

ginning of a powerful new regime based in Egypt—the Mamluks (1250–1517)."[789]

In 1260 the Mongols had conquered all the way from Baghdad to Damascus. "After the capture of Damascus it was clear that the Mongols were threatening Egypt. The Mamluk Sultan of Egypt [Rukn ud-Din Baibars] made a desperate effort. With great difficulty he persuaded his people to follow him, and then met the Mongols in battle at 'Ain Jalut ['the Pool of Goliath'] between Nablus and Baissan [near Nazareth]. There in 1260 a fierce battle was fought, which ended in the complete defeat of the Mongols."[790] For further elucidation about the Mamluks, see Chapter 17 under "Egypt's Christians Ruled by a Slave Dynasty."

In desperation, the Christians on the eastern seaboard of the Mediterranean had sided with the Mongols against the Muslims. "Therefore, the remaining Middle Eastern Christians found their situation dreadfully changed, as they were persecuted as quislings[791] for their actions during the Mongol onslaught."[792] During the nearly three centuries of Mamluk rule in the eastern seaboard of the Mediterranean, their power was challenged not only by several Mongol attacks, the most destructive being that by Tamerlane, but also by the incursion of the Crusaders.

(5) Rule by the Ottomans from Istanbul. In 1516 Selim inaugurated Ottoman rule in Syria. The tide bringing the Ottomans to power turned when "the Ottomans faced the Mamluks with overwhelming power in a decisive battle on August 24, 1516 at Marj Dabiq, just north of Aleppo. As noted earlier, in the Ottoman-Mamluk conflict, the Mamluks were severely hampered by their sneering disdain for firearms, which they refused to carry, regarding them as effeminate innovations."[793] From there, Selim's armies went on to Egypt where they destroyed the remnant of the Mamluk army on January 22, 1517. But, with the arrival of Selim on the eastern seaboard of the Mediterranean in 1516, "a new era began for the Arab world: that of domination by the Ottoman Turks."[794] Ottoman rule did not end till the defeat of Ottoman Turkey in World War I.

Turkish Decline—French and Papal Advance

The Ottoman Empire continued to gain power and territory till 1683 when the Ottomans suffered defeat in their second attempt to conquer Vienna, eastern gateway to Europe. (Their first attempt to conquer Vienna had taken place in

---

789 Fred M. Donner, *Muhammad and the Caliphate, Political History of the Islamic Empire Up to The Mongol Conquest*, The Oxford History of Islam, John L. Esposito (ed.), (New York: Oxford University Press, 1999), p. 57.
790 Laurence E. Browne, The Eclipse of Christianity in Asia, (Cambridge: At The University Press, 1933), p. 154.
791 Traitors
792 Philip Jenkins, The Next Christendom, The Coming of Global Christianity, (New York: Oxford University Press, 2002), pp. 25-26.
793 Peter N. Stearns (ed.), The Encyclopedia of World History, (New York: Houghton Mifflin Company, 2001), p. 129.
794 Philip K. Hitti, History of Syria Including Lebanon and Palestine, (London: Macmillan & Co. Ltd., 1957), p. 658.

1529. See additional details in the Introduction.) From their defeat in 1683, a slow but unmistakable Ottoman decline began. Also, from that point, "French influence in Ottoman affairs was strong and growing stronger, a circumstance which reflected not only the changing balance of power between the Ottoman Empire and Europe but the cordial relations [with France] which common hostility to the House of Hapsburg had bred between the infidel Sultan and [France] the eldest Daughter of the Church."[795] An example of Hapsburg/Habsburg ongoing hostility [against the Ottomans] came in 1908 when "Austria-Hungary annexed Bosnia and Herzegovina, two Ottoman provinces."[796]

The French used their close relationship with the Ottoman Porte, as the government of the Ottoman Empire was called, to vigorously promote the cause of Roman Catholic mission work in Geographic Syria. The Ottomans were pleased to cooperate with the French Catholic Church because France, under Napoleon, had fought against the Habsburg/Hapsburg Empire. It was the Habsburgs who thwarted the Ottomans in their attempts to conquer Europe by entering through Vienna, the Habsburg capital. One procedure became a very effective incentive which the French used to get Christian communities to acknowledge the authority of the Papacy. It was the help they gave to protect from piracy those ships which were owned or operated by individuals and communities which had submitted to Rome. The pirates, for the most part, were based in Ottoman North Africa. "The coast of North Africa right up to Algiers was ruled by the Barbary corsairs in the Sultan's name. ... Algiers remained a hotbed of piracy well into the nineteenth century, when even the Americans primly demanded an end to the pirate's activities."[797] The Ottomans had a tie with the Roman Catholic hierarchy. "The alliance between France and the Porte against the Habsburgs, which was always vague on land became a reality on sea."[798] The Ottomans agreed with the Papacy that they would not molest any ship whose captain had a certificate from the church authorities in Syria and Lebanon! "Inevitably the Syrian Christian whose property was exposed to the depredations of the corsairs, or who sought restitution of property already plundered by them, made his way to the French consuls. The consuls, in effect, then referred him to the missionaries, for the tacit price of French intervention in these matters was unquestionably submission to Rome."[799]

Those who submitted to Rome are called Uniates, that is, those who are united with Rome. The Uniates included the Uniate Melkites, (in contrast to the Or-

---

795 Robert M. Haddad, Syrian Christians in Muslim Society, An Interpretation, (Westport, Connecticut: Greenwood Press, Publishers, 1970), p. 30. On the Ottoman-Hapsburg hostility, see Chapter 27 under the subtitle "Expanding Empire."
796 John Bagot Glubb, Syria Lebanon Jordan, (New York: Walker and Company, 1967), p. 122.
797 Jason Goodwin, Lords of the Horizons, A History of the Ottoman Empire, (New York: Henry Holt & Co., 1998), p. 82 & 126.
798 Jason Goodwin, Lords of the Horizons, A History of the Ottoman Empire, (New York: Henry Holt & Co., 1998), p. 127.
799 Robert M. Haddad, Syrian Christians in Muslim Society, An Interpretation, (Westport, Connecticut: Greenwood Press, Publishers, 1970), pp. 41-42.

thodox Melkites) and especially the Maronites.[800] The word Melkite is a derivative of the Arabic word *malik* which means king or ruler. Thus, the Melkites, theoretically at least, followed the faith which was defined by the imperial Byzantine ruler. Of course, one who came to bear the name Uniate Melkite had a contradictory name, for the Byzantine imperial ruler never acknowledged the Roman Papacy, certainly not after the great schism in 1054.

The Monophysites, "denied that Christ had a double nature and managed to impose this view on the eastern Church at the Second Council of Ephesus. In 451 A.D. the Byzantine emperor reversed this decision at the Council of Chalcedon, and most of the Syrian [i.e. Greater Syria] Church accepted the new decrees. They formed the Melchite [Melkite] Church, accepted the Byzantine rite, and later followed the Patriarch of Constantinople into schism with Rome (1054). Partly owing to the zeal of the Jesuit missionaries, however, the Melchite [Melkite] Church split at the end of the seventeenth century and a group of them formed a Uniate Church with Rome in 1727. They became Greek Catholics and the non-Uniate Melchites became known as Greek Orthodox."[801]

Christians of all persuasions who lived on the eastern seaboard of the Mediterranean remained under Muslim political overlords till the end of World War I. At that point, France and Britain, under a mandate from the League of Nations, began to govern Syria (including Lebanon), Palestine and Iraq respectively.

As we have seen so far in our survey of the impact of Islam on Christianity, in those countries where that withering wind from Arabia has blown, it has gained the ascendancy. Islam has always suppressed those who have sought to give their allegiance to Christ. We will find as we extend our survey into Turkey that the impact on the followers of Christ under Turkish rule has invariably been the same.

છ૨

---

800 Maronites are "an indigenous Church of the area [of Lebanon], originally Monothelete in its views on the nature of Christ but in union with Roman Catholicism since the twelfth century. When the Lebanon later gained its independence in 1943 ... the new republic formulated a constitution carefully designed to balance the interests of Christians against other confessional groups. It succeeded for some three decades, before unraveling in civil war; the consequences of that great break down are still unfolding." – Diarmaid MacCulloch, Christianity, the First Three-Thousand Years, (New York, Viking, 2010), pp. 925-926

801 David Gilmour, Lebanon, The Fractured Country, (New York: St. Martin's Press, Inc., 1984), p. 22.

Chapter 26

ISLAM'S IMPACT ON THE CHURCHES IN TURKEY

One of the many ruined churches of the city of Ani, Armenia, now in Turkey. The Seljuk Turks began the destruction of the churches shortly after the Battle of Manzikert. The destruction continues even in the present time.-- Wikimedia Commons

From the Battle of Manzikert to the Founding of the Ottoman Empire

The bleached bones of defunct empires, which died because they exceeded the "limits," are strewn all over the pages of history. The British Empire, The French Empire, the Dutch Empire, the Japanese Empire and the Soviet Empire provide a few post-World-War-II examples.

It is obvious that individual empires are vulnerable to extinction, however, some have alleged that the "genus," the "category" or the "order" is immune from death. This contention was made not long ago by Aude Lancelin who asserted that the contemporary phenomenon called globalization "should be seen in line with our historical understanding of Empire as a universal order that accepts no boundaries or limits."[802]

---

[802] From his commendation on the back cover of the 2000 paper-back edition of <u>Empire</u>, a book by Michael Hardt and Antonio Negri, published by Harvard University Press.

Perhaps the "genus," the "order" or the "category" is immune from limits and, thus, from death, but individual empires certainly are not. Hitting the limits or breaking through the limits is often called imperial overreach. Think of those imperial limits as restrictions whether imposed by geographic, economic, military, demographic, political or philosophic realities. Once breached, inevitably either an embarrassing retrenchment or total collapse will eventually take place.

Arguably, the United States of America is not, and never has been, a traditional imperial power.[803] Its dogged pursuit of the Vietnam War, handicapped by its then self-imposed doctrine of limited war, ultimately became a case of imperial overreach which forced this great country to pull back with great embarrassment. Fortunately, however, so far it has not resulted in the collapse and death of America!

Ignoring the Limits Proves Costly

It was a foolish case of blatant imperial overreach by Byzantium which wrenched Asia Minor out of its control. As a political power, Byzantium had been sympathetic to Christianity, though extremely severe in its opposition to non-conformist Christian groups. That is one of the reasons why the Byzantine Empire is prophetically portrayed as a rapacious beast emerging from the sea. (Revelation 13:1-10) Ironically, Byzantium, through a foolhardy military misadventure, delivered Asia Minor into the hands of Turkish Muslims, who ultimately became bent on limiting, manipulating, opposing and, finally, eradicating Christianity. Byzantium's imperial overreach took place through their military push to the east, culminating in the Battle of Manzikert[804] on August 19, 1071 A.D. Before that decisive battle "for four hundred years, Asia Minor had stood fast against the Muhammadans, remaining as a province of the [Eastern] Roman Empire, and as part of the European heritage."[805]

The Byzantine "government had so radically changed its policy that it deliberately embarked on a course of military aggression against its Muslim neighbors on the opposite [i.e., its eastern] frontier. From 926, when an East Roman expedition was sent to win territory on the Euphrates, the government persisted for a century and a quarter in pursuing a forward policy which weakened its defenses, exposed its heart to attack, and aggravated the internal social strains

---

[803] Anatol Lieven, senior associate at the Carnegie Endowment for International Peace, writing in the March 2004 issue of <u>Current History</u> (p. 100) alleged that "The United States under George W. Bush is indeed driving toward empire, but the domestic political fuel being fed into the engine is that of a wounded and vengeful nationalism." In contrast, David Halberstam contends that, "Vietnam made us understand in some terrible way that we [who compose the U.S.A.] were no longer a mere democracy; we were a superpower, a democracy become empire. A democracy functions on the basis of shared truths, but an empire is far grander, it is about power, and truth often becomes an obstruction. ... We did not realize that America had become an empire, run by men suited to running empires, men who did not necessarily value the truth. They were far too grand for that; they valued power over truth. They had created their own truth: In power there was truth." – David Halberstam, <u>The Next Century</u>, (New York: William Morrow and Company, Inc., 1991), pp. 66-68.

[804] It is also spelled Manzikurt, Manzikart, Malazkirt or Malazgirt. The site is located about 25 miles northwest of Lake Van in the far southeastern corner of present-day Turkey.

[805] William Montgomery McGovern, <u>The Early Empires of Central Asia</u>, (Chapel Hill: The University of North Carolina Press, 1939), p. 14.

which the Bulgarian Wars [on Byzantium's western borders] had already produced. The virus of militarism ... carried the Empire onwards with an ever-increasing momentum until it precipitated the irretrievable collapse of 1071."[806]

Epochal Folly—Epochal Defeat

The Byzantines felt justified in their aggressive push to the east because the Seljuk Turks had previously invaded Armenia. At that time, the Seljuks comprised the dominant section of the Turks, while the Ottomans (who were later to dominate) were clearly in a subordinate position. Ironically, the Turkish Sultan "Alp Arslan still hoped to make a truce with the Byzantines so that he could concentrate against the Fatimids [in Egypt] but when he heard that Emperor Romanus Diogenus was leading a new offensive to the east, he moved north for a direct confrontation with the Byzantine army, the first time that the Turks had risked such a battle."[807]

The Battle of Manzikert in 1071 was "a historic confrontation between two empires and two faiths, which opened the way for the Turks, once and for all, into Asia Minor."[808] It "was the worst disaster ever experienced by the Byzantines until the final fall of Constantinople to the [Ottoman] Turks in 1453. The imperial army [following the Battle of Manzikert] had virtually ceased to exist and the whole of Asia Minor lay open to the Turkman invaders."[809]

"Despite the capture of the Emperor [Romanus IV] and the annihilation of his troops [at the Battle of Manzikert], all was not yet lost; but the disorganized government at Constantinople failed to initiate any effective resistance. Asia Minor was rapidly overrun, and by 1081 the Turks ruled from the Euphrates to the Sea of Marmora [Marmara], where Nicaea became the first capital of the Seljuk sultanate of Anatolia."[810]

Islam's Banner in New Hands

The epochal Battle of Manzikert ultimately opened the way to supremacy for the Ottoman Turks, the third great ethnic group to ultimately dominate Islam. When the Islamic empire was established, its initial stunning expansion, stretching from India to Morocco, was accomplished through the dynamism of the Arabs. As the Arabs ultimately weakened and lost momentum, their place of dominance was snatched at the Battle of the Great Zab River in 750 A.D. by Iranian aspirants who subsequently, working behind the scenes, initially ruled through the facade of the Abbasid Caliphate. The Seljuk Turks later became

---

806 Arnold Toynbee, A Study of History, (New York: Portland House, 1982), p. 193.
807 Stanford Shaw, History of The Ottoman Empire and Modern Turkey, Volume I: Empire of the Gazis: The Rise and Decline of the Ottoman Empire, 1280–1808, (New York: Cambridge University Press, 1976), p. 6.
808 Lord Kinross, The Ottoman Centuries, The Rise and Fall of the Turkish Empire, (New York: Morrow Quill Paperbacks, 1977), p. 18.
809 John Bagot Glubb, The Course of Empire, (London: Hodder and Stoughton, 1965), pp. 207-210.
810 Norman H. Baynes and H. St. L. B. Moss (ed's.) Byzantium, An Introduction to East Roman Civilization, (Oxford: The Clarendon Press, 1953), p. 28.

dominant in the Abbasid Caliphate but through sensualism and indulgence were weakened and consequently defeated by the Mongols and lost control. Their close cousins, the Ottoman Turks, then rose to dominance to proudly keep the withering wind from Arabia blowing. As devotees of "The Prophet," from their initial domain in Anatolia, they took control of the most sacred Muslim areas of Arabia and the eastern and southern seaboards of the Mediterranean. Ultimately, they also swept across Europe's Balkan Peninsula. Two times, in 1529 and again in 1683, their successful drive to dramatically expand the boundaries of the Muslim world propelled them all the way to Vienna, eastern gateway to Europe. Thus, "the Battle of Manzikert did what the Arabs at the height of their glory had never been able to do, and, by seizing the greater part of Asia Minor, [then following up on that victory, the Ottoman Turks] reduced cultural Europe to the limits of geographical Europe."[811]

Asia Minor Defined

The major portion of the territory of present-day Turkey, except for the section in the northeastern corner of the Balkan Peninsula, which borders on Greece and Bulgaria at Edirne, occupies the area commonly designated as Asia Minor. It is a peninsula jutting to the west from the Middle Eastern mainland.[812] It is bounded by the Black Sea, the Bosporus, the Sea of Marmora [also spelled Marmara] and the Dardanelles on the north, the Mediterranean Sea on the south and the Aegean Sea on the west. When the Greeks looked east across the Aegean Sea, they referred to the opposite shore, present-day Turkey, as Anatolia. The term comes from the Greek word *anatol*, meaning "east." Thus, Anatolia means the land to the east of Greece.

Drought Moves People

To understand the causes of the invasion of Asia Minor by the Turks, one must look back to remote events in the vast Russian Steppe area far to the north of the Caspian and Aral Seas. It was dominated by the virile Japhetic Mongols and their very close relatives, the Turks. Whenever inadequate rainfall reduced the crop of natural grass on which their flocks and herds were dependent, major tribal migrations ensued. The most aggressive tribal competitors forced the weaker ones out of the coveted grazing lands. It was this recurring phenomenon which is thought to have caused the Mongols to drive the Turks south into the Persian homeland of the Abbasid Caliphate.

In their new environment, the Turks were soon converted to Islam. "That made them potential empire builders. By the ninth century, Turkish 'slaves' were serving as guardians of the Caliph in Baghdad, ... Finally, in 1055, a Turkish

---

811 William Montgomery McGovern, The Early Empires of Central Asia, (Chapel Hill: The University of North Carolina Press, 1939), p. 14.

812 "The [geographical term] Middle East [as well as Near East] is a repugnant term to Muslim sensibilities because it defines the Muslim world in relation to the West." – Fouad Ajami, The Arab Predicament, Arab Political Thought and Practice Since 1967, (New York: Cambridge University Press, 1992), p. 134.

horde known as the Seljuks, after a famous chief, overthrew the feeble [caliphal] dynasty in Baghdad and officially took over the rule of Persia. Their leader Tugrul Beg assumed the title of Sultan, meaning the holder of temporal power, to distinguish himself from the Caliph, who ostensibly held the spiritual power. It was his son Alp Arslan who crushed the Byzantines at Manzikert. Malik Shah, the next Sultan, built an empire that reached from Transoxiana to Egypt."[813] It was "the Seljuks—forebears [or elder brothers] of the Ottoman Turks—[who initially] carved the Sultanate of Rum [out of the previous territories of the Byzantine Empire]."[814]

Crusaders Respond

"In 1071, [as a consequence of the Battle of Manzikert] the sovereignty of Palestine passed from the caliphate of Baghdad to a newer branch of Islam, the Seljuk Turks. The Seljuk conquest provoked the First Crusade."[815] Previously, "the Arab conquests had not interrupted the stream of pilgrims [to the Holy Land], for the early caliphs were more tolerant of unbelievers than Christian rulers were of heretics. After the conquests of the Seljuk Turks, pilgrimages became more difficult and dangerous. The stories which floated back to Europe of the outrages on Christian pilgrims and shrines awakened an intense desire to rescue the Holy Land from 'infidels.'"[816]

Sultanate of Rum

"The first wave of the Turkish invasion occurred during the second half of the eleventh century and took the form of nomad raids, migration and settlement, mainly on the east and center of Anatolia. These incursions eventually reduced Byzantium to a few fortified towns—Constantinople, Nicaea [Nicea] and Trebizond—and resulted in the establishment in 1098 of the Seljuk sultanate of Rum centered on Konya.[817] The Seljuks might well have adopted Byzantine ways and become absorbed into the culture in which they settled; instead they chose to erase Hellenistic influence and slowly converted the peoples they subdued to Islam."[818]

Changes in the Church

The central and western parts of the territory governed by modern-day Turkey comprised one of the arenas in which, centuries earlier, the gospel had been proclaimed intensively on each of Paul's three missionary journeys. From those apostolic beginnings, the message of Jesus ultimately was embraced throughout the whole peninsula which is now called Turkey.

---

813 Herbert J. Muller, The Loom of History, (New York: Harper & Brothers, 1958), p. 276.
814 Niall Ferguson, *A World Without Power*, Foreign Policy, July/August 2004, pp. 36-37.
815 Barbara W. Tuchman, Bible and Sword, How the British Came to Palestine, (London: MacMillan, 1985), p. 36.
816 Hutton Webster, World History, (New York: D.C. Heath & Co., Publishers, 1921), pp. 187-188.
817 This was the biblical Iconium. See Acts 13:51, 14:1, 14:19, 14:21, 16:2 and II Timothy 3:11.
818 Youssef Courbage and Philippe Fargues, Christians and Jews Under Islam, trans. Judy Mabro (New York: I.B. Tauris Publishers, 1998), p. 92.

By the time the Turks made their appearance, the form of Christianity in Asia Minor had gone through many changes and had become radically different from the simple biblical form of autonomous congregations which it had in New Testament times. The earliest form of church government is clearly seen in the book of Revelation. There, it is important to note, Jesus deals with churches as individual congregations. There were no district, state or national headquarters involved. In contrast, by the time of the Seljuk invasion, "the church had modeled its administration along the lines of the civil administration of the fourth and fifth centuries. In this manner those cities that were the centers of the provincial administration [also] became the centers of the ecclesiastical organization. The Council of Chalcedon in 451 decreed that cities or *poleis* [plural of *polis*, as in *metropolis*, mother city] would be the seats of bishops, and consequently the concept of a *polis* or city became inseparably associated with the presence of a [metropolitan] bishop. ... The episcopal powers and rule in provincial administrative organization were to remain important until the end of the Byzantine Empire [in 1453] and beyond. By the sixth century the bishops were participating in the elections of local urban officials, were important in city finances, and were often the recipients of imperial gifts bestowed on the city. One can say that episcopal authority became a refuge of the last vestiges of urban autonomy, though the eastern bishops, because of the authority of the centralized state, never attained the power of the western Latin bishops."[819]

Turning Turk

The new hierarchical nature of church organization destroyed local church autonomy. Consequently, "the peasantry in Asia Minor, which had provided the imperial government with tax-payers and with soldiers, was also alienated. When in the eleventh century the heart of Asia Minor was occupied by the Seljuk Turks [ultimately to be superseded by the Ottoman Turks], the peasantry was glad to see the last of the extortionate imperial taxation officers and the land-grabbing local magnates. The peasants now turned Turk and turned Muslim en masse."[820]

The Slaughter Begins

One wonders what many of those who "turned Turk," as becoming a Muslim was called, must have thought shortly after their decision to convert. The Byzantine governmental-ecclesiastical system had been, indeed, repressive but certainly not destructive on the scale of that introduced by Turkish conquest. For example, "when the Muslim Nur al-Din captured the city [of Edessa in 1146 A.D.] ... 30,000 were killed, 16,000 enslaved, and only 1,000 escaped. ...

---

819 Speros Vryonis, Jr., The Decline of Medieval Hellenism in Asia Minor and the Process of Islamization from the Eleventh through the Fifteenth Century, (Berkeley: University of California Press, 1971), pp. 8-9.
820 Arnold Toynbee, A Study of History, (New York: Portland House, 1988), p. 193.

In the mid-twelfth century, Yakub Arslan carried away 70,000 Christians from the [Cappadocian] towns of Gaihan and Albistan."[821]

To further understand the rapacity of the Seljuk Turks one should look at the record of the city of Ani, the capital of Armenia. "No traveler visiting what remains of Ani today can fail to catch his breath in sheer astonishment at the splendor of the site: the towering walls, still partially standing, the rolling plain beyond it from which rise the ruins of some of the most magnificent [buildings of] churches of their time (Matthew of Edessa claims that there were a thousand and one of them) and—invisible until one is at the very brink—the sudden chasm formed by the river nowadays known as the Arpa Cay and one of its tributaries, thanks to which the city enjoyed one of the strongest defensive positions of any in the region. This was, however, of little use against the Seljuks. Unlike many of its neighbors Ani put up a show of resistance, holding out for twenty-five days before it surrendered. ... The Arab historian Sibt ibn al-Gawzi quotes a purported eye-witness of what took place: The army entered the city, massacred its inhabitants, pillaged and burned it, leaving it in ruins and taking prisoner all those who remained alive ... The dead bodies were so many that they blocked all the streets; one could not go anywhere without stepping over them. And the number of prisoners was not less than 50,000 souls. I was determined to enter the city and see the destruction with my own eyes. I tried to find a street in which I would not have to walk over the corpses; but that was impossible."[822]

Mongols Punish the Turks

Anatolia was invaded "by Crusaders, Mamluks and Mongols all against a background of Byzantine resistance organized from the remaining fortresses. The most devastating of these incursions, in the middle of the thirteenth century, was that of the Mongols, who were now Islamized and were led by Tamerlane. The Mongols reduced the Seljuks to vassals and destroyed their state structure. In these centuries of disintegration, borders were eliminated in Anatolia and the plateaux was opened up to further migrations of Islamized Turks who enlarged the area in which they practiced nomadism and created a number of small frontier warrior states, one of which was eventually to become the kernel of the Ottoman Empire."[823]

Emergence of the Ottomans

"But Othman, after the death of the last Alaeddin [the Seljuk royal house under which Othman's father Ertoghrul ruled a part of Asia Minor] in 1307, waged

---
821 Speros Vryonis, Jr., The Decline of Medieval Hellenism in Asia Minor and the Process of Islamization from the Eleventh through the Fifteenth Century, (Berkeley: University of California Press, 1971), p. 28.
822 John Julius Norwich, Byzantium, The Apogee, (New York: Alfred A. Knopf, 1994), pp. 342-243.
823 Youssef Courbage and Philippe Fargues, Christians and Jews Under Islam, trans. Judy Mabro (New York: I.B. Tauris Publishers, 1998), p. 93.

wars and accumulated dominions as an independent potentate. He had become chief of his race twelve years before, on Ertoghrul's death in 1288."[824]

"It was about this time, A.D. 1299, that he [Othman] coined money with his own effigy, and caused the public prayers to be said in his name. These among the Oriental nations are regarded as the distinctive marks of royalty."[825]

As pointed out in Chapter 17, following the Battle of Manzikert, the Seljuks had allowed their junior partners, the Ottomans, to migrate into the western areas of Asia Minor while they retained their dominating oversight of the Abbasid Caliphate, a decision ultimately disastrous to the Seljuks. In 1258 the Mongol Hulagu, grandson of Ghenghis Khan, led his wolves in an almost totally destructive attack on Baghdad, ending the Abbasid Caliphate and simultaneously breaking the power of the Seljuks. These events opened the door of opportunity for the Ottomans who, founding their empire in 1299 A.D., continued to gain strength till they faced (and defeated) the Mamluks with overwhelming power in a decisive battle on August 24, 1516 at Marj Dabiq, just north of Aleppo.[826] Now, those who tried to follow Christ faced even more severe and daunting days!

☙

---

824 Edward S. Creasy, History of The Ottoman Turks, (Beirut: Khayats, 1961), p. 5.
825 Edward S. Creasy, History of The Ottoman Turks, (Beirut: Khayats, 1961), p. 9.
826 See Peter N. Stearns (ed.), The Encyclopedia of World History, (New York: Houghton Mifflin Company, 2001), p. 129.

Chapter 27

THE OTTOMAN TURKS INVITED INTO EUROPE

Note: In conjunction with Chapter 27, be sure to read "Turkish Decline—French and Papal Advance" in Chapter 25.

The all-time unparalleled classic example of inviting the fox to take charge of the hen house took place in 1354 when the Byzantine emperor, John Cantacuzene, invited the Ottoman Turks to cross the narrow waters of the Dardenelles from Asia Minor onto European soil. The emperor hoped the Turks would help defeat the army of the great Serbian king and military leader Dushan, who was threatening Constantinople. "Desperate, the rulers in Constantinople allowed the Turkish armies massing in the east to cross ... into Europe and thus to erect a bridgehead at Gallipoli, in order to stave off Dushan's Serbian troops."[827] But the Turks never withdrew from Gallipoli![828] That put them in position to ultimately conquer and usurp all the territory of the Byzantine Empire in southeast Europe and then in 1453 bring that beleaguered empire to its end by finally conquering Constantinople, its justly-fabled capital city.

The Ottoman Turks, whom Emperor John Cantacuzene invited to protect the empire from Serbian attack, were very closely related blood brothers of the Seljuk Turks. The Seljuks were the ones who previously on August 19, 1071 had wrested Asia Minor from the Byzantines by their victory at the Battle of Manzikert. Following that victory, the Ottoman Turks were the ones who occupied and held captive most of the Byzantine area in far western Asia Minor.

Though inviting the Ottomans into Europe may seem to indicate otherwise, the Byzantine Emperor John Cantacuzene was no fool. Yet, in spite of the obvious danger, out of sheer desperation, he invited the Ottomans to cross the Dardanelles. Emperor John's folly was shortly to be crowned by extreme irony. Before Dushan could launch his planned all-out attack on Constantinople, he died![829] With his death Dushan's forces were thrown into confusion and the military danger to Constantinople from southeast Europe evaporated! But the danger from a Serbian attack from southeast Europe was then replaced by dan-

---

[827] Robert D. Kaplan, Balkan Ghosts, (New York: St. Martin's Press, 1993), pp. 35-36.
[828] Subsequently, Gallipoli again proved to be a site central not only to the founding of the Ottoman Empire, but to its resuscitation during and following World War I. It was there that Mustafa Kemal Ataturk gained fame and leadership of the Ottoman Turks by his audacious generalship of Turkish forces in victory over the Australian-New Zealand invasion army. For a gripping, masterful account, read Gallipoli by Alan Moorehead.
[829] His death took place on December 18, 1356.

ger from the Ottoman Turks whom the Byzantine emperor himself had invited to cross the threshold into Europe!

Because of Byzantium's invitation to the Ottomans to help them fight the Serbs, Islamic armies had once again entered Europe, but this time from the southeast. Previously, other Muslim military forces had entered Spain and southern France. By 711 A.D. Spain had been occupied. Having pushed through Spain, those forces then crossed the Pyrenees with the intent of subjugating France to Islam. Their scheme was thwarted by the victorious forces of Charles Martel at the Battle of Tours in 732 A.D. But the reversal did not stop at Tours. Ultimately, in 1492 the last Muslim power based in Europe had been forced out of Granada, the southernmost province of Spain. They crossed the Strait of Gibraltar to join their fellow Muslims in Africa.[830]

Peril Compounded by Enmity

As we have seen, Byzantine desperation had led them in 1354 to extend an invitation to the Ottoman Muslims to enter Europe. Animosity toward the Western Christian world kept Byzantium from appealing to their Western brethren, the only other source from which help against the Serbs might have come. That animosity had reached a peak in the great East-West Christian schism of 1054. At that juncture, astonishingly, representatives of Pope Leo IX laid "upon the table at St. Sophia [in Constantinople, the greatest church building in all Christendom] a sentence of anathema on the [Byzantine Orthodox] patriarch and his supporters on the ground of evil doctrines and practices. ... The patriarch retaliated by having the name of the pope erased from the diptych[831] of St. Sophia."[832] But that animosity reached much greater intensity because, "The Latin capture of Constantinople in 1204 [by the fourth crusade] left a legacy of bitterness between eastern and western Christendom that was, at times, even stronger than the antipathy felt by Muslims and Christians toward each other."[833]

---

830 For a detailed account of Islam's push through Spain all the way to the heart of France, see Chapter 22 under "A Mountain Lair" and Chapter 23.

831 In Roman antiquity, a two-leaved hinged writing tablet. A similar tablet, containing in one part the names of living and, in the other, those of dead orthodox persons (such as bishops, patriarchs, emperors, and benefactors of the church) for whom commemoration was made in the Eucharistic service in the early church. – Webster's New International Dictionary of the English Language, Second Edition Unabridged.

832 Albert Henry Newman, A Manual of Church History, (Philadelphia: The American Baptist Publication Society, 1933), Vol. I, p. 626.
"On July 16, 1054, Humbert entered St. Sofia during divine service, and laid on the altar the decree of excommunication against the Patriarch and his adherents, after which he with some difficulty made his escape. The event thus accomplished, though often obscured and misunderstood by being regarded as a trivial ecclesiastical dispute, ranks with the foundation of Constantinople and the coronation of Charlemagne as one of the turning-points in the relations of the West and East. Above all, it was for the East of cardinal and doleful import. In it found expression [of] that dull antagonism, that deep-rooted want of sympathy between the two great geographical divisions of Christendom which prevented them from ever combining against the common aggressor, and which thus proved the main cause of the fall of the Byzantine Empire and the establishment of the Turk in Europe." – Charles Eliot, Turkey In Europe, (London: Frank Cass & Co. Ltd., 1965), p. 220.

833 Molly Greene, A Shared World, Christians and Muslims in the Early Modern Mediterranean, (Princeton: Princeton University Press, 2000), p. 6.

It isn't surprising then that a diplomat-historian has written, "They [the Ottomans] gained their first footing in Europe in consequence of the dissensions of Europeans. They have always been numerically inferior to the aggregate of their subjects, and could hardly have maintained their rule had the latter ever been able to unite against them."[834]

Strength To Weakness

The peril to Constantinople coming through the Balkan Peninsula, was, to be sure, extremely grave. It arose from the incursions of, among others, the Avars, the Slavs and the Bulgars. In earlier times the Byzantines managed those problems without inviting help from their enemies. For example, Basil II, who ruled from 963–1025 A.D., was known as the Bulgar-slayer. In harmony with his name, after a great battlefield victory, he brought the Bulgarian threat to an end in 1014 by blinding 15,000 Bulgarian captives and having them led home as a warning to others! "With this terrible vengeance the ruin of the Bulgarian Empire was consummated, and its territories were placed under Byzantine rule."[835]

Under Basil II, the Byzantine Empire had reached its apex. But by the time Emperor John Cantacuzene invited the Ottomans to assist in protecting Byzantine territories in southeast Europe, many events had transpired to weaken the empire. Among those events, one unquestionably stands out for causing the greatest damage to the ability of the empire to defend itself. It was the capture of Constantinople, just alluded to, by the forces of the Fourth Crusade. "The loss of Constantinople in 1204 was a mortal blow to the Byzantines, and although the city was recaptured in 1261, the empire remained a shadow of its former self."[836]

As a result of the Fourth Crusade, "Constantinople was half ruined, deprived of its treasures, and largely depopulated. Its trade with the East had moved elsewhere. ... The reign of the first of the Palaeologue[837] emperors, after the recapture of Constantinople, was followed ... by a dynasty locked in an intermittent civil war ... This disunity played inevitably into the hands of the Turks, united as they were in the holy warfare of Islam."[838]

Plague Strikes

In addition to the chaos and weakness resulting from the fourth crusade, beginning in 1347 Constantinople was smitten repeatedly by the plague of Black

---
834 Charles Eliot, Turkey In Europe, (London: Frank Cass & Co. Ltd., 1965), p. 220.
835 Norman H. Baynes & H. St. L. B. Moss (eds.), Byzantium, An Introduction to East Roman Civilization, (Oxford: The Clarendon Press, 1953), p. 24.
836 Angus Konstam, Historical Atlas of The Crusades, (New York: Thalamus Publishing, 2002), p. 153.
837 "Palaiologos ... often Latinized as Palaeologus, was a Byzantine Greek noble family, which produced the last ruling dynasty of the Byzantine Empire." – Wikipedia.
838 Lord Kinross, The Ottoman Centuries The Rise and Fall of The Turkish Empire, (New York: Morrow Quill Paperbacks, 1977), pp. 37-38.

Death. This further weakened the Byzantine government's ability to resist the attacks of the Ottoman Turks, after those Turks had turned against their hosts and committed themselves to a relentless drive to bring the great Byzantine Empire to an end. A dispatch from a British ambassador in the early 1600s will help one gain a realistic impression of the devastation which had earlier taken place in Istanbul, the former Constantinople, by his description of a later plague. He wrote that the epidemic "had killed one thousand a day ... and forced more than two hundred thousand to flee into the countryside."[839] This was part of a much wider plague. See Chapter 2 under "Empires at War."

For many centuries Southeast Europe, in the area known as the Balkan Peninsula,[840] had been governed by the Byzantine Empire. Today, within this roughly triangular tip of southeast Europe are located nine states as well as part of a tenth, the northwest corner of Turkey. Those nine political entities are, listing them, as closely as possible, from north to south: (1) The Republic of Slovenia, (2) The Republic of Croatia, (3) Romania, the largest Balkan state, (4) The Republic of Bosnia and Herzegovina, (5) present-day Yugoslavia which consists of the federation of Serbia and Montenegro, (6) The Republic of Bulgaria, (7) The Republic of Albania, (8) Macedonia (The Former Yugoslav Republic) and (9) Greece (The Hellenic Republic).

Expanding Empire

As a chronological reference point of great interest, it may be noted that in 1295, "Marco Polo returned to Venice from the East, reporting amazement at Chinese use of petroleum, coal, and asbestos."[841] Just four years later, in 1299, the Ottomans began their career in empire. "With the enfeeblement of the Byzantines, the Ottoman Turks [as has just been mentioned] secured their first foothold on the European continent in 1354 at Gallipoli. They were able to make Adrianople their capital in 1366."[842] Adrianople not only served as their capital but also, "as their base as they moved toward encircling Constantinople."[843]

The Mediterranean Basin was polarized by the rise of contending political entities at both ends of it. The Ottoman Empire was to dominate the eastern end of the Mediterranean while the Spanish Habsburg Empire,[844] from the time of Fer-

---

839 Mark Mazower, Salonica, City of Ghosts Christians, Muslims and Jews, 1430–1950, (New York: Alfred "A. Knopf, 2005), p. 108.
840 The boundaries of the Balkan Peninsula are triangular, one side being in the north basically along the Danube River. Its eastern boundary follows the shore of the Black Sea from the mouth of the Danube to the southern end of Greece. The western side of the peninsula follows the alignment of the west coast of Greece all the way to the city of Munich.
841 Wired [Magazine], January 2002, p. 76.
842 Carlton S. Coon, Caravan: The Story of the Middle East, (New York: Henry Holt and Company, 1956), p. 97.
843 David Fromkin, Kosovo Crossing, The Reality of American Intervention in the Balkans, (New York: Simon & Schuster, 2002), p. 91.
844 "While Ferdinand was absorbed with events in Italy, he was also profoundly occupied with the preservation of his power in the [Spanish] peninsula. In January 1502 his daughter Juana arrived from the Netherlands in the company of her husband the archduke Philip of Habsburg (whom she had married at Lille in 1496). In Toledo and Saragossa they attended the Cortes and were sworn in as heirs to the throne of Spain." – Henry Kamen, Empire How Spain Became a World Power 1492–1763, (New York: Harper Collins, 2003), p. 33.

dinand and Isabella, was to dominate the western Mediterranean. (See Chapter 25 under "Turkish Decline—French and Papal Advance.")

Following definitive victories from a series of significant battles, the Ottomans were in position to threaten Vienna, the eastern gateway to Europe proper. The first of those victories took place June 28, 1389 near Pristina, at Kosovo Polje (The Field of Blackbirds).[845] It was a major encounter in which the Serbs valiantly tried to prevent the Turks from using their base in Gallipoli to expand to the north. Significantly, this battle broke the military power of the Serbs. The Serbian prince Lazar and Ottoman Sultan Murad I both perished in the battle but the victory went clearly and overwhelmingly to the Ottomans. "The Serb leader, Prince Lazar, was captured by the Turks, brought before the Turkish sultan, and beheaded. To this day many Serbs, while celebrating the bravery of their forces, are motivated by a desire to avenge the defeat."[846]

Following the failure of the Serbs to halt Ottoman expansion, the Hungarians led a crusade against the Turks but suffered defeat at Varna in 1444. Despite their military reversal, four years later the Hungarians invaded territory held by the Ottomans but were defeated again in 1448 in what is known as the Second Battle of Kosovo.

The Death Knell

"In 1453, Sultan Mehmed the Conqueror captured Constantinople and ended the [great] Byzantine Empire. Though Byzantium had been declining for centuries, the fall of the last bastion of imperial Rome by a Turkish dynasty was a wrenching moment in Western history. Europe was deeply shaken."[847] One scholar points out that the Islamist Welfare Party in Turkey considers the conquest of Constantinople as "the beginning point of the supremacy of Muslims over Europe."[848]

"With the consolidation of their position, the Turks, who had formerly allowed the European caravans to pass through their territories, now put an end to any direct overland communication between Europe and the more distant East. ... The westward movement of Asiatic merchandise, once a mighty stream, became a feeble and irregular trickle."[849]

What overall evaluation should we give to the fall of Byzantium? "Some historians date the end of the Middle Ages from the fall of Constantinople to the Turks in 1453, others from the invention of printing by movable type in 1454, or from Columbus' discovery of the New World in 1492, or from the revolt against Rome signaled by Luther's nailing his theses to the church door in

---

845 Located west of Pristina in Kosovo, about 48 miles north northwest of Skopje. Between Mitrovice and Skopje.
846 Madeleine Albright, Madam Secretary, (New York: Miramax Books, 2003), p. 379.
847 Zachary Karabell, Parting The Desert, The Creation of the Suez Canal, (New York: Alfred A. Knopf, 2003), p. 93.
848 Elif Batruman, Ottomania, The New Yorker, February 17 & 24. 2014, p. 57.
849 William Montgomery McGovern, The Early Empires of Central Asia, (Chapel Hill: The University of North Carolina Press, 1939), p. 14-16.

1517. Not any one of these events, but the combination and interaction of all within roughly fifty years, brought about the new era."[850]

Deeper Into Europe

Persistently, the Hungarians still blocked the Turks' way to Vienna and on into the heartland of Europe. Leading a 250,000 man army Sulayman [Suleiman] defeated the Hungarians at the Battle of Mohacs on August 29, 1526. "The twenty-year-old King of the Hungarians was killed, a hundred thousand Christians were taken into captivity and the treasures of the palace of Matthias Corvinus went to decorate the Seraglio in Constantinople. The floodgates were opened; and there was nothing now to prevent the Turks from invading Europe in strength."[851] "Hungary never recovered from this defeat. A prolonged civil war (1526–1538 A.D.) ultimately resulted in the incorporation of the central and southern two-thirds of Hungary into the Ottoman Empire (1547) and in the establishment of Transylvania and the eastern Hungarian provinces as an autonomous principality within the Ottoman Empire."[852] "For three centuries Hungary had stood out against the Sultan, but the disaster of Mohacs (1526), in which the king of Hungary was killed, laid that land at the feet of the conqueror. His [Suleiman the Magnificent (1520–1566)] fleets also took Algiers, and inflicted a number of reverses upon the Venetians. In most of his warfare with the [Habsburg] Empire he was in alliance with the French. Under him the Ottoman power reached its zenith."[853] (See "Turkish Decline—French and Papal Advance" in Chapter 25.)

Despite Expanding Evil, There Was Some Good

Catastrophic though it was, the fall of the Byzantine Empire was not entirely negative. "Renewed interest in the literature of Greece dates from the fifteenth century, when the advance of the Ottoman Turks, culminating in the capture of Constantinople, sent a stream of Greek exiles into Italy. Some of them were learned men, and their conversation and lectures greatly stimulated the study of Greek in the West."[854]

---

850 Barbara W. Tuchman, Bible and Sword, How the British Came to Palestine, (London: MacMillan, 1985), pp. 83-84.
851 Robert Payne, The History of Islam, (New York: Dorset Press, 1990), p. 271.
852 Encyclopaedia Britannica, Micropaedia, Vol. 6, p. 967.
853 H.G. Wells, The Outline of History, (Garden City, New York: Garden City Books, 1949),Vol. II, p. 602.
854 Hutton Webster, World History, (Boston: D.C. Heath & Co., Publishers, 1921), p. 242. One must not forget the remarkable work done by Alcuin 671 years before the fall of Constantinople. The work of Alcuin actually antedated the work done in The House of Wisdom in Baghdad. "Charlemagne ordered that reading and writing would be taught in all monasteries. In 782 he brought the Northumbrian scholar Alcuin to his capital at Aachen as, in effect, minister of education. Alcuin founded flourishing schools, and established standards in teaching. At his scriptoria, thousands of books from the ancient world were scrupulously copied. Almost all those Latin classics which have survived in Europe have come down to us through these copyists. The Carolingian Renaissance thus begun was to blossom in the reign of Charlemagne's grandson Charles the Bald." – Michael Worth Davison (ed.), When, Where, Why & How It Happened (London: The Reader's Digest Association Ltd., 1995), p. 81. The main reason this great educational and intellectual initiative did not spark a widespread revival of learning in Europe was because of the economic stranglehold which the Muslim world had on Europe, forcing its people into the direst penury. That stranglehold was not broken till the voyages of Vasco da Gama.

The Ottoman Turks Invited Into Europe ~ Chapter 27

The same perceptive historian wrote, "Conquest was the Turks' one business in the world, and when they ceased conquering the decline set in."[855] But up to this point they certainly had not yet ceased to conquer!

"In subsequent decades, the armies of the sultan ... annexed what are now Bulgaria, Romania, Yugoslavia, and Hungary. The Ottomans kept advancing, all the way to the gates of Vienna in 1529. The siege was unsuccessful [see below], and Sultan Suleiman [Sulayman] the Magnificent ordered his troops to return home before the onset of winter.[856] But the [Ottoman] empire did not recede. It expanded, throughout North Africa, into the Near East as far as Persia, and around the Black Sea, through Tartary, and into the Caucasus, where the Ottomans perennially defeated the soldiers of the Russian tzar."[857]

The retreat from Vienna in 1529, probably more than winter conditions at Vienna, was caused by developments on the eastern border of the Ottoman Empire which demanded that Suleiman focus his attention there. For it was there, on the Ottoman eastern border, that "Shah Isma'il Safavi (reigned 1501–1524), a Turkish-speaking Shi'ite from Azerbaijan, [had] brought all the lands of Iran under a single ruler for the first time since the Arab conquest in the seventh century. ... He made Shi'ism the official religion of the state, and thus differentiated the Muslim realm of Iran sharply from its Sunni neighbors on both sides; to the East, in Central Asia and India, and to the West, in the Ottoman Empire. ... Persia remained a separate, rival, and, for the most part, hostile state. Busbecq, the imperial ambassador in Istanbul,[858] went so far as to say that it was only the threat from Persia that saved Europe from imminent conquest by the Turks."[859]

"In 1683 the Turks [for the second time] made their farthest penetration of Europe, to the gates of Vienna, the capital of Austria. The siege of Vienna was bitterly fought by both sides, but at length the Turks were routed."[860]

Defeat and Pastry

"Remember that croissant at brunch last Sunday? The quintessential French pastry, right? Think again. The crescent-shaped roll, or Kipfel, was invented by a Viennese baker, who mimicked the lunar symbol of Islam to celebrate Austri-

---
855 Hutton Webster, World History, (Boston: D.C. Heath & Co., Publishers, 1921), p. 194.
856 "The Sultan's army was essentially a summer force, limited in its offensive scope by the fact that its feudal cavalry could not face a winter campaign lest their horses perish, hence were confined to a campaigning season of barely six months. Nor could the Sultan himself and the ministers who accompanied him, conveniently remain absent from Istanbul for longer. Thus, now that it was already mid-October and the last assault [on October 14] had failed, Suleiman raised the siege and ordered a general retreat. The Turkish troops set fire to their camp, massacring or burning alive all their prisoners from the Austrian countryside, except those, of both sexes, young enough to qualify for the slave market." – Lord Kinross, The Ottoman Centuries The Rise and Fall of The Turkish Empire, (New York: Morrow Quill Paperbacks, 1977), p. 192.
857 Zachary Karabell, Parting the Desert, The Creation of the Suez Canal, (New York: Alfred A. Knopf, 2003), p. 93.
858 This was Odgier Ghiselin de Busbecq, ambassador both for the Habsburg ruler Ferdinand I and for the Holy Roman Emperor at the Sublime Porte.
859 Bernard Lewis, What Went Wrong?, (New York: Oxford University Press, 2002), pp. 8-9.
860 Richard Horchler, The Fighting Monks, (New York, Walker and Company, 1961), p. 95.

a's triumph over the last invasion by Ottoman Turks in 1683. The grateful locals washed their Kipfels down with coffee from beans the Turks left behind. A century later, Marie Antoinette, daughter of Empress Maria Theresa, took a Viennese pastry cook with her to France, and the Kipfel became the croissant."[861]

Evaluation and Consequences

What was the impact of the rise and expansion of the Muslim Ottoman Empire, individually and corporately, on those who were trying to follow Christ? To begin with, "they converted what they could of the conquered people to Islam; the Christians they disarmed, and conferred upon them the monopoly of tax-paying."[862]

The fate of the Christian citizens of the city of Thessalonica, known as Salonica in Ottoman times, will help one understand why those who tried to follow Christ have largely died out in many parts of the former Ottoman Empire, especially those parts which now comprise Turkey. "'On numerous occasions we saw Christians—boys as well as unmarried girls, and masses of married women of every description—paraded pitiably by the Turks in long lines throughout the cities of Thrace and Macedonia,' wrote the Italian merchant-antiquarian Cyriac of Ancona. They were 'bound by iron chains and lashed by whips, and in the end put up for sale in villages and markets ... an unspeakably shameful and obscene sight, like a cattle market.' ... Some converted to Islam in the hope of better treatment; others, yoked to one another by the neck, could be seen begging for alms in the streets of the capital, Edirne [historic Adrianople], where they were brought to be sold off, or entered the imperial service."[863]

"It is recorded of Suleiman the Magnificent that he converted churches into mosques in every one of the towns and fortresses he had won from Christendom. All churches in towns taken by assault were at the disposal of the conqueror, though the principle was not always insisted on."[864] No wonder, then, that, "Thousands of abandoned and decayed Christian churches were rebuilt as mosques, and medreses [also madrassa—a mosque school] were built around them to serve as centers for the new enlightened ulema congregating in Istanbul."[865]

---

861 Barrymore Laurence Scherer, *On Disc: Tasty Blends of East and West*, <u>The Wall Street Journal</u>, June 3, 2003, p. D5.
862 Bernard Lewis, <u>Islam And The West</u>, (New York: Oxford University Press, 1993), p. 16.
863 Mark Mazower, <u>Salonica, City of Ghosts Christians, Muslims and Jews, 1430–1950</u>, (New York: Alfred "A. Knopf, 2005), 33-34. "The process of enslavement was applied to prisoners of war and the inhabitants of captured places. A law gave to the Ottoman soldier an absolute right to the possession of captives unless they consented to profess and practice Islam. He might keep them for domestic or agricultural employment; he might sell them in the open market, subject to the government's right to a fifth of the market value of the total captured." – Lord Kinross, <u>The Ottoman Centuries The Rise and Fall of The Turkish Empire</u>, (New York: Morrow Quill Paperbacks, 1977), p. 47.
864 F.W. Hasluck, <u>Christianity and Islam Under The Sultans</u>, (New York: Octagon Books, 1973), pp. 6-8.
865 Stanford J. Shaw, <u>History of the Ottoman Empire and Modern Turkey</u>, (Cambridge: Cambridge University Press, 1977), Vol. I, p. 143.

Christians were often held hostage. For example, Sultan Murat, "began a policy of settling many Christian peasants from the Balkans in Anatolia and the environs of Edirne [Adrianople] to assure the obedience of their fellows back home."[866]

Christian women were mere chess pieces in the hands of Muslim rulers. Yet numbers of them tried valiantly to exercise an influence for Christ. For example, "Orhan's wife Theodora, daughter of Cantacuzene, is said to have remained a Christian and to have provided help to the Christians of Bithynia while she was in the Ottoman court. Murat I and Bayezit I had Christian Greek mothers. Murat married the Bulgarian princess Tamara and the Byzantine princess Helena. Bayezit married Despina, daughter of the Serbian prince Lazar. All these women brought Christian advisers into the Ottoman court, influencing Ottoman court practice and ceremonial as it evolved in this crucial century. ... Their influence changed Bayezit I from a gazi leader to an invader of the Muslim Turkoman principalities of Anatolia."[867]

Institutionalized Kidnapping

One of the most despicable practices of the Ottoman period was the long-lived system of systematically shanghaiing young Christian boys and after compelling them to convert to Islam, forcing them, as obligatory celibates, to spend the rest of their lives in compulsory labor for the Ottoman state. These young men became an elite corps of shock troops from which was also formed the palace guard. They were called in Turkish *Yeni Ceri*, meaning "New Troop." The Turkish term has through the centuries been approximated in English by the word, "Janissary." The shanghaiing process was known in Turkish as *devsirme*. "Originally, the term devsirme had been applied to the process of collection of the ruler's pencik (Persian, one-fifth) right to a portion of the booty captured in warfare."[868]

"In the first half of the nineteenth century, both Shiite and Sunni clerics found imperial Great Britain's aggressive opposition to slavery to be morally absurd and offensive. God via the Qur'an had vouchsafed to believers the right, with detailed restrictions laid out in the Holy Law, to enslave other men and women conquered in war or raiding parties."[869]

For additional information on the topic of the Janissaries, see Chapter 19 under the heading of "Meaning of Human Tribute." For a description of the Armenian geno-

---

866 Stanford J. Shaw, History of the Ottoman Empire and Modern Turkey, (Cambridge: Cambridge University Press, 1977), Vol I, p. 19.
867 Stanford J. Shaw, History of the Ottoman Empire and Modern Turkey, (Cambridge: Cambridge University Press, 1977), Vol. I, p. 24.
868 Stanford J. Shaw, History of the Ottoman Empire and Modern Turkey, (Cambridge: Cambridge University Press, 1977), Vol. I, p. 113.
869 Reuel Marc Gerecht, The Islamic Paradox, Shiite Clerics, Sunni Fundamentalists, and the Coming of Arab Democracy, (Washington D.C.: American Enterprise Institute Press, 2004), p. 39.

cide, the most heinous of all Turkish crimes against Christians, please see Appendix B.

In view of the conditions just enumerated, it should not surprise us that "in Anatolia, as in the rest of the Middle East, the conjunction of Muslim state power, the decline of organized Christian societies, and the social and cultural relevance of Islam facilitated mass conversions to the new religion."[870] The rapacity of Turkish Islam reached its apex in a series of the most unspeakable atrocities during the Turkish genocide of the Armenian Christians. On this despicable development, be sure to read Appendix B.

Summary

To summarize the centuries during which the withering wind from Arabia has continued to blow, hear the great Jewish scholar of Islam, Bernard Lewis: "We tend nowadays to forget that for approximately a thousand years, from the advent of Islam in the seventh century until the second siege of Vienna in 1683, Christian Europe was under constant threat from Islam, the double threat of conquest and conversion. Most of the early Muslim converts west of Iran and Arabia were converts from Christianity. Most of the new Muslim domains were wrested from Christendom. Syria, Palestine, Egypt, and North Africa were all Christian countries, no less, indeed rather more, than Spain and Sicily. All this left a deep sense of loss and a deep fear. The beginnings of the study of Arabic and Islam in Europe in the High Middle Ages were certainly linked with the fear of conquest by the Arabs and conversion to Islam. Muslims had no such fear and in consequence felt no such need during the early formative centuries when the character of their civilization was determined."[871]

CR

---

870 Ira M. Lapidus, A History of Islamic Societies, 2nd Ed., (Cambridge: Cambridge University Press, 2002), p. 202.
871 Bernard Lewis, Islam And The West, (New York: Oxford University Press, 1993), p. 127.

Chapter 28

ANSWERING SKEPTICS

In two current books, prominent scholars have given their evaluation of many of the issues and developments that are basic in the account I've given in *Withering Wind From Arabia*. In this chapter I present their most salient points and my response. Hopefully the resultant clash of views will help each one seeking the facts to discern truth and error.

Professor G. W. Bowersock, a scholar of great academic reputation, tells us that the Islamic conquests were remarkably benign. He expressed that view when he wrote, "The era of the four caliphs who were designated in subsequent tradition as orthodox (*rashidun*) marked the irreversible transfer of the center of Islamic administration from Mecca and Medina, first to Damascus, and, in 750, with the Abbasids to Baghdad. Perhaps the most remarkable feature of this era, which terminated in a brief civil war [known as the Battle of the Great Zab River], was the almost imperceptible impact that it had upon the Byzantine culture of the region. The orthodox caliphs simply showed no interest, apart from imposing some taxes to pay for their soldiers and other routine costs, in imposing their own language, religion, or traditions upon the lands into which they had moved. Churches continued to function as before and were treated as holy places."[872]

Consider Archaeology

Dr. Bowersock clinches his historical assertion by saying it is buttressed by archeology. He claims that "it has only recently become clear from the examination of the archaeological record that in Palestine, Syria, and Transjordan hardly anything changed in the patterns of daily life, including religion and cultivation of the land from the beginning of the Muslim invasions right through to the end of the caliphate of Muawiya. ... The only surviving historical text of any length from the late seventh century, the narrative of the Armenian Sebeos (who was writing at a time when the ships of Muawiya were approaching the shores of Constantinople), provides no warrant for assuming major social or administrative changes in the Near East during the tumultuous events that brought down the Persian Empire."[873] Though Dr. Bowersock mentions the prolonged incessant naval attacks by the Umayyad Caliphate on Constantinople, he gives no mention of the resulting dis-

---

[872] G. W. Bowersock, The Crucible of Islam, (Cambridge, Mass.: Harvard University Press, 2017), pp. 129.
[873] G. W. Bowersock, The Crucible of Islam, (Cambridge, Mass.: Harvard University Press, 2017), pp. 132-133.

New Taxes

ruption of daily and church life in that great city as though such results had never occurred.

Professor Bowersock has awesome qualifications, being the professor emeritus of Ancient History in the Institute for Advanced Study at Princeton University and the author of many books. In view of his prestigious experience and qualifications, it is breathtaking that he has made such an inclusive exoneration of Muslim behavior during and after their conquest of the Near East. He does point out, however, that one change was made by "imposing some taxes." According to the Koran, those taxes were rapacious and were to be received in an insulting and demeaning way. The Koranic mandate says: "Fight against such of those who have been given the Scripture as believe not in Allah nor the Last Day, and forbid not that which Allah hath forbidden by his messenger, and follow not the religion of truth, until they pay the tribute readily, being brought low." (Surah 9:29)

That Koranic command must not have been carried out, if as Prof. Bowersock says, "It has only recently become clear from the examination of the archaeological record that in Palestine, Syria, and Transjordan hardly anything changed in the patterns of daily life, including religion." Did that "archaeological record" to which Prof. Bowersock calls attention give any proof that the demeaning tax so clearly mandated by the Koran, which was to be paid by those "who have been given the Scripture" (obviously, Christians and Jews), had been ignored, ameliorated, post-poned, annulled or cancelled?

Alternative Minimum Tax

To get a true picture of the situation for Christians, consider the situation in North Africa. During Muawiya's Umayyad Caliphate,[874] the period to which Dr. Bowersock points us, Muslims demanded that the Louata Berber Christians pay their taxes by giving virgin daughters for whom the Muslims established a price which would be credited to their tax payment. As previously noted in Chapter 19, "Human tribute was a means through which the conquerors obtained slaves, especially slave girls, to cater for the pleasures of the Arab ruling class. This practice seems to have been initiated at the beginning of the conquest. ... Upon conquering Cyrenaica in 642 or 643 'Amr b. al-'As [the Arab military commander who was also conqueror and governor of Egypt] fixed the jizya to be paid by its Berber tribes at 13,000 Dinars. From the Lawata [Louata] tribe he demanded that they should 'sell' to the Arabs a number of the 'sons and daughters' to the value of their share of the total jizya."[875]

---

[874] A list of all fourteen Umayyad caliphs and the years of each one's term in office is given in Appendix H, footnote 1150.

[875] Jamil M. Abun-Nasr, <u>A History of the Maghrib in the Islamic Period</u>, (Cambridge: Cambridge University Press, 1987), p. 34.

Prof. Bowersock also alleges that "churches continued to function as before." Did he not know that as soon as the conquest of Damascus took place (in 661 A.D.), the Muslims demanded that the Christians give one-half of the church of St. John to them to use as a mosque? To quote from Chapter 24 in this book: On that night, just before morning, chosen Arabs scaled the wall, overpowered the skeleton guard and flung the gate open through which the main Muslim army flooded in to overpower the entire city. After the capitulation of the city, the magnificent cathedral of St. John was divided by a wall so the victorious Muslims could use one side as a mosque. That was only a trivial token of the coming impact which Islam would have on the lives of those who wore the name of Christ.

The testimony of Professor Creswell, who at the peak of his career was Chair of Muslim Architecture in the American University in Cairo, flatly contradicts the position held by Professor Bowersock. Creswell wrote, "In these early days, the Muslims, when they conquered a town in Syria, usually took one of the churches and used it as a mosque, or merely *divided* one of the churches if the town had surrendered without resistance. At Homs, for example, they took a fourth part of the church of St. John. At Aleppo, according to Balādhurī, they took half of the churches. How is a church converted into a mosque? One can easily guess. In Syria the *qibla* (direction of Mekka) is due south, whereas churches are turned towards the east. Under these circumstances it was only necessary to close the western entrance (or three entrances), pierce new entrances in the north wall, and pray across the aisles. That this is exactly what happened can be verified in the Great Mosque of Hamā, where the west front of the Kanīsat al-'Uzma (Great Church), which was converted into a mosque in A.D. 636-7, now forms the west end of the sanctuary. Its three western doors have been converted into windows and it is now entered from the north."[876]

Though Dr. Bowersock asserts that church life and activities continued without disruption, his position totally disregards the record left by Christians who experienced the Muslim conquest. For example, Sophronius, patriarch of Jerusalem during the first wave of Arab attacks, described the situation. He wrote, "we are like Adam banned from paradise, 'we do not see the twisting flaming sword, but rather the wild and barbarous Saracen [sword], which is filled with every diabolical savagery.' We are like Moses forbidden to enter the promised land. And our plight also resembles that of David: as once that of the Philistines, so now the army of the godless Saracens has captured the divine Bethlehem and bars our passage there, threatening slaughter and destruction if we leave this holy city and dare to approach our beloved and sacred Bethlehem."[877]

As also mentioned in Chapter 24, in harmony with the theological message of Islamic superiority, which the building of the Dome of the Rock was intended

---

876 K. A. C. Creswell, A Short Account of Muslim Architecture, (Baltimore, MD: Penguin Books Ltd., 1958), p. 7.
877 Robert G. Hoyland, Seeing Islam as Others Saw It, A Survey and Evaluation of Christian, Jewish and Zoroastrian Writings on Early Islam, (Princeton, NJ: The Darwin Press Inc., 1997), p. 70.

to convey to the world, as Schick has pointed out, Muslims did not hesitate or scruple to take the gilded copper dome from a church building in Baalbek to adorn their splendid Dome of the Rock![878] Prof. Bowersock does not bother to tell us about that original dome but, rather, says, "The [current] dome, which radiates a golden glow from miles away, is actually constructed from wood covered with a gilded aluminum alloy."[879] Obviously, "gilded aluminum alloy" was not what originally covered that dome! Therefore, it does not appear, as Dr. Bowersock alleges, that "churches continued to function as before," certainly not the one from which their church building's dome had been looted!

It was not only Christianity toward which the conquering Muslims showed utter disdain but toward Judaism as well. "Tiberias, which was conquered by the Muslims in 635 C.E. became a district capital and a mosque was subsequently built there.

"The mosque's builders made use of accessible building materials that were in the vicinity, and also recycled stones that had symbolic significance—a message of the victory of Islam over the cultures and religions that preceded it.

"Thus Jewish burial doors were exposed in the excavations, which served as bases for the columns of the building."[880]

As noted in Chapter 9 (under "Permission Granted and Canceled" and under "No Reprieve"), the disdain and contempt with which Islam—from the very beginning—regarded Christianity, is also indicated by Koranic quotations displayed inside The Dome of the Rock. The builder, Abd al-Malik, "placed 800 feet of inscriptions that denounced the idea of the divinity of Jesus with a directness that hints at the close relationship between the two faiths of monotheists: they shared much [doctrinally] but not the Trinity. The inscriptions are fascinating because they are our first glimpse at the text of the Koran which Abd al-Malik was having collated into its final form."[881]

"The Qur'anic inscriptions in the Dome of the Rock denounce what Muslims regard as the principal Christian errors: 'Praise be to God, who begets no son, and has no partner' and 'He is God, one, eternal. He does not beget, He is not begotten, and He has no peer' (Qur'an CXII). This was clearly a challenge to Christendom in its birthplace."[882]

---

878 Robert Schick, <u>The Fate of the Christians in Palestine During The Byzantine-Umayyad Transition, A.D. 600–750</u>, (Chicago: A Dissertation Submitted to the Faculty of The Division of The Humanities in Candidacy for the Degree of Doctor of Philosophy, The University of Chicago, 1987) Vol. I, p. 179.
879 G. W. Bowersock, <u>The Crucible of Islam</u>, (Cambridge, Mass.: Harvard University Press, 2017), p. 140.
880 Daniel K. Eisenbud, quoting Dr. Katia Cytryn-Silverman of Jerusalem's Institute of Archaeology and Dept. of Islamic and Middle Eastern Studies, *Menorah Inscribed on Basalt Discovered in Tiberias Mosque*, <u>The Jerusalem Post, Christian Edition</u>, January 2018, p. 14.
881 Simon Sebag Montefiore, <u>Jerusalem, the Biography</u>, (London: Orion Books Limited, 2011), pp. 182-183.
882 Bernard Lewis, <u>The Crisis of Islam, Holy War and Unholy Terror</u>, (New York: The Modern Library, 2003), p. 44.

Prof. Bowersock has assured us that the impact of the Muslim triumph upon Christians on the eastern shores of the Mediterranean, the Levant, was trivial. His assertion flies in the face of the true situation.

Dhimmi Status

The situation for the Christians is made clear in the Pact or Covenant of Umar. "The specifics of the requirements for Christians who enjoyed [!!?] *dhimmi* status [see Glossary] were spelled out in what has come to be referred to as 'the covenant of Umar,' which exists in several versions and most likely was attributed to rather than designed by the second caliph, Umar ibn al-Khattab (r.634–44). The covenant stipulated prohibition of the building of new churches or repair of those in towns inhabited by Muslims, although in some cases when financing was available Christians did construct new places of worship. Beating the wooden clapper that Christians used to call people to prayer was forbidden, as was loud chanting or carrying the cross or the Bible in processions. Dhimmis were allowed to keep their own communal laws, although they could apply to a Muslim judge if they wished. They were not, however, allowed to give testimony concerning a Muslim in a court of law. The recruiting of new Christians was forbidden, as was any insult about Islam or its Prophet. As a means of identification, particular dress, such as a special girdle, was required for Christians. [Though not shown by archeology] Over the first several centuries of Islam, dress stipulations grew increasingly stringent for Christian men and women."[883]

Pact of Umar

"Not many years after the Prophet's death, a disturbing and supposedly authoritative document appeared. It decreed that non-Muslims must stand when any Muslim wishes to sit, that non-Muslims must watch their houses of worship decay without repairing or replacing them, that a Muslim's testimony in court trumps that of a non-Muslim. You get the grim picture. This document was called the 'Pact of Umar.' Who was Umar? Prophet Muhammad's second successor—a decent and thoughtful fellow by almost every account I've read. It's a mystery how his name came to be aligned (or maligned) with a series of such thoroughly supremacist diktats. And since that part isn't clear, the question comes up yet again: Why did Muslims choose intolerance over tolerance through the Pact of Umar?"[884]

"Very clearly does this idea [the idea of the submission of Christians in the Muslim state] appear in the document wherein the Christians lay down the terms of their surrender and submission to the Muslim rule;—terms which Omar [Umar, the second caliph, r. 634–44] expressly confirmed. It runs: In the name of God,

---

[883] Jane I. Smith, *Islam and Christendom Historical, Cultural, and Religious Interaction From the Seventh to the Fifteenth Centuries*, John L. Esposito (ed.), The Oxford History of Islam, (New York: Oxford University Press, 1999), p. 308.

[884] Irshad Manji, The Trouble With Islam, A Muslim's Call for Reform in Her Faith, (New York: St. Martin's Press, 2003), pp. 62-63.

the merciful and compassionate. This is a document addressed to Omar Ibn Khattab, Prince of the faithful, by the Christians of the town N. N. When you entered this land we asked you to afford security to us and our families, our properties and our brothers-in-faith. And you acceded to our prayer on condition that we did not build afresh in our towns or in their neighborhood a cloister or a church, a monastery or a hermitage or restore or reconstruct those that had fallen into ruins in the Muslim quarter of the town; that we did not prevent Muslims from occupying our churches for three nights (indeed we would entertain them at our cost for three nights); that we did not harbor spies in our churches or our dwelling-houses, or receive enemies of the Muslims; that we did not instruct our children in reading; that we did not openly practice idolatry or induce people to adopt idolatrous practices; furthermore, that we did not dissuade any of our relatives from accepting Islam if so minded; that we did not wear caps, *Turbans* or sandals similar to those used by Muslims, or part our hair like them; that we did not talk in their language or assume their names, or use saddles for riding, or carry swords, or purchase weapons or carry them about us, or have Arabic inscriptions inscribed upon our rings, or sell wine; that we would cut off our forelock, keep to our costume and that, wherever we were, we would wear a belt round our waist; that we would not set up a cross on our churches; that we would not hawk about our books in the streets frequented by Muslims or in their *Bazaars* either; that we would slowly toll the bell in our churches; that at our prayers we would not raise our voices too high; that in the public procession on Easter day we would not carry palm leaves or idols; that we would not perform the funeral service loudly nor carry a light with the funeral procession in the streets and Bazaars inhabited by Muslims; that we would not buy slaves which were in the possession of the Muslims nor pry into their secrets.

"When Omar read this document he added with his own hand: that we would not strike Muslims, that we undertake to observe these terms for ourselves and our brothers-in-faith, and, in return, accept security of person and property. Should we violate any of the terms which we have promised to observe;—the protection may be withdrawn and you will be at liberty to deal with us as you please.

"This document describes to us the terms of submission of the Syrian Christians as they were dictated by Omar or possibly as they had been formulated before him by Abu Bakr [the very first caliph]. The Caliph simply approved the terms and by his approval conferred upon them the binding character of a treaty. From this it is obvious that the victorious Muslims had no intention whatever of assimilating or absorbing the subject races, but that they aimed rather at drawing the line as clearly and sharply as possible between the believer and the unbeliever, and strove to keep the two severely separate and apart. The maxim Omar set up, that 'no Arab could be a slave' was quite in conformity with the great political principles inaugurated by him. The Arab, according to Omar, was *ipso facto* free. Only a foreigner could and should be a slave. In his eyes the Arabs were a chosen people, summoned to rule the world. He could not conceive the subjection of the Arabs to any foreign or external power—the subjection either of the individual or of any portion of his people, however small or limited."[885]

As noted in chapter 24, perhaps Meron Benvenisti, a former Deputy Mayor of Jerusalem, who administered both East Jerusalem and the Old City, captures the essence of The Pact of Umar most succinctly. He wrote that Christians "were forbidden to ring the church bells, to wear crosses, or to conduct religious ceremonies in public; non-Muslims were forbidden to bear arms or ride horses; a head tax was imposed, and they were even obliged to shave the front of their heads."[886]

The Situation in Arabia

"The classical Arabic historians tell us that in the year 20 of the Muslim era, corresponding to 641 C.E., the Caliph 'Umar decreed that Jews and Christians should be removed from all but the southern and eastern fringes of Arabia, in fulfillment of an injunction of the Prophet uttered on his deathbed: 'Let there not be two religions in Arabia.'

"The people in question were the Jews of the oasis of Khaybar, in the north, and the Christians of Najran, in the south. Both were ancient and deep-rooted communities, Arab in their speech, culture, and way of life, differing from their neighbors only in their faith.

"The attribution of this saying to the Prophet was impugned by some earlier Islamic authorities. But it was generally accepted, and it was put into effect. The expulsion of religious minorities is extremely rare in Islamic history—unlike in medieval Christendom, where expulsions of Jews and, after the Re-conquest, of Muslims were normal and frequent. Compared with European expulsions, 'Umar's decree was both limited and compassionate. It did not include southern and southeastern Arabia [Yemen and Oman], not seen as part of the Islamic Holy Land. And unlike the Jews and Muslims driven out of Spain and other European countries, to find what refuge they could elsewhere, the Jews and Christians of Arabia were resettled on lands assigned to them, the Jews in Syria and Palestine, the Christians in Iraq. The process was also gradual rather than sudden, and there are reports of Jews and Christians in Khaybar and Najran for some time after the decree."[887]

Prof. Bowersock's reliance on the silence of archaeological evidence to show that there was no significant impact upon Christians in the early Muslim conquests, demonstrably does not give the correct picture. For an additional example, one should be aware of the fact that "in Cyrenaica there is

---

885 Von Kremer, The Orient Under the Caliphs, trans. S. Khuda Bukhsh (Beirut: United Publishers, 1973), pp. 119-121.
886 Meron Benvenisti, City of Stone, The Hidden History of Jerusalem, (Berkeley: University of California Press, 1996), p. 14.
887 Bernard Lewis, The Crisis of Islam, Holy War and Unholy Terror, (New York: The Modern Library, 2003), p. xxix-xxx.

archaeological evidence of the deliberate destruction of churches by the conquerors."[888]

A Catholic Professor's Viewpoint

A second contemporary scholar whose views we should evaluate are those of Dr. Garry Wills. From the biographical data on the book jacket of his most recent publication, *What the Qur'an Meant and Why it Matters*, we are told that he "is a Pulitzer Prize-winning historian and the author of the *New York Times* best-sellers *What Jesus Meant, Papal Sin, Why I Am a Catholic,* and *Why Priests?*, among others. He studied for the priesthood, took his doctorate in the classics and taught ancient and New Testament Greek at Johns Hopkins University. Now professor of history emeritus at Northwestern University, he lives in Evanston, Illinois."

Because his book which surveys the Qur'an was enthusiastically reviewed in the December 24, 2017 edition of *The New York Times Book Review,* it is certain that the viewpoints which Dr. Wills promotes, several of which challenge insights I have given in *Withering Wind From Arabia*, will gain a wide readership. The reviewer, Lesley Hazleton, author of *The First Muslim: The Story of Muhammad,* concludes his evaluation with an accolade, saying that Wills "may not be able to make reading the Quran an easy pleasure, but his encounter with it is a pleasure to read for anyone as open to discovery as he is."

In his review, Hazleton says regarding the general public's knowledge of the Qur'an that "phrases and snippets are taken entirely out of context and even invented out of thin air, like the seventy-two virgins in paradise (I kept waiting for them [in Wills' account] but they never appeared)."[889] Though the number is not given, enticing virgins in paradise are clearly predicted in the Qur'an. Surah 78:31-33 tells us, "Truly the reverent shall have a place of triumph, gardens and vineyards, buxom maidens of like age." (The Study Qur'an by Seyyed Hossein Nasr) In Surah 3:15, in Pickthall's translation, the virgins are translated as being "pure companions." He gives the same rendition in Surah 4:57. This same promise of delightful, sensual rewards in the Muslim concept of heaven is also given in Surah 55:46-60: "There will be two Gardens containing all kinds (of trees and delights); In them (each) will be two Springs flowing; In them will be Fruits of every kind, two and two. The Fruit of the Gardens will be near (and easy of reach). In them will be (maidens), chaste, restraining their glances, whom no man or Jinn before them has touched; Like unto Rubies and coral. Is there any Reward for Good —other than Good?"[890] In sharp contrast to the sensual heaven portrayed in

---
888 (W.M. Widrig and R. Goodchild, 'The West Church at Apollonia in Cyrenaica' in *Papers of the British School at Rome,* 1960, p. 71.) quoted by Patricia Crone and Michael Cook, Hagarism, The Making of The Islamic World, (London: Cambridge University Press, 1977) p. 156, note 33.
889 Lesley Hazleton, *Close Reading*, The New York Times Book Review, December 24, 2017, p. 10.
890 This quotation from the Koran is that given by Ayaan Hirsi Ali in her Heretic, Why Islam Needs a Reformation Now, (Canada: Alfred A. Knopf, 2015), p. 112.

the Qur'an, the biblical New Testament tells us of "a living hope by the resurrection of Jesus Christ from the dead, unto an inheritance incorruptible, and undefiled, and that fadeth not away, reserved in heaven for you." (I Pet. 1:4-5)

Reflecting His Affiliation

Being a devout Roman Catholic, it is not surprising that throughout his book Dr. Wills follows the evaluation of Islam given by Pope Francis which he gave in *The Joy of the Gospel* (Libreria Editrice Vaticana, 2013), par. 253. There, the Pope asserted that "authentic Islam and the proper reading of the Koran are opposed to every form of violence."[891]

Not only asserting that authentic Islam is opposed to every form of violence, Dr. Wills would also have us believe that there are hardly any significant doctrinal conflicts between Islam and Christianity. In upholding that viewpoint he makes egregious denials of the New Testament record. Most fundamentally he says, "There is nothing explicit in the Gospel that says Jesus is divine, or that he is part of a trinity of the divine being."[892]

Dr. Wills must have used a very sketchy edition of the Gospels. Right from the beginning, the apostle Matthew made the reality of Jesus' divinity totally clear by quoting Isaiah 7:14. There, the prophet predicted that "the virgin shall be with child and shall bring forth a son, and they shall call his name Immanuel." Then Matthew translated the meaning of the name Immanuel by saying its interpretation is "God with us."[893] (See Matthew 1:23.) Perhaps Dr. Wills was unaware of the fact that Jesus completely upheld the validity of what Matthew has told us by saying "I and the Father are one." (John 10:30) Dr. Wills also needs to learn the theological lesson which Jesus taught to Philip when he told him, "He that hath seen me hath seen the Father." (John 14:9)

Dr. Wills asks, "Is the Qur'an therefore [because it is Unitarian] 'anti-Christian'? It is more anti-Nicaean. It holds that Trinitarian 'Christians' are not Gospel Christians. This has not prevented Pope Francis from praying to the One God with his beloved Muslims (*The Joy of the Gospel* par. 254). ... The future of ecumenical relations between Muslims and Christians may depend on Pope Francis's claim not only that Unitarians and humanists are right about Jesus but that Trinitarianism should be so defined as to be a monotheistic belief—as Augustine taught."[894]

---

[891] Garry Wills, What the Qur'an Meant and Why it Matters, (NY: Viking, 2017), p. 3.
[892] Garry Wills, What the Qur'an Meant and Why it Matters, (NY: Viking, 2017), pp. 118-119.
[893] From immanu "with us," from im "with," + first person plural pronomial suffix, + El "God." www.dictionary.com/browse/emmanuel (Accessed 1/16/18).
[894] Garry Wills, What the Qur'an Meant and Why it Matters, (NY: Viking, 2017), pp. 120-121.

A One-Way Street

Commenting on the Prophet Muhammad's plea for unity between Muslims and Christians as given in Surah 3:64,[895] Wills tells us that "The solidarity of believers in the One God is reflected in the Qur'an's marriage laws. Muslims may marry Jews or Christians without compromising the religion of any of the parties."[896] What Dr. Wills fails to tell his readers is that while Muslim men may freely marry Jewish and Christian women, Christian and Jewish men may only marry Muslim women by first becoming Muslims. To the present day, throughout the Muslim world, Jewish and Christian men who dare to marry Muslim women without first converting to Islam are killed.

A State Within a State

Dr. Wills asks his readers, "What are the state legislators in America so afraid of that they are banning Shari'ah law (what little they know of it)? And for what practices of Shari'ah are Muslims asking permission? Actually what is desired is not so much permission as noninterference. They want, for instance, to conduct their own marriages, divorces, and interments. Catholics and Jews in America regulate their own practices of this sort without any conflict with the law."[897]

If freedom, which they already have, to conduct their own marriages, divorces and burials were all Muslims desired in their new Western homes, there would certainly be no objection from Western societies and governments. However, why didn't Dr. Wills mention some of the other activities that many Muslim citizens in Western countries want the freedom to practice? Among these issues are honor killings and female circumcision. In many cases Muslims want to establish independent enclaves in the Western countries where Shari'ah will define practice. This is not only a dire problem facing Western governments but confronts many moderate Muslim governments as well. It was precisely this issue which led to the assassination of Salmaan Taseer, governor of Pakistan's Punjab province, in January 2011. Governor Taseer "throughout his career had been outspoken in his belief that democracy and pluralism are inseparable and that all religious minorities should be allowed to vote in general elections—opinions antithetical to the positions taken by hardline Islamic fundamentalists. Recently, Taseer had particularly outraged them by criticizing Pakistan's strict blasphemy laws as unjust and indefensible, arguing that they were abused by extremists and that Islamic law should not supplant the laws of the state."[898]

---

[895] Pickthall rendered it "Say: O People of the Scripture! Come to an agreement between us and you: that we shall worship none but Allah, and that we shall ascribe no Partner unto Him, and that none of us shall take others for lords beside Allah. And if they turn away, then say: Bear witness that we are they who have surrendered (unto Him)."
[896] Garry Wills, What the Qur'an Meant and Why it Matters, (NY: Viking, 2017), p. 127.
[897] Garry Wills, What the Qur'an Meant and Why it Matters, (NY: Viking, 2017), pp. 154-155.
[898] Haroon K. Ullah, Digital World War, Islamists, Extremists and the Fight for Cyber Supremacy, (New Haven, CT: Yale University Press, 2017), p. x.

In contrast to the views of Dr. Wills, a former Muslim sounded a timely warning when she wrote, "Under no circumstances should Western countries allow Muslims to form self-governing enclaves in which women and other supposedly second-class citizens can be treated in ways that belong in the seventh century. ... So long as there are some Muslims who regard Muhammad's teachings in Medina as trumping their loyalty to the states of which they are citizens, there will be a legitimate suspicion that tolerance of Islam endangers the security of those states."[899] Such a danger already exists in France where some of the suburbs of Paris, called *banlieues*, have become so defiantly independent that in many cases French police refuse to enter those areas.

Daniel Silva tells us, "In the near term, Western Europe faces the greatest threat, in no small measure because of the large and restive Muslim populations living within its open borders. ISIS has no need to insert terrorists into Western Europe because the potential terrorists are already there. They reside in the banlieues of France and the Muslim quarters of Brussels, Amsterdam, Copenhagen, Malmo, East London and Luton. ... The security services of Western Europe have proven themselves woefully unprepared—especially the Belgian Sûreté [Security] which has countenanced the creation of a virtual ISIS safe haven in the heart of Brussels."[900]

Though this chapter is not intended to be a critique of Dr. Wills' entire book but only an evaluation of some of his most consequential assertions, still I feel it important to make one further evaluation. He says, "Indeed, 'holy war,' sometimes taken as a definition of jihad is not a concept expressed anywhere in the Qur'an."[901] The broad Muslim body politic, the ummah, has not yet gotten the message that there is no "holy war" in the Qur'an. On the Muslim website *Ask.fm*, "often the interrogatives have to do with living standards for Mujahideen fighters or ISIS members ('are the bugs a problem?' or 'can I buy a smart phone there?'), or how can I go about joining the various conflicts going on in the Muslim world. As with almost all Islamic recruitment and PR campaigns, the focus is less on religious doctrine and more on how jihad is 'cool,' the cutting-edge of modern Islam."[902]

Finally, it is appropriate that I let a very famous Muslim speak to the issue of holy war in Islam. Between Bulgaria's attack on the Ottoman Empire in 1912 and his death in 1938, Dr. Allama Iqbal, highly honored as the poet laureate of Pakistan,

---

899 Ayaan Hirsi Ali in her <u>Heretic, Why Islam Needs a Reformation Now</u>, (Canada: Alfred A. Knopf, 2015), pp. 152 & 210.
900 Daniel Silva, <u>The Black Widow</u>, (New York: Harper Collins, 2016), p. 523.
901 Garry Wills, <u>What the Qur'an Meant and Why it Matters</u>, (NY: Viking, 2017), p. 134.
902 Haroon K. Ullah, <u>Digital World War, Islamists, Extremists and the Fight for Cyber Supremacy</u>, (New Haven, CT: Yale University Press, 2017), p. 20.

wrote his famous poem entitled *Complaint and Answer* [903] from which the following lines, which are addressed to God Almighty, are excerpted:

> Who upraised the sword of battle in Thy Name's most sacred cause,
> Or who strove to right the ruined world by Thy most hallowed laws?
>
> -----
>
> It was we and we alone who marched Thy soldiers to the fight,
> Now upon the land engaging, now embattled on the sea,
> The triumphant Call to Prayer in Europe's churches to recite,
> Through the wastes of Africa to summon men to worship Thee.
> All the glittering splendour of great emperors we reckoned none;
> In the shadow of our glinting swords we shouted, "God is One!"
>
> All our life we dedicated to the dire distress of war;
> When we died, we died exultant for the glory of Thy Name;
> Not to win a private empire did we draw the swords we bore—
> Was it in the quest of riches to earth's frontiers that we came?
> Had our people striven for the sake of worldly goods and gold,
> Would they then have shattered idols they might
> gainfully have sold?
>
> -----
>
> We were rocks immovable when in the field we took our stand,
> And the bravest-hearted warriors by our thrust were swept away;
> It sufficed us to enrage, if any gainsaid Thy command,
> Then we hurled us on their cannons, took their swordpoints but for play.
> Into every heart we struck the impress of Thy Unity
> And beneath the dagger's lightning preached the Message, Lord, of Thee.
>
> -----
>
> Tell us this, and tell us truly—who uprooted Khyber's gate?
> Or who overthrew the city where great Caesar reigned in pride?
> Who destroyed the gods that hands of others laboured to create,
> Who the marshalled armies of the unbelievers drove aside?
> Who extinguished from the altars of Iran that sacred flame?
> Who revived the dimmed remembrance of Yazdan's immortal Name?
>
> Strove there ever other nation in the cause of Thee alone,
> Bore there ever other people battle's anguish for Thy sake?

---

903 The quoted verses are excerpted from the translation of A. J. Arberry, published by S.H. Muhammad Ashraf Publishers in Lahore, Pakistan.

Whose the sword that seized the world, and ruled it as its very own?
Whose the loud Allahu Akbar that compelled the earth to wake?
Whose the dread that kept the idols cowering and terrified
So that, heads cast down and humbled, "He is God, the One," they cried?

In the press of mortal combat if the hour of worship came
Then the people of Hejaz, to Mecca turning bowed in prayer;
King Mahmud, Ayaz the slave—their rank in service was the same,
Lord and servant—at devotion never difference was there,
Slave and master, rich and needy—all the old distinctions gone.
Unified in adoration of Thy Presence, they were one.

In the Hall of Space and Being, at the dawn and eventide,
Circulated we like goblets with the Wine of Faith replete,
Still we roved o'er plain and mountain, spread Thy Message far and wide

-----

Is it known to Thee, if ever we returned to own defeat?
Desert after desert spanning, faring on through sea on sea,
In the Ocean of the Shadows our strong coursers watered we.

We erased the smudge of falsehood from the parchment firmament,
We redeemed the human species from the chains of slavery;
And we filled the Holy Kaaba with our foreheads humbly bent,
Clutching to our fervent bosoms the Koran in ecstasy.

In conclusion, let it be clearly understood that the withering wind from Arabia was not benign in its opening phases as Prof. Bowersock would have us believe, nor did it endorse Christianity as Dr. Wills affirms. On the contrary, Islam has been and continues to be a desiccating, devastating movement which tries either to nullify or eradicate any initiative of those who seek to follow the example and teaching of Jesus Christ. The question of whether Islam's sustained and unremitting hostility to the cause of Christ can be ameliorated reminds us of Jeremiah's question: "Can the Ethiopian change his skin, or the leopard his spots? Then may ye also do good, that are accustomed to do evil." (Jeremiah 13:23)

Chapter 29

THE FUTURE

Previous chapters in this book have documented the impact militant Islam has had on the church in the extensive area from the southwest Indian border all the way to the Atlantic Ocean. Now, Islam embraces a much greater area, exercising major influence throughout the Indian subcontinent and Southeast Asia, especially in Indonesia. (However, it should be noted that Islam is currently facing a powerfully resurgent Hinduism in the Republic of India.) In the west, Islam is also contending powerfully and brutally for dominance in Sub-Saharan Africa. It is making especially gruesome advances in Nigeria through Boko Haram and in Kenya through Shabaab, Islamic jihadists from Somalia.

Additionally, there are many startling predictions that by the end of the twenty-first century, Europe, once a bastion of Christianity, will also be Muslim.[904] In addition to the deep analytical presentations of the power of Islamic advances in Europe to which attention has been called in footnote 904 anecdotically, notice what is currently happening in two outstanding European countries.

First, "a Swedish Bishop has responded to an application to have the Muslim call to prayer broadcast in the immigrant suburb of Araby Växjö by welcoming the move as a positive sign of multiculturalism. ... Another Swedish Bishop expressed her desire to see Christian symbols removed to make churches 'more inviting' for Muslims. Eva Brunne, who is the first openly lesbian bishop of a mainstream church in the world, wants the church to be treated more like a public airport, where prayer rooms are made available to Muslims, by removing Christian symbols and 'marking the direction of Mecca.'"[905]

Secondly, in Great Britain, "around 150 schools have made it compulsory for children to wear the hijab and the government is too politically correct to step in and do anything about it, according to Sir Michael Wilshaw. 'There's something like 150 schools which in short make it compulsory for youngsters to wear a hijab—so what's happening about those schools? The country has enormously changed,' Sir Wilshaw said. The critic of Britain's political correctness

---

[904] For substantiation of the ominous prediction that Europe will become Muslim by the end of the 21st century, see (1) Geert Wilders' America as the Last Man Standing. (2) Oriana Fallaci, The Rage and the Pride. (3) Christopher Caldwell, Reflections on the Revolution in Europe.

[905] Paul Joseph Watson, *Swedish Bishop Welcomes Muslim Call to Prayer as "Good" for Society,* From an email from Christian Media and https://www.infowars.com/swedish-bishop-welcomes-muslim-call-to-prayer-as-good-for-society/

went on to say, 'the government needs to step in. It can no longer say it's up to the head teachers.'"[906]

In view of all this, it is highly important that we try to anticipate the impact Islam will have on the church during the twenty-first century and beyond. Central to that issue is the role America will play. The United States is generally assumed to be the world's leading Christian country. Will it have a significant role in stopping, reversing or minimizing the decimating and desiccating attrition of Islam against Christianity? No one could have answered this vital question more poignantly than Professor Malik did when he wrote, "There is an ingrained culture in Washington's foreign policy establishment that prefers to avoid addressing the existential phobias of the [Middle Eastern] region's Christians. These beleaguered Christian communities have become marginalized in America's strategic thinking and hence expendable next to larger and more pressing economic, political, and security interests."[907] Those more pressing interests continue to keep the United States from giving the sustained, careful attention to the impact of the Islamic world on the followers of Christ which it should.

Up to the time of this writing (March 2018) no amelioration in America's hard-nosed immigration stance toward Middle Eastern refugee Christians has taken place. At the beginning of March we are told, "U.S. closes door on Christians who fled Iran. They sold their homes and possessions, quit their jobs, and left their country—they thought for good. The Iranians, mainly members of their nation's Christian minorities, were bound for a new life in America after what should have been a brief sojourn in Austria for visa processing. But more than a year later, some 100 of them remain stranded in Vienna, their savings drained, their lives in limbo and the promise of America dead."[908]

It is fortunate for everyone living outside the Muslim world that disunity is endemic inside the Muslim world, keeping it from a more powerful challenge to nations beyond its domain. For example, during these opening years of the twenty-first century several mutually exclusive concepts of government are ardently advocated in the Muslim world. The four most prominent of them are:

(1) The concept of the nation-state, a construct of the Western non-Muslim world (beginning at the end of Europe's thirty-year war with the Peace of Westphalia in 1648), is operative and upheld in some Muslim areas, such as Syria under the Assads (both father and son) and, previous to his overthrow, in Mubarak's Egypt and now revived under General el-Sisi.

(2) Kingship is perpetuated in Saudi Arabia, Jordan and Morocco.

---

906 https://www.infowars.com/swedish-bishop-welcomes-muslim-call-to-prayer-as-good-for-society/ Accessed 03/02/18.
907 Habib C. Malik, Islamism and the Future of the Christians of the Middle East, (Stanford: Hoover Institution Press, 2010), p. 55.
908 Miriam Jordan, *U.S. Closes Door on Christians Who Fled Iran*, The New York Times, March 2, 2018, p. A11.

(3) Though there has been no caliph in the Muslim world since Ataturk abolished the caliphate in 1924, many Islamic political theorists, such as the late radical Egyptian scholar Sayyid Qutb, fervently advocate its restoration and imposition throughout the entire Muslim world. Based on Qutb's theological-political philosophy, ISIS has been trying with great cruelty and carnage to establish a universal caliphate.

(4) Finally, there is the vigorous ongoing Shi'ite concept of rule by an imam, which was advocated by Khomeini and is perpetuated through the ongoing dynamism of his 1979 Iranian Revolution.

Thankfully, in the foreseeable future, there very probably will not be a resolution of these conflicting concepts of government. We can be quite certain that the concept of a restored global caliphate will not come to fruition any time in the near future. The frustration of that goal has been one of the successful aims of U.S. foreign policy. The United States currently has two main areas of conflict with the Muslim world: (1) keeping up the fight against the Jihadists who want the restoration of the caliphate and (2) the attempt to keep Iran from becoming a nuclear power.

Regarding those primary areas of U.S. concern, the futurologist George Friedman sees that America's first war aim in the Muslim world has been to thwart that "group of Muslims [the Jihadists] seeking to re-create the Caliphate, ... to disrupt the Islamic world and set it against itself, so that an Islamic empire could not emerge."[909] In evaluating America's military effort, Friedman arguably says, "the strategic [Muslim] challenge to American power is coming to an end. Al Qaeda has failed in its goals [as has ISIS]. The United States has succeeded, not so much in winning the war as in preventing the Islamists from winning, and, from a geopolitical perspective, that is good enough."[910] Friedman made this last point even more clear when he wrote, "The United States wins as long as al Qaeda loses. An Islamic world in chaos, incapable of uniting, means the United States has achieved its strategic goal."[911]

We can be quite certain that, in the foreseeable future, the Muslim world will not be united by a revived caliphate. However, that will not prevent Muslim countries from making an expedient accommodation among themselves, a concord which would allow the Muslim world, despite its competing governmental systems, to work in concert. Also, the absence of a caliphate does not prevent committed Muslim jihadist fighters from migrating to each hot spot, as they did in Chechnya's battle against Russia and as they currently are swelling the ranks of the Taliban's forces in the interminable battle for control of Afghanistan.

Though the caliphate has not been restored, for almost fifty years a transnational Islamic organization, currently consisting of fifty-seven member states, has

---
909 George Friedman, The Next 100 Years, (New York: Doubleday, 2009), p. 5.
910 George Friedman, The Next 100 Years, (New York: Doubleday, 2009), p. 31.
911 George Friedman, The Next 100 Years, (New York: Doubleday, 2009), p. 49.

been in existence. "In September 1969 an Islamic summit conference held in Rabat, Morocco, decided to create a body to be known as the Organization of the Islamic Conference (OIC),[912] with a permanent secretariat in Jedda, Saudi Arabia. This body was duly set up, and it developed rapidly in the 1970s. The OIC was particularly concerned with help to poor Muslim countries, support for Muslim minorities in non-Muslim countries, and the international position of Islam and of Muslims—in the words of one observer, the Islamic rights of man. The organization now numbers fifty-seven member states, plus three with observer status."[913] Since its founding, the OIC has had thirteen regular Islamic summits, the most recent in April 2016,[914] which was held in Istanbul, Turkey. Additionally, there have been five extraordinary conclaves.

Three Views of the Future

It is imperative to evaluate three scenarios for the future of Islam: the first is an elitist initiative, the second is a revolutionary political and ideological reformation and, finally, as a priority concern we should pay close attention to one biblical prophetic portrayal of the destiny of Islam.

First, the view of an elitist movement.

The initiators of this movement are all Muslims and have put forth a challenge to the Christian world to reach a truce between Christianity and Islam based on two concepts shared by both religions. This movement has developed from *A Common Word* proposal which was "launched on October 13, 2007 as an open letter, signed by 138 leading Muslim scholars and intellectuals (including such figures as the Grand Muftis of Egypt, Syria, Jordan, Oman, Bosnia, Russia, Chad and Istanbul) to the leaders of the Christian churches and denominations all over the world, including H.H. Pope Benedict XVI."[915] In essence, its platform, based on verses from the Qur'an and the Bible, affirms that Islam and Christianity share at their core the twin (golden) commandments of the paramount importance of loving God and loving one's neighbor. Based on this joint common ground, it calls for worldwide peace and harmony between Christians and Muslims.

The proponents of this Islamic movement stress its importance by reminding us that "Muslims and Christians together make up well over half of the world's population. Without peace and justice between these two religious communities, there can be no meaningful peace in the world. The future of the world depends on [whether there is] peace between Muslims and Christians."[916]

---

912 On June 28, 2011, the name was changed to Organization of Islamic Cooperation.
913 Bernard Lewis, The Crisis of Islam, Holy War and Unholy Terror, (New York: The Modern Library, 2003), pp. 14-16. "Khartoum hosted a Popular Arab Islamic Conference in 1991, 1993, and 1995, designed as an antithesis to the state-based Organization of the Islamic Conference and Arab League which were dominated by Saudi Arabia and Egypt." – Camille Pecastaing, Jihad in the Arabian Sea, (Stanford, CA: Hoover Institution Press, 2011), p. 65.
914 On December 14, 2017 "Turkish president Recep Tayyip Erdogan convened in Istanbul an emergency summit of the Organization of Islamic Cooperation (OIC) seeking a tough response to the recognition by U.S. President Donald Trump of Jerusalem as Israel's capital." Dawn, December 14, 2017, p. 1. (Accessed 12/15/17.)
915 A Common Word Between Us and You, (The Royal Aal al-Bayt Institute for Islamic Thought, Jordan, 2009), p. v.
916 A Common Word Between Us and You, (The Royal Aal al-Bayt Institute for Islamic Thought, Jordan, 2009), p. 6.

The initiators of this movement affirm that "the basis for this peace and understanding already exists. It is part of the very foundational principles of both faiths: love of the One God, and love of the neighbor. These principles are found over and over again in the sacred texts of Islam and Christianity."[917]

The name for this elitist Muslim initiative is taken from Surah 3:64 of the Qur'an. It says, according to the translation used by the Muslim scholars issuing this challenging invitation to Christians, "Say: O People of the Scripture! Come to a common word between us and you: that we shall worship none but God, and that we shall ascribe no partner unto Him, and that none of us shall take others for lords beside God. And if they turn away, then say: Bear witness that we are they who have surrendered (unto Him)."

Those Muslim leaders assert that "justice and freedom of religion are a crucial part of love of the neighbour."[918] While those elite Muslim leaders appeal for Muslim-Christian unity, they do not hesitate to emphasize some of their anti-Christian doctrines. For example, from Surah 2:194-195, they remind us that "God loveth the virtuous." This is in jarring contrast to "God so loved the world ..." (John 3:16). They also emphasize the necessity of following Muhammad, by quoting from Surah 3:31, in which Muhammad is quoted as saying, "If ye love God, follow me." Further, those leaders also uphold the false and erroneous concept of salvation by good works by quoting a hadith, which tells us that "He who says: 'there is no God but God, He Alone, He hath no associate, His is the sovereignty and His is the praise and He hath power over all things' one hundred times in a day, it is for them equal to setting ten slaves free, and one-hundred good deeds are written for them and one-hundred bad deeds are effaced, and it is for them a protection from the devil for that day until the evening."[919]

Those leaders did not need to quote from a hadith, a secondary source, because the Koran itself states: That "good deeds annul ill deeds." (Surah 11:114) It also asserts that alms will atone for sin: "If ye publish your almsgiving, it is well, but if ye hide it and give it to the poor, it will be better for you, and will atone for some of your ill-deeds. Allah is Informed of what ye do." (Surah 2:271). The concept is, as seen in those quotations, that good deeds have a moral value, a merit or a reward. Further, the Koran says: "Have patience, (O Muhammad), for lo! Allah loseth not the wages of the good." (Surah 11:115); "Lo! Allah wrongeth not even of the weight of an ant; and if there is a good deed, He will double it and will give (the doer) from His presence an immense reward." (Surah 4:40).

Another assertion is that if great sins are avoided, the small ones will be forgiven: "If ye avoid the great (things) which ye are forbidden, We will remit from you your evil deeds and make you enter at a noble gate." (Surah 4:31)

---

917 A Common Word Between Us and You, (The Royal Aal al-Bayt Institute for Islamic Thought, Jordan, 2009), p. 6.
918 A Common Word Between Us and You, (The Royal Aal al-Bayt Institute for Islamic Thought, Jordan, 2009), p. 8.
919 Sahih Al-Bukhari Hadith No. 3329.

Also, martyrdom is alleged to be especially efficacious. The Koran says, "Whoso migrateth for the cause of Allah will find much refuge and abundance in the earth, and whoso forsaketh his home, a fugitive unto Allah and His messenger, and death overtaketh him, his reward is then incumbent on Allah. Allah is ever Forgiving, Merciful." (Surah 4:100) Again, we are told, "Think not of those, who are slain in the way of Allah, as dead. Nay, they are living. With their Lord they have provision." (Surah 3:169)

Obviously, as we have just seen, the Koran assigns merit to good works. It is particularly strange that it should do so since it pictures the relationship of God to man as that between master and slave. Can slaves obligate their masters? Notice, just above, the word "incumbent" in Koranic Surah 4:100.

Is the Koranic viewpoint valid? Let's hear Jesus on the topic of meritorious works. It is particularly appropriate, therefore, that Jesus deals with that question under the concept of the master-slave relationship as he is quoted in Luke 17:7-10 (NRSV): "Who among you would say to your slave who has just come in from plowing or tending sheep in the field, 'Come here at once and take your place at the table'? Would you not rather say to him, 'Prepare supper for me, put on your apron and serve me while I eat and drink; later you may eat and drink'? Do you thank the slave for doing what was commanded? So you also, when you have done all that you were ordered to do, say, 'We are worthless slaves; we have done only what we ought to have done!'" Thus, according to Jesus, when we do what is right, we only do what is expected of us. Since we are always expected to do what is right, none of our activities can possibly generate merit with which we might compensate for our moral and spiritual lapses.

If a person steals from someone or robs someone can he erase that sin by being honest in the future? When one is honest and trustworthy, that is only what is expected all the time from each of us. We have not done anything extra by being honest and trustworthy.

If a person deceives someone by telling him a lie, can that person's record be cleared if he tells the truth in the future? Aren't we supposed to tell the truth all the time? When we tell the truth, we haven't done anything extra which could build up surplus virtue which could be applied to erase the sins of our past.

For example, scripture says, "How does God's love abide in anyone who has the world's goods and sees a brother or sister in need and yet refuses to help?" (I John 3:17 NRSV) If at some time in the past we failed to show pity and help someone in need, can that guilt be eliminated by showing pity to someone else in the future? In the future when we help lift the burden off of someone's shoulders, that is only what God expects of us. We have done nothing extra. We have not generated any merit which might be applied to sins which we committed in the past.

Whether we sin little or sin greatly, we can do nothing to erase our sins. Jesus made that point unmistakably clear when in the house of Simon the Pharisee he told the parable of the two debtors. One had a trifling debt, the other a debt of astronomical proportions. But the key point is that neither debtor could pay what he owed. Simon had considered a sinful woman, who had come in to show gratitude to Jesus, to be an extremely flagrant sinner in comparison to himself. Jesus rebuked his attitude by saying, "A certain creditor had two debtors; one owed five hundred denarii, and the other fifty. When they could not pay, he canceled the debts for both of them." (Luke 7:41-42 NRSV)

Obviously, then, someone else has to pay the debt in which our sin has involved us. That payment was made by Jesus Christ. Being sinless, he had no personal debt to pay. Therefore, when he died by crucifixion on Calvary, he paid our impossible debt. Thus, "He is the atoning sacrifice for our sins, and not for ours only but also for the sins of the whole world." (I John 2:2 NRSV)

On the issue of freedom of religion, the "common word" movement is glaringly out of step with the history of Islam. The compilers of the document entitled "*A Common Word Between Us and You*" cite two Qur'anic guidelines which mandate freedom of religion. In Surah 2:256, it is said, "let there be no compulsion in religion." In Surah 60:8, the Qur'an states that "God forbiddeth you [to harm] those who warred not against you on account of religion and drove you not out from your homes, [and mandates] that you should show them kindness and deal justly with them." Almost the whole history of Islam stands as an indictment, alleging Islamic violation of these benign Qur'anic enactments.

Without acknowledging their violations of those Qur'anic mandates, nor asking the Christian world to forgive the Muslim world for egregious violations of freedom, they conclude their overture to the Christian world by saying, "Finally, as Muslims, and in obedience to the Holy Qur'an, we ask Christians to come together with us on the common essentials of our two religions."[920]

Following are excerpts from some of the many responses to this Muslim outreach to the Christian world:

David Ford, Director, Cambridge Inter-Faith Program, said that the common word appeal "does not claim to be the final word but to be a 'common word.'"[921] Scholars at Yale Divinity School's Center for Faith and Culture said, "In the past (e.g. in the Crusades) and in the present (e.g. in excesses of the 'war on terror') many [of us] Christians have been guilty of sinning against our Muslim neighbors. ... We ask forgiveness of the All-Merciful One and of the Muslim community around the world. ... The future of the world depends on peace between Muslims and Christians. ... What is common between us lies ... in something absolutely central to both: love of God and love of neighbor."[922]

---

[920] A Common Word Between Us and You, (The Royal Aal al-Bayt Institute for Islamic Thought, Jordan, 2009), p. 33.
[921] A Common Word Between Us and You, (The Royal Aal al-Bayt Institute for Islamic Thought, Jordan, 2009), p. 78.
[922] A Common Word Between Us and You, (The Royal Aal al-Bayt Institute for Islamic Thought, Jordan, 2009), pp. 82-85.

The Mennonite Church responded by saying, "We also respect '*A Common Word*' as a courageous expression of good will in the midst of less charitable Muslim voices and in the face of recurrent Christian hostility toward Muslims and misunderstanding of Islam. We repent from our role in perpetrating these unchristian actions and ask your patience and forgiveness as we grow in understanding you, our Muslim neighbors and in practicing Christian love with you. We believe that in any society, the love of neighbor that you have so eloquently written about includes respect for that person's freedom to believe or not to believe, to choose his or her own faith and religion. We would indeed welcome opportunity to talk more with Muslim friends and leaders about the implications of religious freedom for this matter is of profound significance."[923]

The response from the spokesman for the "Supreme Patriarch and Catholicos of all Armenians" was touching indeed. He said, "After the annihilation of 1.5 million of our sons and daughters [by Muslim Turks] during the First World War, the remnants of our nation witnessed the caring love and attention of our [Muslim] Arab brothers, which can serve today as the best example of how Christians and Muslims can live together in harmony, support one another in times of hardship, and enjoy the God-given benefits of a peaceful and creative life."[924]

The response of "Patriarch Alexy II of Moscow and all of Russia" draws a stark contrast. First, he calls attention to "the experience of co-existence between Christians and Islam in Russia. The traditional religions in our country have never come into conflict while preserving their identity for a thousand years. Russia is one of those rare multi-religious multinational states whose history has not known the religious wars that have plagued various regions of the world." Going on, without mentioning the rebellion of the Chechnyans against Russian control nor Russia's pogroms against the Jews, he does call attention to the well-known fact that "in some Islamic countries, the legislation prohibits the construction of churches, worship services and free Christian preaching. I hope that the letter of Islamic religious leaders and scholars proposing to intensify dialogue between our two religions will contribute to establishing better conditions for Christian minorities in such countries."[925]

The Archbishop of Canterbury, Dr. Rowan Williams, on July 14, 2008, addressed a major response to those Muslim leaders who issued the challenge to the Christian world entitled *A Common Word Between Us and You*. Though sensing the cordiality found in the Muslim document, he was not carried away by sentiment. He made it clear that the time had not yet arrived where an agreed and shared understanding had been reached. He said, "Such an affirmation would not be honest to either of our traditions. It would fail to acknowledge the reality of the differences that exist and that have been the cause of deep and—at times in the past—

---

[923] A Common Word Between Us and You, (The Royal Aal al-Bayt Institute for Islamic Thought, Jordan, 2009), pp. 99-101.

[924] A Common Word Between Us and You, (The Royal Aal al-Bayt Institute for Islamic Thought, Jordan, 2009), p. 109.

[925] A Common Word Between Us and You, (The Royal Aal al-Bayt Institute for Islamic Thought, Jordan, 2009), pp. 119-121.

even violent division." He then made it clear that any dialogue would have to be conducted "without compromising fundamental beliefs."[926]

The archbishop went on to say the effort must be made in "discussing differences rather than imprisoning ourselves in mutual fear and suspicion."[927] Getting down to bedrock specifics, he explained that when "we speak of 'Father, Son and Holy Spirit,' we do not mean one God with two beings along side him or three gods of limited power. So there is indeed one God, the Living and Self-subsistent, associated with no other, but what God is and does is not different from the life which is eternally and simultaneously the threefold pattern of life: source and expression and sharing."[928]

Referring to Jesus, the archbishop affirms that "he is in no way different in nature from the Father: there is only one divine nature and reality."[929] He then quotes I John 4:8, which says, "Whoever does not love does not know God because God is love." Then he gives a cautionary statement asserting that "understanding the 'breadth and length and height and depth' of the love of God is a lifetime's journey. ... Two qualities of God's love are crucially important for the Christian: it [i.e., love] is unconditional, given gratuitously and without cause, and it is self--sacrificial. ... To love where we can see no possibility of love being returned is to be vulnerable, and we can only dare to do this in the power of God's Holy Spirit."[930]

Expressing hope for mutual understanding with the Muslim world, the archbishop quotes the verses 1-3, 15-16 and 21 from the 145th Psalm. Then he says, "In words like these we hear many resonances with the language of your letter."[931] He then tells his Muslim correspondents that "we shall want to learn from you more about the understandings of love of God in Islam as we continue this journey. ... We believe we have much to learn from each other."[932]

The archbishop also made it clear that to have fruitful discussions, both parties must be committed to "crossing religious and ethnic divisions and transcending ancient enmities."[933] The archbishop called attention to the historic reality that "despite Jesus' words in John's gospel, Christianity has been promoted at the point of the sword and legally supported by extreme sanctions [though not specifying, he may have been thinking of conditions in Spain during the reigns of Ferdinand and Isabella]; despite the Qur'anic axiom, Islam has been supported in the same way, with extreme penalties for abandoning it [Islam], and civil disabilities

---

[926] A Common Word Between Us and You, (The Royal Aal al-Bayt Institute for Islamic Thought, Jordan, 2009), p. 125.
[927] A Common Word Between Us and You, (The Royal Aal al-Bayt Institute for Islamic Thought, Jordan, 2009), p. 129.
[928] A Common Word Between Us and You, (The Royal Aal al-Bayt Institute for Islamic Thought, Jordan, 2009), p. 133.
[929] A Common Word Between Us and You, (The Royal Aal al-Bayt Institute for Islamic Thought, Jordan, 2009), p. 134.
[930] A Common Word Between Us and You, (The Royal Aal al-Bayt Institute for Islamic Thought, Jordan, 2009), pp. 136-137.
[931] A Common Word Between Us and You, (The Royal Aal al-Bayt Institute for Islamic Thought, Jordan, 2009), p. 141.
[932] A Common Word Between Us and You, (The Royal Aal al-Bayt Institute for Islamic Thought, Jordan, 2009), pp. 145-146.
[933] A Common Word Between Us and You, (The Royal Aal al-Bayt Institute for Islamic Thought, Jordan, 2009), p. 147.

for those outside the faith. ... Transcendent values can be defended through violence only by those who do not fully understand their transcendent character. ... As people of faith, we can never claim that social harmony can be established by uncontrolled coercive power."[934]

The archbishop made a key distinction between Islam and Christianity when he said, "The role of the Qur'an in Islam is not really parallel to the role of the Bible in Christianity. For Christians, God's word was made flesh in Jesus Christ. Our understanding of the Scriptures is that they witness to and draw their authority from Christ, describing the witness of prophets and apostles to his saving work. They are the voice of his living Spirit who, Christians believe, dwells among us and within us."[935]

The Archbishop of Cyprus bluntly pointed out that though there had been "13 centuries of coexistence of especially Eastern Christianity with Islam in a common geographical place," that, unfortunately, had not deterred "Turkey, who invaded Cyprus in 1974 and created between others the conditions for deprivation of main religious rights to the members of our Church, spoliation of churches, destruction of religious artifacts, offense of religious symbols, etc. We are hopeful that your initiative will contribute positively to change this unacceptable situation."[936]

The Baptist World Alliance responded positively to the overture made in *A Common Word* by saying, "We believe that this letter is a unique moment in the history of Christian Muslim relations. ... On this ground [that is, love to God and love to our neighbours] the [Muslim and Christian] scriptures intersect in some way. We wish to follow your example of encouraging each other to read and reflect on passages from the Hebrew Bible, the New Testament and the Qur'an. It is by reading each other's Scriptures that we shall come to understand each other and learn better how we both speak of God. ... A verse from the Qur'an clearly brings together the worship of God with doing good to the neighbour, which seems to be a close parallel to the double love command: 'Worship God; join nothing with Him. Be good to your parents, to relatives, to orphans, to the needy, to neighbours near and far, to travelers in need, and to your slaves.' Surah 4:36 ...

"Through the love of God shown in Christ and in his self-sacrifice, we are enabled to love God and others. The power of this initiating or prevenient [anticipatory] love of God, freely given, is expressed in such New Testament texts as this: 'whoever does not love does not know God, *for God is love* ... Beloved, *since God loved us* so much, we ought also to love one another. No one has ever seen God; if we love one another, God lives in us, and *his love* is perfected in us.' (I John 4:7-12, italics added) ... There are mysterious, unknowable depths to the personal nature of God. ... The church confesses that the life of God, who exists only from

---

934 A Common Word Between Us and You, (The Royal Aal al-Bayt Institute for Islamic Thought, Jordan, 2009), pp. 153-155.
935 A Common Word Between Us and You, (The Royal Aal al-Bayt Institute for Islamic Thought, Jordan, 2009), p. 160.
936 A Common Word Between Us and You, (The Royal Aal al-Bayt Institute for Islamic Thought, Jordan, 2009), pp. 174-175.

God's self, and from no other cause, is composed eternally of loving relationships which have some likeness to the relationships we know between a Father and a Son or a parent and a child, and which are being opened up continually to new depths of love and hope by a reality that our Scriptures call 'Spirit.' ... 'God's love has been poured into our hearts through the Holy Spirit that has been given to us.' (Romans 5:5) ... In your courtesy to us, you have refrained from interpreting the prohibitions of the Qur'an against ascribing any partner to God as a critique of the doctrine of the Trinity. ...

"While some Christians have taken up a completely pacifist position, others have espoused a 'just war' theory which includes proportionate means for justifiable self defense. Such 'just war' is not to be confused with a 'holy war' to advance the cause of Christianity, which we utterly repudiate. ...

"It is not altogether clear to us whether you think that this principle [the right of Christians, Muslims and Jews to freely practice their religion] can also cover the freedom of people to change their religion or to move from a community of one faith to another of a different faith. ... Throughout this response we have drawn attention to matters that we have said we would like to discuss further with you. We believe that this is best done, not by a central commission of the Baptist World Alliance, but by encouraging our regional unions and conventions of churches to engage in joint conversations and practical projects for aid and development with their Muslim neighbours, in ways that are appropriate for their own area."[937]

The response from the United Methodist Council of Bishops is very brief. In part, they said, "While acknowledging differences, we also seek to identify shared theological concepts, moral teachings and spiritual disciplines. ... We believe that it is always appropriate for Christians to seek common ground with people of other faiths, and especially because the critical needs of the world today demand inter-religious understanding and cooperation. ... In your appeal to Christians to find common ground, we sense the call of God to all of us at this moment in human history."[938]

The response from the presiding bishop of the Evangelical Lutheran Church in America, who also serves as president of the Lutheran World Federation, was extremely brief. He said, "I receive this letter [he refers to the Muslim letter entitled *A Common Word Between Us and You*] in the sincere expression of faithfulness intended by its drafters, and with the hopeful expectation for peace that calls to us from the origins of our sacred texts and professions of faith."[939]

---

937 A Common Word Between Us and You, (The Royal Aal al-Bayt Institute for Islamic Thought, Jordan, 2009), pp. 176-207.
938 A Common Word Between Us and You, (The Royal Aal al-Bayt Institute for Islamic Thought, Jordan, 2009), pp. 209-211.
939 A Common Word Between Us and You, (The Royal Aal al-Bayt Institute for Islamic Thought, Jordan, 2009), p. 213.

The elitist movement is certain to fail because the Muslim leaders have not asked for forgiveness from the Christian world for their egregious violations of brotherly love, such as forcing thousands of Christian women into their harems. This is in stark contrast to Christian leaders who have not only expressed regret for violations of brotherly love in the past which were made in the name of Christ, such as the Crusades, but also asked for forgiveness for other horrible violations of the love which should have been shown by the followers of Christ.

The second initiative from Islam is a revolutionary movement.

Bahrain, "Saudi Arabia's tiny neighbor has publicly declared that 'freedom of choice' is a 'divine gift' and that 'every individual has the freedom to practice their religion.' The statement by Bahrain—which was witnessed by leaders from Saudi Arabia, the United Arab Emirates, Egypt, and Israel—'goes way farther than any similar document that I'm aware of,' said National Association of Evangelicals board member Johnnie Moore, who observed its signing. That's partly because it was signed by a head of state, unlike two preceding statements from Morocco and Indonesia affirming religious freedom, which were signed by Muslim scholars. Bahrain's declaration—which also condemns preaching hatred, suicide bombing, sexual slavery, and the abuse of women and children—will be drafted into law in December [2017]."[940]

A glaring contrast is seen in comparing the declaration by the head of state in Bahrain with a statement from Turkey's President Recep Tayyip Erdogan. He "lashed out at the term 'moderate Islam' on Friday, saying the term's only aim is to weaken the religion itself rather than distance it from extremists. ... The patent of moderate Islam belongs to the West. There is no moderate or immoderate Islam: Islam is one. The aim of using such terms is to weaken Islam."[941]

The sentiment expressed by Turkey's President Erdogan will probably prove to be only, as it were, the tip of an iceberg of consternation and rejection by almost the entire Muslim world of Bahrain's declaration. It is highly questionable whether the tiny Muslim country of Bahrain can actually carry out their proposal in the face of the violent reactions which will probably ensue throughout the Muslim world.

Third, and finally, is the divine prophetic, world-changing, revolutionary drama highlighted by the prophet Ezekiel.

Of all the Asian Muslim nations, the Persians/Iranians, highlighted explicitly in Ezekiel 38:5, will almost certainly play a significant role—if not the dominant one—in a future major Muslim move against Israel. They have the resources, the dynamism, the subtlety, the creativity and the determination to lead aggressively. All of that is being powerfully augmented by overt cooperation from Putin's Russia. Also, Iran's initiative is augmented by Hamas (centered in Gaza), by Hezbollah

---

940 <u>Christianity Today</u>, November, 2017, p. 23.
941 https://www.jihadwatch.org/2017/11/erdogan-the-aim-of-the-term-moderate-islam-is-to-weaken-islam.

(centered in Lebanon), and, though not bordering Israel, by the Houthis (centered in Yemen). In them, Iran has loyal, like-minded, brutal proxies, two of them right on Israel's borders.

In chapters 38 and 39 of Ezekiel, it is prophesied that a vast three-continent, thirteen-member coalition of nations, with other participants implied, will invade the nation of Israel, determined to destroy the world's only Jewish state. Leading the coalition will be a power called Gog which will come from the extreme north (Ezekiel 38:14-15). If you would like to identify Gog, follow the line of longitude north from Jerusalem till you come to the Barents Sea. Then you can easily determine which country occupies "the uttermost parts of the north."

In the entire scope of the historic past such a coalition has never existed, let alone having invaded Israel. Either this is an event yet to occur or we must totally discount these two prophetic chapters as nothing more than fantasy. For those of us who believe that Ezekiel "spake from God, being moved by the Holy Spirit," (II Peter 1:21) his book, including chapters 38 and 39, serves as a lamp, shedding light on the future of the momentous times in which we live.

Six members of that huge thirteen-member-invading coalition are clearly Muslim countries. Their citizens are predominantly Muslim people who will be part of the alliance devoted to the destruction of Israel. Since this 29th Chapter explores the future of Islam as seen in Muslim people of destiny, we should first identify the six known Muslim groups which will fill significant roles in the future war prophesied by Ezekiel to take place. These brief notes of identification are excerpted from the author's book entitled, *The Definitive Battle For Palestine*. The six Muslim members of the coalition are:

(1) <u>From the North</u>, **Togarmah** (Ezekiel 38:6). The name points to the Turkish people, including not only those in the Republic of Turkey, but millions of other Turkic peoples, living principally in the five "Stans,"[942] whose territories collectively approximate the geographic area historically known as Central Asia. In addition to the Turks in Central Asia, some twenty-million more Turks live in Chinese Turkestan, home of the Muslim Turkish Uygur (Uighur) people, the predominant people of Sinkiang Autonomous Region in western China. They are also known as the Xinjiang Uygur (Uighur) people.

Part of the confirmation of the identity of Togarmah comes from the writings of the traveler Benjamin of Tudela[943] (died 1173 A.D.), a Spanish Jew who visited not only France, Italy, and Greece in Europe, but Palestine, Persia, the borders of China, Egypt, and Sicily during the period from 1159 through 1173. He

---

[942] The statistics for the five Stans are taken from (1) The CIA World Factbook, 2008 and (2) The New York Times 2009 Almanac and (3) Encyclopaedia Britannica. <u>Uzbekistan</u> (88% Muslim, 74.3% of the people speak Uzbek, a member of the Eastern Turk language group.) <u>Kazakhstan</u>, (47% Muslim, 53.4% speak Kazakh, a Turkic language group) <u>Tajikistan</u>, (90% Muslim but mainly of Persian, not Turkic ancestry.) <u>Kyrgyzstan</u> (75% Muslim, 52.4% speak Kirghiz, a member of the south Turkic language group.) <u>Turkmenistan</u> (85% Turkic).

[943] Tudela is located in Navarra province in northern Spain. It is on the Ebro River 52 miles south of Pamplona. It was conquered by the Arabs in 716 A.D. and re-conquered by Alfonso I of Aragon in 1115.

wrote, "Wealth like that of Constantinople is not to be found in the whole world. Here also are men learned in all the books of the Greeks, and they eat and drink every man under his vine and his fig tree. They hire from amongst all nations warriors called Loazim (Barbarians) to fight with the Sultan Masud, King of the Togarmim (Seljuks), who are called Turks."[944]

(2) From the East, **Persia/Iran** (Ezekiel 38:5). Russia has led in the formation of "an international group which first assembled in 1996. In that year The Shanghai Five [as it was then called], consisting of China, Russia, Kazakhstan, Kyrgyzstan, and Tajikistan was given birth. Originally, the main purpose was to facilitate the demilitarization of the China-Soviet border. In subsequent years, the group not only expanded, it also enhanced its vision. Thus, in 2001 the group took the name of **Shanghai Cooperation Organization** (SCO) and added Uzbekistan to its membership.

By its 2007 meeting, held in August, Russia was ready to "push for the inclusion of Iran" which had previously gained observer status. "We are witnessing a potential tactical realignment here, with the initiative coming from Russia. ... SCO countries house more than a quarter of the world's population and at least a fifth of global oil and gas reserves, plus huge uranium resources. ... But it is Russia [the power from the uttermost parts of the north] that is pushing the latest efforts to give the SCO more muscle."[945]

Many centuries after God, through Ezekiel, made the prophecy about Iran coming from the east to participate in the war against Israel, he gave the apostle John additional information. It is recorded in Revelation 16:12 in which further participants from the east are identified as "the kings that come from the sunrising."

It is clear that these kings are coming for war, for they are included among "the kings of the whole world" who are to be gathered "together unto the war of the great day of God, the Almighty." (Revelation 16:14)

Since the reference point is "the great river, the river Euphrates," it is then obvious that the "kings which come from the sunrising" would certainly include Iran, Afghanistan, and Pakistan, all encompassed in the Iran/Persia of Ezekiel's time, which is mentioned in Ezekiel 38:5. Most probably those kings who shall come from the sunrising will include the rulers of the Far East as well. The rearmament of Japan and the great enhancement of China's military power, along with the Maoist dictum, still current in Communist China, telling us that "political power comes out of the barrel of a gun," are ominous portents of this possibility. The expression "the kings of the whole world" (Revelation 16:14) undoubtedly includes the U.S.A. "Kings" is probably used euphemistically for rulers.

---

944 Benjamin of Tudela, Itinerary, trans. Marcus Nathan Adler (London: Henry Frowde, Oxford University Press, 1907), pp. 12-14. Quoted from Charles M. Brand (ed.) Icon and Minaret: Sources of Byzantine and Islamic Civilization (Englewood Cliffs: Prentice-Hall, Inc., 1969), pp. 103-104.
945 Isabel Gorst & Richard McGregor, *Russia Adds Muscle to Central Asian Summit*, Financial Times, August 15, 2007, p. 6.

The identity of the kings who will come from the sunrising becomes more clear if they are also ideologically defined. That definition will point predominately to the Communist and Islamic countries which lie to the east of the Euphrates. Their philosophical and religious commitments will encourage them in the attempt to eradicate America's main foothold on the eastern shore of the Mediterranean, that is, Israel.

The probability of China exerting its military power to the west of the Euphrates was graphically highlighted by the late Lee Kuan Yew, first prime minister of independent Singapore. He asked, "Why has China's peaceful rise, however, raised apprehensions [while India's rise has not]? Is it because India is a democracy in which numerous political forces are constantly at work, making for an internal system of checks and balances [while China is not such a democracy]? Most probably, yes. ...

"Suppose China were also a democracy with multiple parties and political power bases. Would a multiparty China with a yearly economic growth rate of 9% to 12% be viewed with the same equanimity as India is? Such a China would probably continue to make big strides on the economic, social and military fronts, with more sophisticated capabilities on the ground and sea and in the air and space, and would eventually become a peer competitor, if not an adversary, of the U.S. ...

"What if India were well ahead of China? Would Americans and Europeans be rooting for China? I doubt it. They still have a phobia of the 'yellow peril,' one reinforced by memories of the outrages of the Cultural Revolution and the massacres in Tiananmen Square, not to mention their strong feelings against Chinese government censorship."[946]

Among the countries which will come from the east to participate in "the war of the great day of God the Almighty" will almost certainly be North Korea. That prediction is based on the fact that "on an island in the Suez Canal, a towering AK-47 rifle, its muzzle and bayonet pointed skyward, symbolizes one of Egypt's most enduring alliances. Decades ago, North Korea presented it to Egypt to commemorate the 1973 war against Israel, when North Korean pilots fought and died on the Egyptian side."[947]

(3) <u>From the South</u>, **Sheba** (Ezekiel 38:13) It was the domain of the Queen of Sheba whose grandeur is highlighted in the tenth chapter of I Kings and the ninth chapter of II Chronicles. The name Sheba points us to Yemen. The capital city of Sheba was Ma'rib (also spelled Mareb). The magnificent ruins of that ancient city are located near the modern town of Awwam, almost due east from San'a, the present capital city of Yemen. Since the beginning of the Houthi rebellion, Yemen's foreign policy has been clearly in harmony with Iran's blatant efforts to become the dominant power in the Middle East.

---

946 Lee Kuan Yew, *India's Peaceful Rise*, <u>FORBES</u>, December 24, 2007, p. 33. [Note: The late Mr Yew was, at the time of writing, the Minister Mentor of Singapore.]
947 Declan Walsh, *Missiles Made in Pyongyang Sold in Cairo*, <u>The New York Times</u>, March 4, 2018, p. A1.

(4) <u>Also from the South</u>, **Dedan** (Ezekiel 38:13) This name takes us to southern Jordan. Ezekiel 25:12-13 tells us where Dedan was. It says, "Thus saith the Lord Jehovah: Because that Edom hath dealt against the house of Judah by taking vengeance, and hath greatly offended, and revenged himself upon them; therefore thus saith the Lord Jehovah, I will stretch out my hand upon Edom, and will cut off man and beast from it; and I will make it desolate from Teman; even unto Dedan shall they fall by the sword." From this passage it seems quite clear that Dedan was located in what was ancient Edom. Today, Jordan governs that area.

(5) <u>From the southwest</u>, **Cush** (Ezekiel 38:5) Cush is the ancient name for Ethiopia. Some English translations correctly put Ethiopia in the text. Presently, Ethiopia is 33% Muslim. Neighboring Eritrea and Somalia, both overwhelmingly Muslim, are waiting for the chance to conquer Ethiopia. According to Genesis 10:6, Cush was one of the sons of Ham. Some think the name also includes the area of modern Sudan. Ezana, famous king of Aksum [also Axum], ancient Ethiopia, inscribed the names of areas conquered and ruled by him. Among those names is "Kasu." One scholar writes, "Kasu is Meroe, the biblical Kush, in modern Sudan."[948] Should Sudan, the ancient Meroe, an area now governed from Khartoum, prove, indeed, to be part of the biblical Cush, it is already in the hands of radical Muslims.[949] We can easily visualize the Sudanese joining the coalition in its attack on the tiny state of Israel.

(6) <u>Also from the southwest</u>, **Put**. (Ezekiel 38:5) The word Put is the ancient name for the area now known as Libya. The people of Put were descendants of Ham, (See Genesis 10:6) and they constitute the final member of the cast which shall come from the southwest.

Libya's late dictator, Colonel Muammar Qaddafi came to power by a bloodless military coup in September 1969 which overthrew 79-year-old King Idris. Qaddafi proved to be a radical Muslim leader under whose leadership Libya became a socialist republic. Since the recent overthrow and killing of Qaddafi, al Qaeda and ISIS have largely come into dominance in Libya.

What would motivate Islamic countries to join the coalition in the attempt to destroy Israel? It is axiomatic among Muslims that the nation of Israel is the main impediment to progress in the Muslim world! Those who are unwilling to pay the price for excellence usually look for excuses and scapegoats. Much of the Muslim world is currently doing this by blaming Israel for their own shortcomings. Received Arab opinion was "concisely summed up by [the late] Saddam Hussein, [former] president of Iraq, [when he said] 'Imperialism uses Zionism as a strategic arm against Arab unity, progress and development. This

---

948 Stuart Munro-Hay, <u>Ethiopia, The Unknown Land A Cultural and Historical Guide</u>, (London: I.B. Tauris Publishers, 2003), p. 234.

949 That characterization should be evaluated in view of the most recent estimate by the U.S.A. As of November 17, 2017, the U.S. State Department is considering taking Sudan off its list of countries which support Islamic terrorism.

is a well-known fact.' Even a professor like the Moroccan Abdallah Laroui, a Marxist and therefore alert to historical cause and effect, can be found giving credence to such an interpretation. 'The bare fact, impossible to deny, is that Israel by its very existence has checked the Arabs' progress and has been one of the determining causes in the process of continuing traditionalization.'"[950]

The invading coalition will be headed for disaster. Great pride and arrogance will be brought low. Mr. Ahmadinejad, a recent president of Iran, who repeatedly boasted that Iran would wipe Israel off the face of the earth, has, along with his fellow coalition members, a major shock coming. Though the tiny nation of Israel has repeatedly shown militarily that it can give good account of itself, nevertheless the concentration of military might, which the coalition will amass against it, will be overwhelming. But Israel will not be alone. It will have an ally. God says, "I will call for a sword against him unto all my mountains." (Ezekiel 38:21) As world powers are presently aligned, this almost certainly points to the U.S.A. mobilizing its military might in favor of Israel.

Coinciding with the gathering of those forces, arraying themselves against the coalition under Gog, will occur an outbreak of a deadly pestilence. According to Ezekiel 38:22, God tells us, "with pestilence and with blood will I enter into judgment with him." The pronoun "him" refers to Gog and his invading hordes. This will not be the first time such an occurrence will have taken place in Palestine. We have historical evidence of a similar biological malady destroying a vast army in the account of Sennacharib's forces being destroyed on the mountains of Israel. In just one night, one-hundred-and-seventy-five-thousand invading soldiers died! (See II Kings 19:35-37) Centuries later, in 1799, Napoleon's army was similarly decimated by the plague at the Battle of Acre, an event which decisively helped the British gain the victory in that extremely important struggle for control of the Middle East.

A major factor which will help thwart the expectations of the invading coalition will be internecine strife. The second half of Ezekiel 38:21 tells us that the unity of the invading coalition will break down so badly that elements of their forces will turn their weapons on their fellow soldiers! Thus, the unity of the great coalition will deteriorate to the point that "every man's sword shall be against his brother."

In addition to strife among the members of the attacking coalition, earthquake activity (Ezekiel 38:19-20), pestilence, volcanic and meteorological phenomena will also help defeat the invading alliance's forces. Ezekiel 38:22 tells us, "I will rain upon him, and upon his hordes, and upon the many peoples that are with him, an overflowing shower, and great hailstones, fire, and brimstone." The hailstones will be reminiscent of one of the disastrous plagues which God sent upon Egypt. (Exodus 9:18-26) The fire and brimstone will duplicate an identical occurrence during the destruction of Sodom. (Genesis 19:24)

---

950 David Pryce-Jones, <u>The Closed Circle, An Interpretation of the Arabs</u>, (New York: Harper Perennial, 1991), p. 214.

In addition to the military, economic and political consequences which will inevitably result from the overwhelming defeat which will have been suffered by the invading coalition, great epochal spiritual developments will also ensue. There are five explicit statements about the theological impact which the defeat of the invading coalition will have on the nations which will have participated in the coalition against Israel. Since there will be very broad Muslim participation in the coalition, this prophecy predicts a sweeping fundamental spiritual victory in the Muslim world!

Following are five statements which highlight the fundamental change which will be induced in the hearts of the invading people.

(1) "I will bring thee against my land, **that the nations may know me**." (Ezekiel 38:16b)

(2) "I will magnify myself, and sanctify myself, and **I will make myself known in the eyes of many nations; and they shall know that I am Jehovah.**" (Ezekiel 38:23)

(3) "I will send a fire on Magog, and on them that dwell securely in the isles; and **they shall know that I am Jehovah**." (Ezekiel 39:6)

(4) "**The nations shall know that I am Jehovah, the Holy One in Israel**." (Ezekiel 39:7b)

(5) "**I will set my glory among the nations; and all the nations shall see my judgment that I have executed**, and my hand that I have laid upon them." (Ezekiel 39:21)

If one evaluates these statements about the breakthrough in the Muslims' concept of God in light of John 17:3 and Luke 10:22, it seems it will also have involved a major turning to Christ as Savior and Lord!

Simultaneously, with this major turning to Christ by the Muslim world, also, the Jewish people finally will accept Jesus of Nazareth as their Messiah and Savior. Some of Ezekiel's key statements about this incipient, stunning development are:

"My holy name will I make known in the midst of my people Israel." (Ezekiel 39:7a)

"The house of Israel shall know that I am Jehovah their God, from that day and forward." (Ezekiel 39:22)

"Now will I bring back the captivity of Jacob, and have mercy upon the whole house of Israel." (Ezekiel 39:25)

"They shall know that I am Jehovah their God, in that I caused them to go into captivity among the nations, and have gathered them unto their own land; and I will leave none of them any more there: neither will I hide my face any more from them; for **I have poured out my Spirit upon the house of Israel, saith the Lord Jehovah.**" (Ezekiel 39:28-29)

Another startling consequence of this definitive battle for Palestine will be a major correction in Muslims' evaluation of Jews. Instead of their current denigrating view of Jews, based on fallacious genetic and historical assumptions, they will learn God's true appraisal of them. They will learn that the Jews did not become wandering, homeless refugees because they were inferior, but they shall come to "know that the house of Israel went into captivity for their iniquity." (Ezekiel 39:23a) They will also come to realize that Jewish possession of Palestine was not in violation of the divine order but that God himself had "brought them back from the peoples, and gathered them out of their enemies' lands." (Ezekiel 39:27) (See also the surprising statements in Surahs 2:47, 5:20-21 and 17:104.)

How will the issue of East Jerusalem be settled? The issue of the Temple Mount? The issue of the Wailing Wall? The issue of The Dome of the Rock? The issue of Al-Aqsa Mosque? These issues have been intractable and insoluble from 1948 to the present. The finest, most astute diplomatic minds have pondered helplessly over these questions like a checkmate conundrum. This dilemma will be solved by the King of Kings, the King of the "daughter of Jerusalem," who is "just, and having salvation … shall speak peace unto the nations, and his dominion shall be from sea to sea, and from the River to the ends of the earth." (Zechariah 9:9-10)

It will be a breathtaking landmark change. "To Muslims this splendid structure [Dome of the Rock], built in 691, had both religious and political importance. … By building what they intended to be the most magnificent shrine in Jerusalem over this hallowed rock, the Muslims [intentionally] honored God and the Prophet; and by putting an Islamic shrine on a spot holy to the Jews, they demonstrated their political and spiritual superiority over non-Muslims."[951]

If the noble Islamic structures on Temple Mount survive the violent earthquake activity which will occur in Palestine at the time of the coalition's invasion (see Ezekiel 38:19-20), they will be re-christened as places where Christ is worshiped, as ultimately countless mosques all over the world will be! It will not happen as it did when the Grand Mosque of Algiers was taken by gun point and converted into a Catholic cathedral, but by Muslims themselves who, as a result of this epochal battle, will realize they have been on the wrong side. In a meaningful way, they will acknowledge Jesus of Nazareth as the Messiah!

Muslims, among others, "will come from the ends of the earth" and shall say, "Our fathers have inherited nought but lies, even vanity and things wherein there is no profit." (Jeremiah 16:19-20) Simultaneously, the Jews, because God will have poured out his "Spirit upon the house of Israel" (Ezekiel 39:29) as a result of their having acknowledged Jesus as their Messiah, will no longer seek to rebuild

---

[951] Desmond Stewart, <u>Early Islam</u>, (New York: Time Incorporated, 1967), p. 102.

the temple on Temple Mount. They will have gladly acknowledged that there is no need for sacrifice because they will "have been sanctified through the offering of the body of Jesus Christ once for all." (Hebrews 10:10)

Former Jew and former Muslim, having now become 'one new man' in Christ Jesus, (Ephesians 2:15) will joyously throng together in those noble structures on Temple Mount mutually honoring their common Savior! Then shall be fulfilled the prophecy that "They will beat their swords into plowshares and their spears into pruning hooks. Nation will not take up sword against nation, nor will they train for war anymore." (Isaiah 2:4b)

Evaluating the Withering Wind

As suggested in Chapter 2, there seems to have been a sinister spiritual force which captivated thousands of Arabians and motivated them to join the jihad to conquer the world.

Diarmaid MacCulloch, Professor of "History of the Church" at Oxford University wrote, "In the eighth century of the Christian era, the great new city of Baghdad would have been a more likely capital for worldwide Christianity than Rome. The extraordinary accident of the irruption of Islam is the chief reason why Christian history turned in another direction."[952]

In view of all the incontrovertible realities presented in *Withering Wind From Arabia*, is it possible to reasonably say that the "irruption of Islam" was an "extraordinary accident?" As one considers the political, military, economic, social, philosophical, religious, ecological, agricultural, horticultural, botanical, climatological and genealogical phenomena which all—to some extent—coalesced to make it possible for the great Arabian Prophet Muhammad to bring his vision into reality, can we honestly say it all transpired by "accident," even an "extraordinary" one?

The apostle Paul called the propitious circumstances, which coalesced to make the spectacular birth and early growth of the church possible, "the fullness of the time" (Galatians 4:4). Similarly, an equally conducive set of circumstances made it possible for the concept of Islam to take deep roots in society and to dramatically spread globally.

Seeing not only the initial destruction of Christian communities and institutions caused by the irruption of Islam but also the ongoing suppression of the followers of Christ like those in Iran, like the Copts in Egypt, or the utter extermination of Christians and Christian influence on the pattern of what has happened in Arabia and Afghanistan, can we reasonably imagine that the coalition of so many circumstances resulting in such an international devastation of Christian presence and outreach was brought about by a benevolent power?

---

952 Diarmaid MacCulloch, Christianity, the First Three-Thousand Years, (New York, Viking, 2010), p. 3.

In Revelation 12:17 we are given the vision of the dragon who "became furious with the woman [the church] and went off to make war on the rest of her offspring, on those who keep the commandments of God and hold to the testimony of Jesus." (NIV) It seems incontrovertible that this identifies the malicious power which made it possible for the withering wind from Arabia to blow in such a prolonged, destructive and global manner as it did in the past and as it continues in the present in destroying much of the work of Christ.

We Christians—who have been privileged to live outside the boundaries of those areas where the withering wind from Arabia is blowing most fiercely—must uphold our brothers and sisters who are destined to live under the full force of that wind which comes from <u>a society which has been fashioned to repress the message and the people of Christ</u>.

We must also pray that we may be used of God to keep the message of Christ before the Muslim world for the sake of those in that alien culture who hunger and thirst after righteousness.

ೞ

Appendices

APPENDIX A

The Geography of the Arabian Peninsula

The Name. Islam arose in the vast Arabian Peninsula which gets its name from the word *Arab* which is "derived from a Semitic word that means 'nomad.' The first use of the term occurs in Assyrian annals of the ninth century B.C., when nomads mounted on camelback are reported to have raided the settled villages of Mesopotamia."[953]

Size and Location. The peninsula is enormous, being about the same size as the continental United States east of the Mississippi River.[954] Though "technically part of Asia, [it] is almost a subcontinent unto itself. It is the world's largest peninsula—a 1,176,000-square mile tongue of land that is cut off from the rest of Asia by the Arabian (or Persian) Gulf on the east and by the vast Syrian Desert on the north. It is separated from Africa by the Red Sea on the west. And on the south it is girt by the Gulf of Aden, the Arabian Sea and the Gulf of Oman."[955]

Roger Crowley memorably calls the Red Sea "a fourteen-hundred-mile gash in the desert separating Arabia from the African continent."[956]

Evaluation. Some have seen the Arabian Peninsula as only a wasteland of flinty sand, salt flats, and rock. "The area seemed devoid of the most basic natural resources. Its principal source of income was the Muslim pilgrimage to the holy cities of Mecca and Medina, both located in the western Hejaz district. The British were content to let their Hashemite allies rule the Hejaz and to ignore the rest of the peninsula. The French were utterly indifferent."[957]

Others have seen the Arabian Peninsula as one of the extremely, if not the most, static areas in the world. That was the appraisal of Dr. Harry W. Hazard in 1959, then with Princeton University's Near Eastern Studies Program. He asserted that, "Arabia has changed more during the last forty years than it had over the previous thirty centuries."[958] Dr. Hazard's statement was extremely un-

---

953 Arabian Peninsula, (eds. of Time-Life Books), (Alexandria, Virginia: Time-Life Books, 1986), p. 20.
954 "The greatest length of the peninsula from the northwest to southeast is about 1,600 miles (2,600 kilometers), from north to south not quite 1,400 miles (2,300 kilometers), while from east to west the maximum width is about 1,300 miles (2,100 kilometers). It is narrowest from Rabigh on the Red Sea to Manama on the Persian Gulf—a distance of about 700 miles." – Donald August Holm, *Arabian Desert*, The New Encyclopaedia Britannica, 15th ed., Vol 1, p. 1052.
955 Arabian Peninsula, (eds. of Time-Life Books), (Alexandria, Virginia: Time-Life Books, 1986), p. 20.
956 Roger Crowley, Conquerors, (New York: Random House, 2015), p. 287.
957 Michael B. Oren, Power, Faith, and Fantasy, America in the Middle East, 1776 to the Present, (New York: W.W. Norton & Company, 2007), p. 407.
958 Harry W. Hazard, The Arabian Peninsula, (Garden City, N.Y.: Nelson Doubleday, Inc., 1959, p. 3.

fortunate. Certainly nothing from 1959 to the present has equaled the impact and importance of the rise of Islam. Furthermore, the political geography changed quite frequently during the time in which Dr. Hazard saw comparatively few changes. And Arabian history has certainly not been as static as Dr. Hazard's statement would indicate.

To understand the matrix in which Islam was born and from which it went forth to conquer, we first will look briefly at the geography of the Arabian Peninsula.

Strategic Importance. However, before looking at the details of Arabian geography, we need to understand the strategic importance of the peninsula as a whole. First of all, geographically Arabia dominates three of the world's most important waterways: the Red Sea, The Persian Gulf and the northern part of the Indian Ocean, along with its two gulfs: The Gulf of Aden on the SW and Gulf of Oman on the SE.

Bab-el-Mandeb [Mandab]. At the southern end of the 1,400-mile-long Red Sea, the eighteen-mile-wide strait, or water passageway, separating Arabia and Africa is called Bab-el-Mandeb. It is the sea way between the Red Sea and the Indian Ocean, via the Gulf of Aden. The name of the strait, Bab-el-Mandeb, is Arabic which means the *Door of Tears*, reflecting the grief and sorrow many ship captains experienced as they unsuccessfully tried to maneuver their ships through this crucial choke point. "The island of Perim ... divides the strait into two channels, of which the eastern, known as the Bab Iskender (Alexander's Strait [lit. Alexander's Door]) is 2 miles wide ... while the western ... has a width of about 16 miles. ... Near the African coast lies a group of smaller islands known as the 'Seven Brothers.'"[959] Whoever is able to shut or open the Door of Tears, can control the seaborne trade of all Northeast Africa and the Mediterranean which is scheduled for the Arabian Sea and vice versa.

The efforts to control that door have resulted in a centuries-long seesaw tug-of-war between Southwest Arabia and Northeast Africa. At the time Islam came into being, the struggle for control of the Door of Tears was between ancient Ethiopia, then known as Axum, and the Persians working through their client Yemeni ruler, the Jewish king of Yemen, Dhu Nuwas.

Contention for control of the Door of Tears became even more acute when Europe broke the economic stranglehold Islam had on it and began competing for the Red Sea-Indian Ocean trade. In our day, transit through Bab-el-Mandeb is threatened by al Qaeda which has terrorist cells in Yemen, a country poorly equipped to guard the waterway. Before the Houthi uprising in Yemen, the U.S. Navy was training forces in Yemen to establish a viable coast guard. Also, as given in detail below, Somalian pirates operating in the Gulf of Aden have endangered seaborne traffic in and out of Bab-el-Mandeb.

---

959 The Encyclopaedia Britannica, (New York: The Encyclopaedia Britannica Company, 1910), Vol. III, p. 91.

One modern example of the importance of this choke point came from the account of the Yom Kippur War of 1973. Israel's foreign minister, Abba Eban, in negotiating the cease-fire agreement between Israel and Egypt, said, "A cease-fire would not be valid for Israel unless it contained an agreement for the release of prisoners and the ending of blockade practices at Bab-el-Mandeb, the straits where Israeli shipping trying to enter the Red Sea from the Gulf of Aden had been stopped for many days."[960]

Recent pirate activity by Somalian pirates underline the importance of the Bab-el-Mandeb/Gulf of Aden waterway. "Somalia's pirates are threatening to choke off one of the most strategic waterways in the world, the Gulf of Aden, which 20,000 ships pass through every year. These heavily armed buccaneers hijacked more than 40 vessels in 2008, netting as much as $100 million in ransom. It's the greatest piracy epidemic of modern times."[961]

"The piracy threat to shipping was manageable. There was economic loss, whether in the form of higher premiums or ransom, but the cost was marginal compared to the total value of goods transiting the region. About 20,000 ships cross the Bab-el-Mandeb every year."[962] Since the widening of the Panama Canal has allowed much larger ships to pass between the Atlantic and Pacific Oceans, the number of ships going through Bab-el-Mandeb has been reduced.

Ras Musandam. On the southeastern side of the Arabian Peninsula, Oman swings north around the corner of the peninsula, finally terminating in the Musandam Peninsula. At the very tip of that small peninsula is a promontory known as Ras Musandam, which means 'Anvil Headland.' It forms the southern side of the choke point known as the Strait of Hormuz, the sea route in and out of the 623-mile-long Persian Gulf. Because of the highly strategic position of this northernmost part of Oman, during World War II it was "well described as 'the cork in the Persian-Gulf bottle.'"[963] That promontory, though part of Oman, is separated from the main body of Oman by small intertwined areas of Fujairah, Sharjah and Dubai, all parts of the United Arab Emirates.[964] The promontory itself, known as Ras Musandam, though it was formerly called Ras al-Khaimah, is located at the point "which separates the deeper, cooler water of the Gulf of Oman from the Persian or Arabian Gulf."[965]

Though the Strait of Hormuz "is 34 miles wide at its narrowest point" sea traffic must thread its way, "single-file through the two-mile-wide shipping lanes."[966] The Strait of Hormuz is highly strategic because currently about 40% of the world's seaborne oil goes through that very narrow seaway. All oil cargo

---
960 Abba Eban, Abba Eban, An Autobiography, (New York: Random House, Inc.: 1977), p. 530.
961 Jeffrey Gettleman, *The Most Dangerous Place in the World*, Foreign Policy, March/April 2009, p. 62.
962 Camille Pecastaing, Jihad in the Arabian Sea, (Stanford, CA: Hoover Institution Press, 2011), p. 94.
963 Wendell Phillips, Unknown Oman, (New York: David McKay Company, Inc., 1966), p. 19.
964 For any student who wishes to see the details, there is an excellent and detailed map in Rafic Boustani & Philippe Fargues, The Atlas of the Arab World, Geopolotics and Society, (New York: Facts On File, 1990), p. 25.
965 Wendell Phillips, Unknown Oman, (New York: David McKay Company, Inc., 1966), p. 73.
966 Matt Chambers, *Just in Case*, The Wall Street Journal, August 27, 200, p. R7.

ships are guarded on their trips through the straits by the U.S. Navy or the naval ships of one of its allies. Iran has openly declared that should it be attacked it would, in retaliation, immediately close the Strait of Hormuz. Currently, Iran is in good position to carry out its threat because it controls the island of Abu Musa which is strategically located in the Strait of Hormuz, the narrow checkpoint through which all vessels from Iraq, Kuwait, Qatar, Bahrain and the Emirates must pass to reach the open ocean. It has been occupied by Iran since 1992."[967]

Regions

I. The West Coast

Tihama. [Also spelled Tihamah and Tehama] Between the eastern shore of the Red Sea and the mountain range which runs parallel with it, "is the great coastal plain known as Tihama [a semitic word meaning 'lowland'], bordering the Red Sea. Its width ... varies from 40 miles, at [Yemen's Red Sea port of] Hodeida [now called Al Hudaydah] ... and finally shrinks to nothing at the Gulf of Aqaba."[968] The Tihama is hot, humid and malarial. For example, "the heat [and humidity] of Jedda [Jiddah, Jeddah—Arabia's main port on the Red Sea. Just north of Jedda is the port of Yanbu'.] is such that, at its worst ... matches refuse to strike, and keys rust in the pocket. [Before the days of air-conditioning] heat and insects kept one awake at night."[969] A recent description confirms the rigorous and harsh conditions in the Tihama. A very alert lady recorded her experience: "We were living in a place that was never meant for human habitation. Though Jeddah is on the sea—it is a major port—the desert is ever-present, stony and wild, constantly encroaching on life. It has not even one river, no gentle natural greens, no mellow colors."[970]

The Western Mountain Range. Just behind the coastal plain of Tihama, to the east rises "a steep mountain wall rising to over 9,000 feet at the southern end of Asir, 8,000 feet behind Mecca, [decreasing to] ... 3,000 near Medina." Penetrating this "mountain wall ... are great valleys (*wadis*) reaching far to the east, the largest of which is Wadi Hamdh, south of Wejh. One terminus of this valley comes close to Medina. ... On the east side of the mountain wall, the slopes are much less precipitous, graduating to the great inland [arid] plateau which lies nearly within the confines of the Najd province."[971] The Arabic term *najd* means [a plain,] a "steppe region."[972]

---

967 Michael Slackman & Robert F. Worth, *Tiny Island Surrounded By Tension In the Gulf*, The New York Times, March 30, 2009, p. A10.
968 K. S. Twitchell, Saudi Arabia With an Account of the Development of its Natural Resources, (Princeton, New Jersey: Princeton University Press, 1947), p. 11.
969 Gerald De Gaurly, Arabia Phoenix, (London: George G. Harrap & Co. Ltd., 1947), p. 121.
970 Carmen Bin Ladin, Inside The Kingdom, My Life in Saudi Arabia, (New York: Warner Books, 2004), p. 61.
971 K. S. Twitchell, Saudi Arabia With an Account of the Development of its Natural Resources, (Princeton, New Jersey: Princeton University Press, 1947), pp. 10-11.
972 Wendell Phillips, Unknown Oman, (New York: David McKay Company, Inc., 1966), p. 179.

The Name Hijaz (Hejaz, Hedjaz). Originally the mountain range paralleling the Red Sea was called Hijaz which means *barrier*. Though "this term was originally applied only to the range of mountains separating the coastal plain from the interior plateau of Najd, [it] was later extended to include much of the coastal plain itself. To the east of the Hijaz lies the great inland plateau of Najd, most of it consisting of [the] Nafud desert."[973]

"Eighteen volcanic [lava] fields are scattered through the west, mainly in Hejaz, several of them being more than 10,000 square miles in area."[974]

If one follows the western mountain chain south into Yemen, there peaks reach "a height of over 12,000[975] feet, [and] are drained on the west by torrents plunging towards the Tihamah but rarely reaching the sea, and on the east by streams sloping toward the thirsty sands. ... It is characteristic of Arabia that its streams are seasonal and expire short of the sea. In the whole peninsula [with the exception of Wadi Hajar in the southern Hadramawt/Hadhramaut/Hadramaut[976]] there is not a single real perennial river, nor any sizable lake or navigable stream."[977]

Asir. "In the mountains [toward the] south of the Hijaz is the Asir, culturally a part of Yemen but annexed to Saudi Arabia [after being wrested from Yemen in 1934] by Abdul Aziz. Rugged mountains covered with pine trees rise from the coastal plain. Even in the hottest part of summer, its high altitude keeps the climate delightfully cool, so much so that from early June until mid-October, the royal family moves to the mountain city of Ta'if, taking the government with them."[978]

II. On The North

On the north of the Arabian Peninsula, marauding forces emerging from Arabia have relatively easy access through the Syrian Desert to either Iran on the east or to areas on the Mediterranean seaboard to the west.

"North of the Great Nafud [Desert, see below] is the Syrian Desert, which stretches into Iraq, Jordan and Syria."[979] There is a significant plateau "between the northern extremity of the Great Nafud and the junction of the borders of Saudi Arabia, Jordan and Iraq. This plateau attains an elevation of 1,900 feet and forms the divide between the drainage to the Euphrates on the east and the drainage to Wadi al-Sirhan on the west. [Wadi al-Sirhan runs

---

973 Bernard Lewis, The Arabs in History, (London: Hutchinson's University Library, 1950), p. 22.
974 Donald August Holm, *Arabian Desert*, The New Encyclopaedia Britannica, 15th ed., Vol. 1, p. 1052.
975 The mountain known as "Hadur Shu'ayb reaches a height of 12,336 feet." – Donald August Holm, *Arabian Desert*, The New Encyclopaedia Britannica, 15th ed., Vol. 1., p. 1052.
976 Wadi Hajar in the southern Hadramawt does flow perennially. – cf. Donald August Holm, *Arabian Desert*, The New Encyclopaedia Britannica, 15th ed., Vol. 1., p. 1052.
977 Harry W. Hazard, The Arabian Peninsula, (Garden City, N.Y.: Nelson Doubleday, Inc., 1959), pp. 8-9.
978 Sandra Mackey, The Saudis, Inside the Desert Kingdom, (Boston: Houghton Mifflin Company, 1987), p. 101.
979 Harry W. Hazard, *Arabia*, Collier's Encyclopedia, (Crowell-Collier Educational Corporation, 1969), Vol. 2, p. 378.

northwest to southeast. It lies on the east side of the country of Jordan.] A series of valleys running northeastwards into Iraq is known as al-Widyan, and the terrain through which they pass is scarred by the many tributaries of these water courses. Wadi al-Sirhan, the basin of which is not a water course, is a great depression, 200 miles long, from 20 to 30 miles wide, and 1,000 feet below the elevation of the adjoining plateau region. For thousands of years one of the most important trade routes connecting the Mediterranean and central Arabia passed through Wadi al-Sirhan and the oasis of al-Jauf (Jauf Ibn 'Amir)."[980]

III. The Interior

The Najd. Encircled on the east by the Dahna Desert and abutting the mountains on the west, is a great central interior plateau called the Najd, "most of it consisting of [the] Nafud Desert."[981] Occupying the center of the Arabian Peninsula, its elevation ranges from 762 meters to 1,525 meters. Population, understandably, concentrates around oases such as **Riyadh**, now the capital of Saudi Arabia. The Najd is "a particularly arid region in the center of the Arabian Peninsula."[982]

The Nafud. The interior of the peninsula is dominated by three great deserts. In the north, The Nafud, often thought of as part of the Najd plateau, is a sand desert ranging from 100 to170 miles in width while it is 800 miles from south to north. "In the Nafud there are numerous great parallel ridges of sand interspersed with wind-swept exposures of the underlying rock—generally flat beds of limestone. The dunes are like a sea and show the direction of the prevailing winds by huge crests and combs of sand, like breakers."[983]

Rub' al-Khali. "In the southern part of the present-day kingdom of Saudi Arabia is the immense sand body of the Rub' al-Khali or Empty Quarter. This sand body occupies a basin bordered by the mountains of Oman on the east, the plateau behind the coastal escarpments on the south, and the foothills of the mountains of the Yemen and 'Asir on the west. The Rub' al-Khali is approximately 750 miles long and has a maximum width of nearly 400 miles. It covers an area of about 250,000 square miles, nearly the size of Texas, and is the largest continuous body of sand in the world."[984]

The Dahna. (Also spelled, Dahana) Connecting these two immense deserts is a third desert known as the Dahna. North to south, from the Great Nafud the Dahna curves to the east and then back to the west. It is a crescent shaped, strip of sand bending around the Najd. "It extends approximately 800 miles in a

---
980 Roy Lebkicher, George Rentz, Max Steineke, <u>Aramco Handbook</u>, (Arabian American Oil Company, 1960), p. 273.
981 Bernard Lewis, <u>The Arabs in History</u>, (London: Hutchinson's University Library, 1950), p. 22.
982 Camille Pecastaing, <u>Jihad in the Arabian Sea</u>, (Stanford, CA: Hoover Institution Press, 2011), p. 6.
983 K. S. Twitchell, <u>Saudi Arabia With an Account of the Development of its Natural Resources</u>, (Princeton, New Jersey: Princeton University Press, 1947), p. 13.
984 Roy Lebkicher, George Rentz, Max Steineke, <u>Aramco Handbook</u>, (Arabian American Oil Company, 1960), p. 275.

great arc from the Great Nafud in the north to the Rub' al-Khali [The Empty Quarter] in the south. ... The Dahna is a favorite grazing ground of the Bedouins in winter and spring. Water is scarce, and the Bedouins who herd camels here get along with only a little of it for weeks. Camels do not require water while grazing in green grass and bushes, and the Bedouins live mainly on the camels' milk."[985]

IV. The East Coast /Arabian Gulf Coast[986] *(With this section, be sure to read the description of Ras Musandam given previously in Appendix A.)*

The entire east coast of Saudi Arabia is governed as a single province entitled *The Eastern Province*. Its "lands along the [Arabian/] Persian Gulf are mostly desert—sand, or gravel, or salt, mud, or windswept rock."[987] "No part of this coastal region is more than a few hundred feet above sea level. The elevation of the region as a whole increases gradually, from the coast toward the interior of the peninsula, at the rate of about five feet per mile."[988] Though Saudi Arabia is the dominant political power, five small independent countries are located on the east coast of the Arabian Peninsula. From north to south they are: Kuwait, Bahrain, Qatar, United Arab Emirates and Oman.

These states gained their independence from "Britain's decision to wind up its protectorates in the Gulf and by so doing abandon the position of naval and political paramountcy in these waters which it had exercised for 150 years. **Kuwait** had become independent in 1961, and in 1968 declared that it would no longer be looking to Britain for protection against external aggression. At the beginning of 1968 rulers of **Bahrein**, **Qatar** and the **Trucial Sheikhdoms** agreed to federate and thereby to exchange reliance on the protecting arm of Britain for independence. The only complication about this was the Iranian claim on Bahrein—a claim which the Shah had inherited and felt obliged to take seriously, even if nobody outside Iran did. He called the proposed federation 'a colonist and imperialist manipulation' but in 1969 a face-saving formula involving a mission of inquiry dispatched by the Secretary-General of the United Nations was devised. **Bahrein** became independent in August 1971,[989] **Qatar** following just a month later. In July the six former **Trucial Sheikhdoms** formed themselves into a new sovereign state to be known as the **United Arab Emirates**."[990]

---

985 Roy Lebkicher, George Rentz, Max Steineke, Aramco Handbook, (Arabian American Oil Company, 1960), p. 271.
986 On October 13, 2017, President "Trump called the Persian Gulf the 'Arabian Gulf.' No Iranian—whether religious or atheist, pro-regime or anti-regime—can stomach the body of water separating Iran from its southern Arabic neighbors being called anything but the Persian Gulf." TIME, October 30, 2017, p. 11.
987 Harry W. Hazard, The Arabian Peninsula, (Garden City, N.Y.: Nelson Doubleday, Inc., 1959), p. 10.
988 Roy Lebkicher, George Rentz, Max Steineke, Aramco Handbook, (Arabian American Oil Company, 1960), p. 271.
989 "The Shah [of Iran] agreed to the proclamation of independence by Bahrein in return for Iranian occupation of a number of strategic islands defending the Strait of Hormuz (the two Tunbs and half of Abu Musa)." – Fereydoun Hoveyda, The Fall of the Shah, (New York: Wyndham Books, 1979), p. 76.
990 Mohamed Heikal, The Return of the Ayatollah, The Iranian Revolution from Mossadeq to Khomeini, (London: Andre Deutsch Ltd., 1981), p. 92

Al-Hasa. On the east coast of Arabia, due west from central Qatar is the area of al-Hasa, now usually called al-Ahsa. The name means the sound of water flowing underground. This is because at Hofuf, an oasis, and now the largest city in the region, ironically in this very arid region, are some of the greatest artesian fresh-water springs in the world. The largest spring discharges "22,500 gallons per minute. ... The flows of three other springs in the Hofuf oasis have been estimated at 20,000 gallons per minute each. Five other springs show an estimated discharge of 800 to 4,000 gallons per minute. The Hofuf oasis, by far the largest in Saudi Arabia, has an average elevation of 500 feet."[991]

It is in al-Hasa that crude oil was first discovered in Arabia. Loading of oil tankers takes place on the nearby Arabian ports of Dammam and Ras Tanura. When Saddam Hussein's army invaded and occupied Kuwait at the beginning of August 1990, "the Bush administration interpreted the menacing southward advance of Iraq's elite shock troops as a direct threat to Saudi Arabia, and above all to the oilfields in Saudi Arabia's Eastern Province. The greatest oil production area on the planet was centered around the Eastern Province city of Dhahran, just sixty miles south of the Kuwaiti border."[992] Another unique aspect of al-Hasa is the fact that in it lives the largest concentration of Shia Muslims in all of Arabia.

V. The South Coast

On the west end of the south coast of the Arabian Peninsula is the country of Yemen while on the east end is that of Oman.

A brief look at northern Oman. Oman's principal port is Muscat, the capital of Oman. Together with Muttrah, its northern suburb, Muscat is also Oman's largest city. "The outstanding physical feature in [northern] Oman is [the] ... Hajar [mountain] range which extends south-east in a great crescent roughly paralleling the coast to terminate in the vicinity of Ras al-Hadd, the point of land dividing the Gulf of Oman from the Indian Ocean."[993] Between the Hajar range of mountains and the sea is a coastal plain known as al-Batinah. The al Batinah coastal plain is called the "date garden of Arabia."[994] The principal town of the coastal plain is the seaport town of Sohar [also spelled Suhar], 140 miles northwest of Muscat. There are only eight gorges which pierce the mountain range. They "drain the seaward slope of these mountains (Western Hajar) [and] are sufficiently passable to permit communication and trade between al-Batinah and the interior."[995]

Southern Oman. The southern part of Oman is known as Dhofar. The name Dhofar is probably a corruption of the name "Sephar" in Genesis 10:30. "The

---

991 K. S. Twitchell, Saudi Arabia With an Account of the Development of its Natural Resources, (Princeton, New Jersey: Princeton University Press, 1947). p. 46.
992 Christian Alfonsi, Circle in the Sand, Why we Went Back to Iraq, (New York: Doubleday, 2006), pp. 57-58.
993 Wendell Phillips, Unknown Oman, (New York: David McKay Company, Inc., 1966), p. 39.
994 Wendell Phillips, Unknown Oman, (New York: David McKay Company, Inc., 1966), p. 41.
995 Wendell Phillips, Unknown Oman, (New York: David McKay Company, Inc., 1966), p. 41.

prosperity of Dhofar through the ages has been based on its unexcelled incense [frankincense] which, in fact, formed the major economic pillar of all ancient South Arabia. The steppe region (*najd*) directly north of the Qara mountains, possessing the necessary special combination of geographic and climatic factors, has since ancient times been the major source of these fabulous aromatic riches."[996] About eighty miles east of the Yemen border in Oman is the coastal town of Salalah. The coast has been described as "barren, bare, unsightly, unadorned … from Salalah eastward to Sur, a distance of five hundred miles."[997]

A Brief Look at Yemen

Hodeida, (now called Al Hudaydah) and Mocha, the famous coffee port, are Yemen's two principal ports on the Red Sea. "Almost all the coffee grown in the Yemen mountains was exported through Mocha from the 17th to early 19th centuries."[998] The name of the port means coffee. "For two centuries, the port of Mocha in the Tihamah supplied the world with *Arabica*–Arabian coffee. Maritime commerce in the Red Sea and the Indian Ocean was protected by the Muslim empires, and merchant ships from Surat in Gujarat (India) called regularly at Mocha. The coffee boom ended when Dutch merchants took the African bean to Java and Suriname, and within a few years cornered the European coffee market. Mocha's fortunes endured until the mid-eighteenth century, at which point it started a decline that a century later would reduce the city to ruins."[999] That is still its prevailing condition. In 2015 a Yemeni American seeking to flee from Yemen because of the Saudi bombing and the Houthi rebellion, in desperation made his way to the port of Mocha. He reported that "the road into town was potholed and surrounded by crumbling stone dwellings, many abandoned. The fabled port had once been one of the most important in the world, but all that remained were some fifteen thousand impoverished souls. The city had fallen on hard times."[1000]

Bernard Lewis tells us that the coffee plant was a native of Ethiopia. He wrote, "The journey from a coffee bean to a cup of coffee is long and complex and one can only marvel at the ingenuity of the people of Ethiopia who first brought this gift to humanity. The earliest documentation is from the beginning of the fifteenth century, when we hear about coffee being imported from Ethiopia to Yemen. From the southern end of the Red Sea it spread northward along both sides, reaching Egypt, Syria and Turkey, where it was discovered, with delight, by Western travelers."[1001]

---

996 Wendell Phillips, Unknown Oman, (New York: David McKay Company, Inc., 1966), p. 179.
997 Wendell Phillips, Unknown Oman, (New York: David McKay Company, Inc., 1966), p. 205.
998 Harold Ingrams, The Yemen Imams, Rulers & Revolutions, (London: John Murray, 1963), p. 11.
999 Camille Pecastaing, Jihad in the Arabian Sea, (Stanford, CA: Hoover Institution Press, 2011), p. 38.
1000 Dave Eggers, The Monk of Mokha, (New York: Alfred A. Knopf, 2018), p. 277.
1001 Bernard Lewis, Notes on a Century: Reflections of a Middle East Historian, (New York: Viking, 2012), pp. 97-98.

But, "When the British captured Aden in 1839 and gave it peace and good order, [the port of] Mocha died."[1002] The magnificent Port of Aden became Yemen's principal port on the Gulf of Aden. "We learn from Ezekiel [27:23] that Aden [spelled Eden] was flourishing in 600 B.C."[1003]

In the 1960s the Port of Al Hudaydah was modernized by the Russians while the Chinese connected the port by an asphalt road to San'a, the capital. America, in the same time frame, built a road from the port of "Mocha, the old and [then] almost disused coffee-export port, to Taiz and then through the high mountains up to San'a where it would meet the Chinese road."[1004] "The American road, completed late in 1965 at a total cost of $22 million, was a remarkable engineering achievement. Linking the capital, San'a, to the old diplomatic capital at Taiz and the port of Mocha, with a spur to the South Arabian border, it is profoundly affecting the life of the country."[1005] The distance from Mocha through Taiz to San'a is 313 miles.

The Saudi Arabian Red Sea coastal plain, called Tihama/Tehama, also continues south along the Yemen Red Sea coast for 260 more miles. "The [Yemeni] Tihama is a narrow, hot, humid, semi-desert, and almost waterless strip that extends the entire seacoast from Maydi on the northern frontier with Saudi Arabia to the Bab-el-Mandeb at the country's southern limits and occupies approximately 10 percent of the country. Seven major wadis flow eastward from their sources in the central-western slopes of the interior highlands and permit limited agricultural activity."[1006]

On the southwestern coast of Yemen, "a low maritime plain, similar to the Tehama of the western coast, extends for some 200 miles east of the Straits of Bab-el-Mandeb, backed by mountains rising to 7000 ft. or more; farther east the elevation of the highland decreases steadily, and in the Hadramaut/Hadhramaut/Hadramawt, north of Mukalla, does not much exceed 4000 ft. The mountain chain, too, is less distinctly marked, and becomes little more than the seaward escarpment of the plateau which intervenes between the coast and the Hadramaut/Hadhramaut/Hadramawt valley. This valley runs east and west for a distance of nearly 500 m. from the eastern slopes of the Yemen highlands to its mouth on the Mahra coast near Sihut."[1007]

VI. Cities & Towns & Sites Important in the Rise of Islam

Adulis. It was the ancient seaport of Aksum/Axum, located just south of the present-day port of Massawa, in the Gulf of Zula, an inlet of the Red Sea, now

---

1002 Harold Ingrams, The Yemen Imams, Rulers & Revolutions, (London: John Murray, 1963), p. 16.
1003 Harold Ingrams, The Yemen Imams, Rulers & Revolutions, (London: John Murray, 1963), p. 15.
1004 Dana Adams Schmidt, Yemen, The Unknown War, (New York: Hold, Rinehart and Winston, 1968), p. 41.
1005 Dana Adams Schmidt, Yemen, The Unknown War, (New York: Hold, Rinehart and Winston, 1968), p. 288.
1006 G.W.T., *Arabia*, The Encyclopaedia Britannica, (New York: The Encyclopaedia Britannica Company, 1910), Vol. II, p. 259.
1007 G.W.T., *Arabia*, The Encyclopaedia Britannica, (New York: The Encyclopaedia Britannica Company, 1910), Vol. II, p. 259.

in Eritrea. (See the comments on Adulis in Chapter 2 under "War And The Rise of Islam.")

Mecca. "Located halfway down Saudi Arabia's west coast, forty-eight miles inland from the Red Sea, Mecca was a convenient stopping place for the fabled camel caravans that transported goods from India and Central Africa to Egypt and Palestine, where they were fed into the pipeline of trade to the Mediterranean and the crumbling Roman Empire. The merchants of Mecca thrived from this trade. To promote business, they formed joint stock companies and dominated an annual trade fair at Ukaz, near Mecca. In stark contrast to the austere life of the desert people around Mecca, Ukaz brought together hundreds of merchants, actors, gamblers, prostitutes, and poets in a great festival of vice for the sole purpose of promoting business."[1008]

"When trade went through the Hijaz, by the hands of the Yemeni or Sabaean Arabs, Mecca already had some note as a 'station' or halt upon the route and is so mentioned by Strabo, but its real importance dates from the time when the Hijazi Arabs themselves became carriers and made Mecca their business headquarters. ... Its selection as a halt in the first place seems to have been due to no other reason than the presence of a well known as Zem-zem, a very inferior supply of brackish water, round which the town grew up, whilst its selection as headquarters was mainly due to its being the place where the routes to Yemen, to Syria, and the north, and the cross-route to Gerrha, connected."[1009]

Medina. Before Muhammad's arrival, it was known as Yathrib/Yatrib. The citizens renamed their city in Muhammad's honor calling it, Medina-un Nabi, The City of the Prophet. It was, in addition to Arabs, home of a colony of Jewish agriculturists and artisans.

Taif. It was known as "the Garden of the Hijaz."[1010] It is located about 40 miles east-southeast of Mecca. Its elevation is just over 5000 ft. Now the unofficial summer capital of Saudi Arabia. In 619 Muhammad fled to Taif to escape the ridicule and taunts of Mecca but was rejected in this city as well.

Najran. "The most important Christian settlement in Arabia proper was the town of Najran, on the northern border of Yaman [Yemen]. This town was on the trade route from the East which came up through South Arabia and then ran parallel with the coast through Mecca to Syria. The Christian community in Najran was probably connected with this trade route, and may be regarded as an outpost of Syrian civilization. Other places in Yaman, and even in Hadhramaut/Hadramaut/Hadramawt, had Christian communities. Muslim historians tell of a great church at San'a, a city about halfway between Najran and Aden.

1008 Sandra Mackey, <u>The Saudis, Inside the Desert Kingdom</u> (Boston: Houghton Mifflin Company, 1987), p. 64.
1009 De Lacy O'Leary, <u>History of Arabia Before Muhammad</u>, (Lahore, Pakistan: Alliance Publishers, 1989), pp. 182-183.
1010 Martin Lings, <u>Muhammad, His Life Based on the Earliest Sources</u>, (New York: Inner Traditions International, Ltd., 1983), p. 15.

The capital of the Himyarite kingdom had been moved to San'a from Ma'rib, probably in the fifth century when the great dyke of Ma'rib burst."[1011]

"The caravan traffic and perfumes and spices from the vicinity of Aden is normally assumed to have gone northward to the city of Najran and then to have swung westward over toward Bisha to avoid the inhospitable lava fields that lay above Najran. Mecca was a natural destination in this northward movement, and pilgrims and traders would easily have found Ukaz and Ta'if appropriate way stations to the city because of their regular cycle of fairs."[1012]

A war between Yemen and Saudi Arabia ended on May 20, 1934 when "a 'Treaty of Muslim Friendship and Arab Fraternity' was concluded between Yemen and Saudi Arabia, under the watchful eye of a conciliation committee of representatives from other Arab states. The treaty was called the Treaty of Taif, after the village south of al Hudaydah where it was signed. According to its terms, the disputed areas of Najranand 'Asir were to become fully incorporated sections of the Saudi Arabian Kingdom."[1013]

Badr. A place about 85 miles southwest of Medina near the Red Sea coast. Because of springs being there, it was a major caravan watering stop between Mecca and Damascus. In 624 The Battle of Badr took place there in which 300 Muslim's under the personal generalship of Muhammad utterly defeated a 1000-man contingent sent from Mecca to protect a caravan which the Muslims had planned to plunder.

Mt. Uhud. About two miles from Medina, is the site of the famous Battle of Mount Uhud. In 625 A.D. Mecca sent an army to defeat Muhammad and take vengeance for the humiliating defeat at Badr. Muhammad was badly wounded but not killed. He survived and led his forces victoriously in 627 A.D. at the Battle of the Trench at Medina.

Kheibar/Khaibar. Home of many Jews who were suppressed by Muhammad and later expelled by Caliph Omar. Their expulsion is vividly and menacingly remembered by Muslims to this day. There was "a bitter property dispute over the date-palm orchards of Fardak in the oasis of Khaibar, some 90 miles north of Medina, supposedly gifted to Fatimah after they were seized from their Jewish cultivators by Muhammad's warriors in 629. ... On July 20, 2014, Parisian demonstrators against Israel shouted, 'Remember Khaibar' outside the Val d'Oise Synagogue in Sarcelles."[1014] "At Khaibar there are dams, three hundred feet long and thirty feet high, with hollowed stone conduit pipes called *barbakh*—made, it is said, by the old Jews. 'Yahoud Khaibar' is still a phrase in

---

1011 Laurence E. Browne, The Eclipse of Christianity in Asia From the time of Muhammad till the Fourteenth Century, (Cambridge: The University Press, 1933), p. 11.
1012 G. W. Bowersock, The Crucible of Islam, (Cambridge, Mass.: Harvard University Press, 2017), p. 49.
1013 Manfred W. Wenner, Modern Yemen 1918–1966, (Baltimore: The Johns Hopkins Press, 1967), p. 146.
1014 Edward N. Luttwak, *Omens From the Seventh Century*, Hoover Digest, Winter 2015, p. 47.

the current usage of the Arabs: 'Jews from Khaibar,' by which they mean a lost people or a man of unknown origin."[1015]

Mota. [Mu'tah] (See Chapter 7 under "Two Exploratory Expeditions.") It is a village "which still exists under the same name,"[1016] in what is now Jordan, "east of the southern extremity of the Dead Sea."[1017] Here in September 629 A.D. the Muslims made their first attack on Byzantine territory. The Muslims were badly defeated, the remnant being led back to Medina by Khalid ibn al Waleed who later became one of Islam's greatest and most successful generals.

1015 Gerald De Gaurly, Arabia Phoenix, (London: George G. Harrap & Co. Ltd., 1947), p. 118.
1016 John Bagot Glubb, The Life and Time of Muhammad, (New York: Stein & Day Publishers, 1970), p. 291.
1017 Philip K. Hitti, History of the Arabs, (New York: Macmillan, 1968), p. 147.

APPENDIX B

The Armenian Genocide

In its waning years, the Ottoman Empire emphatically and persistently refused to acknowledge the validity of the genocide indictment repeatedly brought against it. Similarly, the present Republic of Turkey, the Ottoman-successor state, vehemently refuses that indictment to this very moment.[1018] From the following statement by Adolf Hitler, it would seem that the persistent Turkish refusal to accept the indictment of genocide had all but quelled the accusation.

In November 1942, shortly after his deportation by the German Third Reich following decades of reporting from that strategic European country, renowned journalist, Louis P. Lochner (1887–1975)[1019] published a book entitled, <u>What About Germany?</u> In it he tells us that one week before Germany launched its invasion of Poland (September 30, 1939) one of his most reliable and trusted informants gave him a manuscript copy of a speech Hitler had made at Obersalzberg on August 22, 1939 to his Supreme Commanders and Commanding Generals. Hitler told them, "Our war aim does not consist in reaching certain lines, but in the physical destruction of the enemy. Accordingly, I have placed my death-head formations [Death's Head refers to special SS military formations.] in readiness—for the present only in the East—with orders to them to send to death mercilessly and without compassion, men, women, and children of Polish derivation and language. Only thus shall we gain the living space (*Lebensraum*) which we need. <u>Who, after all, speaks today of the annihilation of the Armenians</u>?"[1020] (Underlining mine.)

1018 That reminds one of the United Nations denial of genocide in Darfur province of Sudan. "Kofi Annan managed to persuade the UN to set up a committee to look into what's going on in Darfur. Eventually, they reported back that it's not genocide. That's great news, isn't it? Because if it had been genocide, that would have been very, very serious. As yet another Kofi Annan-appointed UN committee boldly declared a year ago: 'Genocide anywhere is a threat to the security of all and should never be tolerated.' So thank goodness what's going on in Sudan isn't genocide. Instead, it's just 100,000 corpses who all happen to be from the same ethnic group—which means the UN can go on tolerating it until everyone's dead, and none of the multilateral compassion types have to worry their pretty heads about it." – Mark Steyn, *America and the United Nations*, Imprimis, February 2006. Vol. 35, No. 2, p. 6.

1019 In 1924, the well known journalist, Louis P. Lochner (1887–1975), "joined the Berlin staff of the Associated Press. Fluent in German, Lochner quickly established contacts within the Weimar—and later the Nazi—governments, and became the Associated Press' Berlin bureau chief in 1928. ... Lochner interviewed Hitler in 1930 and 1933, and accompanied the Fuehrer to visit Mussolini in 1938. Accepted by the suspicious Nazis as a trustworthy man, they allowed Lochner to accompany the German Army into Poland, the Lowland countries, France, Yugoslavia and Greece. ... In 1939 he received the Pulitzer Prize for distinguished service as a foreign correspondent. ... Lochner made his way into the private quarters of Nazi headquarters as well as accompanied Hitler in a variety of settings." [http://Worcestershire/louislochner.html]

On December 11, 1941 the United States declared war on Germany. All the U.S. correspondents were interned in Jeschke's Grand Hotel in the German town of Bad Nauheim. In May 1942 Lochner along with all other U.S. correspondents were sent by train to Lisbon where on May 12th they sailed for New York, arriving on May 22, 1942. In November 1942 Lochner published <u>What About Germany</u>? (Publisher: Dodd, Mead & Company).

Rather than calling the Ottoman Empire's annihilation policy toward the Christian Armenian people a role model for Hitler, some would broaden the analysis of that policy and call it "the template for most of the genocide that followed in the twentieth century."[1021]

While nothing can ameliorate or justify what the Turks did against the Armenians, it is possible to understand a bit of the psychological impetus which had been building up in the Turkish psyche. The force was like that of accumulated flood waters behind a dam just before the dam collapses. "Since the beginning of the century the country had never known anything but defeat and retreat, and they had grown used but not reconciled to the demoralizing spectacle of the refugees streaming back after nearly every battle. To take only one case out of millions, Mustafa Kemal's mother had been forced to decamp from Macedonia, and he found her penniless in Constantinople. Salonika, the city in which he had grown up and which he regarded as Turkish by right, was now Greek. ... Nor was it only the Greeks, the Armenians and the other foreign minorities who were witnessing the Turk's humiliation; the great Christian powers had established sovereign prerogatives in Turkey. They controlled her foreign trade, they administered her armed services and the police, they granted loans to the bankrupt government according to their judgment of its behavior, and their own nationals residing in Turkey were above the law: under the system of capitulations Western Europeans could only be tried for offenses in their own courts. The obvious implication was that the Turk was not only incompetent to manage his own affairs, he was not yet civilized."[1022]

The Turkish government had sided with Germany in World War I. To take Turkey out of the war, forcing Germany to seek an armistice, Britain, in the early phases of the war against Turkey, in an offensive which came to be known as the Gallipoli Campaign, tried to force a naval flotilla through the Dardanelles and into the Sea of Marmara to confront Istanbul, capital of Turkey. On March 18, 1915, Turkish gunfire and mines succeeded in sinking two old British battleships just before they could break into the open water of the Sea of Marmara. That naval success put the Turkish leaders on an emotional high. Pent up resentments against Christians and the West broke forth in a torrent like a flood from a broken dam.

1020 Louis P. Lochner, <u>What About Germany?</u>, (New York: Dodd, Mead & Company, 1942), p. 2. The Turkish propagandist, Kamuran Gurun in his <u>The Armenian File, The Myth of Innocence Exposed</u> on page viii asserts that "The only thing that is certain is that during the meeting held on 22 August 1939, Hitler did not utter the words attributed to him and no document containing this alleged statement was submitted to the court." Robert Fisk in his <u>The Great War for Civilisation</u> (p. 330) assures us that Gurun has not told the truth. Fisk wrote: "There have been repeated attempts—especially by Turkey—to pretend that Hitler never made such a remark but Dadrian has found five separate versions of the question, four of them identical; two were filed in German High Command archives. Furthermore, German historians have discovered that Hitler made an almost identical comment in a 1931 interview with a German newspaper editor, saying that 'everywhere people are awaiting a new world order. We intend to introduce a great resettlement policy ... remember the extermination of the Armenians.'"

1021 Peter Balakian, <u>The Burning Tigris, The Armenian Genocide and America's Response</u>, (New York: Harper Collins, 2003), p. xiv.

1022 Alan Moorehead, <u>Gallipoli</u>, (New York: Ballantine Books, 1956), p. 82.

The Ottoman Turkish regime barely allowed even a month to go by. They "chose 24 April 1915—forever afterwards commemorated as the day of Armenian genocide—to arrest and murder all the leading Armenian intellectuals of Constantinople. They followed this pogrom with the wholesale and systematic destruction of the Armenian race in Turkey. ... In every town and village, all Armenian men were led away by the police, executed by firing squad and thrown into mass graves or rivers."[1023]

Overwhelming Evidence

The evidence that there was widespread annihilation of the Armenian people carried out by the Ottoman government is beyond any reasonable question. "The proof, [is] based on a wide variety of sources from the period, that a comprehensive mass extermination of the civilian population in various parts of Turkey (and certainly not only in the battle zones) was carried out, on the order of Turkish authorities in Constantinople. While certain facts and details can be legitimately debated, and some of the Armenian claims about the genocide can be questioned, the historical sources create an unequivocal and unshakable picture (unless there has been some fantastic conspiracy to invent thousands of documents and reports from various sources in differing countries, including the United States, which was neutral, and Germany and Austria, which were allies of the Turks, and to fabricate hundreds of newspaper items in numerous countries.)"[1024]

The central fact of the Ottoman attempt to annihilate the Armenian people is confirmed by many diplomatic reports. For example, Henry Morgenthau, United States Ambassador to Turkey in a letter to the Secretary of State dated July 16, 1915 wrote, "Deportation of and excesses against peaceful Armenians is increasing and from harrowing reports of eye witnesses it appears that a campaign of race extermination is in progress under a pretext of reprisal against rebellion."[1025]

Excuses, Excuses

Was the Turkish genocide perpetrated on the Armenians simply a senseless blind rage generated by an insatiable Turkish bloodlust, or were there reasons of state which could have made the vast butchery seem in any way, even remotely, reasonable to Turkish patriots? From a xenophobic Turkish-nationalist point of view, there are some possibilities.

<u>First</u>, the Ottoman fortunes had declined disastrously on their western frontier. Their second defeat at the gates of Vienna in 1683 was a decisive watershed. Only three years later, "in 1686 the Ottomans were driven from their 145-year

---
1023 Robert Fisk, <u>The Great War for Civilisation, The Conquest of the Middle East</u>, (New York: Alfred A. Knopf, 2005), p. 321.
1024 Yair Auron, <u>The Banality of Denial, Israel and the Armenian Genocide</u>, (London: Transaction Publishers, 2004), p. 9.
1025 Peter Balakian, <u>The Burning Tigris</u>, (New York: Harper Collins Publishers, 2003), from reproduction on the tenth page of photos and reproductions following p. 236.

occupation of the Hungarian city of Buda; in 1699, by the Treaty of Karlowitz, the Sultan was forced to relinquish to various European powers Ottoman territorial holdings in Hungary, Poland, Croatia, Slavonia, Dalmatia and the Greek Peloponnesus. Armies that the Ottomans had once despised were beginning to inflict upon them defeat after defeat and whittle away their empire."[1026] The majority of the people inhabiting all these areas which had slipped out of Ottoman control were followers of Christ of one kind or another.

Secondly, as Ottoman dynamism began to wane, the eastern regions of their empire were seriously encroached upon by the forces of Tsarist Russia, then known as the eastern colossus. "Russia possessed an open, 'crumbling' frontier to the south, so that during the early 1770s great advances were made at Turkey's expense."[1027] In the Caucasus the Russians occupied Turkish territory inhabited by Armenian followers of Christ. Following their defeat of Napoleon in 1812 at Moscow, the Russians had become even more of a major player on the world stage.

Changing Status, Changing Environment

"Most tragic was the case of the Armenians, who at the beginning of the nineteenth century were still known as the *Millet-i Sadika*, the loyal community, and were described by a well-informed French visitor as the minority group most loyal to the Ottoman Empire and most trusted by the Turks. The change began with the Russian conquest of the Caucasus in the first quarter of the nineteenth century, and the creation of a Russian Armenia on the eastern border of Turkey, where the Armenian Church was established and recognized and where Armenian governors and generals ruled provinces and commanded armies. A stir of hope passed through Turkish Armenia, where, combining with the new national and liberal ideas emanating from the West, it gave rise to an ardent and active Armenian nationalist movement, seeking to restore an independent Armenia."[1028]

By the Treaty of San Stefano, between Russia and the Ottoman Empire (Ratified March 23, 1878) the areas of victorious Russian incursion both in the Balkans and in eastern Armenia had been ceded to Russia. For the Armenian followers of Christ, Russian rule was much more benign than that which they had experienced under the Ottomans. From an old Armenian adage which says, "Better perish physically in Turkey than spiritually in Russia,"[1029] it is clear that Russian benignity referred to the Armenian people's physical circumstances.

1026 Desmond Stewart, Early Islam, (New York: Time Incorporated, 1967), p. 167.
1027 Paul Kennedy, The Rise And Fall of the Great Powers, Economic Change and Military Conflict from 1500 to 2000, (New York: Random House,1987), p. 119.
1028 Bernard Lewis, The Emergence of Modern Turkey, (London: Oxford University Press, 1966), p. 350.
1029 Franz Werfel, The Forty Days of Musa Dagh, (New York: Carroll & Graf Publishers, 2002), p. 84.

However, the Turks were angry over the losses imposed upon them by the Treaty of San Stefano and "appealed to the British to intervene. Lord Salisbury, Disraeli's foreign secretary, was sympathetic to the sultan's request and demanded that Russo-Turkish issues be settled by the European powers. In Salisbury's mind the Russian gains were a threat to Europe and in particular to British interests in the Near East and Asia."[1030] Consequently, by article 61 of the Treaty of Berlin enacted at the Berlin Congress (June 13–July 13, 1878) two of the Armenian provinces were returned to the Ottoman Empire but with no provisions for the protection of the Armenian followers of Christ following the transfer. Conditions for the Armenians grew much more stringent and difficult.

Armenians, Focus of Concern

"For the Turks, the Armenian movement was the deadliest of all threats. From the conquered lands of the Serbs, Bulgars, Albanians, and Greeks [all in the Balkans], they could, however reluctantly, withdraw, abandoning distant provinces and bringing the Imperial frontier nearer home. But the Armenians, stretching across Turkey-in-Asia from the Caucasian frontier to the Mediterranean coast, lay in the very heart of the Turkish homeland—and to renounce these lands would have meant not the truncation, but the dissolution of the Turkish state. Turkish and Armenian villages, inextricably mixed, had for centuries lived in neighborly association. Now a desperate struggle between them began—a struggle between two nations for the possession of a single homeland, that ended with the terrible holocaust of 1915, when a million and [a] half Armenians perished."[1031]

While Professor Lewis clearly called the Armenian genocide a "terrible holocaust" in the quotation just given, subsequently, he said, "while the Armenians suffered appalling losses, the comparison with the holocaust was misleading"[1032] His repudiation of the term holocaust to describe the mass killing of the Armenians is based on an indictment, which is extremely controversial at best, that the Armenians had risen in revolt against Ottoman Turkey.

The Armenians had lived with such impeccable patience and loyalty for centuries under the severe disabilities of those with *dhimmi* status (See Glossary.) that they were known as *Millet-i Sadika*, (the trustworthy nation). Now because of Ottoman governmental panic they were stripped of their tolerated status as *ahl al-kitab* (People of the Book i.e. people with a revealed religion) and were indiscriminately and en masse classified as *kafirs* (blasphemers) and unbelievers. Additionally, they were all now alleged to be traitors, plotting against the state. It was a sweeping indictment that included absolutely everyone: men, boys, the aged, pregnant women, the infirm, children and infants!

1030 Peter Balakian, The Burning Tigris, (New York: Harper Collins Publishers, 2003), p. 39.
1031 Bernard Lewis, The Emergence of Modern Turkey, (London: Oxford University Press, 1966), p. 350.
1032 Bernard Lewis, Notes On A Century: Reflections Of A Middle East Historian, (New York: Viking, 2012), p. 287.

To Sultan Abdul Hamid II it had become obvious that, "if the Armenians were to follow the example of the Balkan Christians, there might be nothing left of the empire except a truncated Turkish state in western Anatolia."[1033] Consequently, "the sultan had decided that the only way to eliminate the Armenian Question [part of the larger Eastern Question] was to eliminate the Armenians themselves."[1034] Consequently, "He formed tribal regiments among the Kurds, on the lines of the Russian Cossacks. They were a means of co-opting and bribing unruly Kurdish tribes, and they helped keep Armenian nationalists at bay."[1035]

Preliminary Pogrom

"Enraged that the Armenian Question had become an international issue, the sultan by 1890 had created the *Hamidiye*, a well-trained force made up of Kurds whom he armed and had clothed in distinctive uniforms. *Hamidiye* regiments were responsible only to the sultan and were fanatically loyal to him. In forming the *Hamidiye* (literally, 'belonging to Hamid') regiments the sultan could both control the unruly Kurds and at the same time use them to deal with the Armenians as he wished. The lands over which the Kurdish nomads roamed bordered on and often dovetailed with those of the Armenian peasants, whom the Kurds resented for their relative prosperity."[1036]

"By the end of 1896 the sultan's campaign had taken the lives of about two hundred thousand Armenians—approximately one hundred thousand killed by direct massacre and the rest dying of disease and famine."[1037] But that massacre was only a token of what was to come in 1915!

By Ottoman Turkish analysis, there was <u>a third reason for unleashing destruction on the Armenians</u>. If the eastern areas were to slip away permanently, as the western ones had, rich trade routes would be lost further endangering the economic viability of the empire. One of those trade routes was, "the lucrative overland trade route from [the Black Sea port of] Trebizond over Alashkert and Byazit to Persia and beyond."[1038]

Armenian History

The Armenians, whose language is Indo-European, are an ancient people. The first surviving written record of them was made by the famous Persian emperor Darius I (see Appendix H) in his amazing inscription carved in three languages

---

1033 Richard G. Hovannisian, *The Armenian Question in the Ottoman Empire, 1876–1914*, <u>The Armenian People From Ancient to Modern Times</u>, ed. Richard G. Hovannisian (New York: St. Martin's Press, 2004), Vol. II, p. 206.
1034 Peter Balakian, <u>The Burning Tigris</u>, (New York: Harper Collins Publishers, 2003), p. 5.
1035 Andrew Mango, <u>Ataturk The Biography of the Founder of Modern Turkey</u>, (New York: The Overlook Press, 2000), p. 14.
1036 Peter Balakian, <u>The Burning Tigris</u>, (New York: Harper Collins Publishers, 2003), pp. 43-44.
1037 Peter Balakian, <u>The Burning Tigris</u>, (New York: Harper Collins Publishers, 2003), p. 5.
1038 Richard G. Hovannisian, *The Armenian Question in the Ottoman Empire, 1876–1914*, <u>The Armenian People From Ancient to Modern Times</u>, ed. Richard G. Hovannisian (New York: St. Martin's Press, 2004), Vol. II, p. 209.

on a sheer perpendicular rock cliff some 200 feet above ground level at Behistun, in western Iran.[1039]

In Ottoman times the Armenians inhabited a huge swath of Turkish territory which stretched diagonally from Tarsus/Adana in the west to an eastern boundary just short of Baku on the Caspian Sea. Between the Armenians and the Caspian Sea the Azeri people occupied the area known as Azerbaijan. Historically, Armenia has been divided between Greater Armenia to the east of the Euphrates and Lesser Armenia west of that river. "In the Ottoman Empire, Turkish Armenia was comprised of six large provinces called *vilayets*, divided into *sanjaks* (counties) and *kazas* (districts)."[1040] The phrase, "Turkish Armenia" is used to distinguish those Armenians living in the Ottoman Empire from those living in northern Iran, in southern Russia and in Israel.

Beyond doubt, the Armenians are one of the first people outside Palestine itself to have accepted Jesus Christ as incarnate deity, the crucified, risen Savior of the world. There are differing accounts of how the gospel first reached Armenia. One very widely accepted legendary account tells us that the Armenian king Abgar, a sufferer from leprosy, having heard of Jesus, sent a messenger with an appeal to him to come and exercise his power to heal. According to the account Jesus sent a return message in which he said, "When I have been taken up, I will send to you one my disciples to heal your suffering, and give life to you and those with you." Accordingly, "After the Lord's Passion and Ascension, His promise was fulfilled by the Apostles, who sent Addai, one of the seventy-two elect, on a missionary assignment to Edessa [Abgar's capital]."[1041] The conversion of the Armenian people was, for the most part, from Zoroastrianism to Christianity.

With the passage of time, in many cases, personal faith in Jesus as Savior and Lord had been replaced by church tradition and ritual. On average, congregational Christian life was far from Biblical standards. In many cases, "simple Christian worship developed into elaborate, stately ceremonies with all the outward trappings of the old Roman state religion."[1042] Yet, the Armenian followers of Christ were, on the whole, resolutely loyal to their commitment to Jesus. "During the time of the Seljuk invasions, Armenian Islamization seems to have been limited to those obliged to convert to save their lives and to the tens of thousands of Armenian women and children forcibly removed from their

---

1039 "In the trilingual Behistun inscription of the late sixth century, the Semitic Akkadian and Elamite versions still use the name 'Urastu' for the land called 'Armina' in the Indo-European Old Persian text. ... The name 'Armina' given to the entire region in the Old Persian version of the Behistun inscription suggests that these 'Armenoi' were gradually gaining a dominant position by the end of the sixth century B.C. and that this preponderance had been accepted by the Persian authorities." – Nina Garsoian, *The Emergence of Armenia*, The Armenian People From Ancient to Modern Times, ed. Richard G. Hovannisian (New York: St. Martin's Press, 2004), Vol. I, p. 40-41.

1040 Robert H. Hewsen, *The Geography of Armenia*, The Armenian People From Ancient to Modern Times, ed. Richard G. Hovannisian (New York: St. Martin's Press, 2004), Vol. I, p. 16.

1041 Aziz S. Atiya, A History of Eastern Christianity, (Millwood, NY: Kraus Reprint, 1980), pp. 244-245.

1042 Imanda Kardesh, Where Satan's Seat Is, (London: E.M.A. Literature Dept., 1978), p. 5.

homes and sold on the slave markets of the Middle East."[1043] (On the Seljuks, see Appendix H, division V, section C, The Seljuk Turkish Period of Iran's Muslim Era.)

The emphasis on tradition and ritual among the Armenian followers of Christ was partly due to not having access to Scripture. "The Patriarch of Constantinople, Cyril Lucaris (1572–1638) ... had the Bible translated into the common language of the people and began plans to reform the Church after the pattern of the Reformation Churches in Europe. The Catholic Jesuit priests learned of his intentions, however, and accused him to the sultan Murad of treason. Murad had Lucaris strangled by the Janissaries and his body thrown into the sea."[1044]

Multiple Denials

One of the specious arguments which the present-day government of Turkey presents to absolve both the Ottomans and themselves of guilt in the genocide of the Armenian people was recently renewed by a professor of international relations at Ankara's Bilkent University. He asserts that, "when the Armenian diaspora ... tries to blame today's Turks for massacres back in 1915, the Israeli Turks [He refers to Jews of Turkish origin.] come to Turkey's defense, saying, entirely accurately, that what happened then was the outcome of a civil war."[1045] The charge that the Armenians were waging a civil war, or for that matter, any kind of war against the Ottoman Empire is patently false. Obviously, his argument does not deny the genocide, it only tries to justify it!

Those who deny the reality of the Ottoman genocide perpetrated on the Armenian people often hold professional positions which give them the opportunity to know better than to persist in denial. An example is that of Justin A. McCarthy, a history professor at the University of Louisville. He recently said, "I think the Muslims and Armenians killed each other. I don't think there was a central government-directed genocide."[1046] If professor McCarthy would read the Official Proclamation Ordering the Deportation of the Armenians which was issued in June 1915 he could no longer hold the position he has espoused.[1047]

Section one of that Turkish Proclamation clearly says, "**all** Armenians are obliged to leave, within five days from the date of this proclamation, and by villages or quarters, under the escort of the gendarmery." That order not only obliged all men and boys to leave their homes but it included all women, all nursing mothers, all infants, all little children and all the aged and infirm. "A

1043 Robert Bedrosian, *Armenia During the Seljuk and Mongol Periods*, <u>The Armenian People From Ancient to Modern Times</u>, ed. Richard G. Hovannisian (New York: St. Martin's Press, 2004), Vol. I, p. 249.
1044 Imanda Kardesh, <u>Where Satan's Seat Is</u>, (London: E.M.A. Literature Dept., 1978), p. 18.
1045 Norman Stone, *'In Turkey, With Turkey'*, <u>The Wall Street Journal</u>, November 24, 2003.
1046 Randal C. Archibold, *Armenian Furor Over PBS Plan For Debate*, <u>The New York Times</u>, February 25, 2006, p. A17.
1047 The Turkish text is given in full along with the translation by the United States State Department as Appendix B in Leslie A. Davis' *The Slaughterhouse Province*.

Appendix B

U.N. convention officially defines genocide as acts 'committed with intent to destroy, in whole or in part, a national, ethnical, racial or religious group.'"[1048]

With the vulnerabilities which those Armenians encountered who had been ordered to leave their homes, even an imbecile would have known that they were being driven to their deaths! "Banishment did not pass, like an earthquake, which always spares a certain number of people and houses. Banishment would go on till the last Armenian had either been slaughtered, died of hunger on the roads, of thirst in the desert, or been carried off by spotted typhus or cholera."[1049] The Armenians must have left the shelter of their homes, their families, their villages and neighborhoods, as Werfel put it, with a "deeply uneasy sense of the inevitable." The most horrible thing they faced was not death, often by slow and torturous means, but being completely dehumanized in the barbarous way they were driven to their deaths and after death their bodies becoming just manure along side the road, along the banks of the Euphrates or on the shores of Lake Goeljuk.[1050]

Another trite denial that present-day Turkish diplomats throw up in an attempt to exonerate their predecessors is to say the death of well over a million Armenians was not genocide but self-defense of the Ottoman Empire.[1051] After the American Consul, Leslie A. Davis,' arduous and heroic ride around Lake Goeljuk, now called Lake Hazar, he wrote, "That which took place around beautiful Lake Goeljuk in the summer of 1915 is almost inconceivable. Thousands and thousands of Armenians, mostly innocent and helpless women and children, were butchered on its shores and barbarously mutilated. It is hard for one living in a civilized country to believe that such things are possible; yet, as Lord Bryce has said, 'Things which we find scarcely credible excite little surprise in Turkey.'"[1052]

One of the reasons Turkey refuses to acknowledge the reality of the holocaust is because, "some Armenian nationalists say that if Turkey can be forced to

---

1048 Kara Scannell, *Turk-Armenian Fight Over WWI History Goes to a U.S. Court*, The Wall Street Journal, October 27, 2005, p. 1.
1049 Franz Werfel, The Forty Days of Musa Dagh, (New York: Carroll & Graf Publishers, 2002), p. 204. Please see the note at the end of Appendix B.
1050 "April 24 is the Day of Remembrance for the Armenian Holocaust of 1915–1918, when millions were either massacred or forced into exile by the Turks." – J.L. Barnett, *When the Vaults of the Armenians Open*, The Jerusalem Report, March 21, 2005, p. 21.
1051 For example Sukru Elekdag, a former Turkish ambassador to Washington and now a member of the opposition Republican People's Party said, "When I look at this from a legal and historical perspective, it's almost impossible to accuse the Ottomans of committing genocide. There had been a civil war. It was started by the Armenians. The events of 1915 are a typical case of revolt and betrayal." – Yigal Schleifer, *None Dared Call It Genocide*, The Jerusalem Report, May 2, 2005, p 27. If there had been civil war, why didn't the Ottomans distinguish between combatants and non-combatants? In the Vietnam war when, on March 16, 1968, the massacre of "hundreds of defenseless men, women and children" took place, it was found that "the Americans had not come under fire, nor were any Viet Cong found in My Lai." – The New York Times, February 11, 2006, p. B13 Investigations went all the way up to Major General Samuel Koster. Though he was judged not to have shown any intentional abrogation of responsibilities was stripped of a Distinguished Service Medal and demoted one rank, to brigadier general.
1052 Leslie A. Davis, The Slaughterhouse Province, An American Diplomat's Report on the Armenian Genocide, 1915–1917, (New Rochelle, New York: Aristide D. Caratzas, Publisher, 1989), p. 87.

concede that, their next step might be to claim reparations or demand the return of land once owned by Armenians."[1053]

Another reason Turkey resists acknowledgment of the Ottoman genocide perpetrated on the Armenians is that the, "defenders of the old order, including prosecutors, judges and officials with influence in the army and bureaucracy, fear that steps to open Turkish society will weaken national unity."[1054] Turkey has long prized national unity above civil liberties.

Rationalization and Expediency

But while Turkey denied what was happening, others rationalized it. A German councillor attached to the Turkish Foreign Office is said to have absolved himself and his government of responsibility when confronted by the well-known German missionary Dr. Lepsius by saying, "In this Armenian destiny, certain historical forces, too vast for us to control, may be working themselves out. … The Armenians are going under because of their geographical position. It's the fate of the weak, of the hated minority."[1055]

Shamefully, "U.S. administrations continue to fight annual attempts in Congress to pass a resolution condemning modern Turkey for the long-ago Armenian genocide."[1056] Courageously, "President Ronald Reagan publicly called the killings genocide, but his successors, including President Bush, in presidential proclamations condemning the massacres have avoided the term."[1057] In April 2005, "on the 90th anniversary of the killings, President Bush called them a 'terrible event' and a 'human tragedy.'"[1058]

The position of recent American administrations, both Democratic and Republican, comes, in part from threats by the Turkish government. "In 2000, for example, Ankara derailed an American congressional resolution calling the 1915 killings 'genocide' by threatening to cut access to military bases in the country."[1059] In addition to threats, "in the past, the Turkish government, an important ally of the United States in the region, has hired Washington lobbyists to help defeat attempts by Congress to pass resolutions condemning the killings as genocide."[1060]

1053 Stephen Kinzer, *Turkish Region Recalls Massacre of Armenians*, The News York Times, May 10, 2000. However the International Center for Transitional Justice conducted, "a legal analysis of the applicability of the Genocide Convention to the 1915 events. The ICTJ report concluded that the events could be defined as 'genocide,' but because the convention could not be applied retroactively, Turkey would not be liable for any reparations, something Ankara has long expressed fears about having to do if it accepted the Armenian claims." – Yigal Schleifer, *None Dared Call It Genocide*, The Jerusalem Report, May 2, 2005, p 27.
1054 Stephen Kinzer, *Courting Europe, Turkey Tries Some Soul-Cleansing*, The New York Times, December 4, 2005, p. 3.
1055 Franz Werfel, The Forty Days of Musa Dagh, (New York: Carroll & Graf Publishers, 2002), p. 535.
1056 Robert L. Pollock, *The Sick Man of Europe – Again*, The Wall Street Journal, February 16, 2005.
1057 Randal C. Archibold, *Armenian Furor Over PBS Plan For Debate*, The New York Times, February 25, 2006, p. A17.
1058 Kara Scannell, *Turk-Armenian Fight Over WWI History Goes to a U.S. Court*, The Wall Street Journal, October 27, 2005, p. A1.
1059 Belinda Cooper, *Turks Breach Wall of Silence on Deaths of Armenians in World War I*, The New York Times, March 6, 2004.
1060 Randal C. Archibold, *Armenian Furor Over PBS Plan For Debate*, The New York Times, February 25, 2006, p. A17.

The government of the Republic of Turkey not only threatens American administrations but American businesses as well in its unceasing effort to suppress knowledge of the Ottoman Turkish genocide perpetrated on the Armenian followers of Christ. In 1934, "the Turkish ambassador to the United States, Munir Ertegun, protested to the State Department about the purchase by MGM of the film rights to Franz Werfel's best-selling novel, *The Forty Days of Musa Dagh*. Werfel's novel, published in Germany in 1932, was based on a true story about the Armenians of Musa Dagh, who had heroically resisted the Turkish invasion of their mountain town in 1915. (Werfel, a Jew, was forced to flee Germany for his life in 1938, three years after the Nazis agreed to the Turkish government's request to ban *The Forty Days of Musa Dagh*.) Ambassador Ertegun threatened that if the film were released, Turkey would consider it a hostile act that would damage relations between the two countries and result in a Turkish boycott of American films. After a series of exchanges between the two governments, the State Department yielded to Turkey's demand and got MGM to drop the project."[1061]

Even more reprehensible than the persistent denials from American politicians are those from Jewish people. Of all people they should be most ready to show sympathy to another people suffering a genocide or holocaust.[1062] This truism notwithstanding, "the genocide issue has also involved American Jewish organizations, which have put their Washington connections behind Turkey's cause, as well as Israel, which has refrained from recognizing the Armenians' claims, in order not to jeopardize its strategic relations with Turkey."[1063]

Resistance

The Turkish government made an official proclamation entitled, *Ordering the Deportation of the Armenians, June 1915*. In section five of the Proclamation we find that, "those who, in opposition to the Government's decision, refrain from leaving, or hide themselves here and there, if they are sheltered or are given food and assistance, the persons who thus shelter them or aid them shall be sent before the Court Martial for execution."[1064] The American diplomatic

---

1061 Peter Balakian, The Burning Tigris, The Armenian Genocide and America's Response, (New York: Harper Collins, 2003), pp. 376-377.
1062 "When a Holocaust conference was to be held in Tel Aviv in 1982, the Turkish government objected to the inclusion of material on the Armenian slaughter. ... The conference went ahead —with lectures on the Armenian genocide— after Shimon Peres vainly asked Israel's most prominent expert in genocide, Israel Charny, not to include the Armenian massacres. Peres was to go much further—and deep into the moral quagmire of Holocaust denial—in a statement he made prior to an official visit to Ankara as Israeli foreign minister in April 2001. In an interview with the Anatolia News Agency, Peres said that 'we reject attempts to create a similarity between the Holocaust and the Armenian allegations. Nothing similar to the Holocaust occurred. It is a tragedy what the Armenians went through but not a genocide.'" – Robert Fisk, The Great War for Civilisation, The Conquest of the Middle East, (New York: Alfred A. Knopf, 2005), pp. 338-339.
1063 Yigal Schleifer, *None Dared Call It Genocide*, The Jerusalem Report, May 2, 2005, p. 25. In the same article, Yair Auron, a professor at Israel's Open University and the author of The Banality of Denial: Israel and the Armenian Genocide is quoted as saying "Israel committed an original sin by not explaining to Turkey from the start that the Armenian genocide could not be negotiated as part of their relations."
1064 Leslie A. Davis, The Slaughterhouse Province, An American Diplomat's Report on the Armenian Genocide, 1915–1917, (New Rochelle, New York: Aristide D. Caratzas, Publisher, 1989), p. 189.

staff throughout Turkey put themselves in great peril to offer succor to many fleeing Armenians.

Even more surprising, the testimony of Leslie A. Davis, American Consul in Harput, eastern Turkey, 1915–1917, in his book, *Slaughterhouse Province*, tells of numerous Turks and Kurds also, though in general the Kurds made up some of the most vicious killing squads,[1065] who put themselves in extreme mortal danger to help as many Armenians as they could! Robert Fisk, the British journalist, tells us, "It is necessary to remember that Muslims sometimes risked their lives for the doomed Armenian Christians. In almost every interview I conducted with the elderly, blind Armenians who survived their people's genocide, there were stories of individual Turks who, driven by religion or common humanity, disobeyed the quasi-fascist laws of the young Turk rulers in Constantinople and sheltered Armenians in their homes, treating Armenian Christian orphans as members of their own Muslim families. The Turkish governor of Deir es-Zour, Ali Suad Bey, was so kind to the Armenian refugees—he set up orphanages for the children—that he was recalled to Constantinople and replaced by Zeki Bey, who turned the town into a concentration camp."[1066]

Even these days, ninety-one years after the final paroxysm of the Ottoman genocide, a few very courageous Turks put themselves in harms way to tell the sordid history of that holocaust as it really was. Taner Akcam, a Turkish sociologist and historian, "is one of a handful of scholars who are challenging their homeland's insistent declarations that the organized slaughter of Armenians did not occur; and he is the first Turkish specialist to use the word 'genocide' publicly in this context."[1067] Another courageous Turkish professional is the historian Halil Berktay. He is, "one of the first academics to support the genocide case—in which he called the Ottoman plan against the Armenians 'genocide' and 'ethnic cleansing.'"[1068] It is not only Turkish academics, speaking the truth about the Armenian genocide, who face trouble for their courage, "The acclaimed [Turkish] novelist Orhan Pamuk ... is charged with insulting the state in comments he made to a Swiss newspaper in 2005 about the Armenian genocide."[1069] What he said to that Swiss publication [Das Magazine] was, "30,000 Kurds and a million Armenians were killed in these lands and almost nobody but me dares to talk about it." Because of that statement, "Mr. Pamuk faces three years in jail."[1070]

1065 Robert Fisk, The Great War for Civilisation, The Conquest of the Middle East, (New York: Alfred A. Knopf, 2005), p. 324, tells us "The Kurds played the same role of executioners for the Turks that Lithuanians and Ukrainians and Croatians would later assume for the Nazis."
1066 Robert Fisk, The Great War for Civilisation, The Conquest of the Middle East, (New York: Alfred A. Knopf, 2005), pp. 319-320.
1067 Belinda Cooper, *Turks Breach Wall of Silence on Deaths of Armenians in World War I*, The New York Times, March 6, 2004.
1068 Yigal Schleifer, *None Dared Call It Genocide*, The Jerusalem Report, May 2, 2005, pp. 24-25.
1069 Sebnem Arsu, *Publisher Is Charged With Criticizing Turkey*, The New York Times, November 19, 2005.

One of the issues which well may keep Turkey out of the European Union is its insistent denial of the Ottoman genocide. Their denial is in the starkest contrast to procedures in Austria, a prominent member of the Union. On Monday February 20, 2006 in Vienna, "the British historian David Irving pleaded guilty to denying the Holocaust and was sentenced to three years in prison. ... Mr. Irving, 67, has been in custody since Nov. 11, when he was arrested in the southern province of Syria on charges stemming from two speeches he gave in Austria in 1989 in which he was accused of denying the Nazis' annihilation of six million Jews."[1071]

The Ultimate Motivation

"The war [WW I] was a tragedy for the Armenians, who lived on both sides of the Ottoman-Russian frontier: many sympathized with the Russians, most wanted to be left in peace. But whatever their actions and their feelings, they perished in their hundreds of thousands within a year of the outbreak of hostilities."[1072]

When one is confronted by the massive horror of the crime perpetrated on the Armenian people he seeks to understand the full array of motivations which brought it about. Already economic, geographic and strategic reasons for the Turkish annihilation of the Armenian people have been briefly explored. No one of these motivations nor all of them collectively provide an adequate explanation for the massive crime which was committed.

The missing motivation, indeed the main one, is spiritual. "Turkic tribesmen in the frontier zone lived by raiding the Muslims as much as Muslim border defenders lived by raiding them. ... Yet Islam gave a religious justification to this way of life—in addition to earthly booty, a promise of heavenly reward, a promise that probably helped win converts to Islam. The raiders' impact could be traumatic, especially on peoples whose religions, in this case the indigenous Inner Asian cults, made them ineligible for *dhimmi* status."[1073]

"The Islamic concept of 'holy war'[was that] waged by *ghazis*, i.e., special [warrior] champions of the faith, whose courage in battle constituted a sort of sanctity. Warfare across the frontiers of Islam therefore offered rude Turks a highly honorable role that was tailor-made to their warrior traditions. ... In general, the Turkish nomadic background closely resembled that of the first

---

1070 Matthew Kaminski, *Awaiting Trial for His Words, the Novelist Talks Turkey*, The Wall Street Journal, December 15, 2005, p. D8. On January 31, 2006, "'The court dropped the charges not because the trial violated the freedom of speech, ... but because 'there was a missing approval by the Justice Ministry to proceed with the trial.' ... Mr. Pamuk's high profile abroad, in Europe and elsewhere, prompted widespread opposition to his prosecution, an advantage that many intellectuals who face similar charges do not have, said Vecdi Sayar, general secretary of International PEN, a worldwide association of writers." – Sebnem Arsu, *Turkish Court Drops Charges Against Novelist*, The New York Times, January 24, 2006.

1071 *Austria Imposes 3-year Sentence on Notorious Holocaust Denier*, The New York Times, February 21, 2006, p. A11.

1072 Andrew Mango, Ataturk The Biography of the Founder of Modern Turkey, (New York: The Overlook Press, 2000), p. 135.

1073 Carter Vaughn Findley, The Turks In World History, (New York: Oxford University Press, 2005), p. 68.

Arab [Muslim] conquerors. This made it comparatively easy to find an honorific niche for such doughty, if barbarous warriors within Islam and allowed civilized Moslems to deflect the brunt of Turkish military enterprise against their Christian and Hindu neighbors. ... Turks provided a majority of the Moslem rulers and soldiers from the eleventh century onward and constituted the cutting edge of Islamic expansion into both Christendom and Hindustan."[1074]

It is truly astounding that Christianity in any form survived such institutionalized and revered barbarity. The Armenian followers of Christ could have ended their perilous, and often massively fatal, situation at any time by simply repeating the simple Muslim creedal statement: "There is no God but God and Muhammad is his Prophet." Heroically, the vast majority were faithful until death!

Turkish Records Confirm The Genocide

"With his book, *The Remaining Documents of Talat Pasha*, Mr. Bardakci (pronounced bard-AK-chuh) has become, rather unwillingly, part of this ferment. The book is a collection of documents and records that once belonged to Mehmed Talat, known as Talat Pasha, the primary architect of the Armenian deportations.

"The documents, given to Mr. Bardakci by Mr. Talat's widow, Hayriye, before she died in 1983, include lists of population figures. Before 1915, 1,256,000 Armenians lived in the Ottoman Empire, according to the documents. The number plunged to 284,157 two years later, Mr. Bardakci said. ...

"Hilmar Kaiser, a historian and expert on the Armenian genocide, said the records published in the book were conclusive proof from the Ottoman authority itself that it had pursued a calculated policy to eliminate the Armenians. 'You have suddenly on one page confirmation of the numbers,' he said. 'It was like someone hit you over the head with a club.'

"Mr. Kaiser said the before and after figures amounted to 'a death record.'

"'There is no other way of viewing this document,' he said. 'You can't just hide a million people.'"[1075]

Note: "The novel [The Forty Days of Musa Dagh] was translated into English by Geoffrey Dunlop in 1934. But Dunlop, a well-respected translator, decided to cut a substantial part of it: passages about Armenian culture and traditions, as well as 'harrowing' pages about the rape and slaughter of women and children that he considered too upsetting for British and American readers. Surprisingly, nobody seemed to notice and Werfel himself didn't protest: non-German editions were of little interest to him apart from their royalties. Now at last a revision of Dunlop's work and a translation of the excised passages has been made by James Reidel. The American edition

---

1074 William H. Mc Neill, The Rise Of the West, A History of The Human Community, (Chicago: University of Chicago Press, 1990), p. 488.
1075 Sabrina Tavernise, *Nearly a Million Genocide Victims, Covered in a Cloak of Amnesia*, The New York Times, March 9, 2009, p. A6.

carries his long and illuminating introduction, and it's a great pity Penguin decided to drop this from its edition of a 'difficult' novel dense with unfamiliar references." – Neal Ascherson, *Howitzers on the Hill*, (a review of <u>The Forty Days of Musa Dagh</u> by Franz Werfel), <u>London Review of Books</u>, March 8, 2018, p. 30.

ଔ

APPENDIX C

The Spread of Islam in Southeast Asia and Sub-Saharan Africa

Tom Lane, author of *A Measured Look at Islam* in the April 27, 2003 issue of <u>Christian Standard</u>, asserted that, in contrast to the period of Islam's "initial rapid spread by military conquest, ... in Southeast Asia and Sub-Saharan Africa, Islam arrived peacefully through trade connections, an Arab specialty." While the author is correct about Islam spreading through "trade connections," he very incorrectly asserted that Islam "arrived peacefully" in Southeast Asia and Sub-Saharan Africa.

Before looking at the historical record of Islam's penetration into Southeast Asia and Sub-Saharan Africa, we should ask what kind of "trade connections" were practiced as "an Arab specialty." The record tells us that even the trade connections practiced by the Muslims were coercive. For example, "Saladin, the famous Kurdish ruler [and warrior] who followed the [Egyptian-based] Fatimids, was extremely orthodox and renewed many of the ancient discriminatory laws, among them the differential treatment of Muslims and non-Muslims in customs' payments. But under the pressure of European merchants, who frequented the ports of his kingdom, he was forced to change his attitude. It is notable that the edict abolishing the discrimination expressly refers to Jews and Christians, both foreign and local."[1076] Previously, Jewish and Christian merchants had often been tempted to convert to Islam just to be on an even playing field in commerce!

Regarding Mr. Lane's contention that Islam "arrived peacefully" in Southeast Asia and Sub-Saharan Africa, let's look first at the situation in Southeast Asia. In 1293, Marco Polo "observed the beginnings of a great Muslim missionary movement which was to spread throughout the Indonesian islands. During the next two centuries the new religion came to Java along the shipping routes and thrived in the coastal areas. Muslim traders became all-powerful; the Javanese aristocracy inter-married with them and gradually took on the religion of the foreign merchants, while the missionaries of Allah slowly built up an understanding of Muslim tenets. ... So at that date [1413 when a Chinese Muslim visited Java] Islam was still a largely foreign element, but later in the century it became predominant. **In the end, force decided the issue** *[bolding mine]* when the old capital of East Java fell in 1478. Apart from those who fled to Bali, the mass of native Javanese and Madurese people who had believed so devoutly in devils became after 1478 at least nominally Muslim."[1077]

1076 S.D. Goitein, <u>Jews and Arabs, Their Contacts Through the Ages</u>, (New York: Schocken Books, 1967), p. 72.

"By the early fifteenth century, Islam had established itself at Malacca, the nerve-center of Southeast Asian trade routes, whence the new faith radiated to other parts of Indonesia. By the middle of the century, Islam had already reached the Moluccas in the east and, more important still, some of the trading towns on the northern litoral of the island of Java, center for many centuries of a flourishing Hindu-Javanese empire, Majapahit.[1078] **Majapahit succumbed under the armed onslaughts of its rebellious, Islamized vassals**, [bolding mine] leaving the interior of Java in political chaos."[1079]

Now let us look briefly at that alleged peaceful penetration of Islam into Sub-Saharan Africa. First, a glimpse of Nubian history is instructive. By the year 643, "peace now reigned throughout the whole of the [Nile] Delta and the Nile valley as far as the southern border of Egypt at Aswan. But the Sudan ... had no notion of changing their Christian faith to Islam. ... An expedition which 'Amr sent against the Nubians [in what is now northern Sudan] not merely failed to vanquish them, but was forced to retreat, having suffered much loss from the exceptional skill of the Nubian archers, whom the Arabs henceforth distinguished as the 'eye-wounder.' ... The final subjection of Nubia was accomplished in 652."[1080]

Also, on the other side of Sub-Saharan Africa, Islam did not penetrate peacefully. The critical history is part of the "Almoravid destruction of the empire of Ghana and the spread of Islam in the political center of the emerging states of Takrur, Songhay, Soso, and Kanem-Bornu. The empire of Ghana had reached its zenith by the late 11th century. In 1076 the Almoravids conquered Ghana [in 1076] and forcibly converted its people to Islam."[1081] "The Almoravid conquest of West Africa was led by Abdallah ibn Yasin."[1082]

Mr. Lane further lauds Islam by saying that, "In these places [Southeast Asia and Sub-Saharan Africa], Islam prevailed by the superiority of its ethical values, beginning with the honesty of those Muslim merchants." He doesn't tell us with what he is making the comparison when he talks about "the superiority of its ethical values." Presumably, he means Islam's ethical values are superior to those of Biblical Christianity. One must wonder how ethical an ideological/religious system is which imposes itself by force. Compare the first century of Islamic history with the first century of Christian history. It will not be difficult to discern which system was one of persuasion and which one resorted to force, intimidation and cruelty.

1077 David Bentley-Taylor, The Weathercock's Reward Christian Progress in Muslim Java, (London: Overseas Missionary Fellowship, 1967), pp. 9-10.
1078 The Majapahit Empire was a vast archipelagic empire based on the island of Java (modern-day Indonesia) from 1293 to around 1500. https://en.wikipedia.org/wiki/*Majapahit*. 10/17/16
1079 Harry J. Benda, The Crescent and the Rising Sun, Indonesian Islam Under the Japanese Occupation 1942–1945, (The Hague: W. Van Hoeve Ltd., 1958), p. 9.
1080 Alfred J. Butler, The Arab Conquest of Egypt and the Last Thirty Years of the Roman Dominion, (Oxford: The Clarendon Press, 1902), p. 432.
1081 Peter N. Stearns (ed.), The Encyclopedia of World History, (New York: Houghton Mifflin Company, 2001), p.144.
1082 Peter N. Stearns (ed.), The Encyclopedia of World History, (New York: Houghton Mifflin Company, 2001), p.141.

Appendix C

Going further into his very imaginary and presumptive scenario, Mr. Lane asserts that "Today, Islam competes well with Christianity in Africa, and among African-Americans, because it carries no taint of association with colonial powers, and because of its color-blindness."

We must ask, is Islam not itself an imperialistic colonial power? "For Muslims, no piece of land once added to the realm of Islam can ever be finally renounced."[1083] "It was perfectly legitimate for Muslims to conquer and rule Europe and Europeans and thus enable them—but not compel them—to embrace the true faith. It was a crime and a sin for Europeans to conquer and rule Muslims and, still worse, to try to lead them astray. In the Muslim perception, conversion to Islam is a benefit to the convert and a merit in those who convert him. In Islamic law, conversion from Islam is apostasy—a capital offense for both the one who is misled and the one who misleads him."[1084]

Colonialism was not only initiated and consistently practiced by Arab Muslims, it was also perpetuated by their successors who came to power in the Muslim world. A prime example is given by the Turks. "In return [for help in securing the throne] the new [Byzantine] emperor ... allowed [the Turkish leader] Orhan's men to ravage and raid Gallipoli and Thrace without opposition. This was accomplished primarily between 1345 and 1348 by Orhan's son Suleyman." Among the places the Turks conquered was Gallipoli, a key Byzantine area later made indelibly memorable by the historic, bloody battle of the Aussies and the New Zealanders against the Turks which took place there during World War I. Cantacuzene (the Byzantine emperor) vigorously protested this unauthorized conquest to which Suleyman answered, "he could not surrender Gallipoli or the conquered lands in Thrace, since by Muslim law infidel territories conquered by Muslim forces could not be so surrendered. ... Gallipoli then became the first permanent Ottoman base in Europe, from which the initial Ottoman raids into and conquests of the Balkans were made in subsequent years."[1085]

CR

1083 Bernard Lewis, The Crisis of Islam, Holy War and Unholy Terror, (New York: The Modern Library, 2003), p.xxviii-xxix.
1084 Bernard Lewis, The Crisis of Islam, Holy War and Unholy Terror, (New York: The Modern Library, 2003), p. 55.
1085 Stanford J. Shaw, History of the Ottoman Empire and Modern Turkey, Volume I, Empire of the Gazis, The Rise and Decline of the Ottoman Empire, 1280–1808, (Cambridge: Cambridge University press, 1977), p. 16.

APPENDIX D

The Rise of Shiism

Note: As a preface to this appendix, be sure to read "Inception of Islamic Division" and "Lust Skews Succession" in Chapter 24.

Shiism grew out of serious faction, strife and division which broke out during the reigns of the third and fourth caliphs. Those divisions were extensions of older jealousies and strifes between the Hashim and Umayya branches of the Arab Quraish Tribe[1086] to which Muhammad belonged.

At the time of Muhammad's death (June 632 A.D.), many thought Ali should have been selected as the first caliph (successor) to lead the Muslim nation, the *umma*. He was both Muhammad's cousin and son-in-law and second earliest convert to Islam. He had fought valiantly in Islam's cause and had jeopardized his own life to make Muhammad's escape from Mecca (the Hijra) possible. Highly qualified and deserving though he was, his appointment was deferred, probably due to Aisha's hatred. (See "Filling the Void" in Chapter 8.) That allowed two elderly deserving candidates, Abu Bakr and Umar, to serve before their deaths. "Abu Bekr [Bakr] and Umar, the Prophet's two immediate successors, were men utterly devoted to religion and belonged to minor clans of the tribe of Quraish."[1087] Thus, the first two Caliphs were outside the main tribal rivalry and their decisions did not fan old flames of jealousy and animosity back to life.

Uthman, the third one to become caliph, was a member of the Umayyad clan of the Quraish Tribe while Ali was a member of the rival Hashim clan. At Uthman's becoming caliph, those old clan rivalries and suspicions flared anew. Tauntingly, Uthman flaunted his authority by appointing his fellow clan members to fill every one of the regional governorships.

Finally, Ali was appointed caliph immediately following Uthman's murder in 656 A.D. One of his first acts was to demand the resignation of all the governors who had been appointed by Uthman. All of them acquiesced except Mu'awiya, exceptionally talented governor of Damascus. Mu'awiya was willing to resign but on one condition: Ali must make a full investigation of the murder of Uthman and punish the murderers. Stubbornly, Ali refused to order the investigation. Mu'awiya had suspected that Ali was somehow complicit in Uthman's murder

---

1086 "During the fifth and sixth centuries the ruling tribe at Meccah was the Kuraysh. This name is derived from a word which means 'to trade,' many of the leading member's of the tribe having been great traders." – Edith Holland, <u>The Story of Mohammed</u>, (London: George G. Harrap & Company, 1914, Reprinted in Pakistan in 1977 by Al-Biruni, Lahore), p. 24.

1087 John Bagot Glubb, <u>The Empire of the Arabs</u>, (London: Hodder & Stoughton, 1963), p. 31.

and his refusal to investigate confirmed the suspicion in his heart. Muʻawiya refused to resign! Civil war ensued!

The military contest between the forces of caliph Ali and governor Muʻawiya, the first civil war in Islam, took place in July 657 A.D. It is known as the Battle of Siffeen, named after a place on the right bank of the Euphrates in Syria. It was located near the present town of Raqqa, the ostensible capital of ISIS. Seeing his forces losing, Muʻawiya successfully pled for a negotiated settlement. Those negotiations were ultimately indecisive. Because Ali had agreed to negotiate, twelve thousand of his troops defected in protest. They are known as the Kharijites, the Seceders, one of whom assassinated Ali on January 24, 661 A.D. in the mosque at Kufa.

It is important to realize that the Battle of Siffeen began a civil war, not just between Ali and Muʻawiya, but between the House of Hashim and the House of Umayya. Thus the Arab portion of the house of Islam was torn asunder by a rift in which non-Arab Muslims in future centuries were forced to take sides.

The rift in the clans of Muhammad's Quraish Tribe was followed by a rift in the caliphate itself. Even though Ali was clearly and legitimately caliph, "in May 660, Muʻawiya proclaimed himself caliph in Jerusalem on the basis of his assertion that Ali was unfit for the position. This was the founding of the Umayyad Caliphate with its capital at Damascus. Ali was preparing to undertake a [second] campaign against Muʻawiya when he was assassinated in the mosque of Kufa [in present-day Iraq, but then part of Iran] in January 661."[1088] Ali had moved the caliphal capital of Islam from Medina to Kufa.

"Ali's remains were buried at nearby Najaf, and a mosque raised over his tomb soon became an object of pilgrimage as important to the Shiites as Mecca is to all Muslims. To this day Najaf remains one of Islam's most conservative, most mysterious cities. Rarely is it visited by nonbelievers."[1089]

Ali's oldest son, al-Hasan, the one on whom the office of the caliph should have devolved, was a flagrant hedonist. Because of his sensualism he was easily, but not cheaply, bribed by Muʻawiya with a lifetime subsidy so he would not seek the caliphate. Though al-Hasan was the legitimate heir to the throne, as mentioned in Chapter 7 he had "already sojourned too long among the fleshpots. His talents lay in fields other than administration—namely, in the boudoir. Though he died at the age of forty-five, he had by that time succeeded in making and unmaking no less than one hundred marriages and in winning a highly individual title for himself: 'the great divorcer.'"[1090]

1088 Martin Sicker, <u>The Islamic World in Ascendancy, From the Arab Conquests to the Siege of Vienna</u>, (London: Praeger, 2000), p. 19.
1089 Thomas J. Abercrombie, *Early Split Still Divides Moslem World*, <u>Seattle Times</u>, May 27, 1979, p. H-10.
1090 Philip K. Hitti, <u>The Arabs, A Short History</u> (London: Macmillan & Co. Ltd., 1965), p. 59.

In April of 680 Mu'awiya died. He was succeeded in Damascus by his ruthless son Yazid. On the other side of the Arab rift, Ali's youngest son Husain, in the same year, was invited to become rival caliph by invitation of the people of Iraq. That involved making an 800-mile trip from Mecca to Kufa, in August or September. When he received the urgent summons from Kufa to come to rule as caliph, Husain sent Muslim, his cousin, to report on the situation. Muslim reported that thousands of supporters were prepared to join the uprising.

Though there were rumors of danger, Husain, with his family and a few supporters, a total of about fifty people, made their way toward Kufa. He did not know that his cousin, whom he had sent to inquire about conditions, had been arrested and executed by agents of Yazid, Caliph of the Umayyad Caliphate.

The Battle of Karbala

Yazid's agents intercepted Husain's entourage and would not allow it to proceed to Kufa. "On the second day of the month of Muharram (2 October 680), al-Husayn's [Husain's] troops camped at Karbala, 70 kilometers north of Kufa and 20 kilometers west of the Euphrates. ... Under command of Ibn Sa'd, they [Yazid's forces] blocked access to the river, forcing al-Husayn's troops [and his family] to do without water for three days. Further negotiations failed, since al-Husayn refused to pay tribute to the caliph Yazid. On the ninth of [the Arabic month] Muharram, the Kufan troops approached al-Husayn's camp and early the following morning (10 Muharram/10 October 680), hand-to-hand combat and skirmishes ensued. By afternoon, the camp had been stormed. Al-Husayn and almost all the men in his convoy—according to Shi'i tradition, 32 horsemen and 40 foot soldier—had been killed. ... The casualties were buried at the site of the massacre where today, the shrines of Karbala are located. Al-Husayn's head was brought to Kufa, where the governor 'Ubayd Allah ibn Ziyad is said to have knocked out several teeth with his staff."[1091]

To recapitulate, "on the tenth day of the month of Muharram, at a place called Karbala in Iraq, Husayn [Husain], his family, and his followers encountered an Umayyad force and were ruthlessly put to death. Some seventy died in the massacre; only a sick boy, Ali ibn Husayn, who was left lying in a tent, survived. This dramatic martyrdom of the kin of the Prophet, and the wave of anguish and penitence that followed it, infused a new religious fervour in the Shi'a, now inspired by the potent themes of suffering, passion and expiation."[1092]

Husain's severed head was ultimately delivered to the caliph in Damascus. "As Yazid touched the martyr's mouth with the point of his staff, so the story goes, an old man at the court cried out, 'Blasphemy! I have seen the Prophet kiss those very lips.' It was a tragic day for Islam. The believers were irrevocably

---
1091 Heinz Halm, The Shi'ites, A Short History, (Princeton, NJ: Markus Wiener Publishers, 2007), pp. 14-15.
1092 Bernard Lewis, The Assassins, A Radical Sect in Islam, (New York: Oxford University Press, 1967), pp. 22-23.

split, creating a schism that has continued to haunt the Moslem world through the centuries."[1093]

"This martyr's death of Husayn [Husain] ... furthered the religious development of the Shi'ah, the party of the 'Alids [followers of Ali]. ... Today Husayn's grave in Karbala is still the most sacred goal of pilgrimage for all Shi'ites, particularly the Persians, whose most ardent desire has remained that of finding their last resting place at his side."[1094] The fortieth day after the anniversary of his death a special Shiite observance is held.

In Kufa, the partisans of Ali (*Shi'at 'Ali* in Arabic) had assured Husain's cousin, Muslim, that thousands of devotees would rise in Husain's support as soon as he arrived in Kufa to lead the movement. But, when the actual moment arrived, not a single person stepped forward to support Husain's cause!

Following the massacre of Husain and his party, intense collective grief and shame swept over the Shiites of Kufa. That shame and self revulsion led to ghastly ritualized self flagellation which has subsequently been widely practiced by every generation of Shiites every tenth of Muharram. The hope is that such severe self--inflicted punishment will be expiatory and they will be forgiven for the grievous sin of not standing with Husain against the enemies of Islam. Even more, they hope for an expiatory death inflicted by Islam's enemies. This is why men and youngsters by the thousands volunteered to walk into Saddam Hussein's mine fields in the eight-year-long Iran-Iraq War. This is also why soldiers who survived the horrors of that war pled for forgiveness when they visited the grave of Ayatollah Khomeini. Survival was sin! But this has taken us far ahead chronologically.

Just before the dawn of the Muslim era, as we saw, Persia clashed unsuccessfully with the Christian West when it attacked the Byzantine Empire. A bit more than a century after being forced into the great Islamic empire, Persia again clashed with the West, but this time with a Muslim West, the Umayyad Caliphate centered in Damascus. Chafing under Arab rule, some of the Muslims of Persia, descendants of al-'Abbas, an uncle of the Prophet Muhammad, successfully challenged Damascus through founding the Abbasid Caliphate which resulted from the Battle of the Great Zab River, on January 25, 750. "The Abbasids routed Marwan's army, bringing to an end Umayyad rule. The deposed caliph fled to Egypt, but was caught there and killed, and his head sent to the new caliph as a present."[1095]

Though al-Abbas and his descendants were Arabs, we call the founding of the Abbasid Caliphate a Persian-Muslim initiative because, first, "they organized their rebellion against the Umayyads from the province of Khurasan in northeastern Iran."[1096] Secondly, at the beginning, the caliph trusted only Persian soldiers from the province of Khurasan as his palace guards. That caliphate was in

---
1093 Thomas J. Abercrombie, *Early Split Still Divides Moslem World*, Seattle Times, May 27, 1979, p. H-10.
1094 Carl Brockelmann, History of the Islamic Peoples, (New York: Capricorn Books, 1960), p. 76
1095 Desmond Stewart, Early Islam, (New York: Time Incorporated, 1967), p. 64.

power from 750 to 1258, that is from the Abbasid victory at the Great Zab River till the Mongols captured Baghdad, assassinated the caliph and brought the Abbasid rule to a complete and permanent end.

To make sure there would be no future resurgence of the Umayyad Caliphate, members of Mu'awiya's caliphal house were hunted down and killed by the new Abbasid Caliphate. The only survivor was the intrepid Abd al-Rahman, a youth of nineteen who, after an adventurous and perilous five-year flight, made his way to Spain to ultimately found the Umayyad Caliphate of Cordoba.

"The accession of the Abbasids was more than the change of a dynasty: it marked the beginning of a new era. The patriarchal Omaiads [Umayyads] gave way to the absolute Abbasids, beside whose throne lay the executioner's leather spread [to catch the blood and gore]. The Arab-dominated state yielded to a cosmopolitan realm based on religion rather than race. Persians played a predominant part, and any influence that Arabs retained was as Muslims, not as Arabs."[1097]

Following the Battle of the Zab, Iran was invaded by the Seljuk and Ottoman Turks who were committed Sunni Muslims. Shortly thereafter, the Abbasid caliph put the governance of the caliphate into the hands of the Seljuk Turks. The Shiite Persians, understandably, felt betrayed. From that point, they withheld their loyalty and cooperation from the Abbasid Caliphate.

The Shia shifted their emphasis from the caliphate to the immamate, in their view a divinely designated succession of leaders. The title *imam,* leader, comes from the same Arabic root as that for *umma,* meaning the entire Muslim community or body politic. Thus, theoretically, the imam is the leader of the umma, the leader of all Muslims. From that point, in their view, the function of the caliph belonged to the imams. Only Ali, the first Shiite imam, held the dual office of Caliph and Imam.

Numerically, the Shiites grew so rapidly that the Abbasid Caliphs began to see them as a threat. Later, because of their inveterate anti-Sunniism, the Iranian Buyid dynasty (945–1055) began to see the Shiites as a potential ally. It was a timely alliance because by the time the Safavid Dynasty (1501–1722) came to power, Iran's western border was being threatened again by the West, by Constantinople, now called Istanbul, not by the Byzantines but by the Ottoman Turks, totally committed Sunni Muslims. The Shiite Safavids put so much military pressure on the Ottoman eastern border that it became a major reason the Ottomans were obliged to retreat in 1529 from their first attack on Vienna. Then Shiism went from strength to strength under the Iranian Safavid Dynasty. "Within twenty years [from the Ottoman retreat from Vienna] the great Safavid

---

1096 Fred M. Donner, *Muhammad and the Caliphate,* The Oxford History of Islam, ed. John L. Esposito (New York: Oxford University Press,1999), p. 24.
1097 Enno Franzius, History of the Order of Assassins, (New York: Funk & Wagnalls, 1969), p. 12.

ruler Shah Abbas I (1587–1629) wrested Baghdad and the Armenian border provinces from the Turks."[1098]

From the time Shiism gained prominence, two powers have vied for primacy in Iran: the monarchy and the immamate. There have been only twelve imams, the twelfth being Muhammad al-Mahdi. He was the last of those imams who were thought to have gone into concealment. Shiites believe the twelfth imam has been living in concealment since 873 and as *al-Mahdi*, the rightly guided one, will one day return to bring justice on the earth. Through many centuries the monarchy prevailed in the contest with the immamate, till the 1979 revolution in Iran when Ayatollah Khomeini violently wrenched state power out of the hands of the reigning shah, Mohammad Reza Shah Pahlavi.

The day-to-day work of the Hidden Imam has been carried on by a select group of elite Imams, religious scholars who are collectively known as the *ulema*, the plural of the Arabic *alim*, a scholar. In Shiism, the pinnacle of the ulema is given the title of *Ayatoullah* (Ayatollah), meaning the sign of God, a name given to the recipient because his decisions are looked upon as divine. Only one further honor is given. Those who have reached the ultimate peak of clerical achievement are given the accolade of Grand Ayatollah.

The two areas of Shia political success have been Iran in the East and, the Fatimid Dynasty which began near Kairwan in western North Africa and culminated in its centuries-long rule in Egypt. Eventually, the Fatimid Dynasty, after notable successes, suffered internal division and sclerosis. It was brought to a decisive end by Saladin in 1171 A.D.

☙

[1098] Nija G. Garsoian, *The Ottoman Empire*, The Columbia History of The World, eds. John A. Garraty & Peter Gay, (New York: Harper & Row, Publishers, 1972), p. 612.

APPENDIX E

The Five Pillars of Islam

Usually a Muslim speaking on the topic of his faith and practice will recite the five pillars of Islam to his audience. However, these matters are ritualistic and may seem to many non-Muslims to be trivial compared with other matters which Islam embraces such as jihad, the form of government, the role of women, and the position of non-Muslims in a Muslim-dominated state. However, the student of Islam should have a clear understanding of the five pillars which are:

(1) The *Shahada* (giving testimony or bearing witness) is the very short creed which one who wishes to become a Muslim is required to recite. Also, a Muslim who wishes to reaffirm his faith will recite this short creed: "There is no God but Allah and Mohammed is His Prophet."

Some scholars think the *Shahada* in its present form, which emphasizes God as the sole deity and Muhammad as his Prophet, came to be formalized some time after the death of Muhammad. For example, Donner says, "The earliest documentary attestations of the *Shahada*, found on coins, papyri, and inscriptions dating before about 66/685, include only the first part of the later 'double *Shahada*': 'there is no god but God' (sometimes with the addition, 'who has no associate')—Muhammad is not yet mentioned. If this is not merely an accident of preservation, we may see in it yet another indication of the ecumenical or non-confessional character of the early community of Believers."[1099]

Antedating the testimony of early Muslim coins, papyri and inscriptions, the Koran is unmistakably clear that both assertions of the *Shahada* must be embraced. Addressing the Bedouin Arabs with an indictment, the Koran says, "The faith hath not entered into your hearts. Yet, if ye obey Allah and His messenger, He will not withhold from you aught of (the reward of) your deeds. Lo! Allah is Forgiving, Merciful. The (true) believers are those only who believe in Allah and His messenger and afterward doubt not, but strive with their wealth and their lives for the cause of Allah. Such are the sincere." (Surah 49:14-15 from Pickthall's translation, confirmed by the translations of George Sale, A.J. Arberry and Yusuf Ali.)

The vicious *Ridda* War, that is the War of Apostasy, beginning immediately after the death of Muhammad, (see Chapter 8 under "Apostasy Suppressed by Khalid ibn al Waleed") was fought expressly to defeat those who dared to challenge the sole and exclusive prophethood of Muhammad. Though there were

---
[1099] Fred M. Donner, <u>Muhammad and the Believers: At the Origins of Islam</u>, (London: Harvard University Press, 2010), p. 112.

others whom Muhammad considered false prophets, he seems to have considered Musailama to have been the most despicable of those false prophets. Thus the *Ridda* War is another testimony to the fact that both assertions of the *Shahada* were deemed absolutely essential from the beginning of Islam.

(2) Salat (pl. *salawat*) or ritual prayer which is to be recited five times each day. The Muslims are called to these ritual prayers by the muezzin [This familiar word is the Turkish-Persian form for the Arabic *mu'adhdhin*, the man who calls the *adhan*.] from a minaret who cries, "Allah is most great, There is no God but Allah, and Mohammed is His Prophet, Come to prayer, come to salvation, Allah is most great, there is no God but Allah." See Surah 11:114, Surah 24:58 and Surah 62:9-10.

The Call To Prayer:

1. allhā-hō akbar - (4 Xs facing west)
   God is Great

2. aśahādō an lā ilāhā illalāh (2 Xs facing west)
   I bear witness: Indeed there is no God but Allāh.

3. aśahādō annā Muhammad-ar rasul allāh (2 Xs facing west)
   I bear witness: Mohammed is the apostle of God.

4. haiyā alssalā (2 Xs with face toward north)
   Come towards

5. haiyā ilalfilāh (2 Xs facing south)
   Come toward salvation (or betterment)

6. allā-hō akbar (2 Xs facing west)
   God is Great.

7. assalā tō khairūm - minannaum (2 Xs F. w. in Morn)
   Prayer is better than sleep.

8. lā ilāhā illalāh (1 X facing W.)
   There is no God but Allah.

(3) Zakat, the obligatory tax collected from Muslims for the needy. See Surah 2:43, Surah 2:83, Surah 2:215, Surah 4:77 and Surah 72:8.

(4) Sawm, the fast during the month of Ramadan. (See the Koran, Surah 2:183-187)

"The fourth pillar is Sawm or Fasting, which means keeping Ramadan. Ramadan is a month, the one during which it is written that God sent the Qur'an to the lowest heaven where Gabriel received it and whence he revealed it, bit by bit, to Muhammad."[1100]

(5) The ***Hajj***, or the pilgrimage to the *Kaaba*, the shrine in Mecca. See Surah 2:158, Surah 2:189, Surah 2:196, and Surah 22:27-29.

Muhammad's first attempt at leading a pilgrimage from Medina to the Kaaba took place in March 628. (See Chapter 7 under "Daring Theological Inconsistency.") Such a pilgrimage is called *'umrah*—the little or lesser pilgrimage. It can be made in any month and is a minor pilgrimage in contrast to the *hajj*, known as the greater pilgrimage, which can be performed only in the month of Dhu 'l-Hijja. Muhammad "did not inaugurate these practices [of pilgrimages] but only assimilated them to his teaching. This he could do all the more readily as their original significance seems to have become but obscurely understood by his contemporaries. That he allowed them to persist at all is probably less to be attributed to his personal reverence for them than to his political instinct which made him respect the traditions of his conservative fellow-countrymen."[1101]

Students who wish to read captivating and enlightening discussions of the current state of the Hajj should read (1) Basharat Peer, *Modern Mecca, The Transformation of a holy city*, The New Yorker, April 16, 2012, pp. 74-87. (2) Christopher de Bellaigue, *In the Supreme Shrine*, The New York Review of Books, April 26, 2012, pp. 17-18.

☙

[1100] Carleton S. Coon, Caravan: The Story of the Middle East, (New York: Henry Holt and Company, 1956), pp. 112-113.
[1101] R. Paret, *'Umra*, Shorter Encyclopaedia of Islam, ed. H.A.R. Gibb and J.H. Kramers, (Ithaca, New York: Cornell University Press, 1974), p. 605.

APPENDIX F

Did Muhammad Have Access to Christian Scripture?

We know the Jews in Arabia showed Muhammad parchments of the Pentateuch. They are called "The book which Moses brought" (Surah 6:92), but we do not know whether those parchments were in Hebrew or Arabic. In any case, Muhammad seems to have known what was recorded on those parchments since he said, "O, People of the Scripture! Ye have naught (of guidance) till ye observe the Torah and the Gospel and that which was revealed unto you from your Lord." (Surah 5:68) In a further exhortation it would seem Muhammad was dependent upon the Jews and Christians to know what was recorded in the Old and New Testaments. The instruction was, "If thou (Muhammad) are in doubt concerning that which We reveal unto thee, then question those who read the Scripture (that was) before thee." (Surah 10:95)

One may also wonder whether Arabic had developed adequately, before the prophetic role of Muhammad, to convey the full scope of biblical concepts. Shahid tells us that Arabic as a literary poetic language, had "emerged at least a hundred years before Muhammad's 'Hijra' to Medina in 622, as a written language in the large sense, and not only in the restricted sense of a language used for the expression of 'epigraphic' sentiments. This is a fact of crucial importance to such major problems as the existence of an Arabic version of the Bible in pre-Islam and the composition of Arabic pre-Islamic poetry."[1102]

But even more importantly, before the dawn of Muhammad's career, did Arabians have access to the gospel of Christ in written form in their own language? It seems quite certain that there had been a translation of Christianity's oldest harmony of the four gospels, Tatian's Diatessaron, into Arabic well before 622 A.D. However, "The Arabic Diatessaron is not a simple translation from the Syriac, but depends in part upon the Gospel text of the Peshito. The translator, or perhaps better the editor, has permitted himself to make important alterations; and in view of the fact that it was often difficult to find in the original the passages from which the elements of the Diatessaron were taken, the consequence is that, instead of the artistic Diatessaron, there is a rough Arabic work."[1103]

At just about the time Islam came into being, "the Gospels were translated into Arabic from the Greek, Syriac and Coptic versions. Also, Bar Hebraeus speaks

---

[1102] Irfan Shahid, The Martyrs of Najran: New Documents, (Bruxelles: Societe Des Bollandistes, 1971), p. 40.
[1103] T. Zahn, Harmony of The Gospels, The New Schaff-Herzog Encyclopedia of Religious Knowledge, ed. Samuel Macauley Jackson (Grand Rapids, Michigan: Baker Book House, 1953), Vol. V, p. 153.

of a translation made between 631 and 640 [Muhammad died in 632 A.D.] by ... order of an Arab prince. ... [However] the oldest known MSS and fragments of translations from the Greek ... are most probably of the early ninth century. The oldest surviving translation from the Syriac ... is of the same period."[1104]

The same scholar goes on to say, "that passages from the Gospels were put into Arabic at a much earlier date cannot be doubted." In support of that statement, Zahn tells of an Arabic translation of Tatian's famous Diatessaron, the earliest known harmony of the gospels,[1105] "which exists in the Codex Fuldensis, made under the direction of Victor of Capua, c. 546 A.D."[1106] That Arabic translation was made 24 years before Muhammad was born. While this indicates that portions of the four gospels had been translated into Arabic even before the birth of Muhammad, it is very doubtful if copies were easily and widely accessible.

Deliberate Destruction?

The current paucity of Biblical manuscripts in Arabic, dating from before the appearance of Islam, may be due to deliberate destruction of those writings. Christian scriptures in Arabic would have been looked upon as competitive narratives and, therefore, could well have been deliberately destroyed as undoubtedly were variant editions of the Koran.

"It is on record that in the very early days of Islam the different manuscripts of the Qur'an in use in Arabia presented variations of such a nature as to disturb gravely those who believed in the literal and verbal inspiration of the book. The Khalifa 'Uthman, in 644 A.D., took a most drastic step to remedy this scandal. He appointed a committee consisting of three men of the Quraish, with Zaid ibn Thabit at their head; and ordered a new edition of the Qur'an to be made on the basis of the copy compiled by Abu Bakr. He further insisted that if these men differed among themselves on any point, the reading at that place should be [worded according to the rendering] in the Quraishi dialect. When this copy was completed 'Uthman had all previous copies burnt. That is something the Christian Church has never done."[1107]

Professor Donner, of the University of Chicago, also tells us of the struggle to delete textual ambiguity in the Qur'an. He wrote, "Among the most important of Uthman's 'innovations,' however, may have been his decision to codify the Qur'an's text. The stories about this are many and confused; some scholars argue that the Qur'an text as we have it was already codified at the time of

---

1104 B. Carra de Vaux, *Indjil*, Shorter Encyclopedia of Islam, (Ithaca, New York: Cornell University Press, 1974), H.A.R. Gibb & J.H. Kramers, eds., p. 168.

1105 The original Diatessaron was prepared by Tatian in about 175 A.D. "On the basis of the text it uses in its OT citations and certain Semitic syntactic features—present even in the Western witnesses—it seems quite certain that Syriac was the original language of the Diatessaron (Peterson 1986)." – William L. Petersen, *Diatessaron*, The Anchor Bible Dictionary, ed. Astrid B. Beck (New York: Doubleday,), p. 190.

1106 T. Zahn, *Harmony of The Gospels*, The New Schaff-Herzog Encyclopedia of Religious Knowledge, ed. Samuel Macauley Jackson (Grand Rapids, Michigan: Baker Book House, 1953), Vol V., p 153.

Muhammad's death, but many reports tell of people collecting parts of the revelation that survived the Prophet only in people's memories or in scattered partial written copies. One stream of tradition holds that Uthman asked a team of companions led by Zayad ibn Thabit to collect and compare all available copies of the Qur'an and to prepare a single, unified text. This aroused opposition not perhaps because of the procedure itself, but because once the new Qur'anic 'Vulgate' was established, Uthman had copies sent to the main *Amsar* [garrison towns] with orders that they be used there in place of regional versions that were considered authentic by their followers and that these earlier copies be burned. Despite this, several of the earlier versions of the Qur'an survived."[1108]

The validity of the Qur'anic text is of utmost importance, as Ayaan Hirsi Ali, a former Muslim, has written: "There is an enormously important scholarly movement underway to explore the nature of the historical Qur'an. How did the Qur'an come to us? When was it written, and who wrote it? What is the origin of the stories, the legends, the principles in the Qur'an? How do we determine its authenticity? This movement, which is largely an enterprise by secular, Muslim academics, seeks factual answers. Their project is not to discredit or attack Islam, or even to enlighten Muslims. These scholars have no political or religious agenda, only a classical academic approach, just like the one that has long applied historical analysis to the Old and New Testaments. Some of them fear for their lives, however, and have to write under pseudonyms. Their work is vital because, if the Muslim mind can be open to the idea that the Qur'an was written by a committee of men over the two hundred years that followed Muhammad's death, the read-only lock on the Holy Book can be opened. If Muslims can allow themselves to perceive the possibility that a holy book was needed to justify the Arab's conquests, every kind of inquiry and cultural shift is possible."[1109]

Destruction of Christian Scripture would have been consistent with the Muslim view of Christianity which considered "Christianity as an earlier, corrupted version of the true faith of which Islam was the final perfection. One does not go forward by going backward."[1110]

1107 L. Bevan Jones, <u>Christianity Explained to Muslims,</u> (Calcutta: Y.M.C.A. Publishing House, 1952), p. 41. Professor Small rather timorously discusses the Qur'anic text by writing, "After Muhammad's death there were collections of this [Koranic] material in use among his Companions that became authoritative versions in their own right. ... It was the use of these different versions that allegedly caused conflicts so severe they threatened the unity of the empire and prompted 'Uthman to create a single version. The traditions recount that 'Uthman did this using for a basis one Companion's version, 'Umar's, ... 'Uthman had this version edited, possibly including additional material as well as removing some material. This version of 'Uthman's then became the Canonical text form. ... If this action was taken by 'Uthman, it prevented the possibility of fully recovering either the authoritative text-forms of the Companions, or the auto-graphic predecessor text forms of the Qur'an." – Keith E. Small, <u>Textual Criticism and Qur'an Manuscripts</u>, (New York, Lexington Books, 2011), p. 8. Small quotes a noted Qur'an scholar saying, "It is today evident that the real history of the fixation of the Qur'anic text attested in early manuscripts differs in extremely serious fashion from the history preserved in the Muslim tradition." – <u>Ibid</u>. viii.
1108 Fred M. Donner, <u>Muhammad and the Believers: At the Origins of Islam</u>, (London: Harvard University Press, 2010), pp. 153-154.
1109 Ayaan Hirsi Ali, <u>Nomad, From Islam to America</u>, (New York: Free Press, 2010), pp. 206-207.
1110 Bernard Lewis, <u>What Went Wrong?</u>, (New York: Oxford University Press, 2002), pp. 45-46.

Muhammad's Biblical Knowledge

Muhammad certainly knew that Christians had the gospel in written form. This is clear from Pickthall's translation of Surah 7:157 which tells us, "Those who follow the messenger, the Prophet who can neither read nor write, <u>whom</u> they will find described in the Torah and the Gospel (which are) with them." But was that written gospel to which the Koran refers transcribed in Arabic or in some other language?

We know the Gospel and quasi-Gospel writings made considerable pre-Islamic Christian impact because, "The passages in the Qur'an which reflect the canonical and apocryphal gospels can be ... assumed to be derived from the same Christian communities, an assumption which is to some extent borne out by the high proportion of Ethiopic and southern Arabic terms which they contain (e.g. Surah v. 112-115). The great majority of these passages are narratives relating to the birth of Jesus, Mary and John the Baptist, and the mission, miracles and ascension of Jesus (see `Isa, Maryam, yahya). There are also allusions to several of the parables, e.g. of the sower (xlviii. 29) and of the virgins (lvii. 13), to the supposed prophecy of the coming of another Apostle (vii. 157), and to many single phrases. More surprisingly, yet not intrinsically improbable, in view of the rivalry between Jews and Christians in Yaman, there are also echoes of the arguments directed against the Jews in the Gospels and Epistles, which, as pointed out by Andrae and Ahrens ... are sometimes employed in the Qur'an against Christians as well as Jews."[1111]

Christians Surrounded Arabia

Though Christian Scriptures in Arabic were not easily accessible up to the birth of Muhammad, still, they probably existed because congregations of people who followed Christ, in one way or another, were widespread in Arabia at the time Muhammad began preaching. Those Christians undoubtedly would have wanted Scripture to be in their daily language. In fact, "The Christians surrounded Arabia. The Nestorians had bishops in Najran, in San'a, the capital of Yemen, in Socotra, the island of Aloes, in Sohar, the capital of Oman, called Mazoun then, in Khota, in Qatar, in Hagar, on the islands of Deirin, Tharon and Mashmahiq, in Basra, in Hira, in Damascus, in Busra; the Jacobites, who were powerful in Yemen, claimed all of the Arab tribes of the north, from Damascus to the Tigris. Aside from this, the wilderness was traversed by monks and pilgrims, who—in groups of 700 or 800 people—went to Jerusalem and to Sinai; the novels and stories praised proselytism among the Arabs, (and) their trade with India mobilized numerous caravans; the life of a hermit was so well loved, that as a manner of speech there were not any deserts or mountains without dwellers, one could also say that the polytheistic Arabs in Arabia only

---

[1111] B. Carra de Vaux, *Indjil*, <u>Shorter Encyclopedia of Islam</u>, (Ithaca, New York: Cornell University Press, 1974), H.A.R. Gibb & J.H. Kramers, eds., p. 169.

formed a small island, which was traversed by Christians from all directions."[1112]

Recent Discoveries

New dimensions of the early impact of Christ's gospel in Arabia came to light in 1994. In that year, "London University's School of Oriental and African Studies revealed what appears to have been a Christian site on Sir Bani Yas Island,[1113] off the coast of Abu Dhabi, with at least one courtyard and no fewer than 15 rooms.

"When they discovered five intricately carved stucco crosses near a collapsed wall, archaeologists concluded that Christians had been present at the ancient site. ... Though the discovery of a pre-Islamic Christian community was unexpected, finds over the past eight years have revealed the presence of ancient churches in present-day Kuwait, Qatar and Saudi Arabia, according to Geoffrey King, field director of the excavation."[1114]

Additional Information

"The second area where one might have found an Arabic gospel prior to the rise of Islam is in Mesopotamia, particularly in al-Hira, near the southern Euphrates. Christianity came to Hira at an early date; this city became an Episcopal See as early as 410 A.D. Its bishop was called Hosea, and it had a strong Christian (Nestorian) presence. It offered protection to the Christians against Sasanid [sic] Persia. The Christians of Hira had played an important role in the development of the Arabic script, especially in the fifth century. According to Muslim tradition, Zayd b. Hamad, a Christian from Hira was among the first persons *to write Arabic* (*circa* 500 A.D.). His son, 'Adi ibn Zayd al-'Ibadi, was a well known Arab Christian poet. Moreover, Christians of al-Hira sent mis-

---

[1112] N.A. Newman (ed.), The Early Christian-Muslim Dialogue, A Collection of Documents from the First Three Islamic Centuries (632–900A.D.) Translations with Commentary, (Hatfield, Pennsylvania: Interdisciplinary Biblical Research Institute, 1993), p. 18. Hitti says, "Christianity of the Monophysite [The Greek means a single nature. Used of those who hold that there is but a single nature in Christ or that the human and divine in Him constituted but one composite nature] type began to trickle in from the north, particularly Syria, at an early date. Syrian missionaries fleeing persecution may have entered al-Yaman [Yemen] at times unknown to us, but the first Christian embassy to South Arabia that we read of was that sent by the Emperor Constantius in 356 under the leadership of Theophilus Indus, an Arian. The real motive behind the mission lay in the international politics of the day and the rivalry between the Roman and Persian empires for spheres of influence in South Arabia. Theophilus succeeded in building one church at `Adan (Aden) and two others in the country of the Himyarites. Najran, into which Christianity of the Monophysite communion is said to have been introduced by a holy man from Syria named Faymiyun (Phemion), embraced the new faith about A.D. 500. Ibn-Hisham and al-Tabari give us the legend of this ascetic, who was captured by an Arab caravan and brought to Najran. Ya'qub of Saruj addressed a comforting letter in Syriac to the Christians of Najran." – Philip K. Hitti, History of the Arabs, (New York: Macmillan, 1968), p. 61.

[1113] Sir Bani Yas Island is only a short distance off the coast of Abu Dhabi to the north of Jebel Dhanna.

[1114] *Early Christian Community Discovered*, Christian Century, July 27– August 3, 1994, p. 718. French archaeological discoveries also confirm the existence of pre-Islamic churches in Arabia. "Archaeologists have discovered relics of a sixth century church in the Qusur area of Kuwait, a senior official announced here (Kuwait) today. A French expedition found ruins of the building last year, but only after examining the relics and the building's construction features did they claim to have found a church dating back to the sixth century, said Fahd Alweheibi, Deputy Director of the Information Ministry's Archaeology Department. ... The church was still operating during the Moslem Abbasid Empire (750–1258)." – A Xsinhua News Agency item released on December 11, 1989. Also, in 1986 a 4th century church building near Jubail, Saudi Arabia was discovered.

sionaries to various places, including the south of Arabia. They had a strong relationship with the Christians of Najran. They built many churches and convents in and around Hira. The most significant Christian inscription of the pre-Islamic time is found in Dayr Hind in Hira and its text shows, with little doubt, that the Christians of Hira used Arabic in writing and in expressing their religious beliefs. ...

"The third group which might have conceivably produced an Arabic Gospel are the Christians of the Arabian Peninsula, especially those from Najran. Najran accepted Christianity in the fifth century and became the main centre for Arab-Christians in Arabia. It had its first known bishop *circa* 500 A.D., and a missionary, 'Simeon of Bet Arsam,' who was active during the first half of the sixth century. In about 517 A.D., a number of Christians at Najran, about 200 men and 100 women, were killed by the Jewish king of Himyar, Dhu Nuwas. Consequently, this place became a pilgrimage centre for the Arab Christians (and possibly also the Ethiopians). It had a well known bishop and poet, Quss ibn Sa'idah, who met the Prophet Muhammad in Suq 'Ukaz.

"No one denies the significance of this place in terms of its Christian presence in Arabia. The question is whether these Arab Christians were confined to the official and ecclesiastical language, mainly Syriac, or produced an Arabic Gospel for liturgical and missiological purposes. The study of AGM [Arabic Gospel Manuscripts] seems to support the second position, and the Arabic language and script were certainly well developed enough to serve such a purpose."[1115]

○○

1115 Hikmat Kashouh, The Arabic Versions of the Gospels, The Manuscripts and Their Families, (Berlin/Boston: Walter de Gruyter GmbH & Co., 2012), pp. 321-322.

APPENDIX G

The Magi and the Church

Long lines of chained,[1116] mocked,[1117] and sexually molested[1118] Israelite captives were led to the region now known as Iran by the Assyrians and, later, by the Babylonians when they in turn exercised their cruel and tyrannical jurisdiction over the area. No one at that time could have possibly imagined that one day from the progeny of those pitiful captives would come the charter members of the Messiah's church in Iran. But certainly that is what happened. Except for any proselytes who may have been among them, those from Parthia, Media, Elam and Mesopotamia (Acts 2:9) who were present in that audience which heard the first declaration of the gospel of Christ were ethnically all Jews, all descendants of those captives. They were also all citizens of the Iranian empire, known at that time as the Parthian Empire. When those Iranians who had accepted Christ that Day of Pentecost (and were present during those subsequent days of triumphant preaching in Jerusalem) returned to Iran, they constituted Christ's Iranian church.

Those Jewish Christians must have shared their new knowledge and their new faith regarding Jesus with many of their fellows in the Jewish diaspora in Iran and with many "native" Iranians as well. In this way they would have added a new dimension to the fulfillment of Micah's prophecy that "the remnant of Jacob shall be in the midst of many peoples as dew from Jehovah, as showers upon the grass."[1119] In Iran, as well as in the Roman Empire, there were people prepared to accept Christ; for example, many Iranians had become converts to Judaism.[1120] They, along with the ethnic Jews in Iran, would undoubtedly have had some anticipation of the coming of the Messiah through study of the Scriptures.

Merging of Movements?

There may well have been another stream which merged with those Jewish elements to constitute the initial church of Christ in Iran during the apostolic period. It would have been that of the Magi who are mentioned so prominently in the first half of the second chapter of Matthew's gospel account of the life of Jesus. While no one can say with absolute certainty that members of the Iranian priestly class known as Magi were in fact also charter members of the nascent Iranian church, it certainly does not seem presumptive to think that they may have been.

1116 Jeremiah 40:1.
1117 Psalms 137:3.
1118 Lamentations 5:11.
1119 Micah 5:7 ARV.
1120 Esther 8:17.

The Magi With the Emperors

To understand who the Magi were one has to begin his search in the records of ancient Iran. The earliest Iranian empire, the Achaemenid Empire, came into existence when Cyrus the Great[1121] conquered the Median Empire, whose capital was Ecbatana.[1122] During the life of Cyrus the Great,[1123] founder and the first emperor of the great Achaemenian Empire, the imperial capital was Pasargadae. Darius the Great, who succeeded to the throne from a different branch of the Achaemenians, felt the capital at Pasargadae was neither adequate nor appropriately impressive for an empire ruling from the Indus River to the Aegean Sea. So he began construction of Persepolis, the magnificent capital city whose ruins, even after 25 centuries, still awe and overwhelm one with their vastness, beauty and technical perfection.[1124] But Cyrus' capital at Pasargadae was not abandoned. Its three palaces, its Zoroastrian fire altars, the tomb of Cyrus and a mysterious building which well may have been the temporary tomb of Cambyses I, the father of Cyrus the Great, were all maintained in a splendid irrigated imperial garden. Paid Magi were perpetually on duty to guard the tomb of Cyrus and offer the proper sacrifices in his honor. (See Photo 13.)

Alexander Meets the Magi

Two centuries later when that first Iranian empire, the Achaemenian Empire, was conquered by Alexander's Greeks, Magi still occupied high offices. "Early in 324 [B.C.] Alexander [The Great] advanced into Persis by the main road to Pasargadae, leading the Companions, the fittest of the infantry, and a few archers. ... At Pasargadae Alexander was very distressed to find that the tomb of Cyrus, whom he particularly honored, had been broken into and all its contents removed except the golden sarcophagus containing the body of Cyrus and the divan on which it stood. Even the sarcophagus had been damaged in an unsuccessful attempt to remove it and the body thrown out. Aristobulus, who has left us a detailed description of the monument which tallies closely with its extant remains, was instructed to repair the damage and restore the tomb to its original condition, then to wall up the entrance and seal it with the royal seal. The Magi who guarded the tomb were interrogated, but even under torture they neither admitted their own guilt nor implicated others, and Alexander let them go free."[1125]

The Magi Have a Very Ancient History

The origin of the Magi, however, certainly antedates Cyrus the Great. "The Magi were one of the several Iranian tribes who had moved onto the [Iranian] plateau

---

1121 The approximate dates of his life are 585–529 B.C.
1122 This city is mentioned in Ezra 6:2. Many translations render the name Achmetha rather than Ecbatana. See the NIV which gives the correct spelling.
1123 Cyrus is mentioned in many biblical references. See II Chronicles 36:22-23, Ezra 1:7-8, 3:7, 4:3-5, 5:13-17, 6:3, 6:14, Isaiah 44:28, 45:1, Daniel 1:21, 6:28, 10:1.
1124 "Construction was begun by Darius and continued by Xerxes and Artaxerxes III." – Donald N. Wilber, Iran: Past and Present, (Princeton University Press, 1948), p. 24.
1125 J.R. Hamilton, Alexander the Great, (London: Hutchinson University Library, 1973), p. 132.

and were distinguished from the others by having acquired exclusive rights to exercising priestly functions."[1126] Those Magi, having come under the influence of the prophet Zarathushtra, who is commonly known as Zoroaster, "aimed at replacing the pagan gods personifying natural forces and human passions with a universal system based on the unending conflict between good and evil. ... The new doctrine recognized Ahura Mazda, from whose name the religion is often called Mazdaism, as the God of Good, associated also with truth and light, and taught the immortality of the soul and the final judgment of humanity."[1127]

In contrast to the oldest copies of the Christian scriptures which go back to a date very early in the first century,[1128] the oldest copies of the Zoroastrian scriptures, the *Avesta*, were "not written down for many centuries; in fact, the oldest surviving manuscript dates from the thirteenth century A.D."[1129] However, "the power and intensity of feeling in the verses may be sensed even in translation as for example, Yasna 44.3:

> This do I ask Thee, O Lord, tell me truly;
> Who is the creator, the first father of Righteousness?
> Who laid down the path of the sun and stars?
> Who is it through whom the moon now waxes now wanes?
> All this and more do I wish to know, Oh Wise One."[1130]

Christians in Bethlehem Knew Who the Magi Were

The Magi, to whom the gospel record gives great prominence in Matthew 2:1-12, undoubtedly belonged to that fellowship of Iranian priests which had grown out of the early Iranian tribe of Magi. Certainly the church in the village of Bethlehem where Jesus was born understood the Magi to have come from Iran. A period of military and economic weakness in the Byzantine Empire took place just prior to the seventh century A.D. "During the reign of the emperor Heraclius (A.D. 610–641), the Persians took advantage of this situation to sweep into the Byzantine Empire in 611. By 614 they had conquered Jerusalem after a siege of twenty days. Aided by Samaritans and Jews, the Persians perpetrated a widespread massacre of Christians in Jerusalem. They destroyed all the beautiful churches [in Palestine] except the church in Bethlehem, which was spared only because they saw on the front of the church a mosaic picture of the magi whom they recognized as Persians."[1131]

1126 Donald N. Wilber, Persepolis, The Archaeology of Parsa, Seat of The Persian Kings, (New York: Thomas Y. Crowell Company, 1969), p. 36.
1127 Donald N. Wilber, Iran Past and Present, (Princeton: Princeton University Press, 1963), p. 23.
1128 See, for example, Carsten Peter Thiede and Matthew D'Ancona, Eyewitness to Jesus, (New York: Doubleday, 1996).
1129 Donald N. Wilber, Persepolis, The Archaeology of Parsa, Seat of the Persian Kings, (New York: Thomas Y. Crowell Company, 1969), p. 35.
1130 Richard N. Frye, The Heritage of Persia, (Cleveland and New York: The World Publishing Company, 1963), p. 32.
1131 George A. Turner, Historical Geography of the Holy Land, (Grand Rapids: Baker Book House,1973), p. 49.

Five Notable Facts Further Help Identify the Magi

In addition to the history of the church building in Bethlehem testifying to the fact that the Magi were Zoroastrian priests who came from Iran, the Biblical record testifies to the same truth. There are at least five notable facts one may deduce from the gospel account which are compatible with this understanding. Of course, these five facts are in addition to the obvious fact that Matthew clearly calls them Magi, the name for Zoroastrian priests and for no one else.

First is the direction of their travel. If the Magi were, indeed, priests of the Zoroastrian religion in Iran, we would expect them to have come from the direction of Iran. That is precisely what we find in the biblical record. "After Jesus was born in Bethlehem in Judea, during the time of King Herod, Magi **from the east** came to Jerusalem and asked, 'Where is the one who has been born king of the Jews? We saw his star **in the east** and have come to worship him.'" (Matthew 2:1-2 NIV)

Secondly, they all came from the <u>same</u> country. Matthew tells us, "they departed into their own country." (Matthew 1:12) Until the coming of Islam in the seventh century A.D., which caused those Zoroastrians who had the means to do so to flee abroad, the ministry of the Magi was confined to Iran. Thus, the coming of the Magi at the birth of Jesus Christ did not take place as Lew Wallace depicted it in his great novel, *Ben Hur*. He portrayed the Magi as coming from three separate continents, meeting in Syria and then traveling together to Bethlehem.

In the **third** place, the general impact which their appearance in Jerusalem had speaks of men of high position and great authority, which the Magi in Iran unquestionably had. Moreover, if they were indeed Magi from Iran, they were highly esteemed religious dignitaries from a rival empire which was an enemy of the Romans! Obviously, the Magi were recognized to be men of great stature; otherwise, how could they have gotten an audience with King Herod? Certainly not every tourist, business man, or curious traveler was granted such a private audience!

When Alexander the Great conquered Iran he found people in high public office who were called Magi. They were priests of the Zoroastrian religion. In addition to their daily priestly duties they were entrusted by Darius (the Iranian emperor at the time of Alexander's invasion) with guarding the tomb of Cyrus the Great in Pasargadae, the first capital city of the Achaemenid Empire. At the time of Darius and the succeeding Achaemenian emperors, Zoroastrianism was not the state religion in the legal sense which it became under the Sassanians who came to power in 226 A.D. However, the Magi not only were guardians of the royal tombs but offered special sacrifices for the peace of the souls of departed monarchs. They were, then, guardians of Iranian royalty. In view of their standing, it is not surprising they could gain an audience with Herod.

Fourthly, their question caused the kind of political concern which such an inquiry would cause if it came from high dignitaries of an enemy country. They asked, "Where is he that is born King of the Jews?" (Matthew 2:2) The political implications of their question were heavy. Herod seemed to have regarded them as emissaries from a rival enemy empire, and rightly so. After Alexander the Great's conquest, Iran was governed by Greeks till the rise of the Parthian Empire which broke the Greek yoke. They constituted the succeeding Iranian dynasty following the Achaemenians. At the time Jesus was born in Bethlehem, the Parthian Dynasty was ruling Iran.[1132] The Parthian Empire was a fearsome enemy, indeed. For example, they "were the first to administer a crushing defeat to the heretofore victorious Roman armies when in 53 B.C. the consul Crassus lost his life to Parthian horsemen with bows."[1133] It was this very empire which had made Zoroastrianism "an organized state[wide] religion."[1134] It would have appeared to Herod that high emissaries of the neighboring enemy empire had come seeking to establish contact with a king who would challenge his own rule and that of the Romans! No wonder, then, that Matthew tells us, Herod "was troubled and all Jerusalem with him" (Matthew 2:3)

In the **fifth** place, Their decisiveness speaks of men who are decision makers—"We saw his star in the east, and are come" (Matthew 2:2)

Were the Magi Members of the Church?

Is there any evidence that the Magi became members of the Iranian church? We have no direct irrefutable proof that they did. However, there are certainly strong implications that they stayed in touch with the followers of Jesus, the King whom they visited in his infancy. Probably the account of their visit which is recorded in Matthew 2:1-12 comes from an interview conducted either by Matthew or by Iranian Christians who subsequently made the account available to Matthew. God has often used this kind of eye-witness or first-person testimony as the source for the scriptural account.

For example, Luke is very explicit about that type of source material which he incorporated into Scripture. He wrote, "Many have undertaken to draw up an account of the things that have been fulfilled among us, just as they were handed down to us by those who from the first were eyewitnesses and servants of the word." (Luke 1:1 NIV) Luke incorporates one of those accounts in his description of the discussions which took place about the reception of Gentiles into the church. That is obvious by his use of the first-person-singular pronouns for Peter in Acts chapter 11. So, it seems, the account of the visit of the Magi reflects the description which they gave themselves. Thus, the account says, "we saw his star in the east and have come to worship him." (Matthew 2:2 NIV) How could

---

[1132] The Parthian Empire was founded by Arsaces I in 250 B.C. It ended with the rout and death of Artabanus in 226 A.D.
[1133] Richard N. Frye, Iran, (New York: Henry Holt and Company, 1953), p. 41.
[1134] Richard N. Frye, Iran, (New York: Henry Holt and Company, 1953), p. 41.

Matthew have gotten that first-person testimony? It implies that the Magi had kept a connection with the church!

They were men so close to God that God gave them direct revelation. That is obvious from the succinct statement that "having been warned in a dream not to go back to Herod, they returned to their country by another route." (Matthew 2:12 NIV) Not only were they the recipients of divine revelation, they were also responsive and obedient to "the vision from heaven" as Paul was later to his own heavenly vision. (Acts 26:19 NIV) Like Samuel, in essence, they said, "Speak; for thy servant heareth." (Samuel 3:10) Aren't those who are responsive to God's leading the very ones who will ultimately be in the church of God?

Perhaps the Magi who had celebrated the birth of Jesus were personally present on that momentous Day of Pentecost, the first one following Jesus' resurrection. If not, they undoubtedly learned of the universally relevant message proclaimed on that day from those who had been present. This is a reasonable conclusion because as has just been pointed out, it is very probable that they kept in touch with the people of Christ. Since, in sharp contrast to Balaam in Moses' time, they were men who made it their practice to obey God's message at any price, it seems reasonable that they obeyed the gospel and thus became an important part of the church in Iran.

Avenues of Perception

In addition to having received revelation from God, there is also a strong presumption that the Magi were students of Biblical Scripture. Perhaps they had made calculations and computations based on Daniel's prophecy which is recorded in Daniel 9:24-27. If so, from their research they may have realized that the time of the anointing of "the most holy ... the anointed one, the prince" was very near. Insight gained through careful study of the time factor in Daniel's prophecy may have helped them realize the appearance of the unusual star[1135] coincided with the coming of the prince predicted by Daniel.

While it may seem a bit speculative to assert that the Magi followed Biblical prophecy, it is certain that they fulfilled it. It had been prophesied that at the coming of the Redeemer, not only people from the west would "fear the name of Jehovah," but people "from the rising of the sun" would revere his glory. (Isaiah 59:19 NIV) No doubt the Magi were among those people of the nations who were to come to the Redeemer's light and among the "kings [who were to come] to the brightness of [his] dawn." (Isaiah 60:3 NIV)

[1135] A very helpful and informative discussion and analysis of the astronomical phenomenon which the Magi beheld is given by Ernest L. Martin, <u>The Birth of Christ Recalculated</u> 2nd ed; (Pasadena, California: Foundation for Biblical Research, 1980), pp. 6-9.

The Iranian Church Reflected the Virtues of the Magi

Some of the greatest chapters of Christian devotion, virtue and heroism of all time have been written by the church in Iran. One wonders if those qualities may not have been inspired by the example of the Magi, and perhaps by their fellowship within the Iranian church.

Truth Versus Power

The Magi loved the truth, which according to II Thessalonians 2:8-10 is the essential basic condition for becoming an heir of salvation. They loved the truth more than their positions of authority and power. Through all the ages, the enticements growing out of the exercise of power often conflict with the duty to embrace truth. That is one reason that "not many mighty, not many noble, are called." (I Corinthians 1:26) Let us not forget that the Magi were leaders highly regarded by the Iranian state. The struggle between loyalty to power versus loyalty to truth becomes vivid from one interpretation of America's experience in Vietnam. "Vietnam made us understand in some terrible way that we were no longer a mere democracy; we were a superpower, a democracy become empire. A democracy functions on the basis of shared truths, but an empire is far grander, it is about power, and truth often becomes an obstruction. ... We did not realize that America had become an empire, run by men suited to running empires, men who did not necessarily value the truth. They were far too grand for that; they valued power over truth. They had created their own truth: In power there was truth."[1136]

Truth Versus Adulation

Those scholar-priests whom scripture identifies as Magi also loved truth more than positions of adulation. Jesus highlighted the conflict between adulation and truth when he asked rejectionists, "How can you believe if you accept praise from one another, yet make no effort to obtain the praise that comes from the only God?" (John 5:44 NIV) Those Magi were in positions from which they could have demanded groveling adulation from obsequious petitioners. They turned their backs on such opportunities in order to bow before a babe in swaddling clothes whom they knew was the world's Redeemer! We are reminded that, "God resisteth the proud, but giveth grace to the humble." (James 4:6)

Truth Versus Advantage

The Magi loved the truth more than the emoluments which could have accrued to them due to the advantages of their position. They were highly paid by the Iranian state as guardians of Pasargadae. Though many in such circumstances "fall into a temptation and a snare and many foolish and hurtful lusts" (I Timothy 6:9), these men were willing to put their incomes into jeopardy, take significant amounts of their accrued wealth and offer it to a babe whom they knew was Jesus, the Savior.

1136 David Halberstam, The Next Century, (New York: William Morrow and Company, Inc., 1991), pp. 66-68.

God Versus Caesar

The Magi were also faced with the dilemma of the Caesar-vs.-God dichotomy (See Matthew 22:15-22) but because of their love of the truth they chose God over country! God's leading took them into enemy territory on a trip which had the potential of putting them under a cloud of suspicion after return to their own country.

Truth Versus Self

The Magi, seekers after God, certainly loved the truth more than self. In addition to putting themselves under a cloud of suspicion at home, there were the difficulties and dangers of the journey itself. To get some idea of the rigors of such a journey, reflect on a trip by Henry Martyn, the great Bible translator. In May of 1812, having completed his translation of the New Testament in Persian, he set out from Shiraz to Tabriz to give it to the British Ambassador who would formally present it to the Shah. "Twelve days' hard riding brought him to Isfahan"[1137] In November of 1975 I drove the same distance in one long day, even though I took out about three hours to examine the ruins of Pasargadae!

Of course, even in ancient times there were faster means of travel to which the Parthian Imperial Administration doubtless had access. A modern Irani cameleer claims a good riding camel can travel at a ten-mile-an-hour clip for twelve hours and repeat the performance after only a two hour rest.[1138] Frederick Tallberg says that, "To ensure the control and development of his immense empire, Darius (550–486 B.C.) connected his cities by means of a network of ... roads, along which caravans could journey safely and comfortably, in the knowledge that at every twenty-four kilometers was a military post and a caravanserai. The swift post-riders on the famous 'Royal Road' covered a distance of 2,100 kilometers from Susa to Sardis in eleven days."[1139] That works out to a daily average of 118.5 miles, which agrees closely with the cameleer's testimony. However, by any standard, the trip made by the Magi was arduous, but they understood that the trip was essential because it was on behalf of divine truth and in obedience to God.

1137 Robin E. Waterfield, <u>Christians in Persia</u> (London: George Allen & Unwin Ltd., 1973), p. 93.
1138 William Graves, <u>Iran Desert Miracle</u>, National Geographic Magazine, Vol. 147, No. 1 (January 1975), p. 41.
1139 Frederick Tallberg, <u>From Cyrus to Pahlavi, A Picture Story of the Iranian Empire</u>, 2nd ed. (Shiraz: Pahlavi University, 1967), p. 19.

Appendix G

Truth Versus Religion

Like Uriah the Hittite, like Ruth the Moabitess, like Ebed Melech the slave from pagan Ethiopia, those Magi realized the ultimate divine truth was not to be found in their ancestral religion, Mazdaism in their case. They had the honesty and the courage to seek God's truth where it really was to be found. In doing so, undoubtedly they put their lucrative, prestigious careers and their own persons in mortal danger. May each of us have the courage to follow the luminous path upon which those spiritual giants trod!

಄

APPENDIX H

Highlights of Iranian History

Through the centuries Iran, known also as Persia, has been so central in the fulfillment of God's eternal purpose that it seems appropriate to give a brief historical overview of Iran's history from Cyrus to the Iran/Iraq War so we may be able to see current events in their proper perspective.

I. The Achaemenian Period of Persian/Iranian History

(559 B.C.–330 B.C., from the reign of Cyrus the Great to capitulation to Alexander the Great)

The most glorious period of Iranian history was the Achaemenian. It derives that name from Achaemenes, the eponymous ancestor from whom the royal line of emperors descended. Four of the first five of those emperors are mentioned prominently in the Old Testament.

A. Cyrus the Great (r. 559–530 B.C.), founder of the empire, who united the Persians and the Medes under his sway. He is mentioned in II Chronicles 36:22-23, Ezra 1:7-8, 3:7, 4:3-5, 5:13-14, 5:17, 6:3 and 6:14, Isaiah 44:28 and 45:1, Daniel 1:21, 6:28 and 10:1.

B. Cambyses (r. 530–522 B.C.) "There are no biblical references to **Cambyses** because the Jews were unable to continue work on the temple during his reign."[1140]

C. Darius (r. 522–486 B.C.) is also known as Darius the Mede, see Daniel 5:31 and 11:1. "Darius is mentioned prominently in Ezra 4-6, (compare Haggai 1:1, 15; 2:10; Zechariah 1:1, 7; and 7:1) as the Persian monarch under whom the temple at Jerusalem was finally reconstructed after the Jewish return from exile under Cyrus."[1141] He is mentioned also in Nehemiah 12:22 and Daniel 5:31, 6:1-28, 9:1 and 11:1.

D. Xerxes (r. 486–465 B.C.) is mentioned in Ezra 4:6 and Esther 1:1. "Ahasuerus of the Book of Esther is the Hebrew name for Xerxes."[1142]

E. Artaxerxes (r. 464–424 B.C.) is mentioned in Ezra 4:7-8; 4:11; 6:14; 7:1; 7:7; 7:11-12; 7:21 and Nehemiah 2:1 and 5:14. "It is certain that Nehemiah (1:1; 2:1) served as the cupbearer of Artaxerxes I, who ruled from 464–424 B.C."[1143]

1140 Edwin M. Yamauchi, Persia and the Bible, (Grand Rapids, MI: Baker Books, 1996), p. 94.
1141 Edwin M. Yamauchi, Persia and the Bible, (Grand Rapids, MI: Baker Books, 1996), pp. 129-130.
1142 Edwin M. Yamauchi, Persia and the Bible, (Grand Rapids, MI: Baker Books, 1996), p. 228.
1143 Edwin M. Yamauchi, Persia and the Bible, (Grand Rapids, MI: Baker Books, 1996), p. 242.

F. Final Reference. There is only one additional notice of Iran in the Bible. It is found in Ezekiel 38:5 where the prophet refers to Iran by using the name "Persia." The name Persia is derived from Pars, the name of Iran's central province. The Greeks simply put a Greek ending on the name Pars so that it became Parsia. Then, for euphony, the 'a' became 'e,' thus making Persia. The name "Iran" is derived from the word "Aryan" and refers to the ethnic origin of the core people of Persia. Shah Reza Pahlavi issued a decree on March 2, 1935 that foreign delegates should use the name Iran in formal correspondence. Chapters 38 and 39 of Ezekiel (see 38:5) prophetically foresee that Iran will be a central participant in a vast coalition of nations which will attack Israel, bringing upon themselves utter disaster.

Scope of the Empire. "The Persian Empire extended over an enormous area. Its eastern and western frontiers were nearly 3,000 miles apart, or considerably more than the distance between New York and San Francisco. Its northern and southern boundaries were almost as remote."[1144] The military exploits of the empire were invincible till the forces of Darius invaded Greece and aroused the anger of Alexander the Great who then conquered the Achaemenian Empire.

II. The Greek Period of Persian/Iranian History

(From 330 B.C.–248 B.C. from the victory of Alexander the Great to the victory of the Parthians, which ended Greek rule.)

Alexander the Great's blitzkrieg-like military conquest of the vast Persian Achaemenian Empire, known also as the Medo-Persian Empire, had been anticipated prophetically by the Jewish prophet, Daniel. He visualized the campaign of Alexander as a "he-goat [which] came from the west over the face of the whole earth, and touched not the ground: and the goat had a notable horn between his eyes [representing Alexander]. And he came to the ram that had the two horns [representing the Medes and Persians], which I saw standing before the river, and ran upon him in the fury of his power. And I saw him come close unto the ram, and he was moved with anger against him, and smote the ram, and brake his two horns; and there was no power in the ram to stand before him; but he cast him down to the ground, and trampled upon him; and there was none that could deliver the ram out of his hand." (Daniel 8:5-7 ASV)

In approximately 330 B.C., in the moment of his triumph, Alexander the Great ordered Persepolis, the magnificent capital of the Achaemenian Empire, to be burned. The carved-stone ruins of Persepolis, even after twenty-three centuries, are so extensive and uniquely grand that they leave every perceptive visitor stunned and awestricken. That highly regrettable incendiary event marked the indisputable end of the Achaemenian period of Persian history and the beginning of the Greek period of Persian history, consisting of two sections defined unmistakably by notable events.

1144 Hutton Webster, World History, (Boston: D. C. Heath & Co. Publishers, 1921), p. 38.

A. First was that portion of the Greek period of Persian history during which Alexander governed personally. It was surprisingly brief, lasting only seven years. It extended from 330 B.C. when he gave the order to burn Persepolis to his untimely death at Babylon in 323 B.C.

B. The second phase of the Greek period of Persian history began at Alexander's death. At that juncture, the empire was divided among four of his outstanding generals. Persia was in the portion which was allotted to Seleucus Nicator, who, emphasizing his own name, founded the Seleucid Empire. Initially, that empire was enormous, stretching from the Indian border in the east to Greece in the west. Eventually it was conquered, one area at a time, Iran being the first segment to fall. The last portion survived till 63 B.C. The Seleucid Empire had several capital cities. The principal capital, also named after Seleucus, was Seleucia on the west bank of the Tigris River. The main capital in the west was Antioch in Syria, the site from which the apostle Paul initiated evangelism in Anatolia, in the Balkan Peninsula, in Italy and in Spain.

III. The Parthian Period of Persian/Iranian History

(248 B.C. to 224 A.D. from the victory over the Seleucids to capitulation to the Sassanians.)

"The Parthians, also known to history as the Arsacids after their first rulers, were originally a nomadic Saka tribe which moved into the area east of the Caspian and then took over the region which had been Parthava [the name from which the title "Parthian" is derived] of the Achaemenid Empire. Arsaces I, 248–246 B.C., led a successful revolt against the Seleucid governor.[1145] Arsaces II, 246–211 B.C., established the independence of the new kingdom, and Arsaces III, 211–190 B.C., resisted the efforts of the Seleucids to reconquer it. The great leader, Mithradates I, 171–138 B.C., extended Parthian rule over Bactria, Parsa, Babylonia, Susiana, and Media but allowed subject kings to retain their thrones. Crushed between the Romans and the Parthians, the Seleucid power was now broken."[1146]

It is this Parthian Iranian empire to which reference is made in Acts 2:9 in Luke's summary of those countries from which Jews had assembled in Jerusalem to participate in the first festivals of Passover and Pentecost following the resurrection of Christ.

IV. The Sassanian Period of Persian/Iranian History

(224 A.D.–642 A.D. from the victory of the Sassanians over the Seleucids to the victory of the Muslim army at the Battle of Nehawand.)

1145 "The Parthians themselves reckoned the year (autumn) 248–247 B.C. as the first of their empire." However, the reality was contested because "we have authentic record that even in the epoch-year 248–247 B.C., the year of the accession of Tiridates, Parthia was still under the Seleucids." – Henry Smith Williams, ed., The Historians History of the World, Vol. VIII, (London & New York: The History Association, 1907), p. 54.

1146 Donald N. Wilber, Iran Past and Present, (Princeton NJ: Princeton University Press, 1963), p. 28.

"About A.D. 211 Ardashir organized a revolt in the province of Fars [Pars] and in A.D. 224 his forces killed the last Parthian ruler in battle at Susiana. Ardashir soon controlled all of Iran except for the provinces of Armenia and Bactria. The name of his new dynasty, Sassanian, seems to come from the old Persian title, *Sasan*, or 'commanders,' although it was later a family name."[1147]

It was during the Sassanian period of Iranian history that Zoroastrianism became Iran's state religion. From 531–579A.D., beginning with the reign of Khusraw I, "Christians were frequently, often violently, persecuted in the first centuries of the Sassanian period, primarily because of the identification of the [Christian] religion with the rival Roman Empire. After the end of the fifth century, when the Christians within the empire were [alleged to be] members of the eastern Nestorian Church, they were treated with increased tolerance."[1148]

Khusraw II, who ruled from 589–628 A.D., tragically in 602 A.D. initiated an all-out war against Byzantium. It raged for twenty-six years and ended disastrously for the Sassanians at the Battle of Nineveh in 627 A.D. That battle resulted from an amphibious attack through the Black Sea by the Byzantine forces under the leadership of Emperor Heraclius. One year later, events culminated in 628 A.D. with the destruction of Iran's Sassanian royal house. That quarter-century-long war left both Byzantium and the Sassanian Empire exhausted, making them disastrously vulnerable to the unrelenting attacks soon to fall upon them from the nascent Islamic empire.

III. The Muslim Era of Persian/Iranian History

(From 642 A.D. to the present.)

A. The Arab period of Iran's Muslim Era. This period began when Islam was imposed on Iran by "the shattering blow of the Arab conquest"[1149] culminating in the Battle of Nehawand in 642 A.D. That battle destroyed all remaining effective Iranian military power. Following that conquest, Iran was governed by a series of Arab caliphs, first from Medina and then from Damascus. The caliphs ruling from Medina were Umar, Uthman and Ali. Ali ruled Iran from Medina till he shifted his capital to Kufa, in Iraq, where he was assassinated. Then the governance of Iran came under a long series of Sunni caliphs, ruling from Damascus, all of whom occupied the throne of the Umayyad Caliphate.[1150] This oppressive 108-year-long period ended with the Battle of the Great Zab River in 750 A.D.

B. The Abbasid-Caliphate Period of Iran's Muslim Era. It began with a decisive battle on the Great Zab River in 750 A.D. The period ended in 1258 when the

---

1147 Donald N. Wilber, Iran Past and Present, (Princeton NJ: Princeton University Press, 1963), p. 30.
1148 Donald N. Wilber, Iran Past and Present, (Princeton NJ: Princeton University Press, 1963), p. 33.
1149 Donald N. Wilber, Iran Past and Present, (Princeton NJ: Princeton University Press, 1963), p. 88.
1150 The fourteen Umayyad caliphs who ruled Iran were: Muawiya 661–680 A.D., Yazid 680–683 A.D., Muawiya II 683–684 A.D., Marwan 684–685 A.D., Abd al-Malik 685–705 A.D., Al-Walid I 705–715 A.D., Sulayman 715–717 A.D., Umar II 717–720 A.D., Yazid II 720–724 A.D., Hisham 724–743 A.D., Walid 743–744 A.D., Yazid III 4/17/744–10/4/744 A.D., Ibrahim 10/744–12/744 A.D., Marwan II 744–750 A.D.

Mongols under Hulagu destroyed Baghdad, the renowned Abbasid capital. The Persian anti-Umayyad-Caliphate forces were led at the Battle of the Zab by Abbas, a relative of the Prophet Muhammad. His army was manned principally by Iranians. Victory in that critical conflict initiated the Abbasid Caliphate and terminated the Arabian Umayyad Caliphate. Many Iranian Shias helped bring "about the overthrow of the Umayyads and their replacement by the Abbasids, another branch of the family to which both the Prophet and Ali had belonged—but in the hour of their triumph the Abbasid Caliphs renounced the [Shia] sect and the daʿis [evangelists or promoters] that had [largely] brought them [the Abbasids] to power."[1151] This was a significant turning point in Iranian history because "after the victory [at the Zab River] and betrayal of the Shias by] the Abbasids, the Shia concentrated their hopes on the descendants of Ali and, among these, more particularly on those who sprang from his marriage with the Prophet's daughter [Fatimah]."[1152] At this early point they constituted a political, but not yet a religious, movement.

The motivation of the Shias' wholehearted effort to help the Abbasids overthrow the Umayyad Caliphate is easily understood. It was the Umayyads who had killed Husayn, Ali's youngest son, at Karbala. After Hasan, Ali's oldest son, had rejected their call, then Husayn had become the Shias' choice to be the next caliph. He would have ruled from Kufa.

When Husayn/Hussein was killed near Karbala, the pro-Ali Muslims, the Alids, became known also as the Shias (expressed in Arabic as *Shiʿat ʿAli*, The Partisans of Ali). The residents of Kufa had urged Husayn to come and fill the role of caliph in place of his father, Ali, who had been murdered by a Kharijite, a seceder, one who—in protest—had defected from Ali's own army. The assassin had been moved with anger because at the Battle of Siffeen, Ali agreed to a decision through a Koran-based negotiation rather than continuing the war to a definitive conclusion. That battle was being fought to determine whether Ali or Muawiya was to be recognized as the legitimate caliph. (See Chapter 19, "Muslim Civil War.") The Shiite movement continued to be secular till after the Battle of the Zab, in which they fought with great commitment. They fought to destroy the Umayyad Caliphate (which had killed Husayn) and to help give birth to the Abbasid Caliphate.

Culturally, the Abbasid Caliphate made an invaluable contribution when Caliph Harun al-Rashid established The House of Wisdom, a great translation center. (See Chapter 6 under "Translation Center.") The most competent and productive translator was Hunayn ibn Ishaq (808–873 A.D.), a Nestorian Christian. In addition to his translation of the seven books of Galen's anatomy, he translated the Greek Septuagint Old Testament into Arabic. Though he would have been eminently qualified to have done so, unfortunately we do not know if he translated the New Testament into the current, most widely used Iranian language of his time.

1151 Bernard Lewis, The Assassins, A Radical Sect in Islam, (New York: Oxford University Press, 1967), p. 23.
1152 Bernard Lewis, The Assassins, A Radical Sect in Islam, (New York: Oxford University Press, 1967), pp. 24-25.

Following the Battle of the Zab, as just noted, the Abbasid Caliphs alienated the Shiites with great contempt. At that critical juncture, the Alid (a follower of Ali) movement began to take on a religious hue, which slowly intensified until Shiism became the state religion under Iran's Safavid Empire, 1501–1735. Ismail, founder of the Safavid Dynasty, declared the Shia faith to be the state religion when he took the throne. "Wars between the Iranians and the Ottomans [were] a long struggle providing continual encouragement for the Safavids to strengthen the Shi'i identity of Iran. Although conversion was not as rapid as the Isma'ili's forcible policies might suggest, the vast majority of Iranians did identify strongly with Shi'ism by the [effective] end of the Safavid era in 1722 (an end brought on by Afghan Sunni invaders)."[1153] Amazingly, that great Safavid Empire was betrayed into the hands of Mahmud of Ghazni when Sultan Hussein, the Safavid's last ruling sultan, personally handed his crown to the conqueror. In sharp contrast to that moment of surrender, it had been the Safavid Empire in 1529 which had saved Europe from a Muslim invasion by attacking the Ottoman Empire's eastern border. That forced the Ottomans to cancel their incipient attack on Vienna, eastern gateway to the conquest of Europe, and rush their troops to the east.

Superficially, Sultan Hussein's giving his crown to Mahmud of Ghazni seems totally craven and cowardly; however, in his favor we should realize that he was under pressure from daunting factors which were in play. Among them were "disruption by military tribes, the low level of agricultural production, and the gradual change of Western trade routes to the Far East from overland to overseas, [which] ... contributed to economic decline, [which was] reflected in political decline, and to easy conquest by the Afghans in 1722. Frequent wars with the Ottomans also took an economic toll."[1154]

C. The Seljuk Turkish Period of Iran's Muslim Era. (See Chapter 17 under "Egyptian Christians Come Under the Ottoman Turks.") This period partly overlaps the Abbasid period because the fading Abbasid Caliphs invited the Seljuks to help them govern. Early during the Abbasid Caliphate, there had been a major influx into Iran of the Seljuks and Ottomans, two very closely related Turkish tribes from Central Asia. At that point, the Seljuks were clearly dominant over their close cousins, the Ottomans. As the vigor of the decadent Abbasid Caliphs waned, they invited the Seljuk Turks, under their leader Tughril Beg, to fill the resulting vacuum. The Abbasid invitation gave the Seljuks, whose capital city was Rey/Ray/Rayy (now the capital of Rey County in Tehran Province), opportunity to establish their own dynasty which ruled Iran from 1037 to 1157 A.D. "This period became one of the most momentous in the long history of Persian culture, for it was then that the rough illiterate Turks first placed Persians in the highest official posts and then themselves developed into patrons of learning and the arts."[1155]

1153 Nikki R. Keddie, <u>Roots of Revolution, An Interpretive History of Modern Iran</u>, (New Haven, CT: Yale University Press, 1981), p. 12.
1154 Nikki R. Keddie, <u>Roots of Revolution, An Interpretive History of Modern Iran</u>, (New Haven, CT: Yale University Press, 1981), p. 13.
1155 Donald N. Wilber, <u>Iran, Past and Present</u>, (Princeton NJ: Princeton University Press, 1963), p. 45.

In harmony with that analysis it should be mentioned that Omar Khayyam produced his *Rubaiyat* during the reign of Malik Shah of the Seljuk Dynasty. (A *rubaiyat* is a series of rhymed quatrains.)

Beyond their significant impact on Iranian culture, on a broader scale, the most consequential thrust of the Seljuks was their triumph at the Battle of Manzikert in 1071, which largely though temporarily destroyed Byzantine military power, thus opening western Anatolia to occupation by the Ottoman Turks, the Seljuks' subordinate close relatives. The Seljuk Iranian Empire has questionably been deemed by some to have been "the greatest [Iranian] Empire since the advent of Islam."[1156]

D. The Mongol Period of Iran's Muslim Era. The invasion of Iran by the Mongols culminated with the destruction of Baghdad, the Abbasid capital, by Hulagu's marauders in 1258. The city was under siege for one month and then it was stormed by the Mongol troops. "Thousands were slain, the palaces, mosques, and tombs of the caliphs were burned, and a vast store of booty collected. The last of the Abbasid Caliphs was put to death and his line [that of Abbas, founder of the empire] wiped out."[1157]

Did Western Christendom miss a great opportunity? "In 1267 Hulagu died and was succeeded by his son Abaqa, who ruled until 1282. The campaigns against Syria having met with failure [See the Battle of Ayn Jalut in Chapter 17, under "Egypt's Christians Ruled by a Slave Dynasty."], Abaqa revived the earlier idea of sending envoys to the courts of Europe and to the Pope. He proposed, as did several later rulers, a military alliance of East and West against the Moslem Egyptians. Such an alliance might have secured for the Christian nations the holy sites of Palestine, but they showed little serious interest in the plan. Takudar, a brother of Abaqa who succeeded him on the throne, now publicly professed the Moslem faith and took the name of Ahmad. Murdered in 1284, he was succeeded by Arghun, a son of Abaqa. During his reign the Nestorian Christians, long entrenched in northwestern Iran and Iraq, were especially favored and their bishop rebuilt the church at Maragha."[1158]

Had there been a positive response from those countries which made up western Christendom, it is highly probable that the Mongols would never have embraced Islam. Also, a Mongol-Christendom political/military union would have divided the Turkish Muslims in the north from forging links with Muslims in the south, limiting the scope of the Ottoman Empire.

Before the Mongol invasion, the power of the Abbasid Caliphate had been seriously waning, allowing the rise of many local dynasties with overlapping periods and areas of power.[1159] Ultimately, the Mongol destruction of Baghdad not only

---

1156 Frederick Tallberg, From Cyrus to Pahlavi, (Shiraz, Iran: The Pahlavi University of Shiraz, 1970), p. 56.
1157 Donald N. Wilber, Iran, Past and Present, (Princeton NJ: Princeton University Press, 1963), p. 50.
1158 Donald N. Wilber, Iran, Past and Present, (Princeton NJ: Princeton University Press, 1963), p. 51.
1159 "Early in the ninth century strong local dynasties arose and seized control of various parts of Iran from the weak caliph of Baghdad." – Frederick Tallberg, From Cyrus to Pahlavi, (Shiraz, Iran: The Pahlavi University of Shiraz, 1970), p. 45.

ended the Abbasid line of caliphs, it simultaneously also broke the power of the Seljuk Turks. This allowed the Ottoman Turks to rise to unfettered power in Anatolia into which they had moved following the Turkish victory over the army of the Eastern Roman Empire at the Battle of Manzikert in 1071. Their rise eventually culminated in the founding of the Ottoman Empire.

Both the Ottomans, and their close cousins the Seljuk Turks (who had dominated the Abbasid Caliphate) had embraced Sunni Islam. That was an abomination to the Persians and their imams who were partisans to Ali (Arabic *Shi'at 'Ali*) and, thus, they were known as Shias, as well as Alids, followers of Ali. While it was galling for the Shias to be governed by the Sunnis, they had to face stern reality. They had to make a loathsome accommodation because, at that point, they could not triumph over the Turks on the battlefield. In lieu of military strength, Shiism in Iran adopted three aggressive policies of subversion.

First was assassination[1160] which targeted highly placed personnel in the Sunni administration. Initially this was led by Hasan as-Sabbah, who established a nearly inaccessible mountain stronghold at Alamut in which assassins were highly trained and then fortified with hashish (from which the word assassin is derived) before being sent on murder missions against Sunni administrators.[1161] Every attempt by the Turks to eliminate the assassins was a failure. Consequently, they owed a great debt of gratitude to Hulagu and his Mongols for wiping out that initial nest of assassins. "In 1256 [two years before the Mongols destroyed Baghdad] Hulagu carried out a mission against the Assassins [initially at Alamut], razing their fortresses and destroying their power."[1162] However, even though the power of the Assassins was broken, both in Alamut and in Khohistan, they continued to wield power in Syria.

Second, many Iranians adopted the mystical tenets of Sufism, which had been considered heretical in Islam "until Ghazali brought Sufism into the breast of the orthodox Moslem faith by transforming it from a doctrine to an attitude toward life—an attitude of humble faith, boundless love, and pure morals. [It contained] ... a layer of fatalism, passiveness and skepticism."[1163]

Third, in addition to assassination and pacifism, many Iranians heartily embraced a concept of heroism which gave them the courage to triumph in the face of overwhelming odds. It is this kind of unconquerable bravery which is powerfully promoted in the 60,000 quatrains of Firdausi's (b.935–d.1020) *Shahnameh* (The

---

[1160] Wilber also understood this to have been the basic function of the assassins. He wrote, "The core of the Shi'a resistance was the Isma'ili organization led by Hasan as-Sabbah, which has become known to the Western world as 'The Assassins.' From their strong fortresses in northern Iran and farther west they dispatched agents to stir up civil disorder and to carry out political murders. One of their victims was Nizam al-Mulk." – Donald N. Wilber, Iran, Past and Present, (Princeton NJ: Princeton University Press, 1963), p. 46.

[1161] Hitler similarly used hallucinatory drugs such as "methamphetamines distributed to millions of soldiers [which] made possible the blitzkrieg that killed France in 1940. Hitler became dependent on a witch's cornucopia of heroin and other drugs during World War II." – quoted by Marvin Olasky from Norman Ohler's *Blitzed: Drugs in the Third Reich*, World Magazine, June 10, 2017, p. 20.

[1162] Donald N. Wilber, Iran, Past and Present, (Princeton NJ: Princeton University Press, 1963), p. 50.

[1163] Donald N. Wilber, Iran, Past and Present, (Princeton NJ: Princeton University Press, 1963), p. 89.

Story of the Kings), the incomparable, soul-stirring classic of victory over tragedy and hopeless odds. The following tiny excerpt will help us understand the bracing courage Persians imbibed from Firdausi's epic:

> "High in the midst of the embattl'd host
> Young *Hoshung* stood, the royal *Persian's* boast.
> Onward each army rush'd with martial glow,
> Revenge and empire dwell upon the blow.
> Immortal vigour fir'd the *Persian* train,
> And clouds of dust o'ershadow'd all the plain.
> Proud and audacious! dauntful in the fight,
> The demon rov'd, too confident of might.
> His strokes on all re-echo, all engage,
> As when the roaring lion hurls his rage.
> The old king trembled, as he view'd the force
> Of the dire demons mow their dreadful course;
> 'Twas then brave *Hoshung* with undaunted might
> Sought the young demon thro' the thickest fight.
> They met, they fought, the hero's patriot glow
> Gave force and vigour o'er the treach'rous foe.
> Long was the combat, when the prince's arm
> Struck the pale demon, trembling with alarm.
> Then hurl'd him from his courser, as he fled,
> And as he fell, he lopp'd his impious head."[1164]

Debatably, it is claimed that subsequent to the completion of the *Shahnameh*, "the language has changed so little since its composition nine hundred years ago that it can be read with ease by the people of present-day Iran. For centuries it has been recited, and even today thousands of uneducated people can repeat long passages of the poem."[1165]

Triumphant Culture. Long periods of Iranian history have been dominated by a parade of conquerors who were not truly Iranian. The most obvious members in this category were the two very closely related ethnic groups already mentioned, the Turks and Mongols.[1166] In spite of being ruled by many foreigners who could make no claim of being even remotely Iranian, there has been a consistent continuity in the essence of being Iranian. "Examples of this high regard for the past

---

1164 Trans. J. Champion, Persian Poems, An Anthology of Verse Translations, ed. A. J. Arberry, (NY, NY: E.P. Dutton Inc. & Co., no date), p. 187.
1165 Donald N. Wilber, Iran, Past and Present, (Princeton NJ: Princeton University Press, 1963), p. 42.
1166"The Turkish people on the broad plains of southern Siberia and the steppes between the Caspian Sea and the Altai Mountains had emerged out of a racial and linguistic community which in primeval times may also have comprised the Mongols and Tungus." – Carl Brockelmann, History of the Islamic Peoples, (NY, NY: Capricorn Books, 1973), p. 163.

and of efforts to establish identification with it are very numerous. The Parthian rulers thought of themselves as the political heirs of the Achaemenids, and the Sassanian Dynasty proudly traced its lineage to the Achaemenid kings. Firdausi, in assembling all the oral and written material on Iran's early glories, set up a standard for later hero worship. Just a few years ago Reza Shah went back to these national traditions for the name of his new dynasty, and when family names came into general use in Iran, many of those chosen were names of the ancient kings and heroes of the country."[1167] "Iran has vivid memories of its imperial past and the aspirations of great power status that come with them."[1168]

E. The Local Dynasty Period of Iran's Muslim Era. Out of a welter of local dynasties,[1169] which resulted from many invasions and battles, three dynasties emerged to a position of international significance: The Safavids, the Ghaznavids and the reign of Nader Shah.

The Safavids. "Under the Safavid Dynasty, whose noontime lasted from the turn of the sixteenth century until the early 1700s, Persia was united after centuries of fragmentation, its shah a byword for splendor and its people busy trading with and chafing [irritating] their regional rivals, the Ottomans. Enterprising Europeans entered the shah's service as his envoys. Caravansaries, or fortified inns, were built along the main trading routes, and silk—Iran's luxury product par excellence—was transported from the mulberry orchards of the northern provinces to Isfahan, in the centre of the country, and from there onwards to the Persian Gulf for export to Europe."[1170]

A very portentous development took place "in the late Safavid times [when] some mujtahids [qualified jurists in Iran] claimed that they had more right to rule than did the impious, wine-bibbing shahs. They did not yet say they should rule directly, an idea that came forth only with Ayatollah Khomeini, but that the shah should carry out their rulings when given and defend the nation militarily. The political claims of the Iranian ulama developed further from the eighteenth century on."[1171] To understand the fall of the Safavid Dynasty, please read in this appendix the last two paragraphs of section V, division B, "The Abbasid Caliphate Period of Iran's Muslim Era."

The Ghaznavids. They are named for Ghazni, their capital, about 70 miles south of Kabul, Afghanistan which was then still part of Iran. The Ghaznavids were new Turkic converts to Islam who were filled with zeal to promote the cause they had recently embraced. "Islam gave a religious justification [or en-

---
1167 Donald N. Wilber, <u>Iran, Past and Present</u>, (Princeton NJ: Princeton University Press, 1963), p. 86.
1168 Vali Nasr, <u>Iran Among the Ruins</u>, <u>Foreign Affairs</u>, March/April 2018, p. 110.
1169 According to Frederick Tallberg in <u>From Cyrus to Pahlavi</u>, during this period the comparatively weak, local dynasties of note were the Taherids 828–881 A.D., the Saffarids 869–1015 A.D., the Samanids 874–998 A.D., the Ziyarids 932–1043 A.D. and the Buyids 942–1069 A.D. They were followed by the Khorazmshahs 1106–1230 A.D., the Il-Khanids 1253–1355 A.D., the Afsharids 1736–1750 A.D., and the Zand Dynasty 1750–1794 A.D.
1170 Christopher De Bellaigue, <u>The Islamic Enlightenment, The Modern Struggle Between Faith and Reason</u>, (UK: Penguin Random House, 2017), p. 107.
1171 Nikki R. Keddie, <u>Roots of Revolution, An Interpretive History of Modern Iran</u>, (New Haven, CT: Yale University Press, 1981), p. 18.

dorsement] to this way of life [the *ghaza* way of life, i.e. border raiding]—in addition to earthly booty, [there was] a promise of heavenly reward, a promise that probably helped win converts to Islam."[1172] First, they established their brand of Islamic rule in Afghanistan, making it the base from which they projected Muslim military power to the east. After Afghanistan was secure, they brought Islam to what is today northern Pakistan and northern India by the power of the sword. This feat was one which the Arabs, who in 711 A.D. had subjugated the southern drainage basin of the Indus River, the provinces of Sindh[1173] and Baluchistan, did not have the dynamism to carry out. Names of some of the outstanding Turkic Muslim marshal leaders are Sabuktigin, Sabuktigin's son Mahmud of Ghazni, and Babur. These and many others were imbued with military genius. For example, "Babur, the founder of the Mughal Dynasty, was descended from Genghis Khan and Timur (Tamerlane) and was another instance of the extraordinary military potency of Central Asia, Gibbon's source of 'barbarian' vitality."[1174]

An example of that vitality was seen when, "in 997 the Muslim warlord Mahmud of Ghazni stormed through the Khyber Pass and wreaked devastation through the rich provinces of Punjab and Sindh. His Turkic cavalrymen looted all that lay in their path, desecrating temples and smashing sacred idols in their pious, pitiless iconoclasm. There would be 16 more attacks over the next three decades."[1175] The reach of those plundering raids is seen in the fact that "Mahmud of Ghazna, who swept down in Gujarat from eastern Afghanistan ... in 1026 utterly destroyed the sea side Hindu Temple of Somnath."[1176]

"There were nine men of the [ruling] line of the Ghaznavids, whose power now arose in the east of Iran. Alptegin, the first of this Turkish line, had been sold as a slave to Isma'il the Samanid. He became governor of Khorasan, and about 960 proclaimed himself king of Ghazni. Mahmud, the seventh of the line, undertook to extend the limited kingdom of his predecessors, overthrowing the Samanids in 999 and absorbing the Ziyarids. In 1029 he pushed through Buvayhids west of the Iranian plateau so that his rule extended over Muhjara, Afghanistan, Transoxiana, Khorasan, Tabaristan, Sistan, and part of India. In Iran proper, only Kerman and Fars lay outside his rule."[1177]

1172 Carter Vaughn Findley, The Turks in World History, (New York: Oxford University Press, 2005), p. 68.

1173 "Muhammad ibn-al-Qasim, advancing in 710 at the head of a considerable army, of which 6,000 were Syrians, this son-in-law of al-Hajjaj subdued Makran, pushed on through what is now termed Baluchistan and in 711–12 reduced Sind, the lower valley and delta of the Indus (Sindhu)." – Philip K. Hitti, History of The Arabs, (London: Macmillan, 1968), p. 210. "The Arabs were in Makran almost 3-quarters of a century before Muhammad al-Qasim conquered Sind and established the first Muslim settlement on the Indus. Adjacent to the Persian province of Kirman, a western extension of coastal Sind, Makran was first invaded in 644 A.D., the 23rd year of the Hijra, toward the end of the caliphate of Umar." – Andre Wink, Al-Hind, the Making of the Indo-Islamic World, (Boston: Brill Academic Publishers, Inc., 2002), p. 129.

1174 Jeremy Black, War and the World, Military Power and the Fate of Continents, 1450–2000, (New Haven: Yale University Press, 1998), p. 24.

1175 Jonah Blank, *Words into Swords*, U.S. News & World Report, August 16/August 23, 1999, p. 55.

1176 Robert D. Kaplan, Monsoon, (New York: Random House, 2010), p. 102.

1177 Donald N. Wilber, Iran, Past and Present, (Princeton NJ: Princeton University Press, 1963), p. 40.

Nader/Nadir Shah. In 1722 "Iran's serenity was broken by Afghan invaders, who destroyed the old order without creating a new one. The country entered a period of dissolution, violence and horror, as several Transcaucasian provinces were snatched by Russia and Turkey and first one warlord sought to impose his writ on the plateau through the sword and, failing, gave way to the next. The most efficient of these brutes, the tribal freebooter Nader Shah, ravaged the people with his campaigning and depredations, which depopulated huge areas."[1178]

"In 1731 Nadir deposed Tahmasp[1179] and ruled as regent for the latter's son, 'Abbas III, until the death of this last Saffavid in 1736, when he ascended the throne of Iran as Nadir Shah, founder of the Afshar dynasty. As a political move aimed at ending the division of eastern Islam he proclaimed Sunnism the official belief of the country, but neither his proclamation nor his persecution of the Shi'a leaders had any lasting effect. ... Discipline exercised over both the public and the soldiers of his army was very severe. In 1736 he moved into Afghanistan, taking Kandahar, Ghazna, and Kabul; and then on to India where he entered Delhi and robbed the palaces and city of fabulous treasures which included the Peacock Throne. ... His huge army lived off its own country as it marched from west to east and back again, and heavy taxes were levied on the inhabitants. In 1747, in the midst of provincial revolts, he was assassinated by one of his officers."[1180]

F. The Western Imperial/Colonial Period of Iran's Muslim Era. During this period there were five main contending powers which significantly impacted Iran: Tsarist/Soviet Russia, Napoleonic France, Colonial Great Britain, post-World War I Germany and post-World War II America.

Size. One factor which Western powers considered in evaluating Iran's importance is its size. "Iran is four times larger than Iraq—about six-hundred-thirty-thousand square miles to something over one-hundred-forty-thousand for Iraq. To compare it to American or European standards, look at it this way. Texas ... is around two-hundred-sixty-six thousand square miles. This makes Iran two and a half times larger than Texas. And Iran is larger than West Germany, France, Spain, England, Wales and Scotland combined. That's a lot of territory. Does that give you some sort of a picture?"[1181]

Russia. "In 1804 Iran and Russia went to war over tracts of modern-day Georgia, Armenia and Azerbaijan, a conflict that would drag on until 1813 and end in Iranian defeat. In May 1807 Iran and France—the latter was engaged in a major war of its own against Russia in Europe—signed a treaty of alliance directed against St.

1178 Christopher De Bellaigue, <u>The Islamic Enlightenment, The Modern Struggle Between Faith and Reason</u>, (UK: Penguin Random House, 2017), pp. 107-108.
1179 Tahmasp was an influential Shah of Iran, who enjoyed the longest reign of any member of the Safavid Dynasty. (Wikipedia, accessed 08/08/17)
1180 Donald N. Wilber, <u>Iran, Past and Present</u>, (Princeton NJ: Princeton University Press, 1963), pp. 74-75.
1181 Kermit Roosevelt, <u>Countercoup, The Struggle for the Control of Iran</u>, (NY: McGraw Hill Book Co., 1979), p. 25.

Petersburg. No sooner had that happened, however, than the Treaty of Tilsit, signed in July of the same year between Napoleon and Tsar Alexander I, unpicked the Franco-Iranian pact and Britain stepped in with proposals of its own. The British ambition was to prevent Napoleon from gaining influence on India's western border and overseeing military reforms was the obvious way to achieve this. Within a decade of its reunification under the Qajars Iran found itself annexed—like Turkey and Egypt—to the European system of treaty and belligerence."[1182] Tehran had been chosen to be the capital of Iran by Agha Mohammad Khan Qajar, founder of the Qajar Dynasty (1796–1925), who ruled 1796–1797.

During their period of influence, "the Soviet authorities fostered and largely financed a mushroom growth of Communist-oriented political parties and trade unions; the most dangerous group was the Tudeh or 'Masses' party. The Russians refused to cooperate with our civil administrators in the northern provinces, which they completely dominated not only militarily but also politically and economically; the Soviet zone of occupation in fact became almost a separate country and, as later events showed, the Soviets planned that much of it would remain so."[1183]

France. "During the rule of Fath Ali Shah [1797–1834] the first major nineteenth-century European incursions in Iran occurred, as a byproduct of the Napoleonic Wars. Napoleon, along with the short-lived Russian emperor Paul, wished to invade India, which was also threatened by the Afghans. To forestall this, the British sent Captain John Malcolm from India to sign an 1801 treaty with Iran, which promised British military equipment and technicians in return for Iranian support if Afghanistan or France moved toward Iran or India. Soon, however, there was a Russo-British rapprochement, and Iran, still looking for an alliance against Russia, which had taken Georgia from Iranian control, signed the Treaty of Finkenstein with France in 1807."[1184] Napoleon's anti-British aspirations went much further than "influence on India's western border." For example, "after securing Egypt, Napoleon had intended to ally himself with Tipu Sultan, ruler of the southern principality of Mysore and the most effective foe of the British in India at that time."[1185]

Great Britain. British dominance of southern Iran brought about its control of crude oil in the Iranian economy. As Westerners became acquainted with Iran, they realized that a perpetual flame was kept burning in the Iranian Zoroastrian fire temples. Zoroastrians maintained those perpetual flames because fire was the symbol of Ahura Mazda, their god of light and goodness. Westerners suspected that some, at least, of those "eternal fires" were fueled by natural gas. That led to the reasonable assumption that Iran was probably rich in petroleum as well as natural gas. There was also other corroborating evidence for assuming the presence

---

1182 Christopher De Bellaigue, The Islamic Enlightenment, The Modern Struggle Between Faith and Reason, (UK: Penguin Random House, 2017), p. 112.
1183 Mohammad Reza Shah Pahlavi, Mission for My Country, (London: Hutchinson & Co. Ltd., 1974), p. 77.
1184 Nikki R. Keddie, Roots of Revolution, An Interpretive History of Modern Iran, (New Haven, CT: Yale University Press, 1981), pp. 40-41.
1185 Malise Ruthven, *The Islamic Road to the Modern World*, The New York Review of Books, June 22, 2017, p. 25.

of oil in Iran. When the Iranians still controlled the western shore of the Caspian Sea, Geoffrey Duckett, an agent of the Muscovy Company, traveled to Baku in the sixteenth century. There, in his words, he found "a strange thing to behold; for there issueth out of the ground a marvelous quantitie of oile, which oile they fetch from the uttermost bounds of all Persia; it serveth all the countrey to burn in their houses."[1186]

Then in 1892 Jacques de Morgan, a French archaeologist, called attention, "to oil seepages in south-west Persia."[1187] Phenomena like those were tantalizing, beckoning western entrepreneurs to find a way to tap the, all but certain, oil wealth of Iran. The first westerner to gain permission to explore was William Knox D'Arcy, an Australian who had previously made a fortune in gold mining. In 1901 he, "obtained a [60-year] concession from the Persian government for the exploitation of oil resources in all of Iran except the northern provinces."[1188]

In spite of D'Arcy's gold wealth, the cost of exploration almost brought the enterprise to bankruptcy. In the face of impending bankruptcy, D'Arcy's exceptional engineer, G. B. Reynolds, persevered and a copious supply of "oil was struck in January 1908, at the site of an ancient fire temple at Masjid-i-Sulaiman [The Mosque of Solomon], just as the company was ordering Reynolds to give up."[1189]

D'Arcy's enterprise ultimately metamorphosed into the Anglo-Persian Oil Company which built a refinery, at that time the largest in the world, on the Persian island of Abadan. At the same time, Britain was changing its navy from a coal-burning to an oil-burning navy. Consequently, "the [Anglo-Persian Oil, later Anglo-Iranian Oil] company was judged a vital strategic asset and a controlling interest in its shares had been bought by Britain, at Winston Churchill's instigation, in 1913."[1190] The British Navy had just changed from coal to oil to fuel its ships when World War I erupted. Just before hostilities started, Germany had completed the Damascus to Medina hajj (pilgrimage) railway line, the Hejaz Railway. When hostilities began, Germany tried to use that railroad to transport heavy, long-range artillery to the shores of the Red Sea to sink British oil tankers, thus immobilizing the British Navy. It was in that context that the exploits of Lawrence of Arabia took place, successfully thwarting Germany's plans.

The D'Arcy enterprise was the beginning of the oil era in the Muslim world, but certainly only the beginning. The D'Arcy saga was quickly followed in Arabia by another when Frank Holmes, a New Zealander, met "with 'Abd al-'Aziz in al-Hasa in 1922. Holmes returned the following year to al-'Uqayr, where he once again saw the ruler. In May 1923 King 'Abd al-'Aziz signed an agreement with

---

1186 Sarah Searight, The British in the Middle East, (New York: Atheneum, 1970), p. 126.
1187 Sarah Searight, The British in the Middle East, (New York: Atheneum, 1970), p. 126.
1188 Richard N. Frye, Iran, (New York: Henry Hold and Company, 1953), p.70.
1189 Sarah Searight, The British in the Middle East, (New York: Atheneum, 1970), p. 126.
1190 John Keegan, The First World War, (New York: Alfred A. Knopf, 1999), p. 218.

Holmes which entitled the Eastern and General Syndicate to find a company to search for oil in eastern Saudi Arabia."[1191]

The discovery of huge quantities of oil in the Muslim world and the development of world-wide marketing for the product led to a greedy scramble. (Please see the Addendum to this appendix.) For instance, from the time when Leo Amery took over the [British] Colonial Office in 1924, "Iraq's supposedly sovereign assembly was demanding increased authority in most matters, not least an interest in the Turkish Petroleum Company based at Mosul."[1192]

Germany. "Reza Shah [founder of the Pahlavi Dynasty] chafed under British influence, and the British were unpopular with Iranian nationalists. This hostility, combined with a German drive for economic and political influence in Iran, led to a rise in Germany's position in the late 1930s. German firms had a large role in the Trans-Iranian Railroad. The Germans opened sea and air communications with Iran and provided most of the machinery and contractors in Iran's industrial, mining, and building program. Germany was the leading country in Iran's foreign trade from 1939 to 1941, controlling about half of it.[1193]

"Both rulers [King Farouk of Egypt and Reza Shah of Iran] were, like so many others, shocked by the fall of France [June 22, 1940] and assumed that this would lead to a speedy Axis victory. The Shah was in continual contact with the Germans, and Farouk, whose scope in British-occupied Egypt was limited, maintained his contacts with them through a special envoy in Tehran, Youssef Zulficar, his own father-in-law, with whom he communicated directly without going through the Ministry of Foreign Affairs.[1194]

"Seen as a base against the Soviet Union, Iran was penetrated by the Germans militarily and politically. Nazi ideology and agents were prominent, and the Germans declared Iran a pure Aryan country. Reza Shah was not averse to Nazi phrases and methods, as they suited his dictatorial and nationalistic inclinations. On the eve of World War II, Iran housed German economic and political agents, and the government had economic and political commitments tying it to a pro-German policy."[1195]

"After the fall of France the Shah's cooperation with the Germans became more blatant, and the number of German 'businessmen' in Tehran more ostentatious. [Considering the prevailing conditions,] it cannot have surprised him that, when

---

1191 Jane Waldron Grutz, *Prelude to Discovery,* Aramco World, January/February 1999, pp. 31-34
1192 H.V.F. Winstone, Gertrude Bell, (London: Barzan Publishing, 2004), p. 396.
1193 Nikki R. Keddie, Roots of Revolution, An Interpretive History of Modern Iran,(New Haven, CT: Yale University Press, 1981), p. 110.
1194 Mohamed Heikal, The Return of the Ayatollah, The Iranian Revolution from Mossadeq to Khomeini, (London: Andre Deutsch Ltd., 1981), p. 34.
1195 Nikki R. Keddie, Roots of Revolution, An Interpretive History of Modern Iran,(New Haven, CT: Yale University Press, 1981), p. 110.

the Germans invaded Russia in June 1941, British and Russian troops invaded his country and compelled him to abdicate in favor of his son."[1196]

The Rise of American Influence in Iran. During World War II Americans acted as "advisers in almost every branch of the Iranian government. As soon as they became involved in the [second world] war, they had acted in Iran as everywhere else with their customary vigor and thoroughness. Within six months of their first appearance on the scene there were 28,000 American servicemen in Iran, most of them concerned with the delivery of war material to the Russian front, but others with a vast network of ancillary services—signals, road-making, medical and so on, not forgetting, of course, intelligence."[1197]

"Various American advisers were called into Iran in 1942 and 1943. After the United Sates entered the war, American troops came to Iran to help transport war supplies across the Trans-Iranian Railroad. In the war years the American role in Iran became greater than ever before. A major American activity was the second Millsapaugh mission. Millsapaugh was engaged as administrator general of finances in November 1942, and in May 1943, his extensive control over Iranian finances and the economy was clarified by the so-called Full Powers Law. His purview included finances, banking, government industry, commerce and emergency wartime controls. Americans were put in charge of all key economic departments."[1198]

"Throughout World War II the country's destiny was controlled by foreigners; Mohammad Reza Pahlavi (hereafter referred to as 'the Shah') and the traditional political elites were allowed to play only a minimal role in the affairs of their own nation. After World War II, under prompting from key advisers, such as the Foroughi brothers and Ahmad Qavam, the Shah persuaded the United States to expand its role in Iran and force the termination of allied occupation. The British left as scheduled in March 1946, but the Soviets refused to withdraw from Azerbaijan, Iran's northernmost province. The U.S. assisted in forcing out the Russians in May 1946 by taking an uncompromising attitude within the United Nations. This act signaled the beginning of extremely close ties between Iran and the United States, which were to last until the expulsion of the Shah in January of 1979."[1199]

"Although, as has been seen, the American government had early decided that it had a vital interest in keeping Iran out of the Soviet orbit, this was a new part of the world to the American public and to most American officials. As one ambassador in Tehran was to write, 'Most of the world is completely unaware whether Azerbaijan is a river, a mountain or merely a new religion.'"[1200]

1196 Mohamed Heikal, <u>The Return of the Ayatollah, The Iranian Revolution from Mossadeq to Khomeini</u>, (London: Andre Deutsch Ltd., 1981), p. 34.

1197 Mohamed Heikal, <u>The Return of the Ayatollah, The Iranian Revolution from Mossadeq to Khomeini</u>, (London: Andre Deutsch Ltd., 1981), pp. 40-41.

1198 Nikki R. Keddic, <u>Roots of Revolution, An Interpretive History of Modern Iran</u>, (New Haven, CT: Yale University Press, 1981), p. 115.

1199 John D. Stempel, <u>Inside the Iranian Revolution</u>, (Bloomington, IN: Indiana University Press, 1981), p. 4.

G. <u>The Qajar Dynasty Period of Iran's Muslim Era</u>. The Zand Dynasty (1750–1796) came to ruin and its successor, the Qajar Dynasty (1796–1921), was given birth when "Agha Mohammad Khan captured Kerman, the last stronghold of the Zands, and the population was treated with inhuman cruelty. Agha Mohammad Khan found the land in a state of hopeless anarchy. Whole provinces and towns were ruled by petty Khans, who ignored the Central Government, and quarreled among themselves. With an iron hand the new King gradually subdued them all, and while he was unanimously hated for his ruthlessness, greed and cruelty, it is still to his credit that he preserved Iran from total disintegration."[1201]

H. <u>The Pahlavi Dynasty Period of Iran's Muslim Era</u>. Ideologically, this period is defined by the contest between the concept of governance by an imperial Achaemenian-like royalty and that of governance by a "divine" Shia priesthood. Only two monarchs were to occupy the throne of this dynasty. Collectively, their reigns covered a total of only fifty-three years. The opportunity for the rise of the Pahlavi Dynasty grew out of the frustration and disappointments with the waning Qajar Dynasty. In his weakness, the Qajar Shah was forced in 1906 to share power with a parliament, the Majlis, and with the Shia clergy. "The situation in post-war [World War I] Iran seemed totally hopeless, when in February 1921, General Reza Khan, the Commander-in-Chief of the Cossack Brigade of the North, an ardent patriot and a man of strength and courage, marched from Qazvin to Tehran with 3,000 men to save the country. The Coup d'Etat succeeded and marked the beginning of a great national resurgence."[1202]

"As far back as 1879 the Russians, at the [Qajar Dynasty] Shah's request, had raised a gendarmerie force in the north, called the Cossack Brigade, with Russian officers and Persian NCOs and enlisted men. It was this brigade which in 1907 had bombarded the Majlis and re-established the [Qajar Dynasty] Shah in his capital. But when the Russian Revolution broke out in 1917 the Russian officers withdrew, leaving the Brigade in the hands of its Persian NCOs.

"One of the most capable of these was a sergeant called Reza Mirza and it was through the intervention of the commander of the British forces in Persia, General Edmond Ironside—the British being concerned to fill the vacuum caused by Russian withdrawal—that Reza Mirza was appointed deputy commander of the Cossack Brigade."[1203]

The rebirth of the concept of an Achaemenian-style royalty. "General Reza Khan, the Commander of the Cossack Brigade, organized the great Coup d'Etat of 21st February, 1921, and became Shahanshah [King of kings] of Iran on 17th December, 1925 after having been Minister of War and Prime Minister. Reza Shah

---

1200 Mohamed Heikal, <u>The Return of the Ayatollah, The Iranian Revolution from Mossadeq to Khomeini</u>, (London: Andre Deutsch Ltd., 1981), p. 47.
1201 Frederick Tallberg, <u>From Cyrus to Pahlavi</u>, (Shiraz, Iran: The Pahlavi University of Shiraz, 1970), pp. 78-79.
1202 Frederick Tallberg, <u>From Cyrus to Pahlavi</u>, (Shiraz, Iran: The Pahlavi University of Shiraz, 1970), p. 91.
1203 Mohamed Heikal, <u>The Return of the Ayatollah, The Iranian Revolution from Mossadeq to Khomeini</u>, (London: Andre Deutsch Ltd., 1981), pp. 30-31.

brought to an end [the rule of] the weak and decadent Qajars, a sick dynasty which could neither suppress the internal disturbances and banditry up and down the country nor stand up to foreign political pressures."[1204]

"Reza Shah was of peasant origin and quite illiterate, though he taught himself to read and write after he became an officer. To consolidate his throne he had to create some form of legitimacy which might replace that of birth. He did this in a number of ways. He looked back beyond the Qajars whom he had supplanted to an earlier stage of Persian history, taking for the title of the dynasty he hoped to found, the name of the language of pre-Islamic Persia—Pahlavi—and changed the country's name from Persia to an earlier form, Iran."[1205]

It deserves mentioning again that "at the outbreak of [the second world] war, in September 1939, German influence in Iran was paramount. German agents were active and the Shah's sympathy for the Germans was no secret. This sympathy caused concern once the Nazis invaded the Soviet Union in June 1941. After that, the Germans wanted to use Iran as a base against the Soviet Union, and the Allies needed Iran as a supply route to the Soviets, which would be impeded by a German fifth column. The British and Russians sent a note to the Iranian government demanding the expulsion of the Germans. When Reza Shah procrastinated, on August 25 Russian and British troops entered Iran."[1206]

"The next Anglo-Soviet move was to force Reza Shah to abdicate in favor of his 22-year-old son. Though he had greatly strengthened, Iran, Reza Shah was not strong enough to prevent being deposed and was sent into exile on the Indian Ocean island of Mauritius on December 18, 1941. He died in Johannesburg, South Africa on July 26, 1944."[1207]

I. <u>The Shia Clerical Period of Iran's Muslim Era</u>. The Shia clergy formed a power center which challenged the functioning of a revived imperial royal line of shahs. "Shiism's top clerics gravitated to the main shrine towns—Najaf and Karbala in Iraq, Isfahan and Mashhad in Iran—from where they maintained polite but distrustful relationships with the shah and the top princes. The religious foundations of the Shia world constituted almost a parallel state that was innately skeptical of the shah's claim to absolute authority—in Shiism this is reserved for the imams, specially anointed descendants of the Prophet, and in their absence, the most learned clerics. This clerical establishment was too diffuse and autonomous for the monarch to bend it to a modernizing political will, as Muhammad Ali had done [in Egypt] to al-Azhar."[1208]

1204 Frederick Tallberg, <u>From Cyrus to Pahlavi</u>, (Shiraz, Iran: The Pahlavi University of Shiraz, 1970), p. 92.
1205 Mohamed Heikal, <u>The Return of the Ayatollah, The Iranian Revolution from Mossadeq to Khomeini</u>, (London: Andre Deutsch Ltd., 1981), p. 31.
1206 Nikki R. Keddie, <u>Roots of Revolution, An Interpretive History of Modern Iran</u>,(New Haven, CT: Yale University Press, 1981), p. 113.
1207 John D. Stempel, <u>Inside the Iranian Revolution</u>, (Bloomington, IN: Indiana University Press, 1981), p. 4.
1208 Christopher De Bellaigue, <u>The Islamic Enlightenment, The Modern Struggle Between Faith and Reason</u>, (UK: Penguin Random House, 2017), p. 109.

"Over time, however, the factors conducive to an alliance between court and ulama changed. Economic bases for ulama independence of the shahs grew; these were not all specifically Shi'i, but in the last few centuries they have operated more strongly in Iran than elsewhere. Throughout the Muslim world Muslims may make bequests of their property or money as *vaqf* (inalienable endowment). There are two general kinds of vaqf, sometimes called charitable or religious, and private. Charitable vaqf is given for institutions like schools, hospitals, mosques and shrines, all of which are controlled and administered by ulama."[1209]

"Every member of this [Shia clerical] community seemed prepared to engage in endless discussions about the nature of Islamic society and Islamic government. They had respect for only one person— Khomeini. They were prepared to defy President Carter or anybody else. They cared nothing at all for talk of international law, maintaining that the Revolution [which culminated in 1979] had created its own law and so could acknowledge no other authority than itself."[1210]

It had been an incident in 1906 which gave the Shia clergy an opening to defy the authority of the Shah. It was then when a "series of demonstrations and protests [occurred] which forced the [Qajar Dynasty] Shah in 1906 to grant a constitution and to summon the first Majlis (parliament). It is this constitution which the popular movement of 1978–79 insisted the Shah should implement."[1211]

"Khomeini was already demanding the removal of the Shah and the institution of an Islamic republic. The moderate clergy in Iran were calling for the strict application of the Constitution of 1906, notably the provision giving five of them a right of veto over any law judged contrary to the principles of Islam. As for the intellectuals and the eighteen or so parties which had suddenly sprung up, they were demanding total freedom."[1212]

Along with other reasons, the Iranian Shia clergy hated the Shah because of his land reforms. "Discontent had been spurred by charges of electoral fraud in the fall of 1962. It was exacerbated by the clergy's hatred of the land reform program because it took so much income-producing property away from Islamic organizations controlled by the mosques."[1213]

The Shia-Sunni Distinction. "In Sunni Islam it was widely held that after an early date all fundamental legal principles had been decided on the basis of the Qur'an, the reported words and actions of the Prophet (*hadith*), and the consensus

---

[1209] Nikki R. Keddie, <u>Roots of Revolution, An Interpretive History of Modern Iran</u>, (New Haven, CT: Yale University Press, 1981), p. 16.

[1210] Mohamed Heikal, <u>The Return of the Ayatollah, The Iranian Revolution from Mossadeq to Khomeini</u>, (London: Andre Deutsch Ltd., 1981), p. 25.

[1211] Mohamed Heikal, <u>The Return of the Ayatollah, The Iranian Revolution from Mossadeq to Khomeini</u>, (London: Andre Deutsch Ltd., 1981), p. 29.

[1212] Fereydoun Hoveyda, <u>The Fall of the Shah</u>, (New York: Wyndham Books, 1979), p. 47.

[1213] John D. Stempel, <u>Inside the Iranian Revolution</u>, (Bloomington, IN: Indiana University Press, 1981), p. 6.

of scholar-jurists, and that there was no more room for new judgments based on the effort *(ijtihad)* of a qualified jurist [*mujtahid*]."[1214]

The Egyptian writer and newspaper correspondent, Mohamed Heikal, though being a Sunni Muslim, has given what may be the best concise description of the unique emphases of Iranian Shi'ism in contrast to Sunni Islam. He wrote, "Sunnis maintain that the successors of Muhammad were no more than fallible human interpreters of the law; the Shi'is [maintain] that as Muhammad was the imam, or interpreter, while he was still alive, so after him there have been other imams to interpret for the faithful, and that, because the message of God was received with the greatest clarity by Ali and his family *(ahl el-beit)* [literally, the people of the house, thus the family of Muhammad], the imam must be able to prove descent from Ali and Fatimah, the Prophet's daughter. Against the Sunni reliance on consensus among believers *(ijma)* the Shi'is trust in what amounts to divine right of the family of Ali. A majority of Shi'is believe that the imams continued visible in the world until the twelfth in succession disappeared in A.D. 873. [The date 873 is that of the Minor Occultation.[1215]] They await his reappearance as the Mahdi, the infallible guide who will institute the reign of justice in the world and liberate the poor. But until that day some other means for interpretation for the word is required and that is to be found in those who have special knowledge and understanding of religious matters, the *fuqaha* [canon lawyers, from *fiqh*, the spiritual law], who thus become in effect the deputies of the hidden imam. ... Shi'ism found adherents among those who for any reason resented the centralized authority of Sunni orthodoxy—the poor and underprivileged classes, the minorities, and those, such as Persians, who had accepted Islam when the Arab conquerors swept over them but who retained a strong feeling of national identity."[1216]

It will also be useful to gain insight to the essential meaning of Shiism from Fereydoun Hoveyda, a highly educated Iranian Shiite who served, in addition to holding other important positions, as Iran's representative in the United Nations. He wrote, "while Shi'ism professes, like Sunnism, that Mohammad was the 'seal of the Prophecy,' the last prophet, it holds that the final point of the 'cycle of the prophecy' coincides with the initial point of the 'cycle of the imams,' who are seen as the custodians of the 'secret of the emissary of God.' The twelve imams are those who guide their followers on the esoteric spiritual way of the Revelation announced by the Prophet. The first, Ali, the husband of Fatimah, daughter of the Prophet, was stabbed to death in 661. His two sons Hassan and Hussein were also assassinated. [Hassan was killed by one of his own wives.] The period of the holy imams goes up to the 'Great Occultation' in 940 of the twelfth imam, Mohammad

---

1214 Nikki R. Keddie, Roots of Revolution, An Interpretive History of Modern Iran, (New Haven, CT: Yale University Press, 1981), p. 10.
1215 The word 'occultation' is a noun form of the adjective 'occult,' a derivative of the Latin *occulere*, to cover up, to hide. In Shia Islam it is used to refer to the person called Mahdi who is thought to be an infallible male descendant of the Prophet Muhammad. He is alleged to have disappeared and is thus hidden but will one day return and fill the world with justice and peace.
1216 Mohamed Heikal, The Return of the Ayatollah, The Iranian Revolution from Mossadeq to Khomeini, (London: Andre Deutsch Ltd., 1981), pp. 80-81.

al Ghaim, who is to return at the end of time. There then begins the secret history of the hidden imam, which makes Shi'ism into the esoteric branch of Islam. The Shi'ites are those who assume the secrets of the imams and conserve the hidden meaning of the Book. It is precisely the secrecy and mysticism which it has developed in Iran that exercise such a powerful attraction."[1217]

A serious distraction. Attention toward Iran's main ideological contest, that of being ruled by an Achaemenian-like royalty or by a Shia priesthood, was sidelined for several years by a prime minister who was committed to Communism and tried to impose it by backing the Communist Tudeh (Masses) Party. "Dr. Mohammed Mossadegh had served nearly thirty years in the Majlis [the Iranian Parliament] and had become a formidable force. In succeeding years he was to become even more formidable. He put himself above any 'party loyalty' and could well be described as a political megalomaniac. Winning the [reluctant] support of H.I.M. [His Imperial Majesty, a title used only for the Pahlavi Shah], he nationalized the Anglo-Iranian Oil Company. Then he expelled the British from Iran. Growing in confidence, he allied himself with the revivified Tudeh [Communist Party] and their Russian backers and turned on the Shah himself. By now he [Mossadegh] had not only made implacable enemies of the British; he had also alarmed President Eisenhower, who had just assumed office, and the new U.S. Government—most especially John Foster Dulles, Secretary of State, and his brother Allen, Director of the C.I.A. Churchill, then Prime Minister of England, Anthony Eden, Foreign Secretary, and other British elements combined their different concerns. The result was AJAX [the code name for the C.I.A.'s project to overthrow Mossadegh's government]."[1218]

Kermit Roosevelt, C.I.A. leader in Iran for the AJAX project said, "If we were not too blatant about it, we and our Persian associates could underline Mossadegh's alienation from the West, his increasing dependence on the Soviet Union and the obvious fact that if he continued to develop his personal regime as he was presently doing, there could be no continuing meaningful role for a monarch in Iran."[1219] It was this secondary issue, secondary to the confrontation between the Shia clergy and a revived Achaemenian-style royalty, the issue raised by Mossadegh, which for a very brief but tense time captivated the attention of the U.S. State Department and the C.I.A.

The Shah eventually prevailed in a long and hotly fought battle against Mossadegh, his renegade Prime Minister, who was certainly pro-Russian and probably (secretly) a committed Communist. In August 1953 the battle became so precarious that the Shah found it expedient to temporarily flee from Iran. During his absence Kermit Roosevelt and his colleagues successfully led in the overthrow of Mossadegh, allowing the Shah to return with greater power than ever.

1217 Fereydoun Hoveyda, The Fall of the Shah, (New York: Wyndham Books, 1979), p. 44.
1218 Kermit Roosevelt, Countercoup, The Struggle for the Control of Iran, (NY: McGraw Hill Book Co., 1979), p. 56.
1219 Kermit Roosevelt, Countercoup, The Struggle for the Control of Iran, (NY: McGraw Hill Book Co., 1979), pp. 125-126.

As a side note, in the July 24, 2017 edition of *The Weekly Standard,* Ray Takeyh pointed out that in June the State Department released a collection of documents which described events relating to Kermit Roosevelt and the overthrow of Mossadegh. Takeyh claims that those documents undermine Roosevelt's account of events. It is important to note that Takeyh gives not a single quote from those documents in support of his slander of Roosevelt.

The leader of the Shia clerics. The Shia clerical movement was headed up by the astute and wily Ayatollah Ruhollah Khomeini. Though Khomeini had been exiled to Najaf in Iraq and then to France, his propaganda messages were distributed nationally and surreptitiously by cassette recordings which were made available through most of the mosques in Iran.

"After the invasion of the Iranian and Shi'i capital of Isfahan by militant Sunni Afghans [from Ghazni] [See section "E, The Safavids."], the leaders of the Shi'i ulama moved to cities in Ottoman Iraq built around the tombs of the first imams—Najaf and Karbala. This area remained the center of Shi'i leadership from then until the late 1940s, and this gave the Shi'is a new advantage over the Sunni ulama in their growing independence of the government. Financially independent in Iraq, the leading Shi'i ulama were not subject to economic or political pressure from the [Mohammad Reza Shah] Iranian government."[1220]

"Although he [Khomeini] had been obliged [due to an expulsion order] to abandon his *hawza* [his circle of devoted disciples in the holy city of Qom] he still regarded himself as a part of it, and from Najaf [in Iraq to which he had been exiled by the Shah] he used to send every week to his pupils a lesson he had recorded on cassette. These pupils would congregate to listen to his voice, and gradually others from outside the *hawza* came to listen too. Soon the message on the cassettes moved away from theology and became increasingly political. The cassettes were transcribed, the message on them copied and circulated outside Qom, in Tehran and all over the country. These taped messages became known as *i' ilamiyahs,* communiques, or, literally, 'I-am-informing-you.' As someone said, what was happening was a revolution for democracy, against autocracy, led by theocracy, made possible by xerocracy. Or, as one foreign ambassador observed, the right man had appeared at the right historical moment, saying the right things."[1221]

"In less than two months (July and August 1978) Khomeini's hold on the crowd was an established fact. The exile in Najaf was stronger than the ayatollahs in Iran. He became the sole and undisputed leader of the movement that had started nine months earlier."[1222]

1220 Nikki R. Keddie, Roots of Revolution, An Interpretive History of Modern Iran, (New Haven, CT: Yale University Press, 1981), p. 21.
1221 Mohamed Heikal, The Return of the Ayatollah, The Iranian Revolution from Mossadeq to Khomeini, (London: Andre Deutsch Ltd., 1981), p. 139.
1222 Fereydoun Hoveyda, The Fall of the Shah, (New York: Wyndham Books, 1979), p. 50.

"Contraband recordings of Khomeini's speeches in Najaf [in Iraq] were heard by large congregations, which spread the word outside the mosques. Travelers returning from Iraq were bringing back cassettes of Khomeini labeled as Oriental music to outwit customs and police checks. The tapes were on open sale in the shops of Qom and Tehran. So, fifteen years after his exile, Khomeini's voice was heard throughout the land."[1223]

Shia leaders "joined many other socio-political groups in leading a violent popular uprising against the Shah's rule and reforms—particularly the land redistribution, which affected their religious holdings—in the early 1960s. As in the late 1970s, their leader then was Ayatollah Khomeini. Although the Shah succeeded in crushing the uprising, and exiled Khomeini in 1964, he failed to cut off the latter's ties with the Iranian masses. In fact, exile made Khomeini a martyr and a symbol of religious-political opposition to the Shah's rule."[1224]

"Meanwhile, in answer to representations from the Iranian government, and following Khomeini's calls for rebellion, Iraq took restrictive measures against the Ayatollah. Basing their case on the fact that the exiled Khomeini was a kind of political refugee, the Iraqis forbade him to have any contacts with visitors from Iran. These isolation measures led to protests. The opposition in Iran called a general strike for Sunday, October 1, [1978] which was widely observed in Tehran and the main provincial towns. The Iranian Foreign Minister had been in New York attending the General Assembly of the United Nations; he pursued his negotiations with his Iraqi colleague and managed to get Khomeini expelled. ... The Ayatollah of Najaf left Iraq, was turned back at the Kuwaiti frontier, and headed for Paris, where he arrived on October 3."[1225]

"From his lair in Neauphle-le-Chateau [in France] the Ayatollah Khomeini redoubled his exhortations, interviews and maledictions. In palace circles in Iran, as well as in various world capitals, there was astonishment at the attitude of the French government, which was allowing the exiled cleric to incite a rebellion, contrary to the international rules governing political refugees. In fact, when Khomeini arrived from Najaf, the French government had consulted the Shah, and received a request not to turn him out."[1226]

"Political activity was developing in the mosques, the traditional centers of opposition to the state. In a society where discontent finds no outlet in parliamentary institutions, the relative inviolability of the holy places makes them a natural focus of dissidents."[1227]

1223 Fereydoun Hoveyda, The Fall of the Shah, (New York: Wyndham Books, 1979), p. 20.
1224 Amin Saikal, The Rise and Fall of the Shah, (Princeton NJ: Princeton University Press, 1980), p. 193.
1225 Fereydoun Hoveyda, The Fall of the Shah, (New York: Wyndham Books, 1979), pp. 56-57.
1226 Fereydoun Hoveyda, The Fall of the Shah, (New York: Wyndham Books, 1979), p. 179-180.
1227 Fereydoun Hoveyda, The Fall of the Shah, (New York: Wyndham Books, 1979), p. 19.

"The eighty-thousand or so mosques and the 180,000 mullahs constitute a well-organized infrastructure capable of mobilizing the masses whenever necessary against anything seen by the guides, the ayatollahs, as a source of persecution."[1228]

"The Shah [had] curiously underestimated the influence of the priesthood. When Olivier Warin asked him if he still had difficulties with the mullahs he replied, 'Perhaps they grumble now and then, but it has no effect.'... It is fair to say that it was religious unrest which sounded the death knell of the regime. It was under the banner of Shi'ism that the Iranian people mustered the energy and solidarity necessary to bring down the Pahlavi dictatorship. It was religion that gave the masses the strength to stop living normal lives during the long months of strikes and hardships."[1229]

Mutual enmity. "The tight grip of the Moslem clergy over many phases of public life was a challenge to the position of the new ruler, who took steps to break down their power and prestige. The clergy lost direct control of much of its vast trust funds; religious law gave way to civil and criminal codes; licenses were required for the wearing of clerical garb; civil marriage and divorce registers were established; the position of women was improved; non-Moslem foreigners were permitted to visit the splendid mosques of the country; religious passion plays were suppressed; dervishes were forbidden to appear in town; and religious teaching gave way to state schools."[1230]

"Revolution was inevitable: during its last two years the monarchy flouted both law and tradition with unbelievable nonchalance. ... That is what explains the immense hatred he aroused among the masses after 1978. ... Both laymen and clergy rose in rebellion against the absolutism of the Qajars, [and that] revolution led to the dictatorship of Reza Shah. Will the return to strict Islamic law be any more liberating?"[1231]

Mohammad Reza Shah Pahlavi said, "My father's simplicity carried over into his religion. Because he was always hounding certain sections of the clergy, many people thought that he was not religious; but I know that is untrue. He pushed the clergy into the background because at that time many of them were hindering the country's progress and interfering too much in affairs of state. If he had not treated them somewhat roughly, it might have taken three or four times as long as it did to carry out his programme of modernizing the country."[1232]

A Chronology of Culminating Events

January 16, 1979 – In the face of the overwhelming power and velocity of the Khomeini Revolution, Mohammad Reza Shah Pahlavi fled from Iran. "The Shah's departure triggered an absolute carnival of rejoicing in the streets of Tehran. In the

---
1228 Fereydoun Hoveyda, The Fall of the Shah, (New York: Wyndham Books, 1979), p. 44-45.
1229 Fereydoun Hoveyda, The Fall of the Shah, (New York: Wyndham Books, 1979), pp. 105-107.
1230 Donald N. Wilber, Iran, Past and Present, (Princeton NJ: Princeton University Press, 1963), pp. 98-99.
1231 Fereydoun Hoveyda, The Fall of the Shah, (New York: Wyndham Books, 1979), p. 216.
1232 Mohammad Reza Shah Pahlavi, Mission for My Country, (London: Hutchinson & Co. Ltd., 1974), p. 47.

few minutes which elapsed after the radio broadcast the news, just about the whole population of the capital thronged into the streets to cries of '*Shah raft!*' (the Shah has gone). People embraced one another. Cars honked their horns. The scale of the response and the spontaneity of an entire nation's rejoicing impressed every outside observer. The crowd fraternized with the soldiers, while demonstrators pulled down the statues of the sovereign and his father. Slogans rang out on all sides: 'Our party is Allah's party, and our leader is Khomeini'; 'The final victory is the Islamic Republic.'"[1233]

The Shah had hoped first to visit Jordan but King Hussein politely rejected that idea. After that rejection, "the Shah's party flew direct to Aswan, the winter resort on the Nile. ... The Egyptian authorities [under President Sadat] tried to make his arrival as impressive as possible, and some people were persuaded to come into the streets and cheer; but it was a fairly miserable occasion. The Shah himself was a sad and bewildered man, still unable to comprehend what had happened. ... While he was in Aswan the Shah still behaved as if he were a head of state. He had a three-man summit meeting with Sadat and ex-President Ford at which he brought out some of his grievances against the Americans. Carter, he said, had deceived him by continually saying in public that he was giving him full support while he was negotiating with the opposition behind his back."[1234]

January 22, 1979 – After only five days in Aswan, the Shah flew to Marrakesh, Morocco. "With the Iranian Revolution exercising a fascination over Muslims everywhere, the Shah's presence was obviously going to be a liability for any government of an Islamic state. ... After three weeks King Hassan felt obliged to send his ADC to the Shah to explain that, much as the King would like to give him asylum in Morocco, the situation had changed so much that, with regret, this had become impossible."[1235]

February 1, 1979 – "An Air France charter plane flew [Khomeini] the religious leader back to Iran after fourteen years in exile. He arrived to a delirious welcome as millions of people massed along the route taken by the Mercedes van which carried him. The crowd exploded with joy. The procession headed for the Behechte Zahra cemetery, where the graves themselves were buried beneath a flood of humanity. Khomeini mounted the rostrum to a roar of acclamation and spoke in his neutral monotone: 'The parliament and government are illegal. ... I shall shut their mouths and appoint a government relying on the support of the people. ... Bakhtiar will be arrested if he does not resign. ...' He attacked the United States and called on army officers to join hands with the people."[1236]

1233 Fereydoun Hoveyda, The Fall of the Shah, (New York: Wyndham Books, 1979), p. 200.
1234 Mohamed Heikal, The Return of the Ayatollah, The Iranian Revolution from Mossadeq to Khomeini, (London: Andre Deutsch Ltd., 1981), p. 173.
1235 Mohamed Heikal, The Return of the Ayatollah, The Iranian Revolution from Mossadeq to Khomeini, (London: Andre Deutsch Ltd., 1981), p. 175.
1236 Fereydoun Hoveyda, The Fall of the Shah, (New York: Wyndham Books, 1979), p. 204.

February 11, 1979 – Khomeini established an Islamic theocracy; government forces were routed by Khomeini's supporters and the Bakhtiar government fell; during the year thousands were arrested and executed by the religious militia forces.[1237]

February 12, 1979 – "As he took his opponent's last pawn off the board, Khomeini spoke the traditional phrase: *'Shah mat'* [literally means, death to the Shah or the Shah is dead]. Then he leaned back and allowed his tired eyelids to close for a moment. He had won the marathon game started in 1960, interrupted in 1963 and resumed in 1978. From now on the country was his. No one could contest his authority any longer."[1238]

February 13, 1979 – "Armed units loyal to Khomeini found and arrested General Khosrodad. It was the end of the Pahlavis, and the end of two and a half thousand years of monarchy."[1239]

April 7, 1979 – On their way to Mexico from Morocco, the Shah and his entourage flew to Paradise Island in the Bahamas. There, "the Shah and his family swam in the warm waters of the luxury seaside resort, and tanned themselves in the sun. A few days earlier they had let themselves be photographed with smiles on their lips by the international press. ... He went on minding his health and devoting himself to his favorite sports of tennis, water skiing, jogging, golf and so on."[1240]

Despite his frolicking in the Bahamas, in Iran "it was a revolution without precedent, uniting as it did the most disparate social groupings behind the two slogans of 'Allah is great' and 'Death to the Shah!'"[1241]

June 11, 1979 – The Shah arrived for refuge in Mexico. The circumstances leading to this transition undoubtedly marked the most humiliating point of his exile. "One of the actions of the new government in Tehran had been to cancel the light-blue imperial passports on which the Shah and his family had hitherto traveled. The Mexican authorities wanted to know what passports they would be traveling on. The Moroccans were unwilling to provide passports for the Shah and his family, because then the whole of his entourage would expect them too and all might use them to return to Morocco, which was something King Hassan most certainly did not wish so there was an impasse.

"One day the telephone rang in the Geneva office of Sadruddin Aga Khan, the UN high Commissioner for Refugees. His secretary answered and said that it was a long-distance call from somebody calling herself Queen Farah. This sounded im-

---

[1237] "On 11 February (Bahman 22), Khomeini appointed his own competing interim prime minister, Mehdi Bazargan, demanding, 'since I have appointed him, he must be obeyed.' It was 'God's government,' he warned, disobedience against him or Bazargan was considered a 'revolt against God.'" Khomeini, Wikipedia, accessed 08/08/17.
[1238] Fereydoun Hoveyda, The Fall of the Shah, (New York: Wyndham Books, 1979), p. 209.
[1239] Fereydoun Hoveyda, The Fall of the Shah, (New York: Wyndham Books, 1979), p. 208.
[1240] Fereydoun Hoveyda, The Fall of the Shah, (New York: Wyndham Books, 1979), p. 212.
[1241] Fereydoun Hoveyda, The Fall of the Shah, (New York: Wyndham Books, 1979), p. 213.

probable, but Prince Sadruddin picked up the telephone and recognized the voice. 'I'm sorry to trouble you,' said the Empress, 'but we have this difficulty over passports. The bureaucrats in Mexico say we must produce a piece of paper for them to stamp. Can you help us?' She told him that Princess Ashraf was in contact with Kurt Waldheim in New York over the problem, and she hoped that it would be possible for them all to be issued with UN or refugee passports. The wheel of fortune had indeed come full circle, with the Empress of Iran begging for her and the Shahanshah to be granted the status of refugees."[1242]

October 22, 1979 – "Jimmy Carter reluctantly allowed the Shah into the United States to undergo surgical treatment at the New York-Weill Cornell Medical Hospital."[1243]

November 4, 1979 – Militants seized the U.S. Embassy in Tehran and held 62 Americans hostage.

December 15, 1979 – Flight to Panama: "The Shah's departure from American soil sapped the force of the Iranian demand that Pahlavi be returned for trial in exchange for freeing the hostages. ... Administration officials increasingly have become convinced that the Shah's departure was a prerequisite to settlement of the crisis [of the embassy staff being held hostage in Tehran]. The new arrangements for the Shah were negotiated by White House chief of Staff Hamilton Jordan with Panama's strongman, Gen. Omar Torrijos, in secret visits to that Caribbean nation last Tuesday and Thursday. White House council Lloyd Cutler joined Jordan in San Antonio to present the plans and a handwritten letter of invitation from Torrijos to the former Iranian monarch."[1244]

"In December, shortly after he had arrived in Panama, the Revolutionary Council requested their former leader be extradited. Aristides Royo, the president of Panama, indicated that the Islamic Republic would have to file formal papers, meanwhile assuring the Shah that he could not be handed over to the revolutionaries since Panamanian law prohibits extradition for crimes carrying out the death penalty. By the time Iran was prepared to presents its case in mid-March, the exiled ruler had become very uneasy about his future prospects in Panama. Simultaneously, he had been advised that he needed another operation, this time to remove a cancerous spleen. Complications developed when the authorities in Panama insisted that a local surgeon would perform the operation. The Shah wanted his medical team to be headed by Dr. Michael DeBakey of Houston. A hurried trip to Contadora by White House aide Hamilton Jordan for the express purpose of convincing the former monarch he should remain where he was only increased royal suspicions that the Carter administration was using him as a pawn to induce the return of the hostages by dangling the hope of extradition. Thus when Iran an-

---

1242 Mohamed Heikal, The Return of the Ayatollah, The Iranian Revolution from Mossadeq to Khomeini, (London: Andre Deutsch Ltd., 1981), pp. 175-176.
1243 https://en.wikipedia.org/wiki/Mohammad_Reza_Pahlavi#Exile. Accessed 8/21/17.
1244 Don Oberdorfer and Joanne Omang, Shah Thrown to Sanctuary in Panama, The Washington Post, December 16, 1979, accessed online 8/24/17.

nounced it would file the papers on March 24, the Shah found it expedient to leave Panama on March 23. He said that he was accepting Sadat's offer because he desired 'to be among friends' in a Moslem setting closer to Iran and because he wanted 'to avoid medical problems.'"[1245]

April, 1980 – An American military raid failed in an attempt to free the hostages.

July 27, 1980 – The Shah died in Egypt.

July 30, 1980 – "Fallen Shah Mohammad Reza Pahlavi was entombed in a Cairo mosque today after an Islamic funeral with full military honors that sought to surround him for a final moment with the pomp and splendor he once enjoyed as Iran's 'King of kings.' However, most of the world's nations shunned the event. President Anwar Sadat, stiff in a blue field marshal's uniform and knee-high jack boots, saluted solemnly as a row of trumpets blared a funeral march. A long cannon boomed 21 times to signal Egypt's official mourning for the man—widely despised in his own country—whom Sadat called 'my true and dear friend.' Sadat was flanked by former U.S. President Richard Nixon and Crown Prince Reza. Nixon and deposed King Constantine of Greece were the only foreign dignitaries of note to join Sadat in bestowing final honors on the Iranian monarch, who was chased from the Peacock Throne 18 months ago. Sadat was the only serving head of state in attendance. ... The Egyptian president had led several thousand mourners, including members of the Egyptian government, in the solemn funeral procession accompanying the Shah's coffin to the mosque through a crowded low-rent Cairo neighborhood. The coffin, draped with green, white and red imperial Iranian flag, rested on a black caisson pulled by six shining black Arabian stallions. Officers from the Egyptian armed forces and Sadat's presidential guard walked at each corner, and others followed carrying the Shah's medals on gold-braided, black velvet cushions. Ahead marched Egypt's presidential guard band, playing the Imperial Iranian Anthem and a selection of more than 1,000 officers in full-dress uniform. ... 'Loyal Egypt bids farewell to the Shah,' said a sign strung over their heads across the street. Tens of thousand of Egyptians, a small crowd by Cairo's standards, waited along the street to watch the procession pass by. Many thousands more watched the ceremony live on government television, crowding stores displaying sets. ... Sadat, who also has frequently mentioned the Shah's dispatch of Iranian oil to help a desperate Egypt during the 1973 war with Israel, has offered to care for the Shah's wife and four children permanently."[1246]

September 22, 1980 – War erupted between Iran and Iraq which absorbed almost all Iran's revenue, leaving it nearly bankrupt. Saddam Hussein, a Sunni dictator holding the Shia majority of Iraq in suppression through brutality, unleashed the war against Khomeini's Iranian clerical regime. The conflict grew out of an old and very heated dispute over the location of the international boundary between

---

1245 John D. Stempel, Inside the Iranian Revolution, (Bloomington, IN: Indiana University Press, 1981), pp. 238-239.
1246 Edward Cody, *Shah Entombed After State Funeral*, The Washington Post, July 30, 1980, accessed online 8/04/17.

Iran and Iraq in the Shatt al-Arab.[1247] The war raged for eight years (9/22/80–8/20/88), finally leading to a stalemate growing out of mutual exhaustion.

January 21, 1981 – Minutes after Ronald Reagan's inauguration, the American hostages were freed after 444 days in captivity!

January 22, 1981 – Ayatollah Khomeini took over executive power; a new wave of executions followed with political moderates and non-Islamic religious believers among the principal victims.

September 1988 – A United Nations initiative led to a cease-fire between Iran and Iraq.

June 3, 1989 – Ayatollah Khomeini died.

A Summary

In addition to the account given in Chapters 13 and 14 to the status of Christians in Iran, it is appropriate to focus even more attentively on their ongoing situation. Despite the fact that there have been Christians in Iran since the Parthian Empire, the remnant church is now dying out in most places in the Euphrates River basin and to the east throughout all of Iran and Afghanistan due to the dominance of Islam, culminating most recently in the vicious, bestial and destructive attacks of ISIS/ISIL, one of Islam's many factions. Some of the other significant factions are: Boko Haram in northern Nigeria, al-Shabaab in Somalia, the Taliban in Afghanistan and al Qaeda in Yemen.

For many centuries, Christians in Iran served as spiritual beacons in harmony with Philippians 2:15 in which Christians are exhorted to "be blameless and innocent, children of God without blemish in the midst of a crooked and twisted generation, among whom you shine as lights in the world,"(ESV) Minority communities of Christians courageously survived east of the Euphrates River all the way to the Indus River watershed. They served in an environment that theologically, culturally, socially, politically and legally was, and continues to be, very intimidating and harsh for those who follow Christ.

Since 642 A.D., Christians in Iran have had to face the rapacious nature of Islam. Often it did not even recognize the sanctity of Christian homes. For example, "within Iran the [Muslim] conquest spread, spurred on by the Caliph 'Uthman's promises of the governorship of wealthy Khorasan to the first of his generals to reach the province. In A.D. 652 Iranian forces were defeated at Khwarazm on the Oxus River, and within a few years lands in distant Asia were under the Moslems. Bands of Arabs moved to Khorasan and settled there. The famous general Qutayba, who campaigned in the area from 704 until 715, was so zealous in promoting

---

1247 Shatt al-Arab means "The River of the Arabs." It is the Arabic name for the 120-mile-long river which is formed by the combined waters of the Tigris and Euphrates Rivers. The Shatt al-Arab flows into the Persian Gulf south of Basra.

the Moslem faith that he quartered Arabs in every household of the captured towns."[1248]

One of the factors in the decline of organized Christianity in Iran has been the problem of language. As previously noted, Wilber has asserted that the Farsi language "has changed so little since its [Firdawsi's *Shahnameh*] composition nine hundred years ago that it can be read with ease by people of present-day Iran." However, we must be careful not to over-evaluate Wilber's next statement in which he says, "For centuries it has been recited, and even today thousands of uneducated people can repeat long passages of the poem."[1249] That euphoric assessment draws attention away from the fact that for centuries the limited understanding of the uneducated masses of people has been a devastating hindrance to the cause of Christ. As Roosevelt sagely pointed out regarding the loyalty of the Iranian people to the Shah, while "the armed forces are solidly his, however the people at large were not yet truly an effective ally. Loyal they were and proud of their heritage. But they did not share a common understanding of that heritage. The majority of them were illiterate, and worse, they were illiterate in different languages."[1250]

"Both the Arabs of southwest Iran and the Baluchis of the southeast are impoverished, which creates another grievance. There was not, however, the mass Iranian Arab defection to Iraq that the Iraqis expected. These and other minorities for whom Persian is a second language apparently constitute slightly over half of Iran's population, but they again are not united with each other. The Persians are more united. Some among the minority peoples support Khomeini, but his real support comes from lower-class Persians, and also from religious students and ulama."[1251]

In addition to the intricacies of Iranian languages during the periods when Sogdian and Pahlavi/Pahlevi were dominant, Farsi also for a long period was too intricate and convoluted to be understood by the average Iranian. "Qa'em Maqam [a title used by the chief minister of Crown Prince Abbas Mirza, 1804–1828] is known both in administrative and in literary history as the first person in modern times to try, mainly via example, to simplify the flowery and elaborate forms of Persian court prose. This reform was continued by several later figures, so that official Persian became, if not a model of simplicity and clarity, at least more broadly comprehensible than before, and literary Persian was in time simplified even more. (Premodern elaborate forms, as in many countries, helped rulers limit the comprehension of governmental writings to a small elite.)"[1252]

1248 Donald N. Wilber, Iran, Past and Present, (Princeton NJ: Princeton University Press, 1963), p. 37.
1249 Donald N. Wilber, Iran, Past and Present, (Princeton NJ: Princeton University Press, 1963), p. 42.
1250 Kermit Roosevelt, Countercoup, The Struggle for the Control of Iran, (NY: McGraw Hill Book Co., 1979), pp. 69-70.
1251 Nikki R. Keddie, Roots of Revolution, An Interpretive History of Modern Iran, (New Haven, CT: Yale University Press, 1981), p. 265.
1252 Nikki R. Keddie, Roots of Revolution, An Interpretive History of Modern Iran, (New Haven, CT: Yale University Press, 1981), p. 43.

Linguistic problems even hindered the military. For example, "in the officer corps the Shah had created a large elite class, highly paid and privileged and owing everything to him. Other ranks usually served in units far removed from their homes —thus Azerbaijanis would serve in Tehran, Tehranis in Azerbaijan, and so forth. This meant that there was little in common between the troops and the people round them, who could be alien in race and often in language too."[1253]

Linguistic diversity has proven to be a tremendous problem in making Christian scripture available to all Iranians. The absence of a common language created a daunting problem even for those who governed. For example, "there was no elected self-government in villages, towns, districts, or provinces. Officials were appointed from and accountable to Tehran. In 1938, local administrative units were reorganized into a nationwide hierarchy, with divisions often cutting across traditional cultural and ethnic lines. Control was autocratic and distant, separating the administrator and the subject, who might literally speak different languages and have different educations and values."[1254]

The problem of a common language through which the Gospel might be made known throughout all of Iran is highlighted by the fact that "the Azerbaijani Turki[sh] language was not taught or permitted for official business, and there was resentment against forced Persianization."[1255]

The suppression of Christians socially, economically and educationally helps explain why Christians in Iran did not themselves update translations of the Christian scriptures afresh as the national language changed. As we have seen in Chapter 10, when Sogdian was the language of Iran, Christians translated the scripture into that widely-used commercial lingua franca. From the time Iran was forced into the Islamic empire in 642 A.D., as a result of the Battle of Nehawand, conditions socially, economically and educationally for Christians became and have continued to become more and more restrictive. The upshot has been that the Christian community in Iran lacked the needed freedom in which scholars who had the ability, the education, and the resources might work to keep the Christian scriptures abreast with the changes which have come into the common language of Iran. Therefore, to keep the New Testament translation abreast with changes in Farsi, the cause of Christ in Iran has been dependent on the dedicated efforts of men living outside of Iran, like Henry Martyn whose thrilling achievement was briefly recounted in Chapter 14.

Also, as Wilber has pointed out, "Many Persian authors of this time [the time of Firdawsi] and later wrote in Arabic. The Arabic language with its entirely logical and highly evolved grammatical forms appealed to the Persian intellect, while the

---

1253 Mohamed Heikal, <u>The Return of the Ayatollah, The Iranian Revolution from Mossadeq to Khomeini</u>, (London: Andre Deutsch Ltd., 1981), p. 144.
1254 Nikki R. Keddie, <u>Roots of Revolution, An Interpretive History of Modern Iran</u>, (New Haven, CT: Yale University Press, 1981), p. 108.
1255 Nikki R. Keddie, <u>Roots of Revolution, An Interpretive History of Modern Iran</u>, (New Haven, CT: Yale University Press, 1981), p. 119.

Arabic alphabet was far superior to the intricate Pahlavi script, so that Iranian men of learning knew Arabic as their second language. Many Arabic words came into Persian and, of course, the Arabic characters were now used for written Persian. Such notable figures as Saʻdi and Ghazali wrote both in Persian and Arabic, and many authors whose native tongue was Arabic became so absorbed by Iranian culture and thought that their histories, poems, and philosophical and mystical writings are in fact Persian literature, though in another tongue."[1256]

In addition to the difficulties of gaining broad biblical knowledge due to the problems of language, there was also a great lack of general education. "In 1977, when the Shah had dismissed my brother as prime minister after a little over a dozen years of service, the country presented a different face. More than sixty-five percent of the population owned the houses they lived in (and the percentage was even higher in the capital). Per-capita income stood at $2,200 ($300 in 1965). Primary school attendance was over ten million (270,000 in 1960). <u>Illiteracy had fallen from eighty-five to fifty-five percent</u>."[1257]

"In December 1944 he [Reza Shah] told Morris [Leland B. Morris, American Ambassador] of his wish that Iran should be democratic but of his fears that lack of education made this difficult."[1258] Islamic pressure and societal turmoil ended such a beneficial influence. "The social and health conditions of the peasantry were among the worst in the world. Peasants used primitive tools and suffered from lack of water or good seeds. Technological improvements under post-war conditions of land tenure offered them little."[1259]

The Shah gratefully acknowledged that, "gradually our educational system began to be affected by Western example. In 1836 American Presbyterian missionaries opened a school in Rezaieh, in north-western Iran, followed by a number of others in various parts of the country. British, German, French, and Russian schools were over the years also established in Iran. Altogether many hundreds of Persian boys and girls benefitted from the primary, secondary, and introductory college work offered by these schools."[1260] Basing his statements on the work of L. P. Elwell-Sutton in his work entitled <u>Modern Iran</u>, Keddie tells us that in the post-World War II era "foreigners, especially missionaries, ran the first modern hospitals and schools, and Iranian governments did little. Only a bare minority of Iranians were educated."[1261]

The work of the Presbyterians and other Christian groups was carried out in harmony with Christian outreach going back to the end of the fifth century. It was

---

1256 Donald N. Wilber, <u>Iran, Past and Present</u>, (Princeton NJ: Princeton University Press, 1963), p. 42.
1257 Fereydoun Hoveyda, <u>The Fall of the Shah</u>, (New York: Wyndham Books, 1979), p. 73.
1258 Mohamed Heikal, <u>The Return of the Ayatollah, The Iranian Revolution from Mossadeq to Khomeini</u>, (London: Andre Deutsch Ltd., 1981), p. 40.
1259 Nikki R. Keddie, <u>Roots of Revolution, An Interpretive History of Modern Iran</u>, (New Haven, CT: Yale University Press, 1981), p. 124.
1260 Mohammad Reza Shah Pahlavi, <u>Mission for My Country</u>, (London: Hutchinson & Co. Ltd., 1974), p. 240.
1261 Nikki R. Keddie, <u>Roots of Revolution, An Interpretive History of Modern Iran</u>, (New Haven, CT: Yale University Press, 1981), p. 92.

then that "Nestorian Christians had established a thriving medical school and university in what is known as the Lebanon; but persecution by the Eastern Roman Empire forced them first to move to Syria and then, about A.D. 489, to take refuge in Persia. Shah Khosro Nushirwan welcomed the fugitive professors with their books; and in Jundi Shapur, a town in southwestern Iran, they re-established their medical school which was destined to continue for several centuries."[1262]

However, that benign influence had a serious setback because, as the Shah acknowledged, "in 1940, largely to curb the spread of foreign influence in Iran, my father had decreed that the Government should take over all foreign-run schools in which Persian students were enrolled. But during the Second World War the order was relaxed, and soon a number of foreign schools reopened or were started afresh. The best known of them, the Community School of Tehran, is run by the American Presbyterian mission. Many of the student body are Persians, the school has excellent standards, and it prepares students for American colleges and universities. The Armenians, the Jews, and other native religious minorities in Iran also run their own schools, which commonly do very good work."[1263]

As noted in Chapter 1, throughout the vast Muslim world, churches by the hundreds have died and extensive Christian communities have shriveled and vanished! Reasons? Exorbitant and discriminatory taxes, extreme social and economic restrictions, unequal standing before the law, prohibition of Christian evangelism and heavy restrictions on the practice of one's Christian faith. All of these are results from the withering wind which continues to blow from Arabia. "The latest in a string of harsh sentences against church leaders in Iran has been handed down to four Christian converts for promoting Christianity, according to human rights activists. Pastor Yousef Nadarkhani, along with deacons Mohammadreza Omidi, Yasser Mossayebzadeh and Saheb Fadaie, were sentenced to 10 years in prison in a ruling by the 26th branch of the Revolutionary Court in Tehran, according to a regional director of Middle East Concern (MEC), a human rights organization that tracks the persecution of Christians in the region."[1264] Detailed attention to the agony and injustice which took place in the extinction of the evangelistic and missionary activities of the Church of England in Iran have been given in Chapter 14.

Addendum

One might have thought that the unprecedented wealth which flowed into the Muslim world from oil would have quickly lifted that whole society off the social, educational, entrepreneurial and creative low point which may be called "the bottom." However, one must never forget the insight Jesus has given us about the limitations of materialism. Quoting from Deuteronomy 8:3, he said, "Man does not live on bread alone, but on every word that comes from the mouth of God."

1262 Mohammad Reza Shah Pahlavi, Mission for My Country, (London: Hutchinson & Co. Ltd., 1974), p. 239.

1263 Mohammad Reza Shah Pahlavi, Mission for My Country, (London: Hutchinson & Co. Ltd., 1974), p. 245.

1264 *Morning Star News*, July 13, 2017. http://mailchi.mp/morningstarnews/harsh-punishments-meted-out-to-christians-in-iran-as-tehran-sends-chilling-signal?e=400fb797e8 Accessed 7/14/17.

(Matthew 4:4 NIV) The Muslim experience with riches, which oil copiously bestowed on countless people, certainly substantiates Jesus' assertion.

Oil "confirmed devastating social inequalities and injustices between people within a country, and then between countries with oil and those without it. The seven main Arab oil-exporting states account for about three-quarters of the region's gross domestic product but only about one-quarter of its population. Industry is only about 7 or 8 percent of aggregate GDP [Gross Domestic Product]. Ninety-five percent of total Arab exports consist of oil, in itself an unbalancing factor socially and economically, with which none of the Arab regimes are able to cope."[1265]

"If one subtracted the oil revenue of the Gulf countries, 260 million Arabs exported less than the 5 million Finns [i.e., the tiny country of Finland]. Radicalism usually prospers in the gap between rising expectations and declining opportunities. This is especially true where the population is young, idle, and bored; where the art is impoverished; where entertainment—movies, theater, music—is policed or absent altogether; and where young men are set apart from the consoling and socializing presence of women. Adult illiteracy remained the norm in many Arab countries. Unemployment was among the highest in the developing world. Anger, resentment, and humiliation spurred young Arabs to search for dramatic remedies."[1266]

"Neither large wealth nor displays of traditions will arrest the drift toward disorder in vast stretches of the Arab world [as well as the Iranian world]. Wealth has only underlined a painful gap between what a society can buy and what it can be, between the vast means available to buy into things and the limited capacity to create a somewhat autonomous public project, a livable public order. … The self-confidence and the imagination societies need if they are to reinvent themselves are nowhere to be found in Arab political life. So there it is, the world of Araby, in close proximity to Europe, a veritable dumping ground for the high-tech weaponry and pop culture of the West, but a world stubbornly impermeable to any democratic [or Christian Gospel] stirrings."[1267]

☙

[1265] David Pryce-Jones, The Closed Circle, An Interpretation of the Arabs, (New York: Harper Perennial, 1989), p. 264.
[1266] Lawrence Wright, The Looming Tower, al Qaeda and the Road to 9/11, (New York: Alfred A. Knopf, 2006), p. 107.
[1267] Fouad Ajami, The Arab Predicament, Arab Political Thought and Practice Since 1967, (New York: Cambridge University Press, 1992), pp. 24-25.

Glossary

Glossary

Abbasid – The name of the caliphate which defeated and replaced the Ummayad Caliphate at the Battle of the Great Zab River in 750 A.D. It ruled from Baghdad till it was destroyed by Hulagu's Mongol army in 1258.

Africa – The name Africa has an interesting origin. After the Romans destroyed Carthage "they were gradually extending their hegemony in the Maghrib (see Glossary). They had at once annexed the districts which the Carthaginians had directly administered, and had made of them a [narrow coastal] province which they called 'Africa,' from a Punic root meaning 'cut off'; this presumably referred to the fact that Carthage had been 'cut off' from its motherland of Phoenicia, and the word was eventually extended to cover the whole of the continent."[1268]

al-Hilal – A graphic image of a crescent moon. It appears on many Muslim national flags, usually with a star, embraced by the two arms of the moon.

Alim (plural - **Ulema**) – "Scholars of the Islamic religion who fulfill the function of clergy and used also to act as lawyers."[1269]

al-Jawf – the name of the town raided by 1,000 warriors led by Muhammad from Medina in 621 A.D. Its other name was Dumat al-Jandal. It is also the name of "the great plain in the northeast of Yemen."[1270]

al Qaeda – The meaning of the word is "principle," "base," "basis" or "foundation." It was adopted as the name of the terrorist group headed by Osama bin Laden.

Amir – Prince, commander: an alternate title still used for the office of imam is *Amir ul-Mu'minin* or 'Commander of the Faithful.' Rightly or wrongly, the Imam of the Yemen so calls himself Amir.

Anatolia – The term comes from the Greek word *anatol*, meaning "east." Thus, Anatolia means the land to the east, that is, east of Greece, beginning from the eastern shore of the Aegean Sea.

[1268] Geoffrey Furlonge, The Lands of Barbary, (London: John Murray, 1966), p. 73.
[1269] Ali Dashti, Twenty Three Years: A Study of the Prophetic Career of Muhammad trans. from Persian by F. R. C. Bagley, (London: George Allen & Unwin, 1985), p. xvii.
[1270] Manfred W. Wenner, Modern Yemen 1918–1966, (Baltimore: The Johns Hopkins Press, 1967), p. 72.

Ansar – Supporters or helpers. It is the title which was given to the converts to Islam in Medina who welcomed and aided the Muslims from Mecca when they fled from their hometown (their hijra).

Arab Spring – is the name given to a movement in the Arab Muslim world which seemed to be the dawn of a new day, bringing much more justice and freedom to Arab Muslims. It started in Tunisia on December 18, 2010 when a policeman demanded an exorbitant fee from a push-cart seller of fruits and vegetables. The push-cart entrepreneur, Mohamed Bouazizi, was so dispirited and discouraged that he committed suicide by burning himself to death. As word of the poor man's plight spread, the whole country of Tunisia erupted in violent protest against the injustice, harassment and brutality of their Muslim government. The rebellion became so threatening against those in power that the ruler of Tunisia, Zine El Abidine Ben Ali, fled to Saudi Arabia for protection. The same sense of betrayal by government spread to other countries in the Muslim world. It led to the overthrow of Hosni Mubarak in Egypt. It sparked the protest against Bashar Assad in Syria, which led to the outbreak of a five-year-long civil war in which millions died and some five million others fled from Syria. The Arab Spring also quickly spread to Libya, Bahrain and Yemen.

Arabia Felix – That is, *Happy Arabia*, the name the Romans used to describe those lush, irrigated Yemeni lands before the final collapse of the Marib Dam.

Ashura – The day when Shiites everywhere commemorate the martyrdom of Imam Hussain /Husayn, son of Ali. "It is the name of a voluntary fast day on the tenth day of Muharram; a day of mourning, sacred to the Shiites. It is the anniversary of Hussain's martyrdom at Karbala."[1271]

ayatollah – Literally, a sign of God. A title given to leading Shiite scholars.

azan/adhan – The call to Muslims to pray.

barbarian – In the Maghrib (see Glossary), immediately adjacent to Egypt on the west, "were the people whom the Egyptians called 'Libyans' and the Romans 'Barbari'—whence our words Berber and Barbary—and they [still] form one [very important] component of the population of today. ... The Roman appellation 'Barbari, meaning 'uncultured,' was obviously a term of contempt."[1272]

baya – allegiance, oath of allegiance

[1271] Hans Wehr, A Dictionary of Modern Written Arabic, (London: MacDonald & Evans Ltd., 1960).
[1272] Geoffrey Furlonge, The Lands of Barbary, (London: John Murray, 1966), pp. 1-4.

Glossary

Boko Haram – An Islamist sect founded in 2002 by "an obscure preacher by the name of Mohammed Yusuf, born in 1970 and based in Maiduguri, the capital of Borno state [Nigeria], was calling on 'the Muslim community to correct its creed and its behaviours and its morals ... to give children a correct Islamic education' and to undertake jihad in the name of Allah."[1273] The name means that which is foreign (boko), especially Western education, is abominable, or forbidden (haram). It is the name under which a major Muslim jihadist army has decimated northern Nigeria.

caliph – Successor, the one who succeeds the Prophet Muhammad in leading the *umma,* the worldwide population of Muslims. (See also *khalifa*.)

caliphate – The administrative structure used by the caliph to govern and lead the Muslim people.

Chalcedonian – The term refers to a creedal statement about the nature of the human versus divine aspects of the person of Christ. The name Chalcedonian is given to the statement because it was reached at an imperial council held in 451 A.D. at Chalcedon, a city near Constantinople. The council's decision embodied "a carefully balanced definition of how to view the mystery of Christ: 'the same perfect in divinity and perfect in humanity, the same truly God and truly man, of a rational soul and a body; con-substantial with the Father as regards his divinity, and the same con-substantial with us as regards his humanity.'"[1274]

Copt – Copt is an Arabic word meaning Egyptian. Ultimately it came to mean the native Church of Egypt.

dahna/dahana – "A hard gravelly plain covered at intervals with sand-drifts, here, as a rule, water can be reached by sinking wells, but the surface is usually extremely barren."[1275]

Dar al-Islam – The Muslim world.

dhimmi(s) – A subjugated unbeliever. "The pact [of Umar] or contract between the Muslim state and a non-Muslim subject community was called *dhimma*, and the members of such a tolerated community were called *dhimmis*."[1276] Dhimmis had the status of second-class citizens as non-Muslims in traditional Arab society.

dhimmitude – A category which Muslims granted only to Jews and Christians who wished to retain their religion. The Koran gives the legislation authorizing this demeaning status. It says, "Fight against such of those who have been given the Scripture as believe not in Allah nor the Last Day, and forbid not that which

---

[1273] Adewale Maja-Pearce, *Where to Begin?*, London Review of Books, April 26, 2018, p. 20.
[1274] Diarmaid MacCulloch, Christianity, the First Three-Thousand Years, (New York, Viking, 2010), p. 226.
[1275] De Lacy O'Leary, History of Arabia Before Muhammad, (Lahore, Pakistan: Alliance Publishers, 1989), p. 6.
[1276] Bernard Lewis, The Crisis of Islam, Holy War and Unholy Terror, (New York: The Modern Library, 2003), p. 46.

Allah hath forbidden by His messenger, and follow not the religion of truth, <u>until they pay the tribute readily, being brought low</u>." (Surah 9:29) It is obvious that not only did the Christians and Jews as *dhimmis* have to pay a repressive tax, they had to be humiliated, "brought low."

"It is the duty of a Muslim, wherever he may be, to bring the faith to the unbelievers. ... It is, however, strictly forbidden to a *dhimmi* to try to convert a Muslim to his religion, and if by any mischance he succeeds, the penalty for apostasy is death. From a Muslim religious point of view, this discrepancy is both logical and proper. To promote the true faith is a divine commandment. To abandon it, or to persuade another to do so, is both a mortal sin and a capital crime."[1277]

Donatist – The adjective 'Donatist' comes from the name of Donatus, a North African bishop. Donatus objected to Rome's recognition of Caecilian as bishop in North Africa. It headed up a dispute about baptism. "North Africans said that valid baptism could take place only within the Christian community which is the church, the Romans saying that the sacrament belonged to Christ, not to the church, and that therefore it was valid whoever performed it if it was done in the right form and with the right intentions."[1278] "The opposition, furious at what they saw as this final proof of Caecilian's unworthiness, rallied behind the rival bishop, Donatus. The centuries-long Donatist schism in the North African church had begun."[1279]

Dumat – See Al-Jawf.

Dyophysite – see Miaphysite

emir – One who leads/rules a section of the *umma*, the community of believers.

Eurasia – Europe and Asia combined.

Fatimids – The Fatimids ruled Egypt from 969 to 1171 A.D. They "appeared as successors to the sixth imam, even managed to occupy Egypt in 969 and establish themselves in Cairo, their newly founded residence. Although the Fatimid caliphs were not Twelver Shiites but Ismailis (they were descendants of Ismail [the seventh imam], a son of the sixth imam, Jafar), the establishment of a Shia caliphate in Egypt served as a powerful impetus for Shiism in general. The tenth century could almost be characterized as the 'Shia century.'"[1280]

1277 Bernard Lewis, <u>Islam And The West</u>, (New York: Oxford University Press, 1993), p. 53.
1278 Diarmaid MacCulloch, <u>Christianity, the First Three-Thousand Years</u>, (New York, Viking, 2010), p. 175.
1279 Diarmaid MacCulloch, <u>Christianity, the First Three-Thousand Years</u>, (New York, Viking, 2010), p. 211.
1280 Heinz Halm, <u>The Shiites, A Short History</u>, (Princeton NJ: Markus Wiener Publishers, 2007), pp. 96-97. For those wishing for additional information, see John Glubb, <u>A Short History of the Arab People</u>, p. 142 ff.

fatwa – an Islamic religious edict, see mufti.

fiqh – the body of Islamic Law

fitnah – sedition or discord

fuqaha, (singular, faqih) – Theologians, those competent in interpreting *fiqh*.

hadith – The word *hadith* means tradition. Its meaning in Islamic history and theology is the account of the actions or sayings of Muhammad and his companions. Also, the whole body of sacred Tradition of the Muslims is called "*the Hadith*." It is a collection of traditional reports on the actions and sayings of Muhammad. These traditional reports were often carried forward in time only orally for several versions. However by the end of the first century of Islam, perhaps a bit earlier, "the main facts about the prophet's life were written down much as we have them in written works."[1281] In accessing the *hadiths* one must use caution because many fabricated *hadiths*, concocted by unscrupulous people seeking to establish a point or to achieve some end or goal, found their way into the Islamic historical accounts. The most widely accepted account is *Sirat Rasul Allah, The Life of Muhammad*, by Ibn Ishaq.

The hadith is composed of "reports of the Prophet Muhammad's sayings and actions attributed to his companions, his wives, men who knew or saw him, and men who knew his companions. The Shi'ite Islamic *Hadith*, also called *Akhbār* (reports), includes sayings and examples of the *Emāms*. The Hadith supplemented the Qor'ān [sic] as a source of Islamic law and theology, and was written down in the 9th and following centuries in massive compilations which are thought by modern scholars to include material absorbed from many Eastern sources."[1282]

Hakem-e shar – The leading Shiite judge or authority

hakimiyya – the rule of Allah; securing God's sovereignty in the political system

hajj – Pilgrimage. It refers to the annual greater pilgrimage to the ka'ba (see Glossary) which can be performed only in the month of Dhu 'l-Hijja. See "umrah."

hanif – A word originally meaning 'those who turn away' from existing idol-worship, but eventually came to have the sense of 'upright' or 'by nature upright.'

hijaz – barrier (see definition in Appendix A)

[1281] Ibn Ishaq, The Life of Muhammad, Trans. A. Guillaume, (New York: Oxford University Press, 1982) p. xv.
[1282] Ali Dashti, Twenty Three Years: A Study of the Prophetic Career of Muhammad trans. from Persian by F. R. C. Bagley, (London: George Allen & Unwin, 1985), p. xvii.

Hijra (also spelled Hijrah, Hidjra, or in its Latin form, Hegira) – The Muslim or Islamic Era begins with the date of Muhammad's Hijra. The word means "flight" or "escape." It refers to Muhammad's flight from Mecca to Medina, starting July 16, 622.

Hujatol-Islam – Literally a proof of Islam. A title given to leading ulama (see Glossary).

hunafa – plural of hanif

ijtihad – Independent reasoning. "In Islam, there exists a tradition of intellectual interpretation and innovation known as *ijtihad* practiced by jurists and clerics over the centuries to debate the meaning of Koranic teachings as well as their application to modern ideas and situations. ... *Ijtihad* is central to Islamic law, because sharia is more a set of principles than a codified set of rules. A decision or opinion derived from the process of *ijtihad* means that a jurist appraises a given matter (for example, should women be stoned for adultery in the twentieth century?) by applying reason and deduction and weighing the priorities of the concerns involved. In the early years after the revolution, Ayatollah Khomeini ruled that state media could broadcast music despite the severe attitude of the senior clergy toward song. He concluded that otherwise young people would be lured by Western radio and that ultimately this would be more wounding to the Islamic Republic. This was an act of *ijtihad*, in which a seventh-century convention was found unsuitable for the day."[1283]

ilaf – A guarantee of safe passage. A trade agreement. "The secondary literature generally informs us that they [the Meccans] operated in Syria, the Yemen, Ethiopia, and Iraq, linking all four regions in a single commercial network. This claim rests on Ibn al-Kalbi's *ilaf*-tradition, which goes as follows.

"Meccan trade used to be purely local. Non-Arab traders would bring their goods to Mecca, and the Meccans would buy them for resale partly among themselves and partly among their neighbors. This was how things remained until Hashim, Muhammad's great-grandfather, went to Syria, where he attracted the attention of the Byzantine emperor by cooking *tharid*, a dish unknown to the non-Arabs. Having become friendly with the emperor, he persuaded the latter to grant Quraysh permission to sell Hijazi leather and clothing in Syria on the ground that this would be cheaper for the Syrians. Next he returned to Mecca, concluding agreements with the tribes on the way. These agreements were know as *ilafs*, and granted Quraysh safe passage through the territories of the tribes in question. In return, Quraysh undertook to act as commercial agents on behalf of these tribes, collecting their goods on the way to Syria and handing over what they had fetched on the way back. Hashim accompanied the first Meccan caravan to Syria, seeing to the fulfillment of the agreements and settling Quraysh in the towns and/or villages (*qura*) of Syria; it was on this journey that he died in Gaza. His three brothers con-

---
1283 Shirin Ebadi, <u>Iran Awakening, A Memoir of Revolution and Hope</u>, (New York: Random House, 2006), pp. 191-192.

cluded similar treaties with the rulers of Persia, the Yemen, and Ethiopia, enabling Quraysh to trade in safety, and similar agreements with the tribes on the way, enabling them to travel to the countries in question without fear. All died in places implicitly presented as relevant to their trade. It was thanks to the activities of Hashim and his brothers that the Meccans got rich."[1284]

imam/emam – The one who leads the faithful in prayer. The one who leads in prayer is the imam. "The Arabic word *imam* means 'leader of the community;' it is formed from the same root as the word for 'community' (*'umma*)."[1285] "A second title still used for the same office is *Amir ul-Mu'minin* or 'Commander of the Faithful.' Rightly or wrongly, the Imam of the Yemen so calls himself today. A third title is *Khalifa*, with its European rendition, **Caliph. This is the term most commonly understood by non-Muslims. It means literally 'he who is left behind' and hence 'successor.'**"[1286]

ISIS – Islamic State of Iraq and Syria

Islam – The word means submission. It was originally used by Christians in Najran to indicate their commitment to Christ. It was appropriated by Muhammad to indicate submission to Allah through Muhammad.

Ismaili – "descendants [followers] of Ismail [the seventh imam], a son of the sixth imam, Jafar"[1287]

jahiliyya – The historical period of ignorance, the period of world history before Muhammad brought enlightenment. A person living during that time was *jahil*, ignorant, not enlightened by or living in accord with the revelation given by Muhammad.

jihad – The root meaning is endeavor, strive, labor. Jihad often means a religious war fought by Muslims to defend, protect, strengthen or expand Islam. From this word is derived mujahid and its plural mujahideen, the term describing one who fights in a jihad. See *ijtihad*.

jihadi – Jihadi is a Muslim soldier who fights in a jihad.

jizya – A poll tax levied on Christians and Jews living under a Muslim government. One scholar has poignantly expressed the taxation imposed on Christians saying, "they [were] generally granted religious freedom [to exist] in exchange for higher taxes. [It was a] system of taxed tolerance."[1288]

1284 Patricia Crone, Meccan Trade And The Rise of Islam, (Piscataway, N.J.: Gorgias Press, 2004, pp. 109-110.
1285 Heinz Halm, The Shi'ites, A Short History, trans. Allison Brown, (Princeton: Markus Wiener Publishers, 2007), p. 3.
1286 Carlton S. Coon, Caravan: The Story of the Middle East, (New York: Henry Holt and Company, 1956), p. 95.
1287 Heinz Halm, The Shiites, A Short History, (Princeton NJ; Markus Wiener Publishers, 2007), pp. 96-97.
1288 Elif Batuman, *Ottomania*, The New Yorker, February 17 & 24. 2014. p. 51.

ka'ba/kaaba – "The Kaaba was the House of God and had been [according to Muslim belief] built by Abraham, whose religion he [Muhammad] was himself preaching. The Meccans had sinned by placing idols in the Kaaba and these must be removed. But when this had been done, the Kaaba would remain the House of God and pilgrimage to it would be a Muslim obligation."[1289]

kafir – Irreligious, unbelieving, a blasphemer (see *kufr*).

kalima – The Arabic name for the confession of faith one must make to become a Muslim. The confession says "There is no God but Allah and Muhammad is the prophet of Allah."

khalifa – "*Khalifa*, with its European rendition, Caliph, ... [is] the term most commonly understood by non-Muslims. It means literally 'he who is left behind' and hence 'successor.'"[1290] See *Caliph*.

Kharijite (Seceder) – "Ali, quite understandably, refused to accept this verdict. [The verdict was about the outcome of the Battle of Siffeen which had been derived from consultation based on the Koran.] But he was unable to renew the battle with Mu'awiya, as his ranks were torn by discord and rebellion. Many Muslims believed that by submitting to human arbitration he [Ali] had violated the will of God. They abandoned his cause in disgust, joining with other dissidents to form an extremist group called the Kharijites, or Seceders."[1291] It was one of the Kharijites who assassinated Ali.

kuffar – (plural of *kafir*) infidels, those who write or speak *kufr*

kufr – blasphemy, unbelief; see kafir.

Levant – Levant is from Italian *levante*, the east (where the sun rises). Levant is also a derivative of the Latin *levare*, to raise, thus the East, specifically, the countries on the eastern shore of the Mediterranean.

madrasa/madrassa – A mosque school. "Following the fall of the Fatimid dynasty with Salah al-Din's (Saladin's) conquest of Egypt in 1171, there came with the new ruler a new religious institution, the *madrasa* [while new to Egypt, it was not new to the Islamic world], which was equivalent to a private college. This Salah al-Din introduced to reeducate the population in the four schools of Sunni jurisprudence—Shafi'i, Maliki, Hanafi and Hanbali, named after the religious leaders who founded them. Whereas the mosques were open to all, the madrasas received only limited numbers of students. Gone now were the vast enclosures built to hold all the inhabitants of the city. The layout of the madrasa was centered

---

[1289] John Glubb, A Short History of the Arab Peoples, (New York: Stein and Day, Publishers, 1970), p. 39.
[1290] Carlton S. Coon, Caravan: The Story of the Middle East, (New York: Henry Holt and Company, 1956), p. 95.
[1291] Desmond Stewart, Early Islam, (New York: Time Incorporated, 1967), p. 61.

around a much smaller courtyard, which was often surrounded on four sides by deep alcoves (*iwans*), one for each of the schools of jurisprudence."[1292]

Maghreb/Maghrib – North Africa as a whole is known to the Arabs as "Jezirat al Maghrib," or "The Island of the Sunset." They consider it an island because it is bounded by the waters of the Nile on the east, of the Mediterranean on the north and by the Atlantic on the west and by a great sea of sand on the south. Colloquially, the term Jezirat al Maghrib is now shortened simply to Maghrib.

Mahdi – Rightly guided; in North Africa the Muslim Messiah.

Mamluks/Mamelukes – Mamluk in the singular means "owned." The Mamluks were Turkish slave troops hired by the renowned Saladin's successors who were known as the Ayyubids, after Saladin's last name, Ayyub.

Miaphysite – "The label 'Monophysite' has widely been replaced by 'Miaphysite.' That derives from a phrase for 'one nature' (*mia physis*) which Bishop Cyril habitually and undeniably used in writings which retained a wide esteem in both Greek East and Latin West."[1293] "A majority in the Egyptian Church as well as other strongholds of Miaphysitism denounced Chalcedonian Christians as 'Dyophysites' and sneered at them as 'the emperor's people'—and Melchites."[1294]

mihrab – The mark, often an alcove in the mosque wall, showing the Muslim worshiper the direction, the *qibla* (that is, the direction of Mecca), to which he should face when he prostrates himself in prayer.

millat – The word means "nation," "community." Under Islam it came also to mean a permitted religious community, thus, it was applied to the church.

Monophysite – From the Greek μονος (monos-single) + φυσις (phusis-nature) — a single nature. Used of those who hold that there is but a single nature in Christ or that the human and divine in Him constituted but one composite nature.

Monothelite – Realizing that the destructive confrontation between Christians in the Roman Empire had to be brought to an end, Heraclius, with the assistance of a committee of three **bish**ops,[1295] devised the Monothelite concept as a middle position between the warring camps, a position both could hopefully

---
1292 John Feeney, *A City Adorned*, Saudi Aramco World, January/February 2005, p. 26.
1293 Diarmaid MacCulloch, Christianity, the First Three-Thousand Years, (New York, Viking, 2010), pp. 227-228.
1294 Diarmaid MacCulloch, Christianity, the First Three-Thousand Years, (New York, Viking, 2010), p. 233.
1295 They were: (1) Sergius of Constantinople. "With him originated the formula of compromise adopted by Heraclius, whereby it was settled to dismiss the question whether our Lord's nature was single or twofold, but to pronounce positively that there was but one will or operation." Alfred J. Butler, The Arab Conquest of Egypt and the Last Thirty Years of the Roman Dominion, (Oxford: At The Clarendon Press, 1902), p. 136. (2) Paulus, an Armenian church leader and (3) Cyrus, a Nestorian bishop from Phasis in the Caucasus. This is Cyrus who later became simultaneously Patriarch of Alexandria and civil governor of Egypt.

accept without feeling they had compromised. The Monothelite view was "the confession of two natures and *one energy* [or *one will*] in Christ."[1296]

Moors – The collective name for the people who made up the multinational Muslim invasion force which conquered Spain. "The word 'Moor,' the definition of which is 'an inhabitant of North West Africa' and which I shall occasionally use in that sense, comes from an alternative Roman name for the Berbers, 'Mauri,' which at first applied only to the northern Moroccans but was later extended to cover the Algerians also; it was probably derived from a Greek word meaning 'dark-skinned.'"[1297]

mosque – The English rendering for the Arabic *masjid*, the place where *sijda*, prostration, in the worship of God takes place.

mowlana – Derived from *mowla*, "master," the leader of the Dervish Order founded by Jalalediin. Persian for "our master."

Mozarab – Derived from the Arabic *musta'rib*, meaning Arabized or Arabic-speaking. It usually referred to Spanish converts to Islam.

muezzin – The one who calls the faithful to prayer.

Mufti – A Muslim religious leader who has the authority to issue a fatwa (see Glossary), "a jurisconsult in the Holy Law."[1298] "The Mufti is a salaried appointed [officer or authority] of the State who gives legal opinions, *fatwas*, in answer to questions pertaining to Sharia, or the Sacred Law, submitted to him by judges or private individuals."[1299] See also, qadi.

muhajir – One who goes on a hajj, an immigrant. Plural is muhajirun.

muharram – "The Muslim era does not begin exactly on the day when Muhammad left Mecca for Medina. Its beginning was fixed by Umar in such a way that the year begins with muharram and that the first day of that month keeps the date which it had in the year in which the Caliph put into force the new calculation."[1300]

mujahid – See *jihad*.

mujtahid – A jurist, qualified in theology and sacred law, who delivers a legal decision. (See *ijtihad*.)

mullah – (also *maula*) From *vali*, a master or ruler.

1296 Albert Henry Newman, A Manual of Church History, (Philadelphia: The American Baptist Publication Society, 1933), Vol. I, p. 351.
1297 Geoffrey Furlonge, The Lands of Barbary, (London: John Murray, 1966), p. 4 (note).
1298 Bernard Lewis, The Crisis of Islam, Holy War and Unholy Terror, (New York: The Modern Library, 2003), p. 12.
1299 P.J. Batikiotis, The History of Egypt, From Muhammad Ali to Mubarak (Baltimore: The Johns Hopkins University Press, 1985), p. 302.
1300 Encyclopaedia Britannica 11th Ed., Vol. 4, p. 2001.

Muslim – From the same root as *salam,* "peace," plural: *muslimun,* literally, 'those who find peace by submission.' *Islam,* which means submission, is also derived from the same root. Thus, a Muslim is one who submits to Allah and Muhammad. Such a person makes submission by reciting the *kalima*.

Nafud/Nefud – "The land of sand dunes."[1301] It refers to, "a sand region in the northern part of Arabia. In the southern part of Arabia it is called *ramlah*. For example, "The whole area known to Westerners as the Rubʿ al-Khali [the empty quarter] is known to its inhabitants as *al-Ramlah* or *al-Rimal* (the plural of *ramlah*)."[1302] "An area of deep sand which the wind forces into high banks or dunes: sometimes when the sand is piled in very high ridges with only narrow depressions between it is called *ahqaf*, but this is only a particular variety of the *nefud*."[1303]

naqib – a leader

Orthodox – When referring to a church, it was the official state "Orthodox" church. When referring to a doctrine, it was the doctrine of the official state church. The Christology of the Orthodox church was that defined by the Council of Chalcedon which had been convened in 451 A.D.

Ottoman – The name of the junior branch of the Turkish people, derived from Osman the First who established the Ottoman Empire. The Ottomans held a subordinate position to the Seljuk Turks, their close relatives, till the power of the Seljuks was broken at Baghdad by the Mongol destruction of the Abbasid Caliphate in 1258. That epochal event allowed the previously subordinate Ottomans to come to unrestricted power in Anatolia and subsequently to establish the Ottoman Empire.

pasha – A Turkish word used in Egypt for governor.

qibla/qiblah – The direction which points toward Mecca, the direction a Muslim should face when he prays.

Quraysh/Quraish – The Arab tribe to which the Prophet Muhammad belonged. Though Abu Bakr and his successor, Umar (the first two caliphs following the death of Muhammad), were bonafide members of the Quraysh tribe, neither of them were members of the feuding Umayyad or Hashim clans.

Ramadan – the Muslim month of fasting

sabkhah – a salt flat

1301 K. S. Twitchell, Saudi Arabia With an Account of the Development of its Natural Resources, (Princeton, New Jersey: Princeton University Press, 1947) p. 12.
1302 Roy Lebkicher, George Rentz, Max Steineke, Aramco Handbook, (Arabian American Oil Company, 1960), p. 277.
1303 De Lacy O'Leary, History of Arabia Before Muhammad, (Lahore, Pakistan: Alliance Publishers, 1989), p. 6.

Sahel – "The strip of land that stretches between the Sahara desert and sub-Saharan Africa."[1304]

Salafism/Salafist – The Arabic word *salaf* means "patriarch." Those who look to Muhammad and the first four caliphs as epochal figures, whose lifestyles and careers are to be emulated, are known as Salafists. Salafists especially honor and emulate the examples of those Islamic patriarchal personages for an example of aggressive warfare in expanding and maintaining Islam.

Saracen – "The term [Saracens] *sarakenoi* or *saraceni* originally referred to the non-Arab peoples of northern Arabia, but it was subsequently applied to Arabs and then to all Muslims. Its etymology is unclear, but by the fourth century the historian Ammianus Marcellinus noted that it was used to refer to the region's desert nomads."[1305]

Sharia/Shariah – (also S*hari'at*) The religious law of God, law, ordinance, statute.

Shia – The segment of Islam which gives more status to the traditions of Ali, the prophet's cousin and son-in-law.

Sufi/Sufism – The word "suf" means wool. It is used because of the simple, unadorned garment worn by the devotees who are consequently called "sufis." "Sufism emerged gradually in the Muslim world. Beginning in the eighth century, Sufi mystics stressed a direct, individual connection with God. In time, these mystics drew followers, and these followers began to codify the lessons learned from their masters. Eventually, much as monastic orders coalesced in Europe, Sufi orders formed, and were named after their putative founding teacher. As the Muslim world fragmented into numerous warring states and competing sects, Sufi orders filled the vacuum. After the Mongol invasion of the thirteenth century eviscerated Baghdad and other centers of Muslim civilization, Sufism assumed a dominant place in the lives of millions.

"In Egypt especially, the Sufi orders were intimately woven into society. By the time of Napoleon's invasion, the local Sufi shaikh performed Weddings and funerals, adjudicated disputes, offered counsel and advice, doled out loans, and provided spiritual guidance to the inhabitants of the village. Holidays often revolved around the birthdays of notable shaikhs. At Tanta, the largest settlement in the delta, thousands gathered every October for a week-long festival in honor of Shaikh Ahmad Badawi, who had lived in the thirteenth century and whose tomb and shrine became a geographic center of the Badawiyya order. During the celebrations, animals were slaughtered, prostitutes took a working holiday, different social classes mingled, prayers were said, and people consumed an abundance of sugar-coated nuts called *hubb al-Aziz* ('seeds of the beloved Prophet')".[1306]

[1304] Alexander Stille, *The Last Slaves in Mauritania*, The New York Review of Books, November 23, 2017, p. 37.
[1305] Nigel Cliff, Holy War, (New York: Harper Collins, 2011), pp. 16, 426.

sultan – In Arabic the basic meaning is "power" or "authority." In the Turkish concept, the holder of temporal power. The title distinguishes its holder from a caliph or a successor to the Prophet Muhammad.

Sultanat ur-Rum – Arabic for the Roman Empire

Sunna – *Sunna* is "a word meaning practice or precedent and specialized to mean the practice of the Prophet and his companions and other revered early Muslims, sanctified by tradition. The need for an authority to scrutinize, verify, and interpret the immense body of traditions was met by the acceptance of the doctrine of consensus (in Arabic *ijma`*), which might be approximately translated as the climate of opinion among the powerful, the learned, and the pious. Following precedent was *sunna* and was good. Departure from precedent was *bid`a*, innovation – the nearest Muslim equivalent to the Christian notion of heresy."[1307]

Sunni – Members of the majority Muslim division who "accept the authority of the Sunna, the oral tradition of the Mohammedans."[1308] On the Sunni/Shia divide, see Chapter 24 under "Inception of Islamic Division."

Sura/Surah – A chapter in the Koran.

Sus – "The Sus lies inland along the coast of Morocco to the south of Agadir."[1309] It is a remote area close to the desert.

takfir – accusation of blasphemy, see kafir

Taliban – The Persian/Urdu plural of *talib*, a student in a mosque school. It is now also the name of the political/military group of fighters trying to take over control of Afghanistan. "'Allah has promised us victory and America has promised us defeat, so we shall see which of the two promises will be fulfilled,' Mullah Omar, the Taliban founder, once said. He passed away in 2013, but his words are beginning to look prophetic. Indeed, an American retreat [from Afghanistan] would be widely regarded as a vindication not just of Mullah Omar and his Taliban heirs, but of Osama bin Laden and al Qaeda."[1310]

taqlid – emulation, following the pronouncement of a legal scholar

tawhid – The stern, unitary, monolithic monotheism preached by Muhammad.

tihama – A Semitic word meaning 'lowland.' It refers to the coastal plain between the mountain range and the Red Sea on the western side of the Arabian Peninsula.

1306 Zachary Karabell, Parting The Desert, The Creation of the Suez Canal, (New York: Alfred A. Knopf, 2003), pp. 174-176.
1307 Bernard Lewis, Islam And The West, (New York: Oxford University Press, 1993), pp. 44-45.
1308 Kermit Roosevelt, Countercoup, The Struggle for the Control of Iran, (New York: McGraw Hill, 1979), p. 28.
1309 H.T. Norris, The Berbers in Arabic Literature, (New York: Longman, 1982), p. 187.
1310 Thomas Joscelyn, *Unfinished Business*, The Weekly Standard, June 5, 2017, p. 24.

Transoxiana/Transoxania – The vast area northeast of (that is, *trans* or across) the Amu Darya, formerly known as the Oxus River. The area beyond the river extends all the way to western China's Xinjiang Province. It includes the areas comprising Kazakhstan Uzbekistan, Tajikistan and Kyrgyzstan. The area now includes Turkestan and is known as Central Asia.

ulama/ulema – The plural of the Arabic *alim*, a religious scholar.

Umayyad – The name of the caliphate founded in 658 A.D. by Muawiya, governor of Damascus. It governed the Muslim world until the Battle of the Great Zab in 750 A.D., at which point the Abbasid Caliphate came to power.

umma – The community of believers, the body politic of Islam.

umrah – The lesser pilgrimage. It can be made in any month and is a minor pilgrimage in contrast to the *hajj*, known as the greater pilgrimage which can be performed only in the month of Dhu 'l-Hijja.

waqf – Real property given as a perpetual donation to a mosque or Muslim. charitable entity, a religious endowment.

zakat – The annual obligatory tax collected from Muslims for the needy. See Surah 2:43, Surah 2:83, Surah 2:215, Surah 4:77 and Surah 73:20.

zimmi – See dhimmi.

Atlas

Trajan's Canal, Mediterranean via the Nile to the Red Sea

As long as Rome, governing either from the Tiber or from the Bosporus, dominated the Red Sea and Bab-el-Mandeb, the Door of Tears, (the bottle-neck connecting the Red Sea through the Gulf of Aden to the Indian Ocean), it controlled the critical choke point of the southern branch of the world's east-west maritime trade. Rome's control of the Red Sea-Indian Ocean route gave her an end-run around both Iran and Arabia. She also controlled the northern segment of international water-borne trade: the Black Sea-Bosporus-Dardanelles-Mediterranean route.

Iran, Byzantium's greatest imperial enemy, was left with control of only the middle portion of the fabled Silk Road, the multi-branched land-based trade route stretching all the way from China to the border of Byzantium. Up till the rise of Islam, Arabia proved entirely incapable of breaking the Roman stranglehold on the southern branch of international seaborne commerce. Eventually, Iran, in defiance, set bold plans in motion to gain control of Bab-el-Mandeb, in an attempt to deny Rome its long-standing competitive advantage.

Map 1

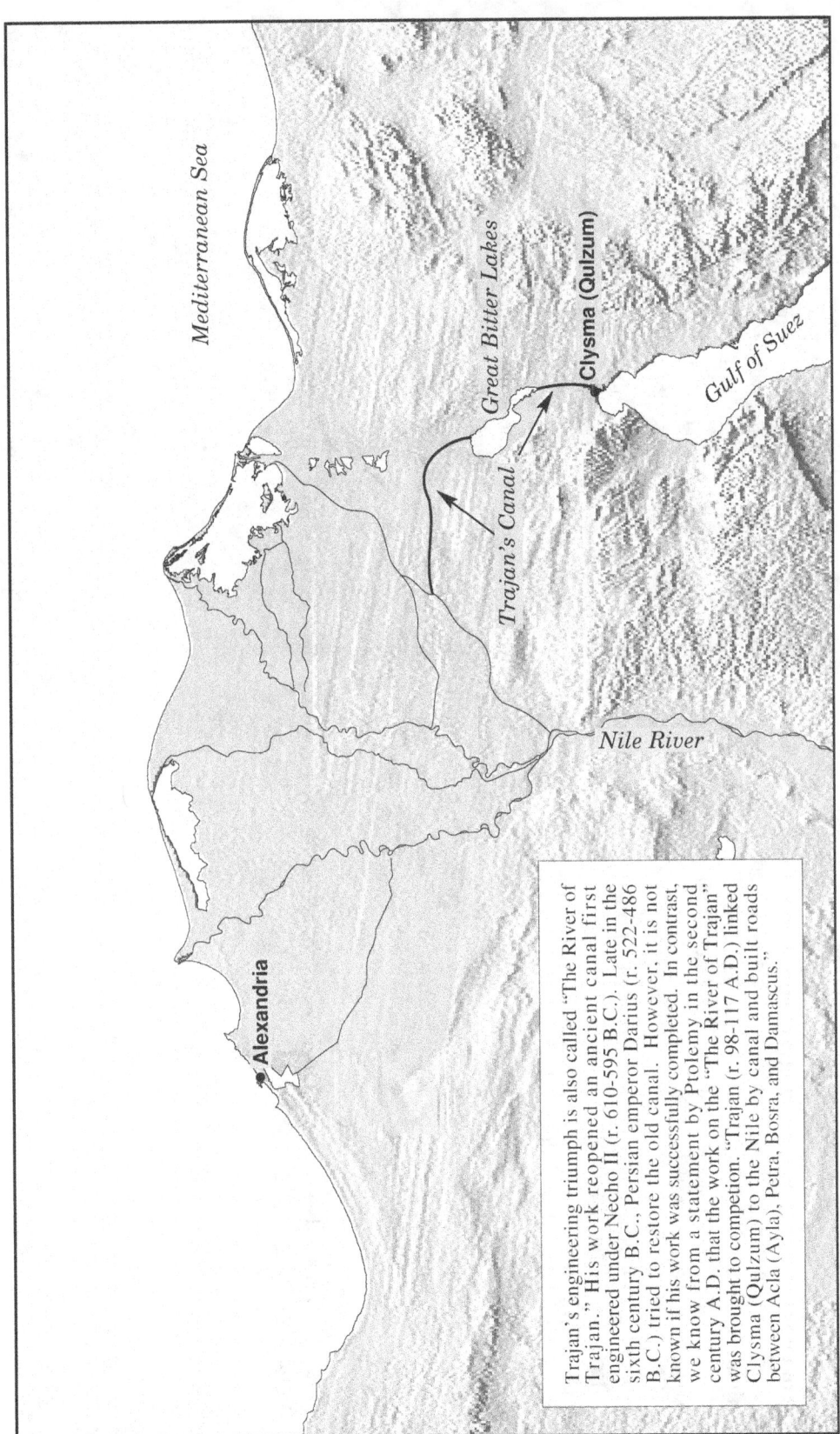

Trajan's engineering triumph is also called "The River of Trajan." His work reopened an ancient canal first engineered under Necho II (r. 610-595 B.C.). Late in the sixth century B.C., Persian emperor Darius (r. 522-486 B.C.) tried to restore the old canal. However, it is not known if this work was successfully completed. In contrast, we know from a statement by Ptolemy in the second century A.D. that the work on the "The River of Trajan" was brought to competion. "Trajan (r. 98-117 A.D.) linked Clysma (Qulzum) to the Nile by canal and built roads between Acla (Ayla), Petra, Bosra, and Damascus."

Trajan's Canal – From the Mediterranean to the Gulf of Suez via the Nile

Trajan's Roads and Other Pre-Islamic World Trade Routes

"Trajan (r. 98-117 A.D.) linked Clysma (Qulzum) to the Nile by canal and built roads between Acla (Ayla), Petra, Bostra, and Damascus."
– Patricia Crone, *Meccan Trade and the Rise of Islam*, (Pliscataway, N.J.: Gorgias Press, 2004, p. 25.

"From the end of the fourth century (B.C.) on, Petra became a key city on the caravan route, linking spice-producing South Arabia with the consuming and marketing centers in the north. It commanded the routes to the port of Gaza in the west, to Busra* and Damascus in the north, to Aila (the Nabataean port on the north shore of the Gulf of Aqaba about three kilometers east of ancient Ezion-Geber**) on the Red Sea, and to the Persian Gulf across the desert. In it [that is, in Petra] the relays of camels were provided." – Philip K. Hitti, *History of Syria*, (London: Macmillan & Co., Ltd., 1957), p. 377.

Palmyra/Tadmor was the anchor point of another major pre-Islamic trade route. It is mentioned not only in the Bible (II Chronicles 8:4) but also in the Indian emperor Ashoka's (r. 268-233 B.C.) inscription at Kandahar, Afghanistan. Its ruins are located "140 miles east of Damascus, 125 miles west of the Euphrates. … The main annual caravan out of Palmyra headed south-east every autumn to the Euphrates, where goods were transferred to rafts that traveled down the river to the Persian Gulf, to be loaded onto ships bound for the Indian Ocean ports. The camels would spend the winter in the pastures of southern Iraq, awaiting the return of the ships in the new year, when they would make the long journey back to their oasis. There were other routes south-west from Palmyra to the Red Sea and east to Mesopotamia and evidence of Palmyrene merchants has been found from India to Rome." Because of the rebellion of Palmyra's Queen Zenobia, "the emperor Aurelian sacked her city in 273 A.D., destroying its trading networks and reducing it to a minor Roman military outpost." – Josephine Quinn, *Nothing Beside Remains*, London Review of Books, January 25, 2018, p. 27.

*Busra [also Bosra and Bostra]: Its ruins are near a village in SW Syria. Known to the Romans as Bostra, it became the capital of the Roman province of Arabia. (Webster's New Geographical Dictionary)
**See Numbers 33:35-36.

Map 2

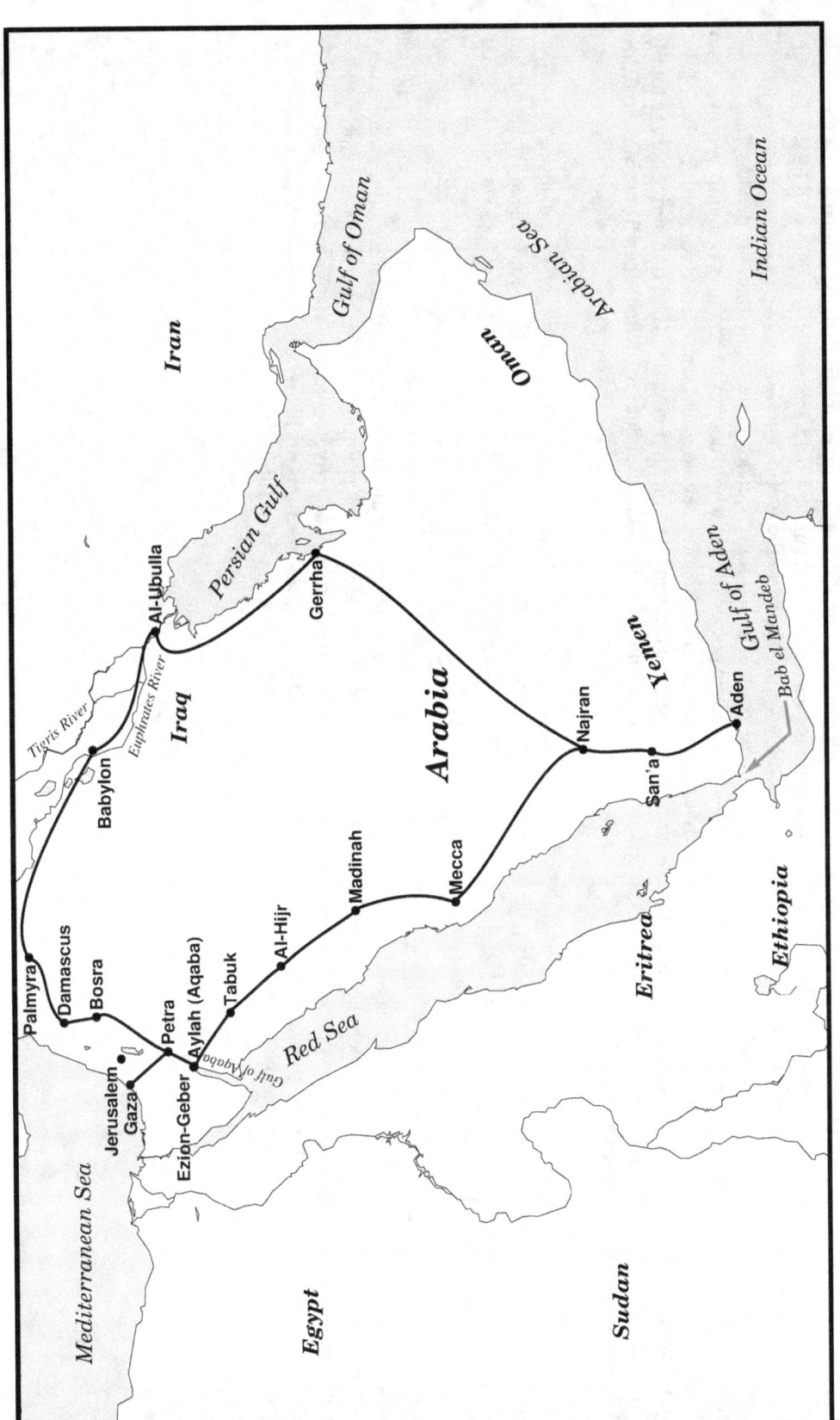

Trajan's Roads and Other Pre-Islamic World Trade Routes

Ethiopia

Two momentous events have put Ethiopia on the threshold of being able to influence affairs in the region at the southern end of the Red Sea as she did centuries earlier in the decades leading up to the birth of Islam. First, construction of the high dam, known as the Grand Ethiopian Renaissance Dam, on the upper reaches of the Blue Nile is nearing completion. "At 6.45 gigawatts, the dam will be the largest hydro electric power plant in Africa when completed, as well as the seventh largest in the world." – *Grand Ethiopian Renaissance Dam*, Wikipedia, accessed 8/28/18. "Addis Ababa wishes to fill the reservoir in about three years or so—a much quicker time frame than the decade-long duration preferred by Cairo." – Stratfor, 6/6/18 It will provide abundant electric power for the whole country. Though it is mainly a power dam, it will also revolutionize some Ethiopian agriculture by providing irrigation. This historic development was carried forward in spite of many threats from Egypt which fears disruption of the water flow in the Nile drainage complex upon which Egyptian agriculture is totally dependent. "The prospect of more electrical power effectively convinced Khartoum [capital of Sudan] to switch sides from Cairo to Addis Ababa—inevitably infuriating Egypt." – Stratfor, 6/6/18

Secondly, the new Ethiopian prime minister, Abiy Ahmed, recently reached out to his counterpart in Eritrea, expressing a desire to peacefully resolve their long-standing border dispute which resulted in war in 1998 in which more than 80,000 people died. To encourage reconciliation, the Ethiopian prime minister traveled to Asmara, Eritrea's capital, on Sunday, July 8, 2018, where he was warmly received by dictatorial president, Isaias Afwerki.

On July 14, 2018, the president of Eritrea visited Addis Ababa, capital of Ethiopia, to an enthusiastic reception, state dinner, and orchestral concert. Each country has re-opened embassies in each others' capitals, restored telephone and air service, and declared, "the war is over." These dramatic developments also open the important Eritrean seaport of Assab (see Map 7) to Ethiopian use. This break-through complements Ethiopia's part ownership of the Port of Berbera on the Somaliland coast. Collectively and cumulatively, these developments point to a dawning period of Ethiopian vigor and power. However, Ethiopia still faces a serious problem in its Ogaden Province which borders Somalia. The province has been infiltrated by Somalis who want to separate it from Ethiopia.

Map 3 473

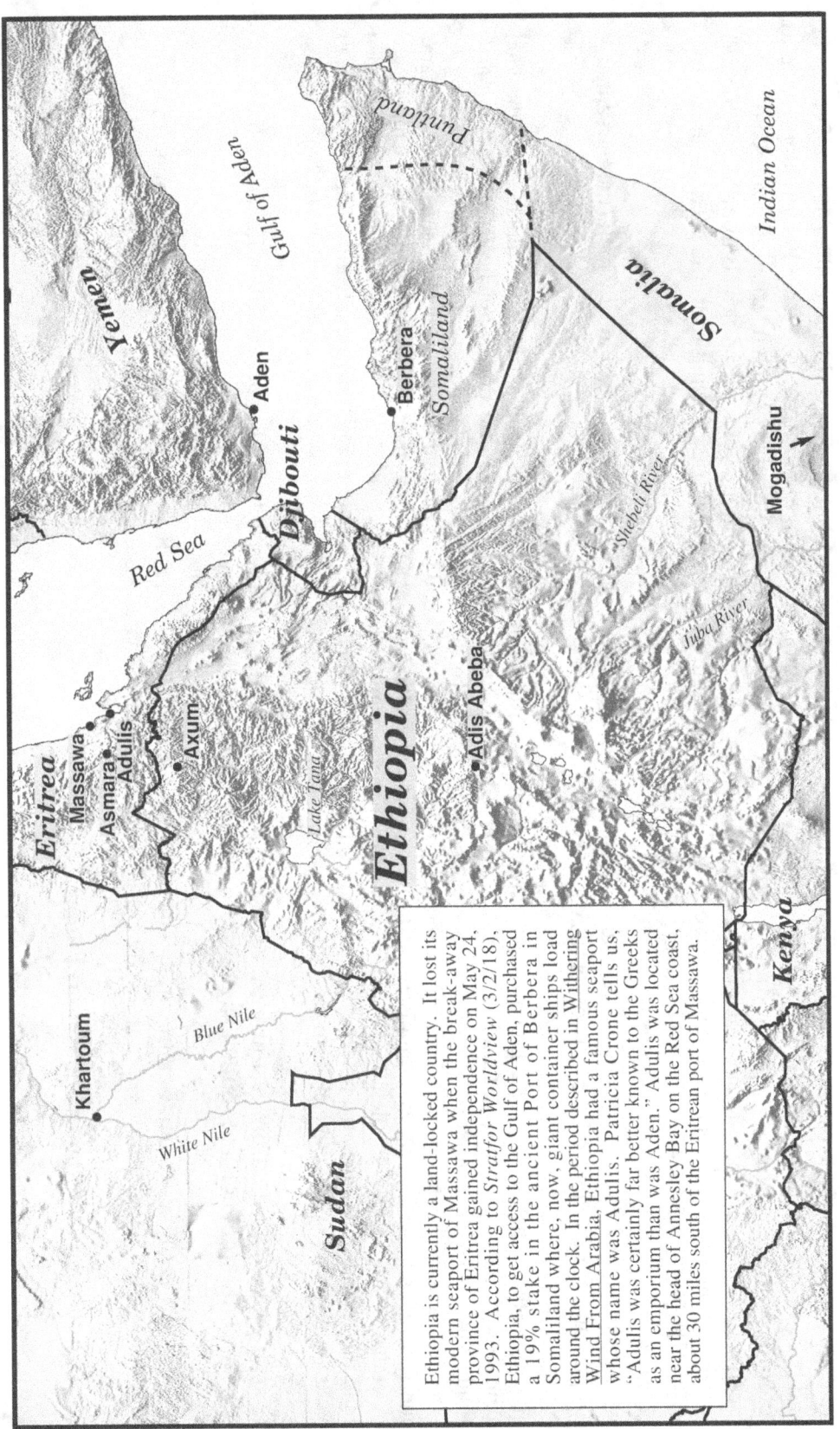

Ethiopia – *(Ancient Abyssinia/Axum – Biblical Cush)*

Competing Empires

When Islam burst forth from its obscurity in the Arabian Peninsula, no one could have confidently predicted its stunning trajectory to the pinnacle of world power. Till the moment of Islam's startling debut on the world stage, the Arabian Peninsula had been distinguished by only four notable realities: (1) It had a region known to the Romans as Arabia Felix (Happy Arabia), referring to the area irrigated by water from a series of dams built by the Queen of Sheba, (2) the international source of incense grown in Oman, (3) being the guardian of the gateway to the southern entrance of the Red Sea (Bab-el-Mandeb), and (4) providing transit routes paralleling the Red Sea/Mediterranean littorals and for those crossing from the Mediterranean to the Tigris-Euphrates watersheds and on to the Persian Gulf.

At the moment when Islam began its epochal expansion, there were three world-class empires, two of which (the Sassanian Empire and the Byzantine Empire) bordered Arabia on the north.

<u>First</u> of the three, the Chinese-Tang Empire was the most stunning. It ruled from its capital of Chang'an and was dominant from the south China Sea all the way west to the Caspian Sea, thus it governed all of Central Asia. In the other direction it stretched from the Pamir and Hindu Kush Mountain complexes, all the way to Taiwan. (See Map 11.) By combining Turkic and Chinese forces, [Emperor] Taizong extended Tang control throughout Central Asia and across the Pamir Mountains and into modern-day Afghanistan. Samarkand, Bukhara, and Tashkent all became Chinese administrative districts. Tibet and Turkic tribes as far west as the Caspian Sea submitted to Chinese suzerainty. Without the nomadic forces behind him, these conquests would not have been possible. Taizong's successors further extended Tang rule, engulfing Manchuria, most of the Korean peninsula, central Vietnam, and parts of present-day Iran. During Taizong's reign, no other empire in the world came close to the Tang in size, population, or military power." – Amy Chua, Day of Empire. (NY: Doubleday, 2007), p. 68.

<u>Second</u>. Sassanian Iran, from east to west, controlled the area from the Indus River to the Euphrates River, including the Persian Gulf. From north to south it stretched from the Caucasus to the Indian Ocean.

<u>Third</u>. The Byzantine Roman Empire stretched east to west from the Euphrates River to the Atlantic Ocean. From north to south it covered the enormous area from the British Channel to the Sahara Desert, giving it control of all of North Africa.

The one comparatively <u>minor</u> empire was Ethiopia.

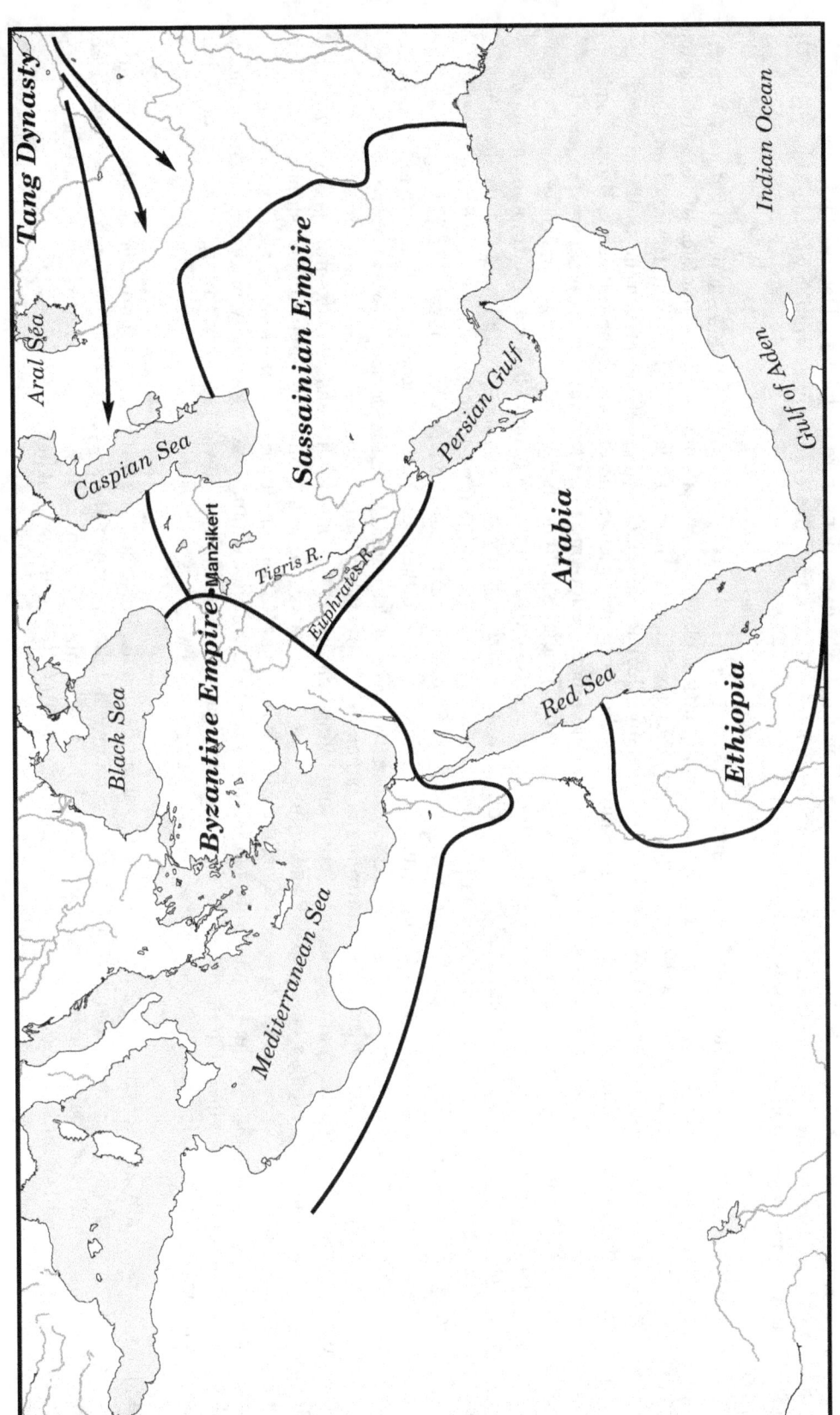

Arabian Peninsula – Political Divisions & Geographic Features

When in 1925 Ibn Saud's forces drove Sharif Hussein out of the holy cities of Mecca and Medina, the overwhelming majority of the vast territory of the Arabian Peninsula came under the rule of Ibn Saud. The exceptions were peripheral. That rule has been continued by Ibn Saud's lineal descendants. In the Eastern Province at al-Ahsa lives the largest concentration of Shia Muslims in all of Arabia. Also, the population of the tiny island of Bahrein is Shia.

In 1903 Yemen was recognized as the "British hinterland of Aden" (Boustani & Farques, The Atlas of the Arab World, p. 24.) but now Yemen is an independent country. Though Saudi Arabia is the dominant political power, five small independent countries of note are located on the east coast of the Arabian Peninsula. From north to south they are: Kuwait, Bahrein, Qatar, United Arab Emirates and Oman. Except Oman, these states gained their independence from "Britain's decision to wind up its protectorates in the Gulf and by so doing abandon the position of naval and political paramountcy in these waters which it had exercised for 150 years. Kuwait had become independent in 1961, and in 1968 declared that it would no longer be looking to Britain for protection against external aggression. At the beginning of 1968 rulers of Bahrein, Qatar and the Trucial Sheikhdoms agreed to federate and thereby to exchange reliance on the protecting arm of Britain for independence. The only complication about this was the Iranian claim on Bahrein—a claim which the Shah had inherited and felt obliged to take seriously, even if nobody outside Iran did. He called the proposed federation 'a colonist and imperialist manipulation' but in 1969 a face-saving formula involving a mission of inquiry dispatched by the Secretary-General of the United Nations was devised. Bahrein became independent in August 1971, Qatar following just a month later. In July the six former Trucial Sheikhdoms formed themselves into a new sovereign state to be known as the United Arab Emirates." – Mohamed Heikal, The Return of the Ayatollah, The Iranian Revolution from Mossadeq to Khomeini, (London: Andre Deutsch Ltd. 1981), p. 92. Since Qabus bin Said took over rule of Oman from his father, he has overseen judicious use of the income from the country's oil exports to greatly improve the country's infrastructure and living conditions for Oman's citizens. One example is the port of al-Duqm. It was "built midway along a largely bleak and uninhabited Omani coastline. A multibillion-dollar rail and shipping complex taking advantage of Indian Ocean traffic between Asia, the Middle East, and Africa, al-Duqm did not even exist a few years ago. … Because al-Dqum lies just outside the Persian Gulf, but is proximate to it, conflict within the Gulf actually increases the importance of al-Dqum, whose rail and pipeline terminuses (in the future originating as far north as Kuwait) will fill waiting ships that dock in safety outside the Strait of Hormuz." – Robert D. Kaplan, The Return of Marco Polo's World, (NY: Random House, 2018), p. 34.

Saudi Arabia, spatially and economically, dominates the Arabian Peninsula. For many years it has also dominated it politically and militarily. However, with the spectacular rise of Bahrein's economy and the influence of its Al Jazeera TV conglomerate, it has been able to seriously challenge Saudi Arabia's leadership. Also, Riyadh's inability to stop the Houthi take-over of Yemen and their attacks on Saudi Arabia's oil infrastructure has highlighted both political and military weakness in Saudi Arabia.

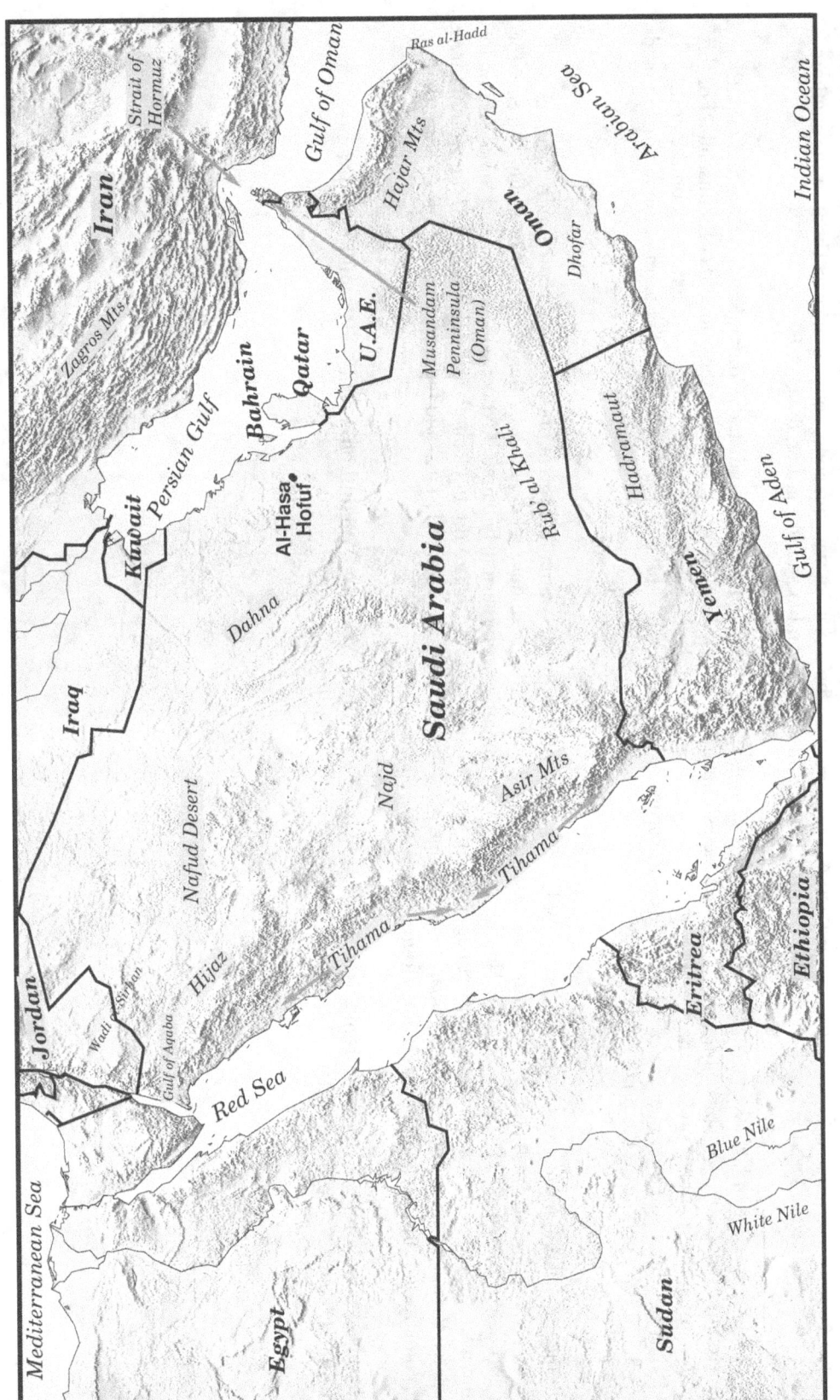

Map 5

Arabian Peninsula – Political Divisions & Geographic Features

Arabian Peninsula – Notable Settlements

At the southern end of the Red Sea currently there is an ironic contrast of conditions. We see this when we consider the recent peace treaty signed between Eritrea and Ethiopia on the east shore compared with the turbulent warring conditions on the east shore of the southern end of the Red Sea, involving war between the Yemeni Houthis and Saudi Arabia and its partner, the U.A.E.

The Houthi movement has taken over Hudaydah, Yemen's largest seaport on the Red Sea. To dislodge them, Saudi Arabia and U.A.E. have committed troops to capture the port. However, the estimated casualties of civilians would be in the hundreds of thousands. For this reason, great international pressure has been brought on Saudi Arabia and the U.A.E. to not unleash their planned attack on the port. Already conditions in Yemen are very grim. "The civil war in Yemen has resulted in the largest outbreak of cholera in human history and left 8.4 million people on the brink of starvation." – Marc Lynch, *The New Arab Order, Power & Violence in Today's Middle East*, Foreign Affairs, September/October 2018, p. 117.)

On the other hand, probably this stand-off will not last for long because Saudi Arabia feels great pressure—their oil export facilities at their Red Sea port of Jizan and their oil pipelines at Najran have been brought under rocket attack by the Houthis. According to a Stratfor report dated July 31, 2018, "last week, the Houthis attacked two Saudi tankers, seriously damaging one, which prompted Saudi Arabia to announce for the first time since the conflict began that it would halt its oil traffic through the Bab-el-Mandeb strait until the Houthi threat ceased. Riyadh's statement was made in part to encourage its allies, especially the United States and the European Union, to commit more diplomatic and military support to its anti-Houthi operations in Yemen."

The latest population statistics are from 2016: Saudi Arabia—32.3 million, Yemen—27.6 million, U.A.E.—9.3 million, Kuwait—4.1 million, Oman—4.4 million, Qatar—2.6 million, and Bahrein—1.4 million.

Map 6 479

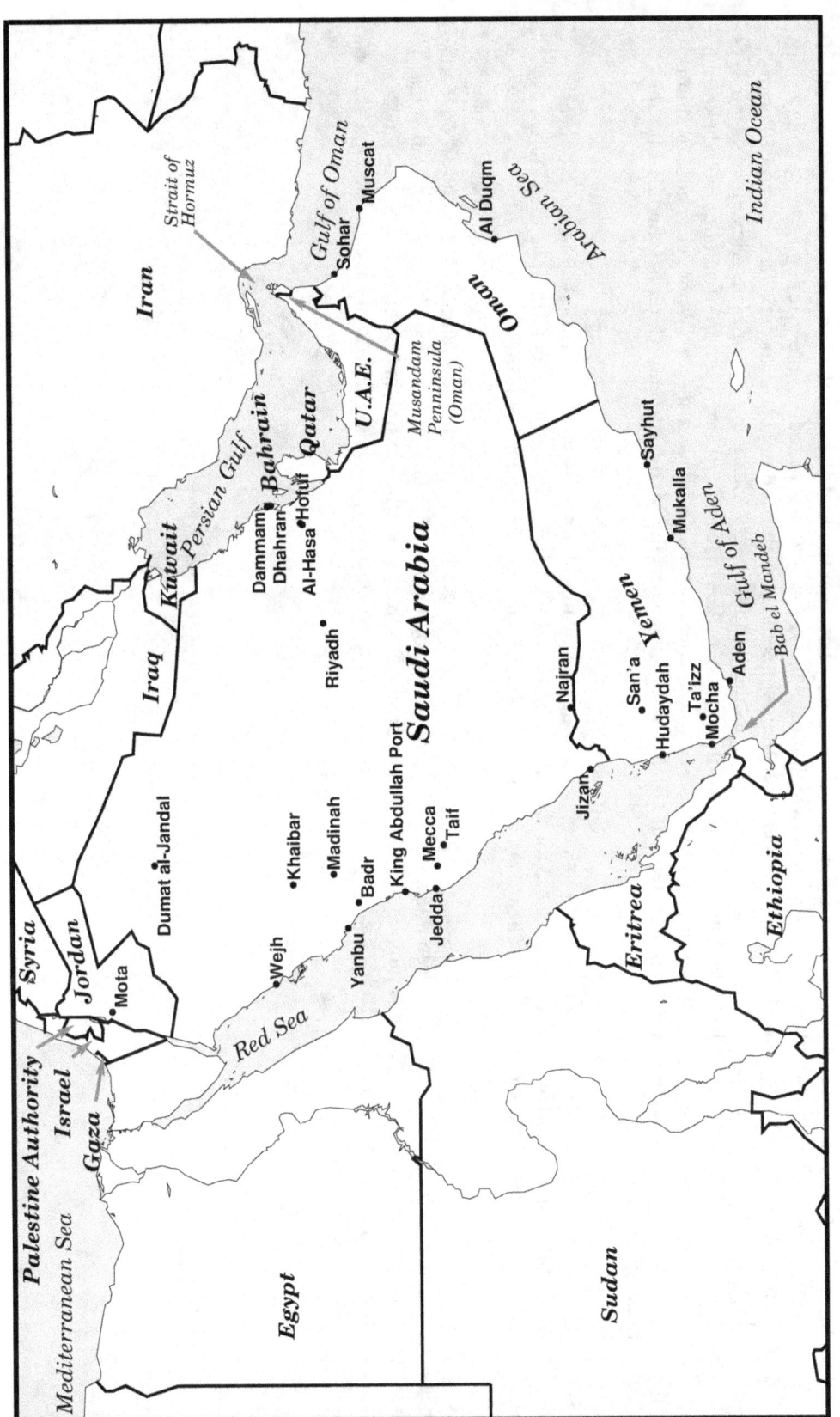

Bab-el-Mandeb

Bab-el-Mandeb/Mandab. At the southern end of the 1,400-mile-long Red Sea, the eighteen-mile-wide strait, or water passageway, separating Arabia and Africa is called Bab-el-Mandeb. It is the sea way between the Red Sea and the Indian Ocean, via the Gulf of Aden. The name of the strait, Bab-el-Mandeb, is Arabic which means the *Door of Tears*, reflecting the grief and sorrow many ship captains experienced as they unsuccessfully tried to maneuver their ships through this crucial choke point. "The island of Perim … divides the strait into two channels, of which the eastern, known as the Bab Iskender (Alexander's Strait [lit. Alexander's Door]) is 2 miles wide … while the western … has a width of about 16 miles. … Near the African coast lies a group of smaller islands known as the 'Seven Brothers.'" – The Encyclopaedia Britannica, (New York: The Encyclopaedia Britannica Company, 1910), Vol. III, p. 91. Whoever is able to shut or open the Door of Tears, can control the seaborne trade of all Northeast Africa and the Mediterranean which is scheduled for the Arabian Sea and vice versa.

The efforts to control Bab-el-Mandeb have resulted in a centuries-long seesaw tug-of-war between Southwest Arabia and Northeast Africa. At the time Islam came into being, the struggle for control of the Door of Tears was between ancient Ethiopia, then known as Axum, and the Persians working through their client Yemeni ruler, the Jewish king of Yemen, Dhu Nuwas.

Contention for control of the Door of Tears became even more acute when Europe broke the economic stranglehold Islam had on it and began competing for the Red Sea-Indian Ocean trade. In our day, transit through Bab-el-Mandeb is threatened by Al Qaeda which has terrorist cells in Yemen, a country poorly equipped to guard the waterway. Before the Houthi uprising in Yemen, the U.S. Navy was training forces in Yemen to establish a viable coast guard. Also, Somalian pirates operating in the Gulf of Aden have endangered seaborne traffic in and out of Bab-el-Mandeb.

Map 7 481

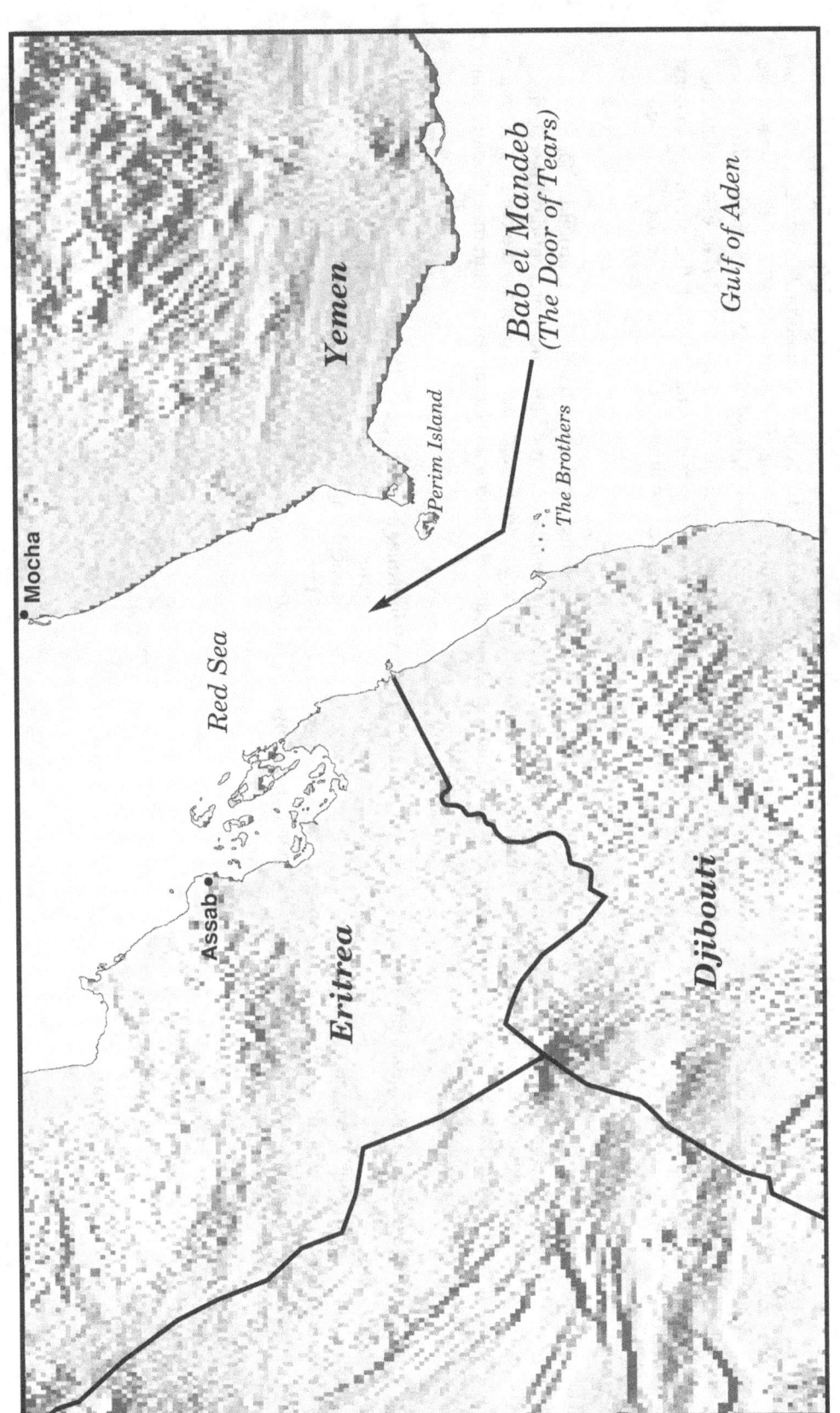

Bab-el-Mandeb

Persian Conquest of Eastern & Southern Arabia

Why had Iran not fully utilized the Persian/Arabian Gulf prior to the beginning of their conquest of eastern and southern Arabia? The Red Sea via Trajan's Canal (see Map 1) and the Mediterranean gave Indian Ocean seaborne trade access to great markets in Europe. In contrast, a route through the gulf would terminate in the north with a landlocked dead end. It became an important export trade route only at the dawn of the oil age. That early static situation changed dramatically with the reign of Ardashir I (226–241 A.D.), the first emperor of the Sassanian Dynasty. Under his leadership the Persians adopted an aggressive policy which used the gulf, not for imports or exports, but as an attack route. That ultimately allowed Iranian military forces success in wrenching from Rome control of Bab-el-Mandeb, the southern gateway to the Red Sea. Implementing their policy, they eventually controlled the Persian/Arabian Gulf, the entire Oman coast, and finally, the entire coast of Yemen. That put Iranian military forces in an overwhelming position to deny Rome the use of Bab-el-Mandeb.

Though Emperor Shapur I (r. 241–272 A.D.) conquered Oman, it subsequently reasserted its independence. Then, around A.D. 570, "during the reign of the Sassanian King Anushiruwan, his General at-Tabari Wahraz embarked at Ubulla [near present-day Basra], first seizing Bahrain, then a dependency of Oman, and disembarked his thousands of Persian troops at Sohar to overrun the country of Oman. The Persian fleet then continued west along the Oman coast, conquering Dhofar and Hadhramaut [Hadramawt, Hadramaut] before taking Aden." – Wendell Phillips, Unknown Oman, (New York: David McKay Company, Inc., 1966), p. 185.

To understand the extent of the Sassanian Persian expansion into the Arabian Peninsula, it should be realized that "by about 570, the Sassanids … had military colonies in Bahrayn [Bahrain/Bahrein], Oman, and the Yemen, as well as commercial colonies in both the Yemen and the Najd. With the exception of [the port of] Shihr, the successor of Classical Cane in the Hadhramawt [Hadhramaut/Hadramaut], they controlled all the major Arabian ports. … The settlements of the Persians were protected by a string of client kings and other proteges, whose influence stretched from [the Persian border town of] Hira through central and eastern Arabia to the Yemen." – Patricia Crone, Meccan Trade and the Rise of Islam, (Piscataway, N.J.: Gorgias Press, 2004), pp. 48-49.

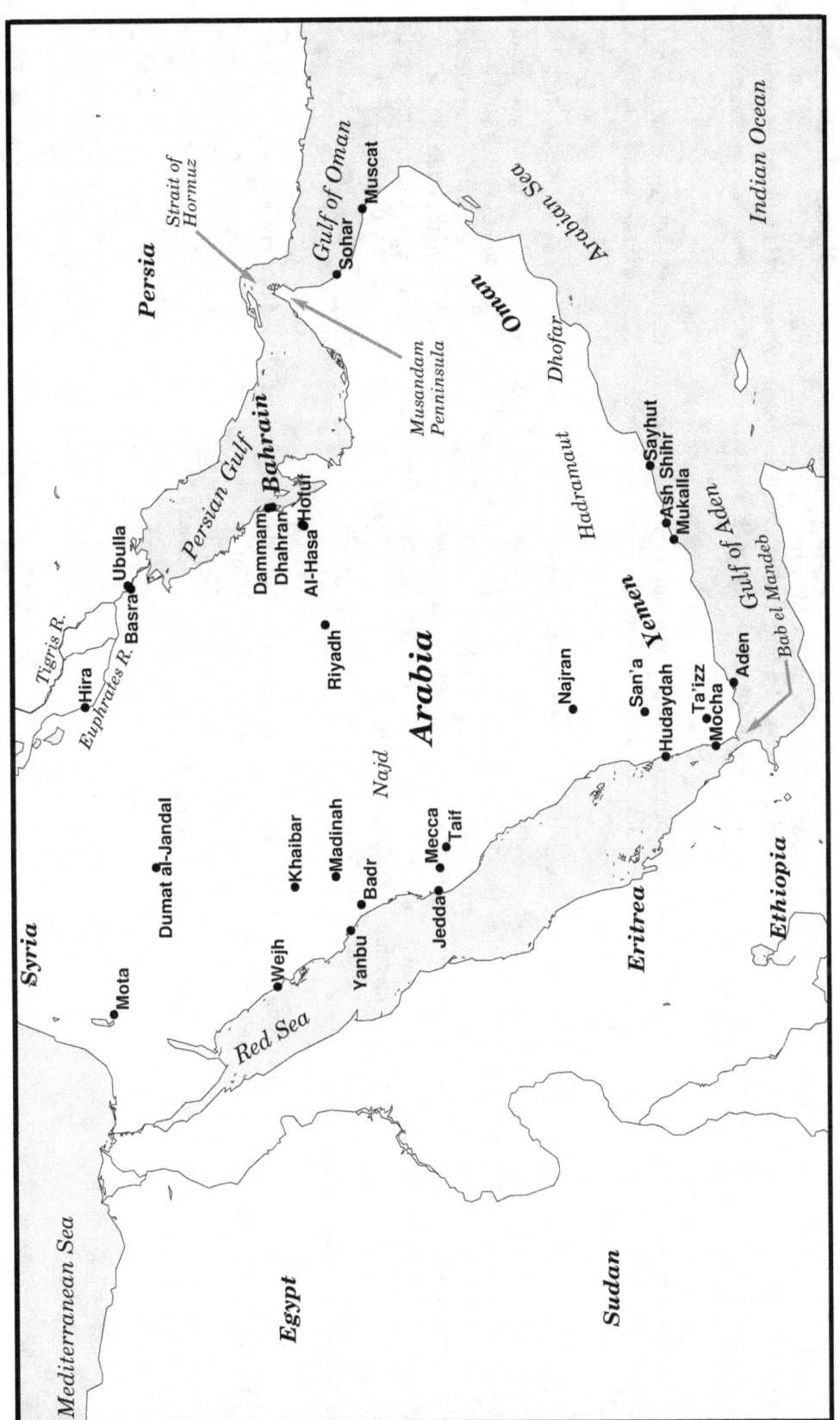

Map 8: The Persian Conquest of Eastern and Southern Arabia

Yemen

"The country [of Yemen] is made up of three regions. The north, the home of the Houthi movement, contains the great majority of the Shiite population and is dominated by powerful tribal alliances. The south of the country, a British colony from 1839 to 1967 and thereafter an Arab communist state until Yemeni unification, is primarily Sunni, with a weak tribal structure that has been eroded by over a century of imperial dominion and then decades of secular communist ideology. Finally, Yemen's eastern region, known as Hadramawt, is inhabited by a sparse Hadrami population that has traditionally enjoyed significant independence." – Asher Orkaby, Yemen's Humanitarian Nightmare, Foreign Affairs, Vol. 96, No. 6, November-December 2017, p. 100.

"Yemen could let Saudi Arabia pipe oil from its wells to the refineries and shipping facilities in Aden, giving the Saudi government a new export route that would bypass the Strait of Hormuz, avoiding the perennial danger of an Iranian blockade." – Asher Orkaby, Yemen's Humanitarian Nightmare, Foreign Affairs, Vol. 96, No. 6, November-December 2017, p. 101.

"Historically, Yemen, when not being invaded or colonized by outside powers, from the Ottomans to the British, was fighting itself. It wasn't until 1990 that Yemen had become the Arabian Peninsula's first multiparty parliamentary democracy. In 1993, elections were held, and in 1999, Field Marshall Ali Abdullah Saleh was elected president of the newly unified country. He was not popular for long, and the Arab Spring swept Yemen up in its dreams of a more democratic and equitable Middle East. Under pressure from within Yemen and from the international community, Saleh eventually resigned. He was replaced by Abad Rabbo Mansour Hadi, but by then the Arab Spring's year-long power vacuum had emboldened insurgent movements. There were the Houthis, a rebel group named after its leader, Husseyn al-Houthi, who were dissatisfied with the leadership in Sanaʿa—who historically ignored their [i.e., the Houthis'] region, they felt—and had been staging raids and seizing land in the north. In the south, with Aden as its capital, there was talk of secession." – Dave Eggers, The Monk of Mokha, (New York: Alfred A. Knopf, 2018), pp. 131-132.

"The Houthis adhered to a branch of Shia Islam called Zaidism, which accounted for about 35 percent of the Muslims in Yemen. Before 1962, the Zaidists had controlled northern Yemen for a thousand years, and the Houthis frequently clashed with their neighbors over territory, with the Saudis to the north and the Yemeni government to the south. In Sanaʿa they were considered a nuisance, uncivilized hillbillies bent on wreaking havoc." – Dave Eggers, The Monk of Mokha, (New York: Alfred A. Knopf, 2018), p. 166.

Map 9

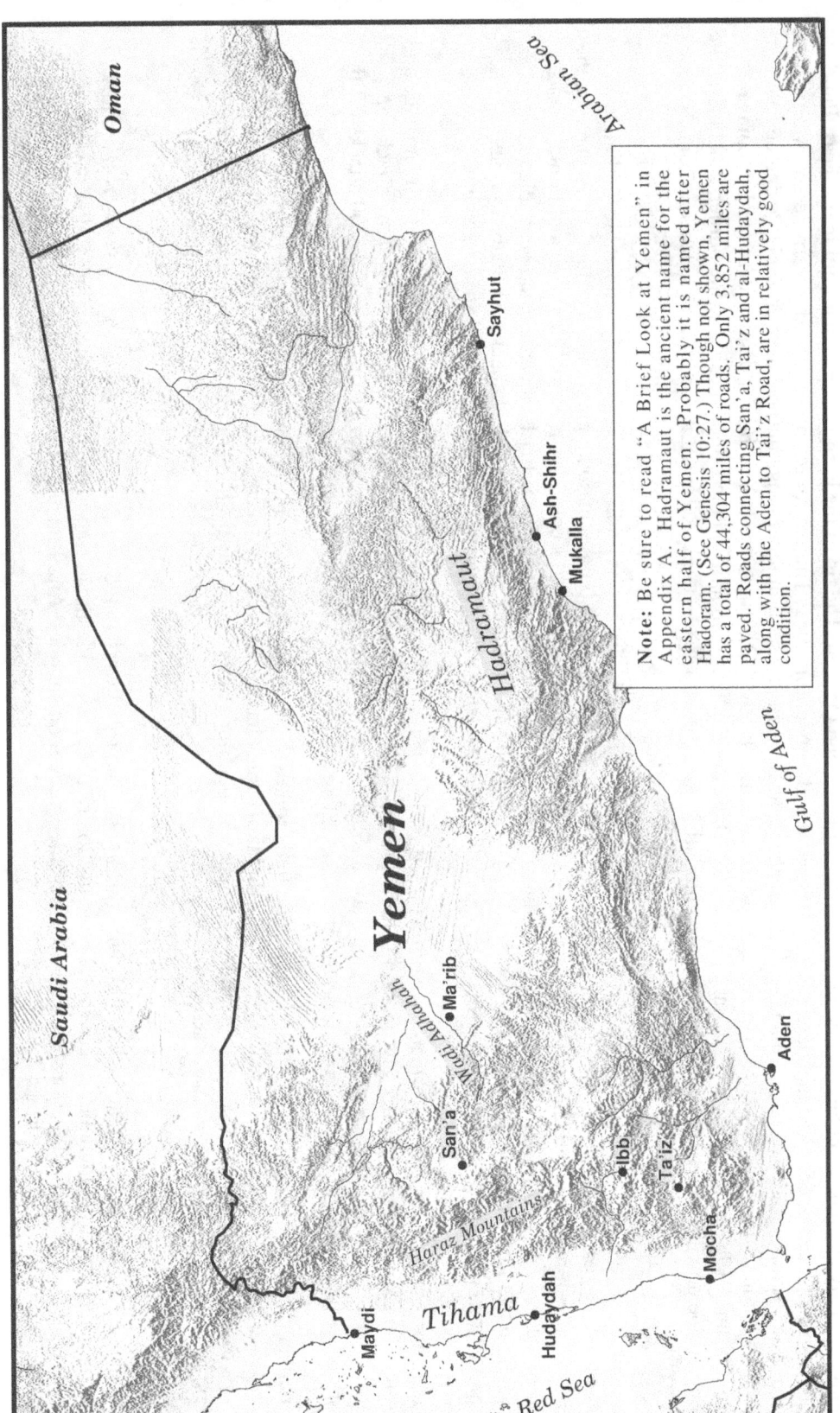

Yemen

Note: Be sure to read "A Brief Look at Yemen" in Appendix A. Hadramaut is the ancient name for the eastern half of Yemen. Probably it is named after Hadoram. (See Genesis 10:27.) Though not shown, Yemen has a total of 44,304 miles of roads. Only 3,852 miles are paved. Roads connecting San'a, Tai'z and al-Hudaydah, along with the Aden to Tai'z Road, are in relatively good condition.

Arabia & the Horn of Africa

The Horn of Africa is the easternmost projection of Africa south of the Gulf of Aden. It includes Somalia along with Somaliland and Puntland. It also includes southeast Ethiopia, comprised of Haud and Ogaden. The tip of the horn is Cape Guardafui in northeast Puntland. Somalia was placed under U.N. mandate in 1945. It became independent in 1951. The weakness of the central government in Mogadishu has allowed semi-autonomous Somaliland with its great port at Berbera and semi-autonomous Puntland to exercise large degrees of autonomy though they are not yet recognized as separate countries by the U.N. There has been a border dispute between Ethiopia and Somalia since 1964. It became outright war in 1977-78. "There are 1,000,000 Somalis on the Ethiopian side of the border, 250,000 on the Kenyan side down to the Tana river and 40,000 in Djibouti." – Rafic Boustani & Philippe Fargues, The Atlas of the Arab World, Geopolitics and Society, (NY: Facts on File, 1991), p. 18.

Somalia is mostly arid, having only two rivers of note: the Shabelle and the Jubba. Its aridity makes it highly vulnerable to climate change. In spite of the fact that Somalia is prone to drought and is largely an arid country, it has a national park known as the Lag Badana "in the fertile southern region, where the Jubba River sustained old-growth forests and visitors could see giraffes, elephants and lions." – Laura Heaton, The Watson Files, Foreign Policy, May/June 2017, p. 49. Failure of rain may trigger ethnic strife. Since herds of camels and goats die due to drought, that situation opens opportunities for radical Muslim groups like the current murderous al-Shabaab. Al-Shabaab is an abbreviation or the short form for the Arabic which means "Mujahideen Youth Movement" or "Movement of Striving Youth."

Facing desperate conditions, fisherman have often turned into pirates who "troll the coastline looking for cargo ships to hold hostage and farmers-turned-insurgents menace civilians on land." – Laura Heaton, The Watson Files, Foreign Policy, May/June 2017, p. 53. "Many of the attacks on transitional authorities and their allies were blamed on al-Shabaab, an al-Qaeda ally. … Pirates carried out more than 200 attacks off the Horn of Africa in 2009." – Sarah Janssen, The World Almanac & Book of Facts 2017, (NY:World Almanac Books, 2017), p. 34.

Somalian piracy is a major threat to the great oceanic trade routes through the Door of Tears and the Red Sea. However, with a Chinese naval base and a major U.S. air base in Djibouti, the threat of piracy has been greatly reduced. Also, currently, "roughly 500 American troops in Somalia, mostly composed of a number of Special Operations units" fight the al-Shabaab and therefore reduce this radical Islamic threat to world trade. – Thomas Gibbons-Neff and Helene Cooper, An American Soldier is Killed and 4 Are Wounded in Somalia Fight, The New York Times, June 9, 2018, p. A6.

"Despite U.N. attempts to initiate peace talks, widespread clan and tribal warfare led to a complete breakdown of government authority in 1991-92. A severe drought helped to create over two million refugees and widespread starvation gripped the nation. Relief workers were prevented by warring armed factions from distributing emergency food supplies. An estimated 300,000 people died in 1991-92." – John W. Wright, ed. The New York Times 2011 Almanac, (London: Penguin Books, 2011), p. 682.

Map 10

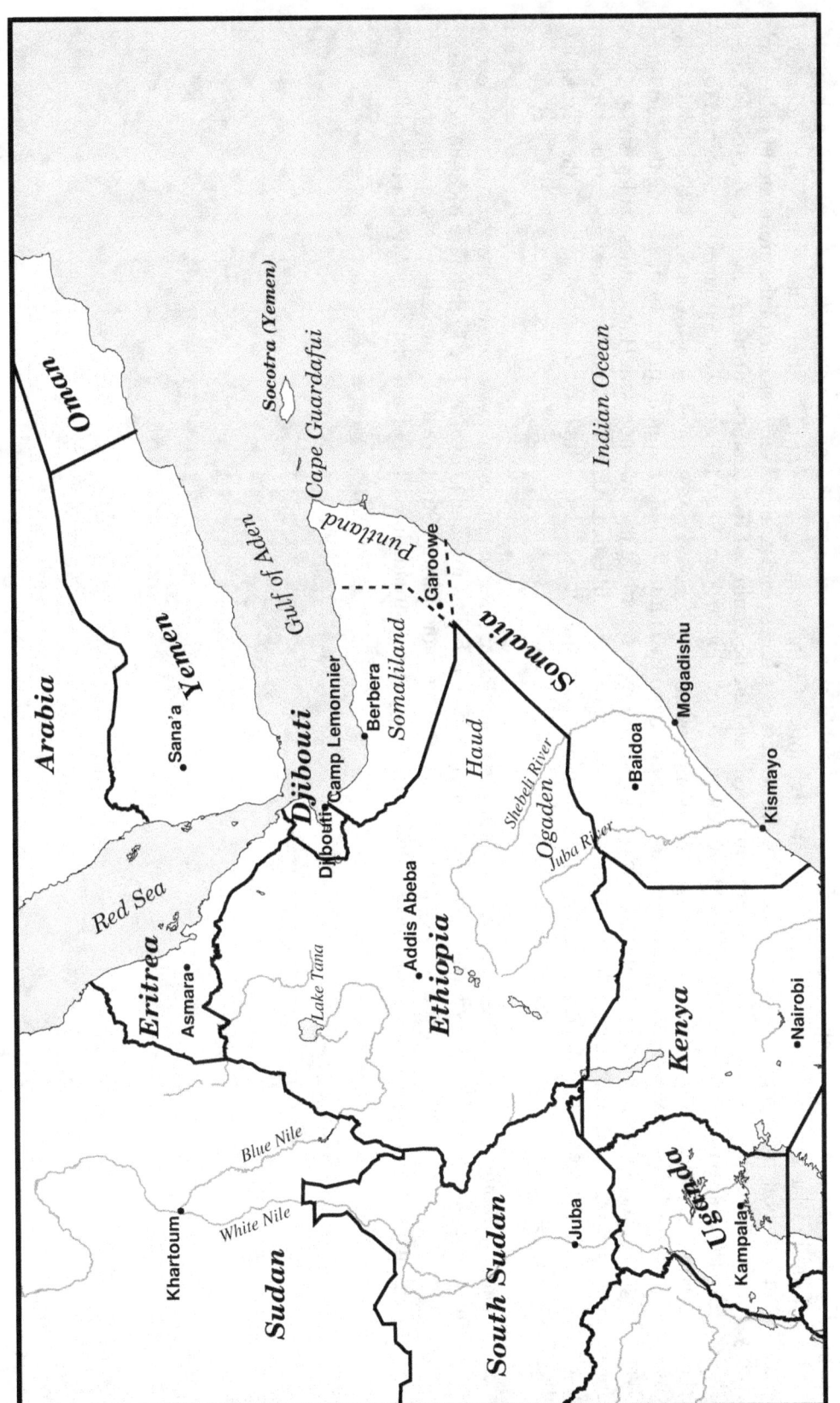

Islam's Two Early Efforts to Win China

The dynamism of the devotees to the Prophet Muhammad who initiated the opening decades of the epochal Islamic movement is astonishing. Turkish converts attempted to bring China into the fold by a sustained attack from the west. "In 751 A.D., [by a decisive battle] at Talas in what is now the isolated central Asiatic Republic of Kirghistan [Kyrgyzstan], … [the] Chinese army was defeated. The encounter, although fought in an area remote from the centers of Chinese and Arab power, was one of the most fateful battles of history. It marked the end of Chinese control over Central Asia and the beginning of five centuries of steady military decline for the Chinese Empire. It also marked the beginning of the Arab conquest of Central Asia. Soon the area was permanently converted to Islam." – Samuel Hugh Moffett quoting E.O. Reischauer in A History of Christianity in Asia, Vol. I: Beginnings to 1500, (2nd ed. rev.; Maryknoll, New York: Orbis Books, 1998), p. 298. The current Chinese government is still trying to blunt that ongoing cultural-ethnic-religious thrust by displacing the Turkish Uygur (Uighur) Muslim people in Xinjiang Province by overwhelmingly resettling the province with Han Chinese colonists. Currently under Communist rule, the Uighur people have very restricted civil liberties. Also, the Chinese central government has built numerous re-education centers in which the Uighur people are forced to submit to classes which are designed to break their Turkish allegiance to Islam.

A corresponding, though less successful, attempt to bring China into Islam's expanding domain was made in the Far East. Very early in the Muslim era, at Guangzhou, previously known as Canton, Muslims built a mosque known as The Lighthouse Mosque because the minaret was used as a navigational reference point by those sailing in the Taiwan Strait. That mosque still exists, having been rebuilt many times. However, Islam never seemed to have made significant inroads into China from that early Muslim toehold.

Map 11

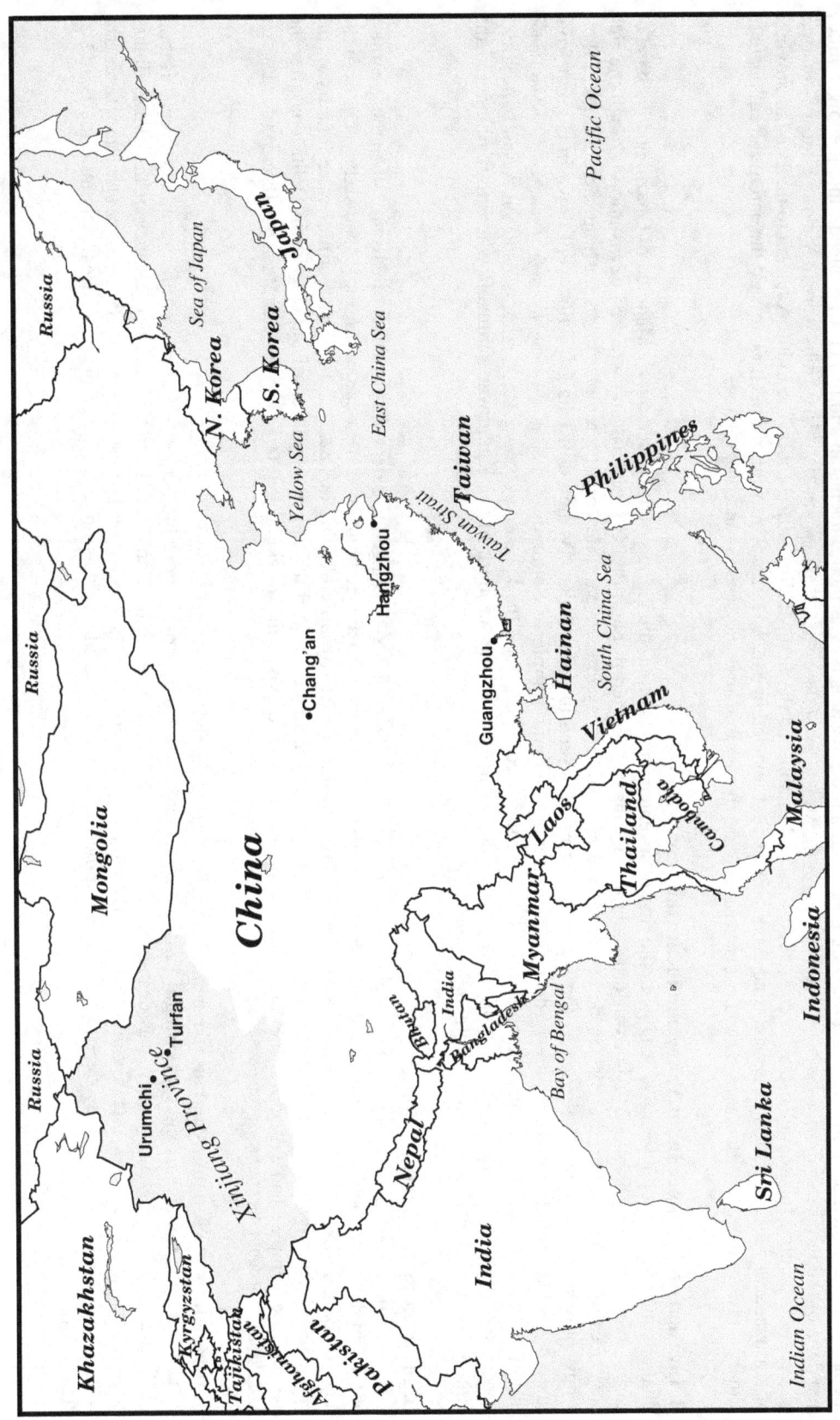

Islam's Two Early Efforts to Win China

Muslim Invasions of India

A. Invasion of Makran, Baluchistan and Sindh/Sind

Muslim invasions of the southwestern area of India, which is now in southern Pakistan, began when Muhammad ibn-al-Qasim, advancing in 710 at the head of a considerable army, subdued Makran, pushed on through what is now termed Baluchistan and in 711-12 reduced Sind, the lower valley and delta of the Indus (Sindhu). – See Philip K. Hitti, History of The Arabs, (London: Macmillan, 1968), pp. 210-212. "The Arabs were in Makran almost 3-quarters of a century before Muhammad al-Qasim conquered Sind and established the first Muslim settlement on the Indus. Adjacent to the Persian province of Kirman, a western extension of coastal Sind, Makran was first invaded in 644 A.D., the 23rd year of the Hijra, toward the end of the caliphate of Umar." – 1511 Andre Wink, Al-Hind, the Making of the Indo-Islamic World, (Boston: Brill Academic Publishers, Inc., 2002), p. 129.

B. Invasion of the Upper Indus Valley and the Kathiawar Peninsula

That conquest began in the year 997 A.D. with the first of seventeen devastating, plundering raids carried out by Mahmud of Ghazni and his band of daring marauders. "In 997 the Muslim warlord Mahmud of Ghazni stormed through the Khyber Pass and wreaked devastation through the rich provinces of Punjab and Sindh. His Turkic cavalrymen looted all that lay in their path, desecrating temples and smashing sacred idols in their pious, pitiless iconoclasm. The reach of these plundering raids is seen in the fact that "Mahmud of Ghazna, who swept down in Gujarat from eastern Afghanistan and in 1026 utterly destroyed the sea side Hindu Temple of Somnath." – Robert D. Kaplan, Monsoon, (New York: Random House, 2010), p. 102. There would be 16 more attacks over the next three decades." – Jonah Blank, Words into Swords, U.S. News & World Report, August 16/August 23, 1999, p. 55.: Those raids took Mahmud's plunderers, in 1026, all the way to the seashore of the Kathiawar Peninsula where they plundered the famous and extremely rich Hindu temple at Somnath.

C. Invasion by the Ghorids/Ghurids

A Ghurid army from Firuzkuh/Firozkoh—"behind the tortoise wall of their shields—managed to defeat the elephants of Ghazni. When the greatness of Ghazni declined, the Ghurids took over. … Firuzkuh, where the minaret [of Djam] remains, was their capital for more than sixty years from the reign of Baha al-Din in A.D. 1149, until conquered in 1210, and finally destroyed by Chingiz in 1222. … Their own armies were infantry of the mountains, helped by bodies of Turkish mercenary cavalry whose generals continued the military tradition of the Ghurids in Delhi long after the overstretched empire had fallen and the last of their sultans had been deposed in Firuzkuh." – 1514 Freya Stark, The Minaret of Djam, An Excursion in Afghanistan, (London: John Murray, 1970), pp. 60-61.

D. Invasion by the Moguls/Mughals (the name is derived from Mongols)

In 1526, Babur, founder of the great Mogul Empire, won victory over northern India at the Battle of Panipat on the Yamuna River. "Babur, the founder of the Mughal Dynasty, was descended from Genghis Khan and Timur (Tamerlane) and was another instance of the extraordinary military potency of Central Asia, Gibbon's source of 'barbarian' vitality." – 1515 Jeremy Black, War and the World, Military Power and the Fate of Continents, 1450-2000, (New Haven: Yale University Press, 1998), p. 24. The power of that Muslim empire was not broken till 1757 by Great Britain at the Battle of Plassey in Bengal.

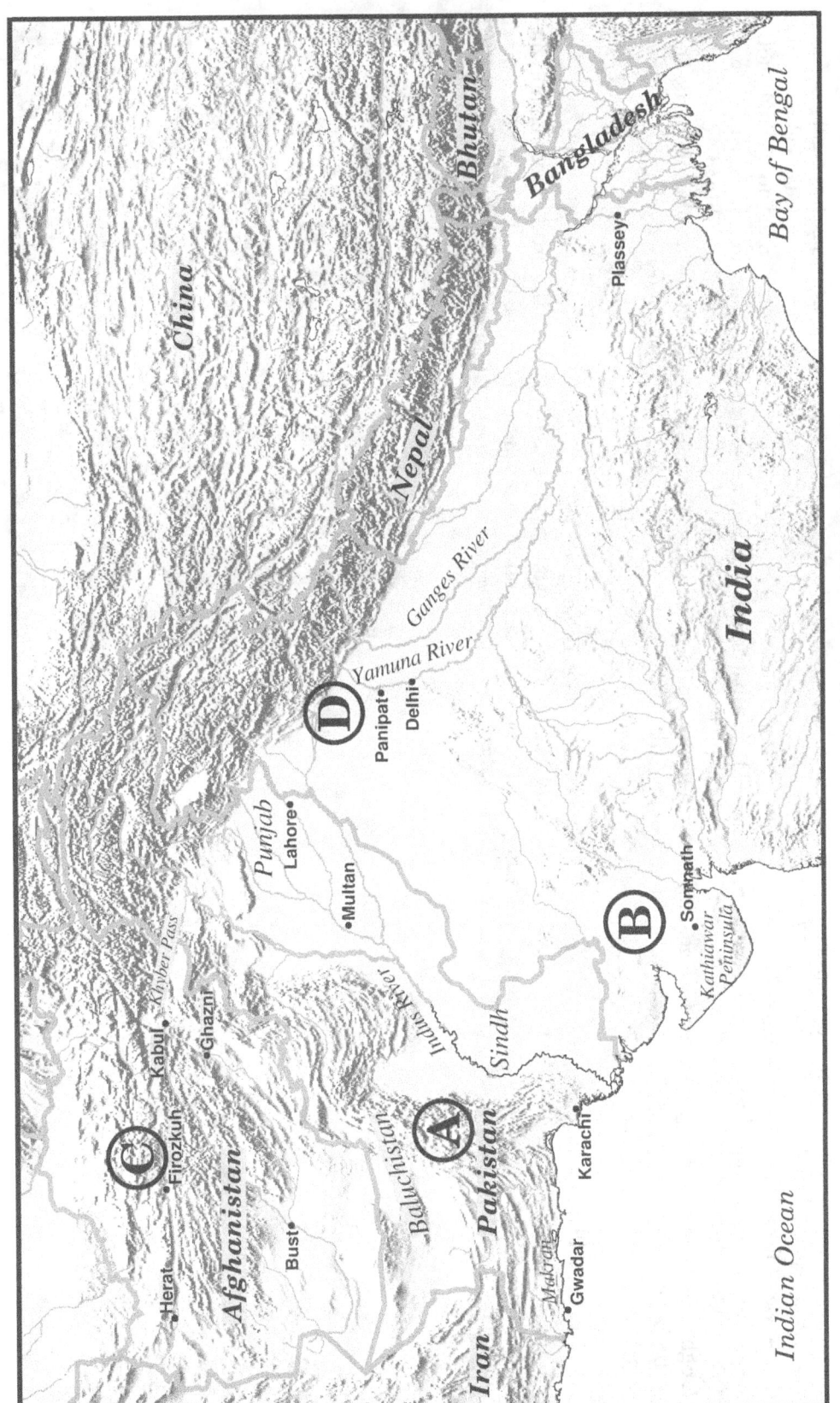

Map 12

Muslim Invasions of India

William Carey – The Bible for Hindu India

Though this map is entitled "William Carey – The Bible for Hindu India," the modern states of Bangladesh and Myanmar (formerly Burma) are shown to help the student grasp some of the current political, spacial and geographic realities of the area. The country of Bangladesh came into existence on May 26, 1971, when it (the former East Pakistan) became independent from present-day Pakistan. Due to the scale of the map, the narrow Indian land corridor between Bangladesh on the south, and Nepal and Bhutan on the north, could not be shown. It is that corridor by which India's state of Assam and the tribal areas to the east are joined to the main area of India to the west of Bangladesh. From the days of William Carey and Henry Martyn, the Ganges' main outlet to the Bay of Bengal has shifted from the Hooghly to the Padma. The great Australian geographer of India, Dr. Spate, tells us that "the cardinal factor in the later history of the Delta has been the eastwards shift of the Ganges waters from a main outlet along the western margins —the Bhagirathi-Hooghly—to the present main course, the Padma-Meghna." – O. H. K. Spate, India and Pakistan, (London: Methuen & Co., 1954), p. 524.

The work of William Carey was indisputably prodigious. He translated the Bible into Bengali, Oriya, Assamese, Marathi, Hindi, and Sanskrit. However, in contrast to the translation work of Henry Martyn, Carey's work "was seriously flawed. If there had been competent Bible translation consultants in Carey's day, they would not have approved for publication much, if any, of the translation work done by Carey and under his supervision." –H.L. Richard, Some Observations on William Carey's Bible Translations, International Bulletin of Mission Research, Vol. 42, Issue 3, July 2018, p. 242.

Map 13 493

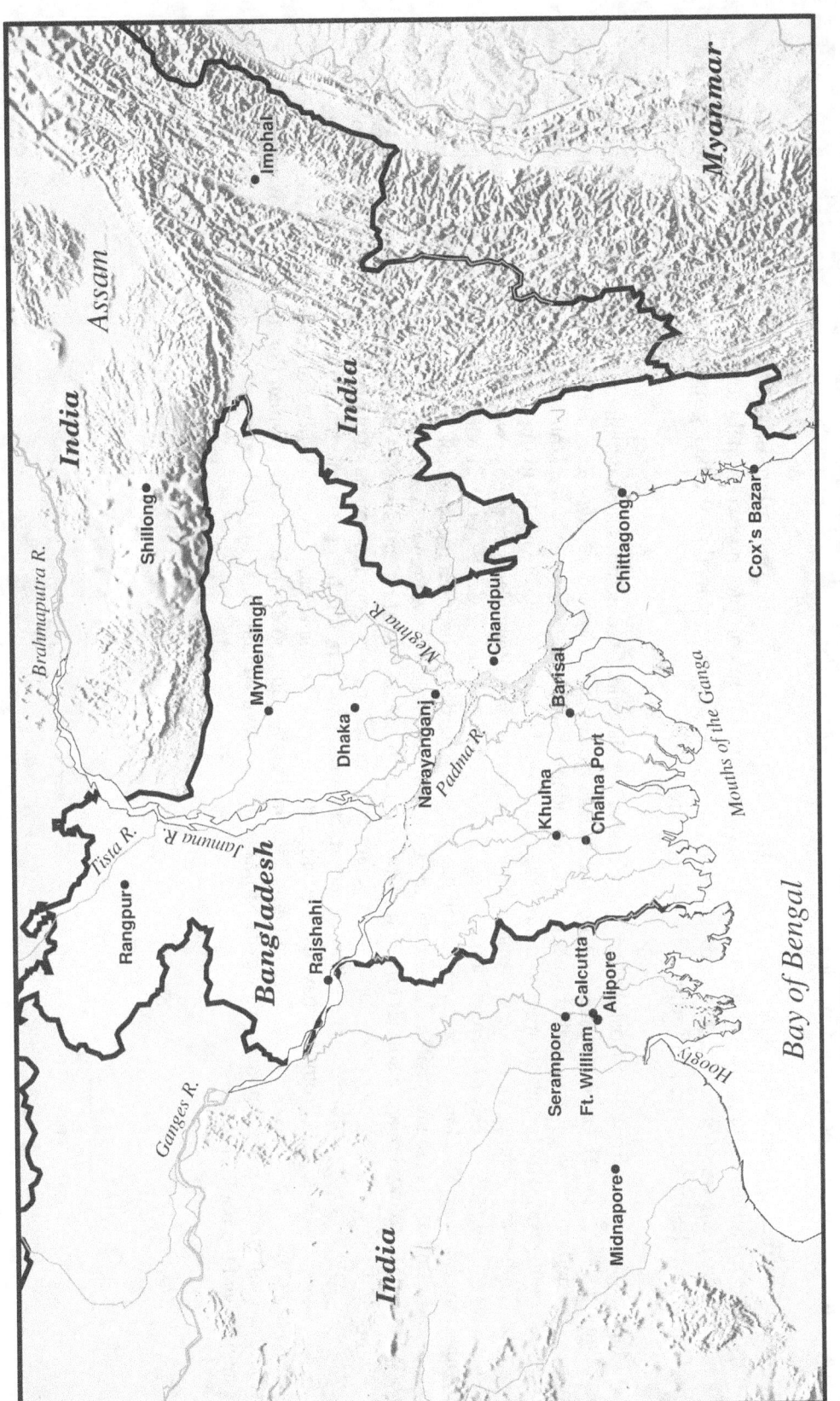

William Carey – The Bible for Hindu India
(See also Henry Martyn – The Bible for Muslim India & Iran)

Henry Martyn – The Bible for Muslim India & Iran

While the borders of Bangladesh and Myanmar (ancient Burma) are shown, the student should be aware that Bangladesh was East Pakistan till 1971 when it became independent.

In spite of suffering from active, out-of-control, advanced tuberculosis, Henry Martyn, in addition to his demanding work in Kanpur as a chaplain in the British Indian Army, devoted himself to completing two translations of the New Testament, one in Farsi (Persian), the other in Urdu. His Urdu translation is generally recognized as the basis upon which current translations of the Urdu New Testament, both in India and Pakistan, are based.

On Martyn's retirement from the British Indian Army chaplaincy, he said, I "sometimes look with interest at the road that leads to Cabul and Candahar." – Constance E. Padwick, Henry Martyn Confessor of the Faith, London: Inter-Varsity Fellowship, 1959, p. 117. He contemplated that road as a possible route to Persia/Iran. Very fortunately that itinerary was not adopted. With his precariously weak physical condition, it is probable he would have died on the way. His friends thought a leisurely sea trip would allow his delicate health to improve. Accordingly, he traveled by raft down the Ganges to Calcutta, where he was able to renew contact with William Carey and those working with him. From there his sea route took him through the Bay of Bengal, south along the east coast of India to Cape Comorin with a short side trip to the island of Ceylon (now known as Sri Lanka) where he visited the cinnamon gardens. His itinerary then took him north along the west coast of India to Goa and Bombay. At Goa he visited the tomb of the great Catholic missionary, Francis Xavier. In Bombay, among other dignitaries, he met Sir John Malcolm who, as "a soldier turned diplomatist, had twice been sent on embassies to establish British trade and prestige in Persia. … In Persia, later travelers took rank in Persian eyes according as they could or could not claim acquaintance with Malcolm Sahib. … He now gave Martyn invaluable help, letters of introduction right and left, much Persian information, and a present of a Chaldee missal." – Padwick, op. cit., p. 135. From Bombay his ship sailed through the Arabian Sea, ("on the morning of Easter we saw the land of Mekran in Persia") – Padwick, op. cit., p. 136. the Gulf of Oman and the Persian Gulf, to disembark at the Iranian Port of Bushehr. With great difficulty, from Bushehr Martyn made his way to Shiraz where he devoted himself to his work on a new translation of the Farsi New Testament and the book of Psalms.

Map 14

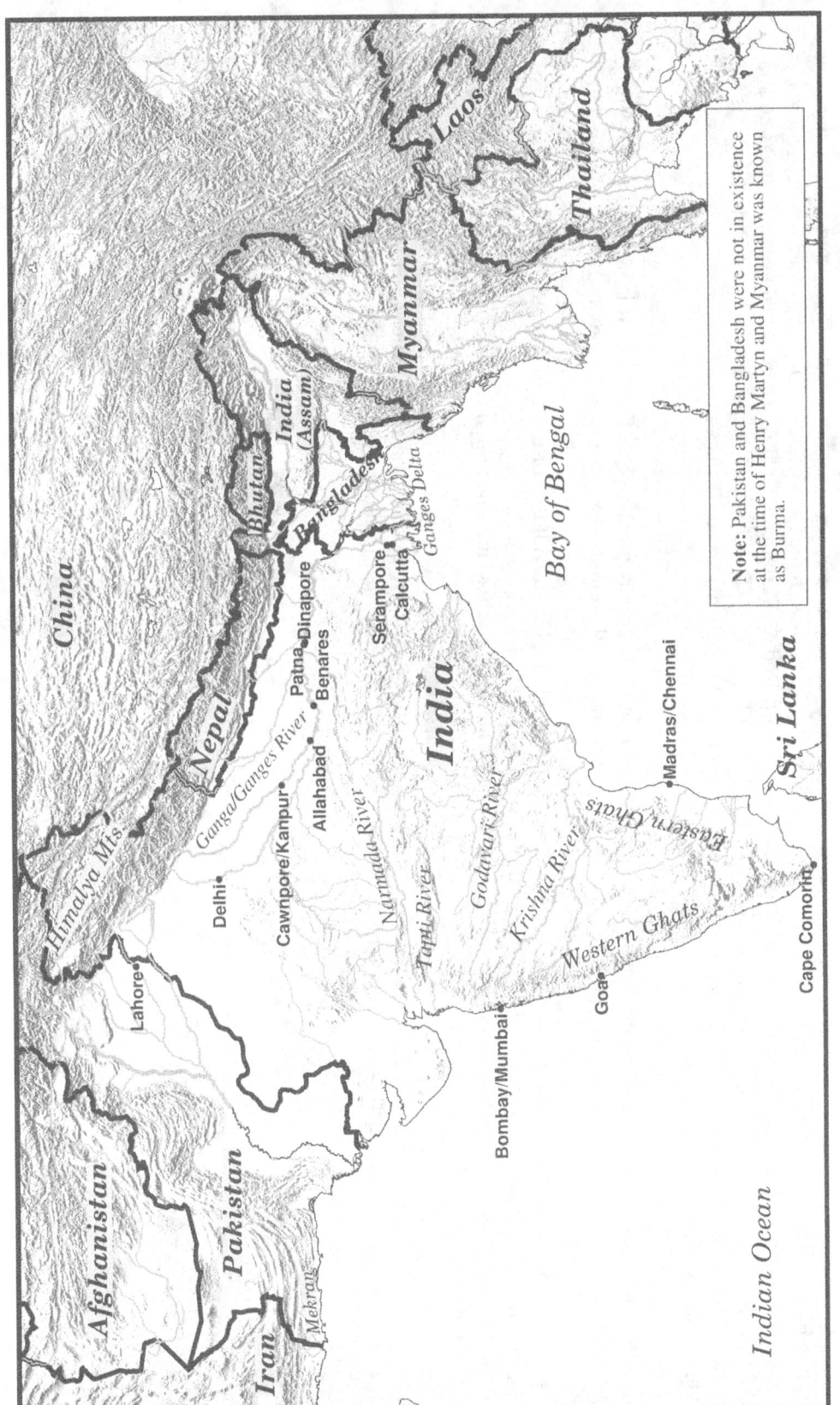

Henry Martyn – The Bible for Muslim India & Iran

Central Asia & Far Western China

Geographically, Central Asia encompasses a more extensive area than the older term "Transoxiana." Transoxiana only described the vast area to the northeast of (i.e., across – *trans*) the 1,628-mile-long Oxus River which arises in far northeast Afghanistan and discharges its waters into the Aral Sea. Ethnically, Central Asia is predominantly Turkish, though the individual country names acknowledge the presence of other ethnic people. It is the area of the five "Stans," comprised of Turkmenistan, Tajikistan, Kazakhstan, Kyrgyzstan and Uzbekistan. Thus, it includes Turkmenistan which was not embraced by the term Transoxiana. Because the name "Central Asia" is ethnically defined by the majority Turkish population, it does not include Afghanistan nor Pakistan which are, respectively, ethnically Afghan and predominantly Punjabi.

"Urumqi [Urumchi], the capital of China's westernmost Xinjiang Province, has a population of 3.8 million. It is bursting with traffic jams on webworks of new highways and overpasses, with gleaming skyscrapers all around. The city is a testimony to Beijing's attempt to dominate its Central Asian minority areas by smothering them with development, even as the Chinese build urban nodes for a post-modern Silk Road of long-distance highways, railways, and energy pipelines linking China with the former Soviet republics nearby. For it isn't only the Tien Shan that manifests the reality of Central Asia deep inside China: It is also the signs in Arabic script, evidence of the Turkic Uighur language spoken by more than a third of Urumqi's inhabitants, a language strikingly similar to Turkish proper. (There are, too, signs in the Russian alphabet, indicating the presence of Kazakh, Uzbek, and other Muslim minorities.) When one adds these ethnic Turkic areas to Tibet, you have a third of China's land area. China is prison house of nations, albeit to a lesser extent than the former Soviet Union. … Kashgar today is a place of new, regimented apartment blocks, with paved streets and a grid pattern, while the animals are kept far from town. It is modernism, deliberately imposed by the Chinese authorities, that is diluting Turkic Uighur culture here." – Robert D. Kaplan, The Return of Marco Polo's World, (New York: Random House, 2018), pp. 255-256.

Map 15

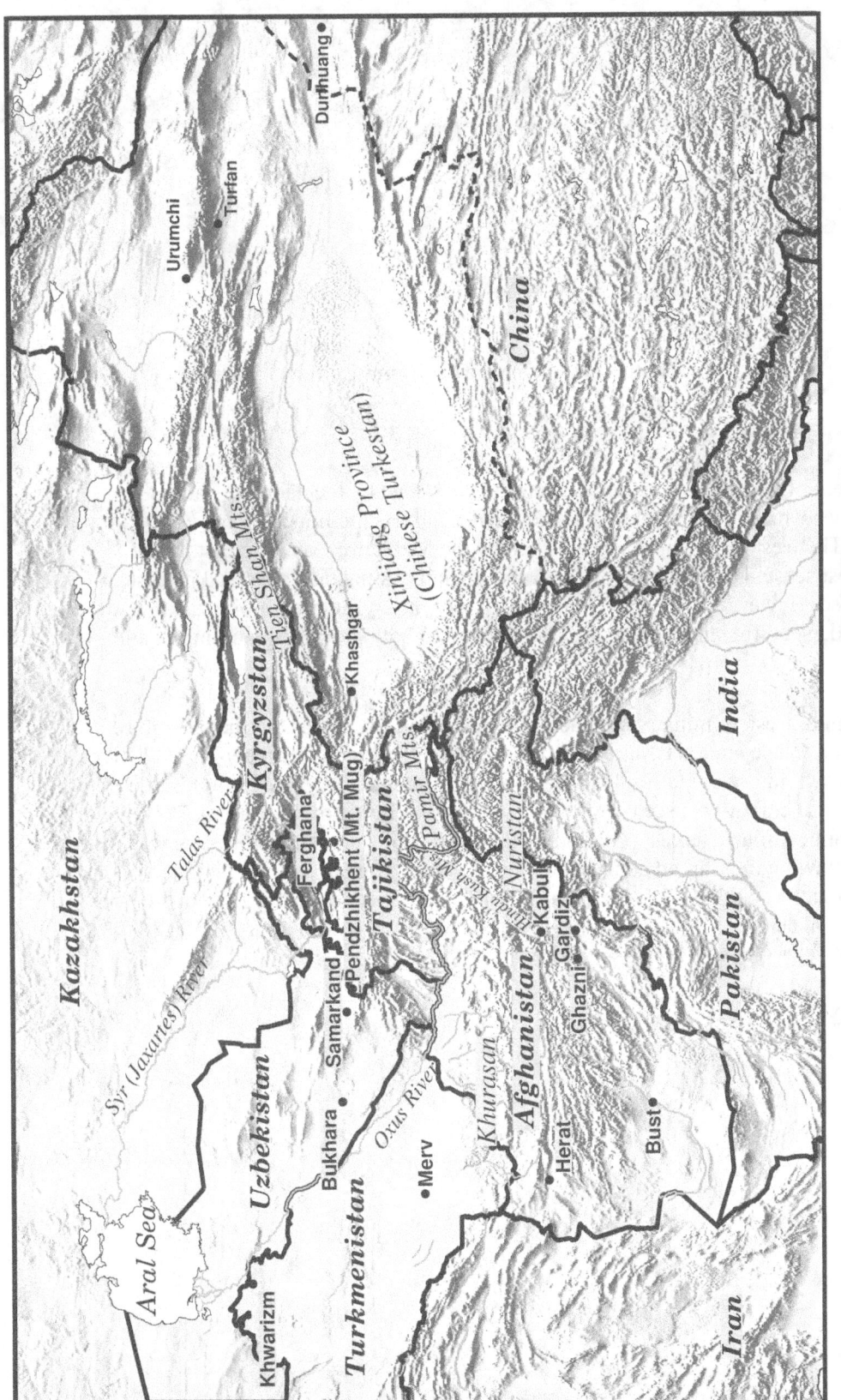

Central Asia & Far Western China

Conquest of the Levant

The term "Levant" is derived from the Italian *levante*, the East (where the sun rises). It is also a derivative of the Latin *levare*, to raise (as in sunrise), thus, the East. Specifically, it refers to the countries washed by the waters of the eastern Mediterranean.

The extent of geographic Levant: the north is bounded by the daunting Taurus Mountains which are in southeast Turkey. The south is determined by the Egyptian border. The west is, obviously, established by the Mediterranean. The east, in the narrowest sense, is determined by the Anti Lebanon Mountain Range and its eastern watershed. However, as the easternmost region of the Byzantine Empire, the Levant extended east till it butted up against the borders of both the Sassanian Empire and Arabia.

In the initial western military conquest by Islam, the Levant was the first area to be conquered. The conquest resulted from two critical battles on the upper Yarmuk River, the largest tributary of the Jordan River flowing from the east. The Second Battle of the Yarmuk was definitive. (See Chapter 8, "The Second Battle of the Yarmuk.") Up to the time Islamic military forces—flushed by their series of stunning victories—raced to the west, following their brutal conquest of Egypt, "the Levant and North Africa [had] constituted the heartlands of Christianity, with most of its population, key institutions, and cultural centers." – Daniel Pipes, In the Path of God, Islam and Political Power, (NY: Basic Books, Inc., 1983), p. 83. Be Sure to read Chapter 25, "Drastic Decline."

Map 16   499

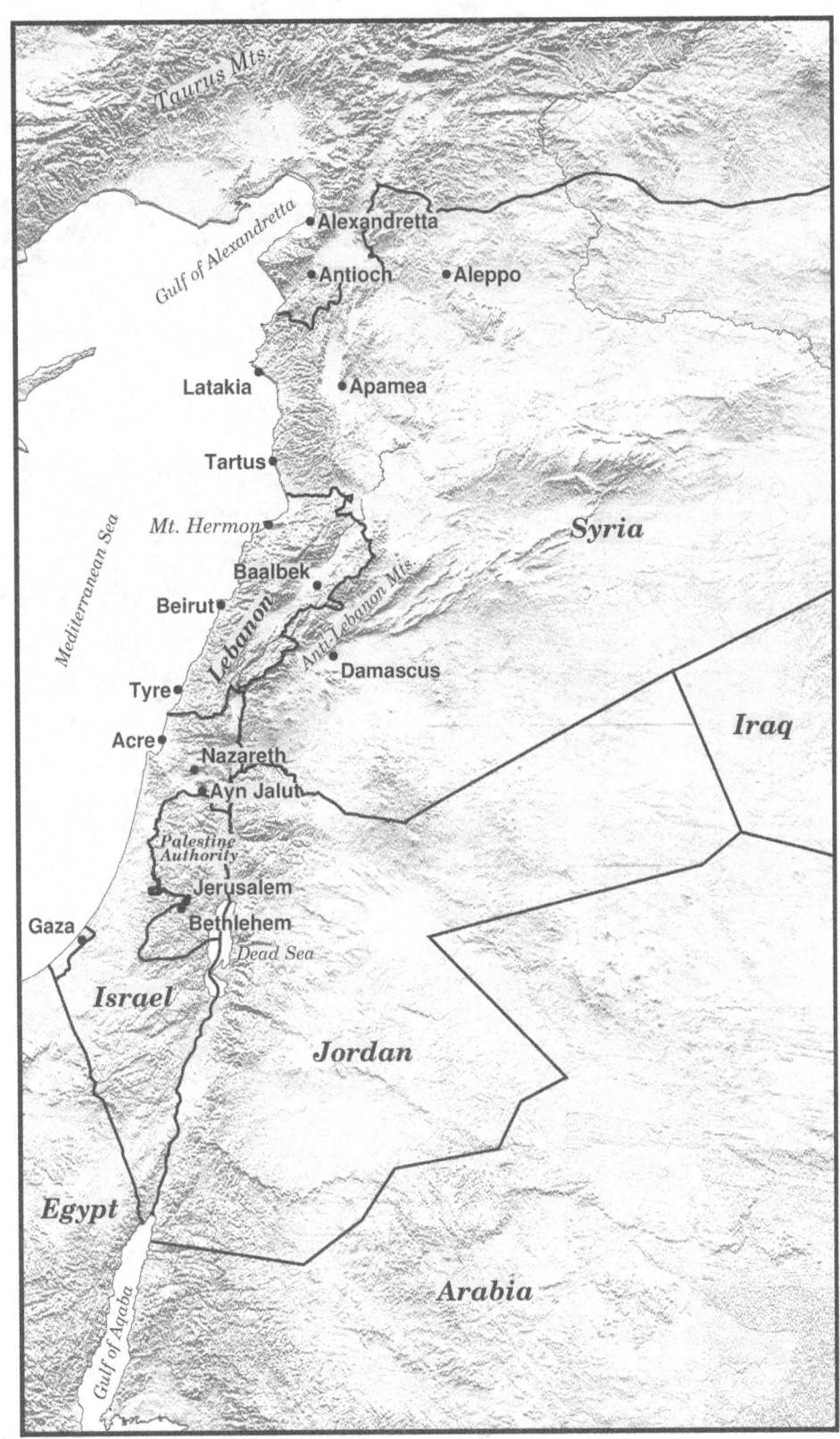

Conquest of the Levant

Muslim Invasion of Iran

This map illustrates the account given in Chapter 14 in the section, "Conquest of Persia/Iran Begins." Though this map of the Muslim invasion of Iran, which progressed from west to east, shows the current political boundaries of the area, the student should realize that (1) all of present-day Iran, (2) all of present-day Afghanistan, (3) a western part of the Makran area, and (4) much of the Euphrates/Tigris drainage basin were part of Sassanian Iran when the Muslim invasion began. The term "Euphrates/Tigris drainage basin" includes the whole watershed of both rivers. That area is far more extensive than that which is included in the name "Mesopotamia," a Greek term which means only the area between the Tigris and Euphrates Rivers.

Though the Afghan people—for whom Afghanistan is named—did not become Muslims until long after the initial Muslim invasion of Iran, the area inhabited by the Afghans was part of Iran at the time of the Muslim invasion.

Today, the western political boundary of Iran follows the Zagros Mountains, eliminating the Euphrates/Tigris drainage basin, and Afghanistan is an independent country. The area now known as Pakistan was culturally and religiously Buddhist until a later Muslim invasion which began in 710 A.D. The Wahkan Corridor which connects northeast Afghanistan to Xinjiang Province in China is not shown due to space constraints.

Map 17 501

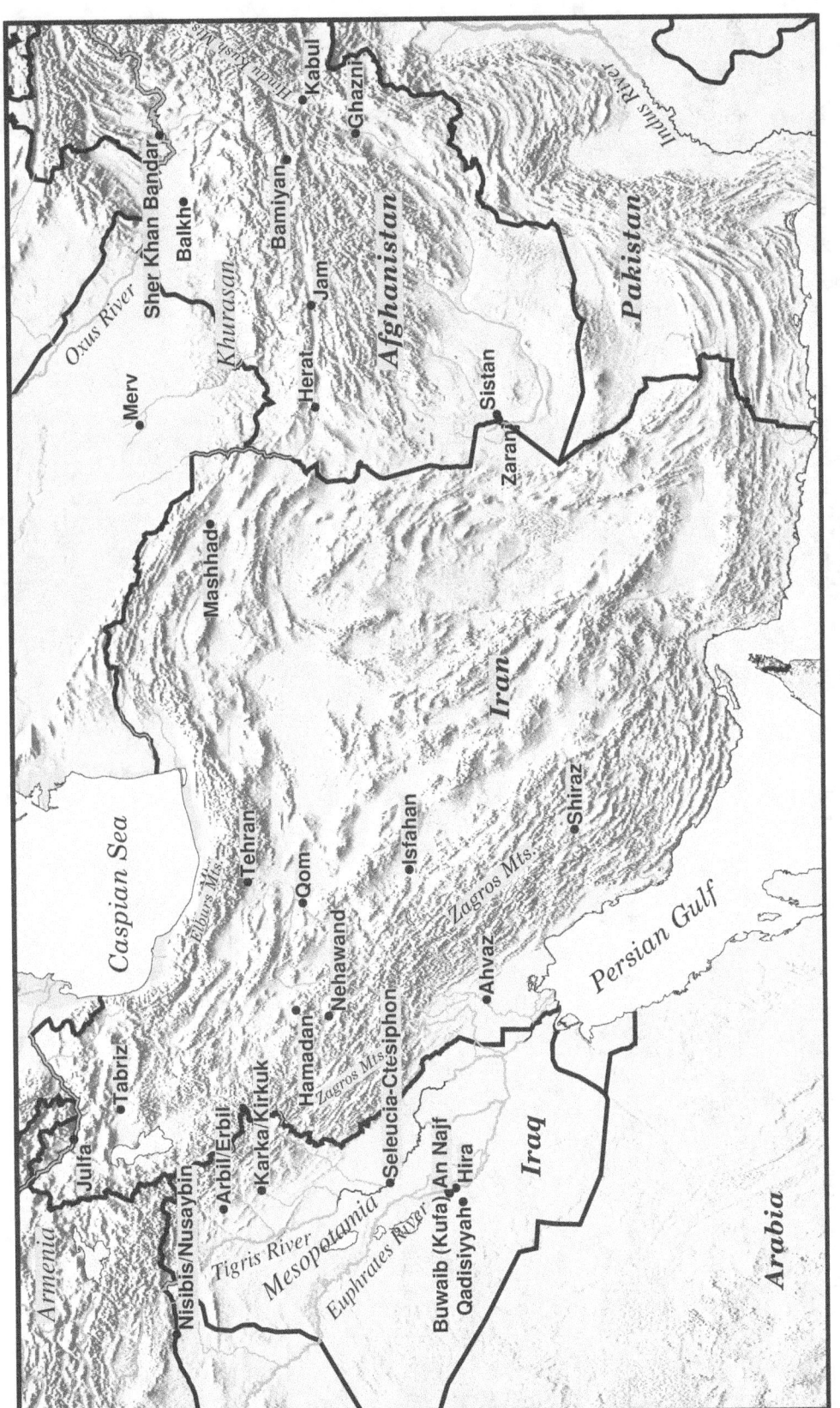

Egypt

Egypt has a very long history. No one could have expressed that fact better than Napoleon did. On July 21, 1798, after marching two weeks through the desert, Bonaparte's armies came in sight of the pyramids. "Soldiers," Bonaparte said, "from the height of these pyramids, forty centuries look down upon you."

That history has been possible only because of the river Nile, which redeems a narrow strip of Egyptian soil from the engulfing desert. The main Nile is approximately 4,199 miles long, making it arguably the longest river in the world. Some, however, think the Amazon River may be longer.

The main Nile is called the White Nile because of the white silt carried in its waters, which in flood season enriches the agricultural soil of Egypt. At Khartoum in Sudan, the waters of the White Nile are augmented by those of the Blue Nile flowing in from Lake Tana in Ethiopia.

The Christians of Egypt are known as Copts, meaning Egyptians. The name comes from the Greek *Aiguptios*, meaning an Egyptian (see the Greek for Acts 21:38). As the soil of the Egyptian Nile valley has produced abundant harvests, so through the centuries the message of Christ has borne much fruit. No other group of national Christians in the Middle East even remotely equals the numerical strength of the Copts. Unfortunately, the Coptic church has deviated from the New Testament ideal. While we applaud their centuries-long tenacity, we must pray for their doctrinal recovery.

Map 18

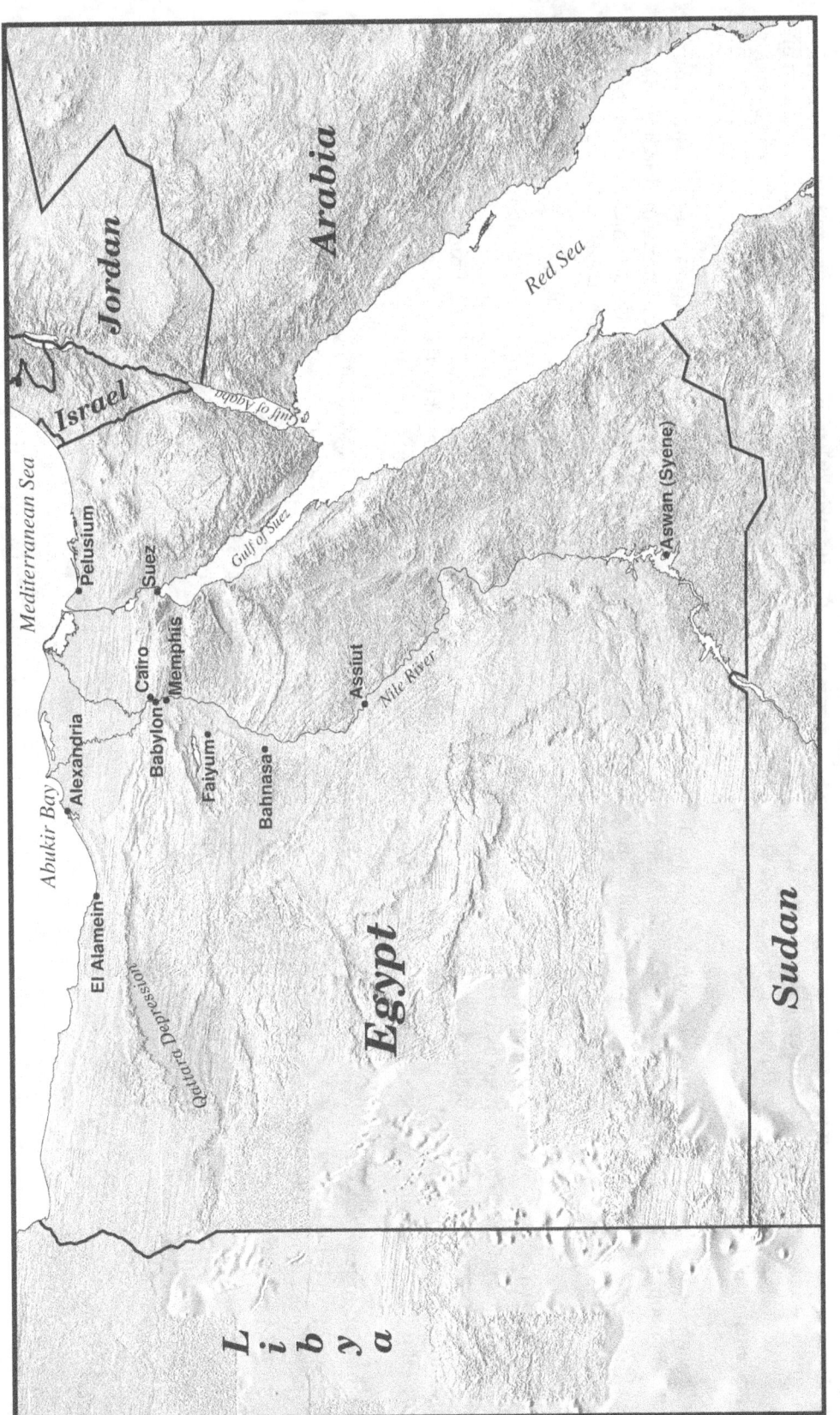

North Africa at the Time of the Muslim Conquest

North Africa as a whole is known to the Arabs as "'Jezirat al Maghrib,' or 'The Island of the Sunset.'" They consider it an island because "the Maghrib is in effect a piece of land surrounded by seas—a 3,000-mile strip of cultivation, pasture and mountain bounded on the north by the Mediterranean, on the west by the Atlantic, and on the south and east by the sand-seas of the Sahara and the 'Western Desert' of Egypt respectively." – Geoffrey Furlonge, The Lands of Barbary, (London: John Murray, 1966), pp. 1-2. Jezirat al Maghrib, is now shortened simply to Maghrib.

"Though the Carthaginians may have known more about the Trans-Sahara than we realize, the knowledge of Africa possessed by the ancient peoples who have left most literary remains was largely confined to the areas participating in, or accessible to, the Mediterranean civilizations, rarely penetrating the colossal barriers of the Atlas Mountains, the Sahara, and the perils of the Upper Nile. … There were Christians in Africa as soon as there were in Europe." – M. A. MacLeod, *Africa*, J. D. Douglas, ed., (Grand Rapids, MI: Eerdmans Publishing Co., 1967), pp. 17-18.

Looking at the human tax levied against the Louata Christians, one can judge how numerically triumphant Christianity had been in North Africa up to the Muslim invasion: "Upon conquering Cyrenaica in 642 or 643 'Amr b. al-'As [the Arab military commander who was also governor of conquered Egypt] fixed the jizya to be paid by its Berber tribes at 13,000 Dinars. From the Lawata [Louata] tribe he demanded that they should 'sell' to the Arabs a number of their 'sons and daughters' to the value of their share of the total jizya." – Jamil M. Abun-Nasr, A History of the Maghrib in the Islamic Period, (Cambridge: Cambridge University Press, 1987), p. 34.

In modern times, "the French Union, like empires of the past, would be built out of different sorts of polities connected to an imperial center in different ways: [1] European France; [2] Algeria, whose territory was fully integrated into France but whose population had been divided into citizens and subjects; [3] 'old colonies,' like those of the Caribbean, whose inhabitants were citizens; [4] 'new colonies,' such as those in Africa, whose inhabitants had mostly been subjects; [5] protectorates, like Morocco and Tunisia, which had their own nationality and sovereignty, having ceded (under pressure) certain powers to France by treaty; and [6] mandates, ex-German colonies that had their own potential nationality for which France was the trustee." – Jane Burbank & Frederick Cooper, Empires in World History, (Princeton, NJ: Princeton University Press, 2010), pp. 420-421.

Map 19 505

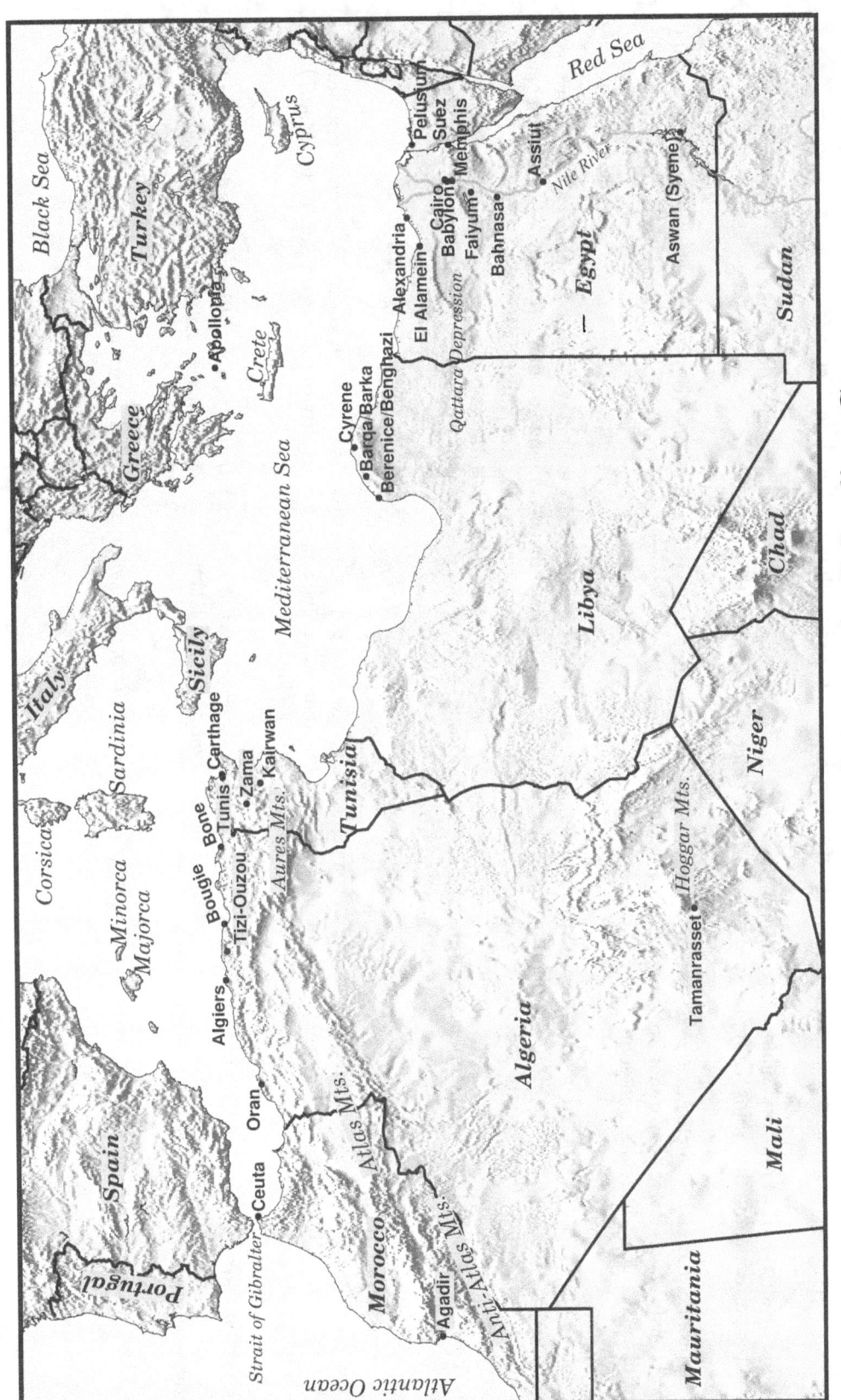

Spain's Future Role

Some appreciation for the importance of Spain in the development of both Christianity and Islam is conveyed by the fact that four chapters (20, 21, 22 and 23) in Withering Wind From Arabia have been devoted to expounding its significant historic role.

While history testifies to the pivotal role Spain has filled in the past, careful study of biblical prophecy leads one to anticipate Spain as a notable participant in the major realignment of world affairs which is currently taking place.

The prophet Ezekiel predicted that an area (then known as Tarshish), longing to share in plunder derived from a war against Israel, would covetously say to the leader of that invasion, "Have you come to plunder? Have you gathered your hordes to loot, to carry off silver and gold, to take away livestock and goods and to seize much plunder?" (Ezekiel 39:13 NIV)

Tarshish most probably should be identified with the ancient city of Tartessus which was located in what is now Spain, on the southwest coast, between Huelva and the Strait of Gibraltar. Tartessus was one of the most renowned mining and metal refining centers of the ancient world. If we connect that with the fact that the word Tarshish comes from a Phoenician word, "for 'mine' 'smeltery'; from Bab. [i.e. Babylonian] word for 'smelting plant'; or 'refinery,'" – Madeleine S. Miller and J. Lane Miller, Harper's Bible Dictionary (New York: Harper & Brothers, Publishers, 1961), p. 727. the identification, though not entirely certain, is very strong. This would indicate that we may expect Spain to be involved in the great developing war which was clearly predicted in Ezekiel chapters 38 and 39.

The murderous train bombings in Madrid on March 11, 2004 (See photo at the beginning of Chapter 23.) brought an ominous and indicative change in Spanish political alignment. First came the sudden and dramatic political upheaval in which then prime minister Jose Maria Aznar, on the questionable accusation that he had lied to the Spanish people about the identity of the perpetrators of the Madrid train bombings, was replaced by Jose Louis Rodrigeuz Zapatero in April, 2004.

Next, "on taking power, Zapatero immediately ordered his country's troops out of Iraq, repudiating Spain's alliance with the United States and launching in its place what he calls an 'alliance of civilizations' with Islam." – Christopher Caldwell, Reflections On the Revolution in Europe, Immigration, Islam and the West, (New York, Doubleday, 2009), p. 272.

In view of this developing situation in our time, participation of a predominantly Catholic area in the war on the side of the Communist forces from the north as envisioned in Ezekiel chapters 38 & 39 would not be surprising.

Map 20

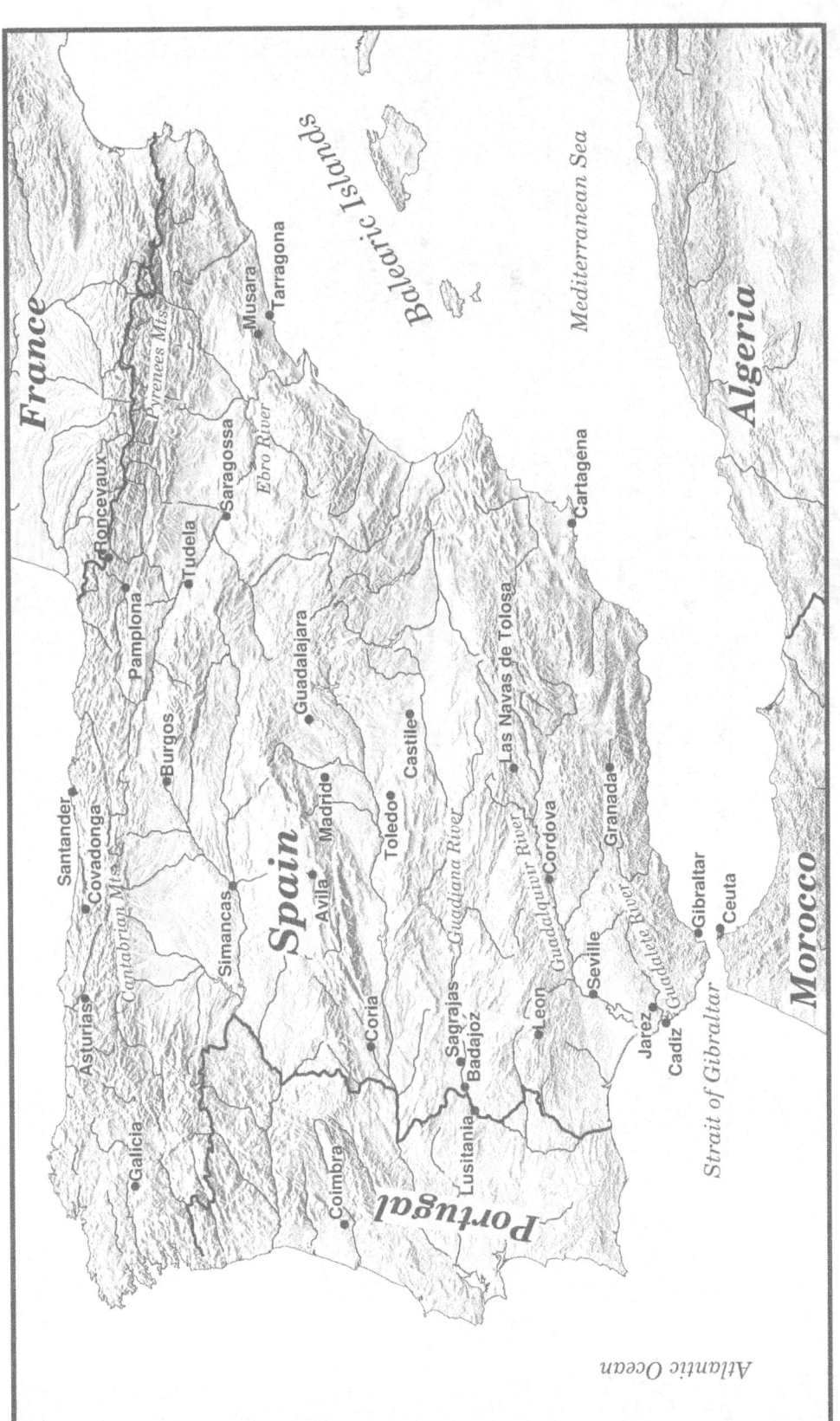

Spain's Future Role

The Islamic Empire – The First 75 Years

Diarmaid MacCulloch, Professor of "History of the Church" at Oxford University wrote, "In the eighth century of the Christian era, the great new city of Baghdad would have been a more likely capital for worldwide Christianity than Rome. The extraordinary accident of the irruption of Islam is the chief reason why Christian history turned in another direction." [Diarmaid MacCulloch, Christianity, the First Three-Thousand Years, (New York, Viking, 2010), p. 3.]

In view of all the incontrovertible realities presented in *Withering Wind From Arabia*, is it possible to reasonably say that the "irruption of Islam" was an "extraordinary accident?" As one considers the political, military, economic, social, philosophical, religious, ecological, agricultural, horticultural, botanical, climatological and genealogical phenomena which all—to some extent—coalesced to make it possible for the great Arabian Prophet Muhammad to bring his vision into reality, can we honestly say it all transpired by "accident," even an "extraordinary" one?

The apostle Paul called the propitious circumstances, which coalesced to make the spectacular birth and early growth of the church possible, "the fullness of the time" (Galatians 4:4). Similarly, an equally conducive set of circumstances made it possible for the concept of Islam to take deep roots in society and to dramatically spread globally.

Seeing not only the initial destruction of Christian communities and institutions caused by the irruption of Islam but also the ongoing suppression of the followers of Christ like those in Iran, like the Copts in Egypt, or the utter extermination of Christians and Christian influence on the pattern of what has happened in Arabia and Afghanistan, can we reasonably imagine that the coalition of so many circumstances resulting in such an international devastation of Christian presence and outreach was brought about by a benevolent power?

Map 21

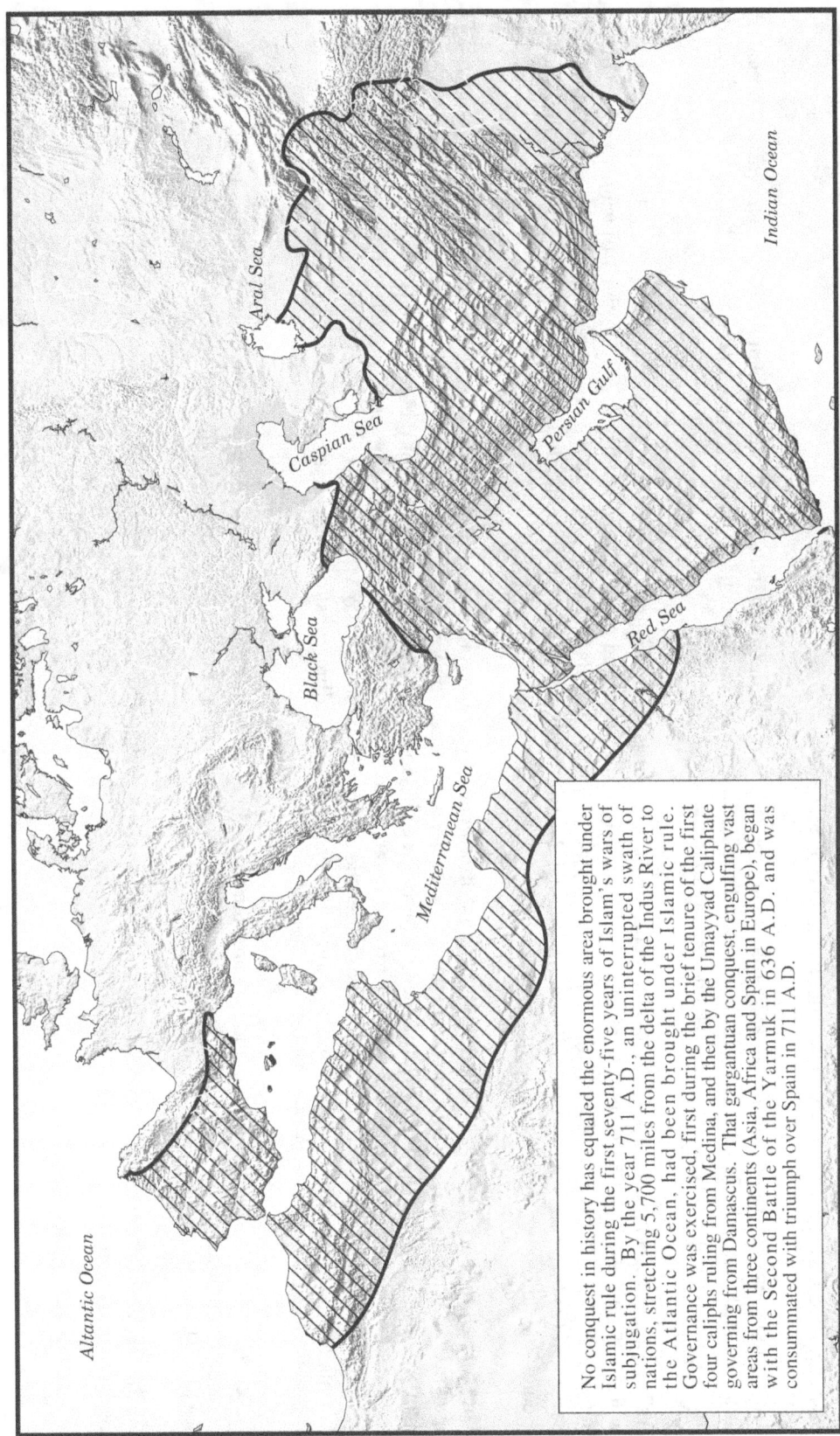

The Islamic Empire – The First 75 Years

No conquest in history has equaled the enormous area brought under Islamic rule during the first seventy-five years of Islam's wars of subjugation. By the year 711 A.D., an uninterrupted swath of nations, stretching 5,700 miles from the delta of the Indus River to the Atlantic Ocean, had been brought under Islamic rule. Governance was exercised, first during the brief tenure of the first four caliphs ruling from Medina, and then by the Umayyad Caliphate governing from Damascus. That gargantuan conquest, engulfing vast areas from three continents (Asia, Africa and Spain in Europe), began with the Second Battle of the Yarmuk in 636 A.D. and was consummated with triumph over Spain in 711 A.D.

The Turkish Assault on Europe Through the Balkans

These comments are complementary to the exposition in two sections of Chapter 27: "Expanding Empire" and "Deeper Into Europe." The route of the Turkish Muslim assault on Europe basically followed the course of the Danube River. Of special interest is the impact those invasions had on the area now known as the Balkan Peninsula.

The boundaries of the Balkan Peninsula are triangular, one side being in the north, basically along the Danube River. The eastern boundary follows the shore of the Black Sea from the mouth of the Danube to the southern end of Greece. The western side of the peninsula follows the alignment of the west coast of Greece all the way to the city of Munich.

As Webster succinctly expressed the development, the Turkish invasion broke up the region into smaller and often hostile areas from which we get the verb to *balkanize*, to break up (as a region) into smaller and often adversarial units. Prior to the Turkish invasion, which began with their occupation of the Gallipoli Peninsula, the Balkan Peninsula had been controlled by two predominate powers, (1) the Serbs and (2) the Hungarians. As highlighted in Chapter 27, two battles were crucial: first, the defeat of the Serbs at Kosovo Polje, and second, the defeat of the Hungarians at Varna.

The Turkish military exploits resulted in planting Islam irreversibly in the Balkan Peninsula. Along with their victories, the Turks also spawned undying hatred for Muslims and Islam. One of the most recent major expressions of this hatred took place in 1995 when "more than 8,000 Muslim men and boys were killed by Serb forces in Bosnia. ... Srebrenica, the site of the massacre [is] in eastern Bosnia. ... By the summer of 1995 Srebrenica and its surrounding area had swelled to 40,000 people, many seeking shelter after the United Nations declared the area a safe haven. But Serb forces under the command of Gen. Ratko Mladic overran the enclave and ordered men and boys to walk across forested hills, pursuing, ambushing and systematically killing most of them." – Barbara Surk, *Hatidza Mehmedovic, 65, Dies; Spoke Out for 8,000 Muslims Killed in 1995 Bosnia Massacre*, The New York Times, July 29, 2018, p. 20.

"Except for the Ottoman progress in the Balkans, the fifteenth century was not favorable to Islam politically or militarily. In all branches of science and philosophy Europe was now clearly in the lead, which has not yet been surrendered." – Harry W. Hazard, Atlas of Islamic History, (Princeton, NJ: Princeton University Press, 1952), p. 22.

For further description of the Ottoman Turkish conquest of the Balkan Peninsula, please see the Introduction to this book beginning with the fifth paragraph.

Map 22 511

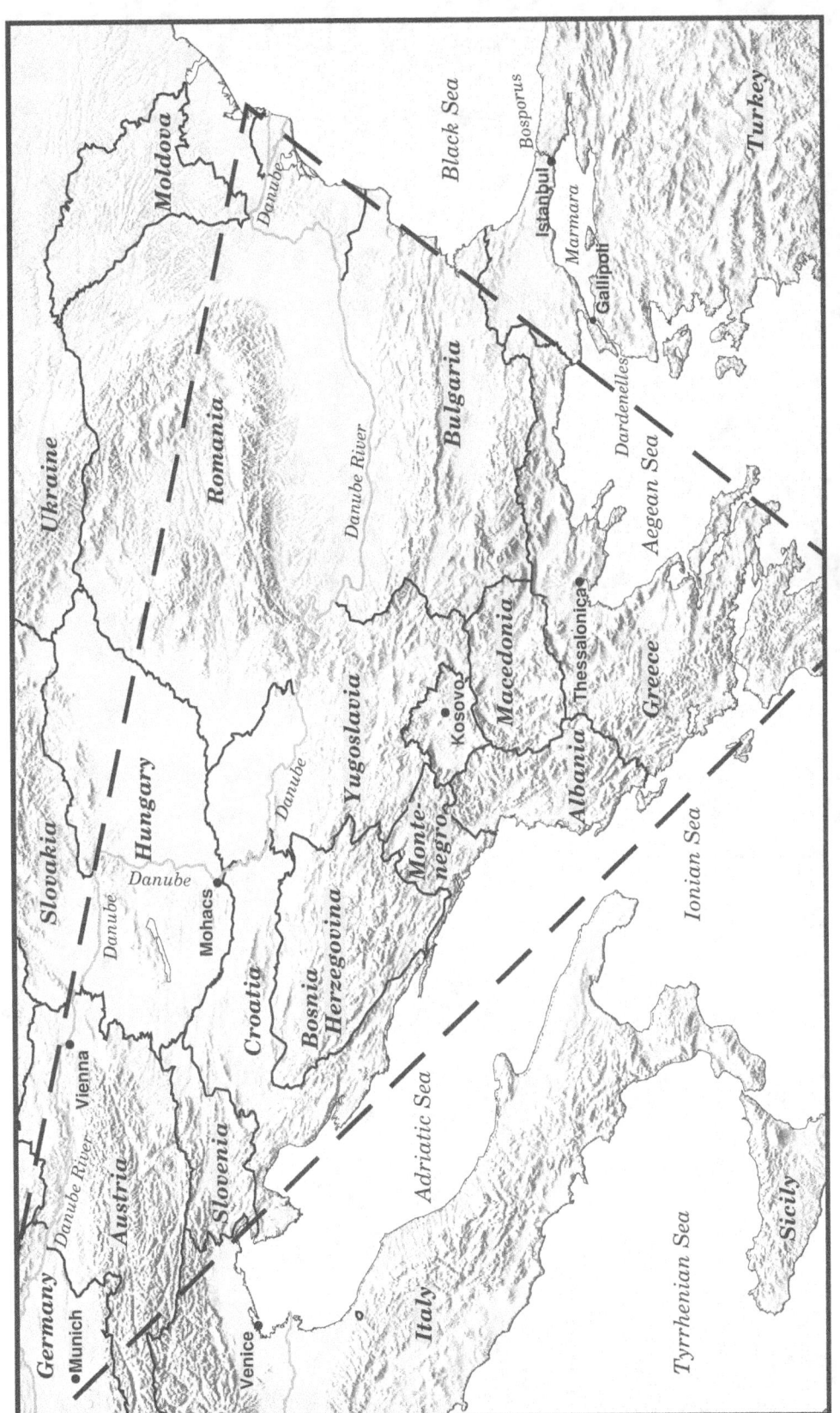

Indexes

Map Index

Abukir Bay	Map 18
Acre	Map 16
Addis Abeba/Adis Abeba	Map 3, Map 10
Aden	Map 2, Map 3, Map 6, Map 8, Map 9
Adriatic Sea	Map 22
Adulis	Map 3
Aegean Sea	Map 22
Afghanistan	Map 11, Map 12, Map 14, Map 15, Map 17
Agadir	Map 19
Ahvaz	Map 17
Al Duqm	Map 6
Al-Hasa/Hofuf	Map 5, Map 6, Map 8
Al-Hijr	Map 2
Al-Ubulla	Map 2
Albania	Map 22
Aleppo	Map 16
Alexandretta	Map 16
Alexandria	Map 1, Map 18, Map 19
Algeria	Map 19, Map 20
Algiers	Map 19
Alipore	Map 13
Allahabad	Map 14
An Najf	Map 17
Anti Atlas Mountains	Map 19
Anti-Lebanon Mountains	Map 16
Antioch	Map 16
Apamea	Map 16
Apollonia	Map 19
Aqaba	Map 2
Arabia	Map 2, Map 4, Map 8, Map 10, Map 16, Map 17, Map 18
Arabian Sea	Map 2, Map 5, Map 6, Map 8, Map 9
Aral Sea	Map 4, Map 15, Map 21
Arbil/Erbil	Map 17
Armenia	Map 17
Ash-Shihr	Map 9
Asir Mountains	Map 5
Asmara	Map 3, Map 10
Assab	Map 7
Assam	Map 13, Map 14
Assiut	Map 18, Map 19
Asturias	Map 20
Aswan/Syene	Map 18, Map 19
Atlantic Ocean	Map 19, Map 20, Map 21
Atlas Mountains	Map 19
Aures Mountains	Map 19
Austria	Map 22
Avila	Map 20
Axum	Map 3
Aylah	Map 2
Ayn Jalut	Map 16

Baalbek	Map 16
Bab-el-Mandeb	Map 2, Map 6, Map 7, Map 8
Babylon	Map 2, Map 18, Map 19
Badajoz	Map 20
Badr	Map 6, Map 8
Bahnasa	Map 18, Map 19
Bahrain	Map 5, Map 6, Map 8
Baidoa	Map 10
Balearic Islands	Map 20
Balkan Peninsula	Map 22
Balkh	Map 17
Baluchistan	Map 12
Bamiyan/Bamian	Map 17
Bangladesh	Map 11, Map 12, Map 13, Map 14
Barisal	Map 13
Barqa/Barka	Map 19
Basra	Map 8
Bay of Bengal	Map 11, Map 12, Map 13, Map 14
Beirut	Map 16
Benares	Map 14
Berbera	Map 3
Berenice	Map 19
Bethlehem	Map 16
Bhutan	Map 11, Map 12, Map 14
Black Sea	Map 4, Map 19, Map 21, Map 22
Blue Nile	Map 3, Map 5, Map 10
Bombay/Mumbai	Map 14
Bone/Annaba	Map 19
Bosnia	Map 22
Bosporus	Map 22
Bosra	Map 2
Bougie/Bijaya/Bejaia	Map 19
Brahnaputra River	Map 13
Bukhara	Map 15
Bulgaria	Map 22
Burgos	Map 20
Bust/Bost	Map 12, Map 15
Buwaib	Map 17
Cadis	Map 20
Cairo	Map 18, Map 19
Calcutta	Map 13, Map 14
Cambodia	Map 11
Camp Lemonnier	Map 10
Cantabrian Mountains	Map 20
Cape Comorin	Map 14
Cape Guardafui	Map 10
Cartagena	Map 20
Carthage	Map 19
Caspian Sea	Map 4, Map 17, Map 21
Castile	Map 20
Caucasus	Map 4
Cawnpore/Kanpur	Map 14
Ceuta	Map 19, Map 20

Map Index

Chad	Map 19
Chalna Port	Map 13
Chandpur	Map 13
Chang'an	Map 11
China	Map 4, Map 11, Map 12, Map 14
Chinese Turkestan	Map 15
Chittagong	Map 13
Clysma/Qulzum	Map 1
Coimbra	Map 20
Constantinople	Map 22
Cordova	Map 20
Coria	Map 20
Corsica	Map 19
Covadonga	Map 20
Cox's Bazar	Map 13
Crete	Map 19
Croatia	Map 22
Cyprus	Map 19
Cyrene	Map 19
Dahna	Map 5
Damascus	Map 2, Map 16
Dammam	Map 6, Map 8
Danube River	Map 22
Dardanelles	Map 22
Dead Sea	Map 16
Delhi	Map 12, Map 14
Dhahran	Map 6, Map 8
Dhaka	Map 13
Dhofar	Map 5, Map 8
Dinapore	Map 14
Djibouti	Map 3, Map 7, Map 10
Dumat al-Jandal	Map 6, Map 8
Dunhuang	Map 15
East China Sea	Map 11
Eastern & Western Ghats	Map 14
Ebro River	Map 20
Egypt	Map 2, Map 5, Map 6, Map 8, Map 16, Map 18, Map 19
El Alamein	Map 18, Map 19
Elburs Mountains	Map 17
Eritrea	Map 2, Map 3, Map 5, Map 6, Map 7, Map 8, Map 10
Ethiopia	Map 3, Map 4, Map 5, Map 6, Map 8, Map 10
Euphrates River	Map 2, Map 4, Map 8
Euphrates Tigris River system	Map 17
Ezion-Geber	Map 2
Faiyum	Map 18, Map 19
Fargana	Map 15
Firozkuh	Map 12
France	Map 20
Ft. William	Map 13
Galicia	Map 20
Gallipoli	Map 22
Ganges River	Map 12
Ganges River Delta	Map 13, Map 14

Gardiz	Map 15
Garoowe	Map 10
Gaza	Map 2, Map 6, Map 16
Germany	Map 22
Gerrha	Map 2
Ghazna/Ghazni	Map 12, Map 15, Map 17
Gibraltar	Map 20
Gilan	Map 15
Goa	Map 14
Godavari River	Map 14
Granada	Map 20
Great Bitter Lakes	Map 1
Greece	Map 19, Map 22
Guadalajara	Map 20
Guadalete River	Map 20
Guadalquivir River	Map 20
Guadiana River	Map 20
Guangzhou	Map 11
Gulf of Aden	Map 2, Map 3, Map 4, Map 5, Map 6, Map 7, Map 8, Map 9, Map 10
Gulf of Alexandretta	Map 16
Gulf of Aqaba	Map 2, Map 5, Map 16, Map 18
Gulf of Oman	Map 2, Map 5, Map 6, Map 8
Gulf of Suez	Map 1, Map 18
Gwadar	Map 12
Hadramaut/Hadhramaut	Map 5, Map 8, Map 9
Hainan	Map 11
Hajar Mountains	Map 5
Hamadan	Map 17
Hangzhou	Map 11
Haraz Mountains	Map 9
Haud	Map 10
Herat	Map 12, Map 15, Map 17
Herzegovina	Map 22
Hijaz	Map 5
Himalayas	Map 14
Hindu Kush Mountains	Map 4, Map 15, Map 17
Hira	Map 8, Map 17
Hofuf/Al Hasa	Map 5, Map 6, Map 8
Hoggar Mountains	Map 19
Hoogly River	Map 13
Hudaydah	Map 6, Map 8, Map 9
Hungary	Map 22
Ibb	Map 9
Imphat	Map 13
India	Map 11, Map 12, Map 13, Map 14, Map 15
Indian Ocean	On many maps
Indonesia	Map 11
Indus River	Map 4, Map 12, Map 17
Ionian Sea	Map 22
Iran	Map 2, Map 4, Map 5, Map 6, Map 12, Map 14, Map 15, Map 17
Iraq	Map 2, Map 5, Map 6, Map 16, Map 17
Isfahan	Map 17
Israel	Map 6, Map 16, Map 18

Map Index

Istanbul	Map 22
Italy	Map 19, Map 22
Jam/Djam	Map 17
Jamuna River	Map 13
Japan	Map 11
Jarez	Map 20
Jaxartes/Syr River	Map 15
Jedda	Map 6, Map 8
Jerusalem	Map 2, Map 16
Jizan	Map 6
Jordan	Map 5, Map 6, Map 16, Map 18
Juba River	Map 3, Map 10
Juba	Map 10
Julfa	Map 17
Kabul	Map 12, Map 15, Map 17
Kairwan	Map 19
Kampala	Map 10
Karachi	Map 12
Karka/Kirkuk	Map 17
Kashgar	Map 15
Kathiawar Peninsula	Map 12
Kazakhstan	Map 11, Map 15
Kenya	Map 3, Map 10
Khaibar	Map 6, Map 8
Khartoum	Map 3, Map 10
Khorasan/Khurasan	Map 15, Map 17
Khulna	Map 13
Khwarizm	Map 15
Khyber Pass	Map 12
King Abdullah Port	Map 6
Kismayo	Map 10
Krishna River	Map 14
Kuwait	Map 5, Map 6
Kyrgyzstan	Map 11, Map 15
Lahore	Map 12, Map 14
Lake Tana	Map 3, Map 10
Laos	Map 11, Map 14
Las Navas de Tolosa	Map 20
Latakia	Map 16
Lebanon	Map 16
Leon	Map 20
Libya	Map 18, Map 19
Lusitania	Map 20
Ma'rib	Map 9
Macedonia	Map 22
Madinah/Medina	Map 2, Map 6, Map 8
Madras/Chennai	Map 14
Madrid	Map 20
Majorca	Map 19
Makran	Map 12
Malaysia	Map 11
Mali	Map 19
Manzikert	Map 4

Marga	Map 15
Marmara	Map 22
Mashhad	Map 17
Massawa	Map 3
Mauritania	Map 19
Maydi	Map 9
Mazandaran	Map 15
Mecca	Map 2, Map 6, Map 8
Mediterranean Sea	On many maps
Meghna River	Map 13
Mekran	Map 14
Memphis	Map 18, Map 19
Merv/Mary	Map 15, Map 17
Mesopotamia	Map 17
Midnapore	Map 13
Minorca	Map 19
Mocha	Map 6, Map 7, Map 8, Map 9
Mogadishu	Map 3, Map 10
Mongolia	Map 11
Montenegro	Map 22
Morocco	Map 19, Map 20
Mota	Map 6, Map 8
Mt. Hermon	Map 16
Mt. Mug	Map 15
Mukalla	Map 6, Map 8, Map 9
Multan	Map 12
Munich	Map 22
Musandam Peninsula	Map 5, Map 6, Map 8
Musara	Map 20
Muscat	Map 6, Map 8
Myanmar	Map 11, Map 13, Map 14
Mymensingh	Map 13
Nafud Desert	Map 5
Nairobi	Map 10
Najd	Map 5, Map 8
Najran	Map 2, Map 6, Map 8
Narayanganj	Map 13
Narmada River	Map 14
Nazareth	Map 16
Nehawand	Map 15, Map 17
Nepal	Map 11, Map 12, Map 14
Niger	Map 19
Nile River	Map 1, Map 18, Map 19
Nisibis/Nusaybin	Map 17
North Korea	Map 11
Nuristan	Map 15
Ogaden	Map 10
Oman	Map 2, Map 5, Map 6, Map 8, Map 9, Map 10
Oran	Map 19
Oxus/Amu Darya River	Map 15, Map 17
Padma River	Map 13
Pakistan	Map 11, Map 12, Map 14, Map 15, Map 17
Palestinian Authority	Map 6, Map 16

Map Index

Palmyra	Map 2
Pamir Mountains	Map 4, Map 15
Pamplona	Map 20
Panch	Map 15
Panipat	Map 12
Patna	Map 14
Pelusium	Map 18, Map 19
Pendzhikent	Map 15
Perim Island	Map 7
Persia	Map 8
Persian Gulf	On many maps
Petra	Map 2
Philippines	Map 11
Plassey	Map 12
Port of Berbera	Map 10
Port of Shihr	Map 8
Portugal	Map 19, Map 20
Punjab	Map 12
Puntland	Map 3, Map 10
Pyrenees Mountains	Map 20
Qadisiyyah	Map 17
Qatar	Map 5, Map 6
Qattara Depression	Map 18, Map 19
Qom	Map 17
Qulzum/Clysma	Map 1
Rajshahi	Map 13
Rangpur	Map 13
Ras-al-Hadd	Map 5
Red Sea	On many maps
Riyadh	Map 6, Map 8
Romania	Map 22
Roncevaux	Map 20
Rub' al Khali	Map 5
Russia	Map 11
Sagrajas	Map 20
Sahara Desert	Map 4
Samarkand	Map 15
San'a/Sana'a	Map 2, Map 6, Map 8, Map 9, Map 10
Santander	Map 20
Saragossa	Map 20
Sardinia	Map 19
Sassanian Empire	Map 4
Saudi Arabia	Map 5, Map 6, Map 9
Sayhut	Map 6, Map 8, Map 9
Sea of Japan	Map 11
Seistan/Sistan	Map 17
Seleucia-Ctesiphon/Medain	Map 17
Serampore	Map 13, Map 14
Seville	Map 20
Shebeli River	Map 3, Map 10
Sher Khan Bander	Map 17
Shillong	Map 13
Shiraz	Map 17

Sicily	Map 19, Map 22
Simancas	Map 20
Sindh	Map 12
Sinkiang Province	Map 15
Slovakia	Map 22
Slovenia	Map 22
Socotra	Map 10
Sohar	Map 6, Map 8
Somalia	Map 3, Map 10
Somaliland	Map 3, Map 10
Somnath	Map 12
South China Sea	Map 11
South Korea	Map 11
South Sudan	Map 10
Spain	Map 19, Map 20
Sri Lanka	Map 11, Map 14
Strait of Gibraltar	Map 19, Map 20
Strait of Hormuz	Map 5, Map 6, Map 8
Sudan	Map 2, Map 3, Map 5, Map 6, Map 8, Map 10, Map 18, Map 19
Suez	Map 18, Map 19
Syr/Jaxartes River	Map 15
Syria	Map 6, Map 8, Map 16
Ta'iz/Ta'izz	Map 6, Map 8, Map 9
Tabriz	Map 17
Tabuk	Map 2
Taif	Map 6, Map 8
Taiwan	Map 11
Taiwan Strait	Map 11
Tajikistan	Map 11, Map 15
Talas River	Map 15
Tamanrasset	Map 19
Tang Dynasty	Map 4
Tapti River	Map 14
Tarragona	Map 20
Tartus	Map 16
Taurus Mountains	Map 16
Tehran	Map 17
Thailand	Map 11, Map 14
The Brothers Islands	Map 7
Thessalonica	Map 22
Tien Shan Mountain Range	Map 15
Tigris River	Map 2, Map 4, Map 8, Map 17
Tihama	Map 5, Map 9
Tista River	Map 13
Tizi-Ouzou	Map 19
Toledo	Map 20
Trajan's Canal	Map 1
Tudela	Map 20
Tunis	Map 19
Tunisia	Map 19
Turfan	Map 11, Map 15
Turkey	Map 19, Map 22
Turkmenistan	Map 15

Map Index

Tyre	Map 16
Tyrrhenian Sea	Map 22
U.A.E.	Map 5, Map 6
Ubulla	Map 8
Uganda	Map 10
Ukraine	Map 22
Urumchi/Ururmchi	Map 11, Map 15
Uzbekistan	Map 15
Vienna	Map 22
Vietnam	Map 11
Wadi a-Sirhan	Map 5
Wadi Adhahah	Map 9
Wejh	Map 6, Map 8
White Nile	Map 3, Map 5, Map 10
Xinjiang Province	Map 11
Yamuna River	Map 12
Yanbu	Map 6, Map 8
Yellow Sea	Map 11
Yemen	Map 2, Map 3, Map 5, Map 6, Map 7, Map 8, Map 9, Map 10
Yugoslavia	Map 22
Zagros Mountains	Map 5, Map 17
Zama	Map 19
Zaranj	Map 1

Index of Koranic References

Surah 2:30	58
Surah 2:30-35	59
Surah 2:40	82
Surah 2:43	401, 469
Surah 2:47	84, 54
Surah 2:65	84
Surah 2:83	401, 469
Surah 2:87	52
Surah 2:122	84
Surah 2:125	99
Surah 2:142-150	73
Surah 2:144	100
Surah 2:158	402
Surah 2:183-187	401
Surah 2:189	402
Surah 2:194-195	340
Surah 2:196	402
Surah 2:215	401, 469
Surah 2:233	43
Surah 2:253	52
Surah 2:256	342
Surah 2:271	340
Surah 3:31	340
Surah 3:45	53
Surah 3:46	54
Surah 3:59	55, 122
Surah 3:64	340
Surah 3:67	42
Surah 3:96	74
Surah 3:120	92
Surah 3:120-199	91
Surah 3:125	92
Surah 3:139-141	92
Surah 3:152	91, 92
Surah 3:165-167	92
Surah 3:169	92, 341
Surah 4	92
Surah 4:31	340
Surah 4:36	345
Surah 4:40	340
Surah 4:46	84
Surah 4:77	401, 469
Surah 4:100	341
Surah 4:157	54, 57, 59
Surah 4:160	84
Surah 4:171	53, 55, 57
Surah 5:13	84
Surah 5:19	54
Surah 5:20-21	84, 354

Surah 5:51	84
Surah 5:57	84
Surah 5:59-60	84
Surah 5:68	404
Surah 5:72	54
Surah 5:72-73	60
Surah 5:73	63
Surah 5:75	54
Surah 5:82	84
Surah 5:97	99
Surah 5:110	52, 61, 62
Surah 5:112-115	62
Surah 6:92	404
Surah 7:157	40, 407
Surah 7:166	84
Surah 7:169	84
Surah 7:191-192	61
Surah 7:191-194	62
Surah 9:1	98, 99
Surah 9:17	101
Surah 9:28	101
Surah 9:29	145, 323, 459
Surah 9:30	64
Surah 9:30-31	54
Surah 9:31	60
Surah 9:33	173
Surah 9:40	71
Surah 10:35	48, 60, 61, 62
Surah 10:38	52
Surah 10:39	52
Surah 10:95	404
Surah 11:114	340, 401
Surah 11:115	340
Surah 12:3	47
Surah 13:7	52
Surah 15:94	49
Surah 16:17	61
Surah 16:103	41
Surah 17:61	56
Surah 17:104	84, 354
Surah 19	64
Surah 19:19	54
Surah 19:20-21	57
Surah 19:20-22	118
Surah 19:21	53, 57, 58
Surah 19:35	64
Surah 22:27-29	402
Surah 22:73	61
Surah 23:91	64
Surah 24:58	401
Surah 29:27	84
Surah 30:2-4	45
Surah 30:2-5	27, 94

Index of Koranic References

Surah 30:42	45
Surah 34:15-19	30
Surah 38:72-79	56
Surah 45:16-17	84
Surah 47:19	55
Surah 48:1-2	55
Surah 48:16	27, 94
Surah 48:28	173
Surah 49:14-15	400
Surah 60:8	342
Surah 61:9	173
Surah 62:9-10	401
Surah 72:8	401
Surah 73:20	469
Surah 78:31-33	329
Surah 81:19-21	52
Surah 81:19-25	48
Surah 85	25
Surah 85:4-10	115
Surah 93:6-8	39
Surah 96:1-5	40, 48
Surah 105	42
Surah 110:1-3	173

General Index

A Common Word	336, 339, 340, 342, 343
A. Guillaume	42
Abba Eban	2, 289, 359
Abbasid	76, 77, 79, 213, 268, 271, 293, 395
Abbasid Caliphate	78, 181, 182, 206, 207, 214, 267, 269, 296, 303, 304, 308, 394, 395, 421
Abbasid Caliphs	204, 207, 233, 296, 395, 421-423
Abbasids	76, 78, 79, 234, 268, 284, 296, 394, 395
Abd al-Rahman	76, 269, 395
Abd al-Rahman I	267, 271, 272
Abd al-Rahman III	270, 272
Abdul Rahman Azzam Pasha	2
Abdul-Muttalib, Muhammad's grandfather	39
Abdullah, al-Mughira b.	135
Abdullah, Muhammad's father	39, 41
Abdullah, Muhammad's son	47
Abode of Wisdom	77
Abraha	25, 26, 28, 29, 42
Abraham	42, 98, 99, 116, 285, 460
Abu 'Ubayd	81
Abu Bakr	70, 71, 73, 75, 88, 102-107, 134, 281, 391, 402
Abu Dhabi	405
Abu Dujana	106
Abu Musa Island	360
Abu Muwayhiba	102
Abu Sufyan	89-91, 99
Abu Talib	39, 40, 44, 65, 66, 88, 233
Abukir Bay	209
Abyssinia	16, 17, 19, 24, 25, 65, 66, 73, 174, 277
Abyssinian	17, 24-26, 33, 40, 115
accident	352
Achaemenian Empire	408, 417, 418
Achaemenid	426
Achaemenid Empire	408, 410, 419
Acre	31, 209, 288, 349
Ad and Iram	67
Ad and Thamud	41
Adam	55, 56, 58
Adam, last	55
Adam, the greater	57-59
Adam, the lesser	57, 59
Addis Ababa/Adis Abeba	18
Aden	18, 19, 23, 30, 366-368, 405

Adhanah..29
Adrianople...312, 316, 317
Adulis...17, 18, 31, 366
Aegean Sea..304, 408
Afghan Christians..141, 154, 157
Afghan Marxists..152
Afghan refugee camps..157
Afghan War...148, 150
Afghanistan............15, 20, 34, 124, 131, 137-145, 147-157, 163, 169, 335, 346, 352, 426-429, 445
Afghanistan Institute of Technology Inc...151
Afghans..429
Africa.....4, 17, 20, 113, 125, 195, 196, 220, 223, 229, 235, 252, 253, 259, 260, 263, 271, 273, 292, 310, 357, 358, 367, 389
Agricultural developments..28
Ahlman Academy..151
Ahmadinejad...349
Ain/Ayn Jalut..206, 297
Aisha..49, 73, 88, 103, 122
Ajyad...43
Aksum/Axum...16, 18, 24, 25, 348, 366
al Amin..44
Al Hudaydah..360, 365, 366, 368
al Qaeda...80, 123, 228, 335, 348, 358, 445
al-'Abbas..69, 394
al-'Aqaba...67-70, 85
Al-Aqsa Mosque..351
al-Banna, Hasan...42
Al-Batinah..364
al-Bukhari, Sahih..47
Al-Hasa...364
al-Hasan..88, 284, 392
al-Husain...88, 89, 284, 393, 394
Al-Huweirith...118
al-Jawf..453
Al-Jawf..94
Al-Kindi..32, 33
al-Mamun...32, 77, 78
al-Mu'tasim..32
Al-Qaeda...453
Al-Salih Ayyub...205
al-Shabaab..445
Al-Zuhri...82
Alamut..206, 424
Albania...209, 312
Albistan...307

General Index

Albright, W. P. 30
Aleppo 174, 208, 277, 295, 297, 308
Alexander the Great 76, 107, 128, 142, 174, 198, 408, 410, 411, 418
Alexandria 17, 34, 165, 175, 191-200, 209, 210, 215, 216, 230, 232
Algeria 200, 213, 216, 218-220, 223, 226, 228, 229
Algiers 218, 220, 228, 298, 314, 351
Ali 70, 75, 76, 88, 101, 103, 233, 234, 284, 391-395, 420-422, 424, 436, 460
Ali Dashti 41
Allah. 41, 45, 47-49, 52-55, 57, 59-64, 68, 71, 72, 82-84, 90, 92, 94, 96, 98, 99, 101, 102, 115, 122, 124, 145, 222, 235, 387, 393, 397, 398, 455-457, 459, 463
Almohad 226, 227, 234, 267, 272, 273
Almoravides 272, 273, 275
Aloes Island 404
Alopen 16, 142, 160, 161, 169
Aluoben 16
Amanullah Khan 137
America 5, 20, 152, 153, 156, 210, 302, 328, 334
American 432
Amina d. Wahb, Muhammad's mother 39, 43
Amr ibn al Aasi 14, 105, 192, 230
Amr ibn al-As 191
Amu Darya River 140, 141, 143, 147
An Najaf 106, 174, 392
Anatolia 108, 207, 303-305, 307, 317, 318, 376, 381, 419, 453
Andalusia 253, 272
Anglo-Iranian Oil Company 187
Ani 307
anointed 54, 412
Ansar 71, 73, 85, 89, 454
anti-Christian doctrines 337
Antioch 20, 21, 164, 165, 199, 206, 215, 216, 231, 283, 293, 419
apostasy 102, 104-106, 125, 145, 175, 227, 294, 389, 456
Arab Empire 130, 161, 210, 268
Arab League 2
Arab Muslim 132, 171, 192, 194-195, 231
Arab Muslims 88, 109, 131, 143, 175, 227, 234, 271, 389
Arab Spring 80, 210, 454
Arabia....9, 10, 12-14, 16-19, 21, 23, 25-34, 43, 49, 55, 64, 67, 70, 74, 81, 86, 87, 94, 96, 101, 104, 106, 113, 114, 116-119, 122-124, 153, 172, 174, 177, 178, 192, 193, 199, 213, 230, 234, 255, 263, 304, 318, 352, 357, 358, 361, 362, 364, 365, 367, 401, 402, 404-406, 449
Arabia Felix 14, 29, 454
Arabian church 56, 114
Arabian Gulf 357, 359, 363
Arabian Peninsula 18, 19, 26-28, 70, 74, 86, 87, 95, 119, 122, 357-359, 361-363, 406, 465
Arabian Sea 24, 357, 358

Arabic....15, 41, 42, 47, 48, 58, 66, 73, 77, 78, 85, 88, 102, 103, 105, 115, 119, 120, 132, 152, 179, 195, 205, 211, 219, 227, 231, 234, 272, 279, 282, 299, 318, 358, 360, 393-396, 398, 401, 402, 404-406
Arabic language...119, 406
Arabic numerals..162
Aral Sea...161, 304
Aramaic..77, 120
Arbela (Adiabene)...164, 168
Arbil (now Erbil)...163
archaeological team...128
Archbishop of Canterbury..340
Archbishop of Cyprus..342
Ardashir..23, 167, 420
Arian Controversy...165-166
Arianism..165, 166, 260-262
Arians...195, 262
Aristotle..77, 78
Arius..165, 200
Armenia..76, 161, 301, 303, 307, 374, 377, 420, 428
Armenian...149, 180, 181, 206, 317, 318, 371-384, 396
Armenian Cathedral...181
Armenian Christians..180, 318, 382
Armenian community..149
Armenian population...180
Armenians..................168, 181, 184, 206, 282, 295, 340, 371-376, 379, 381, 449
Arnaud, Thomas...30
Arpa Cay River..307
Artaxerxes...408, 417
Aryan..418, 431
Asia..20, 292, 357
Asia Minor..1, 145, 207, 233, 293, 302-304, 306-309
Asir Mountains..360-362, 368
Assad..296, 334
Asturias...270, 271
Aswan...199, 211, 388
Ataturk..309, 335
Athanasius..195, 198
Atlantic Ocean..................1, 3, 5, 20, 27, 35, 108, 131, 195, 219, 229, 235, 259, 266, 333, 461
Atlas Mountains..235
Augustine..195, 196, 216, 219, 220, 225, 228, 253
Aures Mountains..224
Austria..125, 298, 315, 334, 373, 383
Aws...66-68
Awwam..347
Axum/Aksum..16, 17, 31, 348, 358, 366

General Index

Axumite Empire	17
Ayatollah Ruhollah Khomeini	189, 438
Ayn Jalut	206, 297
Ayyubids	204-206, 233, 296, 461
Azerbaijan	206, 315, 377, 428
Azores	255
Bab Iskender (Alexander's Strait)	358
Bab-el-Mandeb	16, 17, 23, 24, 26, 28, 43, 113, 358, 359, 366
Babur	1, 144, 427
Babylon	191, 192
Babylonians	407
Bactria	128, 142, 420
Badhan	28, 114
Badr	74, 86, 88-92, 368
Baghdad	35, 76-78, 140, 141, 161, 182, 205-207, 213, 233, 234, 268, 296, 297, 304, 305, 308, 314, 352, 395, 396, 421, 423, 424, 453
Baha'is	189
Bahnasa	192
Bahrain/Bahrein	23, 27, 80, 344, 360, 363, 454
Bahrite Mamluks	205
Baku	377
Balearic Islands	219
Balkan Peninsula	1, 125, 304, 311, 312, 419
Balkans	127, 179, 233, 235, 280, 317, 374, 375, 389
Balkh	141, 142
Baluchistan	144, 427
Bamian	138
Bamian/Bamiyan Valley	137
Bamiyan Valley	140
Baptist World Alliance	342, 343
Bardaisan	163
Barents Sea	345
Barki	139
Basque	256
Basra	23, 295, 404
Battle of Acre	349
Battle of Actium	11
Battle of Ajnadain	20
Battle of Ayn Jalut	423
Battle of Badr	86, 88-90, 92, 94, 368
Battle of Buwaib	175
Battle of El Alamein	230
Battle of Guadalete	266, 267, 270, 271
Battle of Karbala	393
Battle of Kosovo	1

Battle of Kosovo, Second...........313
Battle of Las Navas de Tolosa...........270, 273
Battle of Manzikert...........1, 207, 301-305, 308, 309, 423, 424
Battle of Mohacs...........2, 314
Battle of Mount Uhud...........74, 90-94, 368
Battle of Musara...........267
Battle of Nehawand...........15, 28, 132, 143, 159, 172, 178, 419, 420, 447
Battle of Nineveh...........420
Battle of Panipat...........1
Battle of Plassey...........1, 79
Battle of Qādisiyyah...........177
Battle of Roncevaux...........276, 277
Battle of Siffeen...........233, 234, 284, 392, 421
Battle of Simancas...........270
Battle of Talas...........4, 16, 132
Battle of the Bridge...........175
Battle of the Great Zab River...........76, 268, 269, 296, 303, 319, 394, 395, 420-422, 453
Battle of the Pyramids...........208
Battle of the Trench...........74, 83, 93-95, 98, 368
Battle of the Yarmuk, First...........107, 281, 282
Battle of the Yarmuk, Second...........108, 176, 287, 296
Battle of Tours...........270, 271, 310
Battle of Trafalgar...........182, 183
Battle of Yemama...........105
bedouin...........29, 31, 87, 102, 106, 174, 177, 363, 397
Bengal...........1, 79
Beni Bekr tribe...........177
Beni Ghassan...........13, 30, 96
Beni Haneefa...........105, 106
Beni Hashim clan...........39, 50, 104, 391, 392
Beni Kalb...........31
Beni Umayya clan...........39, 104, 284, 391
Benjamin of Tudela...........345
Benvenisti, Meron...........287, 325
Beraa...........106
Berbers...........132, 214, 220-224, 232, 234, 235, 259, 271, 273
Bethlehem...........19, 286, 409-411
Bible translation...........201
bishop....116, 141, 162, 164, 165, 194, 209, 217, 221, 226, 227, 231, 256, 257, 260, 282, 306, 405, 406
Bishop...........121, 133, 167, 187, 188, 191, 193, 199, 216, 224, 231, 253, 254
Bishop Simon...........164, 165, 167
bishops...129, 141, 163, 164, 168, 193, 196, 198, 199, 216, 217, 221, 224-227, 231, 256, 260, 264, 306, 404, 461
Black Sea...........14, 23, 31, 45, 194, 304, 315, 376

General Index

Black Stone...44, 75, 99, 101
blind..52, 61, 151, 154, 156, 187, 382
Blumhagen, Dr. Jeanne..151
Blumhagen, Dr. Rex..151
Bodhisattva...140
Boko Haram...333, 445, 455
Bone...200, 216
Bosnia...298, 312, 336
Bosporus...14, 23, 252, 304
Bosra/Busra..10, 96
Bowersock, G. W..319, 320
Britain...333, 429
British....................79, 80, 133, 147-149, 183, 187, 209, 211, 294, 312, 349, 357, 366, 372, 375
British Empire..147, 301
British Raj...148
Buda, Hungary..374
Buddha..137
Buddhism...138, 140
Buddhist..127, 137
Buhaira...40, 41, 44
building of new churches..179, 323
Bukhara..15, 134, 135
Bulgaria...261, 303, 304, 311, 312, 315, 317
Burgos...271
Burnes, Alexander...149
Bush, George...153, 156, 302, 364, 380
Busra/Bosra..10, 404
Bust/Bost...131
Byzantine Empire......2, 12, 14, 26, 28, 32, 45, 94, 107, 172, 191, 192, 281, 302, 305, 306, 309-314, 394, 409
Byzantine rite..121, 299
Byzantine Roman...24, 94, 160
Byzantine Rome..12-14
Byzantine/Persian war..27
Byzantines......1, 14, 18, 24-26, 31, 34, 102, 162, 207, 219, 232, 234, 281, 293, 303, 305, 309, 311, 312, 395
Byzantium...13-15, 18-20, 23-27, 30, 31, 43-45, 87, 94, 95, 102, 106-108, 113, 132, 164, 174, 175, 191, 192, 194, 207, 257, 282, 293, 302, 303, 305, 310, 313, 420
cabotage..34
Cadiz...256, 259
Caesar...32, 165, 192, 414
Caesarea..199, 256, 282
Cairo...191, 204, 206, 211, 296
Calcutta..183, 209

caliph....58, 70, 76, 79, 80, 88, 89, 103-105, 122, 132, 134, 205, 232, 233, 251, 268, 269, 272, 281, 284, 323, 324, 335, 391-395, 421, 459

Caliphate....72, 76, 78-80, 89, 109, 181, 182, 204-207, 233, 267-269, 272, 284, 296, 303-305, 308, 335, 392-395, 455

Cambridge Inter-Faith Program...339
Cambridge University...183, 187, 198
Cambyses...408, 417
camel..44, 49, 72, 74, 86, 89 102, 115, 222, 272, 367, 414
Cane..27
Cantabria...255, 256, 271
Cantabrian Mountains...270
Canton..4
Cappadocia..307
caravan trade..31, 86, 128
Carey, William...183
Cartagena (New Carthage)..256
Carthage.....................................195, 196, 217-219, 222, 224, 226, 227, 229, 232, 255, 256, 453
Caspian..14, 15, 31, 129, 130, 142, 143, 147, 304, 377, 419
Caspian area..143
Caspian Sea...14, 15, 20, 31, 129, 130, 142, 147, 304, 377, 430
Castile..272, 273
Catholic Church.....................................125, 196, 217, 221, 225, 226, 262, 263, 266, 298
Catholicos of all Armenians..340
Caucasus...45, 194, 315, 374
Cawnpore/Kanpur...183
Celsus...57
Central Asia 1, 14-16, 20, 124, 126-133, 135, 136, 140, 141, 143-145, 147, 161, 169, 315, 345, 427
certificate..32
Ceuta..254
Chad...336
Chalcedon..134, 162, 175
Chang'an..15, 142, 160, 161, 169
Charles Martel...1, 271, 310
Chechnya...335, 340
China...................4, 14-16, 23, 35, 104, 127-133, 141-143, 147, 161, 169, 206, 345-347
Chinese..............1, 4, 10, 15, 127, 132, 133, 138, 142, 143, 160, 161, 169, 312, 345, 347, 366, 387
Chinese Tang Dynasty...132, 133, 160
Chosroes...33
Chosroes I..28, 175
Chosroes II..175
Christ......... 2, 21, 32, 51-59, 64, 72, 77, 108, 115, 116, 118, 120-126, 129, 130, 132-134, 138, 142, 143, 147, 148, 150, 151, 154-157, 159-166, 168, 169, 171, 172, 183, 189, 192-198, 200, 204, 212, 213, 216, 219, 222, 224, 225, 231, 254, 259-261, 264, 276, 277, 282-285, 288, 292, 293, 295, 299, 308, 316, 317, 321, 350-353, 374, 375, 377, 378, 381, 384, 401, 404, 405, 407, 410, 412, 459, 462
Christianity..334
Christian Arabs..106

Christian communities............3, 19, 21, 119, 226, 227, 235, 288, 294, 298, 334, 352, 367, 404, 449
Christian converts..155, 156, 261, 449
Christian country...334
Christian era..11, 130, 131, 139, 291, 292
Christian minorities...340
Christian mission..4, 141, 186
Christian missionaries..148, 161, 179
Christian missionary..119, 142, 160
Christian preaching..119
Christianity. .4, 5, 16-20, 26, 28, 32, 35, 108, 116, 119-121, 123, 126, 130, 138-143, 145, 153, 156, 161, 163, 167, 171, 178, 189, 195, 196, 199, 200, 215-218, 223-227, 231, 235, 254, 256-258, 262, 266, 267, 276, 279, 280, 283, 285-287, 289, 293, 296, 299, 302, 306, 318, 333, 352, 377, 384, 388, 389, 401, 403, 405, 406
Christians................3, 5, 19, 25, 28, 32, 40, 53, 54, 56, 59, 60, 64, 92, 109, 113, 116, 117, 120, 445
Christmas..137, 149
Christological issues..166
Christotokos...133, 166
Chronicle of Arbil...163
Chrysostom, St. John...197
church in Arabia..124, 126
church in Arabia,...2
Church of the East...129, 133, 134, 160, 167, 171
CIA..108, 153, 156, 188
Cilicia..205, 206
City of the Prophet..72, 367
Clement of Alexandria..198, 199
Clement of Rome..255
Clysma..11
Codreanu..125
Coimbra..271
Colebrook..182
Communist..347
Communist China..346
Constantine...14, 32, 164, 165, 167, 200, 221, 256, 258
Constantine, monk..227
Constantinople.....2, 3, 15, 27, 78, 133, 165, 166, 177, 184, 191, 193, 194, 207, 213, 219, 252, 299, 303, 305, 309-314, 346, 372, 373, 378, 382, 395, 461
Constantius..17, 18, 257, 405
constitution...80-82, 137, 155, 185, 299, 435
Constitution of Medina..81-83
conversion........14, 105, 114, 133, 143, 145, 147, 206, 217, 223, 224, 262, 263, 267, 279, 283, 288, 294, 318, 377, 389
conversion of Turks to Islam...147
converts.........4, 49, 65, 67, 85, 89, 99, 140, 144, 155, 156, 180, 190, 195, 198, 261, 265, 267, 272, 318, 383, 407, 426, 454, 462
coppersmith..137

Coptic bishops..199
Coptic Christians..192, 193, 195, 200, 210
Coptic Church...192-194, 196, 211
Coptic language...201, 207, 223, 401
Copts....................................95, 192-194, 196, 197, 205-207, 209-212, 295, 352
Cordoba/Cordova...234, 256, 269-272, 280, 395
Coria..271
cornerstone..153, 200
corrupt church..124-126
Corsica..219
Council of Carthage..225
Council of Chalcedon...134, 193, 195, 200, 299, 306
Council of Constantinople...165
Council of Nicaea...200, 256
Council of Toledo..260, 262
coup d'etat...188, 190, 433
Crassus...11, 411
Croatia...312, 374
Croatian..125, 382
crucifixion...59, 60, 283
Crusader Jerusalem..203
Crusader states..31, 205
Ctesiphon......................4, 15, 143, 161, 162, 164, 165, 167, 174, 177, 178, 268
Cultural Revolution..347
Cush..348
Cyprus...342
Cyrenaica...230-233, 266, 320
Cyrene...21, 195, 216, 218, 231
Cyril..195, 222, 378, 461
Cyrus the Great..72, 191, 408, 410, 417
Cyrus, Bishop..193, 194, 434, 461
Dahna Desert..362
Dailamite...129
Dalmatia..255, 374
Damascus.........10, 13, 31, 35, 44, 74-76, 79, 89, 108, 177, 203, 233, 234, 251, 263, 268, 269, 271, 282, 284, 288, 296, 297, 368, 391-394, 404, 420
Dammam..364
Danube River...1, 261
Dar al-Harb, the House of War...179
Dar al-Islam, the House of Islam..179
Dardanelles...1, 23, 252, 304, 309, 372
Darius..11, 376, 408, 410, 414, 417, 418
Dark Ages..35
Dashti, Ali..41
daughters of Allah..41

General Index

David	43, 82, 118, 138, 285
Dayr Hind	406
dead	28, 52, 60-62, 92, 121, 180, 205, 212, 307
death penalty	189, 443
Dedan	348
Dehqani-Tafti, Bishop	187
Deirin	404
Delhi	137, 428
Demetrius, Bishop	199
democracy	80, 184-186, 266, 302, 347, 413, 438
Deraa Gap	107
destruction of churches	139, 206, 231, 326
Devastich	132
Dhahran	364
dhimma	179, 455
dhimmi	145, 179, 211, 375, 383, 455
dhimmi status [see Glossary]	323
dhimmis	323
dhimmitude	145, 455
Dhofar	23, 364
Dhu 'l-Hijja	97, 399, 457, 466
Dhu Nuwas	17, 18, 24, 25, 113, 116, 358, 406
Diatessaron	162, 182, 401, 402
Didascalia	199
digital Bibles	184
Dioscorides	78
Disraeli, Benjamin	133, 375
Djam	137
Djibouti	18
Dome of the Rock	120, 286, 321, 351
Donatist	125, 196, 220-223, 225, 226
Donatist Church	196, 220, 225
Donatists	195, 196, 217, 220-222, 225, 226
Door of Tears	17, 23, 358
dragon	353
drinking wine	189, 190
Dubai	359
Dumah	94, 95
Dumat al-Jandal	94, 453
Dunhuang	127
Dutch	79, 301
Dutch Empire	301
Dyophysite	162, 456, 461
East-West caravan route	130
Eban, Abba	2, 289, 359

Ebionite..48, 49, 118
Ebionite church/sect...40, 118
Ebro River...252, 345
Ecbatana...408
Edessa...160, 162-164, 306, 307, 377
Edom..348
Egypt.......14, 20, 76, 77, 79, 80, 83, 95, 109, 126, 132, 141, 165, 169, 175, 191-201, 203-216, 219, 220, 223, 227, 229-233, 235, 268, 282, 284, 297, 303, 305, 318, 320, 334, 336, 344, 345, 347, 349, 352, 359, 365, 367, 388, 394, 396, 429, 431, 454
election...143, 180, 185, 186, 263, 306, 444
elephant...26, 39, 42, 176, 218, 253
elitist movement..336, 344
Emanuel...133
emperor-king...185
England..428, 437
Ephesus...166, 299
Ephthalite...130
Episcopal Church...187
Erbil (formerly Arbil)...163
Erdogan, Tayyip..336, 344
Eritrea..16, 18, 348, 367
Ethiopia.................................16-19, 24-26, 28, 29, 43, 66, 113, 199, 348, 358, 365, 406, 414
Ethiopian-Christian vs. Yemeni-Jewish conflict...24
Ethiopians..17-19, 24, 28, 31, 113, 406
Euphrates River....13, 30, 76, 106, 108, 119, 161, 162, 174, 176, 205, 233, 302, 303, 346-347, 361, 377, 379, 392, 393, 405, 445
Europe.......1, 2, 5, 20, 34, 35, 99, 109, 127, 219, 226, 251, 252, 258, 261, 265, 266, 271, 277, 280, 292, 293, 297, 298, 304, 305, 309-315, 318, 333, 345, 358, 375, 389
European..347
European Union..265, 383
Eusebius...198, 199, 256
Evangelical Lutheran Church..343
evangelism..3, 20, 21, 114, 141, 169, 215, 449
execution of Christian converts..155
expiation..68
Ezana...348
Ezekiel...346
Ezion-Geber..10
Fadak...114
Faiyum...192
Fakhry, Ahmed..30
Far East...129, 130, 422
Far Eastern..127, 130, 161
Fargana..132
Fars...33

Farsi	128, 150, 180, 182, 183, 188
Fatimah	39, 47, 88, 233, 368
Fatimid	213
Fatimid Dynasty	226, 396
Fatimids	77, 79, 204, 214, 233, 303, 387
feudal landlords	185
fijar war	43
Firdausi	424
fire pit	25, 115, 116
First Battle of the Yarmuk	107
First Crusade	204, 278, 305
First Pledge of al-'Aqaba	67, 68
five pillars of Islam, the	397
foreign policy	152, 334, 335
France	1, 18, 182, 209, 210, 213, 218, 228, 259, 265, 267, 270, 271, 276, 277, 288, 298, 299, 310, 316, 345, 371, 424, 428, 429, 431, 438
frankincense	32, 365
freedom of religion	82, 124, 156, 337, 339
French	79, 80, 183, 184, 190, 203, 208, 209, 270, 276-278, 298, 301, 314, 357, 374, 405
French Empire	301
French Republic	208
Friedman, George	335
Friesen, Dr. Herb & Ruth	154
Fujairah	359
Gaihan	307
Galen	77, 78
Galicia	256, 260, 271
Galilee	53
Gallipoli	309, 312, 313, 372, 389
Ganges	183
Gardiz	131
Gaul	257-259, 261, 270, 271, 276
Gaza	10, 108, 283, 344
Ge'ez	16
genealogy	84, 128
General el-Sisi	40, 334
Genghis Khan	139, 144, 207, 427
Genoese	31
geopolitical	3, 335
Georgia	194, 428
German	127, 128, 190, 200, 371, 372, 380, 431, 434, 448
Germanic peoples	257
Germanic tribes	35
Germany	260, 265, 371-373, 381, 428, 430, 431
Ghana	388

Ghassan, Beni..13, 30, 96
ghaza way of life...144, 427
Ghazna...131, 144, 428
Ghaznavids...426, 427
Ghazni..1, 144, 243, 422, 426, 427, 438
Ghur...131
Ghurid Empire..137
Gibraltar, Mt..219, 254
Gilan..129
Gilanian...129
Girgis..207, 209
Gog...345, 349
Golden Horn...14
good deeds..337
good works...119, 228, 337
Gospel Lectionary..128
Gospel of John...160
Gospel of Mark..197, 198, 223
Gospel of Matthew..128, 407
Gouraud, Henri...203
Granada...79, 265, 271, 273, 310
Grand Muftis..336
Great Britain..................1, 147, 148, 182-184, 187, 209, 210, 257, 288, 299, 317, 363, 372, 428
Great Zab River...171, 284, 395
greater pilgrimage...75, 97, 399, 457
Greece...210, 213, 304, 312, 314, 345, 371, 418, 453
Greek.....9, 14, 32, 48, 54, 77, 78, 109, 128, 162, 166, 174, 194, 198, 199, 207, 232, 261, 304, 372, 401, 405, 419
Greek language..109, 197, 198
Greek Orthodox..194, 296, 299
Grimme, Hubert..33
Griswold, Eliza...4
Guadalajara..271
Guadalete River..254, 259, 264
Guadalquivir River..271
Guangzhou..4
guide..52, 55, 71, 90, 98, 224
Guillaume, A...42
Gujarat..365, 427
Gulf of Aden..9, 16, 23, 357-359, 366
Gulf of Aqaba...10, 30, 360
Gulf of Oman...357-359, 364
Gulf of Suez..9, 11
Gulf of Zula..366
Habibia..150, 151

General Index

Habsburg	125, 298, 312, 314, 315
Habsburg Empire	312, 314
Hadhramaut/Hadramawt	19, 23, 27, 113, 361, 366, 367
hadith	20, 102, 122, 457
Hafiz	182
Hafsah	88
Hagar	404
Hajar Mountain range	364
hajj	67, 68, 97, 100, 399
Haleema	43
Ham	348
Hamadan	178
Hamas	344
Han	4, 15
Hangchow	4, 15
Hangzhou	4
Hanif	41, 42
Hannibal	217-219, 252, 255
Hapsburg Empire	2
Harbi	179
Harper, Dr. Howard	151
Harun al-Rashid	76, 77, 182, 421
Hasan	421
Hasan al-Banna	42
Hebrew Bible	342
Hebron	20
Hegira	39, 66, 69, 86, 166, 458
Hejaz	357
Hejaz/Hijaz	361
Hellenic	77, 130, 312
Heraclius	4, 13, 20, 45, 95, 107, 108, 191-194, 281, 282, 409, 420, 461
Herat	137, 139, 140, 142, 147, 156
herdsman	43
Herzegovina	298, 312
Hezbollah	344
Hierapolis	116
Hijaz	25
Hijaz railway	11
Hijra	56, 66, 69, 71-74, 86, 88, 119, 169, 172, 391, 401, 454, 458
Himyar	18, 19, 406
Himyarite kingdom	19, 24, 25, 368
Himyarites	18, 24, 116, 117, 405
Himyaritic	17, 119
Hinayana Buddhism	140
Hindu	14, 124, 138, 144, 161, 384, 388

Hindu Kush Mountains	14, 161
Hinduism	138
Hippalus	9
Hippo	195, 216
Hippocrates	78
Hira	27, 47, 106, 174, 175, 177, 404-406
Hira, Mt.	47
Hispano-Roman Catholic	261
historical documents	138
Hodeida	360, 365
Hofuf oasis	364
Holy Spirit	52-54, 57, 61, 197, 216, 292, 345
Hooghly River	183
hostility towards Christianity	108
house church	188, 189
House of Wisdom	76, 77, 182, 314, 421
Houthi	347, 358
Houthis	345
Hsianfu	142
Hsüan-tsang, Buddhist monk	138
Hsüan-tsung, emperor of the Tang Dynasty	133
Hudaybiyyah	74, 93, 97
Hulagu Khan	206, 207, 308, 421, 423, 424, 453
Hunafa	41
Hunayn ibn Ishaq	77, 78, 182
Hungarians	2, 313, 314
Hungary	125, 235, 298, 314, 315, 374
Hunza	154
Husayn	421
Hussein, Saddam	204, 296, 348, 364, 394, 444
Huweirith	118
Iblis	56, 58
Ibn Hauqal (Hawqal)	139, 140
Ibn Hisham	42, 81
Ibn Ishaq	32, 39, 42, 44, 49, 66, 68, 69, 81, 102, 457
Ibn Khaldun	12, 13, 219
ideological	347
Idris	348
Ignatius of Antioch	164
ilaf	458
illiterate	40
imam	68, 103, 104, 335, 395, 396, 436, 437, 453, 459
imperialism	12, 79, 348
incense	32
Incense Trail	30

General Index

India....1, 3, 5, 9-12, 15, 16, 20, 27, 30, 31, 34, 35, 79, 108, 135, 138, 144, 147-149, 169, 182, 183, 199, 209, 215, 267, 303, 315, 333, 347, 367, 404, 427-429
Indian 15, 148, 218, 333, 419
Indian Ocean 9, 12, 15, 16, 23, 26, 27, 30, 358, 364, 365, 434
Indic 130
Indies 4
Indonesia 3, 11, 80, 333, 344, 387, 388
Indus River 144, 408
inferior status 114
inspiration 48, 49, 53, 120, 223, 402
inter-tribal Arabian warfare 12
International Afghan Mission 151
international market 5
Inviolable Place of Worship 99, 101
Iram 67
Iran........12-15, 17, 19, 20, 23, 27, 28, 43-45, 94, 124, 126, 132, 147, 150, 159-167, 169, 171, 172, 174, 178, 180-190, 206, 315, 318, 334, 335, 345-347, 349, 352, 360, 361, 377, 392, 394-396, 407-413, 417-420, 422-435, 437-449
Iran-Iraq War 190, 394
Iran, division of 147
Iran's budget 186
Iranian....2, 17, 108, 128-130, 137, 140, 141, 143, 159-164, 167-169, 171, 172, 177, 178, 180-182, 185, 189, 190, 303, 395, 407-411, 413, 418, 445
Iranian Christians 160, 168, 182, 189, 411
Iranian nationalism 181
Iranian Revolution 190, 335, 441
Iraq.....15, 20, 32, 76, 88, 89, 123, 163, 168, 174, 204, 268, 284, 288, 296, 299, 348, 360-362, 364, 392, 393, 423, 428
irrigation system 28, 32, 205
Isaac 84, 116, 285
Isfahan 180-182, 184, 187, 188, 414
Ishaq 421
Ishaq, Ibn 32, 39, 42, 44, 49, 66, 68, 69, 81, 102, 457
Ishu 'Yab III 134, 140, 171
ISIS 80, 329, 335, 348, 392, 445, 459
Islam 169, 347, 445
Islam, convert to 65, 145, 180, 266, 317, 387, 391
Islam, converts to 65, 66, 85, 99, 144, 272, 383, 426, 454, 462
Islam, expansion of 3, 5, 175, 178, 180
Islam, history of 77, 269, 284, 339
Islam, rise of 4, 15, 23, 26, 28, 31, 32, 34, 119, 124, 358, 366, 405
Islam, the five pillars 397
Islamic armies 109, 225, 310
Islamic conquest 1, 35, 159, 201, 283, 293, 319
Islamic empire 3, 20, 21, 165, 234, 254, 284, 287, 303, 335, 394, 420, 447
Islamic expansion 5, 384

Islamic history............1, 20, 64, 105, 108, 169, 325, 388, 457
Islamic military............34, 135, 216, 276
Islamic movement............20, 33, 49, 90, 93, 172, 336
Islamic period............14, 139, 141, 182
Islamic Republic............189, 441, 443
Islamic resurgence............136, 190, 266
Islamic revolution............184, 185
Islamic rule............64, 125, 144, 206, 296, 427
Islamic world............105, 190, 213, 280, 334, 335
Islamic-nation-state............80
Islamization............227, 235, 288, 377
Ismaili............195, 204, 422, 459
Israel............54, 60, 61, 82-84, 116, 197, 210, 220, 283, 344, 345, 347-351, 359, 368, 373, 377, 381
Istanbul............15, 78, 79, 208, 280, 297, 312, 315, 316, 336, 372, 395
Isthmus of Suez............208
Italian merchants............31
Italy............30, 152, 214, 255, 258, 261, 277, 312, 314, 345, 419
Jabr............40, 41
Jacob............84, 350, 407
Jafar............95, 204, 459
Japan............346
Java............3, 365, 387, 388
Jaxartes............139
Jedda............336, 360
Jehovah............63, 348, 350, 351, 407, 412
Jerez............254, 259
Jerusalem............19, 20, 73, 74, 80, 81, 96, 113, 120, 138, 159, 197, 203, 204, 282, 283, 285-287, 291, 292, 325, 345, 351, 392, 404, 407, 409-411
Jesus Christ............32, 59, 169, 193, 197, 212, 292, 331, 342, 351, 352, 377, 410
Jesus is a mercy............58
Jesus is a revelation............57
Jesus is like Adam............55-57, 59, 122
Jewish Christians............113, 160, 407
Jewish population............24, 138
Jewish priests............116
Jewish state............345
Jews............2, 17, 24, 57, 59, 60, 64-67, 69, 73, 82-85, 94, 108, 109, 113, 114, 116, 120, 124, 125, 129, 145, 159, 189, 197, 205, 235, 257, 262, 263, 273, 279, 283, 285, 289, 293, 295, 351, 368, 378, 383, 387, 401, 404, 407, 409-411, 449, 455, 456
jihad............34, 85, 152, 273, 275, 277, 352, 397
jihadist............335, 455
jinn............48
jizya............179, 230-232, 320, 459
Johannitius............78
John Mark............197

General Index

Jordan	20, 95, 96, 107, 283, 334, 336, 348, 361, 362, 369, 441
Jordan River	107, 281
Judaism	19, 24, 113, 120, 262, 286, 407
Judaism's virulent anti-Christian stance	24
Judea	410
Julfa	180, 181
Justinian	193, 219
Ka'ba/Kaaba	25-26, 41, 43, 44, 49, 67, 70, 73, 75, 81, 86, 96-101, 399, 460
Kabul	15, 138, 148-157, 426, 428
kafir	79, 157, 375, 460, 465
Kairouan/Kairwan/Qayrawan	227, 268, 269, 396
Kaleb, King of Abyssinia	25
Kandahar	428
Kao, General	133
Karbala	89, 393, 394, 421, 434
Karka (modern Kirkuk)	168
Karzai, Hamid	155, 156
Kashgar	127
Kashmir	15
Kasu	348
Kathiawar Peninsula	144
Kavadh	4
Kazakhstan	20, 130, 135, 346
Kenya	333
Kerak	95
Kerala	144
Khadija	40, 41, 43, 44, 47-49, 65, 73, 118
Khaibar/Khaybar	83, 114, 368
Khalid ibn al Waleed	14, 95, 104, 105, 108, 369, 397
khalifa	58, 104, 455, 459
Kharijite	421
Khartoum	336, 348
Khazaria	133
Khazraj	66-68
Khomeini	182, 185, 189, 190, 335, 394, 396, 426, 435, 438, 439, 441, 442, 444-446
Khomeini Revolution	72, 179, 184-188, 190, 440
Khosrow II (Chosroes II)	175
Khota	404
Khurasan/Khorasan	131, 134, 140, 142, 394, 427, 445
Khusrau	45
Khusraw	420
Khusraw II	420
Khuza'a	98, 99
Khwarizm	135
Khwarizmians	135

Khyber Pass..144
King Farouk...210, 431
King of kings..176, 178, 185, 351, 433, 444
kings...346, 347
Kirkuk..168
Koran. .20, 25, 27, 41, 43, 45, 51-64, 69, 71, 81, 84, 92, 94, 115, 116, 119, 120, 122, 124, 233, 270, 322, 397, 398, 402, 404, 455
Kosovo...313
Kufa...76, 88, 89, 284, 392-394, 420
Kufic..120
Kurdish...163, 168, 204, 376, 387
Kurds..163, 376, 382
Kush..348
Kuwait..24, 360, 363, 364, 405
Kyrgyz..136
Kyrgyzstan..1, 16, 20, 130, 133, 135, 136, 143, 346
Lake Goeljuk..379
Lake Van..207, 302, 379
Lakhm..30
Lakhmids..13
language of Najran..119
Laroui, Abdallah..349
Larsen, Howard...150, 151
Latin..............................109, 166, 207, 209, 217, 220, 222, 223, 227, 257, 294, 306, 310, 314
Latin Vulgate..223
Lebanon...283, 288, 298, 299, 345
lectionary..128, 133
Lee Kuan Yew...347
Legionnaires...125
Leo, Bishop..193
Leo, Pope IX...310
Leon..271
leper..52, 61
Levant..109, 132, 216, 460
Libya..80, 214, 216, 218, 219, 226, 229-233, 348
Libyan Desert..218
Licinius...32
Lighthouse Mosque..4
lights in the world...126, 445
Limes Arabicus...94
literacy...55, 67
living waters...138
Loazim...346
Louata Tribe of Berbers...132, 226, 231, 232, 320
Lusitania..262

General Index

Lytton, Governor General ... 148
Ma'rib ... 19, 29, 347, 368
MacCulloch, Diarmaid ... 352
Macedonia ... 312, 316, 372
Madras ... 183
Madras/Chennai ... 183
madrasa/madrassa/madrassah ... 153, 316, 460
Madrid ... 260
Maghreb/Maghrib ... 229, 230, 232-235, 453, 461
Magi ... 159, 167, 407-414
Magney, Gordon & Grace ... 154, 156
Mahayana Buddhism ... 140
Mahmud of Ghazni ... 1, 144, 422, 427
Mahra Coast ... 366
Majorca ... 219
Malacca ... 388
Malay Peninsula ... 11
Mamluks ... 205, 206, 208, 296, 297, 307, 308, 461
Manichaeism ... 16, 143
Manji, Irshad ... 287
Manzikert ... 305
Mao Tse-tung ... 346
Maoist dictum ... 346
Mar Aksenaya ... 116
Mar Paul ... 116
Marco Polo ... 3, 312, 387
Marga ... 129
Marib ... 29, 30
Marib Dam ... 29, 30, 454
maritime trade ... 23
Marj Dabiq ... 208, 297, 308
Mark, Gospel of ... 197, 198, 223
Marmara Sea ... 14, 303, 304, 372
marriages ... 88, 89, 180, 392
Martel, Charles ... 1, 271, 310
Martyn, Henry ... 182-184, 414, 447
martyrology ... 115
martyrs ... 92, 115, 116, 168, 280
martyrs of Najran ... 117
Marwan ... 76, 268, 394
Marxists ... 152, 154
Mary ... 52-55, 57, 64, 118, 133, 140, 166, 195-197, 212, 404
Mary, concubine of Muhammad ... 73
Mashhad ... 150, 186, 187
Mashiha-zakha ... 163, 164

Mashmahiq..404
Matthew, Gospel of...62, 128, 407, 410, 411
Maydi..366
Maysara..44
Mazandaran..129
Mecca........18, 25, 26, 30, 31, 33, 40-42, 44, 47, 49, 66, 67, 69-71, 73-75, 81, 83, 85-87, 89-91, 93, 95-101, 114, 117-119, 122, 169, 172, 357, 360, 367, 368, 391-393
Medain...15, 174, 177
Medical Assistance Program...151
Medina......15, 28, 35, 47, 56, 64, 66-75, 81-87, 89-91, 93-95, 97, 98, 100, 102-106, 114, 118, 121, 123, 169, 172, 178, 194, 233, 234, 284, 296, 357, 360, 367-369, 392, 399, 401, 420, 453, 454, 458, 462
Mediterranean....14, 15, 20, 21, 24, 26, 30-32, 34, 76, 107, 124, 175, 195, 208, 209, 215, 216, 219, 221, 229-231, 235, 255, 266, 268, 270, 281-283, 288, 291, 292, 295-297, 299, 304, 312, 347, 358, 361, 362, 367, 375, 460, 461
Mediterranean Africa..195
Medyan...41
Mekka...30, 31, 100, 101
Melkite Church..192, 195
Memphis..196
Mennonite Church..340
Meroe...348
Merv...134, 140, 141, 171, 178
Mesopotamia...76, 133, 159, 168, 232, 357, 405, 407
Messiah...26, 53, 54, 59, 60, 64, 118, 226, 231, 260, 350, 351, 407
Miaphysite..162, 456, 461
Middle East............108, 124, 127, 181, 185, 189, 190, 196, 283, 289, 294, 304, 318, 347, 349, 378
Middle Eastern..334
Middle-Persian..128
mihrab...73, 100
Milan..32
millat...164, 461
Minaret of Djam..137
Ministry of National Guidance...187, 188
Minorca..219
miracles...52, 404
mirbad..72
mobeds..130, 167
Mocha...365, 366
Mogul Empire..1, 79
Mohammad Reza Shah Pahlavi.........72, 185, 186, 190, 363, 396, 418, 432, 435, 437-444, 446-448
Mohammed Daoud..152, 154
monarchical bishops...141
monarchy...184-186, 262, 263, 396, 440, 442
monasteries...19, 35, 108, 142, 193, 194, 294, 314
Mongol..79, 127, 128, 139, 161, 206, 207, 297, 308, 423

Mongols..................................181, 205, 206, 213, 214, 296, 297, 304, 307, 395, 423-425
monophysite...192, 194, 200, 282, 461
Monophysites..193-195, 299, 405, 461
monotheism..49, 60, 70, 97, 465
Monothelite...193, 194, 461
monsoon...9, 11, 12, 30
Montenegro...312
monument...16, 120, 138, 142, 160, 161, 286, 408
Morocco.................1, 20, 132, 195, 214, 226, 231, 234, 267, 273, 303, 334, 336, 344, 465
Mosaddegh...184, 186, 187
Moscow..135, 184, 374
Moses..43, 48, 55, 83, 84, 116, 118, 401, 412
mosque.........4, 73, 100, 103, 120, 135, 136, 139, 142, 153, 191, 203, 205, 211, 265, 282, 285, 286, 316, 321, 351, 392, 461, 466
Mosul..163, 171
Mota...94-96, 101-103, 105, 369
Mother of God...166
Mt. Carmel..209
Mt. Hira...47
Mt. Uhud..75, 90, 91, 93, 95, 105, 106, 368
Mu'awiya..72, 75, 89, 109, 233, 251, 268, 284, 391-393, 395
muezzin..68, 398, 462
Mughal...267
Mughal Dynasty...144, 427
muhajir...70, 462
Muhajirun...70, 85, 87, 462
Muhammad.......9, 14, 26-28, 32, 34, 39-41, 43-45, 47-49, 51, 52, 55-57, 64-75, 81-83, 85-99, 101-107, 113-115, 118-124, 169, 172, 177, 194, 207, 222, 276, 281, 296, 352, 367, 368, 384, 391, 392, 394, 396, 397, 399, 401-404
Muhammad Ali..207, 209, 210, 434
Muhammad, the Arabian Prophet...3, 169, 200, 284
Muhammad's wives..73, 93, 103
Muhjara...427
Mujahideen..124, 152-154
Mukalla..366
mullahs...185, 190, 440
Mus'ab..68
Musailama...105, 398
Musandam Peninsula...359
Muscat...364
Muslim......1, 42, 69, 79-82, 85, 86, 88, 90-96, 98, 100, 102, 104-108, 115, 117, 120-122, 124-126, 131-133, 135-137, 139, 143-145, 148, 154-157, 159, 163, 164, 171, 172, 174-180, 183, 185, 189, 191, 192, 195, 203-207, 209, 211, 213, 222, 226, 230-232, 235, 251-254, 257, 266-268, 270-273, 275-277, 280, 282, 284, 286-289, 296, 299, 304, 306, 310, 315, 317, 318, 321, 333-336, 344, 345, 348, 350, 352, 353, 357, 383, 384, 387, 389, 391, 394, 395, 397, 403, 405, 427, 455, 456, 458, 460, 463, 465

Muslim Brotherhood...40, 42, 80, 96
Muslim conquest....................1, 35, 108, 109, 132, 134, 178, 220, 229, 232, 233, 235, 293
Muslim converts...180, 265, 318
Muslim empire..1, 3, 76, 95, 169, 180
Muslim era...................4, 56, 69, 71, 103, 105, 119, 140, 219, 264, 272, 462
Muslim initiative...337, 394
Muslim invasion..262, 268, 271
Muslim minorities...190, 336
Muslim missionary activity..179
Muslim Wars of Conquest..106, 107
Muslim world......1, 51, 72, 76, 79, 80, 126, 163, 178, 180, 191, 203, 213, 268, 280, 284, 288, 304, 328, 329, 334, 335, 339, 341, 344, 348, 350, 353, 389, 430, 431, 435, 449, 455, 466
Muslim-Mecca Treaty..98
Muthanna..175, 177
Muwayhiba, Abu..102
Nabataean...9, 10, 120
nabi..81, 82
Nader Shah...426, 428
Nadir...66, 83, 84
Nafud Desert..361, 362, 463
Nairobi..199
Najaf..392
Najd...12, 27, 360-362, 365
Najran...19, 24, 28, 51, 55, 56, 64, 113-123, 169, 367, 404, 406
Najrani Christians......................................19, 28, 56, 82, 113-115, 117-123, 406
Najrani church...115, 117, 119
Nakhla...87
Namus...48
Napoleon..184, 208, 209, 298, 349, 374, 429
naqib...68
Narbonne..270
nation-state..80, 334
National Association of Evangelicals...344
National Organization of Ophthalmic Rehab..151
Nazarenes...165
Nazareth...54, 130, 159, 206, 297, 350, 351
Negus..65
Nehawand..178
Nestorian..141, 161, 166, 405, 421
Nestorian bishop..193
Nestorian Christian..421, 423
Nestorian Christians..27, 78, 449
Nestorian Church...106, 128, 130, 134, 139, 160, 167, 420
Nestorian controversy...133, 166
Nestorian Monument..16, 142, 161

General Index

Nestorian Patriarch..........141
Nestorians..........4, 95, 127, 404
Nestorius..........133, 134, 166, 167
Netherlands..........184, 265, 312
New Testament.......41, 53, 54, 59, 119, 125, 133, 138, 140, 141, 150, 160, 182-184, 198, 200, 212, 216, 223, 306, 414, 421, 447
New Testament pattern..........141
Newcastle..........218
Nicaea..........200, 256, 303, 305
Nicene Council..........165
Nicene Creed..........165, 166
Nicephorus..........13
Nigeria..........333, 445, 455
Nile River..........9, 11, 191, 198, 205
Nile Valley..........199
nirvana..........140
Nisibis..........162
nomads..........3, 31, 90, 128, 130, 357, 376, 464
Nomads..........131
NOOR..........151, 154
Noorin TV..........155
North Africa..........20, 76, 79, 109, 124, 132, 194-196, 213, 215-235, 251, 253, 254, 257, 259, 261, 263, 265-268, 272, 273, 298, 315, 318, 396, 461
North Asia..........127
North Korea..........347
northern alliance..........156
nuclear power..........335
Numidia..........219, 220, 223, 268
Nur Muhammad Taraki..........152
Nuristan..........132
Nyak..........151
Odes of Solomon..........160, 182
Oman..........23, 24, 27, 32, 113, 336, 359, 362-365, 404
Omdurman..........115
Oran..........218
Organization of Islamic Cooperation/Conference (OIC)..........336
organized Christianity..........5, 126, 163, 235
Orient..........119, 216
Origen..........57, 199, 200, 216
orphan..........39, 382
Orthodox Catholic..........256
Orthodox Christians..........17, 18, 143, 293
Orthodox Church..........18, 24, 95, 192-194, 282, 295, 298, 387
Orthodox Hispano-Catholic..........256
Orthodoxy..........17, 18

Osama bin Laden..136, 153, 156, 203, 228
Othman Bin Al-Huweirith..118
Othman ibn Talha...14, 105
Othman, Caliph...100, 233, 307
Ottoman.........1, 2, 13, 78, 79, 182, 194, 207-209, 233, 234, 280, 294, 295, 297, 298, 303, 305, 309, 315, 316, 373, 376, 377, 379, 380, 382, 383, 389, 463
Ottoman Empire...2, 79, 182, 208, 294, 295, 297, 298, 301, 307, 309, 312, 314-316, 371, 372, 374, 375, 377-379, 384, 422, 423, 463
Ottoman Turkish...373, 376, 381
Ottoman Turks.................1, 15, 207, 213, 288, 297, 303-306, 309, 310, 312, 314, 316, 395, 423, 424
Ottomans...213, 378, 422, 424, 426
Oxus River...130, 140, 142, 143, 445
Oxus Valley...141
Oxus-Jaxartes basin..130, 161
pact of alliance...122
Pact of Umar..123
Padwick..183
Pahlavi Dynasty...433
Pakistan..21, 73, 80, 140, 144, 149, 152-154, 157, 185, 287, 288, 346, 427
Palestine..2, 10, 19, 31, 66, 74, 76, 107-109, 199, 204, 209, 230, 232, 278, 282-284, 288, 293, 299, 305, 318, 345, 349, 351, 367, 377, 409
Palmyra...11
Pamir Mountains..14-16, 128, 130, 133
Pamplona..271, 345
Panama Canal...359
Panch...132
Pantaenus..199, 215
Panthera..57
paradise..60, 67, 103, 224, 278
Parlak..3
Parthia...10
Parthian...142, 414, 419, 420, 426
Parthian Dynasty...28, 159, 161, 411
Parthian Empire...15, 129, 160, 407, 411, 445
Parthian Iran...12, 159
Parthian-Persian Empire...11, 15
Parthians..12, 28, 159, 160, 419
Pasargadae...408, 410, 413, 414
Pashtun..153
Pashtunistan..152
Pashtuns..152
Paul, apostle....................................53, 92, 126, 223, 254-256, 305, 352, 412, 419
peace.....69, 71, 98, 103, 131, 134, 210, 221, 235, 263, 336, 337, 339, 343, 351, 366, 383, 388, 410
Peace of Westphalia..334
Pelusium...191

Pendzhikent..132
Pentecost...159, 197, 216, 283, 291, 292, 407, 412, 419
Perim, Island of...358
persecution.....17, 24, 25, 32, 49, 65, 85, 87, 115, 126, 131, 134, 139, 165, 167-169, 180, 186, 188, 189, 193, 194, 196, 201, 212, 213, 220, 260, 263, 280, 288, 405
Persepolis...182, 408, 418, 419
Persia....31, 45, 72, 107, 113, 140, 142, 143, 164, 165, 167, 168, 171, 174-178, 181, 183, 284, 305, 315, 345, 346, 376, 394, 405, 417-419, 426, 430, 433, 434, 449
Persian......11-13, 15, 23, 27, 28, 33, 35, 45, 74, 77, 93, 94, 106, 107, 113, 114, 128, 134, 142, 143, 148, 160-162, 164, 167, 168, 171, 172, 174-178, 182-184, 186, 192, 304, 317, 358, 359, 363, 376, 394, 398, 414, 418
Persian Gulf..10, 15, 23, 27, 113, 161, 357-359, 363
Persians.......11, 14, 18, 24, 26-28, 31, 32, 45, 76, 113, 175, 177-179, 181, 191, 192, 207, 281, 344, 358, 394, 395, 409
Peshawar...154
pestilence..349
Peter, Apostle..115, 159, 197, 216, 292, 411
Petra..9-11
Phasis..193, 194, 461
Philips, Wendell..30
Philo..198
Philostorgius..18
pilgrimage......25, 43, 49, 67, 70, 75, 97, 98, 100, 101, 118, 138, 159, 186, 305, 357, 392, 394, 399, 406, 466
Pisans..31
plague...27, 311, 312, 349
Plato..77, 78
Pliny the Elder..11
plowshares..352
Poitiers..270, 271
Poland...371, 374
political power...346, 347
polygamists...93
polygamy..92
polytheists...68, 124, 142
Pondicherry..11
Pope Benedict XVI...336
Portugal...271
Portugese..79
pre-Islamic..12, 18, 29, 31, 128, 140, 141, 167, 182, 401, 404-406, 434
Presbyterians...210, 448
Presbyterians, American..187
priests...41, 54, 84, 116, 167, 378, 409, 410, 413
printing press..181
Pristina...313
proclaim...49, 54, 68, 98, 103, 226

Prophet who can neither read nor write	40, 404
prophetic passages in the Koran	27, 45, 94
proselytizing tool	4
Punjab	76, 144, 328, 427
Put	348
putsch	190
Pyrenees Mountains	1, 252, 255, 258, 261, 270, 271, 276, 310
Qaddafi	348
Qādisiyyah	176
Qajar Dynasty	429, 433, 435
Qajars	429, 434, 440
Qara Mountains	365
Qasim	47, 139, 144, 427
Qatar	360, 363, 364, 404, 405
Qattara Depression	230
Qaynuqa	66, 82, 83
Qayrawan/Kairwan	227, 268, 269
qibla/qiblah	73, 74, 96, 99, 100, 321, 461, 463
Quraish Tribe	39, 49, 87, 284, 391, 392
Quraish/Quraysh	43, 65, 66, 70, 82, 86, 97, 98, 104, 105, 177, 402
Quraysh Tribe	49, 458, 463
Qurayzah	66, 83
Qutayba	134, 135, 445
Qutb, Sayyid	335
Rabat	336
Rabi' al-Awal	102
Ramadan	47, 398, 399, 463
Ras al-Hadd	364
Ras Musandam	359
Ras Tanura	364
Rawalpindi	140
razzia	85, 86, 89
Red Sea	9-11, 16, 18, 23, 24, 26, 30, 43, 86, 89, 117, 208, 209, 357-361, 365-368, 465
reference point	346
religion of Abraham	41, 42
Religious Freedom Report	123
religious police	124
remnant	445
restrictions	21, 179, 231, 280, 286, 287, 302, 317, 449
resurgent Islam	135
resurrection	59, 68, 84, 198, 212, 291, 412
revelation	49, 53, 57, 58, 73, 87, 98, 99, 103, 115, 118, 403, 412
Revolutionary Court	187, 449
Revolutionary Guard	188
Reza Shah	426, 431, 433, 434, 440

Rhine River..200, 258
ridda...105
Ridda War...105, 397, 398
righteous..54, 58, 65
Riyadh...123, 362
Roberts, Major General..148
Roman...9-11, 13, 23, 32, 35, 45, 57, 59, 95, 108, 109, 113, 134, 191, 209, 217-220, 227, 230, 253-257, 260, 261, 264, 266, 285, 299, 302, 377, 411, 454
Roman Catholic..125, 217, 220, 225, 226, 253, 266, 298
Roman centurion...293
Roman emperor..132, 133, 167, 191, 220, 257
Roman Empire.......11, 12, 14, 15, 20, 25, 31, 32, 131, 160, 166, 179, 193, 219, 255, 260, 282, 302, 367, 407, 461
Roman Lake...35
Roman persecution..32
Romania..312, 315
Romanian Orthodox Church..125
Romans.............3, 11, 15, 24, 29, 45, 94, 95, 165, 219, 220, 229, 230, 234, 252, 410, 411, 453, 454
Rome..9-12, 23, 30, 32, 35, 94, 119, 258
Roosevelt, Kermit..184, 437, 446
Rub' al-Khali..362, 363
Rumsfeld, Donald...152
Ruqayyah...47, 88
Russia...........................147, 148, 182, 210, 335, 336, 340, 344, 346, 374, 377, 428, 429
Russian embassy...138
Russian invasion..137, 149, 154, 157
Rustem..176, 177
Sa'ad/Sa'd..68, 84, 175, 178, 393
Saba..18
Sabaeans/Sabeans...18, 367
Sabaic...119
Sabuktigin...144, 427
Saddam Hussein..204, 296, 348, 364, 394, 444
Safavid Dynasty...182, 395, 422, 426, 428
Safavids..2, 181, 395, 422, 426, 438
Safed Kuh..137
Saffarid Dynasty..182
Saffarids..137, 426
Saladin...203-205, 213, 288, 296, 387, 396, 461
Salah al-Din al-Ayyub (Saladin)..205
Salalah..365
Salat..398
Samanids...131, 426, 427
Samercand /Samarkand..15, 128, 132, 135, 140-141, 143
San'a..19, 25, 26, 28, 347, 366-368, 404

sanctuary 70, 73, 81, 99
Sanskrit 77, 182
Santander 271
Sapor I 30
Saracen 3, 276, 283, 464
Saracens 3, 13, 19, 108, 124, 263, 285, 286, 464
Sardinia 219
Sardis 414
Sassanian 15, 26, 27, 142, 159, 162, 164, 165, 167-169, 174-176, 178, 182, 420, 426
Sassanian Empire 15, 16, 23, 28, 30, 33, 129, 162, 165, 167, 172, 174, 175, 420
Sassanian Iran 12-14, 32, 94, 95, 106, 107, 129, 167, 172, 192
Sassanian Persians 24, 27, 134
Sassanians 26, 28, 95, 160, 162, 167, 410, 419, 420
Sassanids 27, 161
satrap 28, 114
satraps 113
Saudi Arabia 18, 123, 163, 169, 334, 336, 344, 361-364, 366-368, 405, 431
Saudi Law 124
Saudis 34
Sawda 73
Sawm 398
scriptures 35, 41, 48, 83, 109, 114, 129, 133, 143, 212, 260, 402, 404, 407, 409, 447
Sea of Marmara 14, 303, 372
Second Battle of the Yarmuk 21, 107, 108
Second Pledge of al-'Aqaba 68-70, 85, 106
Seistan 139, 141
Seleucia 15, 161, 162, 164, 165, 167, 174, 177, 178, 419
Seleucid Empire 15, 419
Seleucids 419
Seleucus Nicator 419
Selim the Grim 79, 297
Seljuk Iranian Empire 423
Seljuk Turks 1, 181, 207, 288, 303, 305-309, 346, 377, 395, 422, 424
Seljuks 422, 423
Semitic-Yemenite-derivative language 16
Sennacharib 349
Septuagint 421
Serampore 182
Serbia 312
Serbian 1, 125, 309, 313, 317
Serbs 1, 125, 310, 313, 375
Seven Brothers 358
Severus 162, 220
Seville 254, 262, 263, 271-273
Shah Abbas 180, 181

Shah Khosro Nushirwan...449
Shah, Zahir...150, 152-154
Shahada...397
Shahnameh...424
Shamanism...130
Shanghai Cooperation Organization...346
Shanghai Five...346
Shapur I...23
Shapur II...164, 165, 167
Sharia...80, 155
sharia courts...288
sharia law...288
Sharjah...359
Sheba...29, 30, 347
shepherd...43, 165
Shi'ism...204, 422, 436, 437, 440
Shi'ite...88, 181, 186, 335
Shia...2, 39, 100, 104, 233, 234, 364, 395, 464
Shia Islam...424
Shihr, Port of...27
Shiism...39, 204, 391, 395, 396, 422, 424, 434, 436
Shiite Islam...88
Shiraz...183, 184, 189, 414
Sicily...227, 318, 345
signs...52, 187
Sihut...366
Silk Road...16, 23, 127, 135
Sinai...404
Sinai Peninsula...283, 292
Sindh...21, 144, 427
Singapore...347
Sinkiang/Xinjiang Province...16, 127, 130, 142, 345
sinlessness...54, 55
Sir Bani Yas Island...405
Sirat Rasul Allah...102, 457
Siroes...175
Sistan...139, 427
slaves...44, 62, 83, 205, 206, 232, 296, 304, 320
Slavonia...374
Slovenia...312
social...347, 445
Socotra...27, 404
Sodom...349
Sogdian...127-129, 132, 141, 182, 446, 447
Sogdian language...141

Sohar..23, 364, 404
Solomon...18, 125, 160, 285
Somalia...333, 348, 359, 445
Somalian pirates...358, 359
Somnath...144
Sophronius...19, 283, 285, 286
South Arabia...10, 17, 25, 28, 31, 67, 117, 365-367, 405
Southeast Asia...3, 333, 387, 388
Southwest Arabia.................................16, 18, 19, 24, 26-28, 43, 113, 116, 123, 358
Soviet Central Asian republics..136
Soviet Union...152, 153, 431, 434, 437
Soviets..152, 153, 429, 432, 434
Sozomen...168
Spain....1, 20, 21, 76, 77, 79, 169, 182, 219, 220, 232, 234, 235, 251-263, 267, 269, 271, 273, 345, 419, 428
Spanish Peninsula...264, 270, 271
Springs of Badr...89
Sri Lanka...140
St. Petersburg..147
Strait of Gibraltar..219, 235, 251-253, 272, 310
Strait of Hormuz..359, 360, 363
Sub-Saharan Africa...3, 4, 333, 387, 388
Sudan...115, 348
Suez...209
Suez Canal..211
Sufism...424, 464
Sumatra...3
Sunni.................................1, 2, 39, 104, 195, 204, 205, 213, 233, 234, 315, 317, 395, 465
Sunni Islam...80, 204, 424, 435, 436
supremacy of Christ...56
Sur..365
Surat..365
Suriname..365
Susa...414
Sweden..333
swords...10, 14, 96, 97, 179, 222, 324, 352
Syene, modern Aswan..199
synagogue...73, 113, 125, 138, 368
Synod of Isaac..164
Syr River..139, 161
Syria.......10, 13, 18, 27, 30, 40, 41, 43, 44, 77, 80, 82, 86, 89, 95, 96, 107-109, 117, 122, 123, 134, 176, 177, 205, 206, 208, 210, 216, 232, 266, 282-284, 287, 288, 292, 293, 295-299, 318, 334, 336, 357, 361, 365, 367, 383, 392, 410
Syriac....................................77, 78, 120, 127, 128, 130, 143, 162, 166, 171, 401, 402, 405, 406
Syrian Desert..18, 41, 108, 292, 357, 361

Ta'if	69, 361, 368
Tabaristan	427
Tabriz	184, 414
Tabuk	18
tahanuth	47
Taif	66, 87, 367, 368
Taiwan Strait	4
Taiz	366
Taizong	15
Tajikistan	20, 128, 130, 132, 135, 136, 139, 345, 346
Talas River	1, 16, 133
Talib, Abu	39, 40, 44, 65, 66, 88, 233
Taliban	136, 137, 153, 154, 335, 445, 465
Talmud	57
Tamanrasset	218
Tang Chinese Empire	15, 132
Tang Dynasty	1, 20, 132, 133, 143
Tang Empire	4, 15, 16
taqlid	465
Tarsus	377
Tashkent	15, 135
Tatian	162, 182, 401, 402
Taurus Mountains	107, 282, 292
tawhid	70, 465
tax base	109
taxes	21, 105, 134, 174, 179, 186, 280, 449
Tayyi' tribe	31
Tehran	147, 186, 188, 433, 449
Teman	348
temple	32
Temple Mount	285, 351, 352
terrorism	80, 124, 212
terrorist organizations	136
Thaqif tribe	66
Tharon	404
The Eastern Province	363, 364
theocracy	81, 114, 296
theological	445
theological schools	162, 294
Theophanes	13
theotokos	133, 166
Thessalonica	316
Thomas, Bishop of Marga	129
Thrace	316, 389
throne	17, 59, 88, 89, 175, 181, 210, 263, 269, 272, 312, 389, 392, 395, 408

Tiananmen Square..347
Tiber..23
Tiberius..116
Tibet..15, 132
Tien Shan Mountains...127, 130
Tigris River...................................15, 27, 76, 129, 162, 168, 171, 174, 177, 268, 404, 419
Tigris-Euphrates plains...178
Tihama..360, 361, 365, 366
Tikrit..204
time and chance...125
Timothy, Patriarch...129
Timur/Tamerlane...139, 144, 297, 307, 427
Tizi-Ouzou...220
Togarmah...345
Togarmim...346
Tokat..184
Toledo..254, 260-262, 271, 272, 312
Toledot Yeshu..57
Torah..48, 61, 116, 401, 404
totalitarian...80
Tours, France...1, 270, 310
Toynbee, Arnold..130, 131
trade.......31, 32, 43, 49, 67, 70, 74, 96, 100, 117, 131, 135, 163, 180, 282, 311, 358, 364, 367, 372, 387, 404
trade fairs..43, 67, 70, 74, 86, 96
trade route...117, 362, 367, 376, 388
trading block...4
Trajan, Emperor...9, 10, 12
Trajan's Canal...9, 11
Trans-Iranian Railroad..431, 432
Transcaucasian Trough..31
translation of the Bible...182, 223, 261
Transoxania...131, 132, 143
Transoxiana...305, 427
Transylvania..314
Treaty of Paris..137, 147
Trebizond..305, 376
tribute.....................10, 17, 31, 114, 132, 145, 165, 178, 230, 232, 288, 320, 393, 456
Trinitarian...53, 63
Tripolitania..224
Trivandrum..144
Tsarist Russia..147, 374
Tudeh...429, 437
Tudela..271, 345
Tunisia..80, 196, 210, 214, 219, 223, 224, 226, 227, 229, 235

Turfan..127, 129, 133
Turgesh..131
Turkestan...31, 76, 127, 130, 345
Turkey...160, 162, 184, 189, 207, 265, 297, 299, 302, 304, 305, 312, 313, 316, 336, 342, 344, 345, 365, 371-375, 378-383, 428, 429
Turkic..426
Turkish...372, 422
Turkish language...128, 141
Turkish overlords..130
Turkmenistan..20, 130, 135, 140, 345
Turks. 79, 143, 145, 147, 179, 207, 303, 304, 306, 307, 309, 311, 313-316, 340, 345, 346, 372-375, 378, 379, 382, 383, 389, 396, 422, 424, 425
Tyre..31, 204
U.S..153, 184, 185, 190, 212, 213, 334, 335, 346-349, 380, 432, 437, 443
U.S. foreign policy...152, 335
Ubada b. al-Samit..67
Uhud..90-93, 95, 99, 105, 106
Uighur Turks...4, 16, 127, 345
Ukaz...367, 406
Umar..69, 73, 88, 104, 122, 123, 144, 174, 178, 268, 277, 286, 287, 391, 462
Umar, Covenant of..287
Umar, Pact of..287, 325
Umayyad Caliphate..72, 76, 89, 109, 268, 395, 420
Umayyads..76, 77, 289, 296, 394, 395
Umm Kulthum...47, 88
Umma Document..81
Ummayad Caliphate..214
umrah...97, 98, 399, 466
underground fellowships..156
United Arab Emirates...344, 359, 360, 363
United Methodist Council...343
Urdu..149, 183
Urfa...160, 162
Urumchi..127
Usama..101-103
Uthman..88, 284, 391, 402, 403
Uygur..4, 345
Uzbekistan...20, 128, 130, 136, 345, 346
Varna..313
Venetians...31, 314
Venice..312
Viceroy..25, 29, 58, 59, 259
Vienna..1, 2, 213, 266, 297, 304, 313-315, 318, 373, 383, 395, 422
virgin birth..57, 64
volcanic and meteorological phenomena...349

Wadi al-Sirhan	361, 362
Wadi Hajar	361, 364
Wadi Hamdh	360
Wadi Shibwan	29
Wahhabi	153
Wahhabi spirit	123
Wailing Wall	351
Wallace, Daniel B.	198
war	346
Waraqa bin Nawfal	40, 41, 48, 49, 51, 118
warner	52
Wejh	360
Western civilization	130
Western Europe	1
Western Rome	12
Western world	9, 12, 424
White Revolution	186
William of Tyre	204
Wilson, Christy	149-151, 153
Word of God	55, 224
World War I	79, 127, 288, 297, 299, 309, 340, 372, 389, 430, 433
World War II	5, 20, 79, 137, 186, 230, 359, 431, 432
world's population	100, 336, 346
worship	32
Xerxes	408, 417
Xi'an	142, 160, 169
Xinjiang	4, 345
Xinjiang/Sinkiang Province	4, 161
Yakub	273, 307
Yale Divinity School	339
Yaman	19, 26, 367, 404, 405
Yamuna River	1
Yanbu	4
Yarmuk River	107, 108, 281, 282
Yathrib/Yatrib	66-68, 70, 72, 73, 81-85, 367
Yazdegerd	172, 176, 178
year of the elephant	26, 39, 42
Yemama	105
Yemen	16-19, 24-28, 32, 43, 80, 104, 106, 113, 169, 175, 345, 347, 358, 360-362, 364-368, 404, 445, 453, 454, 459
Yemeni	16, 17, 19, 24, 28, 30, 66, 113, 115, 119, 169, 358, 366, 367, 454
Yemeni Christians	17, 19
Yugoslavia	312, 315, 371
Zab River	129, 171, 284, 395
Zafar	116

Zagros Mountains...175, 176, 178
Zahir Shah...150, 152-154
Zaid ibn Harithah..90, 95, 96, 101
Zakat...398, 466
Zaranj...139
Zaynab..47, 73
Zechariah..138
Zeno, Emperor...162
Zia-ul-Haq, General...185, 287
Zimmi...179
Zionism...348
Zoroastrian...19, 28, 130, 135, 139, 159, 164, 167-169, 408-410, 429
Zoroastrianism...28, 130, 139, 164, 167, 169, 377, 410, 411, 420
Zubair..43

About the Author

The author graduated from San Jose Bible College with a Bachelor of Theology Degree in 1947. In 1956, after having served nine-and-one-half years in evangelistic Christian ministry at Vancouver, Washington, and having taught four years in a Portland, Oregon-based Bible college, he entered the graduate school of the University of Pennsylvania, where in 1959 he completed his M.A. Degree in South Asia Regional Studies. His thesis was *A Contribution to the English Historical Cartography of Iran in the Early Islamic Period.*

Following the completion of his studies at the University of Pennsylvania, he and his family sailed to Pakistan in August 1960 where they spent the next fifteen years in Christian evangelism, both urban and rural. During the early part of his stay in Pakistan, he also studied history and political science at the University of the Punjab in Lahore, Pakistan.

While living in Pakistan, Turner made several study and preaching trips to various sites throughout much of India. Also, due to a war between India and Pakistan in 1971, he and his family spent six months in Afghanistan during which he became acquainted with further aspects of that country's history, geography and current condition.

Toward the end of 1975, the Turners were no longer allowed to renew their residential visas and consequently had to terminate their on-site mission work in Pakistan. On their way back to America, Lee and his youngest son Jonathan, traveling by Jeep, made a six-month study-tour of the Middle East which included Afghanistan, Iran, Turkey, Jordan and Syria. During that tour Lee sent a series of letters home entitled *Travel Letters From The Center Arena of History.* After 1975, Lee made 22 trips back to Pakistan and several additional trips to India. As a board member of IDES, a U.S. Christian relief organization, he visited Sudan and Egypt several times. Also, in India he traveled to war-torn Imphal in the remote, far northeastern corner of that great country, to help implement relief projects.

The ministry, begun by the author, continues to the present day by radio and internet broadcasting of the Gospel, along with staff visits to Pakistan. While still in Pakistan, in 1971, the Turners began a shortwave radio outreach in the Urdu language in order to reach more people with the message of Christ. Those broadcasts have continued uninterruptedly and go out under the name of Awaz-e-Haq (The Voice of Truth). The work has expanded so that the programs can also be heard worldwide on internet radio, available 24/7! The ministry is carried on by a small group of dedicated and skilled brethren under the name of Key Communications, directed by Jonathan Turner. Urdu Christian literature and Bibles are also made available to listeners through local Christians in Pakistan.

For additional information, see www.keycom.org.